STOPPING POWER

From the Authors of *Handgun Stopping Power* and *Street Stoppers*

Evan P. Marshall · Edwin J. Sanow

STOPPING POWER

A Practical Analysis of the Latest Handgun Ammunition

Paladin Press • Boulder, Colorado

Also by Evan Marshall and Ed Sanow:

Handgun Stopping Power: The Definitive Study
Street Stoppers: The Latest Handgun Stopping Power Street Results

Stopping Power: A Practical Analysis of the Latest Handgun Ammunition
by Evan P. Marshal & Edwin J. Sanow

Copyright © 2001 by Evan P. Marshal & Edwin J. Sanow

ISBN 1-58160-128-X
Printed in the United States of America

Published by Paladin Press, a division of
Paladin Enterprises, Inc.
Gunbarrel Tech Center
7077 Winchester Circle
Boulder, Colorado 80301 USA
+1.303.443.7250

Direct inquiries and/or orders to the above address.

Visit our Web site at www.paladin-press.com

Photo credits: Evan Marshall, Ed Sanow, and Melissa Wall

Cover, back cover and spine color photo credit: Tom Burczynski

Back cover black and white photo credit: INS/NFU

TABLE OF Contents

Dedication

Evan Marshall:

This book is dedicated to my wife's parents, Jack and Agnes Stabler, of Mesa, Arizona. In the darkest days of World War II, they stepped forward to serve their country. Putting their own plans on hold, they experienced the horrors and heartbreak of war. At its conclusion, they returned home to become superb parents of exceptional children. America is great because of people like them.

And for my wife, Maryann. "God danced the day you were born!"

And our children and their spouses: John and Marcia Marshall, Kelly and Melissa Wall, Gary and Sara Gudmundsen, Evan and Rebecca Marshall, Matthew and Christianne Marshall, and Mark and Cheiko Marshall.

And our daughter, Martha.

And our grandchildren: Derek , Emily, Lauren, Kate, and Ryan Wall; Catherine, Anne, and yet unborn boy Marshall; Ian Marshall; and Jacob Gudmundsen.

> "The greatest thing a father can do for his children is to love their mother."
>
> Harold B. Lee

Ed Sanow:

This book is dedicated to my wife and best friend, Cindy Jo. The book is also dedicated to the men and women of the U.S. Border Patrol, the real gunfighters of our time, who perform far too critical a job for the appreciation they receive.

Acknowledgments

No work such as this is possible without the help of others. The individuals and organization listed below were critical to the success of this effort.

Tom Burczynski, Experimental Research
Greg Foster, Remington Arms
Fernando Coelho, Triton Cartridge
Jeff Hoffman, Black Hills Ammunition
Peter Pi, Cor-Bon Ammunition
Ron Fine, Mag Tech Ammunition
David, Da, and Shane Keng, Keng's Firearms Specialty
Sheppard Kelly, Federal Cartridge
Roscoe Stoker, RBCD Performance Plus
Bill Forson and Thierry Jacobs, Fabrique Nationale Herstal
Mike Jordan, Larry Turi, and the engineering staff at Winchester-Olin
Georgia Arms Ammunition
PMC Ammunition
Michael Bussard, National Rifle Association
Brian Felter, National Rifle Association
Jessica Sparks, National Rifle Association
Jim Horan, Maryland
Ted Lunger, Virginia
Ed Lovette, Florida
Jeff Duncan and Ed Barton
Gary Runyon, John Jacobs, (ret.), and Carl Michaud, INS National Firearms Unit
Dennis Martin, CQB Services, England
Vince O'Neill, CLET, Oklahoma City, Oklahoma
Greg Kramer, Kramer Leather
Marty and Gila Hayes, Washington
Clint Smith, Thunder Ranch
John Farnam, Defense Training International
Massad Ayoob, Lethal Force Institute
Burt DuVernay and Tom Aveni, Smith & Wesson Academy

The legendary Jim Cirillo
Jan Libourel, *Gun World* magazine
Bruce Cameron, *Law and Order* magazine
Ronnie Paynter, *Law Enforcement Technology* magazine
Denny Hansen, *SWAT* magazine
Kerby Smith, *Handguns* magazine
Dr. Tomas Mijares, Southwest Texas State University
Dr. John Pless, Dept. of Pathology, Indiana University School of Medicine
Dr. Michael Clark, Dept. of Pathology, Indiana University School of Medicine
Dr. Ed Hancock, Mesa, AZ
Nick Roberts and Leigh Kilpack, Salt Lake County Sheriff
Lt. David Spaulding, Montgomery County, Ohio, Sheriff
Cpl. Jim Horan, Howard County, Maryland, Sheriff (ret.)
Detective Billy Stagnitta, NYPD, Firearms Training Unit
Sgt. Bill Queen, Newark, Ohio, PD (ret.)
John Hambrick, Waco PD
Sheriff Ernie Winchester, Benton County, Indiana, Sheriff
Capt. Matt Rosenbarger, Benton County, Indiana, Sheriff
Deputy Matt Shuee, Benton County, Indiana, Sheriff
Sgt. Scott Oldham, Bloomington, Indiana, Police CIRT
Officer Jim Witmer, Bloomington, Indiana, Police CIRT
Sgt. Dave Durant, Marion County, Indiana, Sheriff
Sgt. Mark McCardia, Marion County, Indiana, Sheriff
Sgt. Kelly Weidner, Marion County, Indiana, Sheriff
Cpl. Gary Fry, Marion County, Indiana, Sheriff
Deputy Mark Courtney, Marion County, Indiana, Sheriff
Deputy Dave Whitesell, Marion County, Indiana, Sheriff
Deputy Dave McGunegill, Marion County, Indiana, Sheriff
Master Trooper Dave Young, Indiana State Police (ret.)
Trooper Rich Kelly, Indiana State Police ERT
Capt. Ken Campbell, Boone County, Indiana, Sheriff
Sheriff Jim Wilson, Crockett County, Texas, Sheriff (ret.)
Deputy Jeff Belttari, Markleville, Indiana, Marshal
Deputy Dick Koons, Markleville, Indiana, Marshal
Chief Eric Greenberg, Fowler, Indiana, PD
Chief Al Kasper, Pike Township, Indiana, PD
Chief Mike Russo, Meridian Hills, Indiana, PD
Dr. Paul Whitesell, Ft. Wayne, Indiana, PD
Cpl. Ernie Nybo, South Bend, Indiana, PD

In addition, there are those who contributed valuable information but for obvious reasons cannot be identified by name. They belong to the following organizations, and the authors want them to know how deeply we appreciate their contributions in spite of great personal risk.

The Strasbourg Study staff
FBI Crime Lab
FBI FTU, Quantico, Virginia
FBI HRT
U.S. Border Patrol
Naturalization and Immigration Service (NIS)
U.S. Secret Service CAT
U.S. Postal Inspectors
DEA CLET
DEA, Lima, Peru

DEA, Bogota, Columbia
DEA, Mexico City, Mexico
DEA, New York, New York
FLETC
SOTIC
Royal Canadian Mounted Police
Medical examiner personnel in a variety of cities in the U.S. and overseas
Harvard Medical School
John Hopkins Medical School
University of California Medial School
University of Michigan Medical School
Bellevue Hospital, New York, New York
Wayne State University
University of Utah Medical School
University of Virginia Medical School
Bethesda Naval Hospital
Crane Lab, Indiana
Defense Intelligence Agency (DIA)
Central Intelligence Agency (CIA)
National Security Agency (NSA)
SEAL Team 2
SEAL Team 5
SEAL Team 6
U.S. Marine Corps Force Recon
U.S. Marine Corp Special Ops, Central and South America
U.S. Army 82nd Airborne
U.S. Army 101st Airborne
U.S. Army Rangers
U.S. Army Special Reaction Teams
U.S. Army, Mott Lake
Delta Force
SAS, England
SBS, England
Maryland State Police
Baltimore Homicide
Los Angeles Police Robbery-Homicide
Los Angeles PD SWAT
Los Angeles Sheriff SEB
Los Angeles PD Crime Lab
California Highway Patrol
Orange County Sheriff
San Francisco PD
San Diego PD
Long Beach PD
Pasadena PD
Detroit Homicide
New York PD ESU
Albany PD
New Jersey State Police
Newark, New Jersey, PD
Metro-Dade Homicide
GBI
Atlanta Homicide
Macon PD

Las Vegas PD
Reno PD
Anchorage, Alaska, PD
Washington D.C. Homicide
Waco PD
Dallas PD
Texas DPS
Houston PD
Austin PD
New Orleans Homicide
Chicago PD Narcotics
Chicago Homicide
Phoenix PD
Albuquerque PD
Alaska Highway Patrol
Madison PD
Eugene PD
Seattle PD
Oklahoma City PD
Jackson PD
Boston PD
Salt Lake City PD
Denver PD
Boulder PD
Littleton PD
Dayton PD
Indianapolis PD
"The Mad Hatter," Bosnia
"Mighty Mouse," Bogota, Columbia
"The Night Stalker," Cali, Columbia

And for the men at Desert One and on the Son Tay Raid. History may record those operations as failures, but the valor of those involved is unquestioned. They risked everything to save their brothers. There is no greater cause.

Preface

by Evan Marshall

What follows is the third in a series of books that have generated a great deal of interest and a fair amount of controversy. Actually, their intent was neither. I started the collection of this data for one very simple and critical reason: I was a cop in Detroit, and staying alive was an issue that was both relevant and challenging.

There have been those who have been simpleminded enough to think that if they said something rude or argumentative about this study, I would simply go away. They fail to grasp what should be obvious by now—I am not an ego in search of an intellect. If people find this work of value, that's great. But I didn't start this effort in order to collect disciples or groupies. Since my need to be loved, admired, respected, or even tolerated ends at my youngest grandchild, people are wasting their time attacking me.

When I was teenager, my Dad reminded me that if I was going to stand for something of value, I had better be prepared to be a "majority of one." I also figured out a long time ago that most human truths are fiction to God.

What is presented here is the efforts of several dedicated individuals who feel strongly enough about the topic of handgun stopping power to add their names to this book. They, of course, will be attacked by some because real world results don't square with certain beliefs and theories others have built their imagined fame and reputation on. Unfortunately, there are people in this world who put personal gratification and glory ahead of all else. I'm sure they will continue to attempt to discredit this work. So be it.

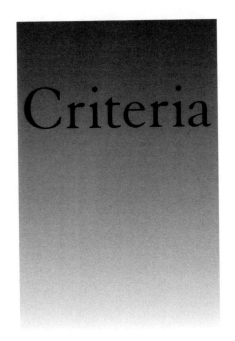

Criteria

Readers of this book need to understand that what follows is the result of almost 25 years of collecting actual shooting data. Both of our preceding books, *Handgun Stopping Power* and *Street Stoppers*, have generated a negative reaction from a small group of individuals who think their opinions carry a lot more weight than they really do.

Street cops and civilians who actually carry a gun on a daily basis have been uniformly positive in their responses. We have received countless phone calls, letters, and e-mails from people who have used the loads that we've reported as successful in the toughest laboratory of all—the street.

The criteria applied, of course, is critical to evaluating the result. Here are our criteria:

1. Only torso hits were used. It is unrealistic to include incidents where a person was hit in a nonvital area and then use that incident to criticize the load as ineffective.

2. Multiple hits were also discarded. Again, we did not think it would be fair if we included an incident where an offender took multiple hits and collapsed.

3. We have defined a stop as follows: if the person shot was assaulting someone when hit, the aggressor must collapse without being able to fire another round or strike another blow. If he or she was fleeing, they collapsed within 10 feet.

4. In order to include a shooting in this study, we insisted on either having or at least being able to review some of the following: police reports on the incident; evidence technician reports; statements by the victim; autopsy reports; officer, civilian, and medical examiner interviews; press videotapes of actual shootings; and photos. Whenever possible we also talked to emergency room personnel.

5. Recovered bullets were either personally examined by us, or we were provided photographs of the bullets.

6. A minimum of 10 verified shootings were required before a load could be included in this study. Fortunately we have been able to accumulate much more than that, and the actual number of shootings at the time of publication is included.

Introduction

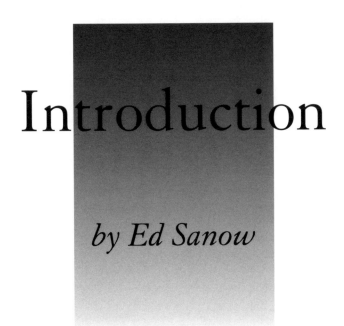

by Ed Sanow

A great deal has happened since Evan Marshall and I published *Street Stoppers* in 1996. By far the most significant was the release of the Immigration and Naturalization Service/National Firearm Unit (INS/NFU) ammunition test protocol, an update of the FBI ammo test protocol. It had become widely acknowledged among cops that too much high-performance ammo was overlooked by the old FBI minimum standard of 12 inches. Of great significance, therefore, the minimum penetration distance in calibrated 10 percent ordnance gelatin under the Border Patrol protocol was determined to be 9 inches.

The attendees at the 1998 INS/NFU conference, which included me and Evan, came from a wide variety of backgrounds, and all had a vastly different experience base. The decision of the attendees in a confidential ballot was unanimous: change the FBI protocol.

In addition to the change of minimum penetration depth, the number of barrier tests was reduced, and some barrier tests were made pass/fail. The Border Patrol protocol also reintroduced the volume of the temporary stretch cavity as a wound predictor, replacing the old FBI emphasis on the permanent crush cavity. In fact, the stretch cavity became a heavily weighted part of the ammo evaluation. Under the new Border Patrol test method, highly effective, high-energy ammo replaces the old deep penetrator subsonic hollowpoints that were so problematic in real life. (For more details on this, see John "Jake" Jacobs' great contribution to this book in Chapter 25.)

Since 1996, a new handgun caliber, the .357 SIG, has gained wide police acceptance. Police departments considering a new caliber or replacing worn-out firearms are now looking at either the .357 SIG or the .40 S&W. The 9mm remains widely used, but few departments since the mid-1990s have gone to the 9mm for the first time.

Other new defensive calibers include the .400 Cor-Bon and Triton's .40 Super. Both of these, like the .357 SIG, are high-performance bottleneck cartridges. The FN 5.7 x 28mm is new to American shooters but so far is restricted to law enforcement.

Since 1996, a number of new bullet designs have been released, and dramatic changes have occurred to many existing bullets. Federal's home defense oriented Personal Defense line is a recent development. So is its police oriented Tactical line of handgun and rifle ammunition. Triton's Quik-Shok has been redesigned, Cor-Bon has introduced its BeeSafe ammo, and RBCD has released its frangible Platinum series with the help of the legendary Jim Cirillo. CCI-Speer upgraded the Gold Dot, and Winchester has introduced Nosler Partition bullets for police handguns and greatly re-engineered its Ranger Talon line.

The most prolific bullet designer of our time, Tom Burczynski, teamed up with Federal to develop the Expanding Full Metal Jacket line of hardball ammunition. We thank him for writing a chapter on how it all came about.

The past four years has seen raised expectations for police and defensive ammo. The bullet must expand reliably after passing through heavy clothes. It must penetrate inside an acceptable range, minimum and maximum, under all shooting scenarios. The load must reliably cycle the auto pistol. For police use, the bullet must be able to defeat glass and steel, then expand and penetrate just as if it was striking bare gelatin. This emphasis on real bullet performance and weapon functioning has shifted the attention away from subsonic and medium-velocity pistol ammo. The new focus, and correctly so, is on full-power, high-energy loads.

As for the actual shooting results, a few new categories have been added. We now have actuals for many .357 SIG loads. The .30 M1 carbine results are new, as are those for the .30-30 Winchester. A wider selection of 12-gauge 00 buckshot, #4 buck, and shotgun slugs are now available, including reduced-recoil and 3 inch magnum loads. We also have many more results for the .223 Remington and .308 Winchester.

We've included chapters to appeal to a wider variety of shooters, including black powder shooters and those who use the 9mm carbine for police work or self-defense. To try to answer some questions raised over the past few years, we've added chapters on nonhollowpoint wound ballistics, short-barrel ballistics, and testing in gelatin versus live animals.

Finally, gunfight veteran Keith Jones and world-class instructor John Farnam have written guest chapters on gunfight survival and the myths of stopping power. These are "must read." In the words of survival tactics instructor Jones, "You must hit them to hurt them."

CHAPTER 1

Gunfight Survival

by Keith Jones

On a cold, raw Midwestern morning, a police patrolman sipped thoughtfully at his coffee and listened as the radio dispatcher gave him his first run of the day. It was another robbery alarm at the 24-hour drugstore a block away. At least twice a week for nearly a month the midnight shift pharmacist had managed to accidentally trip the alarm as he prepared to go off duty. It was getting to be a real annoyance. The patrolman acknowledged the dispatcher and tossed the remainder of his coffee out the window before steering his patrol car toward the drugstore address.

On arrival, the officer parked his cruiser around a corner of the pharmacy building and cautiously approached the front door of the business on foot. As he prepared to quietly scan the interior of the business through the glass storefront, the automatic door thumped open and the officer found himself face-to-face with an armed robber. This sudden arm's length confrontation came as something of a surprise to both men.

The hold-up man instantly reached for a .357 revolver that was shoved down the front of his trousers and jerked it upward toward the blue uniform that was blocking his escape. According to witnesses, the patrolman drew his service revolver and dropped into an Isoceles crouch before hammering a 158-grain softpoint .38 Special +P bullet straight through the armed robber's sternum. The bullet punched a hole, later found to be over .40 caliber, through the robber's heart just to the left of midline before exiting the torso and striking a display case inside the store.

The gunman somehow managed to raise his .357 and fire one shot before collapsing onto his back with a wet-sounding nasal grunt. His bullet struck the officer just above the eyebrow. Astonishingly, the young patrolman toppled forward and fell across the armed robber's legs almost as if to insure, even in death, that a dangerous felon would not go free. The two men were still crumpled in that position when responding officers arrived on scene only seconds later. The robber had a total of $86 stuffed in his coat pocket.

• • • • •

Before you plow any deeper into the text of this book, the authors ask that you keep a few things in mind.

Violent close-quarters combat can be a shattering experience, especially if you are not prepared for it. It is like getting slammed head-long into a cold shower. There is a sudden sensation of shock, and then you are in it. You had better do something, it had better be the right thing, and it had better be quick. It will usually occur at the wrong place, the wrong time, and often for the stupidest of reasons.

Understand that you will react just the way you have been trained to react, even if your only "training" came from watching Hollywood action films. When you don't know what to do, you will do what you know how to do, even if it is only to freeze in your tracks. Guaranteed.

If you have been properly trained, you will be able to flip a switch in your mind and fight to live. If your response to the attacker's threat is immediate and coordinated you will almost certainly prevail, either by thwarting his plan or by wrecking his physical capacity to do you injury. You can expect to be injured, crippled, or even killed, especially if you make mistakes.

Training is the key to avoiding those mistakes. If you do not train, you may end up dead, and dead is forever. You must be alert to your surroundings, think ahead, and do your best to control the many variables that occur both before and during any sort of lethal confrontation. Your survival will depend on your commitment to the time-tested triad of mind-set, tactics, and marksmanship far more than the type of ammunition you have in your weapon. In fact, a case can almost be made that it does not matter what type of bullet you have in your firearm.

A proper combat mind-set is essentially an awareness of your environment combined with the ability to focus and a hard-as-nails commitment to do whatever it takes to prevail. Being constantly aware of your surroundings is a comfortable, natural thing that all of us should strive for. You miss out on too many of the good things in everyday life when you plod from place to place totally oblivious to the world around you. You also make yourself an inviting target for criminals. As former police officer and noted survival trainer Clint Smith says, "If you look like food, you will be eaten."

Awareness and the ability to focus are critical to gaining a survival edge. Good people are needlessly maimed and killed every year by predatory felons. Not because they weren't armed, but because they weren't ready to defend themselves when the time came. You must learn to take a healthy, real-world look at humanity and accept the fact that there are criminal predators among us. It is only reasonable and prudent to expect that you may be targeted by them sooner or later. It is also reasonable and prudent to have a plan and the skills needed to insure your safety and survival.

The ability to focus means, in part, being able to see a situation for what it really is. It means being able to readily perceive impending danger, evaluate its threat, formulate a plan for dealing with it, and, finally, to put that plan into high-speed motion at the right time. Failure to properly implement this survival formula will

Four-time police gunfight winner Keith Jones urges shooters to keep their focus and to strive for the best possible shot placement. You have to hit them to hurt them.

result in a "mental stall" that will delay, perhaps fatally, your ability to respond to a life-threatening attack.

Once you have committed yourself to fending off a criminal assault, you must flip that switch in your mind and focus on carrying out your survival plan regardless of any distractions. Gunfights are won or lost quickly, normally in the space of a very few seconds. There will be no spare time for dealing with distractions if you hope to survive, and there will likely be distractions aplenty.

Be aware, for example, that the muzzle blast of a gun being fired toward you, especially at close range, sounds a great deal different from when you are standing behind or beside a gun that is being fired. If you have never experienced it, it can often be something of shock. The noise itself cannot kill you, of course, but it can cause you to falter and burn precious time that cannot be recovered. You must be prepared for it, and things like it, and strive to maintain your focus.

Regardless of the blast and sting of close-range gunfire or of any injuries you may absorb, you must focus on your plan for survival. Your plan must be effective, flexible, and simple enough to implement under the dire stresses of a homicidal assault. If you allow your adversary to disrupt your plan, the press of time may not permit you to go back to square one and start again.

Your ability to focus and carry out your plan depends in large measure on how quickly you can get control of your emotions. Fear and anger, it is said, are different sides of the same emotion, and recognition of that can often be the key to your success. You should look closely at your emotions and develop an ability to turn your anger on and off at will.

When we speak of the capacity to "flip that switch" in your mind, we are referring to turning your fear into a controlled and intelligently applied anger. Getting angry with someone who is trying to kill you is not only natural, it can pave the way to your survival provided you work to make it an asset instead of a dangerous liability. Anger can be the catalyst that puts all your survival systems in harmony and enables you to stay focused on the things that matter.

People who have gained some experience in close-quarters combat often report that they notice much less emotional stress during subsequent lethal encounters. Retired police officer and gunfight survival instructor Jim Cirillo notes that he eventually experienced only a slight increase in his heart rate while confronting armed robbers during his service with the famed New York City Police Department's Robbery Stakeout Squad. He also notes that it took a half-dozen gunfights for him to gain that much inner composure.

Jim's hard-won experience allows him to speak with great authority on controlling the variables of a gunfight. He will quickly tell you that the first rule of control is self-control. You should strive to control your emotions by turning your fear into a useful anger. It is a simple expedient that will help you to stay focused on your plan and on the fast-changing variables of the situation. That is the first big step in surviving an armed assault on your life.

Knowing how to shoot with a handgun is not enough. You have to know how to fight with one. This is where tactics come in. Good tactics will do far more to keep you alive than the type of bullet you have in your handgun or even the type of wounds you might manage to inflict on your adversary. The story you just read about the young patrolman who died in a drugstore doorway with his attacker is a good case in point. There is no doubt that better tactics would have kept him alive.

You simply cannot rely on the bullet impact from any hand-held weapon to instantly incapacitate an adversary 100 percent of the time. You must never, ever assume or expect that it will. Even with the best shot

placement and the hardest-hitting bullet, it may still be several seconds before your attacker succumbs to his wounds. A lot of bad things can happen in that brief span of time, and good tactics are your only protection.

If you wish to survive, you have to train for it ahead of time. You must learn simple, flexible survival tactics from a competent instructor, and fortunately there are a number of those around. Few of them will have all of the answers, of course, but all of them can help you to learn. The goal of tactical training is to prepare you to fend off an assault on your life with no mistakes and, as much as is possible, with no surprises.

You cannot learn tactics from reading this or any other text. Survival tactics involve what instructors refer to as "psychomotor skills" and can be properly assimilated only in a hands-on learning environment. Good tactical training will teach you to move well and shoot well. Even more importantly, it will also teach you how to recognize and control the many variables of a life-threatening encounter. This can be accomplished, to a great degree, by learning to control another survival triad: distance, cover, and time.

Learning to control distance is critical. The distance between you and your attacker can be the determining factor in his ability to hit you with gunfire. At conversational distances even an untrained felon has a good chance of hitting his victim. The probability of his hitting you, however, will dramatically decrease as the distance between you increases, especially if he is using a handgun. We are talking about an increase in distance of even just a few yards. If you are in motion, his odds of hitting you are even less.

You should be alert and conscious of distances as you approach a potentially dangerous place or situation. If you are aware of your surroundings and alert to the slightest indication of danger, it will be very

difficult if not impossible for your adversary to truly take you by surprise. Be ever mindful of the distance between you and any potential source of danger. Be ready to move at a split-second's notice. Always try to position yourself so that you are never more than a step or so from solid cover.

Cover stops bullets. The old timers used to say that the three most important things in gunfight survival are (1) cover, (2) cover, and (3) cover. We know now that it is a little more complicated than that, but only a little. You must learn to use cover effectively. Any worthwhile survival tactics training will stress the difference between concealment and cover and show you the practical applications for each. Remember that it is not cover unless it is capable of stopping the bullets your adversary is using.

Taking a good position behind solid cover can give you some breathing space while you take stock of your options and prepare for your attacker's next move. It will also make you go from being vulnerable to formidable in an instant and will seriously complicate your attacker's plan. Good cover can minimize your risk of injury and maximize your ability to deliver accurate return fire. Most of all, cover can buy you time when time is in terribly short supply.

If you can make time work for you during an armed encounter, you can be sure that it is then working against your adversary. Under most circumstances this can be accomplished by somehow disrupting his plan of attack and causing his own timing to be thrown off. Like a predatory animal, a criminal must base his assault on the principles of stealth, distance, and timing. If his timetable is destroyed, his plan is then crippled and the risks of his apprehension or injury will skyrocket.

Most of the time a criminal assault is a low-tech affair involving a simple plan, a headlong attack, and a minimum amount of time spent on scene. Normally his goal is to execute the plan and make good his escape. Since your goal is simply to avoid injury, you have time to dig in and make the clock work for you. It is extremely rare for a criminal to have that luxury.

One of the best ways to make time work for you is to capitalize on the extra time that your awareness and actions can buy for you. If your survival sensors alert you to impending danger a few seconds before you are attacked, you can use that time to strike first and neutralize your assailant if need be. You can also use it to increase the distance and seek cover. Cover will greatly increase your chances of surviving any injury you might sustain.

Good cover will also make it possible for you to survive after you have seriously wounded your adversary. Some criminals drop instantly to handgun fire, while others can be nearly shot to hamburger before they stop posing a threat. Most are able to stay on their feet, and dangerous, for several seconds at the very least. You had better have plans for your survival during that interval of time. It will seem like an eternity if you are vulnerable. A good position behind solid cover can set the clock ticking in your favor and allow you to conserve your ammo. You may need every cartridge you have.

Combat marksmanship centers on your ability to reliably hit the vital zone of your assailant in spite of unfavorable circumstances and the fact that he is attempting to kill you. Listen carefully, because this is the part that gets intense. You must keep your head, maintain your focus, and strive for the best possible placement of your shots. *Regardless of caliber, design, or velocity, a bullet can never do its part until you first do yours.* If you do not hit your assailant and hit him hard, you will not hurt him. If you do not hurt him, you may end up dead.

You must be able to pick up your weapon and shoot it well with very little mental involvement. Your

weapon must be simple for you to operate, and you must practice with it until its operation becomes second nature to you. If you are unwilling to find time to practice and bond with the weapon you carry, you may not be able to place your shots well enough to save your life in a gunfight. You must master the basic mechanics of shooting as though your very existence depends on it, because it does. Dead is forever.

During practice, for example, try keeping your shots in the head of a full-sized B-27 silhouette target at 25 yards. This will clearly indicate that you know what the front sight is for. Even more importantly, it will demonstrate that you have a proper grip on the weapon and a good feel for its trigger. A comfortable, natural grip and good trigger control are major factors in getting effective, high-speed hits at very close range. You cannot afford to miss your attacker's vital zone, especially up close. There simply will not be time for it. Good shot placement can cancel out a multitude of other mistakes.

Any solid hit to your adversary's torso is acceptable, particularly if you are using a potent shoulder-fired weapon or a really powerful handgun. To get the most out of your ammunition, regardless of its caliber or design, try to place your shots somewhere between the target's eyebrows and the bottom of his sternum and as close to the midline as possible. Repeated, solid hits to this area of the body are normally very effective. From a practical standpoint, it is probably the most vulnerable section of the human anatomy. This target area is also easy to focus on and large enough to hit reliably in close-quarters combat. If you don't believe that, you aren't shooting enough.

The pelvic area with its heavy bone and broad lumbar vertebrae is also a highly effective target for your gunfire, provided you use a potent cartridge. This is the center of the load-bearing structure of the upright skeleton and the center of balance for a

mobile, hostile adversary. When someone is literally knocked off his feet by the impact of a handgun bullet, it is very often due to a solid hit in the pelvic area.

Additionally, bullet fragments and gunshot-splintered shards of bone can clip major nerves and lacerate major blood vessels of the lower torso. In one recent autopsy, a policeman's bullet was found to have ruptured the apparently distended bladder of an armed robber. The resulting fluid shock explosion nearly severed a large artery in the robber's groin area and put him immediately out of the fight.

The effect of a solid gunshot to the pelvic area is usually the same as a solid kick delivered there. The target will be unceremoniously dumped on his backside and momentarily, even permanently, robbed of his mobility. Granted he may still be highly dangerous from the waist up, but he will also be highly vulnerable. The press of time, his injuries, and your follow-up gunshots will overwhelm him. When he is down and stationary, he will be much easier to hit. If you don't hit him, you won't hurt him. If you don't hurt him, you may end up dead.

Most of the horror stories that you hear about the combat-related failure of a particular medium or heavy caliber bullet are usually the result of poor shot placement. Probably the least effective place to hit your assailant is in his stomach area. While a handgun wound in that area can certainly be lethal, its effect is seldom immediate, and "immediate" is the only thing that really counts. The object of the exercise is to put your attacker out of action now, before he injures you, not to cause his lingering death in a hospital bed next week.

Failure-to-stop horror stories involving powerful handguns, or even shotguns or rifles, almost always involve a primary or initial wound in the mid-section of the torso. Placing your shots to that area of your attacker's body is tantamount to intentionally gut-shooting a grizzly bear. In most cases, nothing of immediate consequence will be struck and your adversary will certainly now have a surge of adrenalin coursing through his system. This can often result in your attacker turning into a "bullet sponge" and continuing to function despite having absorbed numerous additional bullet impacts.

It appears that the central nervous system (CNS) can register the shock of only about two gunshot wounds. After that, it is possible for the adrenalin surge to briefly protect your assailant from the immediate effect of any additional bullets that are not direct CNS strikes. Gunfight veterans and big-game hunters have been noting this for many years. If your attacker is not obviously becoming incapacitated by the time you have fired your second shot, then you must promptly shift your point of aim and concentrate on making a CNS hit.

This is not to say that your adversary will not be seriously, even mortally, injured by poorly placed torso hits. Depending on the circumstances, of course, you may be doing well to hit your assailant anywhere in the torso. Just remember that poorly placed hits can take far too long to take effect. They can burn up too much time when time is in critically short supply. Again, poor shot placement accounts for most of the bullet failure horror stories that you will hear.

Additionally, these horror stories usually involve someone's unreasonable expectations of what a bullet can or should do when it strikes a human target. There is only so much that you can expect out of any bullet, especially a handgun bullet. Most people expect too much, or at least they expect the wrong thing. Your bullets will never explode your attacker into a pink fog, or blast him bodily through an adjacent wall, or even reliably collapse him at your feet. You should never, ever expect that they will. Instead, you should expect to be involved in a high-speed, close-quarters brawl.

A handgun fight is often an elevated, highly dangerous form of a fistfight, especially with regard to what you can or should expect from a handgun bullet. A prizefighter, for example, might hope that the first solid punch will knock his adversary out of the fight, but he does not expect it to happen that way. What he expects instead is simply that his first solid blow will give him a good start on his opponent and lead to an opening upon which he can capitalize.

The limited power available in any handgun cartridge requires that you adopt much the same perspective. Too many people expect a handgun bullet to inflict an incapacitating wound that instantly knocks their attacker to the ground. Instead, you should expect your bullet to inflict an incapacitating wound that instantly wrecks your attacker's mind-set and ability to fight. With good tactics, good shot, placement and an effective bullet, you can achieve that goal.

You have got to hit people to hurt them. To hurt them reliably, you have got to hit them hard. There are bullets now available in certain handgun calibers that can reliably distract your attacker from his focus, or disrupt his plan, or disable his physical capacity to function, or destroy his will to fight. You can often readily see the instantaneous effect, or "impact signature," of your bullets striking your attacker, especially if you have been trained to look for it and, more importantly, to capitalize on it.

In his book *No Second Place Winner*, the late Bill Jordan, a retired U.S. Border Patrolman, World War II Marine combat officer, and gunfight survival instructor, stressed the need for a visibly hard-hitting handgun cartridge. He noted that the impact signature of the standard-velocity .38 Special bullet was "hardly apparent" during gunfights and spoke of the "authoritative" power of the .357 Magnum revolver cartridge. Bill also thoroughly understood that wrecking an assailant's mind-set can be a primary factor in winning a gunfight. He often stated that, "It's rare for a man with a gunshot wound to show an interest in anything other than getting to a hospital."

You will recall the story of the police patrolman at the beginning of this chapter who died after having fatally wounded his adversary. While his tactics were flawed, it would be pretty hard to find fault with his shot placement or the internal damage inflicted by his bullet. As a result of his death, his agency adopted the 125-grain .357 Magnum revolver cartridge and used it for nearly 15 years before transitioning to autoloaders.

In numerous subsequent gunfights, his agency noted that criminals struck in the upper chest area with a .357 Magnum bullet were instantly unable to continue hostile action. Not always killed, mind you, but instantly and decisively taken out of the fight. The .357 Magnum cartridge could also be counted on to wreck a criminal's hand or arm and immediately render it useless. The same could not be said for their previously issued .38 Special bullets.

This agency's officers reported that a criminal always turned away slightly, or was at least briefly staggered by the impact of high-energy .357 rounds, regardless of where he was hit in the torso. They noticed that even if he did not collapse, the criminal was still forced to take an extra second or more to regain control of himself and his plan. These officers quickly learned to capitalize on that time by concentrating on well-aimed follow-up shots or by stepping toward solid cover.

These officers learned to not expect their bullets to blow an attacker into next week. Instead, they learned to look for and capitalize on the impact signature of a hard-hitting handgun cartridge. Today there are a number of bullets in several different calibers that can help you dominate a handgun fight, but only provided that you have good training, effective shot placement, and a realistic expectation of what your bullets can do. Knowing how to shoot your weapon is not enough. You must know how to fight with it. *Distract, disrupt, disable, or destroy.*

This all serves to illustrate the high-speed chaos of a handgun fight and underscores the crucial need for a proper mind-set, good combat tactics, and skilled marksmanship above everything else. It also illustrates the sort of "survival edge" that a properly selected bullet can gain for you. This is the reason that this book and its predecessors, *Handgun Stopping Power* and *Street Stoppers*, were written. These books are based on real-world facts from real-world lethal encounters. The research data needed to improve combat training and bullet performance must come, to a great degree, from the careful debriefing of gunfight participants.

Many useful facts can be gathered at autopsy tables and in laboratory experiments, but they cannot account for the actual dynamics of an armed encounter, or for the varied reactions of a criminal who gets struck by a bullet. To gather those facts you must thoroughly study after-action reports and painstakingly interview witnesses and survivors. Gunfight survivors, like participants in any traumatic event, can make poor witnesses if they are not handled with patience and skill. The knowledge gathered, however, is invaluable as we strive to learn about the variables of armed encounters and about bullet effectiveness.

There are, of course, people who will tell you that this is the wrong approach. These clinical researchers will assure you that any facts or theories that are not subjected to laboratory analysis and peer review are suspect. They will point out that statistics can be skewed and that the facts that the theories are based on are "anecdotal" and cannot be replicated. Curiously though, most of these scientists adhere to the "Big Bang" theory of cosmic creation, which apparently happened only once, was witnessed by no one, and cannot be replicated.

A commitment to scientific research principles is praiseworthy and productive, but you must take real-life variables and human factors into account. Peer reviews are meaningless unless they include those "peers" who are still standing when the echoes of gunfire have died away.

Relying on a handgun to save your life in a close-range brawl can be a frightening prospect, at least to those who have been forced to use one to defend themselves. It is, at its best, a low-powered and inefficient tool for the job. A short-barreled shotgun or rifle-caliber carbine is a much better choice for delivering accurate, decisive, fight-stopping power, especially at short range. You should strive to have ready access to a potent, shoulder-fired weapon whenever circumstances will allow it.

Still, a handgun is often the only thing available, and when it is, you must get the most out of it. Good shot placement is critical at all times, but especially so with regard to handgun bullets. You have got to hit people to hurt them. To hurt them reliably, reliably enough to save your life, you have got to hit them *hard*. This means your shots must dependably strike the vital zone of your assailant. You must practice regularly and discipline yourself to somehow use your gunsights at anything beyond bayonet range. To do otherwise is to trust to luck, and luck is not the thing to rely on in a gunfight.

You should use the most powerful handgun that you can shoot well and carry comfortably. Shooting it well is the key here. Hitting your attacker solidly with a full-metal jacket bullet is far better than missing him with the world's most exotic hollowpoint. You must first be able to dominate your weapon before you can use it to dominate the other variables of a handgun fight.

Bullet performance has always been one of those variables. However, it is one that you can try to control before the fight by doing research and selecting a load that fits your needs. There is no doubt that some bullets perform better than others in defensive shooting applications. The authors hope that the information contained in this book will assist you in your understanding of this vital aspect of street survival. Remember, the only thing worse than being involved in a gunfight is losing one.

CHAPTER 2
A Century of Handgun Stopping Power

People collapse after being shot for a wide variety of reasons. Some of these, like blood loss, are firmly rooted in medical science. Others, like neural shock, are not as well understood. Still other reasons are psychological in nature and vary widely from scenario to scenario. The harsh reality is this: no predictable and reliable medical reason exists for a person to instantly collapse and become incapacitated for a handgun bullet in under five seconds except for a shot to the brain stem or upper spine.

Handgun bullets cannot be depended upon to work in under two seconds. In fact, even strikes to the heart itself by the most devastating handgun bullets still allow up to 10 to 15 seconds of hostile activity. How are you going to survive that long? You will make better survival-oriented decisions if you *expect* your gunfire to have absolutely no effect whatsoever. You will fire from behind cover or get to cover as soon as possible. You will fire numerous times. You will be as precise as possible under the circumstances. You will keep the firearm pointed at the target until you are absolutely sure the action is over.

Blood loss is the most common mechanism of collapse, but it is an extremely slow process. With the heart stopped, the aggressor will have enough oxygen in his brain for 5 to 8 seconds of vision and neural function to the arms. Few handgun bullets are capable of completely stopping the pumping action of the heart. Again, even on a direct heart shot, activity for 10 to 15 seconds is medically reasonable.

A shot to the vascular organs like the liver, spleen, and kidneys will result in blood loss, but the process of oxygen depletion takes *much* longer. It may take 30 to 90 seconds for the person to collapse. A shot to the lungs, the most likely vital organ to be hit, takes even longer to have an effect. The mechanism of blood loss or, more properly, lack of oxygen to the brain, is a long process but is also the process you are most likely to be dependent upon.

The fastest and most reliable way to cause an instant incapacitation is to get a bullet into the cranial vault. But remember: a head shot is not a brain shot. And the skull itself is rounded, hard, and thick. It can be difficult to penetrate this natural armor.

Another mechanism of collapse is when the bullet shatters a support bone in the foot, leg, knee, or perhaps hip. The attacker will appear to be instantly knocked down, but he will be far from incapacitated. Be extremely skeptical of any bullet having instant effectiveness.

In addition to blood loss, damage to the central nervous system, and shattered support bones, people fall from gunshots for other, less reliable reasons. These include the psychological reaction to being shot and the mechanism of neural shock caused by a large stretch cavity. Neither one is dependable nor repeatable. In the laboratory, we can cause a brain wave disruption by a blood pressure spike that leads to a collapse. But we still don't know enough about why it happens to be able to duplicate the effect on the street.

RELATIVE STOPPING POWER

For 100 years we have been trying to predict handgun stopping power. At the turn of the century, the United States Army shot live cattle and human cadavers to get a better understanding of bullet effectiveness. This work by Capt. John Thompson (ordnance) and Maj. Louis LaGarde (medical corps) was later converted to a predictive formula by Gen. Julian Hatcher: the Relative Stopping Power

The Thompson-LaGarde tests, circa 1904, involved shooting 13 head of cattle, 2 horses, and 10 cadavers. The .30 Luger and 9mm were included. The .476 Enfield was the winner.

In the 1970s, the U.S. Justice Department's National Institute of Justice (NIJ) funded a computer modeling based on the stretch cavity in ordnance gelatin and the tissue that cavity would disrupt, calling it the Relative Incapacitation Index (RII). The NIJ/LEAA (Law Enforcement Assistance Administration) work indicated that bullets with more energy and the fastest energy transfer were the most effective. This study was soundly mocked and ridiculed, yet the "Computer Man" gave predictions quite close to what we now know are the right answers based on actual street performance.

The RII had one legitimate shortcoming: all the tests assumed a frontal shot. This makes it perfect for the selection of home defense and off-duty ammo, but for the work to have been more meaningful to police, the tests needed to be run with angular and cross-torso shot placements. The NIJ/LEAA project ran out of funding before this step could be completed. Even still, the RII did a good job of ranking hollowpoint bullet performance.

Julian Hatcher's Relative Stopping Power theory predicted larger caliber, high-momentum bullets like the .45 Colt 255-grain RNL, left, and the .45 ACP 230-grain FMJ, right, would be twice as effective as the smaller caliber, high-energy bullets like the 9mm 124-grain FMJ, center. Street results, however, show the effectiveness to be the same.

The Relative Incapacitation Index from the 1970s, based on the "computer man" studies, favored loads with a high energy and rapid energy transfer. Top loads from that test were the 9mm 115-grain JHP, left, and .357 Magnum 110-grain JHP, right. History has proven the much maligned test to be correct.

(RSP). Hatcher's work indicated that bullets with more momentum and of a larger caliber were the most effective.

The RSP was developed using subsonic and nonexpanding bullets. When restricted to this type of ammo, it does a fairly good job of relative ranking. However, it greatly overstates the differences between calibers and loads. For example, it rates the .45 ACP 230-grain FMJ ball superior to the 9mm 115-grain FMJ ball. The RSP for these two loads is 60.0 and 29.4 respectively, giving the .45 ACP ball twice the effectiveness of 9mm ball. The street results, however, give these two loads ratings of 62 percent and 70 percent, respectively.

THE USE OF ORDNANCE GELATIN

By the early 1980s, the use of ordnance gelatin had gained acceptance in law enforcement as a legitimate bullet test medium. This allowed major police agencies to do testing of their own based on their own theories of how to predict stopping power. This also set the stage for the argument of how to use gelatin to predict effectiveness that would last for the next 20 years.

The volume of the permanent crush cavity is too difficult to measure accurately to be a reliable estimate of stopping power. This .45 ACP 230-grain Black Talon and the .45 ACP 230-grain Hydra-Shok have the same penetration and recovered diameter. However, the fast-expanding Hydra-Shok produces a larger crush cavity and a much higher one-shot stop.

Ordnance gelatin allows us to accurately measure two aspects of wound ballistics: the permanent crush cavity and the temporary stretch cavity. The crush cavity is the amount of tissue actually touched by the passing bullet. This is the tissue that absolutely, positively will be destroyed by the bullet, period. In general terms, the crush cavity is a calculation involving the diameter of the bullet and the length of the bullet penetration. The diameter is squared in the calculation, making it much more influential than the penetration depth.

The volume of the crush cavity is the basis for the FBI Wound Value

For nearly a century, it was widely believed that the shape of the bullet had something to do with stopping power. With thousands of shootings involving everything from rounded bullets to Keith-style semiwadcutters, we now know that the shape of the bullet has no effect at all on stopping power.

method of predicting stopping power (discussed below). This calculation involves not the actual diameter or the peak diameter of the bullet but its recovered diameter. The problem is that the diameter of the bullet changes dramatically during penetration. It may expand and then fragment to a smaller recovered diameter. Even worse, some bullets expand early while others expand late. Even for bullets with exactly the same penetration depth and exactly the same recovered diameter, the differences in *rate* of expansion can affect the total volume of the crush cavity by up to 20 percent. That is an unacceptably large error to be the basis for an entire theory of stopping power.

As a general trend, and all else being equal, stopping power increases as the size of the recovered bullet increases. Even more relevant, a statistical analysis has proven that stopping power *also* increases as the size of the initial bullet diameter increases.

The other unique term used when discussing wound ballistics is the stretch cavity. The stretch cavity is

the result of tissue being pushed out of the way in the wake of the passing bullet. The disrupted organs then return to their original location in less than a second.

This disrupted tissue may or may not be damaged. Elastic tissue like skin, muscle, lung, and intestines will be the least damaged by the stretch cavity at handgun velocities. Elastic organs like the spleen, kidneys, and especially the liver will be the most damaged by the stretch cavity.

Bullets with more energy or with more energy transfer produce larger stretch cavities. Bullets with less energy or with less energy transfer produce smaller stretch cavities. An analysis of comparing gunfight results with the same ammo fired in gelatin shows that stopping power increases as the volume of the stretch cavity increases. This trend continues as the velocity increases into the rifle levels.

Tissue that is disrupted but not necessarily damaged can lead to an instant collapse or even loss of consciousness. This typically happens with only the highest energy handgun loads. The exact medical mechanism is still not fully understood. Put another way, only the loads with more than a 90 percent one-shot stop rating produce a temporary stretch cavity that is most likely to cause instant incapacitation.

For handgun bullets, the stopping power can be predicted by a review of both the crush cavity and the stretch cavity. For rifle bullets, the stopping power is almost exclusively controlled by the stretch cavity.

THE SIFS PROTOCOL

The Dallas-area Southwest Institute of Forensic Sciences (SIFS) was among the first to fine tune the process started by the NIJ. It correctly focused on energy transfer, specifically the amount of energy transferred in 5.5 inches of 20 percent gelatin. This was a takeoff of the method used in the late 1970s by the U.S. Secret Service. The SIFS departed from the NIJ concept in that it wanted a medium rate of energy transfer as opposed to an early energy transfer.

The SIFS protocol was well on the way to leading the research in predicting stopping power. It established a minimum amount of energy (200 ft-lbs.). It required that no less than 75 percent and no more than 90 percent of the total energy be deposited in the denser 20 percent gelatin block. This method produced one of the highest correlations ever recorded for a gelatin-based test in comparison with actual street results. Of course, large numbers of street results were not yet available to show how truly accurate the SIFS method was. At the time, it was just a theory. Unfortunately, the SIFS protocol would immediately become overshadowed by the FBI methodology of 1987.

THE FBI PROTOCOL

The FBI led the police and ammo industry into a dark age of medical rhetoric and intellectual

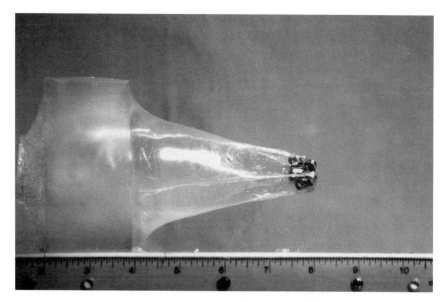

In the early 1980s, the Southwestern Institute of Forensic Sciences checked the amount of energy transferred in a short section of gelatin. It set minimum initial energy levels for police use and a minimum and a maximum amount of energy transfer. They were on the right track.

In the mid 1980s, the FBI developed a series of gelatin and barrier tests that rewarded underexpansion and deep penetration. The two loads to come directly from this methodology, the 9mm 147-grain JHP, left, and the .40 S&W 165-grain medium-velocity Hydra-Shok, right, produce the least actual stopping power among hollowpoints in their respective calibers.

elitism when it ushered in an era of minimum penetration standards. As a result, hollowpoint bullets were designed to suppress expansion in an attempt to increase penetration. Of the FBI's eight ballistics tests, seven required the bullet to defeat some sort of barrier before striking the gelatin.

Yet the tests were represented as a way to select a general-issue police duty round.

The FBI method resulted in a "wound value" which was basically the permanent crush cavity of the bullet factored for a minimum of 12 inches of penetration in 10 percent gelatin. For the next 10 years, the FBI misled the police across America that "subsonic hollowpoints," deep penetration, minimum expansion, and the permanent crush cavity were the keys to stopping power. At this time, however, initial shooting results began to filter in showing that the 9mm 115-grain jacketed hollowpoint (JHP), the "old" load used by the FBI, had an 80 percent one-shot stop record while the agency's "new" 9mm 147-grain JHP had a success ratio of just 69 percent. In the end, the FBI method of predicting stopping power was proven to have the worst correlation to actual shooting results of any method this century.

The hottest topic of debate from the mid-1980s to the mid-1990s was penetration depth. How much was enough? How much was not enough? Was it possible to have too much? City, county, state, and federal law enforcement was completely divided on this issue.

On one side was the high-profile FBI favoring a minimum depth in 10 percent gelatin of 12 inches and, originally, no maximum whatsoever. The load that was the lightning rod for this side of the controversy was the 9mm 147-grain subsonic hollowpoint, with penetration, at the time, of 14 to 18 inches. On the other side were the gunfight veterans at the U.S. Border Patrol favoring the .357 Magnum 110-grain JHP with just 10 inches of penetration. The lightning rod in this camp was the 9mm 115-grain JHP +P+ Illinois State Police load. These +P+ loads penetrated from 8 to 12 inches.

The vast majority of law enforcement followed the lead of the FBI in adopting the 9mm 147-grain JHP. For the 10-year period between the mid-1980s to the mid-1990s, these cops were unwittingly involved in a test of a theory. That experiment is finally over, and so is the controversy surrounding penetration.

The best performance in police and defensive scenarios comes from

The FBI multiple barrier gelatin tests from the mid-1980s led to a decade of low performance subsonic hollowpoints. However, it also correctly showed that some hollowpoints that work great in bare gelatin, like this .45 ACP 200-grain JHP, can plug up with heavy clothes and not expand at all.

bullets that penetrate in the 8.4 to 12.8 inch range. Acceptable, but not the best, performance comes from bullets that penetrate in the 12.8 to 14.6 inch range. The worst street results come from bullets that penetrate more than 14.6 inches.

Experts can theorize as much as they want, but it still remains an *opinion* until the facts are in. In police action and defensive shootings, the facts are in on penetration distances. The 10 to 14 inch range emphasized by Marshall and Sanow in *Handgun Stopping Power* (1992) and *Street Stoppers* (1996) has been validated by street performance.

Over the past 10 years, ammunition companies have slowly but steadily improved even their so-called subsonic hollowpoints. The 9mm 147-grain, .40 S&W 180-grain, and .45 ACP 230-grain JHPs originally penetrated 16 to 18 inches of gelatin. After a decade of improvement, all of these loads now penetrate in the 12 to 15 inch range. Many police departments now penalize ammo for excessive penetration. The Indiana State Police,

for example, disqualified any of the .40 S&W 180-grain JHPs that penetrated deeper than 14 inches. The Border Patrol allows a maximum of 15 inches. Even the group of deep-penetration proponents who urged the FBI to accept ammo that went as deep as 18 inches has now backed off. These self-appointed experts, few of who had any police experience, now accept the reality that ammo with less than 12 inches of penetration can be more effective than ammo with more than 18 inches of penetration.

For personal defense scenarios, ammo that penetrates in the 8 to 12 inch range is ideal. For general-issue police use, ammo that penetrates in the 10 to 14 inch range is ideal.

THE STRASBOURG GOAT TESTS

In the early 1990s, a privately funded research project conducted a high-tech version of the old Thompson-LaGarde stockyard tests. This time the targets were 160 pound French Alpine goats wired with transmitters for blood pressure and

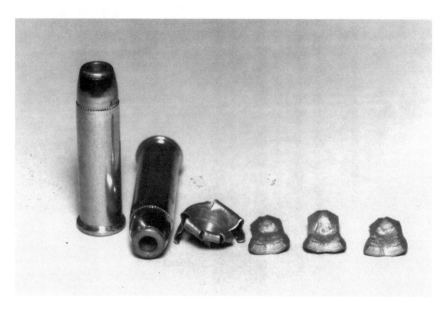

The high-tech Strasbourg Tests involved lung-only shots on French Alpine goats. Like the RII, the results favored the high-energy bullets with the most rapid energy transfer like this Triton .38 Special +P 110-grain Quik-Shok.

bullet either stopped the attacker or it did not. A "stop" was defined as follows: if the subject was shooting, he stopped shooting, period. If the subject ran after being hit, he ran no more than 10 feet. If the attacker stopped shooting or ran less than 10 feet, the load was considered to have stopped the attack, which is the purpose of police and defensive ammo.

The one-shot stop methodology says nothing about lethality. The subject can fully recover. The method says nothing about what happens after the subject's actions are stopped by gunfire. He can resist arrest all the way to the hospital.

This leads to the single largest misunderstanding about stopping power. In a defensive and police scenario, all that counts is what happens in the first five seconds after the bullet strikes. What happens five minutes or

brain wave activity. The Strasbourg Tests attempted to find what bullets caused an instant collapse and why.

The initial report from the tests recorded collapse times after one shot through both lungs. The relative rankings of these rounds had an extremely high correlation with actual shooting results that had then become available. Regretfully, the research team was disbanded before a correlation between an instant collapse, blood pressure spikes, and brain wave activity could be made.

EVAN MARSHALL'S WORK AND THE FULLER INDEX

Evan Marshall's one-shot stop method of predicting stopping power is not a theory about future performance—it is a historical fact about past performance. Marshall simply collected shooting results from all jurisdictions, border to border, coast to coast. He then sorted through the results looking for shootings where the violator was struck somewhere in the torso just one time. Multiple shots

Evan Marshall's "one-shot stop" is not a theory about stopping power—it is a summary of actual events. His methods do not favor either high-momentum bullets, like the .45 ACP 230-grain Hydra-Shok, left, or high-energy bullets, like the .45 ACP 185-grain JHP +P, right. In reality, these have nearly the same one-shot stop rating.

were excluded. So were shots to the head, neck, arms, and legs.

Of the shootings involving one shot to the torso, Marshall then sorted the results into one of two groups: the

five hours later is not relevant to the problem of stopping power.

The same thing applies to the visual examination of the bullet wound in the emergency room or morgue. It simply doesn't matter. It doesn't matter that a trained and experienced gunshot pathologist cannot differentiate between the damage caused by a 9mm and the damage caused by a .45 ACP. It doesn't matter that a highly skilled battlefield surgeon cannot see the effects of the handgun-velocity stretch cavity. All this stuff happens hours after what really matters.

What counts, and the only thing that counts, is the effect of the bullet in the first few seconds after impact. What counts is the real-time record from the in-car video camera and the footage from press cameras. What counts is witness and officer-involved testimony. Did the violator stop shooting after being hit, or did he keep shooting? Did the violator run away from the cops after being hit, or did he slump down? It is really that simple.

In 1992, Evan Marshall published two decades worth of shooting results in the book *Handgun Stopping Power*. Statisticians from all over the country loaded 7,600 shootings, sorted by caliber and load, into their personal and mainframe computers. The result was a wide variety of equations to predict effectiveness. The best of these, developed by programmer Steve Fuller, has become known as the Fuller Index. In time for the 1996 book *Street Stoppers*, Fuller combined over 13,500 shootings into a quadratic and exponential equation.

The Fuller Index can be used to estimate the one-shot stops for any load from the .22 Long Rifle to the .44 Magnum. It requires only three pieces of information: the initial bullet diameter, the muzzle energy of the bullet, and the penetration depth in 10 percent gelatin. The predictive accuracy of the Fuller Index is the same as if 109 actual shootings with that load had been calculated. The crush cavity does not need to be measured—that is covered by the bullet diameter and the penetration depth. The stretch cavity does not need to be measured—that is covered by the muzzle energy and penetration depth.

The Fuller Index is an equation based on Marshall's one-shot stop findings for the .22 Long Rifle up to the .45 Long Colt. It has the same predictive accuracy as if we had 109 shootings with the load in question. The index is able to predict, for instance, that this Winchester 9 x 23mm 125-grain Silvertip will have 93 percent one-shot stops before anyone is shot with it.

Energy is the key to stopping power. Actually, it is energy transfer that is the key. How do we get the bullet to transfer the most energy? The answer is to get the bullet to expand or fragment. And the two keys to getting the bullet to expand, almost independent of energy, are impact velocity and hollowpoint design.

At velocities below 900 feet per second (fps), the bullet needs to have an extremely aggressive hollowpoint design to expand. At velocities above 1200 fps, nearly all hollowpoints expand regardless of design. Put another way, at 900 fps, a Federal Hydra-Shok is more likely to expand than a Hornady XTP-HP due to its design. At 1200 fps, all hollowpoints expand in bare gelatin. At 1400 fps, all hollowpoints and most softpoints expand, even after passing through layers of heavy clothing.

Shooters with short-barreled guns must heed the same advice. As the barrel length on a .45 ACP, for example, drops from 5 inches to 4 1/4 inches to 3 1/2 inches to 3 inches, the bullet weight must also drop in order to maintain enough impact velocity to

expand. A 230-grain JHP will expand at 816 fps from a 5 inch gun but not at 738 fps from a 3 inch gun. You need to drop in weight from 230 grains to 200 grains to 185 grains to 165 grains as the barrel length gets shorter to keep the impact velocity as high as possible.

All hollowpoint bullets have a "threshold of expansion." This is the velocity at which the bullet just begins to expand under ideal conditions. For most handgun hollowpoint designs, it is between 750 and 850 fps. The shooter should select the load with as much safety factor as possible. A bullet that has a threshold of expansion at 850 fps will be an unreliable performer when fired at 900 fps. On the other hand, a JHP with a threshold of expansion at 850 fps will expand every single time when fired at 1350 fps.

The threshold of expansion for the various bullets is not common knowledge, and it is subject to change as the ammo makers make improvements. Select a bullet with as high an impact velocity as you can to be sure the bullet expands. Simply put, in the .40 S&W caliber, for example, the 155-grain JHP at 1200 fps is *much* more likely to expand over a wide cross-section of shooting scenarios than a 180-grain JHP at 950 fps. An extra bonus is that the 1200 fps load also produces more energy. The result is more energy and more energy transfer and more stopping power.

The muzzle energy of the bullet is just the starting point for predicting stopping power. Even more telling is the amount of this energy that is actually transferred to the target. The .44 Magnum and .41 Magnum have much more muzzle energy than the .357 Magnum and .40 S&W. However, the .357 Magnum and .40 S&W have better results in actual shootings. This confuses many people. The reason is that while the .357 Magnum and .40 S&W have less energy, they transfer more of the energy they do have. And they transfer it at a depth that is meaningful to personal defense. Of course, when the target changes from an adult human to a brown bear or a Cape buffalo, all of this changes.

When we compare muzzle energy to stopping power, we find that the best street loads generate at least 400 ft-lbs. of energy. The 9mm 115-grain JHP +P+ with a 93 percent one-shot stop produces 432 ft-lbs. The .40 S&W 155-grain JHP with a 97 percent record produces 495 ft-lbs. The .357 Magnum 125-grain JHP with a 96 percent success produces 580 ft-lbs.

In comparison, the 9mm 147-grain JHP with 295 ft-lbs. is 78 percent effective. The .40 S&W 180-grain JHP with 360 ft-lbs. is 86 percent effective. The .380 ACP 90-grain JHP with 200 ft-lbs. is 69 percent effective.

The street results also show that energy from a handgun bullet over 675 ft-lbs. is nearly wasted. In a practical sense, a police round that produces more than 580 ft-lbs. of energy simply produces more recoil than it should. You do not gain much stopping power; you just slow down the shot-to-shot recovery time.

It is the amount of energy transferred that determines stopping power. This also includes how soon the energy is transferred, how much energy should be considered a minimum, and how much is a practical maximum.

The three general rates of energy transfer are early, medium, and late. The handgun bullet design itself determines how rapidly energy is transferred. The extremely lightweight jacketed hollowpoints and the frangible bullets like MagSafe, Glaser, and BeeSafe all produce an early energy release. In gelatin, the wound profile is spherical (softball) in shape, with an early and well-defined peak. The maximum diameter of the temporary stretch cavity may occur in the 2 to 4 inch deep range.

This kind of ammo is excellent for personal, home, and car defense, police off-duty, and police backup use. It is also an excellent choice for on-duty police work during transit and housing patrol, courtroom and school security, and VIP protection. In those scenarios, the shooter is likely to fire a frontal or near frontal shot and is unlikely to face barriers like glass or metal. The most common barrier in this type of shooting is an upper arm or forearm. On a frontal, upper torso shot, the combination of this type of ammunition, energy release, and wound profile is extremely effective.

The medium-weight hollowpoints and some heavy hollowpoints produce a medium energy release. The term "medium" means medium for the caliber. In the .40 S&W, for example, the 135-grain JHP is considered light, the 150- to 165-grain JHPs are considered medium, and the 180-grain JHP is considered heavy. The same 185-grain JHP is considered light in the .45 ACP, while a 147-grain JHP is considered heavy in the 9mm.

In gelatin, the wound profile from a medium-energy release load is oval (football) in shape, with a deeper and less-defined peak. The maximum diameter may be at 5 inches, but the diameter from the 3 inch mark to the 7 inch depth is about the same.

This kind of ammo is ideal for general-purpose police work. In these scenarios the officer is likely to fire cross-torso through the felon and is very likely to engage glass and sheet metal prior to striking the target. Some police-fired shots will be frontal while others will need to penetrate auto glass, a car seat, and a shoulder bone en route to vital organs.

The ideal police bullet is a compromise. Much like the officer or deputy himself, the police bullet will face a wide variety of shooting scenarios. He or she needs to perform like a SWAT officer in some scenarios, marriage counselor in others, and paramedic in others. The police bullet, likewise, must be a jack-of-all-trades. It may not perform like a specially selected bullet in any one scenario, but it should perform well overall in all scenarios.

The medium-energy bullets work well in this criteria. Some of the energy will be transferred early for something like a frontal torso shot, while some of the energy will be transferred later if the bullet has to defeat a tactical barrier first. We cannot have the police duty bullet dumping all of its energy in the biceps of the upper arm and not retain enough juice for deeper penetration. Likewise, we cannot have the it dump energy so late that it has traveled beyond the vital organs in the upper torso before the bullet starts to work well.

Most heavy hollowpoints and all nonexpanding bullets like the semiwadcutter, full wadcutter, round-nose lead, and FMJ hardball produce a late energy release. In gelatin, the wound profile is cylinder in shape. The stretch cavity doesn't really have a peak—it is the same, or nearly the same, for almost the entire bullet path. This kind of ammo is well-suited for hunting but not very effective for most defensive or police use.

Projectiles with a late energy release, or almost constant energy release, typically expand very little and penetrate very deep. The lack of

Actual street results show that bullet penetration anywhere in the 8.4 to 12.8 inch range is ideal for civilian and police use alike. The worst performance comes from ammo that penetrates deeper than 14.6 inches of gelatin. This Winchester .40 S&W 180-grain Supreme SXT subsonic hollowpoint penetrates exactly 12 inches of gelatin.

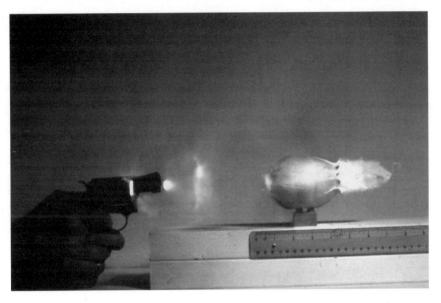

Stopping power is not that hard to understand. It is simply a matter of energy transfer. Bullets that transfer the most energy, regardless of how much they start with and regardless of how they go about doing it, produce the most stopping power.

expansion causes the deep penetration. Heavy hollowpoints that expand well produce a medium energy release, while heavy hollowpoints that do not expand well produce a late energy release.

Two police and defensive bullets were specifically designed as late energy release hollowpoints: the original Winchester Black Talon and the Hornady XTP-HP. In actual police shootings, bullets with both

these designs ended up at the bottom of the chart in terms of effectiveness. This was true regardless of caliber.

Winchester has since redesigned its bullet to produce a medium energy release. The resulting new bullet, the Ranger Talon, or T-series, has extremely promising gelatin performance. The Hornady XTP-HP remains largely unchanged. It works the best only at extremely high impact velocities.

Nearly every handgun caliber has the same differences in street results within the same caliber. Some loads incapacitate the attacker just 60 percent of the time with one hit to the torso. Some incapacitate more than 90 percent of the time with one shot. Thanks to three decades of work by Evan Marshall, we now know for sure which loads give what kind of performance in actual gunfights.

The projectile should stagger the bad guy with the very first shot. The felon should know he is hit. But what is a stagger? What does the bullet have to do to cause this? The purpose of the defensive bullet is to shift the thought process of the attacker. Stopping power, in the defensive scenario, is not what you hit but how hard you hit it. You want the bullet to have an instant effect, and ideally you want it to have a visible effect—you want the attacker's knees to buckle. Most low-energy bullets do not have much of a visual effect. A puffing of the clothes may be the only sign the person is hit.

As Keith Jones stated in Chapter 1, you want your first shot to damage, disrupt, disorient, and distract. The goal is to buy time for the second and third shots that will almost certainly be required. The shooter does not have time to wait for the effects of the gunfire. He needs to keep shooting, change positions, and create time to take better aim and make follow-up shots. Heed the advice from gunfight veterans, especially those involved in multiple gunfights in their police career: use the first shot to buy time for the follow-up shots.

This is where the one-shot stop results are especially helpful. They tell us which caliber and bullet combination is the most likely to stop the fight with one torso hit. These same results also tell us which bullet is the most likely to distract, disrupt, and delay further action by the attacker.

The loads with the highest one-shot stop rating are the most likely to stop the attack outright and the most likely to buy time for follow-up shots.

As we enter the new millennium, the Fuller Index remains the state-of-the-art in predicting stopping power. In turn, the Fuller Index is firmly rooted in Evan Marshall's compilation of actual results. If we want to know how handgun ammo will work against human targets in the future, we must look at how similar ammo has worked against human targets in the past.

CHAPTER 3

.32 ACP Ammo

The .32 Automatic Colt Pistol (ACP) cartridge was designed in 1899 by John Moses Browning for his first successful semiautomatic pistol. The .32 ACP, also known as the 7.65mm Browning, has enjoyed a century of popularity.

John Browning was involved in the design of everything from pocket pistols to antiaircraft artillery. Browning-designed weapons have been produced by Remington, Winchester, FN Herstal, and, of course, Colt. His pistols have been of two basic designs: the pocket pistol with a straight blowback action chambered in smaller calibers, and the military pistol with a locked-breech action in larger calibers. The Baby Browning, the Model 1906, in .25 ACP is one of his most famous blowback designs, while the 9mm Browning Hi-Power and the .45 ACP Colt Government Model are his most famous locked-breech pistols.

The .32 ACP was introduced on a Belgium-made Fabrique Nationale pistol in 1899. The caliber hit American shores when Colt produced a pocket autoloader based on the Browning-patented Model 1903. Colt, Remington, Smith & Wesson, Harrington & Richardson, and Savage

Arms have all made pistols chambered for the .32 ACP. It was even chambered in the German-made Pickert revolver. The most famous modern pistols in this caliber today are the Seecamp and the Beretta Tomcat.

The .32 ACP had been the standard police caliber in Europe for decades. It was as popular there as the .38 Special was here. As European police upgraded to the .380 ACP and finally the 9mm, a number of surplus .32 ACP pistols became available for import.

The .32 ACP is considered by some to be the minimum size that can be "seriously considered" for self-defense. With a muzzle energy of around 130 ft-lbs., this is a curious and provocative statement. Most would argue that the .380 ACP and .38 Special with 200 ft-lbs. are the minimum. The more street-savvy probably point to the 9mm +P+ with 400 ft-lbs. as the minimum. The .32 ACP, like the .25 ACP and the .22 Long Rifle, is what it is: better than nothing.

The .32 ACP operates at a maximum chamber pressure of 16,900 cup (copper units of pressure). This is slightly less than the 19,900 cup used by the .25 ACP. Like the .25 and the

.38 Super Auto, the .32 ACP uses a semirimmed cartridge case.

European versions of the .32 ACP fire a .312 to .314 inch diameter bullet. The true bullet diameter is actually closer to .308 inch. Handloaders have successfully used the Speer .308 caliber 100-grain JSP Plinker and the .30 Luger 93-grain FMJ in the .32 ACP.

The classic and still most popular loading in .32 ACP is the 71-grain hardball. All the ammo makers who load the .32 have a 71-grain FMJ. These loads typically run about 900 fps and penetrate in excess of 18 inches of gelatin. This means the tiny FMJ bullet will almost certainly exit, even on a torso shot. However, the exit energy after 12 inches of 10 percent gelatin is just 23 ft-lbs. The U.S. Army has stated that 58 ft-lbs. of energy is necessary to produce a casualty.

The stopping power from these 71-grain FMJ loads is surprisingly high, even compared to the JHP, semiexotic JHP, and exotic frangible loads. The Fuller Index for the hardball ammo is between 45 and 46 percent one-shot stops; the actual results from 156 shootings with the 71-grain FMJ is 49 percent. The average Fuller Index for all the .32 ACP hollowpoints is 43 percent one-shot

The Winchester .32 ACP 60-grain Silvertip expands to the largest recovered diameter of any JHP in its caliber. The pure aluminum jacketed bullet expands under the most diverse scenarios.

a load with only 120 ft-lbs. of energy that expands to .55 caliber and penetrates just 6 to 7 inches of gelatin. And 66 percent stands in sharp contrast to the Fuller Index, which predicts closer to a 45 percent effectiveness.

Again, the Fuller Index is as accurate in predicting stopping power as if 109 shootings had taken place with a hollowpoint, or 270 shootings had taken place with a solidpoint. Of the more than 13,500 shootings in dozens of different calibers and loads collected by Evan Marshall, the .32 ACP 60-grain Silvertip is the one load

the two popular pocket pistol calibers on either side of the .32. The Fuller Index for loads in these calibers is within 6 percentage points of the actual one-shot stop and equally split between underestimated and overestimated. The one-shot stop on the .32 ACP 60-grain Silvertip is 21 percentage points better than predicted.

Another attempted explanation involves the total number of shootings involved. This might make sense if the .32 ACP Silvertip had been used in only a dozen or so shootings. However, it has been used 110 times,

stops, making the .32 ACP the only caliber where hardball is estimated to work as well as hollowpoints! This is just the first of the oddities with this caliber. There are others.

All hardball ammo is alike. One of the more interesting versions is the 65-grain FMJ from Federal. The company makes two .32 ACP hardball loads: 71-grain and 65-grain. The Norma-based 65-grain is only available in their American Eagle line. It clocks at 845 fps, compared to between 890 and 934 fps for the other 71-grain FMJ loads.

The first of the .32 ACP hollowpoints, and still clearly the best, is the Winchester 60-grain Silvertip. Bullets in the Silvertip line have a variety of jacket materials, including nickel-plated, copper-zinc, and an aluminum-manganese alloy. This particular .32 ACP bullet is the only Silvertip in the line to use a pure aluminum jacket. The Seecamp auto pistol is specifically designed around the overall length, feed profile, and exterior ballistics of the 60-grain Silvertip.

The 66 percent one-shot stop rating from the 60-grain Silvertip is extremely controversial. This street effectiveness equals the 9mm 115-grain FMJ, the .45 ACP 230-grain FMJ, and the .380 ACP 85-grain Silvertip. This seems way too high for

The Winchester .32 ACP 60-grain Silvertip penetrates just 6.2 inches of BB-calibrated, 10 percent ordnance gelatin. Yet this Silvertip is as effective in actual gunfights as the .45 ACP 230-grain FMJ!

that performs the farthest from the Fuller Index prediction.

One possible explanation for this difference is that handgunners with a .32 ACP know that the cartridge is underpowered. As a result, even though the one-shot stop methodology allows one shot anywhere to the torso, perhaps the .32 ACP shooter is more precise in his fire as a way to make up for this lower power.

As good as that sounds, it is not the case for the .25 ACP or .380 ACP,

which is a fairly large number. The Hydra-Shok and the Gold Dot have a 15 and 20 percentage point difference between their Fuller Index and their street record, but this can be partially explained by a lower number of actual shootings.

The incredible success of the .32 ACP Silvertip remains just that: incredible, controversial, and arguable. For this reason, and for an apples-to-apples comparison with other .32 ACP loads, the stopping power of the 60-

The Federal .32 ACP 65-grain Hydra-Shok expands to .47 caliber and penetrates 8.4 inches of gelatin. The low velocity, however, results in a Fuller Index of only 40 percent.

The CCI .32 ACP 60-grain Gold Dot offers reliable expansion and a low felt recoil. This copper-plated bullet has a Fuller Index of 45 percent.

grain Silvertip listed in Table 3-1 is based on the Fuller Index.

Very few .32 ACP hollowpoints expand after encountering heavy clothes. The ones that get plugged up and do *not* expand penetrate like hardball. In this case, the nonexpanding bullet with the most muzzle energy is the best defensive choice.

Ironically, the 60-grain Silvertip is the conventional JHP with the most energy. Even more ironic, the 71-grain FMJ hardball has more muzzle energy than the Silvertip. All of this helps to explain the relative success of hardball but doesn't really explain the success of the Silvertip.

The popularity of the Seecamp and the recent release of the Beretta Tomcat led to the introduction of the Federal 65-grain Hydra-Shok and the CCI-Speer 60-grain Gold Dot. (The

Hydra-Shok is the bullet with a post in the center of the hollowpoint cavity; the Gold Dot is the internally prestressed hollowpoint with a pure copper, electroplated jacket.) Both these loads expand well in bare gelatin. The Hydra-Shok produces slightly deeper penetration than the Silvertip and Gold Dot. The Hydra-Shok and the Gold Dot produce 60 percent one-shot stops in a limited number of shootings but have a Fuller Index rating of between 40 and 45 percent.

The old MagSafe company produced a 50-grain frangible Defender at 1250 fps. In gelatin, it fragmented and released its payload of #4 birdshot, which penetrated up to 7.8 inches. With its 174 ft-lbs. of energy, it had the highest Fuller Index of any .32 ACP load at 57 percent. These loads are now collector's items.

The new MagSafe company now produces a 36-grain Defender, the X-load, which has a velocity of 1215 fps. The new load has much less energy but still saturates the first 7 inches of gelatin with #4 birdshot. It has a Fuller Index of 45 percent.

Dating back to the 1960s, the

Glaser Safety Slug is the original frangible bullet. The Glaser in .32 ACP was introduced in 1983 as a flatpoint; the round-nose version came in 1987. In most calibers, the Glaser comes either as a Blue or a Silver Safety Slug. The Blue version fires a plastic-tipped jacket filled with compressed #12 birdshot. The Silver fires a payload of fused #6 birdshot. The .32 ACP, like the .25 ACP, is only available as a Blue Safety Slug.

Upon impact, the 55-grain Glaser saturates the first 5 inches of gelatin with its #12 birdshot. It has a Fuller Index of 48 percent. With just 5 inches of penetration, the .32 ACP Glaser will perform better than predicted on a frontal, upper torso shot but not nearly as well in the event of a poor shot placement.

Recently, Cor-Bon has entered the frangible market with its BeeSafe ammunition using bullets made by Beeline of Nova Scotia. The .32 ACP 52-grain BeeSafe has a payload of compressed #6 birdshot inside an aluminum jacket. Importantly, the birdshot is capped with a 23-grain, .25 caliber, #3 buckshot pellet to assure

The Glaser 55-grain Blue Safety Slug saturates the first 5 inches of gelatin with #12 birdshot. This load works the best with a front upper torso hit.

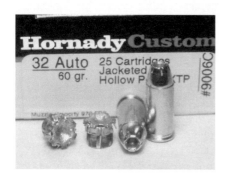

The Hornday .32 ACP 60-grain XTP expands slightly to .39 caliber. This allows it to penetrate deeper. This load has a Fuller Index of 41 percent one-shot stops.

deep penetration. Upon impact, this load fragments slightly—the pellets only disperse an inch or so away from the main bullet path. However, the buckshot pellet and jacket reach more than 10 inches deep. The result is a Fuller Index of 49 percent, among the best in the caliber.

The .32 ACP is an unusual caliber in that the frangible and exotic versions do not seem to be a great deal more effective than standard JHP ammo and hardball. The frangibles have the highest Fuller Index in the caliber, but the margin of superiority is not as high as in other calibers.

One of the most recent .32 ACP hollowpoints is the Hornady 60-grain XTP-HP. The XTP was the first bullet ever designed specifically to pass the FBI eight-media gelatin test protocol. It is also among the most accurate, if not the most accurate, of all handgun bullets. It generally expands less and penetrates more compared to other bullets, a distinct advantage in .25 ACP, .32 ACP, and .380 ACP. Police ammo experts expect a minimum penetration in gelatin somewhere between 9 and 12 inches, and the 60-grain XTP meets this criteria. In fact, the Hornady XTP is the only .32 hollowpoint that penetrates more than 9 inches of gelatin.

The XTP has a Fuller Index of 41 percent, which is a little low for a .32 ACP hollowpoint. However, its 10

inches of penetration sets this load apart. Nine inches is enough for serious defensive use, while more than 18 inches is clearly too much. The Cor-Bon BeeSafe, Triton Quik-Shok, and Hornady XTP are the only hollowpoints or frangibles to meet the 9 inch minimum.

The newest hollowpoint in the .32 ACP caliber is the Triton 60-grain Quik-Shok. Introduced at the 2000 SHOT Show, it is an XTP-style bullet with a prestressed core. The Quik-Shok bullets come in two varieties. The QS1 has longitudinal cuts that start in the

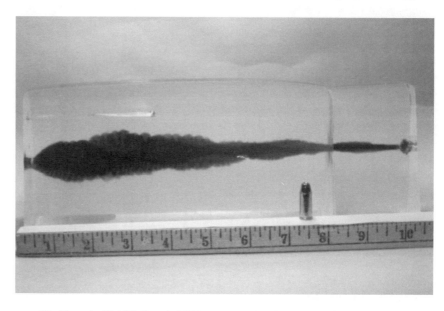

The Hornady .32 ACP 60-grain XTP penetrates 10 inches of BB-calibrated, 10 percent ordnance gelatin. This is the only standard hollowpoint to penetrate more than the police-oriented 9 inch depth.

center of the lead core and go almost to the outside diameter of the core. The QS2 has lengthwise cuts that start on the outside of the core and go almost to the center, leaving a small hub. With both designs, the bullets break into three pieces upon impact, even after passing through heavy clothes.

The .32 ACP 60-grain Quik-Shok at 968 fps uses the QS1 design to assure a uniform split into three 16-grain fragments. In comparison, a .24 caliber #4 buckshot pellet weighs 21 grains. Most of the Quik-Shok bullets in the

higher velocity calibers use the QS2 design, which actually slows down the rate of frag separation. Each of the large Quik-Shok frags penetrates 9 inches of gelatin in a separate wound path, and their irregular shape assures that the projectile will spread out in the gelatin. In the .32 ACP, the three frags fan out to 4 inches apart by the time they come to rest, making the Quik-Shok load one of the best self-defensive choices in this sub-mouse caliber.

In 1998, PMC announced a 60-grain JHP at 980 fps for the .32 ACP. Since then, the company has struggled to get the tiny bullet to perform up to its expectations. With just 125 ft-lbs. to work with, it is very difficult to get a hollowpoint to both expand reliably and penetrate adequately. This problem plagues all .25 ACP and most .380 ACP hollowpoints. As a result, the 60-grain JHP from PMC has been delayed until the design is perfected.

For accuracy testing (see Table 3-2), we fired these .32 ACP loads from a Llama Model X-A with a 3.6 inch barrel. It is hard to imagine actually shooting at anything 25 yards away with any .32 ACP pistol, but that was the distance used to print five-shot groups.

The most accurate loads from this military- and police-oriented single-action pistol were the PMC 71-grain FMJ and the Hornady 60-grain XTP-HP, with group sizes as small as 3.3 inches. The practical accuracy from the true pocket pistols with shorter barrels will not be this good.

The .32 ACP can be used for a wide variety of sporting, plinking, and defensive uses, including concealed carry. The recoil is something anyone old enough to shoot can handle. The pistols chambered in this caliber vary from compact to palm size. These guns really are easier to conceal and carry than the pistols chambered for the larger calibers.

All .32 ACP pistols are accurate enough to hit a man-sized target across a master bedroom. However, they will be much less effective than the .380 ACP pistols and .38 Special snub-nose revolvers. Practice with the .32 ACP pistol until you can achieve a frontal, upper torso shot placement every time. With the .32 ACP the Force is *not* with you!

TABLE 3-1
.32 ACP WOUND BALLISTICS

Make & Load	Velocity fps	Energy ft-lbs.	Expansion inch	Depth inches	Power Factor	Fuller Index %
Cor-Bon 52 gr. BeeSafe	1133	148	frag	10.8	59	49
Glaser 55 gr. Safety Slug	1055	136	frag	4.8	58	48
Triton 60 gr. Quik-Shok	968	125	3-frag	9.0	58	47
PMC 71 gr. FMJ	934	138	.31	19.6	66	46
CCI-Speer 60 gr. Gold Dot	827	91	.50	6.8	50	45
MagSafe 36 gr. Defender	1215	118	frag	7.0	44	45
Remington 71 gr. FMJ	890	125	.31	19.7	63	45
Winchester 60 gr. Silvertip	950	120	.55	6.2	57	45
Federal 65 gr. FMJ	845	103	.31	20.0	55	43
Hornady 60 gr. XTP-HP	883	104	.39	10.0	53	41
Federal 65 gr. Hydra-Shok	827	99	.47	8.4	54	40

TABLE 3-2
.32 ACP 25-YARD ACCURACY

Make & Load	5-Shot Group (inches)
PMC 71 gr. FMJ	3.3
Hornady 60 gr. XTP-HP	3.5
CCI-Speer 60 gr. Gold Dot	3.6
Triton 60 gr. Quik-Shok	3.8
Federal 65 gr. Hydra-Shok	4.2
Winchester 60 gr. Silvertip	4.9
Glaser 55 gr. Safety Slug	6.6
Federal 65 gr. FMJ	7.0
Remington 71 gr. FMJ	7.1
MagSafe 36 gr. Defender	8.6
Cor-Bon 52 gr. BeeSafe	10.2

CHAPTER 4

History of the 9mm

"Parabellum" was the telegraphic address of Deutsche Waffen & Munitionsfabrik (DWM) in Berlin, Germany. The word meant "prepare for war." Parabellum was also the trademark for various DWM weapons, the most famous of which was the pistol developed by Georg Luger. While the new semiautomatic pistol was officially marketed as a Parabellum, it was universally called a Luger.

The forerunner of the Parabellum auto pistol was invented by Hugo Borchardt. Borchardt was born in Germany and immigrated to the United States in 1865, where he became an American citizen. While in America, he worked for Pioneer Breechloading Arms, Colt's Patent Firearms, Sharps Rifle Company, and Winchester Repeating Arms. In 1882, Borchardt returned to Germany to develop his pistol with the Ludwig Lowe Company. He remained with Lowe when the arms company was taken over by DWM.

The Borchardt action was based on the Maxim toggle design. The biggest challenge with this design was the development of a rimless cartridge to work with the action. The bottlenecked and rimless 7.65mm case

The 9mm is flanked by other popular auto pistol cartridges, left to right: .380 ACP, 9mm Makarov, 9mm Luger, .40 S&W, 10mm Auto, and .45 ACP. The 9mm is the most popular military and police cartridge in the world.

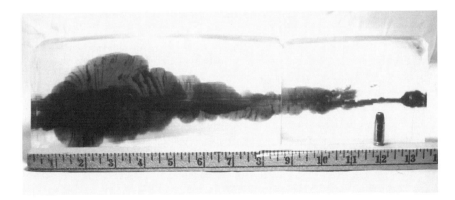

The 9mm is nearly 100 years old and available in four pressure levels—standard, +P, +P+, and NATO—and in bullet weights from 90 to 147 grains. The loads with the most success in actual shootings are the 115-grain +P and +P+ JHPs, like this 1300 fps offering from Black Hills.

The .30 Luger, or 7.65mm Parabellum cartridge, was designed specifically for the toggle-action Parabellum pistol. The 93-grain, .301 caliber FMJ was driven to 1220 fps. Note that this is a bottleneck cartridge.

The German arms maker DWM, simply opened the bottleneck case of the .30 Luger (left) and inserted a .355 caliber bullet. The 9mm Luger (right) was developed in 1902.

was specifically developed by DWM engineers for this new pistol.

Georg Luger worked with Borchardt to improve the auto pistol. Their goal was to make it less bulky, less complex, and more reliable. The first Luger pistol, chambered in the 7.65mm Parabellum cartridge, was adopted by the Swiss Army in 1900. The cartridge used a 93-grain .301-caliber FMJ bullet driven to 1220 fps.

In 1901, the British, Belgian, Dutch, and American armies tested this new .30 Luger pistol. They all rejected it due to its tiny-caliber bullet. At that time, most of the world was oriented to calibers like the .45 Long Colt, .455 Webley, and .476 Enfield.

The Philippine Insurrection of 1899 was still a recent event, and it was the first significant live-fire trial for something other than a big-bore cartridge. The .38 Long Colt, firing a round-nose lead slug, was deemed a total failure from its performance in this on-going war. The double-action revolver "failed to give a good account of itself" against the fanatical Moro tribesmen. This prompted the famous recall-to-duty of the .45 Long Colt in the Colt Single Action Army. Most big-bore proponents fail to mention, however, that the .30-40 Krag rifle didn't always stop the drug-crazed Moros either.

Luger responded to this international demand for a larger

caliber auto pistol in 1902. DWM opened up the neck of the 7.65mm Parabellum bottleneck case and inserted a 9mm .355 caliber bullet. The company indicated that 9mm was the maximum caliber the Parabellum pistol design could easily handle.

In 1903, the U.S. Army traded 50 of its 7.65mm Lugers from the previous testing for bigger 9mm Lugers. Georg Luger himself brought these pistols in various barrel lengths to the United States. In 1904, the German Navy became the first military branch in the world to adopt the 9mm Luger.

The year 1904 is perhaps best known as the date the U.S. Army established a caliber review board. It was led by Maj. Louis LaGarde of the Army Medical Corps and Capt. John Thompson of the Army Ordnance Department. The Thompson-LaGarde tests would influence the next 80 years of small arms decision making.

Nine different calibers were involved in these tests, held primarily at the Chicago stockyards. These cartridges included the .30 Luger, 9mm Luger, .38 Long Colt, .38 Auto, .45 Long Colt, .455 Webley, .476 Enfield, and others. During the wound ballistics tests, Thompson and LaGarde shot 13 hed of cattle, 10 cadavers, and two horses.

Significantly, all of the test bullets were either round-nose lead, jacketed

softpoint, cup point, or FMJ hardball. Nothing like the modern jacketed hollowpoint was tested. All the Lugers fired FMJ bullets, while the revolver cartridges shot soft lead bullets. These lead bullets were later ruled as unacceptable for military use.

In his 1914 book, *Gunshot Wounds*, Major LaGarde concluded, "The tests showed that the .476 caliber lead bullet has the greatest stopping power." This load was the .476 Enfield Mark III, which fired a 288-grain RNL bullet at 729 fps. In the final analysis, Thompson and LaGarde concluded, "No pistol smaller than .45 caliber should be considered for military service." These tests were widely accepted, and as a result, the American military shunned the 9mm.

The U.S. Army really wanted a Colt semiauto like the Model 1900 it had tested in the 1904 pistol trials. However, it did not want the .38 Auto cartridge. With the .45 it wanted firmly in mind, the army set up a new round of pistol trials. In 1906, a handful of Parabellums chambered for a .45 caliber cartridge were hand-built. DWM entered two of these pistols in the 1907 U.S. Army tests, the same tests that would eventually lead to the Colt Model 1911 in .45 ACP.

The .45 caliber Parabellum performed so well in the first series of tests that the U.S. Army wanted to purchase 200 more pistols for later troop trials. The problem with this request was one of timing—in 1908, the German Army adopted the DWM Pistole-08 chambered for the 9mm (setting the stage for worldwide acceptance of both the pistol and cartridge). Because DWM was busy tooling up for the German Army contract, it was unwilling to devote resources to make 200 special-caliber pistols on the calculated chance they would be adopted by the U.S. Army. The American military's enthusiasm for the Colt Models 1900 and 1905 was not lost on DWM (although the army did postpone the tests for months so Luger could compete).

In the final round of tests, conducted in March 1911, the Colt Model 1911 beat the Savage .45 pistol and was awarded the U.S. contract. The Model 1905 fired a 200-grain blunt-nosed .45-caliber bullet at 910 fps. This was the original .45 ACP loading. By 1911, the bullet weight

Pistole). The German Army then insisted on an external hammer. This became the Model HP (Heeres Pistole). In 1938, the German Army adopted the Walther Model HP, calling it the Pistole-38.

In 1927 and again in 1934, Gen. Julian Hatcher converted the

nonexpanding bullets. Modern writers who attempt to update Hatcher's theory to include higher velocity and expanding or fragmenting bullets do the General a grave injustice. They also violate a basic tenant of predictive statistics. Predictive formulas are only good for loads that have velocities and bullet weights and styles within the scope of the loads used to develop the formulas. The Hatcher formulas cannot be validly used for the high-speed expanding bullets we have had since the 1960s.

For what they knew, Thompson and LaGarde, and later Hatcher, were right to avoid the 9mm in favor of the .45 ACP when both fired FMJ bullets. The 9mm hardball has a Hatcher Index between 28 and 30. The non +P .38 Special round-nose lead checks in between 30 and 31. The .45 ACP ball, on the other hand, has a Hatcher Index between 60 and 62.

The actual street results based on 315 shootings with 9mm FMJ hardball and 575 shootings with .45 ACP FMJ hardball, however, do *not* reflect this 2-to-1 difference. The 9mm ball actually has a 70 percent one-shot stop record compared to 62 percent for .45 ACP ball. Even still, the Thompson-LaGarde tests dominated military and police thinking for the next 80 years.

Near the end of World War II, the U.S. Army held meetings to see how well all of its firearms and ordnance were working. It was looking for what improvements could be made and what new equipment was needed. Fresh from battle, the soldiers did indeed have something to say. In no uncertain terms, the Colt 1911 was said to be too heavy and too bulky. The .45 ACP cartridge was said to kick too much. Overall, the complaint was that the single-action, big-bore auto pistol was too difficult to shoot.

In 1945, the Ordnance Department's Infantry Board studied future weapons and wrote up "military characteristics" for the ideal new army pistol. These specs called for a lightweight, double-action auto pistol

This 1914 Pistole-08 made by Erfurt is chambered in 9mm Luger. The P-08 made the 9mm world famous.

was bumped up to 230 grains. The original muzzle velocity was 860 fps, though over the years it was reduced to 830 fps and again down to today's level of 790 fps.

In 1930, Mauser took over production of the Parabellum pistol but retained the DWM toolmarks. Mauser discontinued production of the "original" pistol chambered for the 9mm in 1942.

Also in the 1930s, the German Army began a search for a replacement for the Parabellum. Walther was the first factory to respond with its Model PP now chambered in the 9mm. There was no way any modern army was going to adopt a straight blowback pistol for a cartridge as powerful as the 9mm.

Walther redesigned the Model PP to become the Model AP (Armee

Thompson-LaGarde tests into a formula in order to rank or predict stopping power. At a time when the other countries were adopting the 9mm as a service cartridge, Hatcher's Relative Stopping Power (RSP) scale served to dampen U.S. interest in the 9mm.

In reality, Hatcher's formulas turned out to be quite accurate in ranking near subsonic, nonhollowpoint bullets. In *Handgun Stopping Power* (Paladin Press, 1992), six of the original Thompson-LaGarde loads, including the 9mm, are compared to actual street results compiled by Evan Marshall. The ranking from best to worst for these six calibers is almost identical. The correlation coefficient is excellent.

As a rule, Hatcher was right in his predictions about lower velocity, chambered in the 9mm Luger! The last major purchase of Colt Model 1911 pistols by the military was made in 1945.

In 1953, the army's Springfield Armory made a request for single-action 9mm auto pistols to test for a possible military contract. Smith & Wesson and Colt were among those to supply steel frame autos. The results of this military interest and design effort were the Smith & Wesson Model 39 9mm pistol and the downsized Colt Commander single-action auto. The

In 1953, the U.S. Army's Springfield Armory made a request for a lighter and more compact pistol than the Colt Government Model. The army insisted it be chambered in 9mm. It tested both the double-action S&W Model 39 (shown) and the single-action Colt Commander. The only ammo available was 115- and 124-grain hardball.

aluminum frame Model 39 was introduced in 1954.

The U.S. Army lost interest in the 9mm project due to shifting priorities during peacetime. The expense to replace its large stockpiles of .45 ACP ammo and Model 1911 pistols, holsters, magazines, and spare parts was considered too high for the benefit.

The service pistol controversy was quiet from the mid-1950s until 1963. In that year, the U.S. Air Force abruptly dropped the Model 1911 as its official sidearm and replaced it with

.38 Special double-action revolvers like the S&W Model 15.

In the mid-1960s, the ammunition industry was revolutionized by Lee Jurras and his tiny Super Vel Company in Shelbyville, Indiana. Super Vel produced extremely lightweight hollowpoint bullets and drove them to record velocities for a handgun load.

The big winners in stopping power were to be the .38 Special and 9mm. In the 9mm, the Super Vel 90-grain hollowpoint had an actual 4 inch muzzle velocity of 1485 fps; the 112-grain softpoint had a velocity of 1330 fps. At the time, the .38 Special and .357 Magnum fired 158-grain solid lead bullets, while the 9mm and .45 ACP were only available in FMJ ball. These fully jacketed round-nose bullets were deemed absolutely necessary to achieve absolute feed reliability.

For that time, the use of either lightweight hollowpoints *and* velocities of 1300 to 1400 fps was scandalous. The 1974 issue of *Gun Digest* called

Super Vel cartridges "perhaps the most powerful and destructive of all these calibers commercially manufactured."

It took both a hollowpoint design and a high-speed, lightweight bullet for the 9mm to be effective. Hollowpoints would later be developed to exotic designs like the Hydra-Shok, which would indeed expand at lower velocities, but that was decades down the road.

In the early 1970s, the Super Vel concepts of lightweight and high-velocity hollowpoints were proven to be most effective on the street. It seems every generation of shooters and cops has to learn this for themselves the hard way. At any rate, the entire ammo industry followed Super Vel's lead. Lightweight hollowpoints were soon available in all calibers, tipping the scales in favor of the medium-bore bullets like the 9mm.

Remington became the first of the Big Three ammo makers to produce a hollowpoint for the 9mm in the early 1970s. This was the 115-grain JHP driven to 1160 fps. At that time Winchester had 100-grain "Power Point" softpoints and Federal had only 123-grain FMJ ball. The .38 Special +P 158-grain lead hollow-point was released by Winchester in 1972.

In 1973, the 9mm cartridge was

In the early 1970s, Remington became the first of the Big Three to offer a 9mm 115-grain JHP. These standard-pressure JHPs produce superior wound ballistics comparable to the subsonic hollowpoints developed in the mid 1980s.

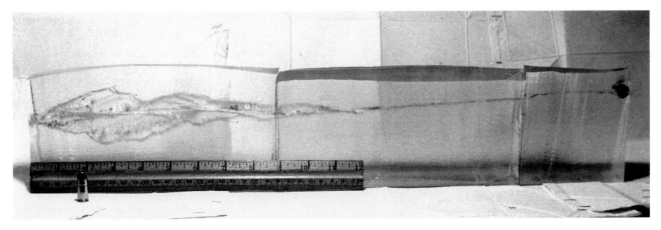

The Winchester 9mm 100-grain "Power Point" softpoint at 1325 fps was one of the first attempts to improve stopping power from the 9mm. This JSP seldom expanded and, as a result, produced excessive penetration.

given its first good press in ages. The National Institute of Justice funded a complex study of wound ballistics and stopping power. The study was released in 1975, and an updated version was published again in 1980. All police and defensive calibers and dozens of loads within each caliber were ranked from best to worst. Shockingly and stirring great controversy, the 9mm 115-grain hollowpoints were ranked better than the .45 ACP hollowpoints. This ranking was based on the Relative Incapacitation Index for each load.

The RII has its roots in the "energy deposit" theory developed by the U.S. Army in the late 1960s, which states that stopping power is related to the amount of energy transferred to the target. Contrary to popular belief, the U.S. Army has been as divided over "energy versus momentum" as the rest of the world's shooters, having been internally split on this issue since the pioneering work of Col. Frank Chamberlin of the Army Medical Corps, a contemporary of Gen. Julian Hatcher.

The army's energy deposit theory did not account for how rapidly the energy was dumped. The RII took into account the effects of both early and late energy transfer. The RII, however, did not account for quartering or cross-torso shot placements; it was based on frontal shots only. Even still, the RII predictions are in close agreement with actual street results compiled by Marshall.

The RII was a computer simulation based on the average marksmanship of soldiers, the relative importance of the organs, vessels, and tissue in various parts of the body, and how much this tissue is disrupted in the wake of a passing bullet. It was the first time most cops had ever heard about either ordnance gelatin or the temporary stretch cavity.

The Thompson-LaGarde tests favored a heaver bullet weight, a larger bullet diameter, and a flatter bullet nose. In today's calibers, the ideal load according to these tests would be a .45 Long Colt firing a 250-grain, cylinder-shaped slug at 900 fps.

The RII, on the other hand, favored a higher bullet velocity, medium bullet diameters, and expanding or fragmenting bullets. The Glaser Safety Slug won the RII outright. In 1992, the Glaser and MagSafe won the Strasbourg goat tests outright. Both are high-speed frangible bullets. According to the RII, the ideal load among conventional ammo in the same recoil range as the .45 Long Colt would be a .357 Magnum 125-grain JHP at 1450 fps. This is where the push came to

develop the 9mm +P+ 115-grain JHP at 1300 fps.

According to the Fuller Index, the .45 Colt 255-grain semiwadcutter at 800 fps will produce one-shot stops 73 percent of the time. The .357 Magnum 125-grain JHP at 1450 fps is up to 96 percent effective. The 9mm +P+ 115-grain JHP has an 89 to 91 percent rating. However, actual results like these were not available until the late 1980s. All we had before then were theories. The bottom line is that the RII added fuel to the energy versus momentum debate and gave a tremendous boost to the 9mm cartridge.

The 9mm had always had the potential to be a credible manstopper, but the load selection didn't release this potential. Around 1978, only a few hollowpoints were available. Winchester and CCI had 100-grain JHPs, and Federal, Remington, and Smith & Wesson had 115-grain JHPs. Most shooters still used FMJ ball.

Perhaps the biggest development during this era was the release of the Winchester 9mm 115-grain Silvertip hollowpoint in late 1978. The 9mm Silvertip was widely available by early 1980. It was originally released with a manganese-aluminum jacket but was soon upgraded to a nickel-plated, copper-zinc jacket.

Out of this first generation of 115-

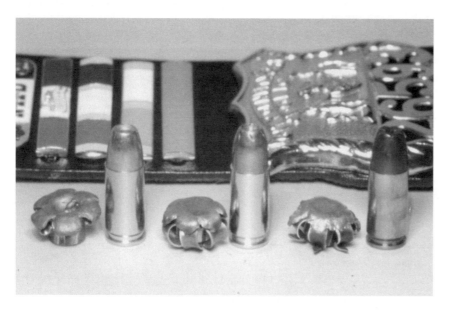

The New York City PD was one of the last major metro departments to adopt a hollowpoint. It tested the Federal 124-grain +P Hydra-Shok (left) and the Winchester 127-grain +P Ranger Talon (right) before selecting the CCI-Speer 124-grain +P Gold Dot (center).

grain JHPs from all ammo makers, the Federal 9mm 9BP emerged as the clear street fighter. To this day you do not hear any of the failure-to-stop horror stories from cops using the Federal 9BP as you hear from cops using variations of the 147-grain subsonic hollowpoint.

Compared to Europe, the adoption of the 9mm by American police was agonizingly slow. In 1980, nearly all cops were still armed with revolvers and debating dump boxes for reloading versus the "new fangled plastic thing" called a speedloader. In 1981, nearly every state police and highway patrol issued the double-action revolver. Troopers in New York, Florida, Indiana, and New Jersey, for example, packed the .357 Magnum, while those in Michigan, Ohio, Delaware, and Virginia carried the .38 Special.

At that time, the *only* state police or major police department anywhere to issue an auto pistol was the Illinois State Police (ISP). The 9mm +P+ cartridge traces its history back to the 9mm High Pressure jointly developed by Federal Cartridge and the ISP.

In 1966, the ISP became the first

The first major police department to switch from the .357 Magnum to the 9mm was the Illinois State Police. It started out with the 124-grain FMJ hardball (left), then went to 95-grain softpoints (center) in an attempt to improve stopping power. It then worked with Federal to develop the 115-grain JHP "high pressure" (right).

major police agency to adopt the 9mm auto pistol when it selected the S&W Model 39. The Remington-Peters 124-grain FMJ ball was the original duty load. Restricted to nonhollowpoints, the ISP set out to improve stopping power in 1969. Its first attempt was the 100-grain "thin-jacket" FMJ developed for the troopers by Winchester. The ISP had hoped to

reduce soft tissue penetration with this 1300 fps load but in reality saw no difference on the street.

Next, the ISP tried the 100-grain "Power Point" JSP also developed specifically for them by Winchester. Even at 1300 fps, the softpoint did not expand unless bone was hit. The Federal 95-grain cup point at 1320 fps performed the same.

In 1978, the ISP received approval to adopt hollowpoints. Its first choice was the new aluminum-jacketed 115-grain Silvertip. Due to accuracy, bore fouling, and stopping power problems, this load was withdrawn and replaced with the Winchester 95-grain JSP at 1355 fps until a solution could be found. In late 1979, the Silvertip received its copper jacket.

In 1980, the ammo contract was awarded to Federal and the ISP issued the 115-grain 9BP. Even so, the agency wanted performance against people and car bodies identical to the .357 Magnum carried by surrounding states.

Since Federal had the ISP contract, it was Federal that pioneered the 9mm High Pressure. This was the forerunner of today's 9mm +P+. The company bumped the velocity from 1160 fps to 1260 for the load it labelled 9BPLE. This load, unchanged since its introduction, has gone on to dominate the 9mm caliber.

In 1982, the ISP developed its own internal standards for the load with a minimum velocity of 1300 fps. Federal declined to push its bullet that fast, which left Winchester as the only ammo maker to meet the spec. Winchester has had the contract ever since. Under the original produce code Q4174 and, more recently, Ranger RA9115HP+, the famous Illinois State Police load has been the envy of nearly every cop and civilian who owned a 9mm auto pistol.

In 1987, Remington joined the other two in offering the 9mm 115-grain JHP loaded to +P+ pressures. Today, Remington, Cor-Bon, Triton, Black Hills, and Georgia Arms all produce a +P civilian version of this

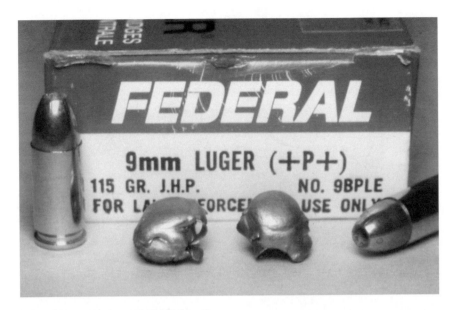

The Illinois State Police began work with Federal to develop the 9mm "high pressure," then perfected the load while working with Winchester. These are the best loads in the caliber.

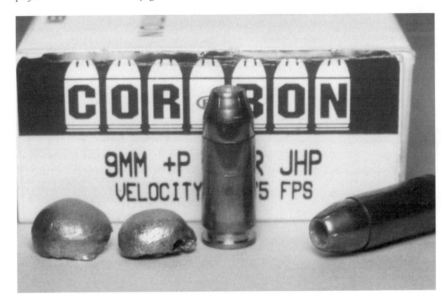

Cor-Bon made big news in the late 1980s by making a 9mm 115-grain +P JHP at 1330 fps for all shooters. Before Cor-Bon, these 1300 fps JHPs were restricted to law enforcement. Now nearly all ammo makers have a +P JHP available for civilians.

great load. The current duty load of the Los Angeles Police Department is the Remington 9mm 115-grain +P hollowpoint.

The standard-pressure 9mm has a product average maximum chamber pressure of 37,400 psi. The 9mm +P is loaded to 38,500 psi, while the limits for the 9mm +P+ are 40,000 psi. As a reference, 9mm NATO has a loading limit of 42,000 psi and 9mm "proof loads" are 49,800 psi.

The 9mm 115-grain JHP cartridge loaded to +P and +P+ pressures with 1260 to 1330 fps velocities produces the most stopping power for the caliber, period. Tests in ordnance gelatin predicted this. The Strasbourg Tests predicted this. Actual results from officer-involved shootings compiled by Marshall confirmed this. With these +P and +P+ loads, the 9mm is nearly equal to the best .40 S&W and .45 ACPs.

In 1976, the U.S. Air Force began to evaluate commercial 9mm auto pistols in an attempt to replace a wide variety of .38 Special revolvers then in use. In 1977, the U.S. Department of Defense asked the House Appropriations Committee for the money to design a new .38 auto pistol cartridge. Instead, the DOD was told to evaluate existing military guns and calibers. At the time, military stockpiles contained 25 different handguns and 100 kinds of handgun ammunition.

In 1978, the job to test and standardize the military sidearm was given to the Joint Services Small Arms Program (JSSAP). After much debate and testing, in 1980 JSSAP recommended the use of a 9mm cartridge for future military use.

The choice of the 9mm was made for both political and practical reasons. Politically, the rest of the free world was standardized on the 9mm. Practically, soldiers did indeed continue to complain that the Model 1911 was too big, too heavy, and too hard to shoot. That was probably the military's best kept secret.

Between 1981 and 1984, numerous tests of eight different 9mm pistols were conducted. These tests all included the Colt Model 1911 in .45 ACP as a control. All the pistols were double action/single action.

In the final analysis, only the SIG-Sauer and the Beretta were considered to have passed the battery of tests and were eligible to bid. Beretta produced the overall low bid. The following was announced January 14, 1985, during the SHOT Show in Atlanta, Georgia:

"The Department of Army as Executive Agent for the Department of Defense today announced the winner of its competition for a 9mm personal defense weapon. The Beretta USA Corporation of Accokeek, Maryland, has been selected to supply the new standard handgun to be used by the U.S. Army, Navy, Air Force, Marines, and Coast Guard. A five-year, multiyear fixed price contract for 315,930 weapons will be awarded to Beretta in approximately 30 days."

"The army's decision was based on a thorough test and evaluation of eight candidate weapons from both American and foreign manufacturers. The Beretta was one of only two candidates to satisfactorily complete a rigorous test program designed to verify both performance and durability under both normal and adverse environmental conditions. It met or exceeded all mandatory requirements and was judged to have the lowest overall costs and provides potential future savings over the life of the weapon due to durability advantages."

"The 9mm Beretta will be the first new military handgun since the introduction of the .45 caliber pistol in 1911. The need for a new standard handgun was reflected in a 1978 House of Appropriations Committee Survey that showed a proliferation of handguns and ammunition among the services. The adoption of a 9mm standard handgun and ammunition will provide compatibility with our NATO allies and result in savings and efficiencies due to its enhanced reliability, better performance, and lighter weight."

The pistol selected was the Model 92 SB-F. This sidearm traces its roots back to the Beretta Model 1934 (itself a refinement of the basic 1915 design) chambered in .380 ACP and to the Beretta Model 1951 Brigadier in 9mm. The Beretta Model 92 SB-F became the military M9. Ammo for the M9 was type classified as M882 in April 1985. The 9 x 19mm cartridge case used a 124-grain 9mm FMJ bullet driven by 9mm NATO pressures. The official muzzle velocity was 1263 fps, plus or minus 45 fps when fired from a 7.8 inch test barrel. When fired from an M9, the actual velocity is indeed 1273 fps.

The military testing and adoption of the 9mm gave this caliber the

credibility that most cautious cops needed. Police departments across the country traded in their .38 Special and .357 Magnum revolvers for 9mm auto pistols. The Connecticut State Police became the second state police agency to adopt the 9mm. In 1983, it selected the Beretta Model 92 SB. Other departments rapidly followed, as did many federal agencies like the Border Patrol.

In the mid-1980s, life was good for the 9mm. The police transition from the revolver to the 9mm pistol was in high gear. Skeptics of the auto pistol in general and the 9mm in particular were being silenced one by one. Then came April 11, 1986, and the FBI shootout in Miami.

Four FBI agents armed with 9mm auto pistols and .38 Special +P revolvers took on two fanatical thugs in a forced vehicle stop gone bad. One of the felons was armed with a Ruger Mini-14 rifle chambered in .223 Remington. In the middle of the protracted gunfight, Special Agent Jerry Dove hit the rifleman, Michael Platt, in the chest with a 9mm 115-grain Silvertip. The bullet first entered the biceps and exited the arm before entering the chest cavity and collapsing the right lung.

The 9mm Silvertip expanded and penetrated exactly as designed. It stopped on the way to, but short of, the heart. Platt continued his deadly rifle fire until he was stopped by a cylinder full of .38 Special +P 158-grain lead hollowpoints fired by Special Agent Ed Mireles into Platt's head and neck.

No one can know if Platt would have been stopped sooner if the lone Silvertip had penetrated an inch or so deeper. In very similar gunfights in Georgia, Indiana, and Montana, through-and-through heart shots still allowed the perps to continue firing for periods of time. Regardless, this one incident in Miami forever changed the police image of the 9mm and overall concepts of police ammunition.

The Miami tragedy ushered in a new era of police bullets, the so called

This Winchester 9mm 147-grain JHP was developed from a 140-grain subsonic sniper load used by the U.S. Navy SEALs. It would not cycle the guns, so the weight was increased to 145 grains, then 147 grains. None of the subsonic hollowpoints expand well in actual shootings.

"deep penetrators." The FBI was advised by a panel of specialists to look at either the hush-hush Winchester 9mm 147-grain subsonic hollowpoint, the Remington .45 ACP 185-grain hollowpoint, or a deep-penetrating load like a 9mm NATO 124-grain FMJ ball.

These loads all shared a common feature in wound ballistics—they did not expand very much. As a result, they generated tremendous soft tissue penetration. The Bureau eventually selected the 9mm 147-grain Olin Super Match hollowpoint from Winchester.

The 9mm subsonic was originally developed for the U.S. Navy SEALs to take out Viet Cong sentries and guard dogs at close range. The first subsonic load was a 9mm 158-grain FMJ ball. After Viet Nam, the Navy changed the emphasis to making 100-yard head and torso shots from submachine guns like the Uzi and MP5.

In the late 1970s Winchester met this accuracy demand with a 140-grain JHP, identified as Type B, but the load was found to produce too little recoil to reliably cycle the weapons. In the early 1980s, the bullet weight was bumped up to 145 grains and again to 147 grains to improve cycle reliability. Now labelled Type L, this was the exact load adopted by the Bureau as an interim until a better one could be developed. A better load was indeed developed, the 10mm Medium Velocity 180-grain JHP, also known as the 10mm FBI.

Cops around the country have used the 9mm 147-grain subsonic hollowpoint of all makes and designs since 1987. Actual police experience has identified four basic problems when using this military match load as a general duty police load. First, the slide velocity could be too low to reliably cycle the police pistols. Winchester has been fighting this problem for a decade, and it has formally warned cops about it. The cops instead misdiagnosed ammo-induced stoppages as being shooter-induced stoppages. Wrong.

The other three failings, however, are being slowly solved by the ammo companies. These are unreliable expansion causing poor stopping power and excessive soft tissue penetration. (The fourth problem is poor penetration against automobile bodies due to soft bullet construction and low bullet energies.) Fortunately, ammo developments like the Golden Saber, Gold Dot, Hydra-Shok, Ranger Talon (police), and Supreme SXT (civilian) have gone a long way to improving wound ballistics from subsonic hollowpoints.

The 9mm cartridge, per se, took a real beating in the wake of FBI/Miami. The 115-grain JHPs were under fire, and the 147-grain JHPs were totally unproven. Law enforcement lost confidence in the cartridges in spite of years worth of good results. The Federal 115-grain 9BP JHP put people on the ground with one torso shot 83 percent of the time. That fact was selectively ignored.

The transition to the 9mm peaked in the late 1980s and then slowed down. Cops were waiting on the "new" FBI caliber. This turned out to be a reduced-velocity version of the 10mm originally chambered in the Bren Ten. The full-power 10mm was too much, but the medium-velocity 10mm was just right. However, the FBI cartridge did not require a full-frame, big-bore auto pistol to tame it. In other words, once again, the duty auto pistol was found to be too big, too bulky, and too heavy. Interest from other police agencies in the 10mm FBI dwindled.

In 1990, a new challenger arose from the ashes of the 10mm. The year before, Winchester and Smith & Wesson teamed up to optimize the medium-velocity 10mm and to make it fit a 9mm-sized auto pistol. This, of course, was the .40 Smith & Wesson, and it is by far the greatest threat the 9mm has ever faced.

An incredible variety of 9mm defense and duty ammo exists today. The 9mm has the greatest hollowpoint bullet weight range of any handgun caliber.

The best of the 9mm combat loads are the 115-grain +P and +P+ JHPs, followed by the 124- and 127-grain +P and +P+ JHPs. Next in effectiveness are the standard-pressure 115 and 124-grain JHPs. The 115-grain JHP

The best standard-pressure loads for the 9mm are the 115-grain JHPs like the Winchester Silvertip (left), the Federal 124-grain Nyclad HP (center), and the 124-grain JHPs like the Federal Hydra-Shok (right).

Medium-weight JHPs like this CCI-Speer 124-grain +P Gold Dot are the future of the 9mm caliber. They produce deeper penetration than the 115-grain JHPs and have better wound ballistics than the 147-grain JHPs. This load produces 88 percent one-shot stops.

remains today as a better defense and police choice than the 147-grain JHP that was suppose to replace it.

In the mid 1990s, the 124-grain loads seemed to be the trend for the future of the 9mm. All of the ammo companies introduced semiexotic 124-grain JHPs like the Golden Saber, Gold Dot, Hydra-Shok, Tactical, Starfire, and Hornady XTP-HP and 127-grain Ranger SXT.

It seemed as if the old energy versus momentum debate was alive and well entirely within the 9mm-caliber! On one hand were the 115-grain +P+ JHPs; on the other were the 147-grain JHPs. The 124-grain standard-pressure and +P+ JHPs seemed like a reasonable compromise. But instead of settling the century-old debate, it was simply called off. Police departments began to abandon the 9mm in favor first of the .40 S&W, then the .357 SIG.

While the 9mm may lead the .40 S&W in current duty use, this does not tell the real story. The real story is which caliber is being selected when pistols are replaced or when transitions occur. Since the mid 1990s, it has been extremely rare for a police department to adopt the 9mm for the first time or to replace worn-out 9mm handguns with new 9mm pistols. Instead, the choice has been evenly divided between the .40 S&W and the .357 SIG.

The .40 S&W and .357 SIG will not make the 9mm obsolete any more than the .357 Magnum made the .38 Special obsolete. In fact, in the late 1990s the mix of 9mm versus .40 S&W is very similar to the mix of .38 Special versus .357 Magnum in the mid 1970s. The reasons for this are exactly the same.

Like the .38 Special, the 9mm can be controlled by nearly all handgunners. This is even more important now than in the 1970s when nearly all police departments had minimum height and weight requirements. The 9mm is an excellent

The 9mm is seeing stiff competition from the .40 S&W and .357 SIG but remains an extremely popular police caliber. The 9mm is the caliber of choice from New York City to Metro-Dade to Los Angeles. The larger the department, the more sense the 9mm makes.

choice for the huge metro departments with the widest imaginable cross-section of police officers. Like the .38 Special +P, the 9mm offers reasonable stopping power. Depending on the load, it is effective 78 to 91 percent of the time. In fact, that is a step up from the popular .38 Special 158-grain lead hollowpoint with its 69 to 77 percent street record.

On the other hand, like the .357 Magnum, the .40 S&W has both more felt recoil and more stopping power than the 9mm. Actually, the .40 S&W from a Glock Model 22 is easier to control than the .357 Magnum fired from a S&W Model 66 revolver. In JHP form, the .40 S&W ranges from 83 to 94 percent effective, an exact overlap of the .357 Magnum caliber.

The .357 SIG is the other caliber today's cops are pursuing. Introduced in 1994, the .357 SIG slowly gained police acceptance to the point where, six years later, it is the fastest growing police duty caliber. This bottlenecked .40 S&W cartridge pushes a 125-grain JHP between 1350 and 1475 fps, depending on the auto pistol. That is a match for the old .357 Magnum. The

Delaware State Police was the first to adopt this retro 1970s caliber; the Texas Department of Public Safety is the largest to date. The New Mexico State Police has been the most recent to trade in a 9mm or a .45 ACP for the .357 SIG.

As we enter the new millennium, American law enforcement is almost evenly divided between the 9mm and .40 S&W. A few cops, waiting to retire, are holding on to their .38 Special revolvers. Others are trying to figure out a way to dump their .45 ACP pistols. An ever-growing number of cops with truly progressive agencies are putting the legendary wound ballistics of the .357 Magnum back into service in the form of the .357 SIG.

Developed in 1902, the 9mm remains a popular police and defensive caliber nearly a century later. It is still the caliber of choice for the New York City Police Department, the largest police force in America. It is the caliber of choice for the Los Angeles Sheriff, the largest sheriff's department in America. And it is the official sidearm of the U.S. military. Long live the 9mm.

CHAPTER 5

9mm Makarov Wound Ballistics

The fall of the Berlin Wall and demise of the Eastern Bloc has made large quantities of inexpensive Russian auto pistols available to American shooters for the first time. The most popular of these calibers is the 9mm Makarov, also known as 9mm Soviet Auto Pistol. With a 9 x 18mm cartridge case, dimensionally the 9mm Makarov is midway between the .380 ACP (9 x 17mm) and the 9mm Luger (9 x 19mm). However, the chamber pressures, velocities, and wound ballistics of the 9mm Mak are much closer to the .380 ACP than the 9mm.

It is clear why the 9mm Makarov has caught on with American shooters—auto pistols of above average quality as well as hardball ammo are available at army surplus prices. The pistols are sized right for concealed carry, and the cartridge is able to produce serious stopping power from a pocket pistol.

The 9mm Makarov pistol was designed by Nikolai Makarov for the Russian high command late in World War II. The exact date of issue for the gun is uncertain. Although some sources list 1951 as the year of military adoption, it is now believed the 9mm Mak may have appeared much earlier.

Since the demise of the Soviet Bloc, two Russian military calibers have been imported in large numbers: the 9mm Makarov (left) and the 7.62 Tokarev (right). The Tokarev, c. 1933, was replaced by the Makarov, c. 1946.

The 9mm Makarov (left) and the .380 ACP (right) have the same overall length. The .380 ACP uses 9mm/.355 inch bullets, while the 9mm Makarov uses larger .364 inch bullets.

Communist political officials were reported to be using it as early as 1946. The Makarov eventually was used for all duties in the Soviet military that called for a pistol.

The 9mm Makarov pistol was adopted by the police and military in several Eastern Bloc countries after World War II. This tapered-wall cartridge replaced the 7.62mm Tokarev, which fired a .30 caliber bullet from what appeared to be a trimmed and rimless bottleneck .38 Special case. The advanced 9mm Makarov pistol replaced the mechanically simple 7.62mm Tokarev pistol, which dates back to 1933.

Both East Germany and China began making the Makarov in the late 1950s. The Germans called their version the Pistole M, while the Chinese Makarov was classified as the Type 59. More recently, the Russians began making their own Makarov pistol. Thousands of these Chinese and Russian Makarovs have been imported since 1989.

The Makarov has been accused of being a Walther PP clone. (During World War II the Americans had captured the Walther pistol plant at Zella-Mehlis and handed it over to the Russians.) The Makarov has a level of accuracy similar to full-size service pistols, but it also has significant improvements over the Walther's highly regarded design.

The Makarov pistol features that are similar to the Walther PP are the double-action lock work and the blowback action with the fixed barrel surrounded by the recoil spring. The different areas include the manual safety decocker where the up position is on safe and the down position is off safe. The down sweep of the thumb to put the Makarov in firing mode is the same as the Colt Government Model but the opposite of most other auto pistols.

The Makarov and Type 59 use the cartridge feedpiece and breechface design of the Walther P38. The Makarov uses its own design of extractor that covers an unusually large arc of the case rim and has a very wide range of movement. The Makarov also has an exterior slide release latch not found on the Walther PP.

At eight rounds, the Makarov holds one more cartridges than the Walther. It uses a heel-clip magazine release, which Europeans feel is less prone to accidental tripping than the Walther's button release. Of course, American auto pistol shooters have a strong preference for the button release. The Makarov also eliminated the loaded-chamber indicator pin

The 9 x 18mm Makarov (left) is loaded to lower chamber pressures and muzzle velocities than the 9 x 19mm Luger (right).Depending on the load, the 9mm Luger produces more stopping power. The 9mm Mak can be made from 9mm Luger cases.

Factory hardball for the 9mm Mak varies from the Chinese-spec 95 grain FMJ at 1060 fps (shown) to the European-spec 94 grain FMJ at 1050 fps to the Russian-spec 92 grain FMJ at 1060 fps. Some 9mm Mak hardball has a steel core and steel jacket.

found on the Walther. Finally, the Makarov uses a leaf-style hammer spring compared to the Walther's coil spring.

Technically, the 9mm Mak is not a true 9mm. The .380 ACP, 9mm Luger, and .38 Super family of cartridges uses .355 to .356 inch diameter bullets. The 9mm Makarov uses .363 to .364 inch diameter bullets. For the surplus hardball shooter and the defensive shooter firing factory hollowpoints this is not an issue. It is, however, a problem for handloaders, as the wide variety of .355 inch 9mm bullets cannot be used with the 9mm Mak case. CCI-Speer and Hornady make both hollowpoints and hardball in .364-inch diameter for the 9mm Mak.

Boxer-primed reloadable cases for the 9mm Mak are available from Starline. Cases also can be easily made from readily available 9mm Luger cases. Both calibers use the same casehead dimensions. Simply trim 1 millimeter off a 9mm Luger case by cutting the .754 inch case back to .713 inch. Use 9mm Makarov reloading dies to expand the case mouth to hold .364 inch bullets. The first firing will form the case to the proper dimensions. No special case forming or reaming operations are necessary.

The official factory load for the 9mm Makarov depends on the factory.

There is no world standard as there is for the 9mm Luger and .45 ACP. Factory 9mm Mak hardball ammo includes the European-spec 94-grain FMJ at 1050 fps, the Soviet-spec 92-grain FMJ at 1060 fps, and the Chinese-spec 95-grain FMJ at 1060 fps. Some references cite the Makarov hardball with velocities as high as 1115 fps, but this ammo is rare.

Some surplus 9mm Makarov military ammo has a mushroom-shaped, mild steel core wrapped with a lead sheet under a copper-washed steel jacket. These dual-core loads were issued specifically for the Soviet Stetchkin selective-fire pistol and Polish Vz63 submachine gun.

Compared to the 1050 fps velocity for the 95-grain 9mm Mak, the 95-grain .380 ACP has a nominal velocity of 950 fps. This 50 to 100 fps advantage for the 9mm Mak comes at a very significant velocity level. As we've noted earlier, all bullets have a "threshold of expansion," the velocity at which the jacket and core just begin to yield. At impact velocities below this threshold, the bullet will not expand. The most reliably expanding bullets are fired at 200 fps or more over their threshold of expansion.

Many handgunners know that .36 to .38 caliber bullets in the 800 to 950 fps range have a hard time expanding in real shootings. The .380 ACP is notorious for having bullets that either expand or penetrate but not both. Exceptions exist, including the Hydra-Shok, Supreme SXT, Golden Saber, and Gold Dot. However, the rule is that most .380 ACP hollowpoints do not expand well because the impact velocity is too close to the threshold of expansion. The 9mm Mak, on the other hand, pushes these same bullets faster than the .380 ACP. With velocities over 1000 fps, they simply expand more reliably than the same bullets with velocities under 1000 fps.

The 9mm Makarov has been frequently compared to the old Browning 9mm Long cartridge. The

A sample of pocket pistol cartridges, all with CCI-Speer GoldDot bullets, is shown left to right: .32 Auto, .380 Auto, 9mm Makarov, 9mm Luger. The 9mm Mak is also known as 9mm Soviet AutoPistol.

9mm Long is actually quite a bit more powerful than the 9mm Mak. Firing a 110-grain bullet at 1100 fps, the 9mm Long is quite close to the 9mm Luger.

In spite of its longer 18mm case, the 9mm Mak has exactly the same .984 inch overall cartridge length as the .380 ACP, giving it somewhat of a stubby appearance. The 9mm Luger has a maximum length of 1.168 inch.

Although the 9mm Makarov uses a cartridge case just slightly shorter than the 9mm Parabellum (aka 9mm Luger, 9 x 19mm, and 9mm NATO), its chamber pressure is much lower. The Luger operates at 35,000 psi maximum, while the Mak has a 24,100 psi pressure limit. In comparison, the .380 ACP (aka 9mm Browning Short, 9mm Corto, 9mm Kurz, and .380 Auto) has maximum pressures of 21,500 psi. CCI-Speer was the first U.S. manufacturer to make 9mm Makarov ammo, establishing the SAAMI pressure limit at a conservative 24,100 psi. The European pressure limits are closer to 26,000 psi.

The 9 x 18mm Makarov is not the most powerful cartridge that can be handled by a blowback pistol design. That honor goes to the Astra 400 in 9mm Bayard, the Astra 600 in 9mm Luger, and the Browning Model 1903 in 9mm Browning Long. The 9mm Makarov does, however, represent the most powerful cartridge around which a concealment-sized blowback pistol has been engineered. These other handguns are all larger service pistols.

It makes sense not to push the pressures of the 9mm Mak because all of the Makarov pistols use a straight blowback design. This weapon design cannot handle the same chamber pressures as the delayed unlocking designs common with the larger auto pistol calibers.

In 1936, the Germans designed the 9 x 18mm Ultra for use in Walther PP style pistols. This cartridge fired a .355-caliber 108-grain bullet at 950 fps. The 9mm Mak fired a .363-caliber 94-grain bullet at 1050 fps. The Ultra had a longer overall length and smaller rim and base dimensions, but it was not a success. In the 1970s, the West Germans developed another version of the 9 x 18mm Ultra called the 9mm Police.

The 9mm Makarov auto pistol is supposed to be able to fire the 9mm Mak, 9mm Ultra, and .380 ACP interchangeably. Again, the 9mm Mak and 9mm Ultra share the same 18mm case length and the 9mm Mak and .380 ACP share the same overall length. However, both the 9mm Ultra and .380 ACP use .355 caliber bullets compared to the .363 caliber 9mm Mak bullet.

We did not have either version of the 9mm Ultra to test in our Russian Makarov, but we had a bunch of .380 ACP ammo. Our Makarov gobbled it all up without any feed, ignition, extraction, or cycle problems.

The smaller .355 inch bullet diameter of the .380 ACP load does not fully engage the .363 inch 9mm Makarov rifling. However, the .380 ACP loads were spin stabilized enough to group into a 4 inch circle from 50 feet with no smudge marks or signs of keyholing.

The average .380 ACP load produces about 10 percent less recoil and 18 percent less energy than a comparable 9mm Mak load. Even still, the .380 ACP loads locked the 9mm Mak slide to the rear every time. We even tried mixing .380 ACP and 9mm Mak ammo in the same magazine. The pistol cycled flawlessly.

With a .355 inch bullet and a .363 inch bore, more than the normal

CCI-Speer was the first U.S. ammo maker to load the 9mm Mak. It established the SAAMI pressure limits. The company's impressive 90-grain Gold Dot has a 69 percent one-shot stop rating.

The CCI-Speer 9mm Mak 90 grain Gold Dot expands to an incredible .75 inch in gelatin. This copper-plated hollowpoint has a 100 percent weight retention.

The 9mm Makarov has been described as the best concealment-size pistol of its era. Our pistol fired 9mm Mak and .380 ACP ammo interchangeably.

amount of gas blow-by occurred. Excess blow-by reduces the bullet velocity and in turn this reduces the slide velocity. Slide velocity is the key to cycle reliability. However, the Makarov pistol had a tolerant enough spring design to easily accept this ammo.

The same held true for the MagSafe 9mm Makarov 71-grain Defender. It produced the least recoil momentum of any 9mm Mak load. We cycled two magazines full of the Defender and a magazine with Defenders and hardball intermixed, again without cycle failures.

A decade after its release on the U.S. market, the 9mm Mak is still limited in bullet weights and styles. It is loaded in 90- to 95-grain hollowpoints and hardball. In comparison, the .380 ACP is available in a wider variety of 88- to 102-grain semiexotic hollowpoints. (Over the past four years, the .380 ACP has been heavily tweaked in response to its use by police officers as a backup pistol.) So the 9mm Mak has the advantage of slightly higher velocities, while the .380 ACP has the advantage of more refined loadings.

The 9mm Makarov is not available from the Big Three: Remington, Federal, and Winchester. However, it is available from CCI-Speer, Hornady, and Cor-Bon. MagSafe and Glaser make a frangible

in this caliber as well. It is widely available in European and Chinese surplus military ball—all of the surplus arms traders and many of the handgun wholesalers carry Geco and Norinco hardball. Federal carries the 9 x 18mm Mak through its Norma affiliates.

We tested the MagSafe Defender, Glaser Blue Safety Slug, Cor-Bon Sierra JHP, CCI-Speer Gold Dot, Hornady XTP, and a hardball load from Norinco. Hardball is hardball. In gelatin it is hard to tell if it works at all. We got 22 inches of penetration and small crush and stretch cavities. Use hardball for plinking, not defense.

The 9mm Mak hollowpoints and frangibles, however, appear to work much better in gelatin than comparable loads in .380 ACP. The .380 ACP 90-grain Gold Dot expands to .60 inch, while the 9mm Mak 90-grain Gold Dot expands to .75 inch. At 69 percent one-shot stops, the 9mm Mak has a critical 2 percentage point advantage over the .380 ACP version.

The Hornady .380 ACP 90-grain XTP expanded to just .44 caliber. The 9mm Mak 95-grain XTP reached an impressive .58 caliber. With a Fuller Index of 68 percent one-shot stops, the

The Cor-Bon 9mm Mak 95 grain JHP expands and then fragments in gelatin. This kind of performance shows this Sierra hollowpoint will at least expand in combinations of soft and hard tissue.

9mm Mak holds a 3 percentage point edge over the .380 ACP load.

The Cor-Bon .380 ACP and 9mm Mak loads were the closest. The .380 ACP Sierra JHP expanded to .58 caliber. The 9mm Mak Sierra JHP expanded and then fragmented into the core and three large pieces of hollowpoint cavity. Both have a Fuller Index of 68 percent. However, a hollowpoint that expands and fragments in gelatin will always at least expand in combinations of soft and hard living tissue.

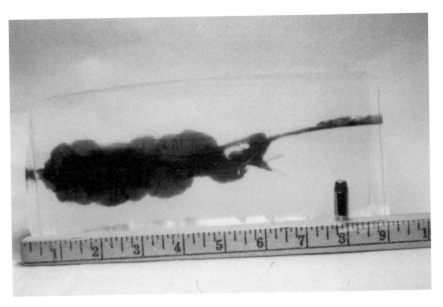

The Hornady 9mm Mak 95 grain XTP expands in gelatin to .58 inch compared to .44 inch for the .380 ACP version. The 9mm Mak ammo produces more stopping power than comparable .380 ACP ammo.

The Cor-Bon 9mm Mak 95 grain JHP transfers 211 ft-lbs. of energy in 9.3 inches. With a Fuller Index of 68 percent, this load is as effective as many .38 Special +P loads.

At 68 to 69 percent effective, the 9mm Mak hollowpoints compare very well against popular loads in other defensive calibers. The 9mm 115-grain FMJ, .44 Special 200-grain SWC, and .45 ACP 230-grain FMJ all produce 63 to 65 percent one-shot stops. The .38 Special +P 95-, 110-, and 125-grain JHPs have proven to be 65 to 73 percent effective. The .40 S&W 180-grain FMJ and .357 Magnum 158-grain SWC are 68 to 72 percent loads.

Among the 9mm Mak hollowpoints tested, the average load expanded to .58 caliber and penetrated 8.6 inches. Similar .380 ACP hollowpoints average .54 caliber and penetrate 9.6 inches. For all loads tested, the 9mm Mak had an average Fuller Index of 70 percent one-shot stops. Similar .380 ACP loads average a Fuller Index of 66 percent. The 9mm Mak indeed produces more stopping power across the board than the .380 ACP.

(Thanks goes to the late Bob Shimek, who provided much of the historical and Walther information used in this chapter.)

TABLE 5-1
9x18MM MAKAROV WOUND BALLISTICS

Make & Load	Velocity fps	Energy ft-lbs.	Penetration depth, inch	Recovered diameter	Fuller Index
MagSafe 51 gr. Defender	1700	327	8.5	frag	81%
Glaser 75 gr. Blue Safety Slug	1300	281	5.6	frag	73%
CCI-Speer 90 gr. Gold Dot	1050	220	7.2	0.75	69%
Cor-Bon 95 gr. Sierra JHP	1000	211	9.3	0.40	68%
Hornady 95 gr. XTP-HP	1000	211	9.2	0.58	68%
Norinco 95 gr. FMJ	1060	237	22	0.36	62%

CHAPTER 6

9mm Carbine Wound Ballistics

The 9mm carbine is rapidly replacing the 12-gauge shotgun in many areas of law enforcement and personal defense. The pistol-caliber carbine is easier to make hits with than the bruising shotgun. The carbine holds more ammo than any shotgun. The carbine shooter is less likely to flinch, making his first-shot hit probability higher. The carbine recoil is negligible, making second and third shots faster and more likely to connect. Semiauto carbines are available in 9mm, 10mm, .40 S&W, .45 Auto, and .44 Magnum. Of all these, the 9mm is the most popular. It also has the widest selection of ammunition types.

The biggest advantage of the shotgun is tissue-shredding stopping power. In terms of wound ballistics from either a handgun or carbine, 9mm loads simply do not compare to 12-gauge rifled slugs, sabot slugs, or 00 buck loads. What makes the 9mm carbine a viable and credible option to the 12-gauge shotgun is not increased power but increased hit probability.

We tested 12 popular hollowpoints in five classes of 9mm ammo. These included the 115-grain +P+ JHPs, 124-grain +P+ JHPs, the standard-pressure 115-grain and 124-grain JHPs, and the 147-grain subsonic JHPs. The auto pistol used for testing a the 4 inch Smith & Wesson Model 439. The carbine was a 16.5 inch Marlin Camp 9.

The +P and +P+ loads were represented by the Cor-Bon 115-grain Sierra JHP. This ammo is similar in velocity to all of the police-only +P+ hollowpoints. In fact, at 1333 fps, only the Winchester Illinois State Police version is faster than the Cor-Bon. The Federal 115-grain 9BPLE +P+, for example, clocks 1,260 fps from a 4 inch pistol.

The two standard-pressure 115-grain loads—the Federal 9BP and the Winchester Silvertip—are the

The pistol caliber is replacing the 12-gauge shotgun in many areas of law enforcement and home defense. The advantages are less recoil, better first-shot hit probability, faster follow-up shots, better accuracy, and more ammo capacity. The carbine does not improve the wound ballistics of the pistol round.

The Federal 9mm 115-grain JHP/9BP is an excellent load from an auto pistol and an outstanding load from a carbine. It fragments in gelatin after nearly a 1400 fps impact.

The Cor-Bon 9mm 115-grain +P JHP produced the largest temporary stretch cavity of the loads tested. All the 115-grain +P and +P+ JHPs will produce better than 90 percent one-shot stops.

The Federal 9mm 147-grain Hydra-Shok had the same penetration and expansion when fired from a 16-inch carbine (left) and a 4-inch pistol (right). The carbine produced slightly higher velocities with this load.

The Remington 9mm 147 Golden Saber has a hard brass jacket. Even with the spiral-cut, camera aperature-style serrations, the bullet expands at a slower rate. This produces a long, debris-tolerant stretch cavity.

workhorses of the 9mm caliber. Both are excellent police and defensive loads in spite of the hype from the 1980s for ultraheavy bullets. The Las Vegas Metro Police department was just one example of a major agency that dropped the 115-grain JHP in favor of a 147-grain subsonic, only to return to the lightweight load for more reliable expansion.

The 124-grain bullet weight is the focus of a lot of attention. This grain weight is seen as an ideal compromise for the auto pistol. As a rule, the 124-grain loads expand more reliably than 147-grain hollowpoints but produce more reliable penetration than 115-grain hollowpoints.

In 1994, Remington released two 124-grain hollowpoints. The test load

was a standard JHP, currently made for the INS/Border Patrol (the other was the dynamic Golden Saber). The second 124-grain test load was the Eldorado Cartridge Starfire. The final test load was the Federal Hydra-Shok. (Federal has given cops and civilians the choice of three 124-grain loads, including a Nyclad lead hollowpoint and a +P+ Hydra-Shok. Cops can also get the 124-grain Tactical HP.)

The veteran load in the 147-grain test weight was also the Federal Hydra-Shok. In the late 1980s and

STOPPING POWER

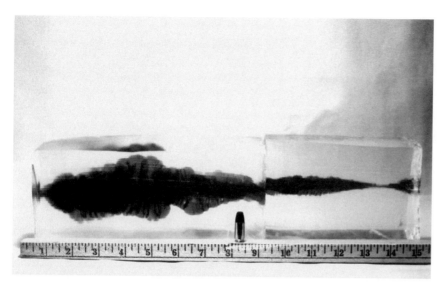

The Winchester 9mm 147-grain Ranger SXT penetrated from 15.8 to 16 inches from a handgun and carbine alike. Note the late energy release wound profile. In the late 1990s, this bullet was redesigned to deliver a faster energy transfer.

Some 9mm subsonic hollowpoints actually go slower from a carbine than from a handgun. The CCI-Speer 147-grain Gold Dot was one such load. Expect the subsonic hollowpoints to under expand and overpenetrate from a carbine.

early 1990s, this was America's police bullet. Since then, the competition has improved and the field has gotten crowded. The Gold Dot and Golden Saber are two of the more recently designed subsonic loads. The Gold Dot has a massive hollowpoint cavity, while the Golden Saber has a carefully engineered, spiral-cut brass jacket with a threshold of expansion of just 620 fps. The 147-grain Ranger SXT is the old Black Talon bullet with a politically correct name. This ammo is still restricted to police use by Winchester and has been since November 1993.

We first compared the muzzle velocity from the 4 inch pistol to the 16.5 inch carbine. Most readers would expect the long-barrel carbine to increase the bullet velocity by at least a couple hundred feet per second. This did not happen. In fact, with two subsonic hollowpoints, the bullets actually clocked slower from the long-barrel carbine.

The muzzle velocity gain, if any, depends on the burning characteristics of the powder. Lighter charges of faster burning powder can generate peak pressure before the bullet exits the carbine barrel. Once this happens,

friction between the bullet and the rifling actually slows the bullet down. In fairness, all 9mm loads have been optimized for handguns and shorter barrel submachine guns, not carbines.

As a group, the +P+ pressure hollowpoints improved the most in velocity from the carbine. The Winchester 127-grain +P+ Ranger SXT gained just 34 fps over the pistol velocity. However, the Federal 124-grain +P+ Hydra-Shok picked up 185 fps when fired from the carbine. The Cor-Bon 115-grain +P JHP improved by 176 fps to reach the 1500 fps bracket.

Likewise the standard-pressure 115-grain Silvertip and 115-grain Federal 9BP went from the low 1200 fps to the high 1300 fps range. Overall, the lightweight and the +P+ types of ammo increased in velocity by 12 percent, or 150 fps.

The medium-weight 124-grain bullets increased by about 60 fps, due mostly to the huge jump from the Hydra-Shok. Overall, this weight class had a 6 percent increase in velocity. However, the Remington and Eldorado loads changed very little.

The heavyweight 147-grain bullets, as an average, did not pick up any velocity. The Ranger SXT and

Hydra-Shok improved only slightly, while the Gold Dot and Golden Saber actually went slower from the longer barrel. As a rule, the subsonic hollowpoints are not any faster from a 9mm carbine than from a pistol.

The average of all 12 9mm police hollowpoints show a mere 6 percent increase in velocity when comparing a carbine to a pistol. This is about a 70 fps increase. To show how insignificant this average increase is, ammo makers certify the muzzle velocity of their loads to be plus or minus 50 fps from the published figures.

With a 70 fps velocity increase, the average 9mm hollowpoint increased in energy by just 50 ft-lbs. Since velocity and energy are tied together, seven of the 12 hollowpoints showed little improvement in energy when fired from the carbine. Five of the loads, however, gained 100 ft-lbs. or more. These were the three 115-grain loads and both 124-grain Hydra-Shok loads.

With 582 ft-lbs. of energy, the Cor-Bon 9mm 115-grain +P JHP from a carbine exactly equals the muzzle energy of the .357 Magnum 125-grain JHP from a revolver. This performance is typical of all makes of

115-grain +P+ hollowpoints, including the Federal 9BPLE and the Winchester/Illinois State Police Q4174.

The 400 ft-lb. level of energy has long been regarded by ammo industry officials as the minimum for an effective and reliable police bullet. The carbine barrel length pushed the 115-grain Silvertip and 9BP and both the 124-grain Hydra-Shok and 124-grain +P+ Hydra-Shok beyond this threshold. The 127-grain Ranger SXT was already there.

Energy is the ability to do work. In living tissue, the work involves penetrating soft and hard tissue to form the permanent crush cavity as well as pushing soft tissue aside to form the temporary stretch cavity. In tactical obstructions, the work is

The Federal 9mm 124-grain Hydra-Shok packs over 400 ft-lbs. of energy when fired from a carbine. The energy is all transferred in 13 inches, for a Fuller Index of 85 percent.

The extra velocity from the 9mm carbine with 124-grain bullets greatly improves the expansion of this Remington 124-grain JHP. The carbine-fired loads (left) are shown in comparison to the pistol-fired load (right).

simply the ability to penetrate objects that are used as cover or concealment.

To test for wound ballistics, we fired all 12 hollowpoints from the carbine into blocks of calibrated 10 percent ordnance gelatin. We then fired them from the auto pistol to serve as a benchmark. Penetration depth, recovered bullet diameter, and the size and shape of the temporary stretch cavity were carefully documented. From this information we calculated the volumes of the crush and stretch cavities.

As velocity increases, so does the reliability of expansion. Beyond a certain velocity, however, the bullet

expands and then fragments to a smaller recovered diameter. Overall, the average recovered bullet diameter decreased from .605 inch for the pistol to .565 inch for the carbine due to fragmentation after expansion from the faster loads and underexpansion from the slower loads. The carbine simply exaggerated the tendencies each class of bullet already had.

Fragmentation in gelatin is not a bad sign. In fact, it is a great sign. A hollowpoint that expands and then fragments in gelatin will at least expand in a variety of clothing-clad combinations of soft and hard tissue. A bullet that fragments in gelatin will expand more reliably under a wide variety of shooting scenarios.

One pistol-fired JHP in this test, the Cor-Bon 115-grain +P, expanded and then fragmented. This performance is typical of nearly all +P and +P+ hollowpoints. From the carbine, the four hollowpoints that reached above 1250 fps, expanded, and fragmented, were the Cor-Bon, the 115-grain Silvertip, the 9BP, and both pressures of 124-grain Hydra-Shok.

Obviously, if the muzzle velocity decreases from the carbine, as in the case of two subsonics, the bullet

expansion will be less. The otherwise excellent CCI 147-grain Gold Dot barely reached the minimum expansion velocity from the carbine as exhibited by the small recovered bullet diameter.

Many police administrators worry that a bullet fired from a pistol-caliber carbine will produce excessive penetration. The 9mm carbine hollowpoints all penetrated between 10.5 and 16.0 inches of gelatin. The pistol-fired 9mm hollowpoints in the test averaged 13.46 inches of penetration; the carbine-fired loads generated 13.27 inches of penetration. There were only two cases in which the penetration depth from the carbine was more than a half inch deeper than the same load from a pistol. With six loads, the penetration was less or exactly the same.

The permanent crush is the volume of tissue actually touched or pulped by the penetrating bullet and fragments of the bullet that leave the main bullet path. This volume is calculated from the penetration depth and the recovered bullet diameter. As a rule, the bullet goes from initial diameter to fully expanded diameter to recovered diameter in just 2 inches of gelatin.

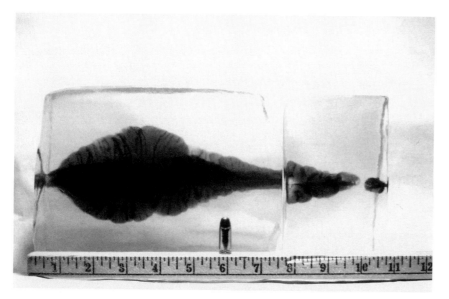

The carbine-fired Eldorado Cartridge 9mm 124-grain Starfire produces a progressive stretch cavity, an above average crush cavity, and adequate penetration.

The Eldorado Cartridge 9mm 124-grain Starfire expanded to .68 caliber from both the pistol and the carbine. This was the largest recovered diameter of the dozen loads tested.

Hollowpoints which expand and then fragment, like this carbine-fired Winchester 115-grain Silvertip, will at least expand in living tissue. The higher velocity from the carbine on this particular load causes the fragmentation.

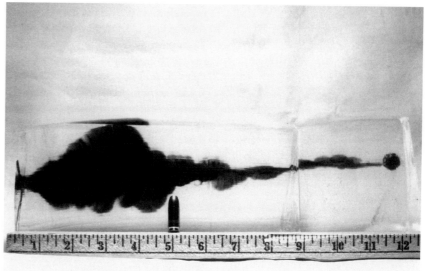

The Remington 9mm 124-grain JHP produced ideal penetration depths and larger stretch cavities when fired from the carbine. All 9mm 124-grain loads benefit from extra velocity.

Compared to the pistol, the average carbine-fired hollowpoint produced slightly less penetration and had a slightly smaller recovered diameter. The pistol's 3.9 cubic inch crush cavity shrank slightly to 3.4 cubic inches for the carbine.

The temporary stretch cavity is the volume of soft and dense tissue that is displaced, disrupted, and occasionally torn in the wake of the passing bullet. The maximum diameter of this stretch and stress cavity is often 10 times the diameter of the bullet. The size and shape of this temporary cavity is where bullets over 1250 fps get their stopping power.

The average carbine-fired hollowpoint produced a slightly larger 32.6 cubic inch temporary cavity, compared to 30.4 cubic inches for the same bullets fired from a pistol. This is only a slight overall change. However, four specific loads produced much larger stretch cavities from the carbine: the 115-grain Cor-Bon, Silvertip, and Federal 9BP and the 124-grain JHP from Remington. The Remington JHP expanded to much larger bullet diameters and the result was a larger stretch cavity.

As a point of reference, .223 Remington loads have stretch cavities ranging from a low of 37 cubic inches

The Winchester 9mm 127-grain +P+ Ranger SXT has 90 percent one-shot stops from a handgun. The talon-serrated bullet expands to .64 caliber and dumps more than 400 ft-lbs. of energy.

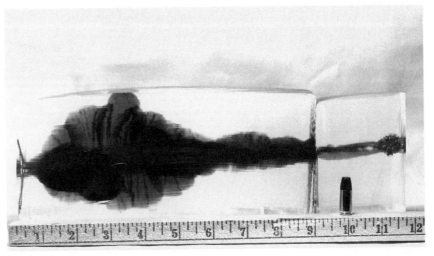

The best load to fire from a 9mm carbine is this Winchester 127-grain +P+ Ranger SXT. It penetrates 12 inches from a pistol (shown) and 14.3 inches from a carbine. The wound profile is excellent for police work.

to a high of 138 cubic inches. Even from a carbine, the 9mm is no .223!

The real eye-opener came when comparing the one-shot stops for the pistol-fired loads to the Fuller Index for these same loads fired from a carbine. These 12 loads from a pistol averaged 82 percent one-shot stops. From a carbine, they have an average Fuller Index of 81 percent.

Based on these 12 hollowpoints, the 9mm pistol and the 9mm carbine produce the *same* estimated stopping power. On the average, the shooter cannot expect *any* overall improvement in *any* aspect of wound ballistics with the 9mm simply by firing this ammo from a carbine.

The good news is that a shooter can still enhance the effectiveness of the 9mm by careful bullet selection. Bullet selection is more important than caliber selection in producing stopping power. The 9mm loads that respond well when fired from a carbine are the obvious choices to select for the carbine, and these are the +P and +P+ 115-grain, 124-grain, and 127-grain hollowpoints. Forget the myth about the 9mm carbine driving the lightweight hollowpoints so fast that they expand too much and penetrate too little. Every single one of these +P and +P+ JHPs easily meets the Border Patrol's minimum penetration standard of 9 inches.

The second choices are the standard-pressure 115-grain loads, of which the Winchester Silvertip and Federal 9BP are ideal examples.

Based on actual police-involved shooting results, the 124-grain hollowpoints work better on the street than the 147-grain hollowpoints from auto pistols. These gelatin results, however, do not show a significant difference one way or the other when these loads are fired from a carbine.

The selection of a 124- or 147-grain 9mm carbine load is best done on a case-by-case basis. The 124-grain JHPs in this test and the 147-grain Hydra-Shok produce a more controlled penetration depth. With otherwise equal wound ballistics, excessive penetration should be avoided.

The carbine's barrel length does not turn the 9mm into a miracle caliber, nor does it turn the projectiles into magic bullets. In fact, the barrel length does not improve the interior, exterior, or terminal ballistics of many popular 9mm hollowpoints at all. It does, however, push some 9mm hollowpoints into the .357 Magnum bracket in terms of velocity, energy, wound ballistics, and tactical penetration.

Ultimately, the original reason to use the 9mm carbine is still valid—it is much easier to get hits with a carbine than a handgun. And you have to hit them to hurt them.

TABLE 6-1
9MM PISTOL VS. CARBINE

Make & Load	Exterior Ballistics				Terminal Ballistics			
	4" pistol vel.fps	16.5" carbine vel. fps	pistol muzzle energy ft-lbs.	carbine muzzle energy ft-lbs.	pistol pene. in.	carbine pene. in.	pistol exp. cal.	carbine exp. cal.
Cor-Bon 115 gr +P JHP	1333	1509	454	582	12.3	10.8	0.55	0.60
Federal 115 gr JHP 9BP	1177	1383	354	488	11.5	12.0	0.60	0.52
Winchester 115 gr. Silvertip	1217	1346	378	463	10.0	10.5	0.67	0.50
Remington 124 gr. JHP	1071	1088	316	326	14.8	12.5	0.52	0.60
Federal 124 gr Hydra-Shok	1099	1253	333	432	13.4	13.3	0.60	0.40
Eldorado 124 gr. Starfire	1083	1101	323	334	12.0	11.0	0.68	0.68
CCI-Lawman 124 gr. Gold Dot	911	826	271	223	14.5	16.0	0.58	0.52
Winchester 147 gr. Ranger SXT	963	993	302	322	15.8	16.0	0.62	0.58
Remington 147 gr. Golden Saber	990	973	320	309	16.0	16.0	0.63	0.65
Federal 147 gr. Hydra-Shok	935	1000	285	326	14.3	14.3	0.64	0.65

TABLE 6-2
9MM CARBINE WOUND BALLISTICS (16-1/2 INCH BARREL)

Make & Load	Muzzle Vel. fps	Muzzle Energy ft-lbs.	Gelatin Depth inch	Recovered Diameter inch	Crush Cavity cu. in.	Stretch Cavity cu. in.	Fuller Index %	Handgun Acutal %
Cor-Bon 115 gr. JHP +P	1509	582	10.8	60 f	3.0	50.0	93	88
Federal 115 gr. JHP	1383	488	12.0	.52 f	2.6	42.9	89	83
Federal 124 gr. Hydra-Shok +P+	1342	495	12.5	.45 f	2.0	30.9	88	89
Winchester 115 gr. Silvertip	1346	463	10.5	.50 f	2.1	37.1	88	83
Winchester 127 gr. Ranger +P+	1254	444	14.3	0.64	4.6	33.8	85	90
Federal 124 gr. Hydra-Shok	1253	432	13.3	.40 f	1.7	28.9	85	83
Eldorado 124 gr. Starfire	1101	334	11.0	0.68	4.0	31.1	81	81
Remington 124 gr. JHP	1088	326	12.5	0.60	3.5	28.3	80	80
Federal 147 gr. Hydra-Shok	1000	326	14.3	0.65	4.7	26.0	78	79
Winchester 147 gr. Ranger SXT	993	322	16.0	0.58	4.2	33.5	75	78
Remington 147 gr. Golden Saber	973	309	16.0	0.65	4.5	32.1	74	74
CCI-Lawman 147 gr. Gold Dot	826	223	16.0	0.52	3.4	16.0	66	66

CHAPTER 7

The Latest .40 S&W Ammo Developments

In the mid-1980s, American law enforcement made a rapid transition in sidearms. Double-action revolvers in .38 Special and .357 Magnum were traded in for higher capacity 9mm auto pistols. As a rule, the 9mm caliber produced more stopping power and tactical penetration than the .38 Special but less than the .357 Magnum. While some exceptions existed, the 9mm was America's police cartridge from the mid-1980s to the mid-1990s.

Beginning in the early 1990s, another transition in police sidearms took place. The 9mm caliber was slowly replaced by the .40 S&W caliber. This transition was fueled by a number of different events.

First, many of the 9mm auto pistols were wearing out. They needed barrels, recoil springs, and other worn parts replaced. Second, there was a strong demand for 9mm pistols among civilians. Gun wholesalers paid a premium for these high-capacity firearms and were often willing to trade used auto pistols for new ones at less than $100 difference. This was especially attractive to police departments faced with a big armorer's bill for repairing their existing auto pistols.

The third factor was the incentive to "upgrade" calibers. The rationale for the need to improve differed from agency to agency, but the reality was the same. In 10 years experience with the 9mm caliber, shortcomings to one degree or another had been documented with a variety of police duty loads. In the late 1980s, the original 9mm 115-grain JHPs were abandoned in favor of the subsonic 147-grain JHPs in an attempt to improve penetration depths. This solution, however, led to other problems: reduced cycle reliability, less tactical penetration against vehicles, excessive soft tissue penetration, and a decrease in stopping power.

In the early to mid-1990s, the 147-grain JHPs were dropped by some departments in favor of 124-grain or +P+ pressure ammo. This was a compromise between very light and very heavy bullets. These loads offered improvements in some areas but not all. The demands placed on a law enforcement bullet appeared to be too diverse for any one 9mm hollowpoint to be an overall success.

Enter the .40 S&W, a caliber not available in the mid-1980s when most police departments made the transition to auto pistols. At that time it was

either the 9mm with its high capacity for ammunition or the .45 ACP with a better reputation for stopping power.

In the minds of many in law enforcement, the .40 S&W resolved the great 9mm vs. .45 ACP debate. In general, .40 S&W pistols hold more ammo than .45 ACP pistols, and .40 S&W ammo produces more stopping power and better tactical penetration than the 9mm. To be sure there is a great overlap in performance among all three of these calibers, depending on the exact load in question. In fact, it is not the caliber that decides much of the bullet performance but the load itself.

Load selection is indeed more important than caliber selection. However, some loads, like the 9mm 147-grain subsonic hollowpoint, had become so widely used by cops and so heralded by the FBI and their advisors that its performance literally defined the performance of the entire 9mm caliber. While this is not true, perception had grown to become reality. As a result, it was thought the only pragmatic way to improve the performance of the 9mm "caliber" was to replace it with a more powerful "caliber." Some agencies opted for a pendulum swing to the .45 ACP, falling right back into the great debate. Most agencies, however, including most recently the FBI itself, opted for the .40 S&W.

The FBI can rightly be credited with development of the .40 S&W. In the late 1980s, the Bureau was heavily involved in police cartridge research and development. In 1987, it introduced the 9mm in a 147-grain JHP version as a knee-jerk reaction to the 1986 shootout in Miami. This was clearly stated by the FBI to be an interim load until a better solution could be found. By 1989, a medium-velocity version of the 10mm Auto firing a 180-grain JHP at 950 fps was developed. By 1990, the 10mm Auto cartridge, in general terms, had been shortened to become the .40 S&W. The original .40 S&W load was indeed a 180-grain JHP at 950 fps. While the Bureau went on to develop a 165-grain JHP at medium velocity in 1993 specifically for its own day-to-day enforcement scenarios, the original 180-grain JHP at 950 fps remains the most popular choice among uniformed patrol officers.

Today, we have seven unique and distinct loads for the .40 S&W: 1) the 180-grain full power, 2) the 165-grain full power, 3) the 165-grain at "police" velocities, 4) the 165-grain medium velocity, 5) the 150- to 155-grain full power, 6) the 135-grain full power, and 7) the 135-grain medium velocity. Importantly, all of these loads are *not* well-suited for personal defense or uniformed patrol duty.

180-GRAIN JHP

The 180-grain JHP is by far the most popular load in .40 S&W. While the has-been 9mm 147-grain JHP has 295 ft-lbs. of energy, the .40 S&W 180-grain JHP has 360 ft-lbs. Again, energy is the ability to do work, such as defeating tactical barriers and achieving adequate penetration from bullets that have expanded aggressively. While the average 9mm 147-grain JHP has a one-shot stop

record of 77 percent, the .40 S&W 180-grain JHP averages 84 percent.

Some departments, including the California Highway Patrol, Ohio State Highway Patrol, Alaska Department of Corrections, and North Carolina Highway Patrol, use a standard version of the 180-grain JHP in their .40 S&W pistols. The original load for the caliber, it established the energy and momentum values around which all of the spring rates and locking mechanisms in the .40 S&W auto pistol were designed. Therefore, a .40 S&W pistol will generally function more reliably with a 180-grain JHP driven to 950 fps. A load with a different bullet weight or muzzle velocity may not cycle as reliably under all gunfight conditions faced.

The original Winchester 180-grain subsonic JHP is the benchmark load in the .40 S&W caliber. It produces 83 percent one-shot stops, low for this caliber. As a result, many departments have adopted some kind of semiexotic bullet design to improve expansion reliability after passing through both street clothes and heavy clothing.

Among the semiexotic versions, the Winchester 180-grain Ranger SXT—the former Black Talon—is extremely popular in law enforcement. This hollowpoint has been restricted to police sales since 1993. However, this bullet has changed, and for the better.

The Winchester Supreme SXT is the detaloned version of the Ranger Talon and is available to all shooters. It is excellent ammo. This 165-grain full-power Supreme SXT expands reliably even after heavy clothes.

In mid-1997, Winchester introduced the Ranger Talon as an across-the-board replacement for the Ranger SXT in .40 S&W. By late 1997, the .45 ACP and 9mm Luger respectively were also upgraded.

The new Ranger Talon is gold or copper in appearance as opposed to the black finish on the Ranger SXT. More importantly, the bullet itself has been redesigned to expand reliably even from shorter barrel auto pistols and especially after encountering heavy clothing. To accomplish both of these goals, the copper jacket of the Ranger Talon received more prominent notches or serrations, the jacket thickness was adjusted, and the hollow cavity was enlarged. While originally designed as a late-energy-release hollowpoint, the Ranger Talon has clearly been redesigned as a medium-energy-release bullet. It is the only bullet currently designed to expand out of guns of all barrel lengths, from 5 inch to 3 1/2 inch. Gelatin tests from a 5 inch Beretta 96G, a 4 inch Glock 23, and a 3 inch Para-Ordnance P10 confirm this claim.

The hollowpoint cavity on the Ranger Talon is both larger in diameter and deeper than the original Ranger SXT. The new design is especially tolerant of heavy clothing. In tests performed for the Indiana State Police, after defeating four layers of denim the Ranger Talon expanded to larger recovered diameters than most other 180-grain JHPs. In fact, the expansion was so aggressive that the jacket occasionally slipped off the core. However, this did not occur until the end of the bullet travel, by which point the jacket had already done its job. In tests performed by the Pennsylvania State Police prior to its adoption of the .40 S&W 180-grain Ranger Talon, the expansion and penetration of the load in bare gelatin and in heavily clothed gelatin were the same. In tests performed by the authors, this .40 S&W load from a Beretta 96 penetrated 13.5 inches and expanded to .68 inch.

Other state agencies using either the Winchester .40 S&W 180-grain Ranger SXT or Ranger Talon include the Massachusetts State Police, Nevada Highway Patrol, New Hampshire State Police, South Carolina Highway Patrol, South Dakota Highway Patrol, and Georgia State Patrol. The sheriffs department or county police in Maricopa County, Arizona, Baltimore County, Maryland, Dallas County, Texas, Prince Edward's County, Virginia, and Bergen County, New Jersey, use these loads too. As evidence of the Ranger SXT's and Ranger Talon's ability to perform after penetrating light and heavy clothing alike, the Miami, Florida, and Anchorage, Alaska, Police Departments both use this ammo.

Another major player in the 180-grain bullet weight is the CCI-Speer Gold Dot. The Seattle, Washington, Police Department is perhaps the largest agency using this load. However, the ammo demos performed state by state by CCI-Speer have converted a large number of small and medium size police departments across the country.

The Gold Dot hollowpoint has recently been redesigned in the 9mm, .40 S&W, and .45 ACP calibers. The thickness of the copper-plated jacket has almost doubled. The number of serrations, or nose cuts in the jacket, have been reduced from eight to six. The hollowpoint cavity profile has been modified to maintain expansion and penetration results with the thicker jacket. And the brass cases are now nickel plated for more positive extraction and cycle reliability.

As a general rule, bullets with eight serrations expand more uniformly than those with six. However, the longer petals of the six-serration bullets result in larger recovered diameters than the shorter petals from the eight-serration versions. When the Gold Dot expands, the lead from the core remains attached to the jacket petals. The thicker jacket can now support the

CCI-Speer redesigned all of its Gold Dot bullets for better accuracy and larger recovered diameters. The new ammo has six jacket serrations and a nickel-plated case.

larger amount of mass on the jacket petals without breaking off.

In order to improve the accuracy from Beretta pistols, the jacket thickness of all .40 S&W Gold Dot bullets was increased from an average of .011 inch to an average of .020 inch. These pistols had variations in the concentricity of the chamber to the barrel, resulting in substandard accuracy. The thicker jacket increased the structural integrity and the column strength of the bullet, which improved the accuracy from nonconcentric chambers.

This is not the first time across-the-board changes were made to the Gold Dot to address problems experienced in only one pistol. A few years ago, a restrike operation to concave the bullet base and resize the bullet diameter was implemented to resolve accuracy problems associated with the polygonal rifling used in Glock pistols.

CCI-Speer was already considering a heavier Gold Dot jacket to assist feed reliability. The thicker jacket will not ding as easily when the bullet nose is slammed into the feed ramp during cycling or rechambering. As a bonus, CCI-Speer recontoured the nose profile with a rounder feed radius to improve feeding up the ramp.

Of all the .40 S&W 180-grain JHPs, the Federal 180-grain Hydra-Shok has achieved the best results in actual shootings with 88 percent one-shot stops. The Hydra-Shok was the first of the semiexotic 180-grain .40 S&W hollowpoints. The post in the center of the hollowpoint cavity amplifies and redirects fluid pressure for reliable bullet expansion and controlled penetration. This is the current duty load of the Federal

The Federal 180-grain Hydra-Shok remains the best .40 S&W load in the original bullet weight. The Hydra-Shok expands fully in as little as 2 inches of gelatin. With 88 percent one-shot stops, this is the only 180-grain hollowpoint in the top ten .40 S&W loads.

Protective Service, Fairfax County, Virginia, Police, and Arlington County, Virginia, Police.

One of the most interesting .40 S&W 180-grain bullet designs is the Remington Golden Saber, currently used by the Iowa State Patrol, Little Rock, Arkansas, Police, and the U.S. Marshal Service. The Golden Saber uses a brass jacket with 30 percent zinc instead of the conventional gilding metal jacket with 5 percent zinc. This makes the jacket very hard. In fact, with the Golden Saber the recovered diameter of the bullet is established by the expanded jacket, not the expanded core. The bullet serrations are cut completely through the jacket to assist in expansion. While most bullets expand by peeling back the jacket, the Golden Saber expands like the aperture of a camera opening. With the 90 degree form of the jacket petals, a recovered Golden Saber bullet shares many of the features of a recovered Winchester Ranger Talon. They should. Both bullets were designed by the same engineer.

155-GRAIN JHP

The first of the lightweight .40 S&W hollowpoints was the Winchester 155-grain Silvertip. Compared to the traditional 180-grain JHPs, these 150- to 155-grain JHPs have more velocity, more energy, more

The Federal .40 S&W 155-grain Hydra-Shok, shown in gelatin, is tied with the CCI-Speer 155-grain Gold Dot in producing 93 percent one-shot stops. The Hydra-Shok penetrates 12 to 13 inches of gelatin.

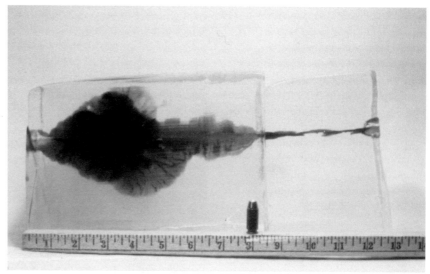

The Triton .40 S&W 155-grain JHP produces a wound profile like the .357 Magnum 125-grain JHP. Like most 155-grain JHPs, this hot JHP should produce about 90 percent one-shot stops.

The Winchester 155-grain Silvertip was the first of the lighter weight .40 S&W loads with a velocity of 1205 fps and 500 ft-lbs. of energy. This is one of the best general-purpose loads in the caliber.

reliable expansion, less penetration, and an overall greater effectiveness in reported shootings. They are arguably the best loads for law enforcement.

The 155-grain loads were originally developed at the request of INS/Border Patrol. This agency remains the largest user of 155-grain JHP ammo made by either Federal or Remington. The Border Patrol load is a standard jacketed hollowpoint and

not the Hydra-Shok or Golden Saber version. The Oregon State Police use a 155-grain Gold Dot, as does the San Antonio, Texas, Police.

Aside from these agencies, relatively few departments have adopted a 155-grain JHP in .40 S&W. Perhaps this will change as more information on this load becomes available. Based on nearly 1,700 officer-involved shootings with the .40

S&W caliber, seven of the top ten most effective loads in the caliber are 155-grain JHPs. Based on over 500 shootings, they average 89 percent one-shot stops.

165-GRAIN JHP

The 165-grain .40 S&W JHP is available in three distinct velocity levels. This has caused great confusion since these differences are not labelled on the box or the cartridge headstamp in any way. The Federal 165-grain medium-velocity Hydra-Shok averages 975 fps. The police-only Winchester 165-grain Ranger SXT and police-only Federal 165-grain Tactical run between 1050 and 1070 fps. The CCI-Speer 165-grain Gold Dot and the Remington 165-grain Golden Saber are full-power 1150 fps loads. The Triton and Cor-Bon versions of the 165-grain JHP are also full-power loads. The Winchester 165-grain Ranger SXT is a lower velocity load, while the Winchester 165-grain Supreme SXT is a full-power 1110 fps load.

The full-power hollowpoints are loaded to standard chamber pressures. They do not have a +P headstamp because they fully comply with all SAAMI requirements for standard-pressure cartridges. The medium-velocity hollowpoints are not identified

A big difference exists among .40 S&W 165-grain JHPs. Left to right, the Remington Golden Saber, CCI-Speer Gold Dot, and Winchester Supreme SXT are full-power loads with velocities more than 1100 fps and one-shot stops of 89 percent or better.

in any way as being different than the full-power loads. Nothing on the packaging nor headstamp tells the shooter that, for example, the Federal 165-grain Hydra-Shok is a medium-velocity load while a Winchester 165-grain Supreme SXT is full power. Perhaps the weenie medium-velocity 165-grain hollowpoints should have a – P headstamp.

With these 950 fps medium-velocity 165-grain JHPs, has the terminal performance of the .40 S&W cartridge been optimized as the FBI intended? Or has one of the lowest performing hollowpoints in the caliber been invented?

The dogma of those who use the medium-velocity loads is this: the 165-grain JHPs do everything the 180-grain JHPs do, except with less recoil and lower chamber pressure. That sounds like something for nothing. Of course, it is not true. The 165-grain medium-velocity JHPs *do not* do everything the 180-grain JHPs do. Instead they do less. They indeed have less recoil and less chamber pressure, but they also have less energy, less bullet expansion, less barrier penetration, less slide velocity, and less stopping power. The medium-velocity 165-grain JHPs turn the .40 S&W pistol back into a 9mm. They are better than all the 9mm 147-grain JHPs, but they are not up to the .40 S&W 180-grain JHPs. And they are certainly nothing like the full-power 165-grain JHPs.

As it turned out, the .40 S&W medium-velocity 165-grain JHPs share many of the problems on the street as experienced with the 9mm 147-grain subsonic JHP. Remember now, these are not theoretical speculations from engineers or surgeons far removed from the realities of street patrol. Instead, these problems are actual experiences and observations taken from real gunfights over 10 years of 9mm subsonic hollowpoint use.

The four problems with the 9mm subsonic hollowpoint are poor stopping power, excessive soft tissue penetration,

poor barrier penetration, and poor cycle reliability. The stopping power is lower than other hollowpoints in the 9mm caliber because of low bullet energy and minimal expansion. Not much tissue is crushed with a bullet expanded to .55 to .58 caliber, and not much tissue is disrupted by .38 Special-size stretch cavities.

The excessive soft tissue penetration comes from small recovered diameters. Between 65 and 75 percent of the bullets that penetrate 15 inches of gelatin will exit on a torso shot. This, of course, becomes a civil liability. The poor tactical penetration is a result of low energy levels. Energy is the ability to do work, like punch through car bodies. These same bullets, therefore, are deep penetrators in soft tissue because of poor expansion and shallow penetrators against barriers because of low bullet energy.

The poor cycle reliability is a result of lower slide velocities than the recoil-operated auto pistols were designed around. Slide velocity is the result of both the energy and momentum of the bullet. The energy must overcome the energy stored in the main and recoil springs. The momentum must overcome the inertia of the slide. A load with lower energy and lower momentum, like the 9mm 147-grain JHP, will produce less rearward slide velocity than one with higher energy and higher momentum, like the 9mm 115-grain JHP +P. A lower slide velocity is more likely to cause stoppages under gunfight conditions.

The .40 S&W 165-grain medium-velocity JHPs have three of these four problems. Compared to all other .40 S&W hollowpoints, the medium-velocity 165-grain JHP produces the least stopping power. The Federal 165-grain medium-velocity Hydra-Shok produces 83 percent one-shot stops. The Federal 180-grain Hydra-Shok is 88 percent effective. The Federal 155-grain Hydra-Shok has achieved 93 percent one-shot stops.

The lack of stopping power is not due to some design flaw with the ammo. Federal Cartridge tests show its medium-velocity 165-grain Hydra-Shok to expand to .60 caliber and penetrate 13.5 inches of gelatin. In our tests, it expanded to .61 caliber and penetrated 13.8 inches. These medium-velocity loads perform exactly as the FBI intended. As a result, they have the worst stopping power potential in the caliber.

The medium-velocity 165-grain bullet is downloaded from 1150 fps to 950 fps, a costly loss of 200 fps. A 200 fps drop from 1450 to 1250 fps like the .357 Magnum medium-velocity 125-grain is one thing—hollowpoint bullets still expand at 1250 fps. A 200 fps drop from 1150 to 950 fps like the .40 S&W 165-grain medium-velocity is quite another. This is close to the theoretical threshold of expansion for many hollowpoints. The safety factor in getting the bullet to expand is now gone.

The download is also a loss of 150 ft-lbs. of energy. With the same initial caliber and the same depth of penetration, this loss of energy alone accounts for a calculated 7 percentage point drop in one-shot stops. In terms of muzzle energy, this is exactly like going from a 9mm 115-grain +P+ JHP to a 9mm 147-grain subsonic JHP, or going from a full-power 10mm Auto 175-grain JHP to 10mm medium-velocity 180-grain JHP. And energy is one of the most significant keys to stopping power.

The medium-velocity 165-grain JHPs do not appear to share the tendency of the 9mm 147-grain JHPs for excessive penetration. Their average penetration is 14.1 inches compared to the caliber-wide hollowpoint average of 13.5 inches. Even though the medium-velocity 165-grain JHPs do not expand much, they don't have much energy and momentum to drive them deeper into tissue either. They perforate the torso during actual gunfights but do not pack much power upon exit.

The medium-velocity 165-grain JHPs have the least energy of any .40 S&W load. As a result, they produce

the least tactical and barrier penetration. They are the least likely of the .40 S&W bullets to get inside a car body. They are the least likely of the .40 S&W bullets to penetrate door and window jambs on a dwelling. They are the least likely of the .40 S&W bullets to defeat laminated or thermopane glass. They are the least likely of the .40 S&W bullets to penetrate a street barrier used by a violator.

Some handgunners have been persuaded that lower chamber pressures will reduce weapon wear. First of all, few civilians and even fewer cops shoot their pistols enough that wear is ever a concern. Secondly, and more importantly, the battering that auto pistols undergo is related to the rearward slide velocity, not chamber pressure. The medium-velocity 165-grain JHPs do indeed produce less weapon wear, but it is due to slower slide velocities, not lower pressures. If you think that this is an advantage, remember that slower slide velocities also cause stoppages due to one-hand shooting, limp-wristing, improper grip, and many other realities of gunfights.

The medium-velocity 165-grain JHPs produce the least energy and the

least momentum of any .40 S&W load. As a result they produce the least slide velocity of any .40 S&W load. This means they are the most likely to cause ammo-induced stoppages during gunfight scenarios where the shooter is not an ideal shooting platform. Such ammo-induced stoppages may not be evident on a highly controlled shooting range where officers shoot on command and take the time to get the proper grip on the pistol and fire from a two-handed stance.

Expansion and cycle reliability questions involving Federal 165-grain medium-velocity Hydra-Shok ammo were raised during a Dayton, Ohio, police gunfight where the wounded officer became less than an ideal firing platform. These questions were answered by a switch to higher velocity ammo. Other agencies using the medium-velocity loads have complained of lack of expansion and poor cycler reliability from short-barrel guns or when fired by officers of small stature.

CCI-Speer originally developed a 975 fps, 165-grain medium-velocity Gold Dot to compete with Federal's 165-grain medium-velocity Hydra-Shok. In March 1997, however, the

The CCI-Speer 165-grain Gold Dot started out as a medium-velocity load. It can be identified by eight jacket serrations. CCI-Speer dropped the low energy load and introduced this full-power Gold Dot, which has better cycle reliability, more stopping power, and more tactical penetration.

STOPPING POWER

load was dropped due to lack of demand from law enforcement departments. Instead, the cops wanted the 1050 to 1150 fps versions, so CCI-Speer completely redesigned its 165-grain Gold Dot for higher impact velocities. This is not just the same bullet driven faster. After the shooting, the Dayton PD adopted the CCI-Speer 180-grain Gold Dot and then became among the first to adopt the full-power 165-grain Gold Dot.

Other handgunners see these low-pressure, medium-velocity loads as a way to reduce the number of casehead ruptures on the firing line. This, too, is a mistake or, at best, a failure to find the root cause of the casehead eruption. If the casehead fails because it is partially unsupported in the chamber, a reduction from 33,000 psi to 25,000 psi chamber pressure may help. If the casehead fails because the auto pistol fired partially out of battery, the lower chamber pressure may not prevent it. In fact, case ruptures have resulted even when medium-velocity 165-grain JHPs were fired out of battery.

The original motivation for the medium-velocity 165-grain JHP, and still the most frequent excuse for its use, is less recoil. Unfortunately, these mid-range loads give up stopping power and tactical penetration to produce less felt recoil. Of course, the obvious question is this: is recoil control a real problem with standard-pressure .40 S&W loads? What level of training would make less stopping power, less tactical penetration, and an increased chance of an ammo-induced stoppage a valid excuse for less recoil? Why not just issue the .32 ACP? The New York City Police issued the .32 S&W to its policewomen for 46 years after its policemen had the .38 Special.

The easiest way to compare the felt recoil from the same auto pistol is to compare the momentum figures from each load. Except for the use of constants and conversion factors, this is exactly how the USPSA/IPSC Power Factors are calculated. It is a widely accepted and completely valid method for comparing felt recoil.

The Power Factor for the typical full-power .40 S&W hollowpoint from 135 grains to 180 grains is 178. This is just barely over the 175 Power Factor that USPSA/IPSC considers to be a major caliber. The .40 S&W is also well under the felt recoil from the average .45 ACP. (This big-bore benchmark of pistol competition has a 190 Power Factor, not counting the +P loads.) In comparison, the .40 S&W medium-velocity 165-grain JHPs have a Power Factor of 157, almost identical to the .38 Special +P 158-grain LHP's 155. The medium-velocity 165-grain JHPs, in fact, have a Power Factor exactly midway between the average .40 S&W load (178) and the average 9mm (142).

The 165-grain medium-velocity JHP is the current duty load for FBI Special Agents issued the newly approved Glock Model 23 and Glock Model 27. Maryland State Police and the Indianapolis Police also use this medium-velocity load. It was developed specifically to reduce recoil and muzzle flip. Recoil is more comparable to the 9mm +P loadings, making it easier to control very light, small-frame auto pistols. Yet it is a little surprising that the felt recoil from a .40 S&W cartridge would have to be lowered to the Power Factor of a .38 Special (155) for FBI agents, Maryland state troopers, and Indianapolis big city cops to control the recoil.

At the same time, some cops say if a .45 ACP had been used at the 1986 FBI/Miami and 1997 LAPD/North Hollywood shootouts instead of a 9mm, those events would have been over sooner. The average .45 ACP produces 20 percent *more* recoil than the medium-velocity .40 S&W and 35 percent more recoil than the average 9mm.

Get the story straight! Either trained law enforcement professionals can handle the recoil of a .45 ACP or they need to have the reduced recoil of a medium-velocity .40 S&W. The answer, of course, is that any well-trained, able-bodied adult male or female of any stature can handle any of the .40 S&W loads from a duty handgun. Those who cannot should have their firearms instructor replaced, not the rest of the police force penalized by being given wimpy ammo.

We fired all the popular .40 S&W duty and defensive loads into gelatin. However as a double check, we also obtained some bullets recovered from tissue. These bullets had engaged a wide variety of bones like the sternum and ribs, and then a wide variety of vital organs, primarily the lungs, heart, and liver. Today's hollowpoint designs perform in combinations of hard and soft living tissue just like they perform in bare and heavily clothed gelatin.

Of specific interest, of course, were the medium-velocity 165-grain JHPs. In gelatin, the low-energy 165-grain Hydra-Shok expanded to .61 inch compared to an average of .60 inch in tissue. One of the Hydra-Shoks recovered after a solid upper chest shot during the Dayton shootout could have been reloaded and fired again according to Montgomery County, Ohio, sheriff officials. A 165-grain Hydra-Shok fired into four layers of denim and gelatin by Marion County, Indiana, Sheriff deputies could also have been reloaded. Therefore, either the Federal 155-grain or 180-grain Hydra-Shok would be a better choice. In fact, nearly any .40 S&W hollowpoint is a better choice.

Both the full-power Remington 165-grain Golden Saber and the full-power Winchester 165-grain Supreme SXT performed exactly as designed in gelatin and tissue. Both are outstanding choices for law enforcement. The 165-grain Golden Saber, in fact, has produced 94 percent one-shot stops.

With all this variety and the confusion over .40 S&W loads in general, which is the best one? Of course, there is no "one" best load. However, certain loads are the best for specific scenarios.

The .40 S&W load with the most documented stopping power in actual shootings is the Remington 165-grain Golden Saber. This brass jacketed ammo produces 94 percent one-shot stops.

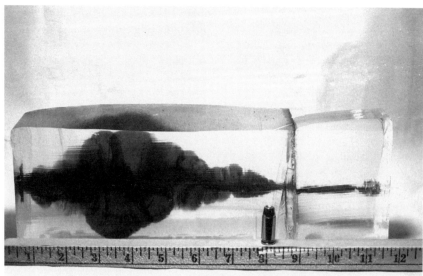

The Remington .40 S&W 165-grain Golden Saber penetrates 12 inches of gelatin and expands to .68 caliber. This wound profile shows the medium energy release ideal for police scenarios.

The latest .40 S&W development is the Winchester 165-grain Partition Gold. Using a Nosler-style Partition bullet, the soft front core expands easily even after heavy clothes. The partitioned rear core maintains enough bullet weight for excellent after-glass performance.

For law enforcement situations in densely populated areas and for personal and home defense, use one of the 135-grain full-power, 150-grain, or 155-grain JHPs. These are the best choices for two reasons. First, they top the stopping power charts with officer-involved shootings, yielding 86 to 93 percent one-shot stops. Second, the average penetration depth in calibrated gelatin from these loads is exactly 13.0 inches, so they provide adequate penetration but are the least likely to exit on a torso shot.

The best loads for less-populated patrol scenarios involving rural sheriff's department activities and interstate vehicle stops by state and county police are the full-power 165-grain JHPs. These loads penetrate an average of exactly 14.0 inches. The most proven of the bunch to date is the Remington 165-grain Golden Saber with 94 percent one-shot stops. (This is the load carried by the author during sheriffs patrol.) Expect similar, top of the chart results from the Winchester Supreme SXT, CCI-Speer Gold Dot, and the brand new Winchester Partition Gold, which may be the ultimate state trooper load. These full-power 165-grain loads also produce a higher slide velocity for more reliable auto pistol functioning in actual shooting scenarios.

The 180-grain .40 S&W loads are acceptable but not really ideal for police or defense. The 180-grain JHP with the best street record is the Federal Hydra-Shok.

For which scenarios are the medium-velocity 165-grain JHPs best suited? These should be used by only the most recoil-shy and muzzle-flip-sensitive handgunners in scenarios where a .40 S&W pistol is issued but only the wound ballistics from a 9mm are needed and only the recoil of a .38 Special can be tolerated. Developed at the request of the FBI hierarchy, rank-and-file FBI field agents deserve better. Other federal agents, like those with the Marshal's Service and Border Patrol, use full-power JHPs.

The Las Vegas Metro Police has been extremely responsive to ammunition issues. Like most police agencies, in the late 1980s it switched from the 9mm 115-grain JHP to the 9mm 147-grain JHP looking to improve performance. When it saw that performance was actually worse with the subsonic load, the LVMPD was one of the few departments with the guts to change back to the 115-grain. Like many departments, it has since adopted the .40 S&W caliber as an across-the-board improvement over the 9mm. Its duty load is the high-velocity version of the 165-grain Gold Dot.

Among the full-power 165-grain JHPs, the most popular appears to be the Remington 165-grain Golden Saber. This load is used by the police departments of Baltimore, Maryland, Rochester, New York, and Woodbridge, New Jersey, as well as the Arkansas State Police and the Utah Department of Corrections.

135-GRAIN JHP

One of the newest bullet weights for the .40 S&W caliber is the 135-grain projectile. This weight was pioneered by Cor-Bon Ammo Company of Sturgis, South Dakota, and quickly released by its arch-rival, Triton Cartridge of Wappingers Falls, New York. Using Sierra and Nosler JHPs, respectively, both companies drive the 135-grain JHP to 1300 fps from duty-length auto pistols.

Based both on initial results from actual shootings and on its expansion and penetration in gelatin, the .40 S&W 135-grain JHP at 1300 fps rivalled the legendary .357 Magnum 125-grain JHP at 1450 fps. In the first dozen shootings, it achieved 96 percent one-shot stops, the best stopping power record in the caliber at that time. Now with many more shootings available, the hot 135-grain JHP has levelled off at 89 percent one-shot stops. These loads are still in the elite top third of the caliber.

The 135-grain JHP expands most aggressively and is least likely to

The .40 S&W 135-grain JHPs from Cor-Bon/Nosler (left) and Triton/Sierra (right) dump over 500 ft-lbs. of energy in 10 inches of gelatin. This controlled penetration is ideal for home defense and court/school security.

overpenetrate in the .40 S&W caliber. It penetrates in the 9.5 to 10.5 inch range in calibrated ordnance gelatin. This bullet is ideal for urban patrol and special assignments such as housing, transit, and courtroom security. It is also ideal for home defense and civilian concealed carry. The police departments of South Bend, Indiana, North Las Vegas, Nevada, and Brockton, Massachusetts

use the Cor-Bon/Sierra version. The Greene County, Tennessee, Sheriff is the largest single customer for the Triton/Nosler version.

Well after the hot 1300 fps, 135-grain loads were released, Federal Cartridge introduced a .40 S&W 135-grain Hydra-Shok in its Personal Defense line of ammo. This bullet is loaded to *much* lower pressures and velocities and should *not* be confused with the high-performance 135-grain JHPs. The 135-grain Personal Defense has a velocity of 1095 fps and 360 ft-lbs. of energy. This compares to 450 ft-lbs. from the full-power 135-grain loads. The result is a Fuller Index of 85 percent one-shot stops for the 135-grain Personal Defense loads compared to 89 percent for the full-power 135-grain loads.

Like all police duty calibers, the .40 S&W can be formidable or feeble. It can be reliable or it can be a liability. It all depends on load selection. Become informed, and be both careful and precise in the load you select for this potent caliber.

TABLE 7-1
.40 S&W WOUND BALLISTICS

Make & Load	Muzzle Velocity fps	Muzzle Energy ft-lbs.	Gelatin Depth inch	Recovered Diameter	One-Shot Stops %
Remington 165 gr. Golden Saber	1150	485	12.0	0.68	94
Federal 155 gr. Hydra-Shok	1140	448	13.3	0.68	93
CCI-Speer 155 gr. Gold Dot	1190	484	12.3	0.70	93
CCI-Speer 165 gr. Gold Dot	1170	501	13.7	0.74	90 est
Federal 155 gr. JHP	1140	448	12.0	0.65	89
Cor-Bon 135 gr. JHP	1300	507	9.8	0.56	89
Winchester 165 gr. Supreme SXT	1110	452	12.8	0.68	89 est
Winchester 155 gr. Silvertip	1205	500	13.5	0.70	88
Remington 155 gr. JHP	1140	448	16.5	0.64	88
Federal 180 gr. Hydra-Shok	950	361	15.0	0.75	88
Winchester 165 gr. Ranger SXT	1070	420	13.6	0.65	87 est
CCI-Speer 180 gr. Gold Dot	960	367	11.6	0.68	86
Federal 165 gr. Tactical	1050	404	14.5	0.62	85 est
Federal 135 gr. Hydra-Shok Pers. Def.	1095	360	9.8	0.64	85 est
Federal 165 gr. Hydra-Shok Med. Vel	950	331	13.8	0.61	83

TABLE 7-2
FELT RECOIL COMPARISON

Caliber & Load	Velocity fps	Power Factor
.380 ACP 90 gr. JHP	1000	90
9mm 115 gr. JHP	1180	136
9mm 124 gr. JHP	1120	139
9mm 147 gr. JHP	980	144
.40 S&W 135 gr. Pers. Def.	1095	148
9mm 115 gr. JHP +P	1300	150
.38 Spl. 158gr. LHP +P	980	155
.40 S&W 165 gr. JHP M.V.	950	157
.40 S&W 180 gr. JHP	950	171
.40 S&W 135 gr. JHP	1300	176
.40 S&W 165 gr. "police"	1070	177
.40 S&W 155 gr. JHP	1140	177
10mm 180 gr. JHP M.V.	1000	180
.357 Mag. 125 gr. JHP	1450	181
.45 ACP 185 gr. JHP	1000	185
.40 S&W 165 gr. JHP	1150	190
.45 ACP 230 gr. JHP	850	196
.45 ACP 185 gr. JHP +P	1140	211
10mm 175 gr. JHP	1290	226

CHAPTER 8

Indiana State Police .40 S&W Ammo Tests

by Keith Jones

In early 1998, the Indiana State Police (ISP) made the decision to transition from the 9mm Beretta 92 to the .40 S&W Beretta 96. The decision of which .40 caliber handgun to use was easy based on the ISP's years of success with the Beretta. The selection of the right .40 S&W ammo was quite another issue.

Many good hollowpoint designs existed at the time, including the Winchester Ranger Talon, Federal Hydra-Shok, Remington Golden Saber, and CCI-Speer Gold Dot. More importantly, the selection of bullet weights was much greater in the late 1990s than in the early 1990s when the .40 S&W gained acceptance. Police

departments could choose from the 135-grain JHP, 155-grain JHP, three velocity levels of the 165-grain JHP, and the original 180-grain JHP.

To decide among all the different loads, a series of ammo tests was conducted by or for the ISP. These tests included clothed and bare ordnance gelatin and clothed and bare hogs.

The ISP was formed in 1933. Troopers were issued the Colt Official Police in .38 Special. They later used the S&W Model 10 and Model 15 in .38 Special, the S&W Model 19 and Model 66 in .357 Magnum, and the Beretta 92G in 9mm. The ISP has entered the next millennium with the Beretta 96G in .40 S&W.

The ISP logs 41 million miles a year patrolling 12 thousand miles of Hoosier road. Each year the average ISP trooper qualifies four times and shoots 750 rounds of ammo.

The service pistols used in the testing were a S&W M39 in 9mm Parabellum and a Glock M22 in .40 S&W. Additionally, a S&W Sigma in .380 was used for some limited testing of the ISP's .380 ACP 90-grain JHP service ammunition. The .380 Sigma was also used initially to euthanize some of the test animals. The ISP's current-issue 9mm 147-grain Hydra-Shok was used during the testing as a "control" round.

The test animals themselves came from the small percentage of feeder hogs that, due to illness or injury, had failed to thrive in a large farming operation. Since these animals had no hope of reaching market weight, it was routine policy to destroy them. These sick and injured animals became available at the rate of about two per month during peak farm population periods. This series of tests was conducted over a 10-month period, based on the availability of test animals.

It was initially hoped to have at least 200-pound animals for these tests. The hogs, however, were sadly dehydrated due to their inability to feed properly and were usually in the 155- to 160-pound weight range. Upon necropsy, it was noted that these animals frequently had little or no fatty tissue between their skin and the underlying muscle and bone structures. On reflection, it may be that these particular animals came closer to replicating human tissue due to their debilitated physical condition.

Realizing that a marked difference in thickness and density between hog skin and human skin would have an effect on bullet performance, I contacted the International Wound Ballistics Association (IWBA). Duncan McPherson of the IWBA research staff advised that, while differences exist, hog skin came the closest to duplicating human skin in their collective experience.

Each test animal was euthanized with brain shots strictly following the

The ISP performed 50 yard accuracy tests using a Beretta 96G duty pistol and a Ransom Rest. The departmental armorer fired two 10-shot strings of a wide variety of .40 S&W ammo.

The ISP set new and tough standards for bullet performance in bare ordnance gelatin. It required a minimum of 12 inches of gelatin and enforced a maximum of 14 inches. The Winchester .40 S&W 180-grain Ranger Talon penetrated 12.9 inches and expanded to .72 caliber.

American Veterinary Medicine Association (AVMA) protocol. The animals were immediately rolled into position and test shots were fired into the torso. The bullets were fired into each animal at its widest point or fired into the animal's shoulder area, allowing the bullets to penetrate the body lengthwise. The bullets engaged a variety of muscle, bone, and other

tissues as they penetrated the carcasses.

The test animals were then necropsied and most of the bullets were recovered. A few of the bullets were simply lost in the viscera. Additionally, on the broadside shots, a few of the bullets perforated the torso through-and-through and were also lost. The bullets fired into each animal were preselected by style, weight, and manufacture so as to make identification after expansion easier.

The recovered bullets were cleaned of extraneous material, identified, then measured, weighed, and cataloged. Notes were made of the location of recovery within each test animal's torso. A precise measurement of the total depth of penetration was not practical due to the inadvertent movement of some of the test bullets during the recovery process. About 10 recovered bullets for each of the test loads were recovered.

The primary goal of these tests was to compare the expansion and penetration of .40 S&W duty ammo in a realistic, live-tissue medium. With this goal in mind, the test bullets were first fired into the bare hog carcasses and recovered. After that, the carcasses were covered with four layers of cotton blue-jean denim in an effort to plug the hollowpoint cavities. The bullet performance differences between the bare-hog test shots and denim-clad test shots were documented.

A secondary goal of these tests was to compare standard-velocity 180-grain JHPs against medium-velocity 165-grain JHPs in a live-tissue medium. The medium-velocity versions of the .40 S&W caliber, developed for FBI use, have been used by some police agencies, including the Indianapolis Police and Marion County, Indiana, Sheriff. The medium-velocity versions were reported to "do everything the 180-grain loadings do," but with less chamber pressure and less felt recoil. However, CCI-Speer has dropped its medium-velocity 165-grain Gold Dot, and a number of police departments have upgraded to a higher velocity version, including the Marion County, Indiana, Sheriff.

Regarding the recovery depth of the bullets fired into the test animal's shoulder area, it would be helpful to visualize the carcass hanging by its head from the ceiling. The 135- and 155-grain bullets, as a group, penetrated "downward and inward" into the torso and came to rest at the base of the lung area. The 180-grain and high-velocity 165-grain bullets, as a group, were recovered in the upper intestinal area. The medium-velocity 165-grain bullets were recovered at a slightly greater depth than the 180-grain bullets in the middle of the intestines.

The Cor-Bon 9mm 115-grain JHP +P bullets were recovered in the base of the lung area. The Federal 9mm 147-grain Hydra-Shok control rounds penetrated the deepest of all, being recovered at the bottom of the intestinal area. None of these test shots exited the animal's carcass.

The Federal 9mm 147-grain Hydra-Shok was the ISP duty load and was fired into the hog as a benchmark. It averaged .50 caliber expansion in the heavily clothed hog. Every .40 S&W load, except the 165-grain medium-velocity Hydra-Shok and the 180-grain subsonic hollowpoint, did better than this.

In gelatin tests and actual shooting results alike, the Federal .40 S&W 165-grain medium-velocity Hydra-Shok consistently turns in the lowest performance. These hog tests simply confirmed that. The load expanded to .58 inch in the bare hog (left), which was well below the .66 inch average for all .40 S&W loads. In the heavily clothed hog, the load expanded to just .42 inch. No duty load did worse.

The test shots fired broadside into the widest part of the carcass successfully penetrated the animal's near-side chest wall, regardless of caliber or bullet weight. The .380 ACP 90-grain JHPs seemingly ran out of energy and were recovered, badly fragmented, in the body cavity. This was also true of the 9mm Cor-Bon 115-grain JHPs when they struck heavy bone upon entering the torso.

The 9mm 147-grain Hydra-Shok and the various .40 S&W rounds, regardless of bullet weight, penetrated much deeper and struck the far-side chest wall. Several of the Remington .40 S&W 180-grain Golden Sabers were recovered just under the skin on the far side of the test animal's torso. About 30 percent of the Federal medium-velocity 165-grain Hydra-Shoks exited the torso on the broadside test shots. A similar percentage of the Winchester 180-grain subsonic JHPs also exited the torso. This through-and-through penetration was mostly associated with test shots into the denim-clad carcasses.

For comparison purposes, an additional test bullet of each type used in the live animal tests was fired into 10 percent ballistic ordnance gelatin. The bullets test-fired into gelatin were from the same lots of ammunition used in the live tissue testing. The gelatin blocks employed were manufactured according to IWBA protocol. The gelatin blocks themselves were calibrated by firing a .177 caliber BB from a Crosman Powermaster air rifle at a velocity between 588 and 603 fps.

Prior to my participation in these tests, you could have never convinced me that a .40 S&W bullet was significantly better than a 9mm bullet. At roughly the same velocities, how could a 1 millimeter increase in bullet diameter make that much difference? Yet during this testing we observed that the various .40 S&W loads struck the carcasses decidedly harder in comparison to the impact delivered by the other calibers. They were, for the

The Remington .40 S&W 180-grain Golden Saber expanded to .79 caliber in bare gelatin and to .75 caliber in the bare hog, larger diameters than any other bullet. However, it was this mere .54 caliber expansion in the heavily clothed hog (shown) that disqualified the load.

The Winchester .40 S&W 180-grain Ranger Talon expanded to .72 inch in the bare hog and a best-in-class .68 caliber in the heavily clothed hog.

most part, also visibly more destructive of tissue, tearing thumb-sized holes through internal organs and often leaving bloodshot tissue trails that the other calibers could not rival. Additionally, the .40 S&W loads handled gristle plates and tough bone joints that sometimes deflected, or even defeated, the other test calibers.

The ISP 9mm service load performed as expected in its role as a control round. This Federal 147-grain Hydra-Shok expanded adequately and reliably defeated heavy bone structures. The load appears to represent the minimum performance needed for an effective police handgun round. The four layers of denim greatly reduced the tendency of the Cor-Bon 9mm 115-grain loads to

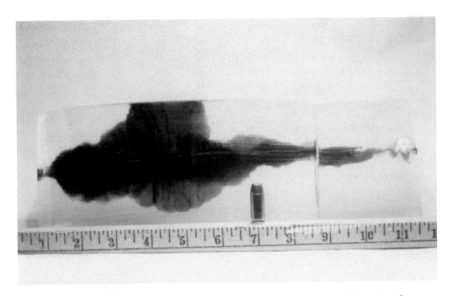

The CCI-Speer .40 S&W 180-grain Gold Dot expanded reliably in a wide variety of test media. The ISP tested the redesigned Gold Dot, which has a thicker jacket for better accuracy and fewer jacket serrations for larger recovered diameters. It expanded to .67 caliber in the bare hog and to an average of .61 caliber in the heavily clothed hog.

The Federal .40 S&W 180-grain Hydra-Shok was one of the finalists in the ISP tests. It is the .40 S&W load with the most one-shot stops, and the ISP had previously had good success with the 9mm 147-grain Hydra-Shok.

fragment. One Cor-Bon 9mm test shot into a bare hog struck the shoulder of the animal and fragmented in the joint area. The surrounding bone was shattered dramatically, but only a few large fragments penetrated into the chest cavity.

The .40 S&W 135-, 155-, and high-velocity 165-grain JHPs expanded well and penetrated adequately. The tendency of the 135-grain JHPs to fragment was also greatly reduced during the denim-clad hog testing. Instead, these bullets expanded to large diameters and held the mushroom.

With the exception of the Winchester 180-grain subsonic JHPs, the .40 S&W 180-grain test rounds performed quite well. The Winchester

.40 S&W 180-grain Ranger Talon repeatedly gave the best expansion performance during the denim testing. Some of the 180-grain Ranger Talon rounds experienced separation of the jacket and core during the testing. The wound tracks indicated a percentage of these rounds had engaged heavy bone during penetration. The jackets and cores were usually recovered within 4 inches or so of each other at a depth of 12 inches or more in the carcass.

The CCI-Speer 180-grain Gold Dot test rounds were noteworthy for their consistency of expansion and penetration. These rounds displayed the least shot-to-shot variance in expanded diameters. They also demonstrated the most consistent penetration. It was not unusual to recover three or more spent 180-grain Gold Dots clustered within about 5 inches of one another inside the test carcass.

Regarding the performance differences between the standard-velocity 180-grain .40 S&W loads and the medium-velocity 165-grain loads, it was clear that the 180-grain versions were superior. In the bare-hog tests, the medium-velocity 165-grain Hydra-Shok rounds expanded to 9mm 147-grain Hydra-Shok levels. The Federal 180-grain Hydra-Shok versions, on the other hand, expanded to the size of a 12-gauge rifled slug.

The reported reduction in felt recoil of the medium-velocity 165-grain JHPs was not readily discernible to the shooters during this testing. In fact, the only perceptible difference in felt recoil among any of the .40 S&W test rounds was the slightly increased recoil of the 135-grain and 155-grain loadings.

Within the parameters of this series of tissue and gelatin tests, it was clear that the .40 S&W caliber was a definite improvement over the 9mm Parabellum. With few exceptions, the .40 S&W test rounds expanded well and exhibited adequate, but not excessive, penetration. The results obtained in these tests also tended to validate the use of calibrated 10

The Federal .40 S&W 180-grain Tactical turned in its trademark consistent performance. It expanded to between .64 and .66 inch in bare media and to .60 inch in the heavily clothed hog (shown).

The ISP adopted the Winchester .40 S&W 180-grain Ranger Talon as its new duty load. The Ranger Talon is an upgraded version of the old Black Talon. The .40 S&W Ranger Talon is also used by the Georgia State Patrol, Pennsylvania State Police, Nevada Highway Patrol, Dallas County Sheriff, and Anchorage Police.

The Federal .40 S&W 180-grain Hydra-Shok expanded to .73 inch in the bare hog (left) and a respectable .60 inch in the heavily clothed hog (right). This was the second best performance of the test.

The Winchester .40 S&W 180-grain Supreme SXT expanded to .66 caliber in the bare hog (left) and to .59-caliber in the heavily clothed hog (right). This was right on the average expansion for all the 155-, 165-, and 180-grain loads.

percent ordnance gelatin as a practical test medium.

Based on this testing, the ISP narrowed its bullet selection to one of three loads: 180-grain Hydra-Shot, 180-grain Ranger Talon, and 180-grain Gold Dot. After bench rest testing for accuracy from the Beretta 96, the Ranger Talon was selected as the ISP duty load.

TABLE 8-1
EXTERIOR BALLISTICS

Manufacturer	Caliber	Weight grs.	Style	Velocity fps
Federal	.40 S&W	180	Hydra-Shok	945
Federal	.40 S&W	180	Tactical JHP	985
CCI-Speer	.40 S&W	180	Gold Dot *	980
Winchester	.40 S&W	180	Sub-Sonic JHP	950
Winchester	.40 S&W	180	Supreme SXT	955
Winchester	.40 S&W	180	Ranger/SXT **	955
Remington	.40 S&W	180	Golden Saber	980
Federal	.40 S&W	165	Hydra-Shok	975
CCI-Speer	.40 S&W	165	Gold Dot ***	980
Federal	.40 S&W	165	Tactical JHP	1050
Winchester	.40 S&W	165	Black Talon	1070
Winchester	.40 S&W	155	Silvertip	1205
CCI-Speer	.40 S&W	155	Gold Dot	1175
Cor-Bon	.40 S&W	135	Sierra JHP	1325
Federal	9mm Para	147	Hydra-Shok	955
Cor-Bon	9mm Para	115	Sierra JHP	1350
Federal	.380 ACP	90	Hydra-Shok	985

* Gold Dot 180-grain with new style 6-petal hollowpoint.

** Ranger/SXT 180-grain with new style 6-petal hollowpoint.

*** Gold Dot 165-grain Medium Velocity is no longer in production. Included for comparison purposes only.

TABLE 8-2
TERMINAL BALLISTICS

Manufacturer	Caliber	Weight grs.	Style	Bare Gel. inch	Bare Hog Inch	Denim Hog Inch
Federal	.40 S&W	180	Hydra-Shok	.74	.73	.60
Federal	.40 S&W	180	Tactical	.66	.64	.60
CCI-Speer	.40 S&W	180	Gold Dot	.69	.67	.61
Winchester	.40 S&W	180	Sub-Sonic	.63	.60	.42
Winchester	.40 S&W	180	Supreme/SXT	.68	.66	.59
Winchester	.40 S&W	180	Ranger/SXT	.74	.72	.68
Remington	.40 S&W	180	Gold. Saber	.79	.75	.54
Federal	.40 S&W	165	Hydra-Shok	.67	.58	.42
CCI-Spee	.40 S&W	165	Gold Dot	.69	.62	.51
Federal	.40 S&W	165	Tactical	.65	.64	.60
Winchester	.40 S&W	165	Black Talon	.67	.65	.61
Winchester	.40 S&W	155	Silvertip	.70	.68	.66
CCI-Speer	.40 S&W	155	Gold Dot	.70	.66	.61
Cor-Bon	.40 S&W	135	Sierra JHP	.59(f)	.57(f)	.72
Federal	9mm Para	147	Hydra-Shok	.64	.56	.50
Cor-Bon	9mm Para	115	Sierra JHP	.55(f)	.53(f)	.66
Federal	.380 ACP	90	Hydra-Shok	.57	.42	.39

CHAPTER 9

.357 SIG Ammo

The .357 SIG cartridge dates back to a 1993 joint effort between Sigarms and Federal Cartridge. Credit for the caliber goes to Alan Newcombe, a bottleneck cartridge enthusiast working for Sigarms who used to work for Federal. The Sigarms .357 SIG P229 auto pistol and the Federal .357 SIG 125-grain JHP were introduced at the NRA Convention in mid-1994.

The demand for the .357 SIG caliber dates back to the mid-1980s transition from the six-shot .357 Magnum revolver to the higher capacity 9mm and .45 ACP auto pistol.

While cops gained a few more shots between reloads, they gave up a lot of stopping power. Cops tried the 9mm 115-grain JHPs, then the 9mm 147-grain JHPs. Disillusioned, some tried the .45 ACP 230-grain JHPs, then the 10mm medium-velocity 180-grain JHPs, then the .40 S&W 180-grain JHPs.

Nothing, it seemed, had the velocity, energy, and ultimately the street effectiveness of the .357 Magnum they used to carry. In fact, the ones most satisfied with the 9mm were the ones who used to carry the .38 Special and didn't know any better.

The .357 Magnum 125-grain JHP produces between 87 and 96 percent one-shot stops. Most other loads tried by the police range from the mid 70s to the high 80s in percent effectiveness.

The idea behind the new caliber was to use the case capacity of a bottleneck cartridge to push a .355 inch auto pistol bullet as fast as a .357 Magnum. The .357 SIG is basically a .40 S&W casenecked down to .355 inch. The .357 SIG fires a .355 inch 9mm bullet, not a .357 inch .357 Magnum bullet.

The original goal was to achieve more than 1300 fps in muzzle velocity

The .357 SIG cartridge was a joint effort between Sigarms and Federal. The first load, introduced in 1994, was the Federal 125-grain JHP.

The .357 SIG, like this Remington 125-grain JHP (center), produces more energy than any 9mm 115-grain JHP +P+ (left) and more velocity than any .45 ACP 185-grain +P (right).

The popular police calibers are shown in comparison, left to right: 9mm, .357 SIG, .40 S&W, and .45 ACP. The .357 SIG is a necked-down .40 S&W that fires a .355 inch bullet as fast as a .357 Magnum.

and more than 500 ft-lbs. of muzzle energy. The hottest 9mm 115-grain +P+ travels more than 1300 fps but only generates 450 ft-lbs. The hottest .45 ACP 185-grain +P is more than 500 ft-lbs. but well under 1200 fps. The only other cartridge to achieve the goals of the .357 SIG is the .40 S&W, but only when loaded with 135-grain JHPs from Cor-Bon and Triton.

The .357 SIG is one of the most powerful bottleneck auto pistol cartridges ever developed. It operates at up to a 40,000 psi chamber pressure. This compares to 35,000 psi for the .357 Magnum, .40 S&W, and 9mm. The 9mm +P is at 38,500 psi while the 9mm +P+ is generally acknowledged to be at 40,000 psi. Only the 9mm NATO, .356 TSW, and 9 x 23mm Winchester have higher pressures among popular handgun calibers. The .44 Magnum is restricted to just 36,000 psi.

According to the Fuller Index and actual street results, the .357 SIG outperforms nearly all of the 9mm +P+, .40 S&W, and .45 ACP loads. It may not produce more one-shot stops than the 135-grain and 155-grain .40 S&W and the 185-grain .45 ACP +P, but the effectiveness is quite close with much less felt recoil. The .357 SIG in its original 125-grain JHP loading is far more effective than the .40 S&W in its original 180-grain JHP loading.

The .357 SIG was specifically developed for law enforcement. Yet the caliber itself absolutely defies the FBI test method for law enforcement ammo. The FBI protocol, geared for cops, has resulted in bleak performing rounds like the 9mm 147-grain JHP and the .40 S&W medium-velocity 165-grain JHP. What cops really want is their old .357 Magnum back. Yet even the .357 Magnum itself does not fare well under the FBI protocol.

The .357 SIG is the answer to cops (and all handgunners) who like the idea of a load that has been proven on the street rather than in the lab. Evan Marshall's street results show the .357 Magnum 125-grain JHP to be the statistically most effective handgun

load ever used in police-action shootings. Since the FBI test protocol points to loads in the opposite direction, it cannot help to identify which new auto pistol load works like the old .357 Magnum, or even how to develop one that does.

The only choice was for Federal and Sigarms to exactly copy the "exterior" ballistics of the .357 Magnum. This would give them the same wound ballistics as the .357 Magnum, no matter what the best-intentioned test protocol indicated.

The .357 SIG and the .357 Magnum fire the same bullet weight (125 grains) with a similar bullet diameter (.355 inch vs. .357 inch) at the same velocities (1400 fps). A felon cannot tell if this bullet came from a S&W Model 686, a Sigarms P226, a Colt Trooper, or a Glock Model 31. The end result is the same: instant incapacitation over 90 percent of the time with one shot to the torso.

Federal and Sigarms only had two real options to achieve .357 Magnum ballistics from a 9mm bullet. One was to make the cartridge longer. For example, the 9 x 23mm Winchester absolutely equals the performance and exceeds the power of the .357

Magnum. However, the grip size on the auto pistol has to be longer to allow the longer cartridge. A police auto pistol has to fit a wide cross-section of hands, and the grip panels on most large-frame auto pistols are simply too big for most shooters.

The other option was to make the cartridge diameter larger. Bottleneck pistol cartridges are *not* new! Bottleneck cartridges like the 7.62mm Tokarev, 7.63 x 25mm (.30) Mauser, 7.65mm Borchardt, and 7.65 x 21mm (.30) Luger have been around as long as the auto pistol itself. In fact, the first "successful" auto pistol calibers were bottleneck cartridges. Other bottleneck cartridges include the .45/.38 Clerke, 9mm Action Express, .357 Auto Mag, and more recently, the 9 x 25mm Dillon.

A little confusion exists on the "true" velocity of the .357 Magnum 125-grain JHP. The muzzle velocity of 1450 fps is frequently cited, yet that is only typical of a 6 inch gun. Some 4 inch revolvers with an especially tight cylinder-to-barrel gap can produce this velocity, but it is the exception. The velocity from a 4 inch .357 Magnum 125-grain JHP varies from 1275 fps to 1465 fps, with an average of 1370 fps.

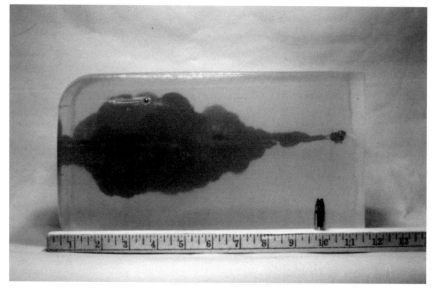

The Federal .357 SIG 125-grain JHP penetrates from 11 to 14 inches of gelatin, depending on the barrel length. This load has produced 92 percent one-shot stops.

The heavy favorite among cops using the .357 SIG is this CCI-Speer 125-grain Gold Dot. This copper-plated JHP expands well and has excellent tactical penetration.

This is from the full-power loads, not from the Remington 125-grain medium-velocity S-JHP or the downloaded Remington 125-grain Golden Saber. The 2 1/2 inch revolvers average 1325 fps with full-power 125-grain JHPs.

Similar confusion exists with the .357 SIG. Federal and Sigarms pushed the chamber pressure of the .357 SIG past the .357 Magnum to achieve a velocity of 1350 fps from a 125-grain JHP out of a 3.9 inch Sig P229. This rivals the .357 Magnum 125-grain JHP from a 2 1/2 to 3 inch revolver. The 3.5 inch Glock 33 produces about the same results. That is okay, and it sure beats the 9mm 115-grain +P+, but it is not "legend" status.

The .357 SIG earns its .357 name when fired from a 4.4 inch Sig P226, 4 inch Glock 32, and 4.5 inch Glock 31. While the makes of ammo vary, these pistols produce muzzle velocities from 1385 fps (P226) to 1465 (G31). These are the 4 inch .357 Magnum velocities that have earned the 125-grain JHP a one-shot stop record of up to 96 percent.

The first loads for the .357 SIG were the Federal 125-grain JHP, the Hornady 124-grain XTP, and the CCI-Speer 125-grain Gold Dot. While Federal got all the early press because it invented the caliber, it was CCI-Speer that captured most of the police market with its Gold Dot bullet.

The .357 SIG caliber was introduced at the peak of two law enforcement concerns: weight retention and tactical penetration. Federal had designed its .357 SIG 125-grain JHP to react in a way totally different from its legendary .357 Magnum 125-grain JHP. The .357 Magnum expanded, then fragmented, and had a 60 percent weight retention. This defined success in police-action shootings. The new Federal .357 SIG load expanded, retained its full mushroom, and had a 100 percent weight retention. In spite of the fact that this was not how the .357 Magnum reacted in gelatin, the prevailing thinking at the time called for maximum weight retention. In fact, nearly all makes of .357 SIG ammo followed this same "high weight retention" theory of stopping power.

The various makes of .357 SIG ammo differed the most in their tactical penetration, especially against car bodies and auto glass. The Delaware State Police was the first major agency to select the .357 SIG 125-grain Gold Dot specifically for its superior anticar ballistics. DPS tactical teams had a hard time getting inside vehicles with their 9mm 147-grain JHPs. The .357 SIG load has 80 percent more energy than the 9mm subsonic hollowpoint, giving it more punch to defeat auto glass.

The Gold Dot bullet is more likely to perform well after tactical barriers than a conventional JHP. This is its true advantage. In bare and heavily clothed gelatin, the Gold Dot works as well as other bullet designs. However, many of these JHPs shed their jackets or suffer extreme weight loss after encountering auto glass. The Gold Dot has a thick electroplated copper jacket that simply will not separate even from a high-energy impact with glass. As a result, most of the major agencies like the Delaware State Police and the Texas Department of Public Safety that adopted the .357 SIG also adopted the 125-grain Gold Dot.

Shortly after the 124- and 125-grain JHPs were released, Hornady introduced its 147-grain XTP and Federal followed with its 150-grain JHP. They were hoping to appeal to agencies that were dissatisfied with the 9mm subsonic hollowpoint yet wanted to keep all the hype with the heavy bullet weight. After all, it would be the same bullet, just driven 200 fps faster. But the cops didn't fall for it like they did in the mid-1980s. Even the FBI

Not even the 40,000 psi chamber of the .357 SIG can push the 147- to 150-grain JHPs fast enough for top performance. This Federal 150-grain JHP produces 85 percent one-shot stops.

itself, which popularized the 9mm subsonic hollowpoint, abandoned it as soon as the 10mm medium-velocity was developed.

As a result, while the .357 SIG 147-grain JHP is vastly superior to the 9mm 147-grain JHP, if an agency wanted to "upgrade" it went to the .40 S&W 180-grain JHP. If, however, it got stung one too many times by the lack of energy from *all* these subsonic loads, regardless of caliber, it went to the .357 SIG 125-grain JHP.

Shortly after the caliber was introduced, Cor-Bon and Triton Cartridge joined the fray. Both released sizzling versions of the 124- or 125-grain JHP and a 115-grain JHP.

CCI-Speer has two very different Gold Dot bullets in this weight and diameter range. One is a .357 inch 125-grain hollowpoint developed for the .357 Magnum. It has a very shallow, V-shaped, "cup" hollowpoint cavity. The shallow cavity does not plug up with clothing or building material debris simply because the cavity is too small. This is the same Gold Dot bullet used in the .357 SIG caliber except the bullet diameter measures .355 inch. What works at 1450 fps from the .357 Magnum also works at 1450 fps from the .357 SIG.

CCI-Speer also has a .355 inch 124-grain Gold Dot developed for the 9mm. It has a larger and deeper hollowpoint cavity designed for reliable expansion between 1150 and 1250 fps. Simply put, the 124-grain Gold Dot has a lower threshold of expansion than the 125-grain Gold Dot. Cor-Bon used to load the 9mm 124-grain Gold Dot in the .357 SIG caliber. When driven to the same 1400 fps, both the 124- and 125-grain Gold Dots penetrate the same 16.5 inches. The Gold Dot developed for the .357 Magnum had a larger recovered diameter than the one developed for the 9mm. Both bullets have a 100 percent retained weight but the 9mm-based bullet broke up and was literally held together only by the copper-plated jacket.

The Cor-Bon .357 SIG 115-grain Sierra JHP has one of the highest stopping power ratings in the caliber. This load dumps nearly 600 ft-lbs. of energy in 12.5 inches of gelatin.

The Triton .357 SIG 125-grain JHP is the most like the original .357 Magnum 125-grain JHP. The wound profile and recovered weight are identical. This may be the best overall load in the caliber.

Cor-Bon originally loaded its .357 SIG with a 124-grain bonded hollowpoint. This bullet was a deep hollowpoint Gold Dot developed by CCI-Speer for its successful run at the New York Police Department contract. This was in the mid-1990s when the NYPD was considering a variety of 9mm 124- to 127-grain +P JHPs. Cor-Bon later transitioned to a 125-grain Sierra JHP for all its 9mm-size loadings, including the 9mm, .38 Super, and .357 SIG. The 115-grain JHP used in its .357 SIG has always been a Sierra bullet.

Cor-Bon's 125-grain Sierra JHP and the 125-grain Rainier JHP used by Triton in its .357 SIG ammo typically expand and then fragment to a 60 percent recovered weight. As such, the

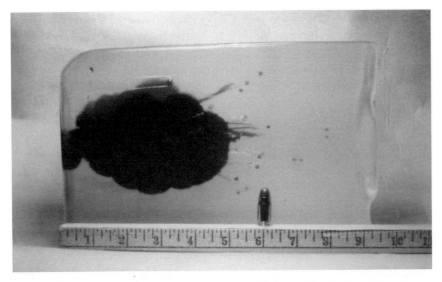

The .357 SIG is available in a wide variety of frangible bullets like this Glaser 80-grain Silver Safety Slug. Frangible and controlled separation bullets, like the Triton Quik-Shok, make excellent home defense loads.

The most recent .357 SIG load is the police-only Winchester 125-grain Ranger T-series, developed specifically for the U.S. Secret Service.

stopping power, cycle reliability, and tactical penetration problem that civilian handgunners did not experience. The .357 SIG gained in use but not nearly as fast as the .40 S&W had in the early 1990s.

One by one, more ammo companies began to produce the .357 SIG. Remington released a 125-grain JHP, then Glaser introduced both a Blue and Silver 80-grain Safety Slug. The MagSafe 64-grain Defender was the first of the frangibles, introduced within a few months of the new caliber being announced.

Each time a JHP was developed, each of the major ammo companies also released a FMJ hardball training round. Federal, CCI-Speer, PMC, and Remington all produced such lower cost hardball training ammo.

Of the nine major ammunition companies, it was Winchester that waited the longest to develop a .357 SIG. In fact, while the .357 SIG caliber and pistols were introduced in 1994, Winchester did not join the party until 1999. By this time, Glock had joined Sigarms in producing auto pistols.

Winchester came late but made the second big splash in this caliber. They announced a me-too 125-grain FMJ, then stunned the ammo industry with a 125-grain JHP developed for the U.S. Secret Service. One week Winchester did not have a .357 SIG hollowpoint; the next it had captured

Winchester makes the most loads for the .357 SIG, including the 125-grain Ranger T-series (shown), the 125-grain Partition Gold, the 125-grain FMJ, and the 105-grain Super Clean NT.

Triton and Cor-Bon .357 SIG 125-grain JHPs are the most accurate duplications of this successful .357 Magnum 125-grain JHP. Many ammo makers strive for the most retained weight to pass certain test protocols. Triton and Cor-Bon are the only ones to exactly follow the wound profile—success frozen in time for all to see—of the .357 Magnum 125-grain JHP. As a result, the Triton and Cor-Bon .357 SIG 125-grain JHPs may be the best overall loads in this caliber.

After the first big splash in 1994, ammo companies large and small sat back and watched the caliber to see if it would become popular. The .357 SIG was more accepted by law enforcement than civilian shooters simply because it solved a combined the 1.6 million round Secret Service ammo contract.

The new Winchester loading developed specifically for the Secret Service is its Ranger T series of ammo and is the same load available to all of law enforcement. The bullet construction and the muzzle velocity are the same. This is not one of the restricted or minimum-buy Q loads. Instead, it is the catalogued Ranger T ammo. Even small departments can get this stuff.

Winchester has changed names and bullet designs on this line of ammo a number of times. First it was the Black Talon. Then it became the police-only Ranger SXT, which was different than the defanged, civilian Supreme SXT. Then the bullet was changed from a late energy release to a medium energy release to work better against heavy clothes and from short-barrel pistols. Winchester renamed these upgraded loads Ranger Talon. For 1999, Winchester again renamed this entire police-only line the Ranger T series. Still the upgraded, full-talon design, the Winchester Ranger T series is probably the best general-issue police duty bullet available.

Immediately after the .357 SIG 125-grain Ranger T, Winchester announced its answer to the police demand for a "tactical" or "bonded" bullet with its Partition Gold ammo. The company already loaded the Nosler Partition bullet in the big-bore hunting calibers. In 1999, it began to load the bullet in the police auto pistol calibers too.

The CCI-Speer Gold Dot was the first of the bonded anticar bullets. This ammo is available to all handgunners at standard JHP prices. Next was the restricted, semiexotic, and expensive Federal Tactical. Based on its Trophy Bonded rifle bullets, this ammo uses a high copper jacket with the lead alloy core literally soldered to the jacket. Remington followed suit in 1999 with a Golden Saber Bonded. Again, the lead core is actually soldered to the hard brass jacket.

The Winchester Partition Gold is perhaps the ultimate anticar, antiglass handgun bullet. The nose and the front core are designed to expand readily in bare and heavily clothed gelatin. Yet the heavy web, or partition between the front and rear cores, allows the bullet to penetrate auto glass and car bodies with a high retained weight and adequate penetration. The Winchester .357 SIG 125-grain Partition Gold hollowpoint (PGHP) has the same 1350 fps (P229) and 1385 fps (P226) as Winchester's other 125-grain loads.

The .357 SIG is so geared to law enforcement that Winchester does not even make a non-police JHP in this caliber. Both its 125-grain Ranger T-series and 125-grain Partition Gold are restricted to law enforcement. The company currently has no plans for a civilian 125-grain Supreme SXT. With the exception of the Federal 125-grain Tactical, all other .357 SIG loadings are available to all handgunners.

With the .357 SIG, all the attention has been on muzzle velocity, muzzle energy, and how similar the .357 SIG is to the .357 Magnum. In addition to .357 Magnum wound ballistics, the new bottleneck caliber also has advantages in the areas of cycle reliability, felt recoil, and accuracy.

The .357 SIG may be the most technically reliable of all the current police auto pistol calibers due to the bottleneck cartridge design. It may have better cycle reliability than a .45 ACP when fed 230-grain ball, and it is certainly more reliable than a 9mm-fed subsonic hollowpoint. The loading cycle involves putting a .36 inch diameter bullet into a .40 inch diameter chamber. It is just about as simple as that. Fully automatic rifles and larger caliber military small arms all use the bottleneck cartridge design. Getting the round extracted and ejected face the same challenges as all other pistol calibers; however, getting a round out of the magazine and into the chamber is much easier than other calibers.

Police academy instructors have

found that recruit classes are the best possible proving ground for any piece of police equipment. Police recruits make more of the same grip and stance shooting errors than veteran officers and civilian enthusiasts. In an acid-test, the Texas DPS Academy staff found that their Sigarms P226 shooting the .357 SIG cartridge would reliably cycle even when the shooter did not lock his wrists or when fired one-handed or with a low grip. The cartridge produces a snappy enough recoil to allow weak hand and broken wrist shooting with no shooter-induced stoppages. No pistol caliber has the same inherent cycle reliability as the .357 SIG.

In the first Texas DPS Academy class to be trained on the .357 SIG, recruits fired a total of 300,000 rounds without a *single* stoppage of any kind for any reason. In another test for cycle reliability, two Academy sergeants fired 640 rounds of duty ammo through one P226 in 12 minutes. The pistol got so hot it could not be held. In fact, the plastic around the night sights melted and the pistol was close to cooking-off chambered rounds. However, not one stoppage occurred. In another test, the staff fired 4,000 rounds of Federal 125-grain JHPs through five Sigarms pistols with no failures to cycle.

Another advantage is in the area of felt recoil. Much of the .357 Magnum level of felt recoil is softened by the .357 SIG overcoming the inertia of the slide and compressing the spring system. The ergonomics of the auto pistol are clearly superior to that of the revolver. Even though the auto pistol may weigh a little less than the revolver, the felt recoil is less and the recoil recovery time is faster than the .357 Magnum. This is true even though both guns fire a 125-grain bullet at 1400 fps.

The .357 SIG 125-grain JHP has a Power Factor similar to the .40 S&W 180-grain JHP and produces less recoil than the .40 S&W 155-grain JHP and the .45 ACP 230-grain JHP. From a P226, the .357 SIG 125-grain JHP has

The Texas DPS Academy firearms staff evaluated the poor effectiveness of the .45 ACP and pushed for the .357 SIG cartridge. This gave the DPS the stopping power and tactical penetration equal to its S&W Model 28-fired .357 Magnum.

a Power Factor of 173 compared to a Power Factor of 190 for the .45 ACP 230-grain JHP from a P220.

This recoil reduction was instantly verified during training sessions with the March 1997 trooper recruit class at the Texas DPS Academy. The class was together for initial training with the S&W K-22 .22 Long Rifle revolver and the S&W Model 586 revolver firing .38 Special ammo. They received the same introduction to the Sigarms auto pistols. Then the class was divided into two groups.

One group trained with the Sig P220 in .45 ACP while the other trained with the Sig P226 in .357 SIG. Then both groups shot for score. At ranges from 7 to 50 yards and 300 points possible, the .45 ACP group averaged 245 points. The .357 SIG group averaged 275 points. The .45 ACP group was then given .357 SIG pistols and their scores promptly came up to match the first group.

In a transition from the 9mm and .40 S&W to the .357 SIG, New Jersey Fish, Game, and Wildlife experienced the same improvement in scores as the Texas troopers. As a surprise bonus,

their percentage of center hits also increased with the .357 SIG.

The Texas DPS Academy firearms staff credits three reasons for the greatly improved qualifying scores. First, less recoil. The March 1997 Academy class settled the question of whether stiff recoil or an intense muzzle blast causes a shooter to flinch. The .45 ACP produces more recoil. The .357 SIG produces more blast. While the tendency of a shooter to flinch might be due to both recoil and blast, the DPS clearly proved in its comparison that the problem with low scores was the recoil from the .45 ACP. From a training perspective, half of the officers that carry the .45 ACP cannot deal with the recoil.

The second factor in the improved scores was the flatter trajectory of the .357 SIG bullet. At nearly 1400 fps, the 125-grain JHP shoots to the same point of aim out to 50 yards. With the slower and heavier .45 ACP bullet, the shooter has to hold over the point of impact from 6 to 12 inches out to 50 yards.

The third factor in the improved scores comes from increased confidence. This is tough to measure,

but it is easy to see when it's there and obvious when it's missing. Even though the .45 ACP had a macho reputation as the legendary big bore, the Texas troopers had lost confidence in it in just three years due to its poor performance. Troopers now have confidence and, in fact, a real sense of pride in their sidearm.

Another advantage of the .357 SIG caliber is accuracy. The first major (100+ man) police departments to adopt the .357 SIG were the LaPorte County, Indiana, Sheriff's Department (LCSD) and the Porter County, Indiana, Sheriff's Police. Porter County carried the .357 Magnum until an auto pistol load was developed that exactly matched its revolver round. They did not go for the 9mm +P+ nor anything in .40 S&W, but they jumped all over the .357 SIG.

LaPorte County was a different story. It had suffered through the dark ages carrying a 9mm subsonic hollowpoint. All the while it wanted a caliber with the stopping power of the .357 Magnum its deputies used to carry. The real issue with LaPorte County, however, was accuracy. Its firearms instructors are competitive PPC shooters. They attend matches in the Hoosier State and all across the midwest. They also serve as adjunct instructors during the Firearms Instructor classes at the Indiana Law Enforcement Academy. The best 9mm 147-grain JHP was nowhere near as accurate at 50 yards as their .357 Magnum. More than wound ballistics, the LCSD wanted long-range accuracy. They got it with the .357 SIG.

The .357 SIG generally uses a slower rifling twist (1:16) than the 9mm (1:10) but a slightly faster twist than the .357 Magnum (1:18). While each gun and each lot of ammo is different, the .357 SIG has established a reputation among police marksmen as the most accurate of all the auto pistol calibers.

One of the components of this accuracy reputation is the longer range and less bullet drop of the .357 SIG compared to all other duty caliber and load combinations. The .357 SIG is the flattest shooting of all these calibers. It requires no holdover out to 50 yards and shoots the closest to point of aim at 100 yards of any duty auto pistol caliber. Texas Highway Patrol troopers can now pick off coyotes at 100 yards. They couldn't do that with either the 9mm 147-grain JHPs or the .45 ACP 230-grain JHPs they used to carry.

The .357 SIG is starting to gain the same street reputation among cops as the old .357 Magnum. With over 500 ft-lbs. of energy, state troopers know the .357 SIG will punch through cars and not ricochet off glass or get defeated by body panels. They know that the round produces enough energy to defeat tactical barriers with enough energy left over to adequately penetrate the human target. City cops know that the 1400 fps bullet will penetrate heavy layers of clothing and still have enough velocity to expand reliably.

The .357 SIG has been used in a number of officer-involved shootings. The early reports from agencies like the Texas DPS are that it is a clear improvement over the .45 ACP 230-grain JHP its officers used to carry and equal to their old .357 Magnum.

Of the available .357 SIG loads, the highest Fuller Index estimates go to the frangibles like Glaser, MagSafe, and Quik-Shok and to the 115-grain JHP from Cor-Bon. These loads have a Fuller Index between 87 and 96 percent one-shot stops. However, none of these have yet been used in enough shootings to publish an actual one-shot stop result. The Fuller Index for all these .357 SIG loads is based on velocities from the 4.4 inch Sigarms P226 and the 4 inch Glock 32. These auto pistols produce the same velocity, which is 50 to 100 fps faster than the shorter barrel auto pistols. The 4.5 inch Glock 31 averages 35 fps more velocity.

The 125-grain JHPs have proven to be fight stoppers 89 to 92 percent of the time with one shot in actual shootings. The 147- to 150-grain JHPs

have actual results and a Fuller Index between 84 and 85 percent. The various FMJ hardball loads will be just 70 percent effective.

New loads continue to be released for this now firmly entrenched police and defensive caliber. CCI-Speer has made a brass case 125-grain totally metal jacketed (TMJ) training load since the beginning. This same TMJ bullet is now available in the aluminum case Blazer line of ammo. Also in training ammo, Winchester has a 125-grain Super Clean NT (nontoxic) loading for the .357 SIG. The Super Clean NT uses a lead-free primer and a jacketed softpoint bullet with a *tin* core. This ammo is intended only for indoor and outdoor ranges, not for police duty or personal defense. The Super Clean NT has one of the shortest bounce-back threat ranges of any load, making it an excellent choice for steel reaction targets.

Other recent developments include a 115- and 135-grain Quik Shok from Triton Cartridge. The Quik-Shok had the fastest incapacitation time of any jacketed hollowpoint during the Strasbourg Tests. On impact, the Quik-Shok breaks into three large fragments, each weighing about 40 grains. In comparison, a .30 caliber, #1 buck pellet weighs 40 grains. These large frags penetrate 9 to 11 inches of gelatin. No less a gunfight authority than the U.S. Border Patrol has determined that 9 inches of penetration is enough for its agents who patrol border-to-border and coast-to-coast.

The U.S. Secret Service has been a long-time proponent of the 9mm 115-grain +P+ JHP. It, too, wanted just 9 inches of penetration from its new .357 SIG load. While a 12 inch minimum may have been the goal from the mid-1980s, the new minimum among police gunfight experts is 9 inches. While the Winchester Ranger T series is arguably the best general-issue police duty load, the Triton Quik-Shok is arguably the best load for home defense and personal protection scenarios.

On the topic of tactical loads, Federal has recently introduced a 125-grain Tactical for the .357 SIG caliber. While the CCI-Speer Gold Dot and Winchester Partition Gold are very good anticar loads, *no* bullet is better against laminated auto glass and thermopane windows than the Federal Tactical. It uses a softer alloy of jacket than gilding metal, 97 percent copper and 3 percent zinc compared to 95 percent copper and 5 percent zinc. The core is dead soft, 0 percent lead. The bullet is then flame annealed to further soften the jacket after the work hardening of the final forming operations. As a result, the nose of the Tactical is extremely soft.

On an angled impact with glass, the nose of the Tactical bullet instantly deforms to the angle of impact. This allows the bullet to push forward with the least change in bullet flight. While other bullets are likely to ricochet or dig into the glass and tumble or be thrown off course during the penetration, the Tactical has the closest point of impact to point of aim after glass of any bullet. The Tactical gives up a little in wound ballistics to gain a lot in after-glass effectiveness.

One sign of success for any new caliber is the adoption by major city, county, state, and federal police departments. The Delaware State Police was the first state agency to adopt the .357 SIG. Then came the Virginia and Connecticut State Police. The Alameda County, California, Sheriff and Springfield, Illinois, Police were next. The Texas DPS is the biggest department to date to go with the .357 SIG. The Dallas, Texas, Police now authorizes the .357 SIG. The U.S. Secret Service has adopted the bottleneck caliber. So has the U.S. Sky Marshals. The New Mexico State Police is the most recent major agency to adopt the .357 SIG.

The caliber continues to grow in popularity, mostly among cops. In the years to come, the .357 SIG could very well replace the 9mm and .40 S&W as America's police caliber.

TABLE 9-1
.357 SIG WOUND BALLISTICS

Make & Load	Muzzle Velocity fps	Muzzle Energy ft-lbs.	Gelatin Depth inch	Recovered Diameter	One-Shot Stop
MagSafe 64 gr. Defender	2275	736	11.3	frag	96% est.
Federal 125 gr. JHP	1430	568	12.7	0.62	92% actual
Cor-Bon 115 gr. Sierra JHP	1515	586	12.5	0.58	92% est.
CCI-Speer 125 gr. Gold Dot	1385	533	16.5	0.68	91% actual
Triton 125 gr. Rainier JHP	1440	576	13.8	.40(f)	91% est.
Federal 125 gr. Tactical	1410	552	12.0	0.65	91% est.
Cor-Bon 125 gr. Sierra JHP	1440	576	13.3	.40(f)	91% est.
Winchester 125 gr. Ranger T	1385	533	11.5	0.75	90% actual
Triton 115 gr. Quik-Shok	1425	519	9.0	3-frag	90% est.
Remington 125 gr. JHP	1350	506	14.3	0.57	89% actual
Glaser 80 gr. Silver Safety	1610	461	9.0	frag	88% est.
Hornady 124 gr. XTP	1395	536	14.5	0.55	88% est.
Glaser 80 gr. Blue Safety	1610	461	8.0	frag	87% est.
Cor-Bon 91 gr. BeeSafe	1525	470	7.0	frag	87% est.
Federal 150 gr. JHP	1140	433	15.0	0.60	85% actual
Hornady 147 gr. XTP	1210	478	16.2	0.58	84% est.

CHAPTER 10

.400 Cor-Bon Ammo

During the 1996 SHOT Show, Pete Pi finalized plans for a powerful bottleneck cartridge bearing his company's name, the .400 Cor-Bon. The new defensive and sporting cartridge is a .45 ACP necked down to .40 caliber and loaded to just over .45 ACP +P pressures. It is safe to fire from any .45 ACP pistol after only a barrel change and requires no spring, guide rod, or magazine changes. The .400 Cor-Bon is available with bullet weights from 135 to 180 grains with velocities from 1200 fps to 1450 fps.

The .400 Cor-Bon cartridge is

The .400 Cor-Bon uses a .45 ACP case necked down to .40 caliber and loaded to 10mm medium-velocity pressures. Bullets include 135-, 165-, and 180-grain JHPs. Stopping power is in the 10mm Auto class.

not the first time a .45 ACP case has been necked down to a .40 or .41 caliber. The 10 Centaur, developed by fellow gun writer Charlie Petty in conjunction with barrel compensator maker Centaur Systems in 1989, was the most recent necked-down .45 ACP cartridge. Petty's goal was to duplicate the ballistics of the .41 Action Express and to come close to the 10mm Auto. He was cautious not to hot rod the 10 Centaur.

With its longer case neck, the 10 Centaur simply did not have the case capacity to achieve 10mm Auto ballistics from .45 ACP pressures. The load used a .250 inch neck that reduced the powder capacity of the case. The .400 Cor-Bon, however, uses a shorter .150 inch neck that leaves the .45 caliber case at a larger diameter for a longer distance. In fact, it has the most powder capacity possible from a necked-down .45 ACP case.

Unlike most auto pistol cartridges, the bullet on the .400 Cor-Bon is roll crimped in place. This is somewhat required by the short case neck. Since the .400 Cor-Bon headspaces off its 25 degree shoulder, a revolver-type roll crimp is a perfectly acceptable way to increase bullet pull. It also increases the efficiency of slow-burning powders that work so well in larger cases.

In spite of the similarities with the 10 Centaur, the design of the .400 Cor-Bon was instead heavily influenced by the .41 Avenger, circa 1979. The .41 Avenger was developed by big-game handgun hunter, SSK Hand Cannon maker, and Outstanding American Handgunner award winner J.D. Jones. Jones used .45 Win Mag and .308 Win cases trimmed back to an overall length of .950 inch to make the .41 Avenger. Long before anyone heard of a 10mm Auto or .40 S&W, the .41 Avenger used a bullet originally made

The new .400 Cor-Bon (center) is based on the .41 Avenger (left) except it has the same overall length as a .45 ACP. The .400 Cor-Bon has a larger case capacity and shorter case neck than the 10 Centaur (right).

for the .41 Magnum. It had a long .275 inch case neck and a sloping 30 degree shoulder. At Pete Pi's request, the legendary Jones had some input into the design of the .400 Cor-Bon.

While the .400 Cor-Bon is not the first necked-down .45 ACP, it is the first necked-down .45 ACP to be a commercial success. The 10 Centaur was more of a pet project than a commercial venture. Its success was limited in part because Centaur Systems kept it as a proprietary wildcat.

The .400 Cor-Bon has advantages over both the standard-pressure .45 ACP and the .40 S&W. First, it has a lot more energy than either of these two calibers, which means it produces more stopping power. The .45 ACP pushes a 185-grain JHP to 1000 fps and the .40 S&W pushes a 180-grain JHP to 980 fps. In comparison, the .400 Cor-Bon pushes its 180-grain JHP to 1150 fps. With 180-grain bullets, the .400 Cor-Bon has 33 percent more energy than the .45 ACP and .40 S&W. The closest comparison to the .400 Cor-Bon in terms of energy is the .45 ACP +P. The .45 ACP 185-grain JHP +P and the .400 Cor-Bon 180-grain JHP both produce the same velocities and the same 530 ft-lbs. of energy.

The .400 Cor-Bon operates in the 29,000 psi chamber pressure range. The .45 ACP +P has a psi chamber pressure of 23,000, while the 10mm medium velocity runs between 29,000 and 32,000 depending on the factory. The only requirement for the 10mm medium-velocity ammo is to be under the 37,500 psi SAAMI limits for the full-power 10mm Auto. At 29,000 psi, the .400 Cor-Bon is far from the 35,000 psi pressures of the .40 S&W, the 37,500 psi allowed for the 10mm Auto, and the 40,000 psi pressures of the .357 SIG. Except for the downloaded 10mm MV, the 29,000 psi pressure of the .400 Cor-Bon is unique among pistol cartridges. The other defensive cartridges are either below 23,000 psi or above 35,000 psi. The .400 Cor-Bon started off with 23,000 psi as a pressure goal, but this did not quite achieve the

Glock was the first firearms maker to express interest in the .400 Cor-Bon (left). Glock wanted to co-develop it and rename it the .400 Glock to compete against the other bottleneck defensive cartridge, the .357 SIG (right).

velocities Pi wanted. Cor-Bon has become famous for successfully pushing cartridges to their safe but absolute maximum limit.

The .400 Cor-Bon has a case capacity 60 percent larger than the .40 S&W and 25 percent larger than the 10mm Auto. This is based on each firing the same 180-grain JHP and each loaded to the SAAMI maximum overall length. The .400 Cor-Bon will continue to be described as a necked-down .45 ACP. However, it is more meaningful to think of it as a large case capacity .40 S&W.

With the extra powder capacity, the .400 Cor-Bon is able to push .40 caliber bullets 150 fps faster than the .40 S&W. In fact, the lower pressure .400 Cor-Bon has enough case capacity to rival the exterior ballistics of the high-pressure 10mm Auto. Both the full-power 10mm Auto and the new .400 Cor-Bon push a 135-grain JHP to 1450 fps. The .400 Cor-Bon achieves these velocity levels by the use of larger amounts of slower burning powders. As a rule, slower powder burn rates produce higher velocities at lower chamber pressures.

The .400 Cor-Bon cartridge case can be made from any .45 ACP case. This is different in concept from the bottlenecked .357 SIG. The .357 SIG starts off with a longer case than the .40 S&W so that after the shoulder

forming operation it has the same overall length as the .40 S&W. The .400 Cor-Bon case was designed specifically to be made from a .45 ACP case. Pi wants the ample supply of .45 ACP cases to be easily converted to .400 Cor-Bon.

The .400 Cor-Bon also headspaces differently than the .357 SIG. The .357 SIG headspaces on the case mouth, making the overall length of the case critical. The .400 Cor-Bon, like nearly all bottleneck rifle cartridges from .223 Rem to .30-06 Springfield, headspaces on the shoulder. A properly resized case always produces the correct headspace regardless of overall case length.

Brass with the .400 Cor-Bon headstamp is being made by Starline. Far from being proprietary to Cor-Bon, the brass is being sold to all shooters through Midway. In addition to loaded ammo, even Cor-Bon is selling new unloaded brass for handloaders.

Significantly, the Starline .400 Cor-Bon brass is slightly stronger than cases formed from existing .45 ACP brass. The case head has a slightly thicker cross-section and the case wall is more tapered. The internal case dimensions are not as beefy as the .45 Win Mag or .45 Super, but the .400 Cor-Bon case withstands higher pressures than the .45 ACP case. Handloaders who plan to do their own load development will certainly want to use these stronger .400 Cor-Bon headstamped cases. Even still, the .400 Cor-Bon is not the right cartridge to hot rod. If you want a true 10mm Auto, buy a 10mm Auto.

Cor-Bon has developed loading data for a number of popular ball and flake powders in all three bullet weights. All of the handloading data published by Cor-Bon is based on reformed .45 ACP brass. Auto pistols like the Glock, which have a lot of unsupported case head, should still use .400 Cor-Bon cases as opposed to the reformed .45 ACP cases.

RCBS and Hornady both produce sizing and reloading dies for the .400

The .400 Cor-Bon 135-grain JHP produces exactly the same felt recoil from this Glock 21 as the .45 ACP 230-grain hardball. With an IPSC Power Factor of 196, this is the most recoil controllable and enjoyable by many handgunners.

Cor-Bon. These dies will neck down any vintage of .45 ACP brass to make the .400 Cor-Bon. The dies will also, of course, resize existing .400 Cor-Bon brass. Unlike the long wait for .40 S&W brass in the early 1990s, the .45 ACP brass to make the .400 Cor-Bon is readily available.

Due to the modest chamber pressures of the .400 Cor-Bon, no changes need to be made to .45 ACP pistols except for a swapped barrel. This is certainly true of the Glock 21 and Sig P220. The recoil spring used in the .45 ACP Glock 21, for example, is exactly the same spring as used in the 10mm Glock 20. All .400 Cor-Bon loads fall within the extremes of both energy and momentum defined by these two calibers. Olympic's Schuetzen Pistol Works indicated that the pistols based on the Colt Model 1911 seem to work better with the .400 Cor-Bon ammo when an 18.5 pound variable-power Wolff spring is used. Many handgunners already use this spring in their Model 1911s instead of the 16 pound straight-rate spring. The Taurus PT-.400, introduced in 1999, is of course designed from the ground up to fire

the potent .400 Cor-Bon cartridge.

The slide velocity and overall wear and tear on a .45 ACP pistol firing the .400 Cor-Bon will be the same as a steady diet of .45 ACP +P ammo. The original press release said the .400 Cor-Bon could use the stock recoil spring, but this was based on it operating at .45 ACP +P pressures. With the slightly higher 10mm MV pressures, a heavier recoil spring will reduce the battering from the slide. While this is not required, it is a good idea. Wolff springs are inexpensive, readily available, and easy to install when changing barrels. Most handgunners keep the correct recoil spring with the drop-in barrel for pistols with interchangeable barrels anyway.

Feed reliability is one of the advantages of the bottleneck cartridge design. It is easier to put a .40 caliber bullet in a .45 caliber chamber than to put a .45 caliber bullet in a .45 caliber chamber. The .400 Cor-Bon produces enough slide velocity to work interchangeably with traditional .45 ACP pistols. It has enough energy in all three bullet weights to overcome the energy stored in the main and

recoil springs. It also has enough momentum in all three bullet weights to overcome the inertia of the .45 slide.

The felt recoil of the .400 Cor-Bon is just slightly greater than the .45 ACP 230-grain hardball. With an IPSC Power Factor of 196, many shootists consider .45 ACP ball as the upper limit of recoil that is either controllable or enjoyable for the average handgunner.

The IPSC Power Factor is really a measure of momentum as opposed to energy or stopping power. Calculated by taking the bullet weight in grains times the muzzle velocity in feet per second and dividing by 1000, it has become a widely recognized measure of felt recoil and controllability. To qualify as a "major" caliber in IPSC or IDPA competition, the load must have a power factor of at least 175. The .40 S&W 180-grain JHP at 980 fps, for example, has a power factor of 176.

The new .400 Cor-Bon 135-grain JHP produces exactly the same felt recoil as the .45 ACP 230-grain hardball. Both have a 196 Power Factor. The .400 Cor-Bon 180-grain JHP produces about 6 percent more felt recoil than .45 ACP hardball. The 165-grain JHP kicks about 9 percent more than .45 ACP ball. Of course, this calculation for felt recoil assumes the use of auto pistols with the same weight and ergonomics, especially grip angle.

From the same Glock 21, we

At 1450 fps, the .400 Cor-Bon 135-grain Sierra JHP expanded violently and spun off fragments of its hollowpoint. This is exactly how the best street loads in 9mm, .357 Magnum, .40 S&W, and 10mm work.

The .400 Cor-Bon 135-grain JHP penetrates 9 inches of calibrated ordnance gelatin and produces a massive stretch cavity. This load equals the stopping power of the 10mm 135-grain JHP.

At 1300 fps, the .400 Cor-Bon 165-grain JHP expands and fragments in gelatin. This promising defensive load packs almost 150 ft-lbs. more energy than the .40 S&W versions.

could not tell any difference in felt recoil or muzzle rise between a .45 ACP 230-grain JHP and a .400 Cor-Bon 135-grain JHP. This .400 Cor-Bon load seemed more controllable in rapid-fire strings than the .45 ACP 185-grain JHP +P (again, from the same auto pistol). In side-by-side tests, we found the .400 Cor-Bon 165- and 180-grain JHPs from a Glock 21 to

kick much less than the full-power 10mm 175-grain Silvertip from a Glock 20.

The .400 Cor-Bon 165-grain JHP would kick about 13 percent more than the .40 S&W 165-grain JHP if both were fired out of the same gun. However, it was tough to feel any recoil difference between the .400 Cor-Bon load fired from the large-frame

Glock 21 and the .40 S&W fired from the medium-frame Glock 22. With power factors of 196, 207, and 214 for bullet weights of 135, 165, and 180 grains, we would not want a general-purpose auto pistol cartridge to kick more than the .400 Cor-Bon.

With 529 to 630 ft-lbs. of energy, the .400 Cor-Bon is in the same energy class as the .357 Magnum, the full-power 10mm Auto, and the .45 ACP +P. No conventional load in 9mm +P+ even reaches 500 ft-lbs. of energy. The most powerful .40 S&W JHPs are under 510 ft-lbs. Yet the .400 Cor-Bon does not get into the wasted energy levels of many .41 Magnum and most .44 Magnum loads.

Many handgun calibers and loads produce more energy than the 584 ft-lbs. Of the .357 Magnum 125-grain JHP. However, no caliber or load produces more stopping power against people in a defensive shooting scenario. The three current .400 Cor-Bon loads average 593 ft-lbs. of energy. Anything over 675 ft-lbs. is nearly wasted.

We checked out the wound ballistics of the .400 Cor-Bon in calibrated 10 percent ordnance gelatin. The result is exactly what we expected when 600 ft-lbs. of energy is transferred to a soft target: stopping power at the upper limit of what is even possible from a handgun.

The .400 Cor-Bon 135-grain Sierra JHP produced 9 inches of penetration in calibrated 10 percent gelatin. This makes it the best choice for scenarios where you do not want bullets to overpenetrate, like home defense, concealed carry, and bank and courtroom security. This load will work the best with an unobstructed, frontal upper torso shot. With a Fuller Index of 93 percent, the 135-grain .400 Cor-Bon ranks with the most effective of all handgun loads.

The .400 Cor-Bon 165-grain Sierra JHP produced an ideal 12.3 inches of penetration, right in the middle of the 10 to 14 inch range recommended for uniformed patrol

At 1150 fps, the .400 Cor-Bon 180-grain JHP has 140 ft-lbs. more energy than similar JHPs in .40 S&W, 10mm MV, and .45 ACP. The .400 Cor-Bon version expands and fragments to a .58 inch recovered diameter even after heavy clothes.

The .400 Cor-Bon 180-grain JHP penetrates 15.2 inches of gelatin. For handgun hunting, this load rivals anything from the 10mm Auto.

Future loads for the .400 Cor-Bon include the 190-grain FMJ Match (left) for competition use and the 155-grain Bonded Hollow Point (right) for defensive use.

and general-purpose defensive use. It produces about the same crush and stretch cavities as the .40 S&W 165-grain JHP. However, the higher energy of the .400 Cor-Bon 165-grain JHP earns it a Fuller Index of 92 percent compared to 88 percent for the .40 S&W version.

The .400 Cor-Bon 180-grain Sierra JHP produced about the same 15.2 inch penetration as many 180- and 185-grain hollowpoints in .40 S&W, 10mm MV, and .45 ACP. However, the .400 Cor-Bon packs a lot more energy and forces larger stretch cavities. With a Fuller Index of 89 percent, the .400 Cor-Bon 180-grain JHP is similar in stopping power to the .45 ACP 185-grain +P. The deeper penetration of this .400 Cor-Bon load makes it a good choice for handgun hunting.

The .400 Cor-Bon has the same felt recoil as a .45 ACP from a large-frame auto and a .40 S&W from a medium-frame auto. It has chamber pressures similar to the medium-velocity 10mm Auto and can be fired out of any .45 ACP pistol without changing springs. It is easily made from readily available .45 ACP brass and a wide variety of .40 caliber bullets. The .400 Cor-Bon has the stopping power equal to the best handgun loads. With all this, the new .400 Cor-Bon cartridge promises to be both a popular sporting caliber and an effective defensive caliber.

TABLE 10-1
.400 COR-BON WOUND BALLISTICS COMPARISON

Caliber & Load	Vel. fps	Energy ft-lbs.	Depth inch	Diameter inch	Crush cu. in.	Stretch Cavity cu. in	Fuller Index %
.400 Cor-Bon 135 gr. Sierra JHP	1450	630	9.0	.58	2.4	66.6	93
.400 Cor-Bon 165 gr. Sierra JHP	1300	619	12.3	.58	3.2	45.4	92
.400 Cor-Bon 180 gr. Sierra JHP	1150	529	15.2	.58	4.0	47.7	89
.400 Cor-Bon 155 gr. Bonded HP	1330	609	14.0	.70	5.4	39.5	91
.40 S&W 135 gr. JHP (C-B)	1300	507	10.1	.57	2.6	64.0	90
.40 S&W 155 gr. JHP (Fed)	1140	448	12.0	.65	4.0	56.9	88
.40 S&W 180 gr. JHP (Win)	980	384	13.3	.66	4.6	32.8	85
.45 ACP 185 gr. JHP (Fed)	1000	411	13.5	.68	4.9	18.3	88
.45 ACP 230 gr. H-Shok (Fed)	850	369	12.0	.78	5.7	28.4	87
.45 ACP (+P) 185 gr. JHP (Rem)	1140	534	12.3	.55	2.9	58.2	91
10mm MV 180 gr. JHP (Win)	980	384	15.0	.68	5.5	33.3	84
10mm 135 gr. JHP (C-B)	1450	630	11.9	.56	2.9	63.1	92

TABLE 10-2
AUTO PISTOL FELT RECOIL COMPARISON
(least to most)

Caliber & Load	Recoil Impulse lb-sec.	IPSC Power Factor
9mm 115 gr. JHP/FMJ	.59	133
9mm 147 gr. JHP	.62	139
9mm 124 gr. JHP/FMJ	.62	139
9mm 115 gr. JHP (+P)	.66	149
.357 SIG 125 gr. JHP	.76	171
.40 S&W 135 gr. JHP	.78	176
.40 S&W 180 gr. JHP/FMJ	.78	176
10mm MV 180 gr. JHP	.78	176
.40 S&W 150 gr. JHP	.80	180
.45 ACP 185 gr. JHP	.82	185
.40 S&W 165 gr. JHP	.84	189
.45 ACP 230 gr. JHP/FMJ	.87	196
400 C-B 135 gr. JHP	.87	196
10mm 135 gr. JHP	.87	196
10mm 150 gr. JHP	.87	196
400 C-B 180 gr. JHP	.92	207
.45 ACP 185 gr. JHP (+P)	.94	212
400 C-B 165 gr. JHP	.95	214
10mm 175 gr, STHP	1.00	225

CHAPTER 11

.40 Super Ammo

In 2000, Triton Cartridge released a full line of ammo for its .40 Super caliber. This hot bottleneck cartridge is the first caliber designed and developed by the New York state ammo maker, famous for its Quik-Shok ammunition and the .45 Super caliber. The .40 Super, announced at the 1999 SHOT Show, is the latest cartridge to be based on a .45 caliber case.

Don't confuse the .40 Super with the .400 Cor-Bon. Where the .400 Cor-Bon is a necked-down .45 ACP, the .40 Super is a necked-down and shortened .45 Win Mag. The .400

The .40 Super is the first caliber designed and developed by Triton Cartridge. It is the latest and most powerful of the calibers based on a necked-down .45 caliber case.

Cor-Bon operates at 29,000 psi; the .40 Super operates at 37,000 psi. Compared to the .400 Cor-Bon, the .40 Super produces 19 percent more felt recoil but 37 percent more energy.

As a caliber comparison, the .40 S&W is a wimp compared to the .40 Super. While the .40 Super has a 37 percent higher Power Factor, it also has 78 percent more energy. The .40 S&W pushes a 135-grain JHP to 1300 fps. The 10mm Auto and .400 Cor-Bon both push a 135-grain JHP to 1450 fps. The .40 Super pushes a 135-grain JHP to a sizzling 1800 fps! That is 507 ft-lbs., 630 ft-lbs., and 971 ft-lbs. of energy, respectively. The .40 Super packs .44 Magnum levels of energy.

Since the .40 Super caliber conversion is based on the .45 ACP auto pistol, it makes the most sense to compare it to the .45 ACP. The .40 Super has 16 to 25 percent more recoil than the +P and standard-pressure .45 ACP, respectively. However, it also generates 150 to 220 percent more energy! With a 200-grain JHP, the .40 Super has more energy at 100 yards than the .45 ACP +P 185-grain JHP has at the muzzle.

In 1994, Triton Cartridge released the .45 Super, a high-pressure version of the .45 ACP. The .45 Super

has the same external dimensions as the .45 ACP, but internally the case is much thicker. The stronger .45 Super case allows higher chamber pressures and much faster velocities. The .45 ACP drives a 230-grain JHP to 850 fps while the .45 Super drives the same bullet to 1100 fps. The .45 ACP +P pushes a 185-grain JHP to 1150 fps while the .45 Super pushes the same bullet to 1300 fps.

With the availability of stronger .45 Super cases, in mid-1995, Fernando Coelho, president of Triton, and Tom Burczynski, inventor of the Hydra-Shok and Quik-Shok, began the

The .40 Super started off as a necked-down .45 ACP (left). For improved feed reliability and superior ballistics, the final cartridge (right) has the same length as a 10mm Auto.

Triton Cartridge president Fernando Coelho is shown firing the .40 Super from a converted S&W Model 4506. The .40 Super has up to 25 percent more recoil than the .45 ACP but packs up to 220 percent more energy.

development of a new cartridge. Their concept was to neck down the .45 Super to accept the wide variety of .40 caliber and 10mm bullets.

The idea to neck down a .45 case to .40 caliber is not new. In 1979, big-game handgun hunter J.D. Jones trimmed .45 Winchester Magnum and .308 Winchester cases to .950 inch and necked down the cases to accept .41 Magnum bullets. The result was the .41 Avenger. In 1989, gun writer Charles Petty worked with the barrel compensator maker Centaur Systems to develop the 10mm Centaur. Petty necked down .45 ACP cases to 10mm in an attempt to duplicate the ballistics of the .41 Action Express. Like the .41 Avenger, the 10mm Centaur remained a proprietary wildcat.

In 1996, Cor-Bon released the first commercially successful .40 caliber load based on a bottlenecked .45 case, the .400 Cor-Bon. With an extremely short (.150 inch) neck, the .400 Cor-Bon has the most powder capacity possible for a necked-down .45 ACP case. It uses a slightly stronger version of the .45 ACP case. While the .45 ACP +P has a 23,000 psi chamber pressure limit, the .400 Cor-Bon

operates in the 29,000 psi range. This is similar to the 10mm Medium Velocity but lower than the 35,000 psi pressure limit for the .40 S&W.

Triton's original concept for the .40 Super involved a much longer (.225 inch) neck than the .400 Cor-Bon, resulting in a lower powder capacity. The Triton load could be driven to much higher chamber pressures, still giving it a velocity edge over the Cor-Bon. By late 1996, Coelho and Burczynski made a major decision: they wanted their new cartridge to feed better and have much better wound ballistics than any other cartridge using a necked-down .45 caliber case. To accomplish this, they bumped the cartridge case from the .45 ACP length of .898 inch to the 10mm Auto length of .992 inch. That gave the .40 Super its clear dominance.

The change to a 10mm length cartridge allowed the .40 Super to have a large powder capacity, a high-pressure case, and a longer neck. No other bottlenecked .40 caliber cartridge has all three features. To maximize bullet pull without a roll crimp and to optimize feed reliability, the .40 Super has a .175 inch neck and 25 degree

shoulder. The overall dimensions of the .40 Super case prevent a nose dive in a standard .45 ACP magazine.

Triton did not simply switch from .45 Super case to a trimmed .45 Winchester Magnum case for its .40 Super. The company replaced the large primer pocket in the .45 Win Mag with a small one and increased the thickness of the case wall from the web area to the shoulder. The result is an extremely strong case. Triton loads the .40 Super to 37,000 psi, which is well below the case strength rating of 50,000 psi. By comparison, the 10mm Auto has a 37,000 psi limit and the .357 SIG operates at 40,000 psi. The .40 Super really does seem to have the best features of the .45 ACP, .45 Super, 10mm, and .45 Win Mag. It has the same recoil as the .45 Super, but the .40 Super packs 25 percent more energy.

The .40 Super is available in seven factory loads, including a 135-grain Hornady JHP at 1800 fps, a 155-grain Quik-Shok at 1500 fps, and a 165-grain Sierra JHP at 1500 fps. All of these loads are based on chamber pressures less than a .40 S&W. In early testing, the .40 Super 135-grain JHP actually reached 2000 fps from a 5 inch auto pistol within the 50,000 psi chamber pressure limits of the cartridge case.

Triton factory loads for the .40 Super use Sierra and custom-made bullets from Hornady, Starline brass

The .40 Super (left) has the best features of the 10mm Auto (center) and .45 Win Mag (right). It is loaded to just 37,000 psi, which is well within the strength of the .45 Win Mag case.

with a Triton headstamp, and Federal small rifle primers. The .40 Super is not a proprietary cartridge to Triton. Federal and Hornady have both expressed interest in producing the ammo, depending on shooter demand, with Hornady likely to be the next one out with a factory load. For handloaders, loading data developed by Tony Rumore is available from Triton Cartridge. It covers 135-, 150-, 165-, 180-, and 200-grain jacketed bullets. Reloading dies are available from RCBS.

The .40 Super is an extremely versatile cartridge. In its various factory loadings, the new caliber can be used for law enforcement, personal defense, IPSC competition, metallic silhouette, bowling pin matches, hunting, and target shooting.

In terms of wound ballistics, the .40 Super outperforms anything from .40 S&W, 10mm Auto, .41 Magnum, .400 Cor-Bon, .45 ACP +P, and .45 Super. Ordnance gelatin looks exactly like it was hit with a .44 Magnum. With impact velocities from 1300 fps to 1800 fps and an average of 800 ft-lbs. of energy, the bullet performance is totally unaffected by heavy clothes. Not even four layers of denim, a harsher test than the FBI-spec heavy clothes, affects expansion of the .40 Super bullets.

The .40 Super 135-grain JHP is capable of incredible energy transfer. It

The .40 Super 135-grain Hornady JHP transfers 970 ft-lbs. of energy in just 6.5 inches. This 1800 fps JHP fragments like a Glaser Safety Slug.

produces 9 to 10.5 inches of penetration when fired from a .40 S&W, 10mm Auto, or .400 Cor-Bon pistol. From a .40 Super pistol, the expansion of this same bullet is so violent and the energy transfer so rapid, the bullet penetrates just 6.5 inches! The result is a Glaser Safety Slug kind of wound profile in gelatin. This 135-grain, 1800 fps load has almost no chance of overpenetration with a solid shot placement. It has a Fuller Index of 97 percent one-shot stops.

The 135-grain JHP used by Triton is custom made by Hornady and is similar to its XTP, but the core is different. The hollowpoint cavity is deeper on the bullet built for Triton and the cavity is more conical. Depending on the caliber, the antimony content may also be different and as high as 3 percent. The Triton bullet jacket has the same thickness, taper, ogive, and serrations as the Hornady XTP jacket. This is good. Regardless of weight or caliber, the Hornady XTP is one of the most accurate bullets made.

The .40 Super 135-grain JHP is an excellent defensive load for those who can handle the recoil, though a better overall load in this caliber is the 155-

grain Quik-Shok. The .40 Super 155-grain Quik-Shok at 1500 fps is a step up from the full-power 10mm Auto 155-grain Quik-Shok driven to 1400 fps. Both loads penetrate in the 10 to 11 inch range, but the .40 Super version dumps more energy.

On impact, the 155-grain Quik-Shok breaks into three well-defined 32-grain fragments that spread out in a 4 inch pattern. The .40 Super 155-grain Quik-Shok has a one-shot stop Fuller Index of 98 percent. This is the highest rating ever given for a handgun load.

The .40 S&W (far left) pushes a 135-grain JHP to 1300 fps. The 10mm Auto and 400 Cor-Bon push the same bullet to 1450 fps. The .40 Super (far right) gets the 135-grain JHP to 1800 fps.

The .40 Super 155-grain Quik-Shok breaks into three large fragments in as little as 1 inch of gelatin. The frags reach over 10 inches deep. This load has a Fuller Index of 98 percent.

The .40 Super 165-grain JHP may be the best overall load in the caliber. It has a Fuller Index of an awesome 98 percent.

The .40 Super 165-grain Sierra JHP expands to .71 caliber in bare or heavily clothed gelatin and penetrates 10.6 inches. That is deep enough according to the Border Patrol.

The .40 Super 200-grain Hornady JHP penetrates a total of 17.5 inches. This is a great deer and wild boar hunting load.

The .40 Super 200-grain JHP (shown) has more energy at 100 yards than the .45 ACP 185-grain JHP +P has at the muzzle. With up to 970 ft-lbs. of energy, the .40 Super rivals the .44 Magnum.

Also with an awesome 98 percent Fuller Index is the .40 Super 165-grain JHP. This may be the best overall load in the caliber and is certainly the top choice in the .40 Super for police work. In ordnance gelatin, the Sierra hollowpoint expands to .71 caliber and penetrates 10.6 inches in bare gelatin. It is extremely rare for a handgun caliber to produce one-shot stops in excess of 95 percent of the time. The .40 Super has three such loads!

The .40 Super 200-grain JHP also uses a Hornady-built bullet. This load penetrates 17.5 inches, expands completely to a .65 caliber mushroom, and makes an excellent hunting load. The auto-pistol-fired .40 Super 200-grain JHP exactly equals the ballistics of the revolver-fired .44 Magnum 240-grain JHP.

Aware of the heavy Power Factor numbers from the .40 Super, Triton has developed two lower recoiling, 1250 fps loads. One is the 135-grain Team Triton Quik-Shok; the other is the 135-grain Team Triton Competitor. Both are loaded to 25,000 psi instead of the full-power chamber pressures of 37,000 psi. The downloaded .40 Super has ballistics similar to the .400 Cor-Bon. These "competition" or "tactical" loads are

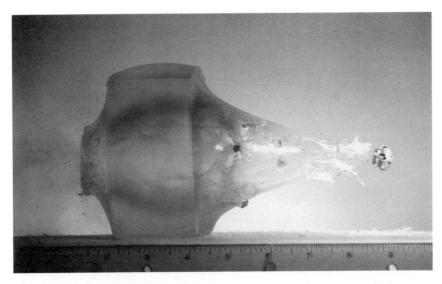

This high-speed photo of the .40 Super 200-grain JHP shows that the bullet expands to its full .65 caliber in just 2 inches. This load produces 89 percent one-shot stops but is more at home in the field than on the street.

also well-suited to personal defense and make an excellent defensive choice for those who are sensitive to recoil or where a short shot-to-shot time is absolutely critical.

The .40 Super 135-grain Team Triton Quik-Shok works just like a .40 S&W 135-grain Quik-Shok. On impact it breaks into three well-defined 28-grain fragments. Each frag penetrates 10.5 inches and spreads out in a 3.5 inch pattern.

IPSC and IDPA shooters will want the 135-grain Team Triton Competitor. This load uses a 135-grain SinterFire frangible with a flatpoint profile, called a Reduced Hazard Flatpoint (RHFP). The copper and tin composite RHFP bullet is very long for its weight. In fact, the 135-grain Sinterfire Competitor is as long as a standard hardball bullet weighing 200 grains. The longer bullet means more rifling engagement for better accuracy, while the lighter weight means less

recoil for faster follow-up shots. With a Power Factor of 169, this 1250 fps load has been sanctioned by IDPA as a "major" caliber. It is currently being used in competition by Mark Redl, Ron Moran, Pat Goetz, and Al Greco, members of Team Triton.

Triton also has a Close Quarter Defense (CQD) load for its .40 Super. The bullet used in this ammo is the same 135-grain Sinterfire flatpoint except drilled with a hollowpoint. The resulting 125-grain bullet is called a Reduced Hazard Hollowpoint (RHHP) and is a good choice for competitive shooting, especially against steel or where a lead-free bullet is preferred. The 125-grain RHHP is a sintered metal, tin, and copper composite bullet that breaks into small particles upon impact with steel reaction targets or back stops. This minimizes the back splash hazard to the shooter.

As a defensive round, the 125-grain RHHP partially fragments in

gelatin and saturates the first 2.5 to 4.5 inches with copper shards weighing 2 to 4 grains each. These frags spread out laterally in a 3 inch diameter pattern. The remaining core, which measures .40 caliber and weighs 61 grains, continues to penetrate as far as 15 inches. The frags actually break off the core in a way that leaves the remaining bullet with a sharp cone point. Most back splash safe frangible bullets do *not* break up in gelatin.

The .40 Super is currently available as a new pistol and as a caliber conversion kit for .45 ACP and .45 Super pistols. New pistols in this high intensity caliber are available from STI International through RSP Wholesale. STI makes both a 5 inch pistol and a 6 inch slide. The auto pistols are available with both steel and polymer frames. The most recent pistol to be chambered in the .40 Super is the CZ Model 97B, which controls the .40 Super's felt recoil through its legendary ergonomics.

Conversion kits for the .40 Super include a reamed barrel and the correct recoil spring. These kits are available for the S&W 4506, H&K USP, Sigarms P220, Glock 21 and 30, and all the variants of the Colt Government Model. Existing .45 ACP magazines can be used with no modifications. Handguns already set up for the .45 Super need only a barrel swap. Our test guns were a converted Glock 30 and a converted S&W 4506. In fact, the first handgun converted from .45 ACP to .40 Super was a Model 4506 using a Bar-Sto barrel and .45 Super recoil spring system.

Think of the .40 Super as an autoloading version of the .44 Magnum. Available in full-power, high-energy loads and in medium-velocity, low-recoil loads, the .40 Super may be the ultimate auto pistol cartridge.

TABLE 11-1
.40 SUPER WOUND BALLISTICS COMPARISON

Caliber	Load	Penetration	Expansion	Fuller Index
.40 Super	135 gr. JHP	6.5 inch	.70 cal	97%
.40 Super	155 gr. Quik-Shok	10.3 inch	3-frag	98%
.40 Super	165 gr. JHP	10.6 inch	.71 cal	98%
.40 Super	200 gr. JHP	17.5 inch	.65 cal	89%
.40 Super	125 gr. RHHP	15.0 inch	.40 cal	91%
.40 Super	135 gr. TT Q-Shok	10.5 inch	3-frag	91%
.40 Super	135 gr. TT Comp.	26.5 inch	.40 cal	66%
.400 Cor-Bon	135 gr. JHP	9.0 inch	.58 cal	95%
.400 Cor-Bon	165 gr. JHP	12.3 inch	.58 cal	95%
.400 Cor-Bon	180 gr. JHP	15.2 inch	.58 cal	89%
.40 S&W	135 gr. JHP	10.1 inch	.57 cal	92%
.40 S&W	180 gr. JHP	13.3 inch	.66 cal	85%
.45 ACP	230 gr. JHP	12.0 inch	.78 cal	88%
.45 ACP (+P)	185 gr. JHP	12.3 inch	.55 cal	94%
10mm Auto	135 gr. JHP	11.9 inch	.56 cal	95%

TABLE 11-2
.40 SUPER CALIBER COMPARISON

Caliber	Load	Muzzle Velocity fps	Muzzle Energy ft-lbs.	Power Factor
.40 Super	135 gr. Hornady JHP	1800	971	243
.40 Super	155 gr. Quik-Shok	1500	775	232
.40 Super	165 gr. Sierra JHP	1500	824	248
.40 Super	200 gr. Hornady JHP	1300	750	260
.40 Super	125 gr. SinterFire RHHP	1450	583	181
.40 Super	135 gr. TT Quik-Shok	1250	469	169
.40 Super	135 gr. TT Competitor	1250	469	169
.400 Cor-Bon	135 gr. JHP	1450	630	196
.400 Cor-Bon	165 gr. JHP	1300	619	214
.400 Cor-Bon	180 gr. JHP	1150	529	207
10mm Auto	135 gr. JHP	1450	630	196
10mm Auto	175 gr. STHP	1285	642	225
.40 S&W	135 gr. JHP	1300	507	176
.40 S&W	165 gr. JHP	1145	480	189
.40 S&W	180 gr. JHP	980	384	176
.45 ACP	230 gr. JHP	850	369	196
.45 ACP (+P)	185 gr. JHP	1140	534	212
.45 Super	185 gr. JHP	1300	694	241
.45 Super	200 gr. JHP	1200	639	240
.45 Super	230 gr. JHP	1100	617	253

TABLE 11-3
CALIBER COMPARISON

Year	Caliber	Neck Length	Shoulder Angle	Case Length	Case
1979	.41 Avenger	.430	30 deg	.950	.308 Win
1979	.45 Win Magnum	n/a	n/a	1.198	.45 Win Mag
1982	.451 Detonics Mag	n/a	n/a	.945	.45 Win Mag
1988	.45 Super	n/a	n/a	.898	.45 Detonics Mag
1989	10mm Centaur	.250	20 deg	.898	.45 ACP
1990	.40 S&W	n/a	n/a	.850	.40 S&W
1994	.357 SIG	.150	25 deg	.860	.40 S&W
1996	.400 Cor-Bon	.150	25 deg	.898	.45 ACP
1999	.40 Super	.175	25 deg	.992	.45 Win Mag

CHAPTER 12

Fabrique Nationale's 5.7 x 28mm

The current standard for a law enforcement patrol rifle is the Colt AR-15 M4 in 5.56mm NATO, while the benchmark firearm for tactical teams is the H&K MP5 in 9mm. Challenging both of these firearms is Fabrique Nationale Herstal with its P90 select-fire bullpup firing the 5.7 x 28mm rifle cartridge.

The P90 is the most recent attempt at the ideal balance between hit probability, firepower, and compactness for police tactical teams. It is shorter than the MP5 and can be used at close and long range alike. In full-auto mode, the P90 is easier to control than the MP5 while having the ability to defeat the soft body armor worn by violators.

The P90 is made by FN Herstal of Liege, Belgium. Located in the heart of gunmaking Europe, FN Herstal has gained a worldwide reputation for military armament since its start in 1889. The company invented the M2 .50 caliber Browning Machine Gun and the dual-core SS109 5.56mm NATO cartridge adopted by NATO forces as the 62-grain M855. It also makes the famous 7.62mm NATO FAL and 5.56mm NATO FNC assault rifles.

In 1897, FN Herstal began working with John Moses Browning. The father of the 9mm Hi-Power and .45 ACP Colt Government Model, Browning invented most of FN's first generation military arms. In 1903, the company released the Browning autoloading shotgun and, in 1935, the legendary Browning High Power 9mm pistol. In 1977, FN Herstal acquired the Browning company and, in 1991, purchased U.S. Repeating Arms from Winchester. In 1980, FN located a manufacturing plant in South Carolina and began production of the 7.62mm NATO belt-fed M240 machine gun for the U.S. Army. Then it captured the contract for the M16A2 rifle from Colt. (FN still makes these A2 series rifles.) In 1996, FN took over production of the 5.56mm NATO

The FN P90 fires the 5.7 x 28mm cartridge developed specifically for the bullpup and pistol. The 31-grain FMJ has a velocity of 2346 from the 10.3 inch bullpup. This SS190 round will defeat Threat Level IIIA armor at 200 yards.

M249 belt-fed Squad Automatic Weapon for the U.S. Army.

In July 1996, the French company Giat Industries made the decision to sell off the Herstal Group. In turn, in December 1996 Herstal Group sold its dominant interest in Beretta, the Italian arms maker. In November 1997, the government of the Walloon Region of Belgium purchased Herstal Group to protect its industrial heritage and the company was immediately restructured.

In the past, FN only dealt with the military forces of the world, while Browning and U.S. Repeating Arms only dealt with sporting firearms. The police, specifically the American police, were left out. This all changed in June 1998 when FN Herstal opened its weapon systems to city, county, and state police forces. Small-caliber weapons for nonmilitary and nonfederal police departments was a major change for a company that sold either to hunters or soldiers but nothing in between. FN's Law Enforcement Branch was introduced at the International Association of Chiefs of Police convention in October 1998.

The 5.7 x 28mm cartridge dates back to a mid-1980s concern about body armor on the battlefield. NATO approached the small arms industry about the possibility of developing a new class of cartridge to replace the 9 x 19mm round, which simply would not defeat soft armor. Depending on the weave and denier, 9mm ball is stopped by as few as five layers of Kevlar fabric. Two companies, Fabrique Nationale of Belgium and Giat Industries of France (before their merger), began the development of two new bottleneck cartridges, taking somewhat different approaches. Giat developed a cartridge similar to the .30 Luger necked down to .22 caliber called the 5.7 x 22mm. FN developed a larger round, the 5.7 x 28mm. Giat halted its development when it purchased FN Herstal.

To replace the 9mm, FN engineers went back to the original work they did on the 5.56 NATO and the Small-Caliber High Velocity (SCHV) program. To increase both penetration against armored targets and controllability, the bullet weight and diameter had to decrease. This would allow the bullet's velocity, energy, and force (energy divided by impact area) to increase. The result was the 5.7 x 28mm cartridge. In 1988, FN Herstal introduced the 5.7mm Weapon System based on the P90 select-fire bullpup with a 50-round magazine and a lightweight, 20-round pistol called the Five-seveN.

In very general terms, the 5.7 x 28mm is a downsized version of the 5.56 x 45mm NATO cartridge. Both fire a .224 inch diameter bullet. The 5.7 x 28mm uses a 31-grain FMJ driven to 2346 fps from a 10.3 inch FN P90 bullpup carbine. The 5.56 NATO uses a 62-grain FMJ fired to 2950 fps from a 16 inch Colt M4 rifle. The 5.7 x 28mm operates at a chamber pressure of 49,000 psi. This is comparable to the 9 x 23mm Winchester handgun round and 5.56 NATO rifle round.

The 5.7 x 28mm is currently available in three loads: SS190 FMJ ball, SB193 subsonic FMJ ball, and L191 tracer. The SS190 uses a 31-grain FMJ bullet with a velocity of 2346 fps. The bullet has a steel penetrator as the front core. (Remember, FN Herstal invented the dual-core SS109 cartridge that was adopted by NATO forces as the M855 ball.) The rear core of the SS190 bullet is aluminum. These dual cores are housed in a *steel* jacket. The subsonic SB193 uses a lead core, 55-grain boat-tail bullet with a velocity of 998 fps.

The 5.7 x 28mm caliber was under development nine years before the LAPD North Hollywood shootout in 1997. However, that was the exact type of scenario for which the cartridge was developed. Ten officers and six civilians were shot by robbers wearing Threat Level III-A body armor covering their torso and legs. One robber was armed with an HK M91 in 7.62 NATO converted to full auto. The other was armed with a ChiCom Type 56 (AKM) in 7.62 x 39mm, also converted to full auto. Their armor stopped a dozen police-fired 9mm bullets in a gunfight lasting 45 minutes. A lot of second-

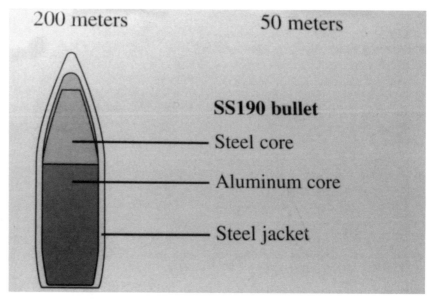

The 5.7 x 28mm 31-grain SS190 FMJ is a dual-core projectile with a hardened steel penetrator in front of an aluminum base plug. FN Herstal based the 5.7mm projectile on their famous 5.56mm SS109 projectile now known as NATO M855.

guessing has happened since then, but the facts are the 5.7 x 28mm can easily defeat soft body armor and yet has a limited down-range threat for use in urban environments.

The small diameter, high velocity, and hardened construction of the SS190 give it outstanding penetration ability. In this regard, the 5.7mm is similar to the 5.56 NATO and far superior to the 9mm and other pistol rounds. The 5.7mm SS190 will defeat Threat Level IIIA soft armor out to 200 meters. It will also defeat the PASGT Kevlar helmet, which carries a Threat Level IIA rating. At close range, the 5.7mm will defeat K-30 rigid ceramic inserts. The 31-grain FMJ will consistently penetrate 48 layers of Kevlar, which will stop all conventional versions of the 9mm, .40 S&W, .45 ACP, and .357 SIG. The 5.7mm will not defeat Threat Level IV hard armor.

The personal armor of the future will be even tougher to defeat. The reference armor for the future is the CRISAT target. It consists of a 1.6mm sheet of rigid titanium backed up by 20 layers of Kevlar. Handgun ammo will

The 5.7 x 28mm (center) is shown in comparison to the 9 x 19mm (left) and the 5.56 x 45mm (right). The 5.7mm produces one-third the recoil of the 5.56mm and two-thirds the recoil of the 9mm. It has a shorter downrange threat than either.

not begin to penetrate this armor, but the 5.7 x 28mm will defeat the CRISAT target.

The NATO definition of maximum effective range is where a weapon's projectile will still deliver 60 ft-lbs. of energy on target. The 5.7mm drops below 60 ft-lbs. of energy at 400 yards. This gives it a lower downrange threat than the 9mm ball and 5.56 NATO ball, which retain higher levels of energy well past 800

yards. The reduced downrange threat of the 5.7 x 28mm ball makes it an especially good choice for heavily urbanized patrol scenarios.

The 5.7 x 28mm is available for two versions of the Five-seveN pistol from FN Herstal. The Five-seveN is a delayed blowback pistol available as the Double Action Only and the Tactical, which is a double action/single action. It is the only patrol-oriented handgun in the world with a magazine capacity of 20 rounds, yet fully loaded it weighs just 26 ounces.

The Five-seveN has a polymer frame and slide cover. The frame has an integral accessory rail for white lights and red lasers. The 4.8 inch barrel is hammer-forged and hard chromed. Even firing steel-jacketed FMJ at chamber pressures of 49,000 psi, the Five-seveN has a minimum barrel life of 20,000 rounds.

The SS190 ball has nearly the same velocity from the Five-seveN pistol with a 4.8 inch barrel as it does from the P90 submachine gun with a 10.3 inch barrel. The 31-grain FMJ clocks 2346 fps from the subgun and 2133 fps from the pistol. The 5.7mm pistol shares the armor penetration advantages of the 5.7mm SMG. The 31-grain FMJ from the pistol will defeat Threat Level III A armor without overpenetration in soft tissue. The Five-seveN pistol is a clear choice for the point man on a tactical team whose primary weapon is typically a handgun and who will be the first one to face an armor-clad violator.

We fired a Five-seveN Tactical pistol, which is quickly identified by an ambidextrous, external safety lever mounted on the frame directly above the trigger. The 5.7 x 28mm cartridge has a Power Factor of 66 when fired from the Five-seveN pistol, giving it a level of felt recoil somewhere between the .32 ACP and the .380 ACP. Of course, the size, weight, and ergonomics of the Five-seveN pistol make it far more controllable than any .380 ACP pistol. The FN pistol is extremely easy

Two type of FN Herstal delayed blowback Five-seveN pistols are chambered for the 5.7 x 28mm cartridge: the double-action-only and this Tactical version, which is a double action/single action. The Five-seveN is the only duty-oriented handgun in the world with a magazine capacity of 20 rounds. Felt recoil from this FN pistol was similar to a .380 ACP.

to control in rapid fire. Pulling the trigger as fast as we could, we got coffee cup size groups at 10 yards.

FN Herstal's rally call for both the P90 and Five-seveN was, "No weapon is effective unless the ammunition is!" The company's goals for its new caliber were a maximum temporary stretch cavity, controlled penetration, no bullet fragmentation, extended range, and improved accuracy. The 5.7 x 28mm is meant to be a direct competitor to the 9mm and the 5.56 NATO currently used by police special teams. In nearly every case, the 5.7 x 28mm offers advantages over both these calibers in tactical and patrol use with few disadvantages.

The 5.7 x 28mm projectiles, when fired from either the Five-seveN pistol or the P90 submachine gun, have very flat trajectories out to around 150 meters. With a 100-yard zero, the 5.7mm and the 5.56 NATO shoot within an inch of each other out to 125 yards. At 200 yards, the 5.7mm prints just 7 inches lower than the 5.56 NATO, while 9mm ball with the same zero impacts nearly 3 feet lower. The 5.7mm is essentially "point of aim equals point of impact" for all law enforcement scenarios.

The 5.7 x 28mm does *not* have the wound ballistics of the 5.56 NATO, as has been reported by some. The 5.7 x 28mm has 379 ft-lbs. of muzzle energy compared to 1300 ft-lbs. for the 5.56 NATO. The 5.7 x 28mm tumbles after impact with gelatin but the bullet remains intact; the 5.56 NATO tumbles in gelatin and then fragments. The 5.7 x 28mm 31-grain FMJ penetrates between 10 and 11 inches of bare gelatin; the 5.56 NATO 55-grain M193 FMJ and the 62-grain M855 FMJ penetrate from 17 to 22 inches of gelatin. The 5.7 x 28mm, however, produces its 10 to 11 inches of penetration in bare gelatin and Threat Level III protected gelatin alike.

Unlike most armor-piercing ammo, the 5.7mm bullet tumbles after impact with a soft target. This both transfers energy to cause incapacitation

The 5.7 x 28mm 31-grain FMJ does not have the terminal ballistics of the 5.56 NATO. It tumbles in gelatin and dumps 380 ft-lbs. of energy in 11 inches. It has a wound profile similar to a 9mm 115-grain JHP +P+, but the peak of the cavity occurs deeper in the target.

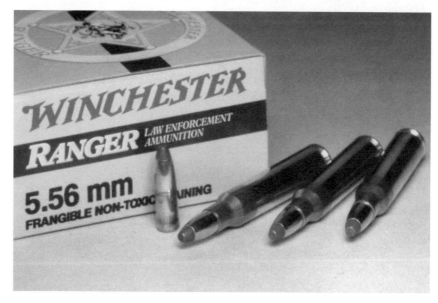

In mid-2000, Winchester began to load the 5.7 x 28mm using components from FN Herstal. Expect Winchester to release a tin core Super Clean NT or Ranger Delta Frangible in 5.7mm. The company already loads these in 5.56 NATO.

and limits the total amount of penetration. When fired from a P90 into ordnance gelatin, the SS190 bullet penetrates about 3 inches and then tumbles one time, base over nose. This tumble transfers energy like a hollowpoint or softpoint but unlike nonfragmenting FMJ ball. The maximum diameter of the temporary

stretch cavity occurs in the range of 4 to 7 inches deep. The bullet continues to penetrate, base first, to a depth of 10 to 11 inches. The diameter of the stretch cavity is comparable to a 9mm 115-grain JHP +P+, though the 5.7mm peak is deeper in the target.

Fired from the pistol, the SS190 penetrated 9 to 9 1/2 inches of bare

The 5.7 x 28mm 31-grain FMJ does not have the terminal ballistics of the 5.56 NATO. It tumbles in gelatin and dumps 380 ft-lbs. of energy in 11 inches. The 5.7mm has a wound profile similar to a 9mm 115-grain JHP +P+, but the peak of the cavity occurs deeper in the target.

gelatin. The same pistol-fired round penetrated 48 layers of Kevlar and still penetrated 8 to 8 1/2 inches of gelatin. The only difference in wound profile between the 5.7mm fired from the pistol and from the P90 was the tumble action. The pistol-fired bullet did not tumble in the gelatin. However, it did form a similar size and shape of temporary stretch cavity.

The 5.56 NATO 55-grain M193 and 62-grain M855 FMJ ammo has produced instant incapacitation with a single shot to the torso between 91 and 96 percent of the time, respectively. In comparison, the 5.7 x 28mm SS190 is estimated to be 71 percent effective, which is comparable to 9mm 124-grain NATO ball.

At the current time, FN Herstal has no plans for either a softpoint bullet or a full-velocity, lead core FMJ. These may become available as American law enforcement demand is better defined. In early 2000 Winchester began loading the 5.7 x 28mm with components produced in Belgium by FN Herstal, a critical step in the American police acceptance of the 5.7mm-caliber. The steel core in the SS190 classifies it as armor piercing, and importation of AP ammo is extremely regulated and requires the use of a Form 6 to be processed through the Import Branch of the BATF. The same components loaded by Winchester requires much less paperwork. Importantly, the Winchester SS190 will also be less expensive than the FN-loaded ammo. Expect the SS190 to be priced in the same range as the 62-grain M855 FMJ. Both use a dual-core bullet—the M855 is steel over lead, while the SS190 is steel over aluminum. However, the SS190 will never be as inexpensive as the 55-grain lead core M193 FMJ.

Winchester is currently developing a training round for the 5.7 x 28mm. This will not necessarily be a low-cost round, but it will be range and environment friendly. Expect a tin core load. Winchester currently makes lead-free, nontoxic ammo in its Super Clean NT line that uses a jacketed softpoint bullet with a tin core for the 5.56 NATO. A frangible load using a composite copper-resin bullet from the company's Delta Frangible line is also possible.

TABLE 12-1
5.7 X 28MM 31-GR. FMJ TEST RESULTS *

Test Phase	Gelatin Penetration, inches
Bare Gelatin, 10%	13.5
Sheet Rock, Gelatin	9.0
Plywood, gelatin	9.8
Auto Glass, Gelatin	8.3
Double Pane Glass, gelatin	11.3
T.L. IIIA Vest, gelatin	12.8

*results courtesy of INS Nat'l Firearms Unit

TABLE 12-2
CALIBER COMPARISON

Caliber	9x19mm NATO	5.56x45mm NATO	FN 5.7x28mm
Class	pistol	rifle	submachine gun
Bullet Weight	124 gr.	62 gr.	31 gr.
Velocity	1240 fps	2850 fps	2346 fps
Energy	423 ft-lbs.	1118 ft-lbs.	379 ft-lbs.
Power Factor	154	177	73

TABLE 12-3
FN 5.7 X 28MM AMMUNITION

Ctg.	SS190 Ball	SB 193 Subsonic	L191 Tracer
Bullet Weight	31 gr. FMJ	55 gr. FMJ	31 gr. FMJ
Velocity, P90	2346 fps	984 fps	2346 fps
Velocity, FN pistol	2132 fps	n/a	2132 fps
Energy, P90	379 ft-lbs.	118 ft-lbs.	379 ft-lbs.
Penetrate Class IIIA	200 meters	50 meters	200 meters

TABLE 12-4
WOUND BALLISTICS COMPARISON
(fired from carbines/submachine guns)

Caliber	Load	Energy ft-lbs.	Gel. Pene. in.	Recovered Dia. Inc.	Est. One-Shot Stop %
5.7x28mm	FN 31 gr. SS190 FMJ	379	10.5	0.22	71
9mm	Winch. 124 gr. M882 FMJ	423	29.0	0.36	70
9mm	Winch. 147 gr. Ranger SXT	322	16.0	0.58	79
9mm	Fed. 124 gr. Hydra-Shok	432	13.3	.40 f	83
9mm	Cor-Bon 115 gr. JHP +P	582	10.8	.60 f	91
5.56 NATO	Winch. 55 gr. M193 FMJ	1305	17.0	0.24	92
5.56 NATO	Winch. 64 gr. Softpoint	1260	11.5	0.32	95
5.56 NATO	Fed. 40 gr. JHP	1185	6.5	frag	96
5.56 NATO	Fed. 69 gr. MatchKing	1380	12.0	0.43	97

CHAPTER 13

Triton Quik-Shok Ammo

One of the most promising defensive bullets is the Triton Quik-Shok. This is the fourth of five major bullet designs by Tom Burczynski, arguably the best bullet designer of all time. His five bullets include the Neutralizer Tunnel Point, the Federal Hydra-Shok, the Eldorado Starfire, the Triton Quik-Shok, and, most recently, the Federal Expanding Full Metal Jacket.

The Quik-Shok is totally unlike any of Burczynski's other bullet designs. It is the only bullet currently in existence to successfully bridge the gap between conventional hollowpoints and fragmenting bullets.

The Quik-Shok first gained prominence in 1992 during the Strasbourg Tests. Two Quik-Shok loads were tested by the Strasbourg researchers against 160-pound French Alpine goats. The 9mm 115-grain +P+ Quik-Shok came in second in that caliber out of 24 hollowpoint and frangible loads. Only the MagSafe beat the Quik-Shok in incapacitation, and only by .1 second. In the .357 Magnum caliber, the 125-grain Quik-Shok hollowpoint came in best in the caliber out of 22 police and defensive loads.

The Strasbourg Tests involved a total of 114 different high-performance bullets in calibers from .380 Auto to .45 Auto, including the .40 S&W and full-power 10mm. Of all these loads, the .357 Magnum 125-grain Quik-Shok produced the most rapid incapacitation of any load in any caliber. This load worked a full three seconds faster in collapsing the 160-pound goats than the .357 Magnum 125-grain JHPs from Remington and Federal.

Overall, based on the 9mm and .357 Magnum calibers, the Quik-Shok produced average incapacitation *more* rapidly than the MagSafe and much more rapidly than the Glaser. The Quik-Shok far outperformed even the

This 9mm +P 115-grain Quik-Shok was as effective during the Strasbourg Tests as the best frangible load. Triton will make 115- and 124-grain versions.

best of the high-energy JHPs. It was one of only eight loads out of 117 fired to produce a collapse in less than two seconds, the long sought-after goal.

Burczynski began his design work on the first variation of the Quik-Shok in 1988. That was the year that Federal Cartridge bought the production rights to the Hydra-Shok bullet. The early development of the Quik-Shok included all-lead, copper-jacketed lead, solid copper, and solid brass (copper-zinc) bullets.

The first Quik-Shok design used a "core intrusion" process. The patented swaging process formed a series of internal radial cuts within the bullet core. These cuts started on the centerline of the bullet but ended before the cuts reached the outside diameter. This process left web areas near the outside diameter where the bullet was not quite completely cut in thirds. The purpose of the web areas was to control the degree and rate of bullet expansion and eventual fragmentation. Very thin web sections allowed the bullet to fragment rapidly.

During this swaging-cutting process, the bullet core grows in length while the outside diameter remains the same. The next operation squeezes the bullet core back to its original length.

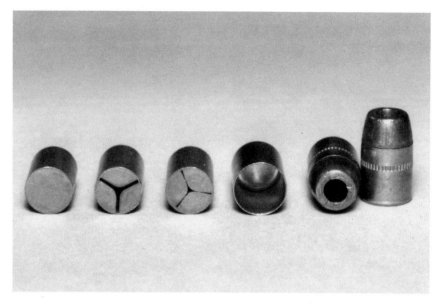

The Quik-Shok One bullet core has internal cuts. After the skive operation, the QS1 core gets compressed back to its original shape. It is then swaged into a hollowpoint. This was the original Tom Burczynski design.

The triangular-shaped portions of the core are swaged together and the air spaces between the sections are eliminated. This leaves a series of visible "parting lines" in the otherwise now solid core. The core is pressed together but it is not fused together.

This reswaged core is then placed in a jacket cup and formed in a profile die to be nearly identical in appearance to a conventional jacketed hollowpoint. Depending on the depth and number of internal parting lines and the thickness of the web areas, the Quik-Shok can be designed to fragment completely into three to six sections. Each resembles a military frag simulator. The Quik-Shok can also be designed to fragment into a number of frontal sections, leaving a solid base portion to continue the penetration.

With the Quik-Shok I (QS1) patented, Burczynski invented the Quik-Shok II (QS2). It had a similar design that produced nearly the same wound ballistics but involved an entirely different manufacturing technique. The QS1 involved a core intrusion process; the QS2 involved a core extrusion process.

With QS2, a series of external radial slots were formed into the bullet core that run the entire length of the core. These cuts penetrated from the outside diameter almost, but not quite, to the center axis of the bullet core. In this design, the webbing between the lead was in the center of the bullet. A hub at the center of the core fanned out into a series of lobes. Again, the hub area or web diameter at the center of the bullet controlled the amount and rate of expansion and fragmentation. Once again, the core with external slots or grooves was compressed back to its original diameter, the lobes were forced together, and the air spaces eliminated. As before, a series of parting lines was barely visible.

In mid-1995, Burczynski's company, Experimental Research, reached a licensing agreement with the New York-based Triton Cartridge to produce the Quik-Shok.

The Quik-Shok is so fundamentally different from other frangible loads that it has a list of characteristics all its own. First, it has better accuracy. It uses standard bullet weights and velocities that are a match for standard handgun rifling twist rates. The Quik-Shok bullet has a true solid core with no air spaces or differences in density across the core.

Second, the Quik-Shok shoots to the point of aim because of these standard weights and velocities. Most frangible loads have half the standard bullet weights and half again as much velocity, causing them to have a point of impact well below the point of aim.

Third, the Quik-Shok has a normal muzzle flash which in most calibers is not visible. Standard bullet weights allow the use of conventional flash-suppressed powder and allows this powder to burn more completely than the lighter weight frangibles.

Fourth, the Quik-Shok produces adequate soft tissue penetration. Some frangible loads have maximum depths of just 5 to 6 inches. The Quik-Shok hollowpoint produces penetration in the 9 to 12 inch range.

Fifth, the Quik-Shok breaks through bones without exploding prematurely. It uses all of its bullet weight to break through the "shell" of the target. The same goes for striking a fleshy upper extremity before entering the torso. Even if the Quik-Shok expands and separates in an upper arm, the exiting frags headed to the torso are much more potent because they have a better chance of hitting something vital.

Triton uses the QS2 design in all of its Quik-Shok ammo. The Quik-Shok Two bullet core has external cuts. The depth of cut controls how rapidly these 9mm and .45 ACP bullets will fragment. The perfectly straight channels of uniform depth guarantee rapid and consistent fragmentation on impact.

The Triton .38 Special +P 110-grain Quik-Shok fragments reliably into three 34-grain segments. A bullet that fragments in gelatin will at least expand in tissue.

To put the Quik-Shok bullet in perspective, the three .38 caliber Quik-Shok frags each weigh 34 grains. In comparison, a single #1 buck pellet weighs 40 grains. The three .40 S&W Quik-Shok frags each weigh 40 grains. The .44-caliber Quik-Shok frags weigh 46 grains each. A #0 buck pellet weighs 48 grains. The #2 birdshot used by MagSafe weighs 5 grains, while the #12 birdshot used in the Glaser Blue Safety Slug weighs 0.2 grains. For another comparison, the .38 caliber Quik-Shok frag is a .28 caliber slug measuring .48 inch long, whereas #2 birdshot is .15 caliber, and #12 birdshot is .05 inch in diameter.

Sixth, the Quik-Shok reacts like a conventional hollowpoint rather than a frangible when it strikes sheet metal. The bullet nose folds in on itself. The same goes for its reaction to building materials like wallboard and plywood. The Quik-Shok expands and produces slightly less tactical penetration than a hollowpoint but more reliable penetration than a typical frangible.

Seventh, the Quik-Shok penetrates auto glass like a conventional hollowpoint—it expands rather than fragments. Due to its conventional bullet weight the Quik-Shok has a better bullet flight integrity than the lighter frangibles, which are easily deflected or simply broken up by glass. The Quik-Shok will, however, fragment or expand when contacting a soft tissue medium after being fired through glass.

When it comes to stopping power, the Quik-Shok also has an advantage over conventional hollowpoints. It unleashes huge pieces of lead inside the target. In this regard, it is similar to a close-range multiple bullet load. Bullet placement of Quik-Shok bullets is less critical than with conventional hollowpoints because of the outward expanding cone-shaped pattern of lead that begins shortly after impact. The segments of the bullet separate and begin separate crush cavities, increasing the chances of striking or affecting one or more vital organs. The Quik-Shok can be most effective even in the event of a poorly placed shot.

These multiple wound paths, compound pressure fronts, and overlapping stretch cavities increase stopping power by way of accelerated bleeding, increased motor interruption, increased neural shock, and a substantially increased system pressure. This increased blood system pressure is what some Strasbourg commentators feel caused the most rapid collapses.

The Triton Quik-Shok challenges the traditional way bullets are reviewed in two specific areas. One,

bullets that expand and then fragment produce more stopping power than those that do not. Two, bullets that penetrate in the 9 to 12 inch range produce more stopping power than those that penetrate in the 12 to 18 inch range.

The potent wound ballistics from the Quik-Shok comes from the fact that the bullet fragments, and fragmentation is a major cause of tissue disruption. The 34- to 46-grain projectiles cause deep and separate wound cavities. It is like a multiple bullet impact since multiple organs can be penetrated with one shot. Multiple organ trauma is the essence of stopping power. It is what people are trying to say when they say shot placement is everything.

In addition to the multiple crush cavities and the overlapping and impinging stretch cavities, fragmentation has another benefit. A bullet that expands and then fragments in 10 or 20 percent gelatin will expand under the widest range of shooting scenarios and in combinations of soft and hard living tissue. In gelatin, the Quik-Shok produces the famous "squid" wound profile: a

The Triton .357 Magnum 125-grain Quik-Shok dumps 487 ft-lbs. of energy in just 11 inches. Bullets that penetrate in the 8.5 to 12 inch range are more effective in actual shootings than deeper penetrating bullets.

TRITON QUIK-SHOK AMMO

The Triton .357 SIG Quik-Shok is available in two other weights: 115 grains and this 135-grain load. The heavier bullet breaks into larger, deeper penetrating frags. Both loads dump 500 ft-lbs. of energy in less than 12 inches.

round stretch cavity, indicating a rapid energy release, followed by long tentacles of penetrating frags.

The greatest man stopping handgun bullet ever documented is the .357 Magnum 125-grain JHP. This hollowpoint fragments violently on impact and has a 40 to 60 percent retained weight, a 25 to 40 percent retained length, and an eroded recovered diameter of merely .55 caliber. This recovered condition absolutely defines what makes the most effective police and defensive bullet performance.

We compared the recovered bullet diameter in gelatin to the number of one-shot stops for the same ammo in 1,800 officer-involved shootings. We found that bullets that fragment have a far better actual street record than their recovered diameter would indicate. Bullets that expand in gelatin to twice their initial caliber sometimes don't expand at all on the street. However, bullets that expand and then fragment in gelatin nearly always expand in tissue. Sometimes one of these bullets will spin off a fragment of lead that will hit vital tissue missed by the main core.

We compared loads that fragment to leave a smaller recovered diameter to the exact same bullets that go slower but retain a plump mushroom. According to 458 officer-involved

shootings, the higher velocity loads that fragment when tested in gelatin actually have an 11 percent better street record than the slower velocity loads that retain a mushroom and do not fragment. That increase in stopping power is extremely significant if for no other reason than it is an increase and not a decrease as some would think.

Fragments can do two things. First, they can put holes in vital tissue that was missed by the bullet. Some experts make a big deal out of one shape of bullet pushing a major vessel aside while another bullet puts a cut in it. And that is a big deal. However, it is an even bigger deal if the bullet core puts a hole in one vessel while one of its fragments puts a hole in another. Fragmentation from handgun ammo that causes secondary injury has been documented by medical examiners.

Second, fragments can put holes in tissue that sets them up for damage from the temporary stretch cavity which instantly follows. In other words, the frags perforate and then the stretch tears. This can in fact dislodge entire sections of tissue. This too has been documented. It is rare for hollowpoints to cause this kind of

damage but extremely common for exotic frangible bullets that totally fragment.

The Quik-Shok is extremely promising. It has better accuracy than a typical frangible. It shoots to the same point of aim as conventional ammo since the bullet weights and muzzle velocities are the same. Its bullet produces fragments as large as numbers 1 buck and 0 buck. And it penetrates auto glass and sheet metal like a conventional hollowpoint instead of fragmenting like a frangible.

What has happened recently to the Triton Quik-Shok? In a surprising move, in 1996 Triton sold the production rights to DKNEES Enterprises. DKNEES elected not to make any centerfire Quik-Shok ammo. In an equally surprising reversal, in mid-1997 Triton purchased back the production rights to the centerfire Quik-Shok! The rimfire Quik-Shok is still produced by DKNEES affiliate MPB-Polywad.

Triton has made a number of changes in the bullet since its first release. The hub diameter, which holds the three lobes of the bullet together, was reduced from .06 to .03 inch. This is a 75 percent reduction in

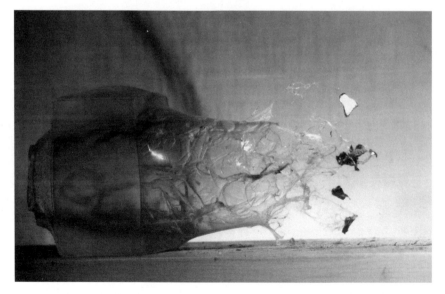

An upper torso involves an inch or two of skin, fat, and muscle and then air-filled lungs. It takes a fragment-prone design like the Quik-Shok to work reliably on these shot placements.

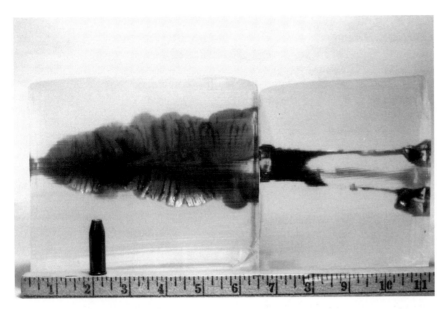

The .44 Magnum caliber is available in two Quik-Shok loads. Shown here is the medium-velocity 165-grain version ideal for personal defense. The full-power 240-grain version is better suited for hunting.

The Triton .44 Special 165-grain Quik-Shok is one of the most effective loads in the caliber. It should produce 88 percent one-shot stops.

ACP, the Quik-Shok bullet breaks into pieces every time, even when fired from very short barrels or after having passed through heavy clothes. Like the original loads, in gelatin tests the new Quik-Shok penetrated between 8.6 and 11 inches. Future Quik-Shok loads include a 10mm Auto 165-grain at 1300 fps, a .44 Special 165-grain at 1100 fps, a .44 Magnum 180-grain at 1250 fps, and a .357 SIG 124-grain at 1350 fps.

The basic concept of fragmenting police duty bullets in general, and the Quik-Shok in particular, has been validated and legitimized by the new Border Patrol ammo test protocol. For the first time, a major law enforcement agency has recognized the benefits of frangible bullets and written them in to a test procedure.

Developed in 1998, the Border Patrol protocol was an update of the FBI test protocol. The number of barrier tests was reduced, different weightings were applied to the tests, and some tests were made pass/fail only. Most significantly, the Border Patrol introduced "controlled separation" projectiles and added the maximum volume of the temporary stretch cavity to the overall analysis.

The Border Patrol *still* emphasizes high retained weight for its duty ammo under the new test protocol. However, its agents understand that controlled separation bullets are the most reliable way to cause multiple organ trauma. This, in turn, can greatly increase the effectiveness of any bullet. With any single shot placement, the controlled separation bullet acts like multiple bullet hits without the stray shots.

The Border Patrol put two constraints on controlled separation bullets. First, the frags *must* still reach the minimum penetration requirements. Second, the individual frags must weigh at least 25 percent of the original bullet weight. This eliminates the frangible bullets filled with birdshot like the Glaser, BeeSafe, and MagSafe. The only load that

the cross-sectional area, making it easier for the bullet to break into three pieces upon impact. The hollowpoint cavity itself was changed from a flat bottom to a sharp, conical V-shape profile. The use of a lower percentage of antimony in the lead forced the change in the cavity profile to maintain the well-defined fragments.

Finally, the antimony content was

dropped from 1.5 percent to either 0.80 or 0 percent. This allows the bullet to perform more like a jacketed hollowpoint at the beginning of its travel and results in a tighter dispersion of the frags. A tighter patterning of the frags can be an advantage when the bullet strikes closer to the intended shot placement.

In calibers from .380 ACP to .45

The Triton .40 S&W 135-grain Quik-Shok expands and fragments into six pieces about the size of #4 buck pellets. After heavy clothes, the Quik-Shok still fragments into three pieces.

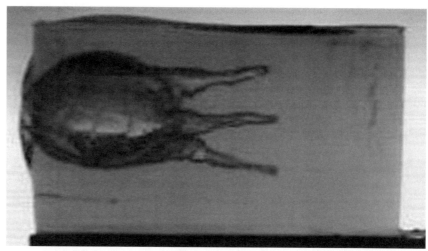

The INS/NFU captured this Triton .40 S&W 155-grain Quik-Shok at 9000 frames per second. The Border Patrol knows that fragmentation is a major source of tissue disruption. Its ammo protocol legitimizes controlled separation projectiles as long as they fall within strict limits.

The Triton .40 S&W 155-grain Quik-Shok was developed to meet U.S. Border Patrol specs. Each of the frags penetrates 9.5 inches in bare gelatin. A 135-grain Quik-Shok is also available in .40 S&W.

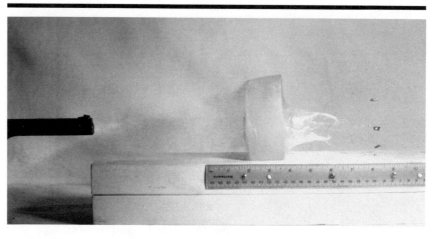

This high-speed photo of the .22 rimfire Quik-Shok shows that the bullet separates cleanly into three frags in as little as 2 inches of gelatin when fired from a handgun. This load tops the caliber with 40 percent one-shot stops.

currently meets the Border Patrol standards for a controlled separation bullet is the Triton Quik-Shok.

In late 1999, the INS/National Firearms Unit tested a number of .40 S&W loads under its new protocol. One of these loads was the Triton .40 S&W 155-grain Quik-Shok newly prototyped specifically for the Border Patrol (see Table 13-2). Expect the Quik-Shok to receive similar serious interest from law enforcement. As for civilian concealed carry and home defense, the Quik-Shok proved during the Strasbourg Tests that it was one of the few loads in any caliber to cause an instant collapse. The Quik-Shok may be the ultimate personal defense load.

The Quik-Shok bullet is also available in .22 Long Rifle and 12-gauge shotgun. (The shotgun load is

covered in Chapter 23.) First appearing in mid-1996, the .22 LR Quik-Shok is made by Magnum Performance Ballistics. The 32-grain frangible has been redesigned recently to expand and fragment at handgun velocities. The original load only performed well from rifles.

The original 36-grain Quik-Shok bullet was made in Mexico by Remington Arms' joint venture Industrias Tecnos. Tecnos is famous for its Aguilla brand of rimfire and centerfire ammo. At the time, the Quik-Shok was imported and

distributed by DKNEES Enterprises. In mid-1997, production rights to the rimfire Quik-Shok transferred to Polywad of Macon, Georgia. Polywad, known for fast-spreading shotshells, had CCI-Speer produce the load. CCI-Speer engineers, led by Gold Dot co-inventor Brett Olin, dropped the bullet weight to 32 grains and ran the Quik-Shok on the same bullet-making and ammo-assembly equipment that produces the legendary CCI Stinger. The Quik-Shok and Stinger share the same special Stinger case, which is longer than a standard Long Rifle

The second generation of the .22 rimfire Quik-Shok weighs 32 grains and is made on the same equipment that produces the CCI-Speer Stinger.

Future plans at Triton include a Quik-Shok for the .308 Win (shown) and the .223 Rem. The .308 Win Quik-Shok could be the ideal hostage rescue load.

case. Both have the same bullet weight and muzzle velocity. We got 1228 fps from a 4 inch S&W Model 34 Kit Gun and 975 from a 2.5 inch Beretta Model 21 Bobcat. The new 32-grain version is an average of 200 fps faster than the old 36-grain version.

The Polywad Quik-Shok penetrates 7 to 8 inches of gelatin. After about 2 inches of penetration, the bullet breaks cleanly into three very distinct fragments, each weighing about 11 grains. These spread out in the target to form a 4 inch diameter pattern by about 8 inches deep. The most impressive part of the second generation Quik-Shok was the absolute reliability of fragmentation. We fired more than a dozen rounds into gelatin from handguns. Every single bullet broke cleanly into exactly three sharply defined frags. The penetration depth for each frag was always between 7 and 8 inches in 10 percent gelatin.

A couple of changes were made to get this kind of consistent performance. One was in the reduction of the hub diameter (the section in the center of the lead core that holds the three lobes of the bullet intact until impact). This diameter was reduced from 0.06 to 0.05 inch. The hollowpoint cavity on the CCI-Speer version was made roughly 5 percent deeper and the hollowpoint opening was made roughly 55 percent wider, which more than doubled the hollowpoint cavity volume. The larger cavity, the smaller hub, and the shorter and faster bullet made all the difference. At 34 percent one-shot stops, the rimfire Quik-Shok maximizes the stopping power from this mini caliber.

TABLE 13-1
TRITON QUIK-SHOK AMMUNITION

Caliber	Weight	Velocity fps	Energy ft-lbs.
.380 ACP +P	90 gr	1050	220
9mm +P	115 gr	1325	448
9mm +P	135 gr	1200	432
.38 Special +P	110 gr	1175	337
.357 Magnum	125 gr	1450	583
.357 SIG	115 gr	1425	518
.357 SIG	135 gr	1300	507
.40 S&W	135 gr	1325	526
.40 S&W	155 gr	1250	538
10mm (full)	155 gr	1400	674
.40 Super TT	135 gr	1250	468
.40 Super	155 gr	1500	775
.44 Special	165 gr	1100	443
.44 Magnum	165 gr	1250	572
.44 Magnum	240 gr	1285	878
.45 ACP +P	165 gr	1250	572
.45 ACP +P	230 gr	950	461
.45 Super	165 gr	1400	718
.30 Carbine	110 gr	1950	929

TABLE 13-2
TRITON .40 S&W 155 GR QUIK-SHOK
(BORDER PATROL TESTS)

velocity	1145 fps
energy	451 ft-lbs.
Power Factor	177
accuracy, 25 yards	2.30 inch (Beretta 96D Brigadier)
accuracy, 50 yards	1.42 inch (test barrel)
cycle reliability	1 jam in 4500 rounds

Gelatin Penetration Averages

bare gelatin	9.5 inch
heavy clothes	16.4 inch
auto glass	8.6 inch
wallboard	13.0 inch
sheet steel	8.6 inch
retained weight	91.5 grain, 59% (per protocol)
Temporary Stretch Cavity	36.5 sq.in. (area)

CHAPTER 14

EFMJ Development

by Tom Burczynski

AUTHORS' NOTE: *Tom Burczynski is the most prolific bullet designer of our time. He designed the Hydra-Shok bullet now used by Federal Cartridge, the Starfire bullet now used by Eldorado Cartridge, and the Quik-Shok bullet now used by Triton Cartridge. The Expanding Full Metal Jacket bullet, currently loaded by Federal, is his fourth commercially successful bullet design.*

The Expanding Full Metal Jacket (EFMJ) concept provides a number of advantages: the bullet feeds like hardball, does not depend on external fluid to initiate expansion, expands faster than a conventional hollowpoint, does not clog up with fabric or dry barrier media, and produces a large permanent wound cavity and ample penetration.

When the EFMJ concept was first introduced to Bruce Warren, Director of Research at Federal Cartridge (Blount Sporting Equipment Group) and man in charge of the most advanced new products, he initially viewed it as a made-to-order product for the European market. Bruce's line of reasoning was based primarily on the facts that hollowpoint bullets were

illegal in that corner of the world and that the police there were saddled with hardball ammunition seriously lacking in the ability to incapacitate quickly. In short, they needed help, which was unavailable to them via other manufacturers. When Bruce ran the EFMJ concept by Dave Longren, Senior Vice President of Marketing and Product Development (Blount Sporting Equipment Group), he was intrigued and concurred with his target-market reasoning. I'd be remiss if I didn't point out that while Bruce is forward-thinking and in charge of R&D of new products, Dave possesses the power to terminate the development of *any* product with the stroke of a pen. I was elated to learn that Dave had sanctioned further development of the EFMJ design.

The EFMJ was not always so named. The original code name was "CSP" (Captive Soft Point). The CSP moniker served more as a temporary in-house designator than as a seriously considered marketing name. Interestingly, the original name is still used in-house from time to time. The name EFMJ is self-descriptive and one based on simple facts: (1) a full-metal

jacket surrounds its contents, and (2) the bullet expands rapidly when fired into any material, wet or dry.

The basic idea for the EFMJ (a soft material held captive in the nose of a FMJ-style bullet) was conceived nearly 20 years ago. Time constraints prevented me from developing the concept to the point of marketability back then, as nearly all my time was consumed developing and promoting other designs.

In its present form, the EFMJ utilizes a gilding metal jacket with six scores * on the interior of its ogive. The weakened jacket houses an elastomer in its nose area. Seated behind the elastomer is a lead hollowpoint core. The rear or open end of the jacket is crimped or "heeled over" the rear of the lead core just like a hardball round. Externally, the finished EFMJ bullet looks very much like a typical full-metal jacket (FMJ) bullet, but of course, this is where the similarity ends.

After gaining approval for the project, I began the rather arduous and drawn-out task of designing dozens of experimental dies and punches. This hardware was needed to weaken the

---

* It was established early on using an *unscored* jacket containing the same elastomer in the nose area that no expansion whatsoever was produced on impact with soft targets—not even when the bullet was driven to 1400 fps.

jackets sufficiently so that bullet expansion would be initiated in a consistent and repeatable manner. Some of these early dies were relatively simple units having generally cylindrical bores. The punches, on the other hand, were extremely intricate and difficult to machine using a non-CNC mill. My uncle, Stan Burczynski, was responsible for machining all of the dies and punches used to make the initial prototypes.

As there are trade secrets involved, I can't elaborate here on the very first die and punch system used or the jacket modification that it produced except to say that it proved that the EFMJ concept was viable.

The second approach used to modify EFMJ jackets utilized an adjustable bottleneck die having 7/8 x 14 threads and a six-bladed scoring punch. Each punch blade maintained a sharp edge over its entire length, and each blade terminated in a sharp-edged radius at the leading end of the punch. These six radii proved instrumental in eliminating any adverse curling of gilding metal that would have otherwise occurred ahead of the blades during the scoring process. The scoring punch had a spring-loaded plunger which prevented the jacket from being pulled out of the die along with the punch as it retracted.

The first step in the process consisted of slipping a drawn 9mm jacket (.011 inch wall thickness) over a proportionally scaled-down bottleneck punch and forcing it base first into the die. This created a "necked down" or bottleneck jacket having a reduced-diameter nose area which was still essentially cylindrical in shape. A mild transition angle separated the full-diameter shank portion from the bottlenecked area. The jacket was ejected from the die using a flat-ended knock-out punch.

The second step involved slipping the bottlenecked jacket over the end of the scoring punch and forcing it into the same bottleneck die. This action formed isolated scores within a select

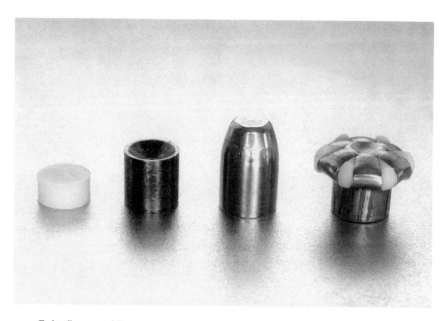

Federal's patented Expanding Full Metal Jacket (EFMJ) bullet utilizes a rubber core in the nose area ahead of a hollow point lead core. Deep scores on the interior of the jacket allow the bullet nose to collapse/expand on impact with any media, wet or dry. Shown at far right is a 200-grain +P .45 Auto round recovered from calibrated 10 percent ballistic gelatin.

The EFMJ looks and feeds like a FMJ round but expands to maximum diameter faster than a conventional hollowpoint under all conditions. Unlike a hollowpoint, it doesn't depend on external fluid for expansion. The captive rubber core acts as the "fluid." The main advantage of the new round is that it can't clog up with such things as fabric and therefore expands consistently when fired through dry media like heavy clothing, wallboard, and plywood.

portion of the jacket (i.e., on the interior of the yet unformed—nonogival—nose area). The score depth was fixed at .010 inch using this particular punch. In contrast, as the die was fully adjustable, the score *length* could be varied. The scores could be as short as a few thousandths of an inch or as long as the nose itself. A thin "web" of unscored jacket material

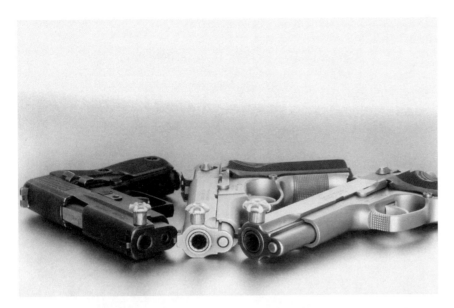

The first three EFMJ calibers available from Federal will be 9mm, 40 S&W, and .45 Auto. Other law enforcement calibers will undoubtedly follow. At some point, Federal may introduce a Personal Defense line of ammunition as well. These bullets were recovered from gelatin after penetrating heavy clothing.

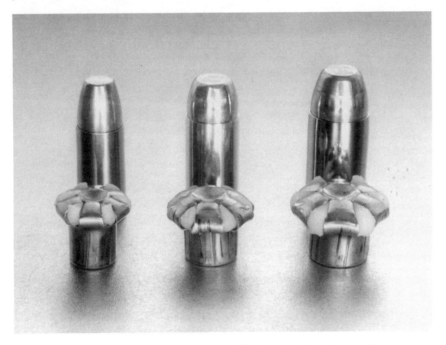

Federal elected to go with the heaviest practical bullet weights in order to maximize penetration. Its goal for law enforcement was 12+ inches after barriers. From left to right: 124-grain 9mm, 165-grain 40 S&W, 200-grain .45 auto.

existed directly in line with and just outside the scored areas. Again, the jacket was ejected from the die using a flat-ended knock-out punch.

The third step entailed inserting a 5/16 inch plastic ball into the jacket, followed by a flat-ended core of pure lead. Both "cores" were then "hard-seated" inside the jacket as the entire component assembly was forced into a profile die (bullet swaging die). The internal pressure created during the seating process forced both the plastic and the lead core to expand radially. This forced the jacket's plastic-containing nose area to fully conform to the ogive portion of the profile die. As the plastic expanded radially, it caused the web areas along each score line in the jacket to split. This resulted in the formation of six narrow slits over a portion * of the ogive area as well as a portion of the forward shank area. At the same time, the seating action formed a recess at the open base of the bullet between the jacket mouth and the rear of the core. The bullet was then forced into a crimping or "heeling" die, base first. This die had a radius machined into its interior which forced the jacket mouth inwardly, forming the same basic radius in the bullet heel area. The bullet was then final-swaged in the profile die. During the final swage operation, this rather large radius collapsed, consequently forming a smaller, more conventional radius at the heel of the bullet.

The resulting 9mm prototypes appeared surprisingly smooth and very different than a conventional truncated cone FMJ due to the slits. Although the slits in the jacket's ogive area were extremely narrow, portions of the translucent plastic and the lead core were visible to the naked eye. The bullets actually *looked* like they would work.

Upon firing these rather light

---

* The reason the slits didn't extend over the entire length of the nose was because the scores were produced (first step) while the jacket nose area was still in cylindrical form. When the jacket was forced into the profile die, its closed end was constricted inwardly and reduced in diameter. What had previously been the outer area of the closed jacket base became the forward portion of the ogive area. As a natural consequence of reshaping the jacket base, a short area (.090 inch in length) behind the meplat was unscored.

(100-grain) bullets into light clothing and calibrated 10 percent gelatin it was discovered that they did in fact expand in a very uniform manner. When viewed from the expanded end, six spoke-like "straps" of gilding metal connected with and radiated outwardly from the still intact meplat. Six triangular sections of the now expanded plastic were visible between the straps. The whitish plastic had been crushed to such a thin state that it had become almost transparent. When viewed from the side, light was visible between the curved jacket straps and the expanded plastic. A space was present in this area because after the bullet came to rest, the plastic, due to its elastic nature, attempted to return to some semblance of its original, undeformed size and shape. This attempt was axially frustrated because it was held captive by the jacket straps. The face of the expanded EFMJ was relatively flat. Weight retention was 100 percent.

Unfortunately, due to the physical properties of the particular plastic used, mainly its hardness and its relatively high tensile strength, the impact velocity had to be quite high in order to initiate meaningful expansion in fabric-clad gelatin. These first bullets were driven to 1200 and 1275 fps. Expanded bullet diameters were .580 and .671 inch respectively. Penetration depth in fabric-clad gelatin was 10 inches and 8.75 inches.

The main problem encountered using this combination of thin-walled (.011 inch) jacket and relatively tough plastic was that when the bullet was fired through 20-gauge sheet steel, the jacket would rupture. When the jacket ruptured, both cores were lost. After a rupture occurred, the substantially expanded lead core continued to penetrate, albeit not as deeply as desired.

Although the slits made the bullet excessively weak, the main culprit was the plastic itself. Its particular

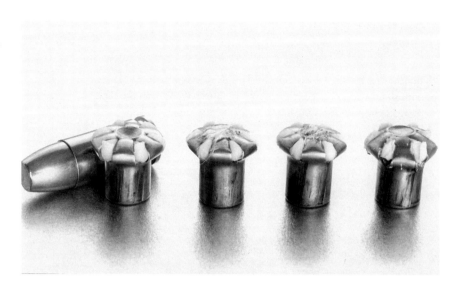

EFMJ nose profiles were designed for ultrareliable feeding through semiauto pistols and sub guns. From left to right: expanded 9mm bullets fired into bare gelatin, heavy clothing, wallboard and 3/4 inch plywood using the FBI test protocol.

Many EFMJ bullet weights in each caliber were tested at different velocities. Expanded .45 Auto bullets were recovered from heavy clothing/gelatin. From left to right: 135 grains, 185 grains, 200 grains, 230 grains. Heavier/slower bullets provide tactical penetration.

durometer * was too great when used with a thin jacket. Further testing substantiated that if the nose core material used in the EFMJ (older *or* newer designs) was too hard, substantially more shock was imparted to the jacket on impact with hard barriers. Hard core materials lacked the "cushioning" effect needed to

prevent jacket ruptures. A kinder, gentler buffer material was needed in the nose.

To complicate matters, an *opposing* problem existed—penetration needed to be increased. What at first seemed totally doable was now looking downright impossible. We needed a bullet that was weak enough to expand

* At higher velocities (both pistol and rifle calibers), even harder materials such as Nylon, polypropylene, polystyrene, and High Density Polyethylene (HDPE) provide sufficient expansion if the appropriate jacket wall thickness is used.

in relatively light resistance and one that would remain intact when fired through steel while providing adequate penetration. I was beginning to think that unacceptable terminal ballistic compromise might provide the only solution.

A search was begun for alternative nose core materials. A relatively soft material was needed that would minimize the stress imposed on the jacket during deformation. The material had to be yielding but not overly compressible. If the material was too soft it would be crushed completely, causing the bullet to overexpand. Such a situation would limit the bullet's ability to penetrate to an acceptable level. With these thoughts in mind, rubber companies were contacted, engineers were grilled, and quotes were obtained. After talking to an engineer from a Minnesota company, a decision was made to obtain some gum rubber balls of appropriate hardness. These .325 inch diameter spheres were black in color and had a somewhat sticky feel to them. I later learned that they also had a tendency to stick in the molds, which is one reason their cost was so high. In fact, most companies try to persuade their customers not to use natural gum rubber but one of the synthetics instead. Synthetic rubbers are generally less expensive and are more compatible with the injection molding process.

Soft nose core materials aside, to end up with a more robust bullet, the jacket had to be strengthened. This meant eliminating the slits. Since the slits were formed as a result of the bottleneck jacket expanding radially inside the profile die, the logical thing to do was to eliminate the bottleneck shape. This meant that a new scoring punch had to be designed—one that was based on the internal shape and dimensions of the profile die.

The switch from straight blades to slightly curved blades compounded the difficulty associated with machining the scoring punch. In spite of the

intricate configuration, my machinist managed to make a nice looking punch using a manual mill. The profile of the new blades was compatible with the die. A proportionally scaled-down pointing punch was also machined which maintained the general contour of the profile die. The existing core-seating punch was used.

The first step in the new process consisted of slipping a drawn 9mm jacket (.011 inch wall thickness) over the pointing punch and forcing it base first into the profile die. This action constricted the closed end, forming a jacket having the general nose profile of the finished bullet. The jacket was then ejected from the die using a flat-ended knock-out punch having a meplat-wide diameter.

The second step involved slipping the ogival-shaped jacket over the end of the ogival-shaped scoring punch and forcing both into the profile die. As the punch blades were contoured to the outside of the jacket ogive, this linear action manifested itself radially. Six scores were formed on the interior of the jacket's ogive area. The score depth could be regulated by the amount of force that was applied. The scores in these prototype jackets were relatively deep using the new punch concept and this particular punch. The score depth could be increased beyond this if desired. The score length could be shortened slightly but at the expense of a shallower score depth. The scores were nearly as long as the ogive itself. As was the case with the bottlenecked jacket (prior to radial expansion), a "web" of uncut jacket material existed directly in line with and just outside the scored areas. The existence of a solid web area substantially strengthened the jacket. Again, the jacket was ejected from the profile die using the knock-out punch.

The third step entailed inserting a gum rubber ball into the jacket, followed by a flat-ended core of pure lead. Both cores were then hard-seated inside the jacket as the component

assembly was forced into the profile die. The internal pressure created during the seating process forced both the gum rubber and the lead core to expand radially. This in turn forced the nose area to fully conform to the contour of the profile die. As the nose of the jacket was tightly confined within the profile die, radial stretching of the jacket was minimized. The web areas remained intact and no splits were formed in the jacket nose. The only evidence that scores were present at all consisted of six faint longitudinal lines on the exterior of the nose. Again, the seating action formed a recess at the open base of the bullet. Insertion of the bullet in the heeling die produced a large radius which was later reduced in size when the bullet was final-swaged.

Using the FBI's test protocol, 115-grain prototypes using the new EFMJ jacket concept and the new nose core material were fired into calibrated gelatin clad with both light and heavy clothing. Impact velocities were 850, 900, 950, 1050, 1100, and 1150 fps. The terminal results were very encouraging using these light bullets. Dozens of expanded bullets having the classic "mushroom" appearance were recovered from gelatin. These looked even better than the previous bullets with jacket slits. The expanded bullets were almost clone-like, regardless of their velocity or the material penetrated. If it hadn't been for their unique look, the consistency of expansion would have been monotonous. Expanded diameters ranged from .534 (850 fps) to .644 (1150 fps) inch. Penetration depth varied from 10.25 to 11.87 inch. The stronger jacket and heavier bullet had gained us some needed penetration. None of the jacket straps snapped in two, and weight retention was 100 percent. But the real test of bullet robustness was yet to come— hard barriers.

The results of these tests were received well by key personnel: Dave Longren, Bruce Warren, Bob Kramer (now Director of Product Engineering), Kris Ostman (principal development engineer), Shep Kelly (Director of Law Enforcement and Military Sales at the time), and of course, Craig Pilarski and Don Bretl, the two R&D engineers I worked closest with regarding new products.

One of Craig's goals was to find a way around the intricate geometry of the scoring blades present on the original punch I had designed. The blades of the original comprised a compound angle that assisted in release. Craig's new design consisted of six relatively sharp ridges flanked by tapered "facets" rather than thin-edged blades. This punch was certainly less complex and costly to machine and did create stress risers on the interior of the jacket nose. However, the angle separating the ridges on this experimental punch proved to be too great. The wide angle didn't allow the ridge edges to penetrate deeply enough into the gilding metal.

The second punch Craig designed more closely matched the basic geometry of the original, although the blades were altered slightly. After incrementally shortening the tip of the punch bit by bit, Craig was able to approximate the score depth I had been working with. This punch worked quite well, and many in-house 9mm tests were conducted with EFMJ bullets made from the jackets it modified.

During this punch design phase, Craig became concerned about the cost of the nose core material. The gum rubber spheres we were using worked exceptionally well and required no orientation but were expensive—disproportionately so when compared to other materials. Craig and I discussed other materials and means of feeding. This, of course, required more research.

Working independently of one another, Craig and I made contact with a number of rubber companies, getting general information and short-

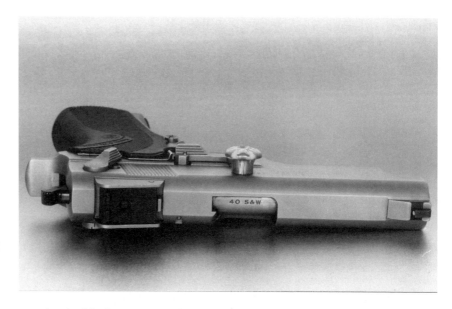

A major federal agency expressed interest in the EFMJ design and asked if .40 S&W bullets could be made as heavy as 165 grains. The 165-grain round provides excellent accuracy and ample penetration through barriers.

This expanded 165-grain 40 S&W bullet was recovered from 10 percent gelatin after penetrating 3/4 inch plywood and light clothing. Size of the exit hole reveals the high rate of expansion. Conventional hollowpoints don't create large exit holes in plywood due to little or no expansion.

run prices. After many hours of poring over the Thomas Register, rubber samples were ordered from several companies. An engineer from one of these companies appeared very knowledgeable and was extremely helpful in explaining shelf life, altered property characteristics (under temperature extremes), the effects of

long-term compression, etc. As it turned out, I ordered several samples of .312 inch diameter rubber in various materials and durometers from this company. Among these materials was Nitrile and EPDM (a nonmarking grade of Ethylene Propylene—"EP" rubber) used as tie-down material. This elastomer is used primarily for making gaskets and O-rings and has an excellent shelf life, as do several others. EPDM was highly resistant to ozone, flame, weather, oxidation, alcohol, solvents, lubricants, etc., and could handle high temperature extremes. When isolated in its own environment (such as a bullet jacket) and removed from light, its "shelf life" extends to decades. Importantly, it was more cost-effective than gum rubber.

The above materials and others were tried and it was found that the turquoise-colored EPDM gave us a good balance of value and the favorable material properties we were looking for. EPDM was also available in a variety of colors.

Tests were conducted in upstate New York using 9mm bullets (117 grains) based on .011-inch-walled jackets scored with the original punch. Bullet velocity ranged from 850 to 1150 fps. Expanded bullet diameters ranged from .444 to .662 inch when fired through heavy clothing and gelatin. The expanded bullets were nearly as uniform as those using gum rubber. Penetration ranged from 10 inches to 13 inches. EFMJ penetration still had to be increased.

When compared to the EPDM results, bullets tested using another slightly softer elastomer known in-house as "R2" produced larger expanded diameters at the lowest velocity (.548 inch at 850 fps compared to .444 inch). The softer core material automatically lowered the expansion threshold. Interestingly, at 1150 fps, the expanded bullet diameter using R2 was actually smaller (.632 compared to .662 inch) than the harder EPDM-based bullets. It was obvious that the softer material was forced to extrude between the expanding jacket straps at a higher rate (using this particular jacket) than that of the harder EPDM. As the R2 rubber bled through, the internal resistance offered by this nose core material was lessened. Something was learned. Application time in relation to nose core hardness was relevant. These results seemed to

dictate that we remain with EPDM, at least temporarily.

Over the next several months, a great deal of experimentation and testing was conducted in both New York and Minnesota. Experimental variables included score depth, rubber volume, and jacket properties.

During this period of experimentation, hard barrier tests (20-gauge steel, windshield glass, 3/4 inch plywood, and wallboard) conducted in New York gave every indication that a thicker (stronger) jacket was needed. One or more jacket straps snapped upon impact with plywood, steel, and glass when fired at typical 9mm velocities. When recovered from post-barrier gel, these bullets were pretty gnarly looking—especially when compared to the classic mushroom-like expansions produced after penetrating heavy clothing.

Several new wall thicknesses were tried. Jackets having relatively thin walls still ruptured on impact with steel. Unacceptable expanded bullet diameters resulted using very thick-walled jackets. Penetration was also greater than desired. The thicker jackets held up well to the resistance offered by steel, however, I felt that there had to be a happy medium somewhere. Federal personnel had begun designing new draw punches which would give us more jacket choices.

The EFMJ project now transitioned to Larry Head, inventor of Federal Cartridge's new Deep-Shok™ bullet. Larry was analytical, resourceful, and creative. He was also open-minded with regard to new ideas and didn't appear to suffer from "NIH" (Not Invented Here) syndrome. I sensed that it would be a pleasure working with him as it had been with Craig. In accordance with Bruce's wishes, we worked closely together from that point on and communicated regularly.

From my perspective, the first thing that we needed to address was the hard barrier issue. A jacket having an optimum wall thickness was

needed. Larry expedited the machining of draw tooling, which provided us with a more robust series of jackets. Larry sent jackets with varying wall thicknesses. Meanwhile, he experimented with other jacket properties. He was also instrumental in designing new scoring punch tooling in 9mm, .40 S&W, and .45 Auto. Larry sent me a couple of the punches in each caliber. Other than custom grinding their outside diameters (to match the inside diameter of a particular jacket) and re-radiusing the blade tips, these scoring punches were just about perfect, as they had been exquisitely ground using a CNC machine. The scores they produced were extremely uniform because of the tight fit inside the jacket. The tighter the fit, the better the alignment and the more uniform the score depth. Unfortunately, the extra time spent on the EFMJ project was getting Larry further behind in his other work. Prior to having the EFMJ production project tossed on his desk, he had been diligently focusing on designing a rifle bullet utilizing the new jacket-locking feature that he invented.

Although working independently of one another, every few days Larry and I would swap war stories regarding any progress with respect to the 9mm version of the design. Bullet weight had been increased to 124 grains, and both New York and Minnesota tests confirmed that the thicker jackets were paying off. The bullets were holding up well when fired through hard barriers *and* penetrating deeper. EFMJ performance in wallboard, the material that causes a universal problem for conventional hollowpoint bullets, was exceptional, although there was a commensurate but small decrease in expanded diameter. The decreased diameter allowed the bullet to penetrate deeper in gelatin, however, even though the wallboard had decreased its momentum. Thanks to the nose core material, it was almost as though the wallboard wasn't there. And unlike a hollowpoint, which depends heavily on *external* fluid to initiate expansion, the "fluid" (rubber) was already present and accounted for in the nose of the EFMJ. The cavity of a standard hollowpoint has a tendency to clog immediately with wallboard dust, transforming it into a softpoint. Oftentimes, no expansion at all occurs. This was not the case with the EFMJ design. The fact that it could expand very quickly through extremely heavy clothing and other dry media gave it a unique advantage over conventional bullets.

With respect to 3/4 inch plywood, we were actually getting *larger* expanded diameters than bullets fired through heavy clothing. The bullets expanded so rapidly that 2+ inch holes were blown out the back of the plywood. The recovered bullets weren't as beautifully mushroomed, but all the jacket straps were intact. In spite of the larger diameter, penetration wasn't unduly affected because the general shape of the expanded bullet nose was more rounded. In effect, these bullets (after penetrating plywood) had a better "*terminal* ballistic coefficient" than the same bullets fired through heavy clothing.

Tests under a wide variety of end use conditions led to refinement of the rubber material selection, with the result that a proprietary rubber was found which was very robust with respect to all operational circumstances.

Good progress was being made by combining features but Larry wanted even greater expansion in order to compensate for the velocity loss which occurred over distances (e.g., 25 yards). I suggested that a hollowpoint core of pure lead might help increase expansion and reduce jacket stress in the process. Larry said that it would have to have a special configuration to eliminate problems of orientation under actual production conditions. The core would also have to have a

"rim" of suitable thickness to withstand deformation caused by normal, in-house handling. I had my machinist make a hollowpoint core-forming punch and a new knock-out punch. Bullets made using these hollowpoint cores did in fact increase expansion. Larry later designed several punches that produced different hollowpoint configurations. It was found that some of these were too aggressive, causing excessive expansion which affected penetration. The current hollowpoint cavity provides a good balance of expansion and penetration and actually helps the bullet hold up against hard barriers as it acts as an additional buffer.

Obviously, improvements continue that expand upon the possible applications for this new and exciting bullet technology (some of which provide deep penetration). I am not at liberty to discuss them all, but rest assured that there is no shortage of good ideas for improvements within the framework of the existing patent and patents applied for.

Both Dave Longren and Bruce Warren have keen vision when it comes to new products, and they intuitively recognize market potential. In late 1998, after the 9mm product had been thoroughly tested, Dave presented the EFMJ concept to top Blount officials. The idea was well received and the general consensus was that it had potential in several areas.

After a number of unscheduled delays and a great deal of experimentation, the 9mm part of the project was nearing completion. Larry had figured out a way to form very consistent scores in the jacket without using a nitrogen cylinder system. A rotary mechanism had been developed to feed the rubber cores into the jackets. Other special equipment was in place. Things were looking up.

About this same time, Bruce began receiving a considerable amount of feedback from a number of agencies that had become interested in the

design in 9mm and other calibers. There was an unusual amount of interest in the EFMJ as fodder for MP5 submachine guns. In response, Bruce requested that the entire project be expedited. As Larry's hands were now completely full working on a dozen projects, he asked me to do the initial development work on the .40 S&W and the .45 Auto. Due to its increasing popularity in law enforcement circles, the .40 was the main priority. Larry was good about sending all the needed support material: carbide profile dies, scoring punches, larger diameter rubber, jackets having various wall thicknesses, hollowpoint cores pre-bled to the approximate weight needed. Of course, all of these materials didn't appear overnight.

Long, sometimes grueling hours were devoted to expediting the project. The profile dies had to be modified to work in a compound leverage press. The outside diameters of the scoring punches had to be ground to snugly fit a particular jacket. Some of the jackets had to be trimmed using a lathe since none of us yet knew what length was required (primarily because the nose core dimension hadn't been established via gel tests). Cylindrical core-seating dies had to be designed and machined for the new calibers along with hollowpoint punches and heel-crimping dies. New core-seating punches had to be machined as well as new pointing punches. Equipment had to be modified in order to handle the larger rubber diameters. My machinist was a lifesaver insofar as getting the parts machined, often in record time.

Larry set forth what he felt were ideal parameters for bullet weight, chamber pressure, velocity, expanded bullet diameter, and penetration depth. Then he told me what we could live with. Larry was surprisingly realistic regarding his ballistic expectations due to our previous experience with the limitations of the design. The main limitation of the EFMJ design is its length. EFMJ bullet length is greater

EFMJ bullet length is greater than a conventional bullet due to the difference in density between lead and rubber. Muzzle velocities are somewhat lower for this reason. However, EFMJ's compensate by expanding to full diameter much faster.

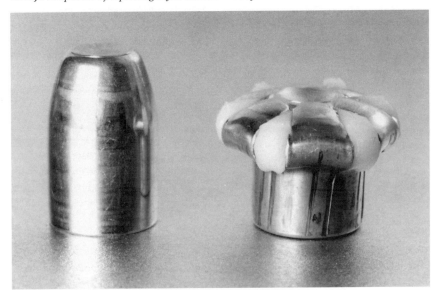

Federal has not ignored police officers who favor big, heavy bullets. The 200-grain .45 Auto bullet provides well over 12 inches of penetration in post-barrier gelatin as well as good expansion. A lighter weight civilian version is always a possibility.

These bullets were driven to 1140 fps, expanded too quickly, and lacked the mass to penetrate as deeply as we wanted them to (12+ inches). Larry asked me to see if the bullet weight could be bumped up to 155 grains while still remaining within SAAMI pressure limits. The heavier bullets were made and tested. Penetration was increased over an inch and the bullets were expanding nicely and working well through various barrier materials.

Shortly before this, a major federal agency expressed interest in the design and asked if .40 S&W bullets could be made as heavy as 165 grains. Larry asked me to give it a try and I complied. After reducing the rubber core volume, the 165-grain bullets were about the same length as the 155s. Maintaining the same bullet length conserved what we now viewed as precious case capacity. The bullets were loaded to 1106 fps. These bullets worked well through barrier materials. The average expanded diameter of the recovered bullets was .664 inch and the bullets penetrated to a depth of 12.29 inches. I was more than content that a bullet this long and heavy could be launched at *this* velocity and still remain within SAAMI pressure specs.

As of this writing, Larry is working on a very similar in-house version of the .40 caliber EFMJ and is testing various propellants in an effort to increase velocity.

The first EFMJ bullets tested in the .45 Auto weighed 165 grains. Bullet velocity was 1045 fps. Chamber pressure was well below the +P level. The maximum expanded diameter obtained using these bullets was .763 inch. The helical fractures created in gelatin were impressive—4+ inches at the widest point. As was the case with the lightest .40 caliber bullets, these didn't penetrate as deeply as we wanted them to, and Larry asked me to bump up the weight to 185 grains.

The heavier 185-grain bullets utilized a hollowpoint lead core, a rubber nose core of less volume, and a

than a conventional bullet due to the vast difference in density between lead and rubber. The rubber eats up jacket volume quickly and that was one of the reasons we were intent on minimizing the amount of nose core material used. A longer bullet consumes more cartridge case capacity. At an equivalent pressure level, a +P EFMJ

bullet will exit the muzzle at a somewhat lower velocity than a conventional bullet. On the plus side, the EFMJ expands *much* quicker than a conventional hollowpoint and provides more control (less recoil) in rapid fire. High velocities are not requisite.

The first EFMJ bullets tested in the .40 S&W weighed 135 grains.

thicker jacket wall. They were launched at 980 fps. While the penetration depth achieved exceeded the minimum established by the Immigration Naturalization Service (INS) using its new test protocol, we were still shy of the minimum standard as defined in the FBI protocol. Average penetration depth (aggregate, all media) was only 11.51 inches. The chamber pressure was still low, however, and Larry again asked me to increase the weight—this time to 200 grains. We were both somewhat concerned that the combination of extra weight, greater bearing surface, and reduced case capacity might bump us up into an unacceptable pressure range. It didn't. In fact, we were still below +P pressure. Penetration was again increased.

Without prompting, I trimmed jackets to the proper length and made up a number of 230-grain EFMJs using the same nose core volume and a heavier lead core. Expanded diameters were more modest, but penetration was 14+ inches—enough to satisfy anyone's needs. Chamber pressure had moved into the +P range. Everyone was surprised and pleased that these big, heavy bullets performed at an acceptable pressure level.

Extremely light .45 bullets were also tested. Bullets weighing 135 grains were fired at very high speeds. Massive expanded diameters were obtained at the expense of an attendant reduction in penetration. These lightweight rounds produced very mild recoil and were very pleasant to shoot.

Using new technology, good progress is being made with respect to increasing the penetration level achieved by high velocity, *lightweight* EFMJ bullets in all calibers. There is a great deal of optimism surrounding the possibilities in this area.

At one point, it appeared that the EFMJ was being viewed more as a niche product than as a mainstream product. The primary target market being considered was Europe. However, after the first article hit the stands (*Guns & Weapons for Law Enforcement*, April 2000), Federal received an unprecedented deluge of calls, letters, and e-mails from U.S. police departments and private citizens expressing interest in the product. The interest expressed by many of these departments stemmed from the fact that they were prohibited from carrying hollowpoint ammunition. Individuals were begging for a civilian version of the round for personal defense. Contact was also made by police departments and government agencies from non-European countries. It was quickly realized that there were a large number of domestic and foreign law enforcement agencies out there in need of such a product. On the domestic side, many departments like the Detroit Police Department are still only allowed to carry hardball ammunition. Canadian law enforcement agencies represented still another market for the same reason. Word gets around quickly in the industry, and many agencies contacted Federal before the article broke and even before the 9mm was in full production. Limited markets were the last thing Federal personnel were thinking about after the flood of inquiries. Thoughts turned rather quickly to production capacity and how the company might meet demand in a timely manner.

The EFMJ concept has received unanimous in-house support from both the law enforcement sales staff and engineering.

I especially valued the opinion and input from one individual in particular. On the sales side, Shep Kelly, Federal's former Director of Law Enforcement and Military Sales, was eminently qualified to make recommendations regarding the real-world weapon and ammunition needs of police and has supported the basic EFMJ concept from the beginning. Shep's background includes employment as a law enforcement officer at both state and federal levels. He served as the Agent in Charge for Firearms Training for the U.S. Department of State Office of Security (now Diplomatic Security Service) and conducted extensive research in the area of law enforcement ammunition performance. Recognizing the shortcomings of conventional ammunition and drawing on his years of experience in the field, Shep has offered useful advice with regards to what constitutes a more effective police bullet. Shep is genuinely concerned about the safety of law enforcement officers. He sugarcoats nothing, and one can always expect an honest and objective answer from him. If a particular design poses a threat to an officer, he'll let you know. This is really the kind of opinion a designer needs to hear. Fortunately, Shep saw increasing merit in the EFMJ design over the course of its development.

Bernie Ness, Senior Law Enforcement Specialist at Federal with 16 years experience; Wade Plucker, Senior Law Enforcement Specialist, formerly with the FBI (26 years experience) serving at Quantico in the areas of firearms training, training in firearms, street survival training, ammunition and weapon testing and evaluation, and writing contract specs; and Ted Hollabaugh, Law Enforcement Specialist with 23 years experience as ordnance gunsmith for the Marine Corps shooting team and former FBI gunsmith and ballistician (15 years), each viewed the EFMJ design as street-worthy and a cut above other designs. The common thread of assent was basically due to the bullet's ability to expand without fail when fired through heavy clothing and dry barriers. As FBI ballistician, Ted had seen it all and was all too well-acquainted with the fluid-dependency of conventional hollowpoints. In his estimation, the new round was a major breakthrough.

On the engineering side, Bob Kramer, Director of Product Engineering at Federal, and Kris Ostman, Principal Development Engineer for the company,

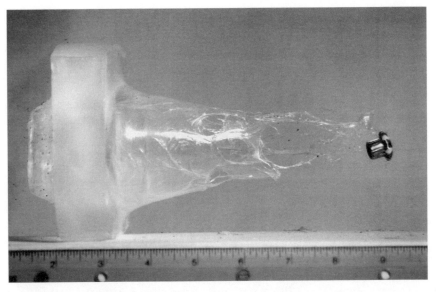

High-speed photo of .45 Auto bullet exiting a 1 inch slice of 10 percent gelatin reveals just how rapidly the EFMJ expands to full diameter. A bullet that expands this fast produces a large permanent wound channel as well as a large temporary cavity.

A reduced-velocity .45 Auto round fired through 3/4 inch plywood produces good expansion even prior to contacting gelatin. The more rounded shape of the expanded nose promotes deeper penetration in ultimate target.

creative and appears to possesses total recall with respect to every process that has ever been used or tried at Federal. Bob's opinion carries major weight at Federal.

Kris is both analytical and practical—and therefore cautious. He is also highly creative. Like Bob, he is a product of experience. Because of this and previous conversations with him, I considered him the quintessential "hard sell." The new design would have to have *real merit* in order for him to accept it. Happily, after due deliberation, both Bob and Kris adjudged the design a significant improvement over conventional bullets and one that was economically feasible. I was relieved when they gave it their stamp of approval.

An initial patent was recently granted which covers slits in the jacket as well as internal and external scores. All 59 of the original claims were approved. Additional EFMJ patents have been applied for. These cover new nose core materials as well as new rear core materials. All current and future EFMJ patent rights have been assigned to Federal. Patent and trademark duties have been turned over to Product Development Engineer Doug Carr. We are working closely together to further expand EFMJ coverage.

In summation, the EFMJ concept provides a number of advantages. It looks and feeds like hardball and expands to maximum diameter faster than a hollowpoint under all conditions. Unlike a hollowpoint, its main advantage is that it never clogs up and therefore invariably expands when fired through dry media like heavy clothing, wallboard, and plywood, and it provides tactical penetration against hard, intermediate barriers. It expands completely in less than an inch of fabric-clad gelatin and provides a wider permanent wound cavity than conventional hollowpoints (that is, *when* said hollowpoints work). Bullet expansion can be obtained at lower velocities than conventional rounds

scrutinized every aspect of the design before rendering their opinions. Their opinions count. By virtue of their positions, they automatically assess and analyze every facet of a new design such as ease of manufacture, the complexity and cost of required tooling, tool life, component cost and future availability, in-house material flow, and square footage consumption of the equipment required. Bob is a veritable mine of information and, in the opinion of many, an indispensable company asset. He draws on many years of experience in dealing with difficult problems, which enables him to solve new problems that continually crop up. He is highly and thus, lower recoil is generated. This translates to greater weapon control and more accurate bullet placement in rapid-fire situations.

Improvements in EFMJ technology continue at Federal. Many core materials have been tested. Many others are being tested. Other applications for the new round are being contemplated. And while it may not materialize, Federal has considered offering a Personal Defense version to civilians. If this were to happen, bullet weights would probably be lighter than those offered to law enforcement and loaded to higher velocity.

Detractors will inevitably surface, but I believe field usage will prove that Federal has a winner here.

CHAPTER 15

Cor-Bon BeeSafe Ammo

Cor-Bon has introduced a line of frangible bullets for home defense and concealed carry. The company's goal for its BeeSafe ammo was to roughly equal the performance of its existing hollowpoints, except do it with less chamber pressure, less blast, and less recoil. Most of the frangible ammo on the market is loaded to +P, +P+, or greater than +P+ pressures in all of the calibers. All of the Cor-Bon BeeSafe ammo is loaded to standard pressures.

Cor-Bon's BeeSafe ammo uses projectiles made by Beeline Custom Bullets of Nova Scotia, Canada. Beeline currently makes three kinds of bullets: Close Quarter Totally Fragmenting (CQTF), Close Quarter Penetrating Fragmenting (CQPF), and Police Ordnance Penetrating (POP).

The Beeline series of bullets was invented by Russell LeBlanc of Nova Scotia. According to LeBlanc, these frangible bullets were inspired by the book *Handgun Stopping Power.* LeBlanc saw both the high performance and the tactical drawbacks of frangible bullets, so he set out to get the stopping power without the shallow penetration problems.

LeBlanc began gunsmithing in the

early 1980s. In 1989, he began experimenting with different bullet designs. By 1991, he was making swaged lead bullets for Canadian IPSC shooters. In mid-1992 LeBlanc purchased bullet jacket-making equipment. By late 1992 he had developed his first jacketed, frangible bullet called the Shocker, available in all defensive calibers. By 1995, the Beeline series of bullets had grown to four: Shocker, CQTF, CQPF, and POP. Each of these are covered by patents. In early 1997, Cor-Bon adopted the Beeline CQPF for its new line of self-defense ammo.

Like the MagSafe (left), the BeeSafe is a frangible bullet loaded with large diameter birdshot (right). Unlike the MagSafe, the BeeSafe is capped with a buckshot pellet for deeper penetration.

All four Beeline bullets have a similar construction. They start off with jackets made from strips of copper. The jackets are punched into circles, then drawn into jacket cups in a series of operations using Corbin dies.

For more than 100 years, most bullet jackets have been made from gilding metal. This is a copper alloy with 95 percent copper and 5 percent zinc. LeBlanc joins a growing number of bullet designers who have selected a different jacket alloy. The Remington Golden Saber, for example, uses a jacket made from cartridge brass. With 70 percent copper and 30 percent zinc, this is the same material used to make cartridge cases. The Winchester Ranger SXT (Black Talon) and Supreme SXT use a copper-rich version of gilding metal with 97 percent copper and 3 percent zinc.

The Beeline bullets use a 110 series, pure copper jacket. The CCI-Speer Gold Dot also uses a pure copper jacket, though it is electroplated onto the lead core, not swaged around the core. While made from a softer alloy than traditional bullet jackets, the Beeline jacket is thicker. The thickness varies by caliber and bullet, but in general the jacket is .017 to .018 inch thick. The Beeline bullet needs to have such a thick jacket for structural integrity. Most frangibles have fused lead shot or epoxy-embedded lead shot as a core. The main part of the Beeline core is just a polyethylene (plastic) ball that simply serves as a filler. It offers no bullet shank rigidity.

Commercial jackets were too thin for the Beeline design—they tended to expand and break up too fast, and the whole projectile came apart too soon. This was one of the drawbacks with frangible ammo. The thick and pure copper jacket helped to delay the bullet fragmentation. This resulted in deeper pellet penetration than expected for a #5 or #6 birdshot pellet.

One exception exists to the Beeline use of a pure copper jacket. The .32 ACP 52-grain BeeSafe uses a 1100 series, pure aluminum jacket. This is similar to the Winchester use of aluminum and aluminum-manganese jackets for some of its lower velocity Silvertips.

For the next step in the Beeline bullet-making operation, the poly ball is placed in the jacket cup. Then the payload of birdshot is hand-placed over the plastic ball. The purpose of the ball is to lighten the projectile for the same rifling bearing area. Put another way, the Cor-Bon 9mm 91-grain BeeSafe bullet is as long, and has the same rifling engagement area as a 9mm 147-grain JHP. This long bearing area gives it better accuracy than the average frangible bullet.

The birdshot pellets are crushed on top of the poly ball and fused together. This same high-pressure swaging, or core seating, operation also expands the jacket in the bullet die to its final diameter.

The size of the birdshot used in the core is the primary difference between the Beeline Shocker, the CQPF used in the BeeSafe, and the police only POP. The Shocker used #9 birdshot compared to #5 and #6 in the CQPF and #2 in the POP. The Shocker bullet is no longer being produced.

The Cor-Bon BeeSafe ammo uses #5 and #6 birdshot just like the Glaser

Silver. In comparison, the Glaser Blue uses #12 birdshot, while the MagSafe Defender uses #2 and #4 birdshot. Cor-Bon's Peter Pi considered the use of the Beeline POP bullet with its larger #2 shot. However, the POP bullets themselves are heavier across the board than the CQPF bullets. Cor-Bon selected the lighter CQPF bullets because this put the BeeSafe ammo in the desired velocity brackets while still using standard rather than +P chamber pressures.

The number and size of the birdshot pellets in the Beeline payload varies by caliber. The 9mm 91-grain BeeSafe, for example, has eleven #6 birdshot pellets. The .40 S&W 101-grain BeeSafe has seven #5 pellets, six #6 pellets, and a single BB pellet in its core. The .45 ACP 107-grain BeeSafe packs seven #5 pellets. These birdshot pellets are "magnum hard" or "extra hard" as opposed to "chilled" shot, but they are not copper or nickel plated.

In an age of high-speed, computer-controlled automation, it is surprising to find out the birdshot pellets are placed in the core by hand and one at a time. Simply dumping the shot in the jacket results in a core that is unbalanced. Heavy or light areas across the same cross-section cause the bullet to yaw in flight or, even worse, to tumble. Hand-placing the pellets in layers and in the proper sequence results in excellent accuracy for a frangible. LeBlanc also tweaked the exact height of the poly ball. Shorter filler heights move the payload closer to the rear of the bullet and cause stability problems. Taller filler heights move the weight of the bullet forward like a badminton shuttlecock for better stability and accuracy.

As a rule, Beeline uses #5 and #6 birdshot as the primary payload in the CQPF core. Two exceptions exist: the 52-grain bullet used in the .32 ACP and the 67-grain bullet used in both the .380 ACP and the .38 Special. These projectiles use #7 1/2 birdshot and a #2 buck nose pellet.

Of course, the most significant

difference between the BeeSafe and all the other frangibles is the lead nose pellet. With the lead birdshot collapsed and crushed into the poly filler, the next operation is to place a large buckshot pellet on top of the birdshot payload. The bullet jacket is then crimped around the buck pellet at the same time the final profile of the bullet is established.

The size of the buckshot pellet in the CQPF bullet used in the BeeSafe varies by caliber. The 9mm 91-grain BeeSafe is topped with a 24-grain, .21 caliber #4 buck pellet. The .40 S&W 101-grain BeeSafe is sealed with a 40-grain, .30 caliber #1 buck. The .45 ACP 107-grain BeeSafe uses a 54-grain, .33 caliber #00 buck. These buckshot pellets are very low in antimony but are not dead soft pure lead.

The soft buckshot pellet flattens out on impact but penetrates 9 to 14 inches of calibrated gelatin. This penetration occurs along the line of impact, which is something no other frangible bullet does. With the BeeSafe, the shooter knows at least one big pellet will penetrate deeply and in a straight line. It may be the only frangible bullet to reach the spine or the pelvis on a frontal shot. The impact with bone by a 54-grain, .33 caliber 00 buck pellet is certain to cause more damage than a 5-grain, .15 caliber #2 birdshot pellet.

As a side note, the Beeline CQTF bullet has the same jacket, poly core, and birdshot payload as the BeeSafe CQPF. The penetrating fragmenting CQPF gets a buckshot pellet crimped in the jacket to make it a jacketed softpoint. The totally fragmenting CQTF is final formed without the buck pellet. The CQTF is a true open-tip jacketed hollowpoint.

The true round-nose profile of the BeeSafe assures reliable feeding in auto pistols and rapid speedloading in revolvers. This profile is a positive feature the BeeSafe shares with the Glaser. The natural lubricity of lead may or may not be an advantage over the plastic nose cap used on the Glaser

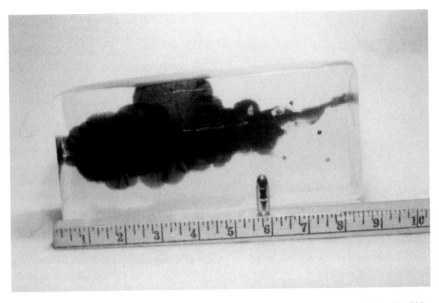

Even with smaller crush and stretch cavities than most frangibles, the BeeSafe, like this .380 ACP 67-grain version with 65 percent one-shot stops, is equal to the best hollowpoints. On impact with gelatin, the single buckshot pellet forms the main wound channel, while smaller birdshot penetrates up to 7 inches in a pattern up to 3 inches in diameter.

The BeeSafe bullet, like this 9mm 91-grain version, is not affected by heavy clothes. After glass, the BeeSafe becomes an effective combination of birdshot and buckshot. The BeeSafe is the only frangible to penetrate plywood and sheet metal like a jacketed softpoint.

as the round slides up the feed ramp. Neither cartridge has the same "bounce" as hardball when the bullet nose hits the feed ramp to guide the bullet into the chamber. However, any round-nose design will feed better than any non-round-nose design.

We conducted two different kinds of ballistics tests on the Cor-Bon BeeSafe. Both involved calibrated Kind & Knox ordnance Type 250 A gelatin. In the first test, we fired through the chronograph into bare 10 percent gelatin. This is the standard procedure that gives us the data to calculate the Fuller Index for one-shot stops.

The eight loads from .380 ACP to .45 ACP BeeSafe all expanded on impact and fragmented as designed. In each caliber, we recovered the buckshot nose pellet, pieces of birdshot, the polyethylene spacer, pieces of jacket that peeled away during expansion, and the circular piece of the jacket which was all that was left of the bullet base. The crush cavities were somewhat smaller than the other frangible loads due to the lower pellet count, while the stretch cavities were somewhat smaller than the other frangibles due to the lower energy levels. However, the penetration was generally in the ideal 8.4 to 12.8 inch range.

The BeeSafe, Glaser, and MagSafe all have different rates of pellet dispersion, different pellet penetration depths, and different pellet patterns or dispersion diameters. The Glaser spreads out rapidly to produce a 3 inch diameter pattern. The #12 shot in the Glaser Blue penetrates 5 to 6 inches starting after 2 inches. The #6 shot in the Glaser Silver penetrates 7 to 8 inches also starting at 2 inches. The MagSafe Defender fragments early too. Its #2 or #3 shot penetrate 10 to 13 inches in up to a 4 1/2 inch pattern.

In contrast, the BeeSafe lead nose cap greatly delays the fragmentation. Instead of separate shot cavities as early as 2 inches, the various BeeSafe loads begin the separate wound cavities at the 4 to 5 inch depth. While some of the BeeSafe loads produce shot penetration as deep as 8 inches, most of the pellets end up in the 5 1/2 to 7 inch range.

The BeeSafe lead nose cap also serves to reduce the diameter of the final shot pattern. Instead of the 3 to 4 1/2 inch diameters of shot, the BeeSafe pellets remain much closer to the main bullet path. With most BeeSafe ammo the pellets come to rest within an inch of the main wound channel, for a 2 inch diameter. Only the .357 Magnum and .357 SIG produced a 3 inch diameter pattern.

If the bullet strikes closer to

where the shooter intended, then less dispersion about the main channel is better. If the bullet strikes farther from where the shooter intended, then greater pellet dispersion is better.

Cor-Bon's goal for the BeeSafe was to come close to the wound ballistics of its high-pressure hollowpoints but to do it at standard pressures. The Fuller Index for these eight BeeSafe loads indicates they did it.

The second ballistics test involved shooting into gelatin after passing through tactical barriers. Tactical barriers like glass, sheet metal, and wood or plastic are very hard on most frangibles because the bullets can start to break apart in these intermediate targets. This is not an issue if the barrier is very close to, or in contact with, the main target. However, it is a serious problem when the main target is a few feet behind the intermediate target.

We fired the BeeSafe into gelatin after a layer of 1/4 inch laminated glass, then after two layers of 3/8 inch plywood, then after a cross-section of leather, denim, and down-filled clothing. The performance against tactical barriers is where the BeeSafe holds a clear advantage over other frangible loads. Unlike all the other frangibles, on impact with tactical barriers the BeeSafe bullet acts like a jacketed softpoint. It is simply not affected by heavy clothes. It performs the same in gelatin whether or not it has to defeat clothing. On impact with wood, the buckshot nose pellet gets pushed into the jacket. It penetrates wood and steel like a softpoint or hardball. The performance in gelatin after wood is also like that of a softpoint or hardball. The 9mm BeeSafe frangible penetrated 18 inches of gelatin *after* defeating two layers of plywood, the only frangible to do so. While the traditional frangibles break up while penetrating the walls of mobile homes and apartments, the Beeline holds together and, in fact, may penetrate more building materials than some jacketed hollowpoints.

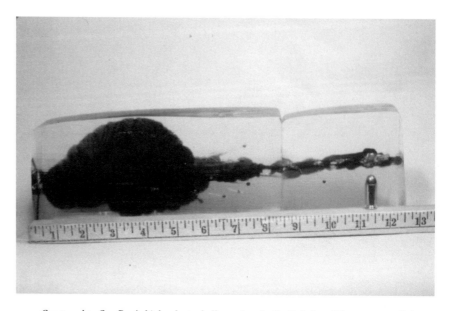

Compared to Cor-Bon's high velocity hollowpoints, its BeeSafe frangible ammo uses lighter bullets and standard chamber pressures. The stopping power is about the same. The BeeSafe, like this .40 S&W 101-grain bullet, uses numbers 5 and 6 birdshot. These pellets are smaller than the MagSafe Defender and larger than the Glaser Blue.

The performance after glass is even more impressive. On impact, the soft lead buck pellet deformed or flattened but the bullet remained intact. On impact with the gelatin after glass, the 9mm BeeSafe expanded to .68 caliber and had a recovered weight of 88 percent. Again, the BeeSafe is the only frangible to do that. As a rule, glass breaks up all forms of frangible bullet into their lead components. The Glaser becomes small or medium birdshot. The MagSafe becomes large birdshot. The Beeline becomes a combination of medium birdshot and buckshot.

The BeeSafe bullet has been classified as a softpoint by the noted independent ballistics lab, H.P. White Labs. This means it can be carried in states like New Jersey, countries like Canada and Germany, and local jurisdictions where hollowpoint ammo has been banned. Yet the BeeSafe produces the same stopping power as hollowpoint ammo and is less likely to overpenetrate on a soft torso shot or pose a downrange ricochet problem.

The BeeSafe frangible ammo produces less recoil and muzzle flip than Cor-Bon's high-pressure

hollowpoints. From the same firearm, felt recoil is directly related to bullet momentum. Without factoring in the weight of the gunpowder ejecta, the formula for momentum is the bullet weight in grains times the muzzle velocity in fps divided by the conversion factor 225,120.

Given the same chamber pressure, lighter bullets produce less felt recoil than heavier bullets. The BeeSafe line uses lighter bullets and lower pressures than Cor-Bon's JHP line. On the average, the BeeSafe produces 23 percent less recoil than the company's high-pressure hollowpoints.

Muzzle energy and muzzle momentum work together to produce the terminal slide velocity of the auto pistol. The bullet energy overcomes the energy stored in the main and recoil springs. The bullet momentum overcomes the inertia of the slide. The resulting rearward slide velocity must be high enough to reliably cycle the pistol. In all six auto pistol calibers, the BeeSafe fed, ejected, and cycled without any problem. However, we fired less than 100 rounds of each caliber. With any ammo using nontraditional bullet weights, the auto pistol shooter is urged to fire at least 200 rounds of ammo through his particular gun using a wide variety of stances and grips.

Cor-Bon released three additional frangible loads in the fall of 1997. These included a .25 ACP 34-grain BeeSafe, a .32 ACP 52-grain BeeSafe, and a .44 Special 105-grain BeeSafe. A CQPF bullet is under development at Beeline for the .223 Rem and .308 Win.

The Cor-Bon BeeSafe feeds like full-metal jacket ammo but performs like hollowpoint ammo. It cannot plug up on heavy clothing. It is safer than either hardball or hollowpoints in the event of a ricochet, yet it works well after defeating common tactical barriers. With standard chamber pressures and low recoil, this ammo is ideal for the common concealed-carry handguns. With hollowpoint-like wound ballistics, the latest ammo from Cor-Bon helps the handgunner to "be safe."

TABLE 15-1
BIRDSHOT USED IN FRANGIBLE AMMO

Size	Diameter	Weight	Ammo
No. 12 Bird	.05	0.2	Glaser Blue
No. 9 Bird	.08	0.7	Beeline CQTF
No. 7 1/2 Bird	.095	1.3	BeeSafe
No. 6 Bird	.11	1.9	BeeSafe, Glaser Silver
No. 5 Bird	.12	2.6	BeeSafe
No. 4 Bird	.13	3.2	MagSafe
No. 2 Bird	.15	4.9	Beeline POP, MagSafe
No. BB	.18	8.8	Omega Star
No. 4 Buck	.24	21	BeeSafe
No. 1 Buck	.30	40	BeeSafe
No. 00 Buck	.33	54	BeeSafe

TABLE 15-2
9MM BEESAFE VS. TACTICAL BARRIERS

Tactical Barrier	Gelatin Penetration	Recovered Diameter
Bare Gelatin	9.7 inches	frag
Heavily Clothed Gelatin	9.7 inches	frag
Plywood then Gelatin	18.0 inches	.38 cal.
Plate Glass then Gelatin	6.7 inches	.68 cal.

TABLE 15-3
COR-BON BEESAFE WOUND BALLISTICS

Caliber	Load	Velocity fps	Energy ft-lbs.	Gelatin Depth	Recovered Diameter	One-Shot Stop %
.380 ACP	67 gr. BeeSafe	1150	197	9.8 f	frag	65
.38 Spl	67 gr. BeeSafe	1450	313	13.0	frag	78
9mm	91 gr. BeeSafe	1400	396	9.7	frag	84
.357 Mag	91 gr. BeeSafe	1650	550	8.5	frag	90
.357 SIG	91 gr. BeeSafe	1525	470	9.0	frag	88
.40 S&W	101 gr. BeeSafe	1350	408	13.8	frag	86
.400 CorBon	101 gr. BeeSafe	1525	522	11.5	frag	90
.45 ACP	107 gr. BeeSafe	1500	535	13.0	frag	91

CHAPTER 16

Federal Personal Defense Ammo

Federal Cartridge was the first major ammunition company to act upon the real differences between the typical police shooting scenario and the typical home defense and concealed carry shooting scenario. The company developed separate ammo lines for each situation and labels them as such: Personal Defense (PD) for civilian shooters and Tactical for the special needs of law enforcement (see Chapter 17).

The typical police shooting scenario involves cross-torso shootings and tactical barriers. The typical civilian shooting scenario involves frontal and near frontal shots almost without exception. In fact, it involves so many frontal shots that bullets seldom strike the upper arm before entering the torso. If an extremity is hit, it is the thinner forearm. This makes sense. The forearm is in the line of sight on a perp holding a firearm, impact weapon, or knife.

Tactical barriers are rare to nonexistent in lawful civilian shooting scenarios. So are cross-torso shooting scenarios. These obstacles for the bullet are so uncommon in self-defense and concealed carry situations that Federal did not compromise its Personal Defense ammo in order to handle them. In fact, that is the best way to think about Federal's two very different lines of ammo: the compromise, police only Tactical ammo and the no compromise, civilian only Personal Defense ammo.

Federal's Personal Defense loads were developed specifically for short-barrel, handguns for home defense and concealed carry scenarios. It uses light to medium weight bullets driven to high, but not the highest, velocities. As a rule, PD ammo has a velocity 15 to 20 percent higher than conventional ammo and packs about 20 percent

Federal's line of Personal Defense ammo uses lighter bullets with faster velocities, more energy, more expansion, less penetration, and less recoil than patrol loads.

more energy. The felt recoil from Personal Defense is an average of 10 percent less than conventional ammo.

Federal Cartridge understands that heavier bullets generally have more felt recoil than lighter bullets. Federal officials watched a number of applicants for concealed carry permits try to qualify and saw that recoil control was a problem. This was made worse when applicants used concealable guns with small frames and short barrels and grips. The .45 Auto 165-grain PD Hydra-Shok produces 17 percent less felt recoil than the 230-grain Hydra-Shok. The .40 S&W 135-grain PD Hydra-Shok produces 13 percent less felt recoil than the 180-grain Hydra-Shok. In both calibers, the Personal Defense load produces much more energy than the heavier Hydra-Shok. These are not medium-velocity loads—they are full-power loads that produce less recoil through lighter bullet weights.

Federal specifically elected not to follow the FBI's eight-media test protocol in developing its PD ammo. This means the company did not use glass, metal, and plywood in front of the gelatin during testing. The only two test media were lightly clothed gelatin and heavily clothed gelatin,

Federal did not use the full FBI multiple-barrier protocol to design its Personal Defense ammo. Instead, the company used only the light clothing and heavy clothing phases. The 9mm 135-grain load is shown.

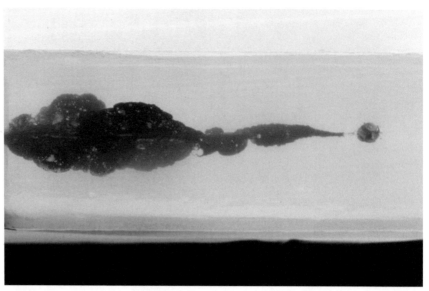

Federal designed all its Personal Defense ammo, like this 9mm 135-grain load, to penetrate between 10 and 11 inches of ordnance gelatin.

Like all Personal Defense ammo, the .380 Auto 90-grain load uses the Hydra-Shok bullet. These loads were all designed to expand after passing through heavy clothes.

The Federal 9mm 135-grain Personal Defense uses the same size hollowpoint cavity as its 124-grain Hydra-Shok but has a much shorter center post.

which are more applicable to civilian self-defense scenarios.

Federal also specifically ignored the FBI's minimum penetration distance of 12 inches. The company designed its PD ammo to penetrate between 10 and 11 inches after clothing. The rationale was simple— this ammo was for civilians, not police. The fact that ammo with less than 12 inches of penetration tops the 9mm and .40 S&W calibers further strengthened their case. Federal also used the work of Steve Fuller as justification for this depth. According to the Fuller Index, with the same initial diameter and muzzle energy, stopping power is equal with penetration distances between 8.4 and 12.8 inches. Beyond this range, stopping power drops off as bullet penetration increases. (For more on the Fuller Index, see *Street Stoppers*, Paladin Press, 1996, Chapter 28.)

Personal Defense ammo does not give up anything so it can perform better after glass and metal. Put another way, PD loads perform worse after barriers than do the police-specific bullets. However, the loads perform far better than these compromise police bullets when the target is frontal torso, even if protected by heavy winter or leather apparel.

While the Personal Defense ammo was specifically developed for civilian scenarios, Federal is certain it will spill over to police officers. Specifically, it is excellent for back-up, investigator, and off-duty guns. The scenarios where these concealed guns are likely to be used is nearly identical to civilian scenarios. Other possible police uses include courtroom security and where recoil control is a major issue.

At the 1997 SHOT Show, Federal announced Personal Defense loads in five calibers: .380 Auto, .38 Special +P, 9mm, .40 S&W, and .45 Auto. Each uses the incredible Hydra-Shok bullet.

The .380 Auto 90-grain PD Hydra-Shok at 1000 fps is mostly a carryover from the company's Premium line. The Personal Defense center post is slightly taller and slightly smaller in diameter. This Hydra-Shok load currently leads the .380 Auto caliber with 69 percent one-shot stops. The PD version expands to .50 caliber and penetrates 11.0 inches of calibrated 10 percent ordnance gelatin. This load does everything right. It has already proven itself to be the definitive choice for everything from the Colt Mustang to the Beretta 84F. Federal did not tamper with success.

The 9mm Personal Defense load is the 135-grain Hydra-Shok. At 975 fps and standard pressures, this Hydra-Shok bullet expands to .60 caliber yet drives to 11.0 inches in gelatin. This load was not specifically developed for the Glock 26, but Federal indicated the mini Glock heavily influenced the bullet's development. Compared to the 124-grain Hydra-Shok, the 135-grain PD Hydra-Shok bullet has the same cavity size but a much shorter center post.

Federal has recently redesigned some of its Hydra-Shok hollowpoints to increase the percent of retained weight and reduce the amount of fragmentation. It used this same strategy for the development of Personal Defense ammo. In our testing, we found the new ammo line to have an average weight retention of over 99 percent.

Federal adopted some nontraditional bullet weights for its 9mm, .40 S&W, and .45 Auto PD loads. The company simply adjusted bullet weight, the resulting bullet energy, and the resulting penetration depth to get the ideal load.

With a Fuller Index of 77 percent and an actual effectiveness of 81 percent in 21 shootings, the 9mm 135-grain Hydra-Shok rivals the street record of the current crop of 115- and 124-grain jacketed and lead hollowpoints when fired from short-barrel pistols. The 9mm 135-grain Personal Defense has a better street record than *every* 9mm 147-grain JHP.

The .40 S&W 135-grain Personal Defense Hydra-Shok is a promising load, but it is not to be confused with the 1300 fps JHPs from Triton and Cor-Bon. The 135-grain PD Hydra-Shok has a 1095 fps muzzle velocity. The 1300 fps velocity of other 135-grain JHPs can be a handful out of short-grip guns like the Glock 27. In fact, these other 135-grain JHPs produce more recoil than the 180-grain JHPs. One of Federal's priorities was recoil control, and its 135-grain PD Hydra-Shok produces 15 percent less recoil than traditional 135-grain JHPs.

At 165 grains, the Hydra-Shok bullet in the .45 Auto Personal Defense is the lightest hollowpoint ever loaded in this caliber. It expands to an impressive .72 caliber.

However, it still produced enough slide velocity to cycle my Glock 27 off-duty gun when shooting one-handed. (Again, the Glock 27 was used in the development of the load.)

The .40 S&W 135-grain Personal Defense Hydra-Shok expanded to .64 caliber and penetrated 9.8 inches of gelatin. This gives it a Fuller Index of 85 percent from a mini pistol.

The .45 Auto 165-grain PD Hydra-Shok is also a departure to extremely light bullet weights for the Personal Defense line. The 165-grain weight is the lightest hollowpoint ever loaded in the .45 Auto. In fact, this was something of an engineering challenge for Federal. The bullet has such a short rifling bearing area in relation to its diameter that Federal had to use the Hydra-Shok design for accuracy reasons as much as wound ballistics. Accuracy would suffer if the 165-grain bullet used a standard hollowpoint cavity. The Hydra-Shok post-in-cavity design shifts some of the bullet weight forward. Federal advises that its .45 Auto 165-grain Personal Defense ammo is nearly as accurate as its 185-grain semiwadcutter FMJ ammo when both are fired from test barrels.

In terms of wound ballistics, the 165-grain Personal Defense Hydra-Shok has a muzzle velocity of 985 fps from a Colt Officers ACP. It expanded to .72 caliber and penetrates 10.0 inches of gelatin. The result is a Fuller Index of 88 percent.

As originally announced, the .38 Special Personal Defense Hydra-Shok was supposed to weigh 125 grains. Late in the project, Federal engineers dropped the weight to 110 grains to increase the velocity. The result was much better performance from snub-nose guns and outright excellent performance from duty-length guns. The average velocity of this .38 Special standard-pressure 110-grain Hydra-Shok from a 2 inch revolver is 838 fps. The bullet expands to .63 caliber and penetrates 9 inches of gelatin, ideal for the frontal shots typical of citizen-involved shootings.

Future loads in the Personal Defense line are unlikely. Federal specifically considered the .25 Auto and .32 Auto and decided not to develop a load for these calibers. Instead, the company focused only on what it considered to be reasonable self-defense calibers. Federal does not think these calibers have enough energy and momentum to function reliably in a pocket pistol that may have to overcome interference from lint and gum wrappers.

Federal also considered the .357 Magnum and .44 Special, but while these calibers may be used by enthusiasts and purists, they are not widely used by the average CCW holder. Some average or infrequent shooters may have tried these big-bore or magnum snubbies, only to find they don't like them and won't carry them. Federal geared its efforts toward the calibers actually carried by CCW holders.

Federal's Personal Defense line of ammo does not compromise bullet performance to give the civilian shooter something for scenarios he likely will not face. Instead, it is no-compromise ammo geared specifically for self-defense, concealed carry, and police off-duty and back-up use. For once, civilian only ammo really is the best choice for the civilian shooting scenario.

TABLE 16-1
FEDERAL PERSONAL DEFENSE AMMO

Caliber	Load	Muzzle Velocity fps*	Muzzle Energy ft-lbs.	Gelatin Depth inch	Recovered Diameter inch	Fuller Index
.380 ACP	90 gr. Hydra-Shok Pers. Def.	1000	200	11.0	0.50	68%
.38 Special (non +P)	110 gr. Hydra-Shok Pers. Def.	838	171	9.0	0.63	65%
9mm	135 gr. Hydra-Shok Pers. Def.	975	285	11.0	0.60	77%
.40 S&W	135 gr. Hydra-Shok Pers. Def.	1095	360	9.8	0.64	85%
.45 ACP	165 gr. Hydra-Shok Pers. Def.	985	356	10.0	0.72	88%

* velocity, energy and gelatin results are from short barrel handguns

STOPPING POWER

CHAPTER 17

Federal Tactical Ammo

In 1996, Federal Cartridge released its Tactical handgun and rifle line of ammunition geared for law enforcement use. Tactical loads were designed specifically to perform well after defeating tactical barriers. The line was developed in response to tactical and patrol officer demands for better penetration ability against all kinds of barriers, especially glass. Tactical ammo is currently available in 9mm, 10mm Medium Velocity, .45 Auto, .40 S&W, .357 SIG, .223 Rem, and .308 Win.

As discussed in the previous chapter, Federal was the first major ammunition company to recognize the fact that typical shooting scenarios faced by the police officer and the private citizen can be very different. In response, the company designed two different bullets to work the best in these two different scenarios. The Hydra-Shok line is still one of the best for home defense and concealed carry scenarios. It performs the best in bare and heavily clothed gelatin. That is why Federal used the Hydra-Shok design in its line of Personal Defense ammo.

The typical police shooting scenario, on the other hand, involves a wide variety of bullet challenges. The bullet rarely strikes the front of the torso. Instead, it often impacts the torso at an angle or will strike the forearm or upper arm on the way to the torso. These fleshy intermediate targets can rob a great deal of stopping power from a bullet that expands too rapidly and dumps energy too early. A bullet with a medium energy release is the best for this scenario.

If the police-fired bullet strikes at so much of an angle that it is actually cross-torso, the total penetration depth can be a problem. Bullets that expand so rapidly that they cannot penetrate 10 to 12 inches of tissue may fail to penetrate as deeply as needed. The heart and major vessels are an average of 7.9 inches deep under a cross-torso shot placement, not counting possible interference from the upper arm.

The police shooting scenario can

Federal's new Tactical line of handgun and rifle ammo was developed specifically for the police scenario. The fusion-bonded bullet expands well after auto glass.

get even tougher. Depending upon the patrol jurisdiction, a bullet may engage glass, metal, and building material barriers prior to striking the target. The bullet must be able to defeat these tactical barriers and still expand as designed once it reaches tissue. It must not shed its jacket in glass or metal. The hollowpoint must not get plugged up by wood or heavy fabric, which will cause a failure to expand. Obviously, the ammo used by courtroom security and urban police officers will face much different challenges than the ammo used by rural police and highway patrol.

The police-action shooting may well be fully frontal; however it could also be a nightmare shot. Consider the typical traffic stop. The officer approaches the driver's window and faces a threat requiring lethal force. His bullet's path is likely to be through glass or sheet metal. The bullet is then likely to face the heavy bones of the shoulder socket or the upper arm. Then it must continue its angled penetration to the vital organs and vessels inside the torso. This may be the toughest scenario any bullet may face.

Now consider the same scenario, except the driver simply exits the car to face the officer before the engagement. Now the police-fired bullet must penetrate only a T-shirt prior to slipping by a rib into the air-filled lungs. This same officer now needs a bullet that expands almost in air and will not overpenetrate to endanger bystanders. Same police officer. Same perp. Yet in the span of 10 seconds, the scenario changed from one demanding extreme penetration to one demanding extreme expansion.

The Tactical line of police only ammo is a compromise bullet to meet the unique demands of law enforcement shooting scenarios. It gives up a little bit of wound ballistics in bare gelatin but is an incredible performer in gelatin after passing through tactical barriers.

The key to the Tactical bullet is a dead soft bullet nose. The jackets in

The Federal 12-gauge Tactical slug easily defeated this quarter inch pane of laminated tempered glass. It remained on course and penetrated 20 inches of gelatin.

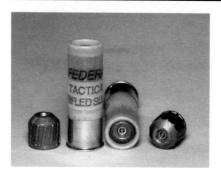

The Federal 12-gauge Tactical slug is a 1 ounce, Foster-style, rifled slug with a Hydra-Shok centerpost. It has 22 percent less recoil than a full-power slug for faster follow-up shots.

The Federal 12-gauge Tactical slug is shown recovered from bare gelatin (far left), unfired (center), and recovered from gelatin after striking auto glass. The slug penetrated a controlled 12.8 inches of bare gelatin and expanded to 1 inch in diameter.

the bullets are dead soft from a full anneal. This soft nose in the handgun hollowpoint and rifle softpoint easily deforms to take on the angle of the barrier that it hits initially. This allows it to strike hard objects at oblique angles, penetrate the barrier, and stay on trajectory after barrier penetration. A hard-nose bullet is likely to either ricochet off the barrier or penetrate it but fly off course. The soft nose gives Federal's bullet flight integrity after passing through barriers.

The projectile used in the Tactical line is an exception to Federal's bullet-making process. All the rifle and handgun Tactical bullets share the same basic construction: they are all copper-jacketed, but the lead core is chemically fused to the jacket.

The jacket cup for the Tactical rifle bullet is made from bar stock on a screw machine instead of extruded from sheet in an extrusion press. This allows the jacket to have a very thick base and tapered walls with a precision

The .308 Win 165-grain Tactical and the 168-grain Match were fired from this Remington 700-P for trajectory and accuracy. At 200 yards, the groups overlapped.

The flight of the Federal .308 Win 165-grain Tactical was not affected at all by an impact with this angled windshield or with angled thermopane glass. The Federal .223 Rem Tactical is the least affected by glass barriers of any load in this caliber.

into the jacket. The bullet assembly is then heated in a process that literally melts the lead core and solders it to the copper jacket. The jacket is then swaged around the core and the hollowpoint, softpoint, or Hydra-Shok is formed in the final operation.

The hollowpoint cavity's depth, width, and shape; the height and shape of the Hydra-Shok center post; the hardness, thickness, and alloy of the jacket; and the 0 antimony content of the lead core were all specially tweaked for the police scenario. *No* bullet works better after glass or sheet metal. But many bullet designs work better against just an exposed torso.

To use the FBI test protocol as an illustration, the Tactical loads did worse in bare gelatin and heavily clothed gelatin than standard hollowpoints, especially Hydra-Shok. However, they did far better in gelatin after glass, metal, plywood, and drywall than any bullet ever designed.

All Federal Tactical ammunition uses nickel-plated brass for reliable extraction and basic lead styphnate primers for the best ignition reliability. All Tactical ammo uses a lacquer sealant on both the primer and case mouth.

The fused-core Tactical police bullet is a spin-off from Federal's Trophy Bonded Bear Claw line of hunting bullets. In fact, tactical teams using rifle calibers other than the .223 Rem and .308 Win, where Tactical ammo is not available, would be best served to use the Trophy Bonded Bear Claw. One rural Midwest SWAT team deploys with the Tactical for its .308 Win and the Trophy Bonded Bear Claw for its .270 Win and 7mm Magnum.

However, Tactical police loads are slightly different than Trophy Bonded hunting loads. Both bullets use a bonded core. However, the .308 Win Tactical cartridge is loaded to a longer overall length, and it does *not* have a cannalure. Both differences are geared for the police bolt-action rifle as steps to improve accuracy. The alloy of

not possible from impact extruded or coined parts. This partly explains the increased expense of Tactical ammo.

The Tactical handgun loads use a dead soft lead core with 0 percent antimony. The jacket is deep drawn from a copper alloy (90 percent copper, 10 percent zinc), with six internal stress risers in the jacket. These

internal scores or serrations assure both reliable and uniform expansion.

The lead core of the Tactical bullet is made from extruded lead wire swaged into preformed slugs like the other handgun and rifle cores. However, before the jacket is formed around the core, solder paste is placed in the bottom and the core is inserted

The Federal Tactical load in .223 Rem is a 55-grain softpoint. The fusion-bonded bullet has a 100 percent weight retention in gelatin. It shoots 3 MOA after striking laminated glass.

The Federal 9mm 147-grain Tactical JHP shows excellent expansion and controlled penetration in ordnance gelatin. This particular Tactical Load uses a Hydra-Shok post.

the Tactical jacket contains more copper than the Trophy Bonded bullet, which makes it softer regardless of a post-forming anneal.

The .308 Win 165-grain Tactical softpoint is ballistically matched to the exact trajectory of the .308 Win 168-grain Sierra MatchKing. We fired both from the same Leupold-equipped Remington 700P at 100 yards to check the matched trajectory. We got .5 inch three-shot groups from the MatchKing and 1.0 inch three-shot groups from the Tactical, but they did overlap. These were then fired from a V-block-bedded test barrel at 200 yards. The result was 1.7 inch 10-shot groups from the MatchKing and 2.3 inch 10-shot groups from the Tactical. Both groups had exactly the same elevation at 200 yards. These two loads could not have been matched any closer.

In .223 Rem, the 55- and 62-grain Tactical softpoints are intended to duplicate the trajectory and point of impact of the 55- and 62-grain softpoint, hollowpoint, and hardball loads so widely used in law enforcement. In the .223 Rem caliber, Federal did *not* intend to duplicate the trajectory of its MatchKing HPBT with its Tactical softpoint like it did in the .308 Win caliber. In .223 Rem, the 69-grain MatchKing HPBT is not the definitive load in the caliber like the 168-grain MatchKing is in .308 Win.

While most .308 Win rifles used

by police tactical teams are bolt-action, most .223 Rem police rifles are autoloaders. For this reason, the .223 Rem Tactical bullets have a rolled cannalure and the case mouth is rolled into this cannalure. This grip is required because occasionally a bullet nose will get caught on the AR-15/M16 locking lug recess. Without the crimp, which increases bullet pull, the bullet could be pushed back into the case and cause a stoppage. Match shooters cringe at the thought of adding a cannalure to a bullet. However, Federal engineers

indicate this knurl opens the 200 yard, 10-shot group by a maximum of 0.4 inch, or roughly a 0.2 MOA penalty for reliable cycling.

We fired the Tactical handgun and rifle loads into bare BB-calibrated ordnance gelatin. Then we fired the same Tactical loads through quarter-inch panes of laminated tempered glass into gelatin. These panes were set at a 45 degree angle tilted at a 15 degree compound angle.

It is one thing to penetrate well in gelatin after glass. Any JHP with suppressed expansion, a small hollowpoint, and a high antimony core can do that. It is quite another thing to stay on course after glass and then expand reliably and produce acceptable depths of penetration in gelatin. It is the most difficult of all to expand and penetrate to acceptable limits *both* in bare gelatin and in gelatin after glass. Remember the nightmare traffic stop. Yet that is what the Federal Tactical ammo does.

The 9mm 147-grain Tactical HP expanded to .58 inch and penetrated 13.2 inches of gelatin. This is a controlled depth for any 147-grain

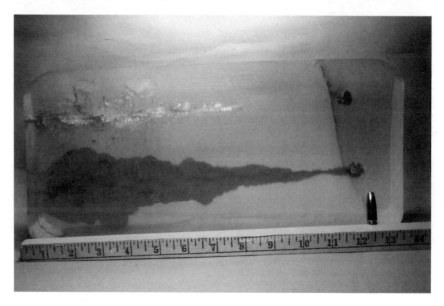

The Federal 9mm 135-grain +P Tactical penetrates 12.5 inches in bare gelatin (lower bullet) and 11.7 inches in heavily clothed gelatin (upper bullet). The bullet deforms to the exact impact angle when striking glass, allowing it to penetrate in a straight line.

The Federal 9mm 124-grain Tactical expands to .67 caliber. All Tactical bullets have the dead soft lead soldered to the soft copper alloy jacket.

hollowpoint. After impacting the compound angle windshield glass, the 147-grain Tactical HP still penetrated 8.3 inches. The average adult male human torso is just 9.4 inches thick. The .45 Auto 230-grain Tactical HP penetrated 14.5 inches of bare gelatin and 9.7 inches of gelatin after the windshield. The most impressive performance was the original 10mm 190-grain Tactical HP. This medium-velocity load penetrated 14.9 inches of bare gelatin and 13.1 inches of gelatin after auto glass.

The Tactical handgun loads expand with extreme reliability because they are so soft. However, as a rule they don't have as large a recovered diameter as the Hydra-Shok, Gold Dot, Golden Saber, or Ranger Talon. Also as a rule, the Tactical handgun loads produce comparatively small temporary stretch cavities.

The good news about the barrier-busting Tactical loads is their penetration depths. In bare gelatin, they penetrate the opposite of how some may expect for a no-holds-barred, antivehicle police bullet. All of the Tactical handgun loads penetrate in the 10 to 14 inch bracket. Where have you read that penetration range before? How about *Handgun Stopping Power* (Paladin Press, 1992), which was written during a time of intense pressure to produce police ammo that penetrated 12 to 18 inches, with 20 inches being even better! In fact, today it is extremely difficult to find police duty ammo that penetrates deeper than 15 inches of 10 percent gelatin, including the "deep penetrator" JHPs.

We tested both the .223 Rem 55-grain and the .308 Win 165-grain Tactical from 85 yards. The tests were into bare gelatin and gelatin after quarter-inch laminated tempered glass. The .308 Tactical penetrated 21.0 inches of bare gelatin, 20.2 inches after a 90 degree impact, and 20.5 inches after a compound 45 degree side and 15 degree tilt impact with the auto glass. Even after the compound angle impact, the .308 Win Tactical had an 83 percent weight retention.

The .223 Rem Tactical loads have 100 percent weight retention in bare gelatin and in gelatin after heavy clothes. They have an 85 percent weight retention after sheet steel and gypsum board. In the test that typically destroys .223 softpoint and hollowpoint bullets—compound angle auto glass—these Tactical bullets still retain over half their original weight. This, in turn, allows adequate penetration after glass.

The .223 Rem 55- and 62-grain Tactical softpoints perform reliably under the FBI multiple barrier test protocol. In bare gelatin and in gelatin after heavy clothes, sheet metal, gypsum board, and auto glass, the 55-grain Tactical SP ranges from 12.5 to 16 inches of penetration; the 62-grain ranges from 14.5 to 17 inches. This is excellent, police-oriented performance for this caliber. These are unquestionably the best overall loads for the police patrol rifle. They are also the clear choice for tactical teams that use the .223 Rem against glass.

While the Tactical rifle loads have adequate penetration, double caliber expansion, and high weight retention after auto glass, their biggest advantage is the bullet flight integrity after glass. FMJ ball and even the Sierra MatchKing can penetrate glass, but these projectiles will *not* stay on course after the impact. Even the traditional "brush busting" heavyweight round-nose softpoints veer well off course after penetrating glass. And so do most "partition" style and solid-copper bullets that work so well against dangerous game.

This wound profile of the Federal 9BPLE 9mm 115-grain JHP +P+ clearly shows that the Tactical bullets give up wound ballistics to gain effectiveness after glass.

The key is to have the bullet nose as soft as possible so it deforms to the exact angle of impact *while* it is still penetrating in a straight line. Of course, it is even more important for a rifle bullet to stay on course after glass than a handgun bullet. Most countersniper shootings take place with the target well behind the glass.

In a test for bullet flight integrity, a .223 Rem sniper rifle was zeroed with the 55-grain Tactical at 50 yards. A 1 inch, three-shot group was fired. Panes of quarter-inch laminated tempered glass were placed at 30 degrees, 45 degrees, and 90 degrees to the bullet flight. The glass was 20 feet, or the width of a room, in front of the target. The three-shot group of the 55-grain Tactical 20 feet after each pane of laminated glass was just 3 inches. Most importantly, the center of each group was the same as the group with no barrier in the way. In a similar test the .308 Win 165-grain Tactical fired *exactly* the same 1 inch group before and after the glass obstacles.

A worst-case deflection test proved that the Federal Tactical bullets have overcome one of the biggest weakness in police scenarios with the .223 Rem caliber. A zero was

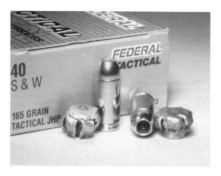

Three different bonded Tactical hollowpoints are available for the .40 S&W: the 155-grain, the 180-grain, and this medium-velocity version of the 165-grain. This kind of bullet is the future of law enforcement.

established with both the 55- and 62-grain Tactical SPs. Then auto glass was placed 5 feet in front of the target at different angles, including perpendicular to the bullet path. At impact angles of 20, 30, 45, and 90 degrees, both loads struck an average of just 0.5 inch from the original zero.

Federal has made a few subtle changes to its Tactical handgun ammo since its introduction in 1996. The 10mm Medium Velocity caliber was originally released with a 190-grain Tactical hollowpoint. While this gave

outstanding performance, sales were too low to justify a separate bullet. The 10mm now uses the same 180-grain Tactical HP as the .40 S&W. The .45 ACP 230-grain Tactical HP has been increased to +P pressures and now achieves an honest 950 fps from a 5 inch pistol.

In 1999, Federal coated its Tactical rifle bullets with molybdenum disulfide. This moly coating reduced barrel fouling and made cleaning easier, and the reduced friction improved ballistics. The coating also slightly improved accuracy with no drawbacks. While this was clearly a good step, the .223 Rem Tactical SPs are still just 1 MOA accurate from a V-block-bedded test barrel rigidly mounted to a test stand.

The two most recent Tactical handgun loads—the .40 S&W 155-grain HP and the .357 SIG 125-grain HP—are arguably the best in the lineup. The future of all law enforcement ammo are loads like these two. They deliver both maximum wound ballistics from high-energy bullets and superior performance through and after tactical barriers.

TABLE 17-1
BARRIER TEST RESULTS
FEDERAL .223 REM TACTICAL AMMO

test phase	55 gr. Tac SP		62 gr. Tac SP	
	penetration	expansion	penetration	expansion
bare gelatin	15.0	0.48	15.5	0.50
4 layers denim	15.0	0.44	17.0	0.44
sheet metal	12.5	0.50	15.0	0.44
gypsum board	16.0	0.41	15.0	0.48
auto glass	14.0	0.31	14.5	0.35

Impact Deflection after Auto Glass
(distance from true zero)

impact angle	55 gr. Tac SP	62 gr. Tac SP
perpendicular	.75 inch	0 inch
20 degrees	.75 inch	.87 inch
30 degrees	.50 inch	.25 inch
45 degrees	.50 inch	.50 inch

	200 yard Accuracy	
load	55 gr. Tac SP	62 gr. Tac SP
10 shot group	2.2 inch	2.3 inch
rifling	1 in 12 twist	1 in 7 twist

TABLE 17-2
FEDERAL TACTICAL POLICE-ONLY AMMUNITION

Caliber	Load	Velocity fps	Energy ft-lbs.	Expansion	Penetration inch	Fuller Index
9mm	124 gr. Tactical HP	1160	370	0.67	10.6	83%
9mm +P	135 gr. Tactical HP	1060	335	0.66	12.5	80%
9mm	147 gr. Tactical HP	980	314	0.59	13.2	78%
.357 SIG	125 gr. Tactical HP	1350	505	0.65	12.0	90%
.40 S&W	155 gr. Tactical HP	1140	445	0.64	12.8	89%
.40 S&W	165 gr. Tactical HP	1050	405	0.62	14.5	85%
.40 S&W	180 gr. Tactical HP	980	384	0.63	14.0	84%
10mm MV	180 gr. Tactical HP	1050	440	0.60	14.9	86%
.45 ACP +P	230 gr. Tactical HP	950	460	0.66	14.5	90%
.223 Rem	55 gr. Tactical SP	3100	1175	0.48	15.0	93%
.223 Rem	62 gr. Tactical SP	3050	1280	0.50	15.5	93%
.308 Win	165 gr. Tactical SP	2600	2475	0.66	21.0	95%

CHAPTER 18

New Winchester Police Ammo

In the late 1990s, Winchester released a number of new defensive and police-only loads. This included the Ranger Partition Gold and a major redesign of the original Black Talon, now called the Ranger T series.

RANGER PARTITION AMMO

In 1999, Winchester released its Ranger Partition Gold ammunition. This new police ammo is a joint development between Winchester and Nosler Bullets. Winchester already loaded hunting-oriented Nosler Partition bullets in its .357 Magnum, .44 Magnum, .454 Casull, and .45 Winchester Magnum. The police-oriented Partition Gold hollowpoints (PGHP) are available in 9mm, .40 S&W, .357 SIG, and .45 ACP. The Indiana State Police may be the first major police department to adopt the .40 S&W full-power 165-grain PGHP.

The Partition Gold ammo is a response to the police demand for "bonded" bullets. The CCI Gold Dot, the first of the bonded bullets, outperforms all conventional JHPs against tactical barriers like auto glass and car bodies. The Federal Tactical, the next of the bonded bullets, actually

has the lead bullet core soldered to the copper jacket. In 1999, Remington introduced its Golden Saber Bonded. Again, the lead core on this bullet was actually soldered to the brass jacket.

The Partition Gold is Winchester's answer to police need for a tactical bullet. Engineered for law enforcement by Todd Eberhart, the PGHP allows Winchester to balance penetration and expansion in a way not possible with conventional JHP designs. It is one of the few bullets that produces both reliable expansion and deep penetration. It is also one of the few bullets that has both a high level of

Winchester recently introduced its Ranger Partition Gold police ammo. The 9mm 124-grain PGHP (left) and the .40 S&W 165 grain PGHP (right) expand reliably even after four layers of denim.

energy with rapid energy transfer and still penetrates deeply.

The Nosler Partition bullet was originally designed as the ultimate hunting rifle bullet. It has a center web, or partition, cold-headed into the jacket. (The cross-section of the bullet shows the "H" profile.) The thick copper partition separates the front core from the rear. Winchester engineers adjusted the exact position of the partition in the PGHP to tweak bullet performance and weight retention. A partition closer to the bullet nose produces less expansion, more penetration, and more retained weight. A partition closer to the base of the bullet produces more expansion, less penetration, and less retained weight, all else being equal.

The Partition Gold bullet uses pure, dead soft lead in both the front and rear cores. The soft front core assists in expansion at low velocities from short-barrel, subcompact pistols, and it assists in accuracy because it allows the bullet to upset into the barrel rifling more completely.

Grain for grain, the Partition Gold is a longer bullet than a traditional JHP. The copper web weighs less than lead, and the copper jacket thickness at the rear of the

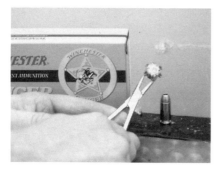

The soft front core on the Partition Gold assists in expansion at low velocities from short barrel, subcompact pistols and after heavy clothes. This .40 S&W 165-grain PGHP fully expanded after heavily clothed gelatin and four layers of denim alike.

The Partition Gold is the load of choice from a police carbine. Even at extremely high velocities, the PGHP bullet produces acceptable penetration and actually penetrates deeper as the impact velocity increases.

The Partition Gold has three different bullet jacket thicknesses to promote expansion, then limit expansion, then retain rear core integrity. Winchester engineers adjust the position of the partition to balance expansion and retained weight. The front and rear cores are both dead soft lead.

The Partition Gold is an extremely tolerant bullet design. After defeating wallboard, the bullet still expands and penetrates just 13.5 inches. Many other designs plug up and overpenetrate.

bullet is far thicker than a normal JHP. This extra copper forces the Partition bullet to be longer in order to weigh the same as an all-lead core JHP. In the .40 S&W caliber, the 165-grain Partition Gold bullet is as long as the 180-grain Ranger T series bullet. The longer bullet, in turn, has more rifling bearing area and improved accuracy.

The Partition Gold actually has three different bullet jacket thicknesses. The jacket near the bullet mouth is very thin to encourage initial expansion. The section near the rear of the front core is thicker, which serves to slow down the rate of expansion but

also to lock the front lead core in place. Finally, the jacket wall in the rear section is very thick to protect the rear core and to positively lock it in place.

The front of the Partition Gold bullet is formed and notched to produce reliable expansion at low velocities and to resist petal fragmentation at high velocities. The partition absolutely prevents the

separation of the jacket from the rear core under even the harshest police shooting scenarios.

The PGHP has one of the largest "operating windows" of any bullet design. This window starts at the velocity at which the bullet just begins to expand and ends at the velocity at which the bullet fragments or loses its jacket. For most JHPs, this range is

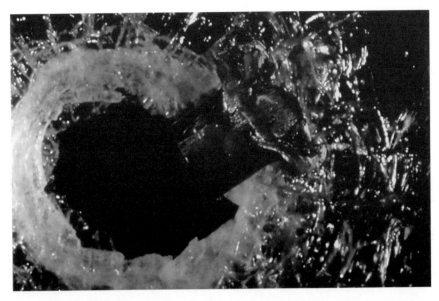

The Partition Gold is the clear choice when the police bullet will strike auto glass or car bodies. The PGHP produced excellent after-glass penetration in this test. The bullet retained 80 percent of its weight while the front core penetrated separately.

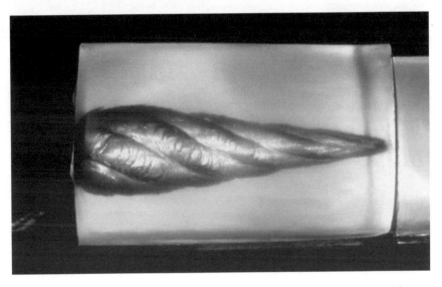

The Partition Gold hollowpoints are lighter than the Ranger T series hollowpoints. They carry and transfer more energy, yet the penetration is the same. The wound profile from the 9mm 124-grain PGHP is shown after four layers of denim in bare ordnance gelatin.

just 300 fps. On the PGHP, it is 1000 fps wide. The 9mm 124-grain PGHP, for example, begins to expand at velocities as low as 600 fps. This means it will work reliably when fired from a compact pistol like the Glock 26. Yet the 9mm 124-grain PGHP still produces acceptable penetration and has acceptable weight retention at impacts up to 1600 fps. This means it

will be a reliable performer from a 9mm carbine.

With most JHPs, penetration decreases as the impact velocity increases. That's because the bullets expand to larger diameters and transfer more energy or actually break into small pieces and rapidly lose penetration energy. Many 9mm hollowpoints produce less than 10

inches of penetration when fired from a carbine. The Partition Gold is different. Its penetration *increases* as the impact velocity increases. Again, this is because the PGHP expands to a certain diameter and then stops expanding. It will not fragment. At the highest velocities, the front section of the hollowpoint erodes away but the rear section remains intact. With the front section gone, the PGHP penetrates like a semiwadcutter bullet.

Since the Partition Gold is designed to readily expand, Winchester has set new retained weight standards for these bullets. The average weight retention in bare and heavily clothed gelatin is 97 percent. Winchester set a goal of 70 percent weight retention after the harshest and hardest tactical barriers, namely auto glass. Retained weight in a traditional JHP assures adequate penetration. This is not an issue for the Partition Gold because adequate penetration comes from the rear core, not the retained weight of the bullet itself.

Tactical barriers are extremely hard on handgun bullets. They either flatten the hollowpoint, as in the case of glass and steel, or they plug the hollowpoint, as in the case of wood, plaster, and heavy clothes. To make matters worse, these barriers actually rob a bullet of its velocity. Steel, plywood, and plasterboard lower bullet velocity by 75 to 100 fps. Auto glass lowers velocity by a whopping 400 fps. Of course, auto glass also sheds bullet jackets.

The Partition Gold has more consistent expansion in bare gelatin and barrier gelatin than most other semiexotic JHPs. More consistent expansion results in more consistent penetration depths. The FBI heavy clothes test protocol is well on its way to being replaced by a test consisting of four layers of denim. The denim plugs the hollowpoint cavity more and generally results in smaller recovered diameters and thus deeper penetration. The PGHP is only one of the four test bullets to expand after four layers of denim. All the others failed to expand at all and penetrated 22 to 23 inches of gelatin. The PGHP still expanded to .57 caliber and held penetration to just 16 inches.

Winchester conducted some pretty unconventional tests during the development of the Partition Gold. In one test, it imbedded the rear leg bone from a cow in a block of 10 percent gelatin. The 2 inch diameter bone was under a half inch of gelatin, providing an obstacle as severe as the auto glass test. In this particular test, the 9mm 124-grain Hydra-Shok and the Golden Saber failed to penetrate the bone about half the time. The Gold Dot got through and averaged 5.3 inches of penetration (same for the Golden Saber and Hydra-Shok slugs that were able to defeat the bone). The 124-grain Partition Gold defeated the bone each time and penetrated an average of 7.9 inches of gelatin.

RANGER T SERIES

Also in 1999, the entire Ranger Talon series of police ammo was redesigned and renamed the Ranger T series. This ammo traces its heritage back to the Black Talon, introduced in 1992. In 1993, this round received a great deal of unfavorable (and unfair) national publicity, so Winchester withdrew it from sale to civilians. In 1994, a civilian version, a defanged Black Talon, was released under the name Supreme SXT. The police-only Black Talon was then renamed Ranger SXT and quickly unseated the Federal Hydra-Shok as America's police bullet. However, the Hydra-Shok was still the better bullet with more reliable expansion and more stopping power based on actual shootings.

In 1998, Winchester redesigned the Ranger SXT for better bullet performance. The new design, briefly called the Ranger Talon, expanded better after heavy clothing and expanded better from shorter barrel pistols. The new loads had a medium rate of energy release compared to a

Winchester recently redesigned its Ranger Talon series of police ammo. The new bullets in 9mm, .40 S&W, and .45 ACP have thinner jackets, deeper serrations, and a revised hollowpoint cavity. The new bullets have the gold bullet color, replacing the black color.

Heavy hollowpoints, like this .40 S&W 180-grain Ranger Talon, now expand more reliably after heavy clothes and when fired from short-barrel pistols.

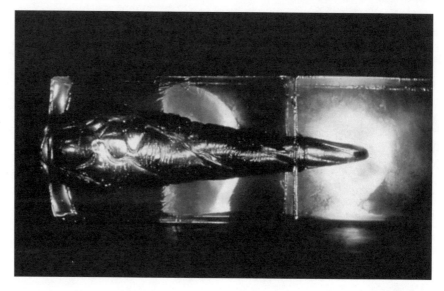

The new Ranger T series has been changed to a medium energy release load. The original Black Talon was a late energy release load. The 9mm 147-grain Ranger T series, shown in gelatin, now expands more reliably.

late energy release of the original version. Renamed the Ranger T series, it is easily recognized by its copper bullet color (the Black Talon and Ranger SXT bullets were, of course, black) and is a real and genuine improvement over the old Ranger SXT. It is now fully equal to, and arguably superior to, the Federal Hydra-Shok.

Compared to the Ranger SXT, the Ranger T series has a thinner jacket and deeper jacket serrations. The

profile of the hollowpoint cavity was also changed from a V to a U shape. The new shape gave the T series hollowpoint cavity a very distinct hinge point. All these changes resulted in a bullet that expands at lower velocities, expands to larger diameters, and retains the maximum weight. The T series keeps many of the features of the previous designs, including the six jacket pedals that expand to become exposed and the reverse-taper jacket that locks the core in place.

The Ranger T series involves heavier bullet weights than the Partition Gold line of ammo. These are the bullet weights associated with the "subsonic hollowpoints." Once a code phrase for nonexpanding and excessively penetrating bullets, the Ranger T series now gives the term a good name.

The first of the new Ranger T loads was the .40 S&W 180-grain. This load has been out long enough to have been tested and adopted by numerous police departments. The 9mm 147-grain and .45 ACP 230-grain Ranger T series were next. All T series loads have a nickel-plated case for positive extraction. All of the loads in the Ranger SXT product line will eventually be upgraded to the T series.

The Partition Gold and the Ranger T series are two very different lines of ammo intended to give law enforcement a choice of performance and advantages. One will not replace the other. The Partition Gold is the clear choice for highway patrol, state police, and rural sheriffs departments where the bullet will be likely to strike auto glass or car bodies. The Texas Highway Patrol estimates that 50 percent of its officer-involved shootings involve vehicles. The Kentucky State Police engage vehicles in over 90 percent of its shootings.

The Partition Gold bullets are generally lighter and carry more energy than the Ranger T series bullets. The result is more energy and more energy transfer for the Partition Gold, with penetration equal to the Ranger T series. The lighter, higher energy Partition Gold penetrates as deeply as the heavier, subsonic Ranger T series, all else being equal. The Ranger T series produces more controlled penetration and works extremely well against heavy clothes, making it the better choice for city police and urban sheriffs departments.

The Ranger line of handgun ammo, including the Partition Gold and the upgraded T series, is restricted to law enforcement. The Partition

Gold bullets in police auto pistol calibers will not be sold as reloading components. Partition bullets for the .357 Magnum, .44 Magnum, and .454 Casull will continue to be available to reloaders from Nosler. This decision to restrict will irritate some handgunners, just like it did when Federal Cartridge restricted its Tactical ammo to police sales.

The civilian version of the T series ammo is the Supreme SXT. The Supreme SXT has a T series hollowpoint cavity but does not have the jacket pedals. Handgunners other than police are actually better off with the Supreme SXT ammo. This seriously tweaked ammunition is ideal for civilian carry and home defense scenarios that seldom involve tactical barriers like auto glass, building materials, and car bodies.

.357 SIG

In 1999, Winchester released its first loads for the incredible .357 SIG cartridge. Winchester was clearly late in releasing a .357 SIG load. However, it made up for lost time by capturing the prestigious U.S. Secret Service contract (1.6 million rounds) with its very first hollowpoint in this caliber, the 125-grain Ranger T series. The .357 SIG 125-grain Ranger T series developed for the Secret Service is the same load available to all of law enforcement. The bullet construction and muzzle velocity are identical. The Ranger T series produces 1350 fps from a SIG P229 and 1385 fps from a SIG P226. The load gives 11.5 inches of penetration in gelatin, which is perfect performance.

NONTOXIC AMMO

Also in 1999, Winchester released a unique line of nontoxic, lead-free training ammo. The WinClean line joins the Super Clean NT, Super Unleaded, and Delta Frangible to round out the array of low-lead, no-lead ammo on the market. All four

lines cycle reliably through semiauto and fully automatic weapons. All have lead-free and heavy-metal-free primers. The result is no airborne lead generated at the firing point by either the primer or the bullet base. The main difference between each low-lead line is the projectile.

In 1992, Winchester introduced its lead-free primer in the Super Unleaded line. The bullet is a full metal jacket with the addition of a brass baseplate. This base closure disc prevents the burning powder from vaporizing lead from a normal exposed lead-base FMJ bullet. An estimated 80 percent of airborne lead comes from the lead styphnate primer and the vaporized exposed lead base of FMJ bullets. The remaining airborne lead occurs at the bullet trap or backstop.

Winchester's lead-free and heavy-metal-free primer uses dinol, tetrazene, boron, and potassium nitrate. The by-products of combustion are carbon dioxide, nitrogen, water vapor, and potassium borate. The primer is lead-free, strontium-free, barium-free, and antimony-free. This is the lowest toxicity primer in the ammunition industry.

The lead-free primer is nonhygroscopic and is tested for ignition sensitivity at minus 40°F and plus 125°F, just like mil-spec ammo. Even still, lead-free primers are slightly less impact sensitive than lead styphnate primers. The shelf life of lead-free primers is also less than lead styphnate primers. Under cool and dry storage conditions, shelf life is estimated at five years.

In 1997, Winchester teamed with Delta Frangible to add a new line of ammo that uses a thermo-plastic (polymer) bullet made of copper powder, tungsten powder, and nylon. The Ranger Delta Frangible breaks into powder when it impacts steel, yet the handgun-fired Delta Frangible penetrates 14 inches of ordnance gelatin. The Delta Frangible has proven to be safe against steel from distances as close as 6 inches. It is the best choice for close quarter battle training with an accuracy and trajectory similar to FMJ hardball out to 25 yards.

At the request of the Federal Law Enforcement Training Center (FLETC), in 1998 Winchester developed its Super Clean NT (nontoxic) line. These bullets are totally lead-free. The projectile looks like a jacketed softpoint except the bullet core is tin instead of lead. Tin has been used in the food industry for over a century—it is totally nontoxic. Tin is also soft like lead, although not as dense. The tin core allows for a minimum back splash distance. The shooter cannot get as close to steel reaction targets with the Super Clean NT as with the Ranger Delta Frangible, but the tin core ammo has half the back splash range of zinc core lead-free ammo.

Since tin is lighter than lead, the Super Clean NT bullets are longer than regular JSPs. They are so accurate that the Super Clean NT is used in competition at the police nationals. At 50 yards, 9mm 115-grain FMJ averages 3.6 inch groups, while the 105-grain Super Clean NT prints 0.9 inch 10-shot groups.

The fourth low-lead, reduced-hazard line of ammo, introduced in 1999, is the WinClean line. The WinClean was developed as a low-cost, low-lead round with traditional bullet weights for practice use in indoor ranges. It uses a traditional jacketed softpoint bullet with a lead core. This load has no airborne lead at the firing point. Instead of the standard CA210 "gilding metal" jacket material, it uses the lower cost CA260 brass. This explains the Brass Enclosed Base (BEB) name given to the ammo. The WinClean ammo with BEB lead core bullets will eventually replace the Super Unleaded with closed-base FMJ lead core bullets.

Winchester is going down four different development paths, so it is prepared for any direction low-lead

ammunition takes in the next five years. Each line has different costs, different amounts of lead, and unique advantages and disadvantages. The Ranger Delta Frangible is the most expensive option and is currently restricted to law enforcement. The Super Clean NT is next in terms of cost. Both the Delta Frangible and Super Clean NT are completely lead-free. The original Super Unleaded and the new WinClean are lead-free at the firing point and are just slightly more expensive than hardball.

RIFLE LOADS

In 1999, Winchester released what could be its most accurate .308 Win rifle load, the S308J. Like the Partition Gold, the Winchester match bullet is a join effort with Nosler Bullets. The Supreme Competition load uses the 168-grain Spiveco J4 match bullet. This competition bullet uses the long 13 degree boat-tail for reduced drag and improved downrange velocity. The pure lead core easily obturates in all barrel types.

The Nosler 168-grain J4 bullet exactly equals the trajectory of the

Sierra 168-grain match bullet formerly loaded by Winchester. The Nosler version is as accurate as the Sierra load. In one test, from a 24 inch tactical rifle off a benchrest, the Nosler J4 averaged .53 inch three-shot groups compared to .58 inch groups for the Sierra MatchKing. The group sizes ranged from .35 to .80 and from .30 to .90 inches respectively. In comparison, the Winchester 168-grain Ballistic Silvertip averaged .98 inch, while the 150-grain FailSafe printed just under 2 MOA. Police countersniper ranges are an average of 78 yards. Even still, many tactical teams rely on the bullet with the maximum accuracy instead of the bullet with the best performance against tactical barriers. The so-called "tactical" loads, like the FailSafe, are not as accurate as the Nosler J4, and accuracy is still the name of the game with many tactical teams.

Winchester gives police teams three different loads in 7.62 NATO to cover all the scenarios. The Nosler J4 is the most accurate of these. It has a unique wound profile in gelatin, remaining stable and intact for the first 5 inches, then tumbling and breaking up. The maximum energy dump is

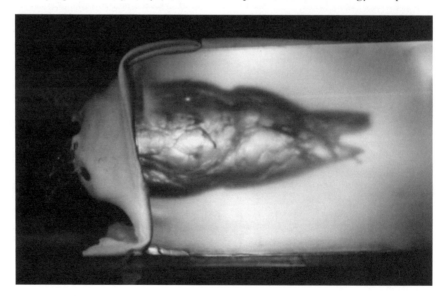

Winchester recently teamed up with Nosler to load the J4 Match bullet in .308 Winchester. Many police tactical teams still rate accuracy higher than defeating tactical barriers. The J4 is seen penetrating 10 inches of gelatin after defeating angled auto glass.

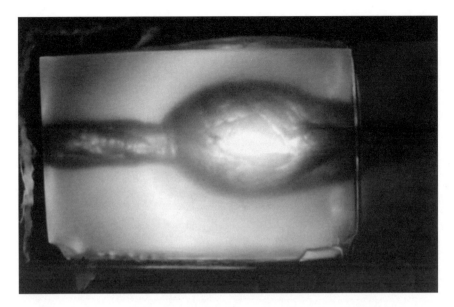

The Winchester .308 Win 168-grain J4 produces a unique wound profile in gelatin. It remains stable for a few inches and then suddenly tumbles. It penetrates a total of 20 inches of heavily clothed gelatin.

Winchester performed the entire battery of FBI tests on its .308 Win. 168-grain J4 Match bullet during development. The 168-grain HPBT bullet is shown passing through a thick layer of wallboard.

Of the rifle loads, the FailSafe performs the best in tactical barriers. It is basically a copper hollowpoint with a rear lead core. The lead core has two steel inserts to prevent the rear of the bullet from bulging on impact. The FailSafe penetrates 31 inches of bare gelatin and is the least affected by tactical barriers like auto and residential glass and car bodies. The hollowpoint is annealed to a soft condition for rapid expansion and the best on-course performance after barriers.

SHOTGUN LOADS

In 1999, Winchester released a number of low-recoil 12-gauge shotgun duty and training loads. The first was a reduced-recoil 1-ounce 12-gauge slug. Winchester lowered the velocity from 1600 fps to 1345 fps in 1997. In 1999, it lowered the velocity *again*. The new low-recoil, Foster-style slug has a velocity of just 1200 fps. The 1345 fps slug was identified by its white hull with a traditional brass casehead; the 1200 fps slug is identified by a white hull but a zinc (silver) plated casehead. The 1345 fps slug expands to 1.05 inches and penetrates 16.5 inches of gelatin. The 1200 fps slug expands to .90 inch and penetrates 11.5 to 14 inches of gelatin.

The slug itself is the same Foster-style hollowpoint slug used in the two higher velocity loads. Only the powder charge is different. The 1200 fps slug

Winchester recently released a low-recoil 12-gauge 1 ounce slug and a low-plated, low-brass case head. Now at 1200 fps, this is the second velocity reduction for the Winchester slug.

between 5 inches and 10.5 inches. Total penetration depth is 20 inches. However, the Nosler J4 penetrates 10 inches of gelatin after auto glass.

The Ballistic Silvertip (BST) made by Nosler is a good intermediate choice. It is the Winchester version of the traditional Nosler Ballistic Tip. The BST bullet is made by Nosler. Available in both 50-grain 5.56 NATO and 168-grain 7.62 NATO, the BST has a silver plastic nose tip with a black oxide-coated bullet. The base of each bullet is especially thick. The .223 version has a pure lead core and a single taper jacket for the most rapid expansion possible. The .308 version has a harder lead core alloy for tactical use and a dual taper core for more controlled expansion.

produces 20 percent less recoil energy than the 1345 fps slug and 46 percent less recoil energy than the earlier 1600 fps slug. At 1200 fps, any adult shooter, male or female, of any stature, can control this load. It takes the pain away from shooting shotgun slugs and is sure to produce the least tendency for a flinch. Yet the wound ballistics are good enough for duty use.

The reduced-recoil slug, like all lower velocity shotgun loads, will *not* reliably cycle all autoloading shotguns. The Remington Model 11-87 will certainly cycle with this ammo better than the Remington Model 1100. The facts are, no reduced-recoil loads from any manufacturer cycle as well as full-power loads. This is not as big a deal as it sounds. In police work, pump shotguns outsell autoloaders seven to one. The autos can use the higher velocity loads and still feel like a reduced recoil load from a pump gun.

Also new from Winchester in 1999 was a reduced-recoil eight-pellet 00 buck load. Again, the load can be identified by a zinc-plated, low-brass casehead. The eight-pellet load was developed specifically to improve patterns. It has long been known that the nine-pellet 00 buck load throws eight tightly grouped pellets and one flyer. Winchester simply eliminated the ninth pellet. This load was developed specifically for 18 inch cylinder bore shotguns.

One of the keys to the improved patterns is a new shot cup with a base wad that is 2.5 times thicker. The cup is also made from a stiffer resin. The 00 buck pellets themselves are made from magnum-hard, high antimony lead, not the dead soft, pure lead.

One less pellet, of course, reduces recoil. So does the reduced velocity. The 1145 fps, eight-pellet load produces 40 percent less recoil than the standard 1325 fps, nine-pellet load. Even for the shotgun-shy, this load is a pleasure to shoot.

Also new for 1999 was an improved version of the low-recoil nine-pellet 00 buck load. The improvement

The new Winchester low-recoil eight-pellet 00 buck load was developed for the best groups from an 18 inch, cylinder bore riot gun. This load patterns tighter than the nine-pellet load.

came in the heavy-duty plastic shot cup, which provides tighter patterns. This load is also identified by the silver color of the zinc-plated, low brass casehead. This 1145 fps nine-pellet load produces 30 percent less felt recoil than the standard 1325 fps nine-pellet load. Again, these pellets are made from extra hard, high antimony lead.

In the shotshell line, Winchester announced a number of future developments. All are lead-free, nontoxic, reduced-hazard loads. All involve a lead-free shotshell primer.

Two of the experimental loads, the low-recoil buckshot and the low-recoil slug, have tin projectiles. Winchester views tin as a great alternative to lead. Tin weighs 66 percent of lead yet is soft like lead. Tin projectiles can be made from the very same equipment and tooling used to make lead projectiles. The tin slug can be driven as fast as lead and still produce 30 percent less recoil.

Since tin has less mass than lead, the tin 00 buck pellets and Foster-style slug will retain less velocity and energy at longer ranges. At the close ranges typical of police scenarios, tin 00 buck and the tin slug should perform the same as lead. The

penetration distances may be less, but both 00 buck and rifled slugs have penetration to spare at close ranges. At longer ranges, the penetration ability of tin projectiles will be much less than lead, which will reduce the downrange threat of these loads in the event of a miss. The 00 buck pellet should still have enough punch at extended ranges, while smaller buckshot pellets certainly will not.

Both nine-pellet 00 buck and 27-pellet #4 buck tin projectile loads are under development. The nine-pellet 00 buck load has promise as a duty load. The 27-pellet #4 buck load may be suitable for home defense scenarios where its lack of penetration in building materials is an advantage. The #4 buck load would not be a good police duty choice. Even the lead versions of #4 buck have suffered from too little penetration when needed in street scenarios.

Regardless of whether tin 00 buck and Foster slugs are used for duty work, both would make excellent training loads. The close-range trajectory is roughly the same, and they do not contaminate the range with lead. The accuracy from the tin slug and the pattern from the tin 00 buck are the same as lead projectiles at normal training distances.

The other experimental shotgun load released by Winchester was the Ranger Delta Frangible 12-gauge slug. The copper-tungsten-nylon composite slug weighs 1 ounce. It has the profile of a Foster slug except it has a solid instead of a hollow base. The 1200 fps Delta Frangible slug has a reduced recoil, making it a good training load. Since the slug is solid, it is not as accurate as lead or tin Foster slugs.

In addition to use as a no-lead training load, the Delta slug holds great promise as a door-breaching round. Tactical teams occasionally have a need to break locks, latches, bars, and hinges prior to entry. The Delta Frangible is perfect for this role whether the door is solid wood or a metal-clad hollow door. In demonstrations at Thunder Ranch, the loads worked equally well on open-in and open-out doors.

The Delta Frangible easily disrupts locking mechanisms and then breaks into powder. While the solid Delta Frangible slug penetrates 20 inches of gelatin, the downrange threat on the far side of a door after breach is very minimal. Like all Ranger Delta Frangibles, this composite slug breaks up completely on steel targets, making it an excellent close-quarter training load.

TABLE 18-1
12-GAUGE FREE RECOIL ENERGY COMPARISON
(BASED ON 8 POUND SHOTGUN)

Winchester Low Recoil, 8-pellet 00 Buck	13.4 ft-lbs.
Winchester Low Recoil, 1-ounce lead slug	15.6 ft-lbs.
Winchester Low Recoil, 9-pellet 00 Buck	15.8 ft-lbs.
Winchester Standard, 9-pellet 00 Buck	22.5 ft-lbs.
Winchester Standard, 1-ounce lead slug	29.1 ft-lbs.

TABLE 18-2

Barriers	.308 Winchester 168 grain Ballistic Silvertip		.308 Winchester 150 grain FailSafe	
	Gelatin Penetration	Retained Weight	Gelatin Penetration	Retained Weight
heavy clothes	17.5 inches	70%	31 inches	100%
auto glass	9.5 inches	59%	18.5 inches	88%

TABLE 18-3

Barriers	.308 Winchester 168 grain Nosler HPBT Supreme Competition J4		.223 Remington 50 grain Ballistic Silvertip	
	Gelatin Penetration	Retained Weight	Gelatin Penetration	Retained Weight
heavily clothed gelatin	20 inches	79%	13 inches	26%
auto glass, then gelatin	10 inches	54%	9.5 inches	24%
wallboard, then gelatin	12.5 inches	77%	8 inches	23%
plywood, then gelatin	14 inches	53%	13.5 inches	27%
sheet steel, then gelatin	9 inches	35%	6 inches	25%

TABLE 18-4
WINCHESTER PARTITION GOLD POLICE AMMUNITION

Caliber	Weight	Velocity	Energy
9mm	124 grain	1130 fps	352 ft-lbs.
.45 ACP	185 grain	1000 fps	411 ft-lbs.
.40 S&W	165 grain	1130 fps	468 ft-lbs.
.357 SIG	125 grain	1350 fps	506 ft-lbs.

TABLE 18-5
9MM 124 GRAIN JHP COMPARISON

Load	Velocity fps	Energy ft-lbs.	Bare Gelatin inches Penetration	Exp.	Heavy Cloth Gel inches Penetration	Exp.	Fuller Index %
Winchester Partition Gold	1077	319	12.3	.67	13.7	.65	79
CCI-Speer Gold Dot	1178	382	12.7	.65	16.0	.54	83
Remington Golden Saber	1109	339	12.3	.63	12.7	.60	81
Federal Hydra-Shok	1101	334	10.8	.59	13.2	.53	81

TABLE 18-6
WINCHESTER RANGER T SERIES POLICE AMMUNITION

Caliber	Weight	Velocity	Energy
.380 ACP	95 grain	955 fps	192 ft-lbs.
9mm	147 grain	990 fps	320 ft-lbs.
.40 S&W	180 grain	985 fps	388 ft-lbs.
.45 ACP	230 grain	880 fps	396 ft-lbs.
.40 S&W	165 grain	1070 fps	420 ft-lbs.
9mm +P+	127 grain	1250 fps	440 ft-lbs.
.357 SIG	125 grain	1350 fps	506 ft-lbs.
.45 ACP +P	230 grain	1070 fps	585 ft-lbs.

TABLE 18-7
WINCHESTER RANGER T SERIES

Load	Velocity fps	Energy ft-lbs.	Gelatin Pen., inch	Exp.	Fuller Index %
9mm 147 gr. Ranger T series	912	272	12.8	.62	75
.40 S&W 180 gr. Ranger T series	944	356	14.1	.68	83
.45 ACP 230 gr. Ranger T series	820	343	12.6	.77	86
.357 SIG 125 gr. Ranger T series	1385	533	11.5	.67	91

CHAPTER 19

RBCD Platinum Plus Ammo

The greatest gunfighter of the 20th century has designed a line of police and defensive ammunition. Are the bullets slow and heavy, or are they light and fast? Do they expand or do they fragment? Are they deeply penetrating or do they penetrate near the minimum? What can we learn about the way bullets should perform from an American law enforcement legend?

Jim Cirillo was born in Manhattan and grew up in Queens. After serving in the army during the Korean War, Cirillo joined the New York City Police Department in 1954 as a street officer. In 1961, he joined the staff of the NYPD Firearms Unit on Rodman's Neck as an instructor. The NYPD requires its firearms instructors to have at least 5 years of street experience. While with the NYPD, Cirillo won three state PPC championships and tied the PPC national record.

In the late 1960s, New York City suffered from a string of deadly robberies. In response to this trend, the NYPD formed the now-famous Stakeout Unit in 1968, a specialized squad within the elite Emergency Services Unit. Cirillo was a charter member. The Stakeout Unit was made

up almost exclusively of NYPD firearms instructors. Over the next five years, its members arrested 242 perpetrators. Of these, 43 were shot to death in bloody confrontations with the police.

By the time it was disbanded in 1973, Cirillo had the highest number of hits in the unit. This included shooting three perpetrators in one incident just two hours into his first stakeout. In his many gunfights, Cirillo has killed more than a dozen armed offenders. In fact, he has a better gunfighting record than most of the famous gunfighters of Wild West fame.

During his tour with the Stakeout

While with the NYPD Stakeout Unit, Jim Cirillo learned the tactical advantages of high-speed ammo. Cirillo is the greatest gunfighter of the 20th century.

Unit, Cirillo was required to attend each post mortem in order to assist the forensic investigation. In addition to his own gunfighting experience, these autopsies showed Cirillo what worked and what didn't in actual shootings.

After 22 years of service, Cirillo retired from the NYPD and joined the U.S. Customs Service as a firearms instructor. As captain of the U.S. Customs pistol team, Cirillo and his partner won the two-man National Championships. Cirillo then took his skills to the Treasury Department, where he served as a firearms instructor at the Federal Law Enforcement Training Center.

The "Sage of the Stakeout" retired from federal law enforcement in 1991, but he continued to tinker with different bullet designs. It is important to know that Cirillo was a peer of Lee Jurras of the original Super Vel Company. Super Vel made 90-grain hollowpoints for the 9mm and 125-grain JHPs for the .357 Magnum at a time when the major factories loaded only hardball and lead semiwadcutters. In fact, many of the .38 Special 110-grain cup-point jacketed hollowpoints used in NYPD stakeouts were hand-made by Jurras for Cirillo.

Cirillo's first patented bullet design was a modification to the Kaswer PinGrabber. He put a large slot across the sawtooth wadcutter hollowpoint and installed a round plastic nose cap. The .45 ACP version of this 185-grain JHP expanded to a rectangle measuring .64 inch by 1.22 inch. It remains the largest recovered diameter for any bullet fired from the .45 ACP and the largest permanent crush cavity. With an average of 13.5 inches of penetration, this 1075 fps sabertooth bullet had a Fuller Index of 92 percent one-shot stops.

Political timing was not on Cirillo's side. He perfected the nose-capped sawtoothed bullet in 1993, just as the Winchester Black Talon became the center of an intense public controversy. While the major ammo companies were considering Cirillo's first bullet, he set out to design an even more aggressive version. This time he teamed up with Roscoe Stoker at Performance Plus. Stoker was a regional ammo loader who supplied the police in the San Antonio, Texas, area and who dabbled in high-performance bullets. In the mid-1990s, he experimented with Beeline frangible bullets made in Nova Scotia, but Beeline eventually teamed up with Cor-Bon to make the BeeSafe line of ammo.

Cirillo and Stoker have developed two very different versions of their Platinum Plus ammunition, a Standard version for personal defense and a Special Application version available only to law enforcement. Both types use Total Fragmenting Soft Point (TFSP) and Epoxy Hollow Point (ExpHP) bullets. Compared to conventional loads, bullets in the RBCD Platinum ammo have half the weight and twice the velocity. For example, the Standard load in .40 S&W is a 77-grain TFSP at 2000 fps. In .45 ACP, the Standard load is a 90-grain TFSP at 2036 fps and a 115-grain TFSP at 1650 fps.

The Platinum Plus Standard loads penetrated an average of 8.8

RBCD produces two very different bullets in its Platinum Plus line. The Totally Fragmenting Soft Point (TFSP) has a buckshot pellet on top of an epoxy core.

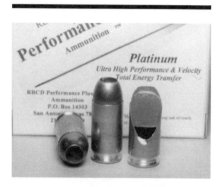

The other RBCD bullet design is the Epoxy Hollowpoint, ExpHP. It has powdered metal mixed in with the epoxy core.

inches of gelatin. This ranged from the 6.5 inch low from the 10mm 77-grain TFSP to the 15 inch high from the .45 ACP 115-grain TFSP. The police-only Special Applications Ammo averaged 5.5 inches of penetration in bare gelatin and 6 inches of penetration after defeating soft body armor. This means the Standard loads, available to all shooters, are better choices for personal defense than the restricted Special Applications loads.

Some people prefer high momentum, high weight retention, and deep penetration. The greatest gunfighter of the 20th century wants high energy, bullet fragmentation, instant energy transfer, and limited penetration. Let's take a look at Cirillo's load.

A Competition Electronics chronograph confirmed the RBCD claims for incredible velocity. The slowest load in the lineup was the .380 ACP 45-grain TFSP at 1500 fps from a Beretta 84F. The fastest of the Standard loads was a tie between the .357 SIG 60-grain TFSP and the 10mm Auto 77-grain TFSP at 2400

With 50 percent more energy than conventional loads, the Platinum Plus ammo gives explosive performance. The 10mm 77-grain TFSP is shown.

Platinum Plus ammo is available in most pocket pistol calibers, including the 1500 fps .380 ACP 45-grain TFSP and 1825 fps .38 Special +P 60-grain TFSP. A .44 Special version is in the works.

Platinum Plus ammo is also available in all the popular duty calibers like the 2000 fps 9mm 60-grain TFSP, 2000 fps .40 S&W 77-grain TFSP, and 2000 fps .45 ACP 90-grain TFSP. The .44 Magnum and .45 Long Colt loads are in the works.

fps. That is about twice as fast as conventional ammo in these calibers. RBCD Performance Plus does indeed make the world's fastest handgun ammunition.

Since energy is based on the square of velocity, all of these Platinum loads have extremely high levels of energy. The 9mm 60-grain TFSP has 539 ft-lbs. of energy. This compares to just 295 ft-lbs. for the 9mm 147-grain subsonic hollowpoint. The .40 S&W 77-grain TFSP has 683 ft-lbs. of energy. Compare this to just 290 ft-lbs. for the .40 S&W 180-grain JHP. Remember, energy is the ability to do work like disrupt tissue and penetrate barriers.

While energy goes up with the square of velocity, felt recoil only goes up linearly with velocity. With lighter bullets, Cirillo and Stoker can pack more energy at the same level of recoil. The .40 S&W 77-grain TFSP has a Power Factor of 154. This compares to 153 for the 180-grain JHP. The .45 ACP 115-grain ExpHP with 700 ft-lbs. of energy and the .45 ACP 230-grain JHP with 348 ft-lbs. of energy have an identical 190 Power Factor.

The same felt recoil as conventional ammo and more energy explains why the Platinum ammo cycles auto pistols so reliably. Functioning is a complex combination of the energy of the bullet overcoming the energy stored in the recoil and main springs as well as the momentum (Power Factor) of the bullet overcoming the inertia of the slide at rest.

It is not enough for a round to have more energy than the round used to design the spring system in the firearm. The round in question must produce enough energy *and* enough momentum. The Platinum loads do. In one series of cycle tests, the Platinum .40 S&W 77-grain TFSP and 37-grain ExpHP both functioned reliably in an H&K USP 40 pistol and an MP5/40A2 submachine gun.

Each bullet is developed specifically for the caliber, but the construction between calibers is similar. All Platinum loads use a special copper-rich alloy for the jacket. Made of five different metals, the jacket material was developed to control bullet expansion and to be ductile enough to better fill the barrel rifling. RBCD claims its jacket has 30 percent less friction than the gilding metal used in most bullet jackets.

The TFSP bullet uses a soft lead alloy pellet made of lead, aluminum, and zinc on top of a mixture of polymer and powdered metal. The ExpHP has a core made entirely of an epoxy mixture. The percentage varies by caliber, but the powdered metals mixed with the epoxy or the polymer include lead, iron, tungsten, and

With a muzzle velocity more than 2400 fps, the .357 SIG 60-grain TFSP penetrates up to 7.5 inches of ordnance gelatin. Most Platinum Plus loads penetrate in the 6.5 inch to 10 inch range.

Three Platinum Plus loads are available for the .357 SIG, including the 28-grain ExpHP, the 50-grain TFSP (shown), and the 60-grain TFSP.

titanium. While it may not look like it, the ExpHP core is 10 to 30 percent powder metal. All of the Platinum loads use Winchester lead-free primers and flash-suppressed Noel/Adco/St.Marks ball powder. The cartridge cases vary by caliber but include IMI Match, Winchester, and Starline.

Both the TFSP and the ExpHP bullets fragment on impact, though Stoker prefers the term "disintegrate." Fragment implies that pieces of the bullet with some real weight will be recovered, even if the frags only weigh 5 to 10 grains. Disintegrate implies almost nothing will be recovered, and this, in fact, is closer to reality with these loads. On impact with gelatin, both the TFSP with the softpoint lead ball and the

With a muzzle velocity of 1650 fps, the .45 ACP 115-grain TFSP penetrated 15 inches of gelatin. This gives it a Fuller Index of 94 percent one-shot stops.

ExpHP with the epoxy and powder metal core totally fragment on impact. Tiny pieces of jacket, lead, and plastic are all that are recovered.

Large fragments of lead from the nose pellet are recovered from the TFSP bullets. The lower impact velocity calibers and loads, like the .45 ACP 115-grain TFSP at 1650 fps, end up with larger pieces of lead and bigger sections of jacket. The higher impact velocity calibers and loads, like the .357 SIG 60-grain TFSP at 2410 fps, have smaller pieces of lead and jacket.

The rapid energy transfer from all these Platinum loads results in temporary stretch cavities with very large diameters. The shape is almost spherical, which is the wound profile that gives the best results in typical personal defense scenarios involving near-frontal bullet impacts and few tactical barriers.

Rapid energy transfer and short penetration distances are perfectly acceptable for ammunition geared for personal defense. These scenarios generally involve near-frontal shot placements and rarely involve tactical

The .45 ACP 115-grain TFSP is shown recovered from gelatin. The lead, aluminum, and zinc nose pellet remains intact with this load but disintegrates on faster loads.

barriers. The 9 inch and 12 inch minimum penetration distances established by the Border Patrol and the FBI, respectively, are for police duty ammo. The street success of the Glaser Safety Slug has proven that ammo for civilian defense can penetrate as little as 5 to 6 inches of gelatin.

In terms of wound ballistics, the RBCD Platinum ammo has a Fuller Index at, or near, the top of their respective calibers. With their high levels of energy and an average of 9

inches of penetration, the Platinum loads in 9mm and above all have a Fuller Index of 90 percent one-shot stops or better.

Two of the more interesting Platinum loads are the 90-grain TFSP and 115-grain TFSP, both in .45 ACP. The 90-grain TFSP packs over 800 ft-lbs. of energy and dumps it all in 9 inches of gelatin. This works out to a Fuller Index of an astonishing 99 percent one-shot stops with a Power Factor less than 230-grain ball. The 115-grain TFSP at 1650 fps penetrates 15 inches of gelatin and has a Power Factor equal to 230-grain ball and a Fuller Index of 94 percent. This may be the best overall load in the entire ammo lineup.

We fired the standard Platinum loads for accuracy from a sandbag rest. At the same time, we compared its point of impact versus the point of aim with conventional hollowpoints.

The Platinum loads proved to be more accurate than many exotics because both the TFSP and ExpHP bullets have a uniform cross-section. Frangible bullets with a mixed core of birdshot pellets and plastic can be harder to spin-stabilize. The Platinum loads placed five shots into group sizes from 3.5 inches to 5.7 inches at 25 yards, depending on caliber, from duty-length handguns. This is clearly accurate enough for personal defense.

We fired two very different calibers to compare the point of aim to the point of impact. One test was the 2400 fps, .357 SIG 60-grain TFSP versus the 1400 fps, .357 SIG 125-grain FMJ. The other was the 1650 fps, .45 ACP 115-grain TFSP against the 790 fps, .45 ACP 230-grain FMJ. As a rule, lighter and faster bullets impact lower on the target than slower and heavier bullets. Given the same felt recoil, the faster bullet generally exits the barrel at a lower point on the recoil arc than a slower bullet. This is less of an issue at close combat ranges but can be a real problem at longer ranges.

From 50 feet, the center of the .357 SIG TFSP group was 1 1/2 inches from

The Platinum Plus ammo is very accurate for a hyper-speed frangible. Even with velocities twice that of conventional ammo, the TFSP bullets have nearly the same point of impact as ball ammo.

Two Platinum Plus loads are available for the 9mm, including the police-only 50-grain TFSP (shown) and the 60-grain TFSP. RBCD really does make the fastest ammo on the market.

the center of the FMJ group. The center of the .45 ACP TFSP was 3 1/2 inches from the center of the FMJ group. This, again, is close enough to the conventional ammo for personal defense.

Future plans at RBCD include a hostage rescue load for the .223 Remington and the .308 Winchester. A 12-gauge is not planned, but loads for the .44 Special, .41 Magnum, and .44

Magnum have been discussed. The .44 Special caliber would benefit the most from a Platinum bullet.

TABLE 19-1
PLATINUM AMMO WOUND BALLISTICS
(SPECIAL APPLICATIONS AMMO)

| Caliber | Load | Gelatin Penetration | | |
		bare gel	after glass	after IIA armor
9mm	50 gr. TFSP	4.5 in	2.5 in	10.0 in
.357 Magnum	50 gr. TFSP	7.0 in	4.0 in	7.6 in
.40 S&W	37 gr. ExpHP	5.0 in	2.5 in	4.0 in
.357 SIG	28 gr. ExpHP	5.0 in	2.5 in	4.0 in
.357 SIG	50 gr. TFSP	5.0 in	3.5 in	6.5 in
.45 ACP	45 gr. ExpHP	5.0 in	3.0 in	4.0 in

TABLE 19-2
PLATINUM AMMO WOUND BALLISTICS (STANDARD AMMO)

Caliber	Load	Penetration inches	Fuller Index %
.32 ACP	37 gr. TFSP	7.0	69
.380 ACP	45 gr. TFSP	8.1	76
.38 Special +P	60 gr. TFSP	10.0	84
9mm	60 gr. TFSP	8.0	90
.357 Magnum	60 gr. TFSP	8.0	90
.40 S&W	77 gr. TFSP	7.0	95
.357 SIG	60 gr. TFSP	7.5	95
10mm	77 gr. TFSP	6.5	97
.45 ACP	90 gr. TFSP	9.0	99
.45 ACP	115 gr. TFSP	15.0	94

TABLE 19-3
RBCD PLATINUM AMMO

Caliber	Load	Velocity fps	Muzzle Energy ft-lbs.	Power Factor	Class
.32 ACP	37 gr. TFSP	1815	271	67	std
.380 ACP	45 gr. TFSP	1500	285	68	std
.38 Special +P	50 gr. TFSP	1825	370	91	std
.38 Special +P	60 gr. TFSP	1705	385	102	std
9mm	50 gr. TFSP	2160	518	108	saa
9mm	60 gr. TFSP	2010	539	121	std
.357 Magnum	50 gr. TFSP	2355	614	118	saa
.357 Magnum	60 gr. TFSP	1975	520	119	std
.40 S&W	37 gr. ExpHP	2550	534	94	saa
.40 S&W	77 gr. TFSP	2000	683	154	std
.357 SIG	28 gr. ExpHP	2820	477	76	saa
.357 SIG	50 gr. TFSP	2470	678	124	saa
.357 SIG	60 gr. TFSP	2410	774	145	std
.45 ACP	45 gr. ExpHP	2550	650	115	saa
.45 ACP	90 gr. TFSP	2036	828	183	std
.45 ACP	115 gr. TFSP	1650	700	190	std
10mm	77 gr. TFSP	2420	1015	186	std

CHAPTER 20

"Reduced Hazard" Frangible Ammo

The 1990s brought the ammunition industry into a new era of bullet design and development: lead-free frangible ammunition. For years, it had been common practice to shoot at the local range with cast or swaged lead reloads or factory full-metal jacket ammunition. This allowed us to get out to the range and improve our marksmanship without breaking the bank purchasing ammo. Many shooters remember the days of gathering up old lead fishing sinkers and melting them down to make their favorite semiwadcutters. The downside has always been the exposure to airborne lead from both the primers and the projectiles.

Since the time when Remington first introduced Klean-Bore primers in the early 1930s, the common ingredient in primers has always been lead. Compounds like lead styphnate, lead nitrate, lead dioxide, and lead ferricyanide, not to mention barium nitrate and other heavy metals, all make up the stuff that is not at all good to inhale or ingest. Unfortunately, these same heavy metals are the basis for the incredibly reliable ignition that we have come to expect from our primers.

With our population increasing in leaps and bounds, local outdoor ranges are decreasing at the same rate. Those that remain are facing greater levels of scrutiny by federal regulatory agencies. And indoor ranges have brought on a host of problems to the shooter. Many suffer from poor ventilation systems and poorly designed or antiquated bullet traps. If you spend any amount of time at one of these ranges, you will end up with raised levels of lead in your system or scars from bullet fragments splashing back at you.

The first move toward making primers lead-free began in the 1980s, with little success. The biggest problem was reliability. By the mid-1990s, Remington, Federal, CCI, Winchester, and Fiocchi began

Airborne lead is a problem on outdoor ranges, like the NYPD's facility at Rodman's Neck, as well as indoor ranges. Of course, lead in the backstop or bullet trap is a severe problem on all ranges.

Smith & Wesson was the first ammo company to make a low-lead training round with its Nyclad bullet. The Nyclad starts off as a lead hollowpoint, which then gets coated in nylon powder. The nylon is cured to fully encapsulate the bullet.

An early entry in the no-lead market was CCI-Speer with its Lead Free Solid, or LFS. The bullet, made from fully annealed, pure copper, greatly deformed on impact with steel plates, Pepper Poppers, or bullet traps. The LFS is no longer available.

CCI-Speer also produced its Clean-Fire ammo using a copper-plated, totally metal jacketed bullet. This is the same process that makes Gold Dot bullets. No lead is exposed.

offering more reliable and stable lead-free primers. Unfortunately, they still did not possess the same reliability as conventional lead-based primers. These new primers were sensitive to moisture and harder to ignite than their lead-based counterparts. Failure rates of 3 to 5 percent were typical.

More recently there have been two unexpected sources for the newest generation of lead-free primers: Germany and Russia. These new primers are purported to be as stable and consistent as standard lead-based primers without the sensitivity problems inherent with earlier versions.

The move to make bullets safer for the shooter began in the 1970s with the old Smith & Wesson Ammo Company in Rock Creek, Ohio. It was S&W that brought us the Nyclad bullet. In the 1980s, when S&W was divesting itself of products, it sold the production rights for the Nyclad to Federal. The Nyclad bullet had a lead core completely surrounded by a thin layer of nylon. Federal dramatically improved both the accuracy of the Nyclad and the expansion reliability, but for the record, Smith & Wesson was "first" with a "green" bullet.

Next came CCI-Speer with its totally metal jacketed (TMJ) bullets. These bullets featured a copper jacket that is electroplated to the core, thus totally encapsulating the lead. Other bullet companies like Rainier Ballistics and Berry's Bullets followed with their own versions of plated bullets. Still others stepped up by taking existing full-metal jacket bullets with their exposed lead bases and sealing the lead with a brass closure disk. This is a modern version of a gas check that prevents combustion gases from vaporizing the lead core from the heel of the bullet.

With a lead-free primer and any style of totally encapsulated bullet, the shooter is not exposed to any airborne lead at the firing point. However, a few major problems exist.

First, these bullets still contain lead. When they engage the steel backstops they typically tear apart, exposing the lead core. This is the equivalent of a plain lead bullet when it comes to range cleanup and disposal. It also exposes the shooter to airborne lead near the impact point. Ventilation systems that have air returns near the impact point—and there are some—simply move this contaminated air right back to the shooter.

Another problem is the increased wear on steel targets. Full-metal jacket bullets are more punishing on backstops and increase the chance of ricochet or back splash. This is less of an issue for the shooter who typically engages a target 25 or 50 yards away.

For those that shoot closer, such as during IDPA, GSSF, and IPSC matches, it is a major concern. For the indoor range owner it means increased liability and maintenance.

The next generation of lead-free bullets introduced two important features: bullet frangibility and the absence of a lead core. Eliminating the lead core was no easy task. A scan of the periodic table of elements shows that very few elements come close to the specific gravity, or density, of lead.

The first company to introduce such a bullet was Delta Frangible Ammunition. The first bullets from Delta were comprised of powdered tungsten, copper, and a nylon polymer. These ingredients were compressed together using a technique commonly referred to as sintering, which had been used for years in the automotive industry. Metal powder is compressed under high pressure to make a solid part. This so-called green part is then sintered under extreme heat, which is nearly the melting point of the metals. (These parts can also be heat-treated for additional strength or hardness.) The Delta Frangible bullets, because they use a polymer binder to hold the metal powders together, are sintered at temperatures just high enough to cross-link the plastic binder.

The Delta bullet was adopted by Winchester and released in its Ranger

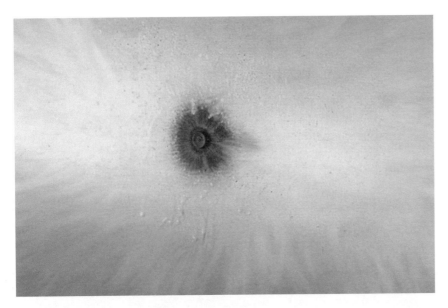

Winchester's Ranger Frangible uses a composite Delta Frangible bullet. The composite bullet completely disintegrates against steel but penetrates gelatin like hardball.

The Winchester Ranger Frangible is available in all duty calibers. The tin and copper composite bullets have the same close-range point of impact as duty ammo and penetrate gelatin almost like hardball.

Federal Ballisti Clean ammo uses a lead-free primer and a jacketed softpoint bullet. Instead of a lead core, the Ballisti Clean bullet features a zinc core.

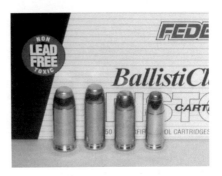

Like all major ammo manufacturers, Federal's reduced-hazard ammo is available in all defensive and duty calibers. The Ballisti Clean zinc core bullet does not expand in tissue.

Longbow and Delta in that the bullet was made up of compressed copper.

Federal stepped into the market using a different approach when it released the BallistiClean line of ammunition. BallistiClean utilized a jacketed softpoint bullet with a core made of zinc. The BallistiClean bullet, while nontoxic, was not a frangible design. If anything, it filled the gap between the totally encapsulated jacketed or plated bullets and the frangible, lead-free products. Federal later released the BallistiClean CQT (Close Quarters Training) to the law enforcement market. Consisting of twisted strands of zinc, it breaks up upon impact with steel.

Remington's offering utilizes another approach. Its Disintegrator line of ammunition features a plated

Frangible Law Enforcement line of ammunition. This was the first step by a major ammunition manufacturer toward a totally lead-free frangible cartridge. It was also the first step toward law enforcement and military applications of such technology. The frangible nature of the Delta bullet made it ideal for engaging steel targets at close distances, the distances normally encountered in close-quarter battle (CQB) training.

With Winchester marketing the Ranger line of frangible ammunition, Delta released its second designs. This time the main ingredient in the bullet was copper. Other companies began to follow suit with their own versions or interpretations of lead-free ammunition. Longbow released its Longbow NTF (Non-Toxic Frangible). The Longbow NTF is similar to the Delta bullet in that it is comprised mostly of copper powder with a polymer binding agent. Simunition, a division of SNC Industrial Technologies of Canada, released the Greenshield line of frangible ammunition. The construction of the bullet was similar to

bullet with a core made of compacted iron particles. The plating is kept to a thin (.005 inch) in order to insure the frangibility of the bullet. Upon impact with steel, the bullet breaks up into tiny particles and slivers of jacket.

Speer introduced ZNT (Zinc Non-Toxic) under its Lawman series of ammunition. The Lawman ZNT bullet was a jacketed design, similar to Federal's BallistiClean, with a core that was cast, not swaged. The core was made up of a blend of mostly zinc with small amounts of aluminum and magnesium. The construction made

Remington's Lead Less training ammo uses Total Encapsulated Metal Case (TEMC) bullets and lead-free primers. The Lead Lokt bullet uses a captive closure disc to prevent the flame front from eroding the bullet base of the FMJ bullet.

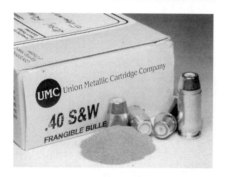

Remington's frangible ammo uses a copper-plated, powder metal bullet. The bullet penetrates gelatin like hardball but breaks up after an impact with steel.

Winchester leads the industry in options for reduced-hazard ammo. Super Unleaded uses a lead core bullet with a closure disc. Super Clean NT has a tin core bullet. Win Clean ammo uses a lead core softpoint.

The lead-free Triton CQD Frangible is a good choice for competition, especially where steel plates or Pepper Poppers are used. The tin and copper composite bullets are accurate and fully disintegrate against steel with no splash back.

the bullet very brittle. When impacting steel it breaks into small pieces, minimizing backsplash.

Winchester came out with the Super Clean NT (nontoxic). The construction was also similar to the Federal BallistiClean, with the difference being the use of tin instead of zinc for the core.

Up to this point, all lead-free frangible ammunition on the market was designed to break apart against steel. When shot into ordnance gelatin these rounds acted like FMJ bullets and did not expand. Then, Triton Cartridge entered the lead-free frangible market with another approach. The introduction of its CQD Frangible, later renamed CQ Frangible, marked the change of the potential roles for lead-free frangible ammunition. The CQ bullet was based on sintered technology and was made of a copper, tin, and lubricant blend. What made it different from other bullets on the market was a hollowpoint design. Upon impact, its nose fragments violently, similar to a Glaser Safety Slug, while the shank area remains

intact and continues to penetrate beyond 12 inches in gelatin even after penetration of heavy clothing.

This approach opened up new possibilities for the role of lead-free frangible ammunition. Law enforcement agencies could requalify with the same ammunition they use on duty. The ammunition is also ideal for urban environments where the risks for ricochets are high.

One departure from the norm for Triton was the use of standard primers instead of lead-free, which stemmed from the concerns of reliable ignition. For a law enforcement agency deciding to adopt lead-free ammunition for duty use, this is a major concern. Triton's answer was to offer its CQ Frangible with a standard primer and make the lead-free primer an option. Ammunition loaded with the lead-free primer has a label on the carton warning of the potential failure rate.

Shortly after the release of the CQ Frangible ammunition, Triton released the Team Triton Competitor line. The Competitor line utilized a frangible flatpoint bullet of the same construction as

The Triton CQD Frangible .40 S&W 125-grain Reduced Hazard Hollowpoint (RHHP) is shown in ordnance gelatin. The CQD Frangible is one of the few reduced-hazard loads to also have a hollowpoint-style wound profile and controlled penetration.

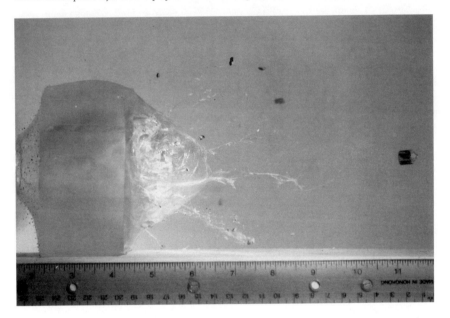

This high-speed photo of the Triton CQD Frangible .40 S&W 125-grain RHHP shows the bullet to partially fragment in the first 2 inches, shredding the surrounding tissue. The remaining bullet core penetrates an adequate but controlled 15 inches.

has an imprint on its nose to designate it as lead-free frangible.

Military and federal agencies have taken a serious look at the role of lead-free frangible ammunition. For the military, lead-free frangible 9mm and .223 Remington fill many needs. They offer our elite soldiers a round for training where close-up shooting on steel targets no longer brings the risk of injury from back splash. Millions of rounds can be expended at military ranges throughout the country with no ground contamination. For law enforcement departments the same holds true. Any size agency can benefit from a lead-free frangible practice load. Some departments that recently constructed new indoor ranges only allow the use of lead-free frangible ammo. By eliminating the lead and using a bullet that is frangible, thinner steel can be utilized for the backstop and much smaller air handling units and filtration systems can be in place, not to mention the lead clean-up every year. All things combined, an indoor lead-free-only range can save departments hundreds of thousands of dollars over the years.

The applications for lead-free frangible ammunition are becoming widespread, but this has also led to problems. The two biggest are testing protocols and product classification. The term lead-free is correct for the ammunition on the market, as is the term frangible. But when the term "nontoxic" comes into play, things change.

What exactly is nontoxic? We know that lead is toxic in nature, but by definition, so is copper. In addition, some materials that compose these lead-free bullets have traces of lead or other heavy metals. Even the polymer used in one of the designs contains trace amounts of lead. At what point is a bullet considered nontoxic or at the very least lead-free? That is something the industry is attempting to settle.

The National Firearms Unit (NFU) with the Immigration and Naturalization Service (INS) was the

that used in the CQ Frangible. Instead of being hot rodded, as Triton typically does, the Competitor was loaded to meet International Defensive Pistol Association (IDPA) power factors, making it ideal for practice or competition.

With the release of the Competitor line, two more companies went to the same sintered metal bullet construction. Federal is coming out with its version and Speer released its Lawman RHT line. Both utilize the same bullet design and construction as the Triton bullet, with the only exception being that the Speer bullet first agency to step up and try to address these issues. They held a symposium on lead-free ammunition in 1999. The purpose was to invite the major ammunition manufacturers and bullet makers to a round table session that would result in a clear understanding on this new wave of ammunition. Terms like nontoxic, lead-free, and frangible were discussed. One term that everyone agreed on for the time being was "reduced hazard."

The INS/NFU has also been the most progressive agency when it comes to lead-free frangible testing. Protocols currently being used include bare and clothed gelatin, steel, glass, and multiple layers of gypsum board. New methods of testing are being evaluated based on the demands encountered by the law enforcement community.

Another area of debate is the level of frangibility these bullets have. As mentioned earlier, some lead-free bullets are designed as an alternative to their lead-based counterparts. They break up upon hitting a backstop but they are not designed to be completely frangible. This raises the question of how many rounds of lead-free ammunition can a steel backstop take before it can no longer stop the bullets effectively. Indoor ranges that are designed for lead-free frangible

ammunition sometimes utilize thinner steel in an effort to cut costs. While this may be fine with frangible ammunition, many lead-free rounds out there are just as punishing on a backstop as their lead counterparts.

The bullets that are considered frangible vary greatly in their ability to break apart. To be clear, they all break up when hitting a backstop. The true test is when they engage steel at a 0 degree angle of obliquity. We have the least frangible designs that need at least half an inch of steel to stop them. The more fragile ones come apart on less than 1/8 of an inch of steel. The biggest question the industry is pondering is what thickness and hardness of steel must a frangible bullet *not* be able to defeat?

For reference, the hardness of steel is measured in two scales: Brinell and Rockwell. Mild steel, like an I-beam or pipe, is 112 to 163 Brinell. T-1 steel, the most popular type used for backstops, has a Brinell hardness of 235 to 293. The hardest is armor plate at 500 Brinell.

For private security, law enforcement, and military applications the concern is not what a frangible bullet will do to T-1 or armor plate but what it will do to a steam pipe in a nuclear site, the deck and walls of a ship, or the inside of an

aircraft. Thus, the thinner and softer the steel the frangible bullet cannot defeat, the better.

The downside with making frangible bullets even more frangible is their reliability. Bullets that are made from cold compaction or sintering are the most prone to this problem. When cycling through a semiauto, being loaded into a magazine, or simply shipping between the manufacturer and the dealer, they can fracture or even break. A move by some of the manufacturers to plating these bullets or utilizing a jacket may solve that problem.

The designs for lead-free frangible ammunition are changing constantly. It can be compared to the personal computer industry—by the time you buy a computer and set it up at home, an even faster and better one is on the market. At this pace, lead-free frangible ammunition will soon be fine tuned to the point where it equals the terminal attributes of its lead counterparts with a greater level of frangibility and safety to the shooter.

What does the future hold? There are designs in the works right now that are completely nontoxic. There is also a design that is very frangible in nature and will not break apart in the gun. The future is looking very bright for the lead-free frangible market.

TABLE 20-1
TRITON CARTRIDGE REDUCED HAZARD WOUND BALLISTICS
.40 S&W 125 GRAIN RHHP/CQD

Test Media	Gelatin Penetration	Fragment Depths	Retained Weight	Fuller Index
bare gelatin	15.5 inch	2 to 4 inch	72 grain	89%
heavy clothes	17.7 inch	3.5 to 4.5 inch	96 grain	
sheet steel	12.4 inch	0 to 1.5 inch	63 grain	
glass	5.2 inch	0 to 4.5 inch	20 grain	

TABLE 20-2
.223 REM 42 GRAIN CQD

Test Media	Gelatin	Penetration Description
bare gelatin	20.3 inch	bullet broke cleanly into two pieces, two wound paths
heavy clothes	20 inch	bullet broke cleanly into two pieces, two wound paths
sheet steel	10.4 inch	near total bullet fragmentation
plywood	18.1 inch	bullet remained intact
auto glass	13 inch	many bullet frags in first 3 inches
3/8 inch steel	none	bullet competely disintegrated, no penetration

TABLE 20-3
TRITON CARTRIDGE CQD FRANGIBLE AMMUNITION

Caliber	Weight	Velocity fps	Energy ft-lbs.
9mm	95 grain RHHP	1325	370
9mm	100 grain RHFP	1270	358
.40 S&W	130 grain RHHP	1350	526
.40 S&W	135 grain RHFP	970	282
.357 SIG	95 grain RHHP	1500	475
.45 ACP +P	160 grain RHHP	1200	527
.45 ACP	165 grain RHFP	1025	385
.40 Super	130 grain RHHP	1450	607
.40 Super	135 grain RHFP	1250	468
.223 Rem	42 grain taper	3100	896

RHHP: Reduced Hazard Hollowpoint
RHFP: Reduced Hazard Flatpoint

CHAPTER 21

Nonhollowpoint Wound Ballistics

What is the most effective handgun load using nonexpanding bullets? Exactly how far do these solid lead and fully jacketed bullets penetrate? Do softpoints expand from handguns? With nonexpanding bullets, will a larger caliber bullet produce more stopping power? Will a bullet with more energy be more effective? How about one with a higher Power Factor?

Many handgunners carry the 9mm and .45 Auto loaded with full-metal jacket (FMJ) bullets in total confidence. Same goes for those who carry a .38 Special revolver stuffed with semiwadcutter (SWC) or full wadcutter (WC) ammo. Some handgunners carry FMJ, SWC, and round-nose lead (RNL) ammo out of indifference or because it is inexpensive. Some use FMJ bullets because of feed reliability concerns. Handgunners in New England, Canada, and Europe use FMJ bullets because hollowpoint ammo is restricted or hard to find.

All of these solid bullets have serious drawbacks. Nonexpanding bullets of all designs produce the least stopping power, the least energy transfer, the least momentum transfer,

the smallest permanent crush cavities, the smallest temporary stretch cavities, and the greatest chance of overpenetration.

The 9mm 115-grain FMJ, for example, has one of the poorest stopping power records of all serious defensive handgun loads. It produces just 70 percent one-shot stops compared to 82 percent for the standard-pressure 115-grain JHP and

92 percent for the +P pressure 115-grain JHP.

Energy is the key to stopping power. Not muzzle energy, per se, but the amount of energy actually transferred to the target. Nonexpanding bullets transfer the least energy. The two most important questions are: how much total energy does the bullet have, and how much of that energy is transferred to the

Energy transfer is easy to measure. Check the muzzle velocity to get a five-shot average. Then check the average velocity again as the bullet exits 12 inches of gelatin.

Stopping power increases as energy increases. Loads that average 200 ft-lbs. of energy, like the .380 ACP 90-grain FMJ, average 52 percent one-shot stops. Loads with 400 ft-lbs., like the 9mm 124-grain FMJ, average 67 percent.

Compared to hollowpoints, nonexpanding bullets like the .38 Special 148-grain wadcutter (left) and the .44 Special 240-grain SWC (right) produce small crush and stretch cavities and provide much less stopping power.

Nonexpanding bullets, like the .45 Super 185-grain FMJ (left) and 10mm Auto 180-grain FMJ (right), transfer an average of 63 percent of their energy in 12 inches. Hollowpoints transfer 95 percent of their energy.

target? All else equal, bullets with more energy will produce more stopping power than bullets with less energy. The real issue is how much energy can be transferred in the first 12 inches of gelatin.

We measured the amount of energy deposited in 12 inches of gelatin by chronographing the bullet both on impact and after exit. The velocity lost in the block can easily be converted to the energy transferred to the block.

The critical issue is how rapidly the bullet should transfer energy. If the adult male human torso is an average of 9.4 inches thick front to back, where should the defensive handgun bullet dump the most energy?

The LEAA study from the 1970s called for the maximum energy to be transferred in the first 9 inches of 20 percent gelatin. The study from the Southwestern Institute for Forensic Sciences in the 1980s took a different approach. Its protocol called for at least 200 ft-lbs. of energy and no more than 80 percent of the bullet energy being transferred in 5.5 inches of 20 percent gelatin. The FBI studies of the late 1980s totally ignored the effects of energy transfer. In fact, its protocol encouraged underexpansion to achieve penetration as deep as 18 inches.

In the late 1990s, the U.S. Border Patrol entered the fray. As described in

detail in Chapter 25, the Border Patrol is involved in more gunfights than all other federal police agencies combined. Among the feds, they are the true gunfight experts. The Border Patrol calls for a minimum of 9 inches of penetration, ignoring bullet penetration deeper than 12 inches. In its view, penetration in excess of 12 inches in 10 percent gelatin greatly increases the probability of overpenetration.

All else equal, bullets that penetrate in the 8.4 to 12.8 inch range produce roughly the same stopping power. Bullets that penetrate deeper than 12.8 inches produce much less stopping power. Regardless of the handgun ammo in use, it must release the maximum energy in the first 12 inches of 10 percent gelatin. For a quick comparison, hollowpoint bullets in 9mm, .357 Magnum, .357 SIG, .40 S&W, and .45 ACP all transfer 350 to 500 ft-lbs. of energy in 12 inches of gelatin. Only the .357 Magnum and .44 Magnum did that in our test with nonhollowpoint bullets.

Loads with more initial energy also transfer more energy. Those that average 200 ft-lbs. of muzzle energy transfer 150 ft-lbs. in 12 inches. Loads that average 475 ft-lbs. of muzzle energy transfer 260 ft-lbs. in 12 inches. However, loads with more initial energy transfer a lower percent of their

initial energy. Loads that average 200 ft-lbs. of muzzle energy transfer 75 percent of what they had in 12 inches. Loads that average 475 ft-lbs. of energy transfer just 55 percent of their initial energy in 12 inches.

Does stopping power increase as muzzle energy increases? Absolutely. With *hollowpoint* handgun bullets, stopping power increases rapidly as muzzle energy increases. However, with hollowpoint handgun bullets, energy beyond 675 ft-lbs. simply does not result in much more stopping power. It is not quite like that with solid bullets. With them, stopping power slowly increases as energy increases. It continues to increase slowly even as energy levels exceed 1000 ft-lbs.

With solid, nonexpanding bullets, muzzle energy is the single key to stopping power. It is much more significant than bullet caliber or bullet shape. Loads with 200 ft-lbs. of energy produce 52 percent one-shot stops, whereas 300 ft-lbs. produces 60 percent one-shot stops, 400 ft-lbs. results in 67 percent stops, and 500 ft-lbs. produces 72 percent stops.

So although loads with more energy transfer produce more stopping power, loads with more initial energy generally transfer more total energy.

One of the big exceptions is the .38 Special +P 158-grain SWC. While

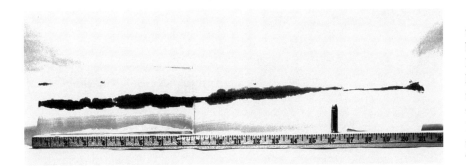

The .38 Special non +P 158-grain RNL averages 23.5 inches of penetration. Between 65 and 70 percent of bullets that penetrate more than 15 inches of gelatin exit the body on a torso shot.

The .38 Special 148-grain Target wadcutter penetrates 17 inches of gelatin. This load produces the same stopping power as the non +P 158-grain loads and the same as .380 ACP hardball.

this load has much more energy than the non +P loads, it is very inefficient, transferring just 43 percent of what it has. All of the non +P loads actually transfer more energy, and can be expected to have more stopping power, than this +P load!

Solid bullets require about twice as much energy to produce an 80 percent one-shot stop as hollowpoint bullets. This makes sense. Solid bullets transfer an average of just 63 percent of their energy in the first 12 inches of gelatin. Hollowpoint bullets transfer 95 percent of their energy in the same 12 inches.

Of course, this is the key to

success for hollowpoints. Hollowpoints and solid bullets may have exactly the same muzzle energy but hollowpoints transfer more of it, and in many cases, all of it, to the target. This is seldom the case for solid bullets.

Softpoints do not expand from handguns. They just don't travel fast enough. The 9mm 95-grain softpoint at 1229 fps did not expand in our tests. Neither did the .357 Magnum 158-grain softpoint at 1230 fps. Neither did the .44 Magnum 240-grain softpoint at 1277 fps. Neither did the .357 Magnum 125-grain softpoint at a whopping 1395 fps. Softpoint bullets do *not* expand from handguns!

Bullets that enter the target and tumble transfer more energy than bullets that remain nose forward. Pointed and rounded bullets are more likely to tumble than flatpoint and truncated cone bullets. However, this varies by caliber and load. The 9mm 115-grain FMJ tends to tumble while the .45 ACP 230-grain FMJ does not. The .38 Special 158-grain and 200-grain Super Police round-nose lead both tumble while the SWC versions do not.

Does stopping power increase as the caliber of solid bullets increases, all else being equal? Believe it or not, no. The 9mm 147-grain FMJ, .40 S&W 180-grain FMJ, and .45 ACP 230-grain FMJ have similar energy and similar Fuller Index ratings. In this case, the smaller caliber bullet had slightly less muzzle energy but actually transferred slightly more energy! Larger caliber bullets typically mean heavier bullets. Lighter bullets simply slow down faster, transferring energy as they slow down.

Larger caliber solid bullets don't result in more stopping power. Given the fact that lighter and smaller bullets can be driven to higher velocities and higher energy levels, with solid bullets, the stopping power advantage may go to the smaller caliber bullets.

Does stopping power increase as the shape of the bullet becomes blunter or flatter? Surprising, the answer is no. The shape of the bullet greatly affects ricochet resistance and stability inside the target, but it does not affect stopping power at all.

Evan Marshall collected 549 shootings with the .38 Special non +P 158-grain RNL and 389 shootings with the .38 Special non +P 158-grain SWC. Both loads produced exactly the same 50 percent one-shot stops. The flatpoint SWC had no stopping power advantage whatsoever over the round-nose lead.

In our tests we found the .38 Special 158-grain RNL and the .38 Special 158-grain SWC to transfer almost exactly the same energy in 12

Softpoint bullets do not expand from handguns. The .357 Magnum 125-grain JSP at 1395 fps (left) did not expand. Neither did the .44 Magnum 240-grain JSP at 1277 fps (right).

With solid bullets, stopping power does not increase with flatpoint bullets. The .38 Special 158-grain RNL and SWC both transfer the same energy to the target. Both have exactly the same 50 percent one-shot stops.

inches of gelatin. Actually, the .38 caliber RNL transferred slightly more energy. It is not surprising that the street results for the RNL and the SWC are the same. A real shock was the .44 Special. While the 246-grain RNL and 240-grain SWC started out with about the same energy, the .44 caliber RNL transferred almost *twice* the energy as the SWC.

On impact with gelatin, round-nose bullets generally tumble one time, base over nose. Jacketed or all lead, these bullets almost always end up base first in the gelatin. This is especially true of the 9mm 115- and 124-grain, .38 Special 158-grain, and .44 Special 246-grain round-nose loads. This half tumble occurs less frequently with bullets having a shorter length-to-diameter ratio, like the .32 ACP, .380 ACP, and .45 ACP.

As the round-nose bullet gets sideways in the target, it dumps much more energy. As a result, RNL and FMJ-RN bullets may actually transfer more of their energy than a similar SWC and FMJ-FP bullets. The total penetration of these rounded bullets is also less than blunter bullets, which drill straight.

The same thing happened with the 9mm 115-grain FMJ-RN and the 9mm 147-grain FMJ-FP. Both had the same muzzle energy, transferred the same amount of energy, and had the same Fuller Index. Same goes for the

.40 S&W 180-grain FMJ-FP and the .45 ACP 230-grain FMJ-RN, which have roughly the same energy, energy transfer, and Fuller Index.

U.S. Army tests conducted in the Chicago stockyards in the early 1900s indicated a flatter bullet was more effective than a rounder bullet. After studying thousands of officer-involved and police action shootings, the facts are that bullet shape really does not matter in terms of stopping power.

Does stopping power increase as the Power Factor increases? Generally, yes. Significant exceptions are the .44 Special loads and the .45 ACP 230-grain FMJ. As a rule, stopping power increases with felt recoil. However, the amount of the increase with Power Factor is not as much as a similar increase in muzzle energy.

Does stopping power increase as the velocity of solid bullets increases? Yes. This makes sense because energy increases with the square of velocity, and stopping power increases as energy increases.

The subcalibers—.22 LR, .25 ACP, and .32 ACP—are the big exceptions to this trend. Loads that average 860 fps have a Fuller Index that averages 55 percent. Loads that average 1190 fps have a Fuller Index that averages 69 percent. However, velocity is not the best indicator of stopping power since many loads have a very different velocity but the same energy. Energy is the key, not velocity.

In addition to poor stopping power, nearly all nonexpanding bullets have another serious problem: overpenetration. The 9mm 115-grain FMJ, for example, penetrates 24 to 28

The .45 ACP 185-grain Target wadcutter penetrates 28.5 inches of gelatin while producing a tiny stretch cavity and a low rate of energy transfer. The 230-grain hardball is a better choice.

inches of penetration in 10 percent gelatin compared to 10 to 12 inches for the 115-grain JHPs. Noted police researcher and prolific author Massad Ayoob has documented a real-life problem with these deeply penetrating loads. The New York City Police has more details of its gunfights than any other major police department. Ayoob found that in one two-year period, 25 people, including 17 police officers, were shot with police-fired 9mm hardball and subsonic hollowpoints that had gone through-and-through other people first.

It is not just American police that have had problems with FMJ and nonexpanding ammo. In Germany, a police officer fired on a man brandishing a knife. His 9mm 115-grain FMJ exited after a head shot and killed an innocent bystander behind the violator. This became controversial enough to have the German government consider alternative bullets for police use.

FMJ, RNL, and SWC ammo is very likely to overpenetrate a human target. The U.S. Army concluded in the 1950s that a bullet with 58 ft-lbs. of

energy is enough to cause a casualty. This was affirmed in the 1970s by the U.S. Secret Service. The key to understanding the threat of overpenetration is to keep the bullet energy less than 58 ft-lbs. after penetrating 12 inches of gelatin. This is the reason why many police departments, now including the NYPD, use hollowpoint bullets.

The depth of 12 inches was selected because the U.S. Border Patrol established this distance to equal a human torso. Specifically, according to its new ammo test protocol, bullets that penetrate more than 12 inches are likely to exit with a torso shot placement. Far from being a minimum penetration depth, like the FBI established, the Border Patrol felt that bullets start exiting in the real world at depths beyond 12 inches.

Of the 30 FMJ, SWC, RNL, and JSP loads tested for this chapter, 23 exited with more than 58 ft-lbs. of energy. With the exception of the 9mm 95-grain JSP, all the loads that exited with *less* than 58 ft-lbs. of energy are also seldom used defensive loads that start out with less than 175 ft-lbs.

What is the best caliber for a shooter restricted to FMJ hardball or solid lead bullets? For the pistol, it would be one of the high-energy calibers like .357 SIG, 10mm Auto, and .45 Super. Of these, the .357 SIG is clearly the easiest to control. With 72 percent one-shot stops, the 125-grain FMJ works about like a .38 Special +P 158-grain LHP. For the revolver, it would likewise be one of the high-energy calibers like the .357 Magnum, .41 Magnum, and .44 Magnum. Remember, the key is energy, so do *not* pick one of the reduced-velocity loads in these magnum calibers.

As a rule, as muzzle energy increases, stopping power increases. Also as a rule, as Power Factor increases, stopping power increases. Exceptions exist. The combat shooter should try to increase muzzle energy *without* increasing recoil. Lighter bullets and smaller calibers produce more energy and less recoil than heavier bullets and larger calibers.

The key to a good defensive load is to pick one with a high Fuller Index and a low Power Factor. For example, the .357 SIG 125-grain FMJ and the .44 Special 246-grain RNL produce almost exactly the same recoil. This .357 SIG, however, produces 72 percent one-shot stops while the .44 Special load is rated at just 57 percent. The .357 SIG load is a much combat-smarter choice. The .357 SIG 125-grain FMJ and the .40 S&W 155-grain FMJ have roughly the same recoil but the .357 SIG has a higher Fuller Index. Same goes for the 9mm +P+ 124-grain FMJ and the .45 ACP 170-grain JSP, with the stopping power advantage to the 9mm +P+. Same goes for the 9mm 95-grain JSP and the .38 Special 158-grain SWC. Both produce a mild recoil, but the 9mm has much more stopping power.

Put another way, some loads produce the same level of stopping power but have a very different level of recoil. The 9mm 115-grain FMJ, .40 S&W 180-grain FMJ, and .45 ACP 230-grain FMJ all produce

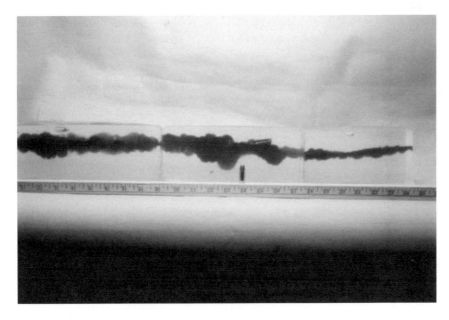

The 9mm 115-grain FMJ penetrates 24.5 inches of gelatin. It exits after 12 inches with 135 ft-lbs. of energy. Only 58 ft-lbs. is required to cause a casualty.

The .357 SIG 125-grain FMJ (left) and the .40 S&W 155-grain FMJ (right) have the same felt recoil, but the .357 SIG load produces more stopping power.

The key to selecting a good defensive load is picking one with a high Fuller Index and a low Power Factor. For handgunners required to use nonexpanding ammo, the .357 SIG is an excellent choice.

The top gun among auto pistol calibers is the .45 Super. The Triton SEAL load has a much higher Fuller Index than .45 ACP ball with just 20 percent more recoil.

nearly the same stopping power. However, the Power Factor for these loads is 131, 174, and 196 respectively. Again, a lower recoiling load with the same stopping power is the smartest choice. The 9mm 95-grain JSP and the .45 ACP 230-grain FMJ have a similar Fuller Index but the .45 ACP load produces nearly 70 percent more recoil. The 9mm 124-grain JSP, 10mm MV 200-grain FMJ, and .45 ACP 230-grain FMJ also have about the same Fuller Index. However, the Power Factors are 143, 166, and 196 respectively.

The no-holds-barred "top gun" among conventional auto pistol calibers is the .45 Super pioneered by Triton Cartridge. The .45 Super 185-grain FMJ developed by Triton for the Navy SEALs outpowers the original, full-power Norma 10mm 200-grain FMJ. It also transfers more energy, has a lower Power Factor, and is readily available. The recoil is just 20 percent more than .45 ACP 230-grain hardball with a Fuller Index of 77 percent, compared to 63 percent for the .45 ACP.

TABLE 21-1
SOLID POINT WOUND BALLISTICS

Caliber	Load	Muzzle Velocity fps	Total Depth inch	Power Factor	Fuller Index %
.22 Long Rifle	40 gr. RNL	739	11.5	30	36
.25 ACP	50 gr. FMJ-RN	765	17.5	38	38
.32 ACP	71 gr. FMJ-RN	890	19.0	63	45
.38 Spl. Non +P	148 gr. HBWC	697	17.0	103	49
.380 ACP	95 gr. FMJ-RN	907	17.0	86	50
.38 Spl. Non +P	158 gr. RNL	696	23.5	110	50
.38 Spl. Non +P	158 gr. SWC	710	28.0	112	50
.45 ACP	185 gr. FMJ-SWC	745	26.5	138	55
.38 Spl. +P	158 gr. SWC	800	30.0	126	55
.44 Spl.	240 gr. SWC	678	27.5	163	56
.45 ACP	170 gr. JSP-FP	827	33.5	141	57
.45 ACP	185 gr. FMJ-FP	779	27.9	144	57
.44 Spl.	246 gr. RNL	680	26.0	167	57
9mm	95 gr. JSP-FP	1229	20.0	117	62
9mm	115 gr. FMJ-RN	1137	24.5	131	62
9mm	147 gr. FMJ-FP	1003	28.7	147	62
9mm	124 gr. JSP-TC	1155	29.0	143	65
.40 S&W	155 gr. FMJ-FP	1042	24.0	162	65
.40 S&W	180 gr. FMJ-FP	967	25.0	174	65
.45 ACP	230 gr. FMJ-RN	851	30.5	196	65
9mm +P+	124 gr. FMJ-RN	1181	33.0	146	66
10mm MV	155 gr. FMJ-FP	1071	24.0	166	66
9mm +P+	124 gr. FMJ-FP	1200	34.5	149	67
.357 Mag.	180 gr. SWC	1056	37.6	190	69
10mm MV	200 gr. FMJ-FP	1008	27.1	202	69
.357 SIG	125 gr. FMJ-FP	1344	38.5	168	72
.357 Mag.	125 gr. JSP-FP	1395	28.5	174	73
.357 Mag.	158 gr. JSP-FP	1230	31.0	194	73
.45 Super	185 gr. FMJ-FP	1272	42.5	235	77
10mm Auto	200 gr. FMJ-FP	1201	29.8	240	77
.44 Mag.	240 gr. JSP-FP	1277	29.0	306	82

TABLE 21-2
SOLID POINT ENERGY TRANSFER

Caliber	Load	Muzzle Velocity	Final Velocity	Muzzle Energy	Final Energy	Energy Transfer
.22 Long Rifle	40 gr. RNL	739	0	49	0	49
.25 ACP	50 gr. FMJ-RN	965	285	65	9	56
.38 Spl. +P	158 gr. SWC	800	607	225	129	96
.32 ACP	71 gr. FMJ-RN	890	385	125	23	102
.38 Spl. Non +P	158 gr. SWC	710	437	177	67	110
.380 ACP	95 gr. FMJ-RN	907	536	174	61	113
.44 Spl.	240 gr. SWC	678	482	245	124	121
.38 Spl. Non +P	158 gr. RNL	696	325	170	37	133
.45 ACP	185 gr. FMJ-FP	779	511	249	107	142
.38 Spl. Non +P	148 gr. HBWC	697	50	160	1	159
.45 ACP	170 gr. JSP-FP	827	483	258	88	170
.45 ACP	230 gr. FMJ-RN	851	624	370	199	171
.40 S&W	180 gr. FMJ-FP	967	689	374	190	184
9mm	124 gr. JSP-TC	1155	764	367	161	206
9mm +P+	124 gr. FMJ-FP	1200	834	397	191	206
.40 S&W	155 gr. FMJ-FP	1042	686	374	162	212
10mm MV	200 gr. FMJ-FP	1008	727	451	235	216
10mm MV	155 gr. FMJ-FP	1071	690	395	164	231
.44 Spl.	246 gr. RNL	680	180	253	18	235
9mm	147 gr. FMJ-FP	1003	525	328	90	238
9mm	115 gr. FMJ-RN	1137	591	330	89	241
.357 Mag.	180 gr. SWC	1056	713	446	203	243
.357 SIG	125 gr. FMJ-FP	1344	901	501	225	276
9mm	95 gr. JSP-FP	1229	423	319	38	281
10mm Auto	200 gr. FMJ-FP	1201	887	641	349	292
9mm NATO	124 gr. FMJ-RN	1181	569	384	89	295
.45 Super	185 gr. FMJ-FP	1272	924	665	351	314
.357 Mag.	125 gr. JSP-FP	1395	618	540	106	434
.357 Mag.	158 gr. JSP-FP	1230	434	531	66	465
.44 Mag.	240 gr. JSP-FP	1277	500	869	133	736

STOPPING POWER

CHAPTER 22

Short-Barrel Wound Ballistics

Powerful, short-barrel auto pistols are the wave of the future. In the late 1980s, the .38 Special snub-nose revolver was challenged by the .380 ACP auto pistol as the ideal concealable handgun. Today, auto pistols in 9mm, .40 S&W, and even .45 ACP are made as small as the average .380 ACP pistol.

Auto pistols with shorter barrels produce less muzzle velocity than longer auto pistols firing the same load. Less velocity means less energy and less momentum. Less energy means smaller stretch cavities and less stopping power. Less velocity also means less reliable hollowpoint expansion and expansion to smaller recovered diameters. Less expansion means deeper soft tissue penetration, which also means less stopping power. Finally, less energy means less tactical penetration. As far as wound ballistics and terminal performance goes, everything about lower velocities is bad.

In the late 1990s the three main police and defensive auto pistol calibers were the 9mm, .40 S&W, and .45 ACP. How much velocity, expansion, and stopping power are lost when going from a 5 inch duty gun to a 3 inch pocket pistol in these same

calibers? Which of the auto pistol calibers loses more velocity and energy when going to shorter barrels? How can the velocity, expansion, and stopping power losses be regained when going to shorter barrels? Do the duty calibers, especially the slower .45 ACP, ever lose so much velocity and stopping power that the handgunner is

just as well off with a potent .380 ACP in a less bulky pistol?

To answer all these questions and others, we tested the complete spectrum of .380 ACP, 9mm, .40 S&W, and .45 ACP hollowpoints from a variety of auto pistols. The ammo included light, medium, and heavy JHPs in each caliber. Where

The biggest difference in wound ballistics between compact and duty auto pistols is the size of the stretch cavity. High-velocity hollowpoints like this Winchester 9mm 115-grain Silvertip were the least affected by the shorter barrel.

possible, we also fired both +P pressure ammo and medium-velocity JHPs. The pistols ranged from 5 inch duty pistols to 4 inch compacts to 3 inch pocket pistols.

Every combination was fired through a chronograph to get the exact muzzle velocity. From this we got muzzle energy and felt recoil. We then picked the test pistol that produced the most, the least, and the midway velocity in each caliber. These pistols represented the typical duty, compact, and subcompact concealable handguns. All of the ammo was fired into calibrated 10 percent ordnance gelatin from these three pistols in each caliber.

The chronograph and the gelatin showed definite changes in performance as the barrel length changed. As a rule, it showed that lighter bullets lost more sheer velocity when going to a shorter barrel compared to heavier bullets. However, the lighter bullets still produced the highest velocity. The heaviest bullets still produced the lowest velocity.

The three duty calibers lost about the same average velocity when dropping from a 4 1/2 or 5 inch duty gun to a 3 inch pocket pistol. All three calibers lost between 115 and 132 fps, an average of a 10 to 13 percent loss. The 9mm and .40 S&W lost about the same amount of velocity, while the .45 ACP lost more sheer velocity and a larger percent of its velocity.

The most extreme velocity loss was the Triton .45 ACP 165-grain JHP. The difference between the 5 inch S&W 4506 and the 3 inch Para P10 was 187 fps. Even still, at 1063 fps from a 3 inch pistol, this lighter load has a higher velocity than any other in the caliber even when the other loads were fired from a 5 inch pistol.

The loss in velocity causes more than a proportionate loss in energy. Energy varies by the square of velocity while momentum or felt recoil changes linearly with velocity. The 9mm lost an average of 71 ft-lbs. of energy, or 19 percent. The .40 S&W

Some .40 S&W hollowpoints like the Federal 180-grain Hydra-Shok (left) and Remington 180-grain Golden Saber (right) have perfect expansion only from long barrel pistols. From compact guns, the expansion suffers.

lost an average of 86 ft-lbs., which was also 19 percent. The .45 ACP was lowered by an average of 107 ft-lbs., or 24 percent. The lower velocity and lower energy .45 ACP suffered both a greater velocity loss and energy loss than the 9mm and .40 S&W.

The recovered bullet diameter from longer barrels was, on the average, larger than from shorter barrels. However, far too many exceptions existed for this to be a general conclusion. In some cases, the bullet clearly underexpanded from shorter barrels, perfectly mushroomed from medium-length barrels, and expanded then fragmented from longer barrels. In other cases, the bullet expanded to about the same diameter regardless of barrel length or expanded and fragmented to about the same diameter regardless of barrel length. In still other cases, the bullet kept expanding to larger diameters as the barrel length got longer.

A couple of trends were evident. Lightweight, fast-moving bullets that expand and then fragment out of longer barrel guns also expand and fragment out of shorter barrels. Bullets that expand and fragment in gelatin are the most likely to at least expand in combinations of soft and hard living tissue. These are the ones that will expand under the widest diversity of shooting scenarios.

The other general trend is that

many heavy or slow-moving bullets need duty-length guns to expand well. Subsonic hollowpoints that expand to 1.7 times their initial caliber from a 5 inch pistol expand to only 1.4 times their initial caliber from a 3 inch gun. Bullets with this little expansion in gelatin under ideal situations frequently fail to expand in tissue under adverse situations.

The threshold of expansion is the velocity where the bullet just starts to expand. At impact velocities below this threshold, no expansion whatsoever occurs even under ideal circumstances. At impact velocities above this threshold, expansion occurs, but to varying degrees. Consider a .45 caliber JHP bullet designed with an 850 fps threshold of expansion. At 950 fps the bullet may expand to .60 caliber. At 1050 fps, it may expand to .70 caliber and even fragment. However, at 900 fps the JHP may only expand to .50 caliber, and at 825 fps the bullet would not expand at all.

The handgunner must understand this issue in order to pick the correct JHP for the short-barrel auto. The bullet with the most velocity in excess of its threshold of expansion will be the most likely to expand under the widest variety of scenarios. The bullet with the muzzle velocity the closest to the threshold will be the least likely to expand even under ideal situations. Pick the load with the largest margin of error and the largest safety factor. This is the one with the highest velocity. You want to be able to give up 200 fps and still expand reliably. Only the highest velocity JHPs will permit this kind of loss.

According to FBI protocol tests conducted by Winchester, the steel in auto bodies, plywood, and plasterboard lowers the bullet velocity by 75 to 100 fps. Auto glass lowers it by a whopping 400 fps!

All three duty calibers have heavier JHPs with lower velocities and lighter JHPs with higher velocities. As a rule, the 9mm 147-grain, .40 S&W 180-grain, and .45 ACP 230-grain

The Federal .45 ACP 230-grain Hydra-Shok is typical of most heavy hollowpoints. As barrel length decreases, the recovered diameter decreases and the penetration increases. A lighter bullet makes up for these problems.

The most stopping power from subcompact pistols comes from lighter and faster bullets, like this Winchester 9mm 115-grain Silvertip. Load selection remains more important than caliber selection regardless of barrel length.

The best loads for the compact 9mm auto pistols are the same as for the duty 9mm pistols. High-energy hollowpoints like the Cor-Bon 115-grain JHP +P (shown) produce 84 percent one-shot stops.

bullets need to be fired from duty-length handguns to expand reliably. Each of these heavy bullets expands much less reliably when fired from a very-short-barrel auto pistol. At the other extreme, the 9mm 115-grain +P, .40 S&W 135-grain, and .45 ACP 185-grain +P bullets all expand and fragment when fired from duty-length handguns. From short-barrel pistols and travelling up to 200 fps slower, all these JHPs still expand to very large diameters or expand then fragment.

The key to improving both the diameter and the reliability of bullet expansion when going to shorter guns is to maintain as much velocity as possible. This means using a lighter bullet or a higher pressure load or both.

The Winchester 9mm 115-grain Silvertip from the 5 inch Beretta and the Cor-Bon 9mm 115-grain JHP +P from the 3 inch Para-Ordnance have exactly the same velocity and energy. The use of the same bullet weight but higher pressures results in exactly the same stopping power even from a much shorter barrel.

The Federal .45 ACP 230-grain Hydra-Shok from the 5 inch S&W 4506 and the Remington .45 ACP 185-grain JHP from the 3 inch Para-Ordnance have exactly the same stopping power. The use of a lighter bullet regained the loss in velocity from the shorter barrel.

The Triton .40 S&W 135-grain JHP from the 3 inch Para-Ordnance actually produced *more* stopping power than the Federal .40 S&W 165-grain medium-velocity Hydra-Shok from the 4 1/2 inch Ruger. (This particular Ruger P91DAO produced higher velocities than either the 4 1/2 inch Glock or 5 inch Beretta.) The use of both a lighter bullet and a higher pressure load result in more stopping power from a pocket pistol than the other load from a duty gun.

With the particular cross-section of JHPs selected in 9mm and .40 S&W, on the average the penetration depth increased as the barrel length decreased. The bullets expanded less with the slower impacts from the shorter barrels. Less bullet expansion means more soft tissue penetration even if the bullet energy is less.

The exception was the .45 ACP caliber, due more to the particular loads tested than to the caliber itself. Bullet fragmentation caused the exceptions in this caliber. The Remington 185-grain JHP expanded and fragmented from short, medium, and long barrels. How times have changed. In the late 1980s, this exact load was selected by the FBI Wound Ballistics Workshop because it did not expand much at all and as a result produced the deep penetration the FBI was told it needed. Remington engineers did not appreciate the honor

of having the one .45 caliber hollowpoint that didn't expand so they redesigned it. Today it offers explosive fragmentation even from a 3 inch Para-Ordnance. Pushing this load faster from longer barrels simply results in deeper penetration.

The other exception is the CCI-Speer 200-grain JHP. This is the famous "flying ash can" bullet, so-named for its massive hollowpoint cavity. This load expands to .76 caliber from a 3 inch pistol. Higher velocities from longer barrels simply cause bullet fragmentation and drive the bullet deeper. For similar energy levels, bullets with expanded mushrooms penetrate less than bullets that have expanded and then fragmented back to smaller diameters. Whether the reason for the small diameter is underexpansion or fragmentation, bullets with less expansion penetrate deeper, all else equal.

In actual terms, however, the total penetration from both duty guns and pocket pistols was quite similar. The 5 inch duty guns averaged 12.1 inches penetration in calibrated ordnance gelatin. The 3 inch pocket pistols firing the same ammo averaged 12.5 inches.

The differences in velocity, energy, expansion, and penetration all come down to one issue: stopping power. How much difference exists between the full-size duty pistol with

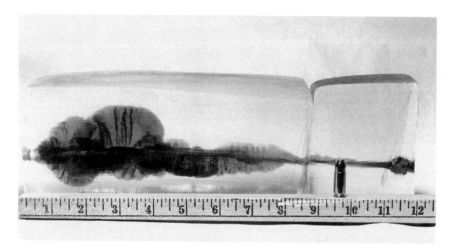

The 9mm Remington 124-grain Golden Saber penetrated 11 inches from both a 5 inch and 3 inch barrel. However, the loss in velocity lowered the one-shot stops from 79 percent to 70 percent.

the most velocity and the pocket pistol with the least velocity? As a surprise to some, the average difference for all three duty calibers is just 4 to 5 percentage points in one-shot stops.

In 9mm, the one-shot stop rating with the Cor-Bon 115-grain JHP +P goes from 87 percent from a 5 inch Beretta to 82 percent from a 3 inch Para-Ordnance. In .40 S&W, the Triton 135-grain JHP goes from 91 percent from the duty gun to 88 percent from the pocket pistol. In .45 ACP, the Triton 165-grain JHP from the 5 inch S&W has a 93 percent rating compared to 89 percent from the 3 inch Para-Ordnance.

From this cross-section of 12 duty loads, three loads lost 3 percentage points, four lost 4 percentage points, and two lost 5 percentage points. Three loads were especially affected when fired from short barrels: Federal .40 S&W 180-grain Hydra-Shok (6 point loss), Federal .40 S&W 165-grain medium-velocity Hydra-Shok (7 point loss), and Remington 9mm 124-grain Golden Saber (9 point loss).

The slower velocity, medium weight, and heavy hollowpoints did not necessarily suffer the biggest loss when going from long to short barrels. Some lost 6 to 9 percentage points in the Fuller Index. However, the Federal 9mm 147-grain Hydra-

Shok and the CCI-Speer .45 ACP 200-grain JHP only lost 3 points. The higher velocity lightweight hollowpoints generally retained more of their stopping power when going to very short barrels. However, one load, the Cor-Bon 9mm 115-grain (+P), had a 5 point loss. Even still, this was right on the average for all 12 of these duty loads.

Overall, the loss in stopping power was nowhere near what many firearms authorities have claimed. In fact, depending upon the load used in the large frame duty gun, the pocket pistol of the same caliber can produce as much or even more stopping power.

In .45 ACP, the Federal 230-grain Hydra-Shok has a Fuller Index of 85 percent from a 5 inch duty pistol. The CCI-Speer 200-grain JHP has the same 85 percent rating from a 4 inch compact pistol. The Remington 185-grain JHP has the same 85 percent one-shot stop from a 3 inch pocket pistol. With proper load selection, this is no loss in stopping power at all, even though the auto pistol is much smaller.

How about an improvement? In .40 S&W, the Federal 165-grain Medium Velocity Hydra-Shok has an 85 percent rating from a large frame duty gun. The Triton 135-grain JHP from a 3 inch pocket pistol improves the stopping power to 88 percent.

Same goes for the 9mm. The Federal 147-grain Hydra-Shok from a 5 inch pistol has a 75 percent rating. Improve upon that when using a 3 inch pistol by using the Cor-Bon 115-grain JHP +P at 82 percent.

The loss of 4 to 5 percentage points when going from a duty gun to a pocket pistol is no big deal. A difference of more than that is possible by using different ammo with the same gun. The best to worst among hollowpoints in the large frame 9mm varies by 12 percentage points! The extreme spread from the duty guns in .40 S&W and .45 ACP is 7 points and 8 points respectively.

Do these three duty calibers ever lose enough velocity and stopping power by going to pocket pistols that the shooter is just as well off with a good .380 ACP hollowpoint? No.

Compare the lowest performing loads from the 9mm, .40 S&W, and .45 ACP out of the 3 inch pistol with the best performing load from the full-size .380 ACP pistol. The Fuller Index from the three duty calibers, at their worst, varies from 72 to 80 percent. The best load from the 4 inch .380 ACP Beretta is 69 percent. And why select the lowest performing loads from the duty calibers? The best performing ones from the short-barrel pocket pistols varies from 82 to 89 percent. This far exceeds the stopping power from any .380 ACP, period.

The .380 ACP Remington 102-grain Golden Saber expanded to .62 inch from a longer barrel and .65 inch (shown) from a shorter barrel. The one-shot stops, however, dropped from 64 percent to just 52 percent.

The same fate that happens to duty calibers when going to a pocket pistol happens even more so to the .380 ACP when going to a shorter barrel length. We fired the medium frame Beretta 84F with a 4 inch barrel against the small frame Colt Mustang with a 2 3/4 inch barrel.

The duty calibers lost an average of 122 fps when going to the pocket pistol. The .380 ACP lost an average of 144 fps when going from the long-barrel Beretta to the short-barrel Colt. That is a 15 percent loss compared to 11 percent for the bigger calibers. The duty calibers shed an average of 21 percent of their energy. The .380 ACP lost 27 percent of its energy. Hollowpoints from the duty calibers had an average of 6 percent less expansion. The .380 ACP hollowpoints had 13 percent smaller recovered diameters. Compared to 5 percent deeper penetration from the duty calibers, going to a shorter barrel in the .380 ACP resulted in 14 percent deeper penetration. While the duty calibers lost between 4 and 5 points in one-shot stop effectiveness, the average for the .380 ACP caliber was an 11 point loss in stopping power.

The grand average one-shot stops from the 3 inch Para-Ordnance in all three duty calibers is 81 percent. The average from the 4 inch Beretta is 65 percent one-shot stops. The average from the 2 3/4 inch Colt is 54 percent one-shot stops.

For the best overall performance from a pocket pistol, carry one of the bigger calibers, especially the .40 S&W and .45 ACP. However, the argument for the carry of a short-barrel pistol is also an argument for the use of lighter, faster hollowpoints. Once the caliber has been selected, load it with one of the lightweight JHPs.

One final conclusion. In all four calibers, the most effective loads from the duty pistols were also the most effective loads from the pocket pistols.

The .380 ACP Remington 102 Golden Saber penetrates 10 inches from a longer barrel and 10.3 inches from a shorter barrel pistol. This load had more tolerance to barrel length changes than any other .380 ACP load.

For the best performance from a pocket pistol, carry one of the bigger calibers, like this .45 ACP Glock 36. The argument for a subcompact pistol is also an argument for lighter, faster JHPs.

While some of the lower performance loads blended together or swapped ranks among themselves, as the barrel length got shorter, the top two loads in each caliber remained the top two regardless of barrel length. These tests prove, once again, that load selection is much more important than caliber selection when it comes to stopping power.

TABLE 22-1
.380 ACP MUZZLE VELOCITY VERSUS BARREL LENGTH

Pistol		Cor-Bon 90 gr. JHP (+P)	Federal 90 gr. Hydra-Shok	Remington 102 gr. Gold. Saber	Winchester 85 gr. Silvertip
Beretta 84 F 4 inch broach cut	Velocity	1063	967	922	989
	Energy	226	187	193	185
Colt Mustang 2 3/4 inch broach cut	Velocity	940	826	760	841
	Energy	177	136	131	134
Extreme spread in velocity (fps)		123	141	162	148
Percent loss in velocity (%)		12	15	18	15
Extreme spread in energy (ft-lb.)		49	51	62	51
Percent loss in energy (%)		22	27	32	28

TABLE 22-2
9MM MUZZLE VELOCITY VERSUS BARREL LENGTH

Pistol		Cor-Bon 115 gr. JHP (+P)	Winchester 115 gr. Silvertip	Remington 124 gr. Gold. Saber	Federal 147 gr. Hydra-Shok
Beretta 92 5-inch broach cut	Velocity	1334	1188	1080	973
	Energy	455	360	321	309
Glock 17 4 1/2-inch polygonal	Velocity	1305	1152	1051	975
	Energy	435	339	304	310
S&W 5906 4-inch broach cut	Velocity	1272	1134	1036	968
	Energy	413	328	296	306
Glock 26 3 1/2-inch polygonal	Velocity	1230	1110	1021	970
	Energy	386	315	287	307
Para P10 3-inch broach cut	Velocity	1186	1095	919	901
	Energy	359	306	233	265
Extreme spread in velocity (fps)		148	93	161	74
Percent loss in velocity (%)		11	8	15	8
Extreme spread in energy (ft-lb.)		96	54	88	44
Percent loss in energy (%)		21	15	27	14

TABLE 22-3
.40 S&W MUZZLE VELOCITY VERSUS BARREL LENGTH

Pistol		Triton 135 gr. JHP	CCI-Speer 155 gr. Gold Dot	Federal 165 gr. (MV) Hydra-Shok	Federal 180 gr. Hydra-Shok
Beretta 96 5-inch broach cut	Velocity	1296	1179	962	921
	Energy	504	479	339	339
Glock 22 4 1/2-inch polygonal	Velocity	1308	1208	988	939
	Energy	513	502	358	352
Ruger P91 4 1/2-inch broach cut	Velocity	1329	1218	1012	952
	Energy	530	511	375	362
Glock 23 4-inch polygonal	Velocity	1269	1167	968	916
	Energy	483	469	343	335
S&W 4046 4-inch broach cut	Velocity	1278	1170	971	906
	Energy	490	471	346	328
Glock 27 3 1/2-inch polygonal	Velocity	1230	1127	948	892
	Energy	454	437	329	318
Para P10 3-inch broach cut	Velocity	1190	1096	897	867
	Energy	425	414	295	301
Extreme spread in velocity (fps)		139	122	115	85
Percent loss in velocity (%)		10	10	11	9
Extreme spread in energy (ft-lb.)		105	97	80	61
Percent loss in energy (%)		20	19	21	17

TABLE 22-4
.45 ACP MUZZLE VELOCITY VERSUS BARREL LENGTH

Pistol		Triton 165 gr. JHP	Remington 185 gr. JHP	CCI-Speer 200 gr. JHP	Federal 230 gr. Hydra-Shok
S&W 4506 5-inch broach cut	Velocity	1250	1023	932	816
	Energy	573	430	386	340
Colt Commander 4 1/4-inch broach cut	Velocity	1169	964	902	785
	Energy	501	382	361	315
Glock 30 3 1/2-inch polygonal	Velocity	1120	923	871	751
	Energy	460	350	337	288
Para P19 3-inch broach cut	Velocity	1063	877	815	738
	Energy	414	316	295	78
Extreme spread in velocity (fps)		187	146	17	78
Percent loss in velocity (%)		15	14	13	10
Extreme spread in energy (ft-lb.)		159	114	91	62
Percent loss in energy (%)		28	27	24	18

TABLE 22-5
.380 ACP WOUND BALLISTICS VERSUS BARREL LENGTH

Load		Beretta 84 4" bbl	Colt Mustang 2 3/4" bbl
Cor-Bon 90 gr. JHP (+P)	Expansion	.60	.59
	Penetration	10.8	9.8
	One-Shot Stop	69	61
Fed. 90 gr. Hydra-Shok	Expansion	.70	.42
	Penetration	9.8	15.0
	One-Shot Stop	63	51
Rem. 102 gr.Golden Saber	Expansion	.62	.65
	Penetration	10.0	10.3
	One-Shot Stop	64	52
Win. 85 gr. Silvertip	Expansion	.61	.53
	Penetration	8.0	9.4
	One-Shot Stop	63	53
Average Expansion		.63	.55
Average Penetration		9.7	11.1
Average One-Shot Stop		65	54

TABLE 22-6
9MM WOUND BALLISTICS VERSUS BARREL LENGTH

Load		Beretta 92 5" bbl	S&W 5906 4" bbl	Para P10 3" bbl
Cor-Bon 115 gr. JHP (+P)	Expansion	.56f	.56f	.56f
	Penetration	9.9	10.4	10.9
	One-Shot Stop	87	85	82
Win. 115 gr. Silvertip	Expansion	.68	.69	.63
	Penetration	8.2	8.9	9.7
	One-Shot Stop	82	80	78
Rem. 124 gr. Golden Saber	Expansion	.68	.65	.65
	Penetration	11.2	13.7	11.2
	One-Shot Stop	79	76	70
Fed. 147 gr. Hydra-Shok	Expansion	.57	.58	.55
	Penetration	16.0	13.1	15.3
	One-Shot Stop	75	77	72
Average Expansion		.62	.62	.60
Average Penetration		11.3	11.5	11.8
Average One-Shot Stop		81	80	76

TABLE 22-7
.40 S&W WOUND BALLISTICS VERSUS BARREL LENGTH

Load		Ruger P91 4 1/2" bbl	Glock 23 4" bbl	Para P10 3" bbl
Triton 135 gr. JHP	Expansion	.63f	.62f	.59f
	Penetration	11.0	11.1	11.6
	One-Shot Stop	91	90	88
CCI 155 gr. Gold Dot	Expansion	.80f	.88	.68
	Penetration	12.2	12.9	13.4
	One-Shot Stop	90	89	86
Fed. 165 gr. MV Hydra-Shok	Expansion	.67	.64	.60
	Penetration	13.2	14.0	15.1
	One-Shot Stop	85	82	78
Fed. 180 gr. Hydra-Shok	Expansion	.71	.67	.56
	Penetration	12.0	13.0	16.1
	One-Shot Stop	84	82	78
Average Expansion		.70	.70	.61
Average Penetration		12.1	12.8	14.1
Average One-Shot Stop		88	86	83

TABLE 22-8
.45 ACP WOUND BALLISTICS VERSUS BARREL LENGTH

Load		S&W 4506 5" bbl	Glock 30 3 1/2" bbl	Para P10 3" bbl
Triton 165 gr. JHP	Expansion	.82f	.84	.83
	Penetration	8.5	8.9	9.5
	One-Shot Stop	93	91	89
Rem. 185 gr. JHP	Expansion	.72f	.71f	.72f
	Penetration	12.5	11.7	10.8
	One-Shot Stop	89	86	85
CCI 200 gr. JHP	Expansion	.64f	.68f	.76
	Penetration	15.1	12.4	11.0
	One-Shot Stop	86	85	83
Fed. 230 gr. Hydra-Shok	Expansion	.80	.68	.62
	Penetration	12.8	13.8	15.1
	One-Shot Stop	85	81	80
Average Expansion		.75	.73	.73
Average Penetration		12.2	11.7	11.6
Average One-Shot Stop		88	86	84

CHAPTER 23

Shotgun Slug Wound Ballistics

Proof of the longevity of the shotgun in police work is the continual release of new duty-oriented shotgun loads. In the mid and late 1990s, a variety of 12-gauge slugs were introduced. Two of the most interesting sabot slugs were the deeply penetrating, French-made Balle Fleche Sauvestre (BFS) and the Polywad Quik-Shok antipersonnel load.

The BFS produces the most wound ballistics of any conventional 12-gauge shotgun slug. However, its real advantage is the fact that it gives the most tactical penetration from any conventional 12-gauge slug. The North Hollywood, California, shootout proved that rifle levels of penetration are sometimes required from a duty riotgun. For this reasons, the BFS has caught the attention of both patrol and tactical officers across the nation.

The Balle Fleche Sauvestre was invented by Jean-Claude Sauvestre. The name "Balle" is French for the word slug, and "Fleche" translates to the word arrow. Sauvestre was the chief engineer in charge of munitions development for the French Defense Ministry. For 30 years, he pioneered the development of tank-killer sabot ammunition. The Sauvestre shotgun

The Balle Fleche Sauvestre expands on impact with gelatin and then spins off numerous lead fragments. It has a small recovered diameter.

The Balle Fleche Sauvestre was developed using antitank technology. The Balle Fleche Sauvestre produced the most tactical penetration of any shotgun slug. The BFS has a high antimony core and the most surface energy of any slug.

ammo incorporates many of the same principles used in modern antitank munitions. These include a fin-stabilized, high-energy projectile and an advanced, wadless sabot design with an auxiliary gas flow diameter to promote better combustion.

Like so many police tactical loads now in use, the BFS was originally designed for big game hunting and is in fact the result of Sauvestre's interest in hunting wild boar. The 12-gauge BFS has been used to take game as large as the Greater Kudu and Cape buffalo in addition to a wide variety of elk, deer, and wild boar.

The Sauvestre sabot is a four-piece assembly made up of the lead alloy slug, threaded steel rod, plastic fin, and two sabot half-shells. The advanced polymer sabot and tail fin completely eliminate the need for an over-powder pusher wad. This in turn frees up additional space in the shotshell for a larger powder charge.

The lead alloy used in the BFS has 3 percent antimony, making the slug very hard. In comparison, most sabot and Foster-style slugs are made with dead soft lead containing no antimony. Lead with 3 percent antimony is considered in the "hard cast" category. In fact, the antimony content in the BFS is too high to allow the slug to be cold swaged like nearly all commercial projectiles are made. The BFS slug is hot cast or, more precisely, hot injected using an automated process similar to hand bullet casting. Evidence of the hard, high-antimony lead in the BFS is the razor sharp fragments that result on impact.

The Balle Fleche Sauvestre has been in full production since 1993. The projectiles are made and the shotshells are assembled at the plant in Bourges, France, about two hours south of Paris. Sauvestre uses primed, high brass cases from NobelSport, a leading European supplier of high-end shotshell components and powder.

Keng's markets the Sauvestre rounds under the trade name Sledgehammer. Four loads are currently available for police, defense, and hunting purposes: the 12-gauge in both 2 3/4 and 3 inch Magnum and the 20-gauge in 2 3/4 and 3 inch Magnum.

Of the readily available sabot and Foster-style slugs, the BFS has the highest muzzle velocity, the second most energy, and clearly the most surface energy. The average 12-gauge sabot slug has a velocity of 1375 fps, while the Balle Fleche Sauvestre clocks around 1675 fps. Energy increases with the square of velocity.

The BFS has the deepest penetration of any shotgun slug and the best chance of defeating tactical barriers for a number of reasons. First,

The Balle Fleche Sauvestre produces the largest diameter and the deepest wound profile of any shotgun slug. This is a .308 Winchester-size wound cavity.

The Wincheter low-recoil Foster-style slug penetrates just 16.5 inches of gelatin, but it also generates a very large and early stretch cavity.

Winchester's version of the reduced-recoil, Foster-style slug expands to 1.05 inches in gelatin.

it has roughly the same energy as a full-power Foster-style slug and 35 percent more energy than other sabot slugs and low-recoil Foster slugs.

More than just sheer energy, the BFS has the most force. Force is generally defined as energy focused over a certain area. At .46 inch in diameter, the BFS has a smaller surface or impact area than the other

sabot slugs, which average .54 inch in diameter. The non-sabot, Foster-style slug typically has a .75 inch diameter. So the BFS spreads nearly the most energy for a shotgun slug over the smallest surface area. The French call this surface kinetic energy. It is expressed in terms of foot-pounds of energy per square inch. The BFS has the same energy of a full-power rifled

Reduced-recoil shotshells are a big help in weapon control, especially from short-barrel riot guns like this 14 inch Remington 870 Synthetic.

The amount of penetration among reduced-recoil slugs varies widely. The Federal version penetrates 12.8 inches, the Winchester version 16.5 inches, and the Remington load, shown here, 27 inches.

slug but spreads it over less than 40 percent of the surface area.

Not counting projectile hardness, the higher energy and the smaller surface area of the BFS result in almost twice the penetration force of the semiexotic sabot slugs, 2.5 times the force of a full-power Foster slug, and 3.5 times the force of a low-recoil Foster slug. At 110 yards, the BFS holds an even larger advantage, having 1.9 times more energy and three times more surface energy than other sabot slugs.

The clear trend in shotgun ammo for law enforcement is toward lower recoil. As a rule, the new generation of American-made sabot slugs produce just slightly more recoil than the reduced-recoil Foster slugs. The BFS slug produces a felt recoil about midway between the sabot slugs and the full-power Fosters. While the BFS has roughly the same muzzle energy as the full-power Foster slug, it kicks less due to its lighter weight.

In terms of wound ballistics, all 12-gauge sabot and Foster slugs are extremely destructive. All of them generate temporary stretch cavities the size of a .308 Winchester softpoint and permanent crush cavities larger than any other shoulder-fired small arm. All of the test slugs had a maximum stretch cavity of between 6 and 8 inches in diameter, which peaked between 4 and 8 inches deep. The largest diameter and the longest stretch cavity was generated by the BFS, followed by the full-power Foster-style slug and then the Federal Barnes-X.

Upon impact with gelatin, the various shotgun slugs responded in unique ways. The Hydra-Shok, Barnes-X, and Foster slugs expanded to impressive recovered diameters. The Federal Barnes-X mushroomed to an awesome 1.4 inch diameter, which also limited its penetration to 16.6 inches.

The Remington Copper Solid expanded upon impact and blew off the four pieces of the hollowpoint cavity wall. These became active secondary missiles. Each 15-grain frag penetrated 4 to 6 inches away from the main bullet path.

On impact, the BFS expanded slightly. With an initial diameter of .46 inch, the recovered mushroomed slugs measured .54 inch. The high antimony content of the slug results in fragmentation of the leading edge instead of expansion, so while the slug does expand somewhat, it is limited by design. Less expansion results in more penetration, and at 36 inches, the BFS produced the deepest soft tissue penetration of any slug in the round-up.

We checked the 100-yard accuracy from all these slugs using a TarHunt bolt-action rifled-barrel shotgun. This professional-grade

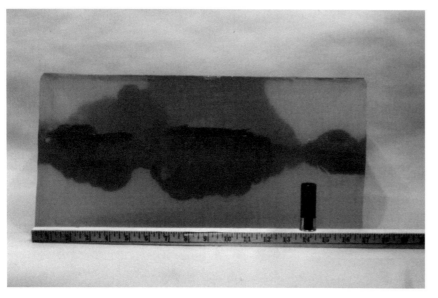

The Federal Barnes-X produces a wound cavity with a large diameter but controlled penetration. The large recovered diameter of the slug limits penetration.

The Federal Barnes-X expands on impact to the largest diameters ever recorded for a shotgun slug. This soft copper slug has a recovered diameter of 1.40 inch and a 100 percent weight retention.

The Remington Copper Solid produces the smallest diameter stretch cavity of any test slug and nearly 27 inches of penetration.

The Remington Copper Solid expands on impact with gelatin and spins off four large pieces of copper. The main core, now a solid copper cylinder, continues to penetrate.

shotgun with a 21.5 inch barrel and Kevlar stock was fitted with a 1.5-6X Burris Signature Series scope. We sandbag-rested the TarHunt and fired four five-shot groups with each of the test rounds.

By a clear margin, the most accurate slug of the round-up was the Federal Hydra-Shok with an average five-shot, 100-yard group size of just 2.9 inches. The Federal Barnes-X was close behind, followed by the Sauvestre Sledgehammer and Remington Copper Solid. All of the sabot slugs were more accurate than the Foster-style slugs from the rifled shotgun.

All of the BFS ammo can be fired in shotguns with cylinder bores to full chokes and in shotguns with rifled barrels and with rifled choke adapters. As with all sabot loads, the best accuracy clearly comes from rifled barrels. The use of a smoothbore shotgun roughly doubles the group size of a sabot slug compared to the use of rifled-barrel shotgun.

Compared to traditional rifled slugs, sabot slugs shoot flatter and drop less. At 125 yards, for example, the BFS drops 9.5 inches compared to 14.5 inches for the Foster-style slug and 18 inches for the Brenneke slug.

The BFS has nearly all of its weight near the front. The center of gravity well forward of the center of pressure allows the slug to fly true even if it is not spin-stabilized. All shotgun slugs, except the Remington Copper Solid and the Federal Barnes-X, use this same "badminton birdie" approach to stability. Of the various sabot, Foster, and Brenneke-style slugs available, the BFS has the most flight integrity.

All else being equal, tactical penetration usually depends on three

The most accurate of the slugs from the TarHunt rifled barrel shotgun was the Federal sabot Hydra-Shok. As a rule, sabot slugs need rifled barrels for best accuracy.

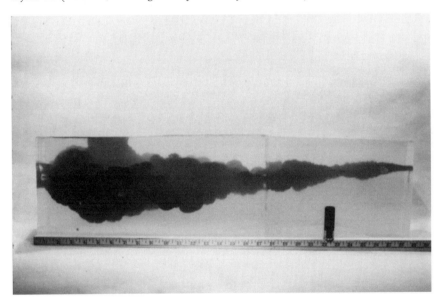

The Federal Hydra-Shok produces impressive wound ballistics with a large stretch cavity and over 28 inches of penetration.

The Federal Hydra-Shok expands to diameters of .86 inch and has a 100 percent weight retention. The expansion is extremely reliable.

Tactical penetration is a matter of energy, diameter, and hardness. Sabot slugs penetrate deeper than Foster-style slugs. Shown recovered from sheet steel, left to right, are the Copper Solid, Hydra-Shok, Barnes-X, and Sauvestre.

factors. The first is impact energy. Slugs with more energy produce more tactical penetration. The second factor is the caliber of the impacting projectile. With 12-gauge shotgun ammo, this is either the .50 caliber sabot slugs or the .75 caliber Foster slugs. Smaller caliber projectiles penetrate deeper in tactical objects than larger caliber projectiles.

The third factor is projectile hardness. Again, all else being equal, the harder bullet will deform less in tactical materials and penetrate more. Among the loads in this round-up, we had softer lead (Hydra-Shok, Foster slugs), high antimony lead (BFS), softer copper (Barnes-X), and harder brass-bronze (Copper Solid). However, the hardness issue is more complex than simply the material used in the projectile. Given the same hardness, a projectile that is less likely to deform, expand, or collapse in on itself will penetrate deeper than a projectile with less structural integrity.

The tactical penetration test was against layers of .50 inch, or 16-gauge, steel separated by 1 inch. This is 60 percent thicker than the .032 inch, or 20-gauge, steel used in the FBI test protocol. The test involved firing five rounds per load.

The shotgun load with clearly the most anticar and tactical penetration was the Balle Fleche Sauvestre. This high-energy, high-antimony, small-caliber slug penetrated an average of 8.5 layers of .050 inch steel. It produces the most tactical penetration of any conventional 12-gauge slug. This is the reason so many police departments are looking at the BFS.

And this performance was from

The Federal 12-gauge Tactical slug expands to a 1 inch diameter in gelatin. It has an extremely controlled penetration depth of just 12.8 inches.

the hunting-grade slug. Sauvestre has other slugs in development specifically for police use. The Sauvestre product line includes five different BFS loads for the 12-gauge, 2 3/4 inch shotshell, including 200-, 290-, and 400-grain slugs driven to velocities from 1315 fps to 1970 fps. The training-oriented LM version is a 200-grain slug loaded to 1315 fps. The 400-grain, 1675 fps hunting-oriented version, called the IAC, combines expansion with penetration. This is the slug currently imported as the Sledgehammer.

A 290-grain, 1970 fps P version is intended for the deepest penetration against armored targets. Compared to the IAC tested in this round-up, the P version has a larger diameter threaded steel rod in the core, and the lead used in the projectile has an even higher antimony content. This perforating slug has been classified as war material and requires both a French authorization of export and an American authorization of import. As of mid-1999, this has not yet been achieved. Based on these tests, such a specialized slug is simply not needed.

The 3-inch magnum version of the hunting-grade IAC load is readily available. It fires the same 400-grain projectile at 1900 fps, producing 3230 ft-lbs. of energy. This is 30 percent more energy than either the 2 3/4 inch BFS or the 2 3/4 inch Foster-style slug. The BFS 3 inch magnum produces roughly 7 percent more felt recoil than a full-power Foster-style slug. Police

departments needing more tactical penetration than is generated by the 2 3/4 inch BFS (and that is hard to imagine based on these tests), should simply use the 3 inch magnum version of the same load.

Among the major agencies, the BFS has been tested by the FBI Firearms Training Unit, the California Highway Patrol, and the Los Angeles County Sheriff. California-area law enforcement is especially interested in the BFS—no one wants a repeat of the North Hollywood bank robbery incident.

The biggest advantage of the BFS slug is penetration. The biggest advantage of the Quik-Shok sabot slug is stopping power. In the late 1990s, Magnum Performance Ballistics (MPB) released a 12-gauge shotshell using the 1 1/8 ounce Quik-Shok slug. Bullets with the Quik-Shok design are available in a .22 Long Rifle rimfire and a 12-gauge slug from MPB-Polywad. The exotic design is also available as a centerfire handgun round in calibers from .32 Auto to .45 Super from Triton Cartridge.

During penetration, the prestressed Quik-Shok projectile expands rapidly and then splits into

three even sections that penetrate in separate directions in an ever-widening pattern inside a soft target. The slug itself has an initial penetrating velocity of nearly 1500 fps, giving each fragment nearly 800 ft-lbs. of energy. Each of the three 164-grain fragments has more momentum and more energy than any .357 Magnum hollowpoint. Each frag penetrates between 13 and 18 inches of 10 percent gelatin, which also is like the .357 Magnum hollowpoints.

Once separated into three segments, the 12 gauge Quik-Shok fragments are irregular shaped and not spin stabilized. This means they transfer energy at a higher rate than a semiwadcutter bullet but not quite as fast as a lightweight hollowpoint. Overall, the terminal effect is something like three simultaneous hits with a .357 Magnum 145-grain Silvertip.

Quik-Shok 12-gauge slugs are made by cutting off a blank of lead wire. The slug, like most Foster-style rifled slugs, is made from pure lead with 0 percent antimony. The blank is formed in the precise shape of a cylinder of lead, then pierced 80 percent of its length by a three-blade punch. The three slots begin at the

The Remington 12-gauge reduced-recoil slug expanded to .77 caliber and penetrated 27 inches of gelatin. The point of impact at 50 yards is the same as the full-power slug.

On impact, the 1 1/8 ounce 12-gauge Quik-Shok breaks into three lead fragments. Each segment weighs 164 grains, and each packs the energy of a .357 Magnum hollowpoint. Each penetrates on its own and forms a separate wound cavity, increases the chance of hitting vital tissue.

The 12-gauge 164-grain Quik-Shok fragments (center) are shown in size comparison to the 000 buck pellet (left) and a .40 S&W 165-grain JHP (right). The Quik-Shok frags produce the same penetration as 00 buck and most handgun hollowpoints.

centerline of the projectile but do not quite reach the outside of the lead core. The thickness of the web and the depth of the three-blade pierce controls the rate of expansion and fragmentation.

The next step is to form the overall shape of the slug, including a large hollow base and a small hollowpoint. Finally, the heel at the hollow base of the slug is bevelled to assist in the high-speed loading of the cartridges. Once fully formed, the knit lines in the Quik-Shok bullet are impossible to see; the rimfire and centerfire Quik-Shok look exactly like a conventional hollowpoint. Similarly, the Quik-Shok shotgun slug looks exactly like a Foster-style slug without the rifling splines.

The 12-gauge Quik-Shok slug itself is made by Hornady Manufacturing under an exclusive license from Polywad, Inc. The Quik-Shok slug is not available as a reloading component. The shotshell is loaded by MPB-Polywad.

The Quik-Shok slug is fully contained by a four-petal polyethylene cup to prevent barrel leading. At the base of the cup is a nylon pusher disk that acts as a buffer between the cup and the soft slug. Without the pusher disc, the wad column would be pushed into the base of the slug and hurt accuracy. As designed, the slug

separates from the cup within 2 feet of the muzzle.

The Quik-Shok is technically a sabot slug. However, most sabot slugs measure .50 caliber in initial diameter. The Quik-Shok has an initial diameter of .68 caliber. Upon firing, the slug swells outward inside the shot cup and is final swaged to diameter in the bore. This gives it an ideal fit to the bore and choke regardless of differences between shotguns.

On impact, the Quik-Shok slug dumps a large amount of energy in a relatively short distance spread over a wide area of the target. It has the energy and initial penetration of a rifled slug, but once inside a soft target it breaks up and acts like a load of very large buckshot pellets. The 00 buck pellet is .33 inch in diameter, weighs 54 grains, and at close range penetrates from 16 to 19 inches of gelatin. Each of the three Quik-Shok segments average .52 by .75 by .34 inch in diameter and 164 grains in weight, and each penetrates 13 to 18 inches.

The 12-gauge Quik-Shok fired from a 20 inch S&W Model 3000 began to separate into three pieces on impact with calibrated 10 percent gelatin. By 1.5 inches deep, the projectile had completely separated into three equal pieces, and each piece began to penetrate independently of the others. By 6 inches, the pattern of

the three frags had grown to 2.5 inches. By 9 inches, the pattern was 5 inches in diameter. At the 12-inch depth, the three-shot group measured 6.5 inches in diameter. At 15 inches, the three segments were 8 inches apart from one another.

The biggest advantage of the Quik-Shok slug in terms of wound ballistics and stopping power is the three independent bullet paths all occurring at the same time. The advantage of three different crush cavities is an increased chance of hitting vital tissue or, better yet, causing multiple organ trauma. The advantage of three simultaneous stretch cavities is that they can overlap one another, causing blunt trauma on the tissue trapped in between.

At close ranges, like 25 yards, the Quik-Shok segment dispersion was up to 8 inches. At longer ranges, like 150 yards, the impact velocity slows to 890 fps. While each Quik-Shok slug still reliably broke into three segments at long ranges, the rate of break-up was less aggressive. As a result, the segment dispersion was reduced to a 4.5 inch pattern. Even still, at impact velocities from 1500 fps to under 900 fps, the 12-gauge Quik-Shok works exactly as designed. This means it will perform reliably at closer ranges even from short-barrel shotguns like the 12.5 inch Witness Security.

Based on the performance in calibrated ordnance gelatin and in a limited number of deer, the Quik-Shok may be the most effective of all 12-gauge loads in law enforcement scenarios. It should certainly exceed the effectiveness of both the 12-gauge Foster-style slug and 12-gauge 00 buck, providing an estimated 98 percent one-shot stops.

The 12-gauge Quik-Shok slug proved itself to be a worthy police duty load during tests conducted by the FBI. It averaged 17.5 inches of penetration in bare gelatin and heavily clothed gelatin alike. Heavy clothes do not affect shotgun slugs like they do subsonic handgun bullets.

SHOTGUN SLUG WOUND BALLISTICS

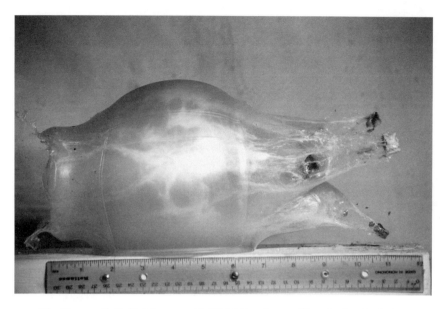

The 12-gauge Quik-Shok impacts with 2500 ft-lbs. of energy like a slug but shreds the target like a load of buckshot. The three frags penetrate 13 to 18 inches and spread out in a 4 to 8 inch pattern.

The real surprise came during the barrier test involving windshield glass and lightly clothed gelatin. Glass can be especially hard on dead soft shotguns slugs. However, the Quik-Shok defeated the compound angle of the windshield and still broke into three segments once in the gelatin. The three frags penetrated 15 to 17 inches and spread out in an 8.5 inch pattern. Not even auto glass changes the performance of the Quik-Shok slug.

One of the biggest advantages of the Quik-Shok slug is controlled penetration. No one doubts the stopping power of a 12-gauge slug. The real issue with most Foster and sabot slugs is their excessive soft tissue penetration. Most Foster-style slugs penetrate up to 24 inches of gelatin, while the Brenneke and sabot types can penetrate up to 30 inches. This may be acceptable for hunting applications but is simply too deep for most law enforcement scenarios. A projectile that penetrates more than 15 1/2 inches of 10 percent gelatin will exit on a torso shot about 70 percent of the time.

One of the chief reasons for using buckshot in police shotguns is the limited pellet penetration compared to the rifled slug. Number 4 buck pellets penetrate 8.5 to 13 inches of gelatin, while 00 buck penetrates 16.5 to 19 inches. The Quik-Shok slug penetrates 13 to 18 inches of gelatin, just like buckshot and not like a conventional slug.

The 12-gauge Quik-Shok weighs 1 1/8 ounces, or 492 grains, and has a muzzle velocity of 1500 fps. On paper this means it has enough energy and momentum to reliably cycle a wide variety of autoloading shotguns. Some of the new reduced-recoil buckshot and slug loads do not always cycle all recoil-operated and gas-operated autos, so we tested the new Quik-Shok in a variety of autos just to be sure. We found it had plenty of power to cycle the Remington Model 11-87P, Beretta 1201-FP3, and Benelli M1 Super 90 Tactical.

With a felt recoil impulse of 3.3 lb-sec., the Quik-Shok has a kick comparable to other full-power 12-gauge loads. In comparison, the 12-gauge nine-pellet 00 buck load produces an impulse of 2.9 lb-sec., while the 12-gauge standard rifled 12-gauge 1 ounce Foster-style slug generates a felt recoil at 3.1 lb-sec.

We found the 12-gauge Quik-Shok to produce only average accuracy from smoothbore shotguns. From a 20 inch S&W Model 3000 wc got very traditional 6 inch groups bench-rested from 100 yards. We were able to achieve consistent off-hand head shots from 30 yards. The best accuracy, as good as 2 MOA, comes from scoped shotguns with rifled barrels. When sighted-in at 50 yards, the Quik-Shok slug impacts within 2 inches of that zero from very close ranges out to 75 yards. By 100 yards, it drops about 5 inches below the zero. This is typical bullet drop from all full-power 1 to 1 1/4 ounce slugs.

TABLE 23-1
SHOTGUN SLUG EXTERIOR BALLISTICS

Load	Weight Grains	Initial Diameter	Muzzle Velocity fps	Muzzle Energy ft-lbs.	Recoil Impulse lb-sec
Balle Fleche Sauvestre	399	.46 inch	1678	2495	2.97
MPB Quik-Shok	492	.68 inch	1500	2458	3.23
Federal Hydra-Shok	427	.51 inch	1430	1939	2.71
Federal Barnes-X	437	.58 inch	1388	1870	2.69
Remington Copper Solid	457	.53 inch	1325	1782	2.70
Winch. Foster slug (low recoil)	435	.74 inch	1370	1813	2.65
Remington Foster slug (full power)	435	.74 inch	1625	2550	3.14

TABLE 23-2
SHOTGUN SLUG WOUND BALLISTICS

Load	Recovered Diameter inch	Gelatin Penetration	Stretch Cavity dia @ depth	Layers of .050 sheet steel	5-shot groups 100 yards (rifled)
Balle Fleche Sauvestre	0.56	36.0 inch	8.0 @ 6"	8.5	3.8 inch
MPB Quik-Shok	3-frag	15.0 inch	9.0 @ 4"	5.5	4.1 inch
Federal Hydra-Shok	0.86	28.5 inch	6.5 @ 5"	6.0	2.9 inch
Federal Barnes-X	1.40	16.6 inch	7.0 @ 8"	7.5	3.4 inch
Remington Copper Solid	0.53	26.6 inch	6.0 @ 7"	6.0	4.3 inch
Federal Tactical slug (low recoil)	1.00	12.8 inch	n/a	n/a	n/a
Winch. Foster slug (low recoil)	1.05	16.5 inch	7.5 @ 4"	4.5	4.7 inch
Remington Reduced Recoil slug	0.77	27.0 inch	n/a	n/a	n/a
Remington Foster slug (full power)	1.20	27.5 inch	7.5 @ 6"	5.5	5.6 inch

CHAPTER 24

Cap and Ball Wound Ballistics

The popularity of cap and ball revolvers has been as explosive as the black powder used by these mid-1800s firearms. Newly made replica handguns are widely available in calibers from the concealable .31 Pocket to the massive .44 Walker.

How did these percussion cap firearms from the U.S. Civil War era really perform? What was the real, measurable stopping power from the pure lead round ball and the conical or elongated ball? How does their effectiveness compare to the smokeless-powder-driven solid lead and hardball bullets from the early 1900s? Was the Colt .44 caliber Walker really as potent as today's .44 Magnum? What is black powder anyway?

Gunpowder—what we now call black powder—was developed so long ago that the exact origin is unknown. We simply do not know enough about events from the 600s to 1200s to know when gunpowder was invented and who or what nation did it. It may have been developed as early as the 8th century. The mixture of saltpeter, charcoal and sulfur has been alternatively credited to the Chinese, Greeks, Hindus, and Arabs.

For certain, the Chinese had a

version of black powder in the 1200s. It was three parts potassium nitrate, two parts charcoal, and two parts sulfur. The first military employment of black powder is generally agreed to have taken place at the Battle of Crecy in 1346, although it did not see widespread military use until the 1500s.

The chief ingredient of black powder is potassium nitrate, called saltpeter or niter. Saltpeter, KNO(3), supplies the oxygen necessary to burn the sulfur and charcoal. The products of combustion are sulfur dioxide, carbon monoxide, carbon dioxide, nitrogen, and hydrogen sulfide. It is the hydrogen sulfide that gives the smell of rotten eggs.

With an oxygen content of nearly 40 percent, potassium nitrate is the oxidizer, or the power, behind black powder. The fuel of black powder is the charcoal—it is the source of carbon and is important to the burning nature of the powder. Sulfur is not an active part of black powder; in fact, black powder can be made without it. Sulfur acts as a binding agent, providing consistency in the burn and lowering the ignition temperature of the final mixture.

Compared to smokeless powder, black powder is very inefficient and very tolerant of variations in charge

weights. It takes much more black powder to achieve the same velocities as smokeless. Black powder also operates at much lower chamber pressures than smokeless. Most black powder guns operate at 15,000 to 20,000 psi compared to 30,000 to 35,000 psi for smokeless powders.

Black powder has historically come in seven different particle sizes: FFFFg, FFFg, FFg, Fg, Life Saving, Whaling, and Cannon. FFFFg is the finest grind of powder and is intended for use as a primer in the flashpan of a flintlock. FFFg is the standard granulation for use in all pistols and revolvers and in muzzleloading rifles up to .36 caliber. During all of the testing for this chapter, we used FFFg powder. FFFg particle sizes vary from .0170 to .0376 inch. FFg is a coarser grind intended for black powder rifles up to .58 caliber. The larger grain sizes are used in large caliber rifles and muskets and in cannons.

FFFg produces higher chamber pressures and higher energy product than FFg. The smaller FFFg particles have three times more surface area exposed to the ignition than FFg for the same weight of powder. Put another way, the FFg powder charge has to be 35 percent greater than the FFFg charge to achieve the same velocities.

Cap and ball revolvers got their slang name from the fact they use percussion caps to fire round balls. Percussion caps were a significant development in the history of all firearms.

In the early 1800s, a Scotsman by the name of Alexander Forsyth became frustrated with the flintlock primer. The separate primer charge would ignite and scare wild fowl before the main charge could be ignited. He wanted instantaneous ignition. As an amateur chemist, he knew of the explosive properties of fulminates of mercury. His concept was to preform a small clump of impact-sensitive explosive material and place it in the hole leading to the main powder charge.

In 1807, Forsyth got a patent for the percussion cap and set about to design a lock to use it. From Forsyth's concept, Joseph Manton developed the percussion cap as we know it in 1818. A lock was designed for the percussion cap by Samuel Colt in 1835. The first use of these firearms in battle was at the hand of British troops in China, circa 1841.

The percussion cap and lock was the first truly dependable firearm ignition system. While it took nearly 30 years to develop, the switch from flintlock to percussion cup was the fastest transition from one major design to another in the history of firearms.

The percussion principle was arguably the most significant innovation in the history of firearms. It led to self-contained metallic cartridges (first rimfire, then centerfire), breechloading firearms, and eventually to fully automatic firearms.

To close the account on percussion caps, in 1857 British Col. Edward Boxer developed a primer with an integral anvil for use in single flash hole centerfire metallic cartridges. American Col. Hiram Berdan developed a primer teamed with a metallic case using an extruded anvil and twin flash holes. Both Berdan and Boxer style cartridges exist to this day, with Americans favoring the British design for its ease of reloading.

In the mid-1800s, two bullet designs were available for handguns: the round ball and the conical ball, also called the elongated bullet. At this point, a sharp distinction must be made between the solid base conical bullet used in breechloading revolvers and the "Minie ball" conical bullet used in muzzleloading rifles.

The conical ball or conical bullet used in revolvers was identical in every way to the round-nose lead bullet still in use today. It was a round-nose, flat-base, full caliber bullet. The Minie ball was a round-nose, hollow-base bullet with a bullet diameter smaller than the caliber. Just like today's hollow-base wadcutter, the skirt on the Minie ball expanded upon ignition to fill the lands and grooves of the rifling.

The conical-profile Minie ball was used in combat because with it a black powder firearm could be fired more times before the barrel was too fouled to accept a projectile. The weight-forward, shuttlecock-style Minie bullet would fly true even if fouled rifling prevented it from being spin stabilized. The conical Minie ball was not better than the round ball in terms of sheer wound ballistics. It was, however, much better in terms of combat readiness. Revolvers did not use Minie balls.

The round ball has the reputation of losing half its velocity and two-thirds of its energy in the first 100 yards. Round ball does have poor aerodynamics, but it is not quite that bad.

The section density of a bullet is the ratio of the bullet's weight to the square of its diameter. Bullets with the same shape but with more weight for their caliber retain their velocity and energy better. The round ball has the lowest weight to caliber ratio and the lowest sectional density of any bullet.

It also has the least rifling bearing area of any bullet design.

The ballistic coefficient is the ability to overcome resistance in flight. It is the ratio of the bullet's sectional density to its so-called form factor, or how sleek the bullet is. The round ball has roughly half of the ballistic coefficient of a semiwadcutter bullet and roughly a third the ballistic coefficient of round-nose lead or conical ball. It may be hard to believe but the round ball has far worse aerodynamics than a full wadcutter bullet!

In comparison, the vintage conical bullet was as sleek as today's hardball. It holds its downrange velocity and energy much better. However, this is not an issue for black powder handguns, even those used for hunting. Velocity and energy loss in the first 100 yards is not the issue, velocity and energy loss in the target is! Just as round ball sheds more energy in air than conical ball, it also dumps more energy in tissue. The fluid physics is the same. Tissue is simply 800 times denser than air. Wound ballistics is where the round ball turns the tables on conical ball.

Conical or elongated bullets were developed in an attempt to improve long-range capabilities. At the time, the key to muzzleloaded wound ballistics was believed to be the heaviest bullet weight driven by whatever velocities the rifle or handgun could muster. The slow and heavy theory of stopping power did not begin with the .45 ACP in 1905, nor with the failure to stop the Moros in 1901!

Muzzleloaders had only two ways to gain bullet weight. One was to increase the bullet diameter or bore size. A .36 caliber round ball weighs 79 grains compared to a .44 caliber round ball at 141 grains. The only other way to increase mass if the bore size cannot change is to elongate the projectile by using a conical bullet, or conical ball. The .36 caliber conical tested for this chapter weighed 125 grains. This is almost as much as the increase from .36 to .44 caliber round ball.

The change from round ball to conical ball did not increase bullet energy. In fact, when maximum loads of each are used, the conical bullet has up to 33 percent less energy. However, it had 5 to 20 percent more momentum.

Unknown to some shooters, the great energy versus momentum debate was resolved before the dawn of smokeless powder. The high-energy round ball was the clear choice of early handgunners over the momentum-latent conical ball unless the deepest possible penetration was needed. Read what the legendary Elmer Keith said in his book *Sixguns:* "The conical bullets gave more range and penetration than round balls, but never were as accurate, nor did they kill game as well as the round ball. The pointed bullets seemingly slipped through game with a very small wound channel while the blunt round ball at high velocities tore a good wound channel all the way."

On impact, round ball deformed from a little to a lot and destroyed a lot of tissue. The penetration was plenty deep but the ball was frequently recovered, melted down, and used again. The conical bullet, however, formed a very long and narrow wound cavity and almost always exited. Unlike some modern round-nose lead bullets that tumble after impact, the blunt conical bullet drove straight through the target like a modern semiwadcutter.

Since the times of buffalo hunting, round ball has been made from the softest lead available. This was not always pure lead, but most of the time it was.

Pure lead upsets in the rifling better than lead alloys for better accuracy. It is denser than lead alloys, meaning better downrange velocity retention. It flattens more upon impact than lead alloys to transfer more energy. The flattened lead ball is less likely to exit and more likely to be recovered by the hunter for reuse.

Pure lead has a higher molecular adhesion than lead alloys. It also flattens to larger diameters without fragmenting. Finally, pure lead melts at a lower temperature (612°F) than lead alloys so the hunter can melt the bullet by campfire for recasting. While modern buckshot pellet contains varying amounts of antimony, the round ball made today by Speer and Hornady is pure lead.

For all of our muzzle velocity and wound ballistics testing, maximum powder charges were used. This means as much FFFg powder as would fit in the cylinder and still allow the round ball or conical to be seated deep enough to permit the cylinder to rotate. These maximum charges may be different than other published maximums. For example, 15 grains of powder is cited as a maximum for the .31 Colt. That amount of powder ended up flush with the cylinder face leaving no room for the round ball! A charge of 12 grains is the most the .31 caliber Baby Dragoon would accept. The same was true of the .31 Navy. While charges of up to 29 grains of FFFg are cited for use with the .375 caliber round ball, our 1851 Colt Navy

would accept a maximum of 22 grains.

The maximum load for the .44 Army appears to be between 35 and 37 grains of FFFg. This applies to both the open top 1861 Colt and the top strap 1858 Remington. This is the most powder that will fit in the chamber and still accept the round ball. This is very different from the modernized Ruger Old Army in .44 caliber, which accepts 40 to 45 grains of FFFg. The new Ruger also uses a .457 caliber round ball compared to the historically correct .454 caliber ball.

As a rule, maximum charges are used for hunting and battle. They are seldom used for plinking and target shooting, as they distort the soft lead bullet, producing the worst accuracy. Maximum charges also, of course, produce the most recoil. However, they produce the most velocity and energy too. They also produce the most stopping power and the least excessive penetration.

Gelatin analysis and the Fuller Index allow us to cut through the myth, superstition, and bravado associated with cap and ball revolvers. We now know exactly how these various black powder guns performed

In one test, the muzzle velocity of the .44 caliber round ball was increased through larger charges of black powder. As the velocity goes up, penetration becomes less and stopping power goes up.

The .44 Army round ball and the .44 Special lead hollowpoint are equal manstoppers. Both are effective with one shot about 75 percent of the time.

during gunfights. We know exactly how one compared to the other. We also know exactly how handguns and ammo of around 1850 compared to the handguns and ammo of today.

The first of the obvious comparisons is how the .44 caliber revolvers like the Remington 1858 Army, Colt 1860 Army, and Colt 1861 Army compared to the .36 caliber revolver like the Colt 1851 Navy. Union troops in the Civil War widely used the .44 Army, but the .36 Navy was also used by Yankee soldiers and was preferred by officers. Almost without exception, Confederate troops used the .36 Navy. The Rebel .36 caliber pistols were based on the Colt 1851 Navy but built by manufacturers like Griswold & Gunnison, Leech & Rigdon, Spiller & Burr, and Augusta Machine Works, all in Georgia.

The Navy designation typically meant .36 caliber while the Army name inferred .44 caliber. In reality, far more of the .36 caliber revolvers were carried by army soldiers than navy seamen. The steel frame .36 Navy was used by the North while the South generally used a brass frame version.

With both cap and ball revolvers using maximum powder charges behind round ball, our tests showed the .44 Army to be clearly superior to the .36 Navy. The .375 caliber 79-grain round ball had about a 100 fps muzzle velocity advantage over the .454 caliber

141-grain slug. However, the big-bore bullet packed 45 percent more energy.

Both loads produced the same very deep, 18 to 20 inch penetration depths. Neither of the round balls deformed much upon impact. The .44 Army ball produced almost twice the permanent crush cavity and more than twice the temporary stretch cavity.

In the final analysis, a round ball from a .36 Navy with a maximum charge has a Fuller Index of 59 percent one-shot stops. In comparison, the maximum loaded round ball from the .44 Army produces 75 percent one-shot stops. That is an incredible advantage for the soldiers armed with the .44 Army. It is like comparing the average .380 ACP hollowpoint to the .357 Magnum or .41 Magnum lead semiwadcutter. A 16 point spread in one-shot stops is like the actual street difference between the 9mm 115-grain JHP +P+ and the 9mm 147-grain subsonic JHP. Or the difference between the 9mm 115-grain JHP and the 9mm 115-grain FMJ hardball. Or the difference between the best .38 Special +P lead hollowpoint and the best .357 Magnum jacketed hollowpoint. Or the difference in

actual results from the best .45 ACP hollowpoint to the best .38 Special +P hollowpoint.

The .454 caliber round ball is so superior to the .375 caliber round ball that the big-bore ball can be downloaded from 35 to 30 grains of powder and fired from a short-barrel .44 Sheriff and still produce the same number of one-shot stops as a maximum loaded .36 Navy. The .36 Navy was an immensely popular revolver in the mid-1800s. However, the .44 Army was the superior manstopper by a margin that is hard to imagine.

The next of the obvious comparisons is between the round ball and the solid base conical bullet when fired from a handgun. Two comparisons from this test are possible. The first is the .36 caliber conical, which is almost a button nose wadcutter. The second is the .44 caliber conical, which is every bit a round-nose lead bullet.

Again the trends are clear. From a revolver, a round ball is profoundly more effective than a conical bullet of any design.

In gelatin, all of the round balls

This .44 caliber Sheriff is a short-barrel version of the Colt 1860 Army. The .44 Sheriff and the full-length .36 Navy have the same stopping power.

The .44 Army can fire (left to right) the 141-grain round ball, 200-grain conical, and 191-grain conical hollowpoint. The round ball was the top performer.

The .31 Pocket round ball produces the same stopping power as the average .22 Long Rifle lead hollowpoint. Its 30 percent one-shot stop rating beats all the .25 ACP loads.

deformed slightly. None were recovered as a perfect sphere. The dead soft balls upset in the rifling to form a short bearing area. The leading and trailing edge of the lower velocity round balls remained fully round. However, the higher velocity impacts flattened the ball to some extent. The balls that hit the gelatin at over 1000 fps could best be described as a flat point round-based, flat nose, or blunt nose bullet. Of course, the base of the bullet is easy to tell. It has the deep indentations from the burning black powder.

From the .36 Navy and .44 Army,

the round ball was an average of 40 percent faster and packed an average of 30 percent more energy with 8 percent less recoil. The conical ball from these two revolvers penetrated almost 4 inches deeper in gelatin. This was wasted. The 19 inch average from the round ball in these two calibers is more than enough.

The real issue is, of course, stopping power. From the .36 Navy and .44 Army, the round ball was 11 to 14 points more effective in one-shot stops than conical ball, according to the Fuller Index. The .36 Navy 79-grain round ball was 59 percent effective. The 125-grain conical was merely 45 percent effective.

The conical bullet from the .44 Walker was exactly the same story even though the Walker revolver was specifically designed to accept the long-range conical bullet. And even though the 141-grain round ball and 200-grain conical generated the same muzzle energy, the round ball turned this energy into tissue damage and massive disruption. The conical bullet turned the same energy into extremely deep penetration. In the final analysis, however, the round ball from the .44 Walker held the same kind of 16 point

one-shot stop advantage over the conical as the round ball in .36 Navy and .44 Army held over their conical bullets. Conical bullets offer the handgunner no advantages whatsoever over the round ball for either defensive use or hunting game up to the size of whitetail deer or the toughness of wild boar.

The next of the obvious comparisons is between the various black powder calibers and their closest smokeless powder counterparts. We start with the Colt .31 Pocket. The .31 caliber five-shot revolver was popular during the Civil War era and the Gold Rush days. It was very small and concealable compared to the .36 and .44 caliber six-shot revolvers of the day. From an 1848 Colt Baby dragoon with a 6 inch barrel (made by Armi San Marco and imported by Dixie Gun Works), the 46-grain round ball driven by 12 grains of powder reached 821 fps. The 69 ft-lbs. of energy and 12.9 inch penetration depth resulted in a 30 percent one-shot stop rating.

The modern cartridge with wound ballistics closest to the .31 Pocket is the .22 Long Rifle with 36- to 38-grain lead hollowpoints. These rimfire loads when fired from a handgun pack a bit more energy than the .31 Pocket, but the .31 Pocket penetrates 2 to 3 inches deeper in gelatin. The rimfire hollowpoints have one-shot stops from 27 to 30 percent.

The .31 Pocket outperforms all of

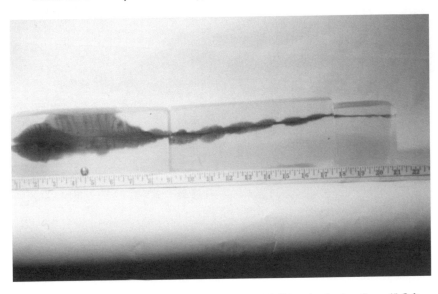

The stretch cavity from the .44 Army 141-grain round ball is twice the size of any .45 Colt hollowpoint. The .44 Army is the better manstopper.

The recovered and unfired .31 Pocket 46-grain round ball is shown with the .32 ACP 71-grain hardball. The .31 Pocket produces just half the energy of the .32 ACP.

The .36 Navy 79-grain round ball is as effective as the average .380 ACP jacketed hollowpoint. This black powder bullet has a 59 percent one-shot stop rating.

The recovered and unfired .36 Navy 79-grain round ball is shown with the .380 ACP 95-grain hardball. The round ball bullet is a much better manstopper than the hardball bullet.

the loads in .25 ACP. The black powder round ball has a little more energy than the .25 ACP hollowpoints and produces about the same penetration in gelatin. However, its larger caliber and greater energy give it the edge. The .31 Pocket far outclasses all of the .25 ACP hardball loads.

On the other hand, the .31 Pocket falls well short of the .32 ACP. While the 46-grain round ball has a Fuller Index of 30 percent, the .32 ACP 71-grain hardball checks in at 42 percent. Of course, the .32 ACP has almost twice the energy of a maximum loaded .31 Pocket. Overall, the .31 Pocket is most similar to the .22 Long Rifle, better than the .25 ACP, but quite far from the .32 ACP.

The .36 caliber is next. This was an extremely popular revolver for soldiers, lawmen, gunfighters, and ordinary citizens alike. U.S. Marshal Wild Bill Hickok carried a pair of .36 caliber 1851 Colt Navy revolvers. Gen. George Custer carried a pair of .36 1861 Colt Navy revolvers.

Fired from a F.Lli Pietta-made 1851 Colt Navy imported by Navy Arms, the 79-grain round ball driven by 22 grains of FFFg hit 1038 fps. This load produced 189 ft-lbs. of energy, 18.3 inches of penetration, and 59 percent one-shot stops.

The .36 Navy 79-grain round ball performs almost exactly like a .380 ACP hollowpoint. In general, it has the same energy and crush cavity

volume, a slightly larger stretch cavity, and much deeper average penetration. The wound ballistics on the .36 Navy calculate to 59 percent one-shot stops. The actual stopping power for the various versions of the standard-pressure .380 ACP hollowpoint averages 61 percent one-shot stops. Like it or not, old Wild Bill was packin' a .380 Auto.

The black powder .36 Navy enjoyed the reputation of being a better manstopper than the smokeless powder .38 Special. Again, Elmer Keith: "For its size and weight nothing

is so deadly as the round ball of pure lead when driven at fairly good velocity. The .36 Navy with full loads was a far better man killer than any .38 Special used in gunfights."

Our tests in gelatin confirmed those locker room and battlefield stories. In standard-pressure loadings, the .38 Special 158-grain round-nose lead and semiwadcutter varied from 45 percent to 53 percent effective. This is significantly less than the 59 percent from the .36 Navy. The 158-grain lead fired from the standard-pressure .38 Special almost exactly matches the

The 46-grain round ball from the .31 caliber Baby Dragoon penetrates 12.9 inches of gelatin. The .31 Pocket outperforms the .25 ACP but not the .32 ACP.

The 79-grain round ball from the .36 Navy makes a very deep wound cavity. The stretch cavity is similar to a .38 Special +P hollowpoint.

With a flash of fire, sound of thunder, and cloud of smoke, this .44 caliber Remington 1858 Army pushed a 141-grain round ball to 935 fps.

wound ballistics from the .36 Navy 125-grain conical bullet. The .36 Navy, however, falls well behind .38 Special jacketed and lead hollowpoints driven by +P pressures. These have 65 to 78 percent street records, but of course the .38 Special +P also generates 30 to 50 percent more energy than the .36 Navy.

Other modern cartridges near the 59 percent one-shot stops of the .36 Navy round ball include both the 9mm 115-grain hardball and the .45 ACP 230-grain hardball. Both of these FMJ auto pistol bullets have an actual street record of 63 percent one-shot stops.

Overall, think of the .36 Navy as somewhere between an average .380

ACP hollowpoint and 9mm hardball. In today's thinking, that kind of effectiveness is the absolute rock bottom in terms of personal defense. Most of us would opt for the .44 caliber, and that is next.

The .44 caliber revolver was the big bore of its day. It was to the mid-1800s soldier and lawman what the .45 Colt became in the late 1800s and what the .45 ACP has been since the early 1900s. It was the most popular revolver with Union troops during the War Between the States.

From both an 1861 Colt Navy and an 1858 Remington Army, the 141-grain round ball driven by 35 grains of black powder was clocked at 935 fps. This gives the dead soft .454 caliber slug 274 ft-lbs. of energy. The result was 19.8 inches of penetration and a Fuller Index of 75 percent one-shot stops.

This is the same energy level as the .38 Special +P but below the .44 Special, .45 ACP, and .45 Colt. The 75 percent one-shot stop rating from the .44 Army round ball is a near-match for the .38 Special +P 158-grain SWC-HP, .357 Magnum, 158-grain SWC, .44 Special 200-grain SWC-HP, .44 Magnum medium-velocity 240-grain SWC, and the actual results for the .45 Colt 225-grain JHPs and LHPs.

In terms of bullet design, the .454 caliber 141-grain round ball was more effective during gunfights than .45 ACP hardball, .45 Colt round nose, and .44 Special round nose even though these loads generated up to 50 percent more muzzle energy. The reason for the superiority, once again, is that round ball is a better manstopper than conical bullets like hardball and round-nose lead. The black powder results themselves bear this out. The .44 Army 141-grain round ball is 11 points more effective in one-shot stops than the .44 Army 200-grain conical bullet.

If forced to pick one cartridge and load that is the modern day equal to the .44 Army, it would be the Federal .44 Special 200-grain semiwadcutter HP. This lead hollowpoint and the .44

Army round ball have similar energy levels, almost identical penetration depths, similar recovered diameters and crush cavities, and the same stopping power potential. The high-drag round ball, however, generates over three times the stretch cavity of the .44 Special hollowpoint.

One of the most enjoyable black powder revolvers of this test was the .44 Sheriff, a short-barrel version of the 1860 Colt Army. The term Sheriff was generic for any shortened version of any caliber revolver. Then as now, the sheriff was the highest ranking law enforcement official, but it was the deputy sheriffs who did the most gunslinging. The sheriff carried a shortened version of a black powder revolver often concealed much like today's police brass carry short-barrel concealable guns. Our .44 Sheriff had a 5 inch barrel, while the 1860 Colt Army upon which it is based originally had an 8 inch barrel.

The 141-grain round ball powered by 30 grains of FFFg had a modest 756 fps muzzle velocity, but it produced the deepest penetration of any round ball in this test. The .44 Sheriff kicked about 30 percent more than the .36 Navy, but both produced 59 percent one-shot stops. Of all the cap and ball revolvers tested, the .44 Sheriff was the author's favorite.

In the mid-1800s, the next step up in power from the .44 Army was a big one—the .44 caliber Colt Walker and later the .44 Colt Dragoon. The Walker could handle 60 grains of black powder while the Dragoon was typically loaded with 50 grains. Remember now, the Ruger Old Army with its 40- to 45-grain powder charges was not available in the 1800s. It was either the .44 Army with 35 grains of powder or the Dragoon with 50 grains. Also remember that the vast majority of shootouts with handguns involved either the .36 Navy or .44 Army. The Walker and Dragoon were simply too big to carry. They were called "horse" revolvers since only mounted troops would carry them.

The .44 caliber 1847 Walker is the largest production revolver ever made by Colt. This heavy 9 inch barrel revolver was carried only by horse-mounted troops.

The .44 caliber 1847 Colt Walker was the magnum of its day, with round ball velocities averaging 1287 fps. This 150 year old cap and ball revolver is a better manstopper than most of today's police loads.

So much has been written about the Walker it is often overlooked that only 1,100 were ever made. The 1847 Colt Walker, which celebrated its 150th anniversary in 1997, was replaced by the 1848 Colt Dragoon. The Walker was the first revolver adopted for use by the U.S. military and the largest production revolver ever made by Colt.

From a .44 Walker with a 9 inch barrel made by Aldo Uberti packed with 60 grains of powder, the 141-grain round ball reached an impressive 1287 fps. That translates to 519 ft-lbs. of energy, more than any 9mm +P+,

The .44 Walker round ball produces the same 87 percent one-shot stops as a .41 Magnum jacketed hollowpoint. The .44 Walker and the .44 Dragoon are extremely powerful, even by today's standards.

The .44 Walker-fired 141-grain round ball expands to .53 caliber in gelatin. Neither the conical bullet nor the conical hollowpoint expanded.

.40 S&W, .44 Special, .45 Colt, .44 Magnum medium velocity, and standard-pressure .45 ACP. This energy level is similar to the .357 Magnum 158-grain and the .45 ACP 185-grain +P ammo.

In spite of this energy level and the use of solid round ball bullets, the .44 Walker penetrated just 17.8 inches of gelatin. In the process it generated a stretch cavity rivaling the best from the .357 Magnum, 10mm Auto, and .41 Magnum.

The .44 Walker was considered the "magnum" of its day. While that is correct, it also understates the power of this famous sidearm. In real manstopping terms, the .44 Walker 141-grain round ball produced an estimated 87 percent one-shot stops. That makes the 1847 Colt Walker more effective than any other handgun until the introduction of the .44 Magnum in 1956.

The .44 Walker round ball had more stopping power than any of the early loads in .38 Special, 9mm, .38 Super, .357 Magnum, .44 Special, .45 Colt, and .45 ACP. In fact, it even outpowered the original 240-grain SWC version of the mighty .44 Magnum. Only the somewhat recent development of high-performance hollowpoints has allowed some of these smokeless calibers to outperform the black powder Colt Walker.

The closest comparison to the .44

Walker 141-grain round ball in terms of muzzle velocity, penetration depth, stretch cavity, and one-shot stops is the .41 Magnum hollowpoint. The overall wound ballistics are the same even though the .41 Magnum hollowpoints have 20 to 50 percent more energy. As an aside, the .44 Walker round ball is far and away more effective than the .41 Magnum 210-grain SWC, .44 Magnum 240-grain SWC, and .45 Colt 250-grain SWC. In fact, the Walker is similar in many ways to the average .44 Magnum 240-grain hollowpoint.

The one exception to the dominating .44 Walker wound ballistics is when conical bullets are used. The gun was specifically designed for conical bullets. The 200-grain conical at 1082 fps exactly equalled the energy of the 141-grain round ball. However, when conical bullets were used from the .44 Walker, the stopping power dropped dramatically from 87 percent to 71 percent.

Perhaps the ultimate nostalgic comparison is between the .44 Army firing the 141-grain round ball and the .45 Colt firing the 255-grain round-nose lead. The metallic cartridge, smokeless-powder big bore has a

muzzle velocity of 860 fps and 419 ft-lbs. of energy. This means it is 75 fps slower than the .44 Army but 145 ft-lbs. more powerful. However, the .45 Colt does not turn energy into wounding like the .44 Army. The 255-grain round nose penetrates 28.5 inches compared to 19.8 inches for the round ball. The stretch cavity of the round ball is 75 percent larger.

In the final analysis, the .45 Colt 255-grain round nose has an actual street record of 69 percent, with the Fuller Index in close agreement at 68

The .44 Walker 141-grain round ball produces a stretch cavity as large as many .44 Magnum jacketed hollowpoints and larger than most .357 Magnum hollowpoints.

CAP AND BALL WOUND BALLISTICS

percent. The .44 Army is a 75 percent effective load. It must be considered the better manstopper.

One of the comparisons was done more for wound ballistics education than anything else. This was the step-up analysis taking the .454 caliber 141-grain round ball and increasing the muzzle velocity in five increments from 756 fps to 1287 fps. The only variable was impact velocity. Everything else was the same.

The first step showed the effects of shorter barrel lengths with black powder. A 30-grain charge from an 8 inch barrel revolver resulted in an 840 fps muzzle velocity. The same powder charge from a 5 inch Sheriff produced 756 fps. That's an 84 fps loss in velocity, a drop in energy of 42 ft-lbs., and an eight point drop in one-shot stops. Overall, that's a pretty big change.

As we increased the powder charge from 30 to 40, then to 50, then to 60 grains, the results were absolutely predictable. Muzzle velocity steadily increased. The penetration from the round ball steadily decreased. The crush cavity remained almost unchanged but the stretch cavity greatly increased. From the .44 Sheriff to the .44 Walker, the energy almost tripled; however the stretch cavity increased seven-fold.

The stopping power went up as it always does when velocity is increased even with nonexpanding bullets. We picked up eight points in the one-shot stops for every increase of 10 grains of powder up to 50 grains. This levelled off at the .44 Dragoon. The 10 grain increase from the 50 grains in the .44 Dragoon to the 60 in the .44 Walker only increased the stopping power from 85 percent to 87 percent.

Thanks goes to thank Butch Winter of Dixie Gun Works, Maria Uberti of Uberti USA, and Paul Reed of Navy Arms for supplying a wide cross-section of cap and ball revolvers for this chapter.

TABLE 24-1
CLASSIC CAP & BALL WOUND BALLISTICS

Caliber	Firearm	Bullet	FFFg	Vel. fps	Energy ft-lbs.	Gel. Pene. inches	Recovered Diameter inch	Stretch Cavity inches	One-Shot Stop
.31 Pocket	Colt 1848 Baby Dragoon	46 gr. Round Ball	12 gr	821	69	12.9	.31	6.3	30%
.36 Navy	Colt 1851 Navy	79 gr. Round Ball	22 gr	1038	189	18.3	.37	17.5	59%
.44 Army	Colt 1861 New Army	141 gr. Round Ball	35 gr	935	274	19.8	.48	38.8	75%
.44 Walker	Colt 1847 Walker	141 gr. Round Ball	60 gr	1287	519	17.8	.53	79.6	87%

TABLE 24-2
.44 CALIBER ROUND BALL BALLISTICS

Caliber	Firearm	Bullet	FFFg	Vel. fps	Energy ft-lbs.	Gel. Pene. in.	Rec. Dia. in.	Stretch Cav. in.	One-Shot Stop
.44	Colt 1860 Army Sheriff	141 gr. Round Ball	30	756	179	21.8	.45	1.6	59%
.44	Colt 1861 New Army	141 gr. Round Ball	30	840	221	20.5	.48	35.2	67%
.44	Ruger Old Army	141 gr. Round Ball	40	1031	333	19.0	.48	42.4	79%
.44	Colt 1848 Dragoon Round	141 gr. Ball	50	1181	437	18.2	.51	66.7	85%
.44	Colt 1847 Walker	141 gr. Round Ball	60	1287	519	17.8	.53	79.6	87%

TABLE 24-3
ROUND BALL VS. CONICAL BULLETS

Caliber	Bullet	FFFg	Vel. fps	Energy ft-lbs.	Gel. Pene. inches	Recovered Diameter inch	One-Shot Stop
.36 Navy	79 gr. Round Ball	22	1038	189	18.3	.37	59%
.36 Navy	125 gr. Conical	18	695	134	21.0	.37	45%
.44 Army	141 gr. Round Ball	35	935	274	19.8	.48	75%
.44 Army	200 gr. Conical	25	726	234	24.0	.45	64%
.44 Army	191 gr. Conical HP	30	934	370	25.0	.45	73%
.44 Walker	141 gr. Round Ball	60	1287	519	17.8	.53	87%
.44 Walker	200 gr. Conical	50	1082	520	28.0	.45	71%

TABLE 24-4
PERCUSSION CAP VS. CENTERFIRE AMMO

Caliber	Bullet	Vel. fps	Energy ft-lbs.	Gel. Pene. inches	Recovered Diameter	Stretch Cavity inches	One-Shot Stop inch
.31 Pocket	46 gr. Round Ball	821	69	12.9	.31	6.3	30%
.22 Long Rifle	37 gr. Lead HP	975	78	10.3	.22	5.6	29%
.36 Navy	79 gr. Round Ball	1038	189	18.3	.37	17.5	59%
.380 ACP	88 gr. JHP	1000	196	17.0	.36	9.1	58%
.44 Army	141 gr. Round Ball	935	274	19.8	.48	38.8	75%
.44 Special	200 gr. Lead HP	810	292	19.0	.48	11.1	73%
.44 Walker	141 gr. Round Ball	1287	519	17.8	.53	79.6	87%
.41 Magnum	175 gr. JHP	1250	608	14.0	.64	83.2	89%

CHAPTER 25

Ammunition Evaluation and Selection:

U.S. Border Patrol, 1970-2000

by John Jacobs

The jackrabbit was about to die, and I did not feel good about it. The shot was not challenging: the big jack was no more than 10 yards away sitting perfectly motionless, angled slightly away from me and presenting a shot that would allow the 110-grain .38 Special +P+ "Treasury" load to strike behind the left front leg, through the heart, and out forward of the right shoulder area. It was not the type of shot that a sportsman would take unless hunting for the sole purpose of adding meat to the freezer. Even with that in mind, most would pass the shot, for the desert jack is long on sinew and short on meat.

The year was 1980, and the need for the shot was urgent. The U.S. Border Patrol had been issuing .357 Magnum 158-grain softpoint ammunition to field agents since the early 1970s, and it was now being replaced by the .38 Special 110-grain jacketed hollowpoint "T" load. We were delighted that we were finally allowed to carry hollowpoint projectiles.

We were well aware of the shortcomings of the heavy softpoint slug that was being replaced. While it was above average in its ability to incapacitate assailants, it could also

The INS is the largest federal law enforcement agency in America. The Border Patrol is the uniformed branch of the INS. INS officers are involved in more gunfights than all other federal agencies combined.

Over time, the Border Patrol has used (left to right): .45 ACP ball, .38 Special RNL, .357 Magnum JSP, .38 Special +P+ JHP, .357 Magnum JHP, .38 Super JHP, 9mm +P+ JHP, and .40 S&W JHP.

Border Patrol agents during quarterly qualifying in the late 1950s. In 1958, the Border Patrol upgraded from the .38 Special to the .357 Magnum.

easily penetrate through the human torso or limbs and create a lethal hazard for other agents and innocent bystanders. It also had a curious delayed effect at times. In an incident that had occurred on the border in California, an agent had handcuffed two aliens together and they had managed to overpower him. They began to drag him by the arm back toward a hole in the international fence. The agent knew that he would not survive if they were to drag him into Mexico. He managed to get his revolver out and fired one shot up toward one of the assailants. The shot startled the two, and the one who had not been shot at anxiously asked his amigo if he had been hit. His friend replied with a laugh, " No, he is shooting blanks!" They continued to drag him several more feet before the one who had made this comment collapsed and died. The projectile had angled up through his chest, causing massive damage and internal bleeding, but he had not even realized he had been hit!

Still, we were disturbed by the fact that we were being forced to give up the .357 Magnum and were ordered to carry a .38 Special that was touted as being just as good or better than our softpoint magnums. This claim was based on the extensive testing done primarily by the U.S. Army Aberdeen Test Center and the National Bureau

This Border Patrol agent, circa 1951, is guarding a point near El Paso on the Rio Grande. He is armed with a Colt .38 Special revolver firing 158-grain RNL.

of Standards through funding provided by the Law Enforcement Assistance Administration (LEAA). This testing continued through most of the 1970s. It was unquestionably the most scientific and analytical evaluation of handgun ammunition wounding effectiveness ever undertaken by the federal

government. It was the first evaluation that was specifically tasked with examining ammunition for use in the law enforcement mission.

Although this evaluation had been conducted with the highest degree of scientific integrity, the published Relative Incapacitation Index (RII) resulting from this study

These Border Patrol agents are shown during night training with their .357 Magnum revolvers, circa 1972. Officers practiced one-hand shooting in case the other hand was holding a flashlight.

From 1982 to 1986, the Border Patrol used this .38 Special +P+ 110-grain JHP "Treasury Load." This load has produced 83 percent one-shot stops.

contained disturbing anomalies. These anomalies, combined with considerations of both practical and political natures, resulted in the adoption of the .38 Special 110-grain +P+ by many federal, state, and local law enforcement agencies. I will cover this issue in more depth at a later point. Back to jack!

My only purpose for shooting the jackrabbit was to test our new duty load. I was apprehensive about the capability of this light, fast-moving projectile to perform at a level anywhere near that of any of the .357 Magnum loadings. I was about to be surprised.

The shot struck the jack and the

results were instantaneous. The rabbit fell on the spot and immediately went into its death throes. He never knew what hit him. I had shot quite a few animals with a handgun both in hunting and euthanasia situations, and I had rarely seen such an instant and permanent reaction to a hit. I was impressed, but I was about to get a second surprise.

I went forward to inspect the jack, which had ceased all movement in less than five seconds after the shot had been fired. The bullet had struck the animal just in front of the left forequarter as intended. It had angled through the heart and lungs, destroying them completely as I later discovered during a quick autopsy of the animal. I was starting to get excited about the possibility that this new round might indeed be effective until I turned the rabbit over to inspect the exit wound. My blood ran cold. There was no exit wound. The bullet had expended all of its energy after traveling less than 4 inches through an animal that was far easier to penetrate than a human assailant. I quickly enlightened other agents regarding this strange performance. The initial result had been excellent on a rabbit, but the lack of penetration was downright frightening.

During the four year period that the INS issued the .38 Special 110-grain +P+ JHP, results were erratic. The velocity of the round was supposed to be in the vicinity of 1200 fps. The actual velocity from a Service issued revolver with a 4 inch barrel never reached 1200 feet per second and averaged between 1050–1125 fps. Most importantly, when the ammunition was carried in a plainclothes revolver with a barrel length of 2.5 to 3 inches, the projectile velocity fell well below 1000 fps and expansion of the projectile was not reliable.

From my point of view, the worst characteristic of the round was its inability to penetrate soft cover such as the brush encountered in our desert environment as well as automotive sheet metal and windshield glass. We had fired into many a junked automobile and found that while penetration might occur, the remaining projectile energy was not sufficient to provide any reasonable expectation of assailant incapacitation.

The issue finally came to a head during shooting incidents in Texas in 1983. In the first of these, an assailant armed with a 9mm Browning Hi-Power and ball ammunition had engaged an agent armed with a 4 inch revolver and the .38 Treasury load. The assailant was in the driver's seat of a pick-up truck and was attempting to fire at a downward angle at the agent, who had ducked down several yards behind the tailgate of the truck. The agent had instantly recognized the tailgate as potential cover between himself and his assailant. As the two exchanged shots, the 9mm projectiles penetrated the tailgate, with one of the rounds wounding the agent in the arm. The agent, attempting to fire back through the tailgate, was dismayed to see his rounds bouncing off it. Fortunately, he survived the confrontation.

In another incident, a mental case on a detention bus snatched a revolver loaded with the .38 +P+ from an INS officer's holster. One round was fired at the officer as he fled from the bus, striking him high in the right tricep. The round pulled the officer's shirt into the wound and did not penetrate enough to cause any serious damage. A second shot was fired at point blank range downward into the back of a detainee on the bus. This round struck the shoulder blade and bounced back. The shoulder blade was not broken and the damage amounted to a minor flesh wound. A third shot was fired and struck another detainee in the head. This one penetrated the skull, instantly killing the subject.

As the deranged suspect got off the bus and behind cover, one of my former students got into a position of cover about 15 yards behind him and ordered him to drop the gun. The

suspect turned and raised his weapon. The agent fired a careful shot dead center on the suspect but was amazed when he showed no signs of being hit. He fired two more well-aimed shots that brought the suspect down.

As a testimonial to the importance of using one's sights, I asked the agent how he had known that he had scored a center hit if the suspect had not reacted to the impact of the projectile. He stated, "Well Mr. Jacobs, you know I'm a pretty good shot, and the sights never moved from the center of his chest when the shot broke. I knew it was a good hit." He was right. The demand for better ammunition was insistent, and something had to be done.

ADOPTION OF THE .357 MAGNUM 110-GRAIN JHP CARTRIDGE

In 1984 I had been transferred from my duty station on the border in Nogales, Arizona, to the firearms division of the U.S. Border Patrol Academy in Glynco, Georgia. Although this transfer brought me a reduction in pay, I considered this easily offset by the opportunity to work with Supervisory Patrol Agent Kent Williams, one of the most knowledgeable law enforcement firearms and ammunition experts in the United States. He is also one of the finest law enforcement trainers I have ever known and is still gifting others with his talents as a firearms training officer at the U.S. Border Patrol Academy in Charleston, South Carolina.

It was not long after my arrival at the Border Patrol Academy that Kent, Supervisory Border Patrol Agent Bob Rogers, and myself were tasked by Border Patrol Headquarters to evaluate ammunition and make a recommendation to either stay with the .38 Special Treasury load or change to something else. The only limitation placed on us was that the recommended ammunition had to be capable of being fired in Service issue

.357 Magnum revolvers. Since there was a policy being adopted to allow agents to carry personally owned semiautomatic pistols, we were also asked to provide ammunition recommendations for reliable DA/SA semiautomatic pistols.

This was the first opportunity that the U.S. Border Patrol had to conduct tests with the purpose of selecting duty ammunition for its agents. Thanks to the LEAA tests of the 1970s, we were no longer limited to ball or softpoint ammunition. We accepted this challenge from Border Patrol Headquarters with great enthusiasm.

1984 AMMUNITION SURVEY

We began our quest by making a telephonic survey of federal, state, and local law enforcement agencies. The purpose of this survey was to identify which handgun calibers and ammunition were performing well and why. Kent, Bob, and I spent countless hours on the phone during this phase of the project. We interviewed subject matter experts within most federal agencies. We also interviewed personnel from many state police and highway patrol organizations as well as municipal agencies as large as the NYPD and as small as three-officer departments. The information came in from California to Maine, from the Florida Keys to Alaska. We additionally interviewed many officers who had been involved in two or more shooting incidents. These officers were able to provide us with invaluable information concerning the reality of armed confrontations in a law enforcement environment and how ammunition can and cannot be expected to perform.

Several of these individuals had been involved in four or more shooting incidents. While they confessed to having somewhat blurred recollections of details from their first experience, they had very concise and detailed recollections about the incidents that followed. Of all the information that we gathered from this survey, the feedback from these heroic individuals was the most consistent and was remarkably free of ambiguities. Their testimony also helped us to formulate doctrines regarding the delivery of multiple shots, a definition of stopping power that we will discuss later, and identifying when and why officers stop firing at a suspect they have engaged.

Our survey included agencies that were using everything from .380s to .44 Magnums. We were even fortunate enough to find agencies that were using revolvers in .45 Long Colt and numerous others that were using 9mm and .45 ACP automatics.

We were confident that this survey would provide us with some clear-cut answers regarding handgun ammunition performance. We were right, but not in the way we had anticipated.

The survey results were dismaying. For every one agency or subject matter expert who felt a particular caliber or ammunition effective, there was another equally reputable resource that had found almost identical caliber and ammunition ineffective.

Some of these anomalies were for obvious reasons. Ammunition that worked well in Florida or Texas might not work well in Alaska or Minnesota because of the difference in clothing worn by assailants in these different climes. Unfortunately, in most cases these anomalies were not as obvious and many times did not seem to exist.

Although it appeared that all of our efforts had gained us little, I decided to review the results one more time using a different approach. I took all of the notes we had accumulated and started over again. This time, I decided to look only for similarities between ammunition that agencies and individuals had listed as consistent and reliable performers in the law enforcement context.

Suddenly, we had some surprising but logical answers.

Our problem was that we had started out expecting to find particular calibers and loadings to be more effective than others. We assumed that considerations of caliber, bullet weight, bullet velocity, and expansion capability would provide the answers we were looking for. In fact, they did, but not in the way we had expected. When we examined the individual characteristics of a cartridge, the consistencies in performance were clouded by our attention to the physical characteristics of the ammunition. When we reviewed the data a second time, the one factor that was present in the majority of reliable performers was dramatically consistent and deceptively simple. All of the ammunition that was trusted by these law enforcement officers developed levels of kinetic energy (Ke) that started at about 400 ft-lbs. and went as high as 750 ft-lbs. The most reliable caliber, regardless of bullet weight, velocity, or nose configuration, was the .357 Magnum that developed energy levels ranging from 415 ft-lbs. to 550 ft-lbs. Even rounds that failed to develop a minimum of 400 ft-lbs. of energy supported kinetic energy as a mathematical constant for performance. It appeared that 185-grain and 200-grain .45 ACP projectiles were favored over 230-grain projectiles. High-velocity 9mm ammunition had established a higher confidence level than standard-velocity 9mm ammunition. Most importantly, there was not another single factor within this survey that could be identified as a constant for reliable performance.

THE PENETRATION ISSUE

Although we had expected penetration to be an issue, it had not surfaced in our interviews. Few of the persons interviewed indicated lack of penetration as a causative factor in a failure to stop an assailant. This was quite surprising to us because we were deeply concerned about the lack of penetration we had experienced with the .38 Treasury load and had erroneously thought this concern would be exposed as an important factor in ammunition failures. Surprisingly, many agencies that were using the .38 110-grain +P+ had a fair amount of confidence in it even though they stated a preference for a more powerful round.

We agreed that projectile penetration was an issue for the Border Patrol even though it did not appear to be a critical factor for other agencies. We knew that our ammunition had to provide penetration through soft cover and heavy clothing. We also knew that the majority of our shooting incidents were taking place in areas of thick brush or during traffic stops involving such hard cover as automotive sheet metal and windshields. Penetration had to be an important factor in our ammunition recommendations.

ADVERSE EFFECTS OF THE LEAA LAW ENFORCEMENT AMMUNITION STUDIES

As I noted earlier, the LEAA studies of the 1970s legitimized the use of hollowpoint ammunition by law enforcement officers. This was a major step forward in providing officers with the proper tools for surviving deadly force confrontations. This one step alone fully justified the tremendous efforts and expenditures that were poured into this project. I, for one, will always be grateful to those who firmly stood their ground and insisted that law enforcement officers needed expanding ammunition even when it was most politically unacceptable to suggest such a radical change in national policy.

While these studies brought us the expanding bullet, they denied us the necessary attribute of sufficient projectile penetration. As in many such endeavors that break new ground, the project evolved from sound logic based on premises that were adversely, fatally flawed. No scientific endeavor is immune to this vulnerability, and the LEAA study was no exception to the rule. Unfortunately, when a premise is flawed, then all that follows is also flawed no matter how conscientious the scientist or how flawless the procedure. The Relative Incapacitation Index (RII) that resulted from the criteria established for these tests was awash in obvious anomalies that defied natural law. The RII was heavily ridiculed and hotly contested by many organizations and individuals and has never been accepted in the ballistic community as a valid gauge of projectile effectiveness. So what went wrong?

Keep in mind that the study that resulted in the RII was conducted in a political atmosphere of extreme civil unrest. In the decade from 1965 through 1975 the United States experienced a level of civil disobedience not seen since the Civil War. With this unrest came acts of extreme violence against law enforcement officers, who were the visible representatives of the establishment. While the LEAA study resulted from a need to protect the protectors, it was also duly influenced by the political perception that the country could ill afford a repeat of Kent State.

The LEAA study was embraced by law enforcement because it promised the potential for dramatic improvement in law enforcement ammunition "stopping power." It was embraced by the politically liberal because five of the seven criteria for the study focused on reducing the risk of injury to both the involved felon and third innocent parties. In other words, the study was heavily slanted to protect not the police officer but everyone else who might be in the vicinity of the officer should the use of deadly force occur!

Without getting into the

particulars of this study, it is sufficient to say that overpenetration of a suspect was considered unacceptable performance for law enforcement handgun ammunition. The scientific evidence proved convincingly that expanding ammunition greatly reduced the potential for overpenetration. At the same time, it was argued that this ammunition would expend enough energy to "incapacitate" a suspect while causing less permanent injury then would conventional ball ammunition. It was proposed that the violent disruption of tissue and organs caused through the vehicle of temporary cavitation resulting from the rapid dispersion of kinetic energy released by an expanding projectile would neatly resolve the concerns of all parties on both sides of this political issue. The icing on the cake, and the source of the dramatic anomalies in the RII, was the belief that the retained energy of the projectile was most efficient in its incapacitation effect if dispersed within the first 6 inches of travel through human tissue. While the "computer man" model used for these tests provided convincing evidence that deep penetration was also an effective means of incapacitation, it was the low penetration/large temporary cavity model that become the basis for the RII.

The published findings of these tests were to become the guiding force for the selection of law enforcement handgun ammunition for many years to come. It was from the results and recommendations of these tests that the Border Patrol had been mandated to discontinue the use of the deeply penetrating 158-grain .357 Magnum and initiate the use of the .38 SPL +P+ Treasury load. In all fairness to the study, it never recommended a 110-grain +P+ .38 Special as the most efficient projectile. The .38 +P+ evolved from the reality that most agencies were armed with .38 caliber firearms. The 110-grain jacketed hollowpoint projectile traveling at a

velocity of 1200 fps appeared to be a significant improvement over the commonly issued .38 158-grain ball round issued by most law enforcement agencies. Later in this chapter I will reveal actual recommendations of the test personnel. I have yet to find anyone who can disagree with these findings, including even the strongest proponents of the FBI test protocol!

THE 1984 BORDER PATROL DILEMMA

Kent Williams, Bob Rogers, and I all knew that we could not totally ignore the mandates resulting from the LEAA tests. In spite of this, we decided that now was the time to gather as much data as possible regarding caliber and projectile performance. We had only three criteria established for performance. They were, in order of importance: (1) must have proper ergonomic interface with the shooter (controllability), (2) must produce a minimum of 400 ft-lbs. of muzzle energy, and (3) must provide penetration at least 50 percent greater than that demonstrated by the .38 SPL +P+ 110-grain Treasury load.

Our dilemma was simple. If our recommendation for ammunition was accepted and someone was injured or killed as a result of penetration beyond the parameters of the LEAA study, our careers were history. We even had to consider the possibility of facing civil or criminal prosecution. We had no illusions as to how well our credibility would fare when compared to the millions of dollars invested in the LEAA study by our own mother agency, the Department of Justice. Fortunately, our fears had no basis in reality and our recommendations were accepted and adopted by the Border Patrol and the INS without any condemning incident. The U.S. Marshal's Service followed suit and adopted the same ammunition as the Border Patrol.

BACK TO THE 1984 TESTS

As stated earlier, we decided to test any reasonable caliber with potential for use by the U.S. Border Patrol in either revolvers or semiautomatic pistols. We also decided that we would test the full spectrum of loadings within those calibers from the lightest to the heaviest projectiles and the slowest to the fastest projectiles. We would use military ball, state-of-the-art hollowpoints, and exotic ammunition such as the THV and Glaser Safety Slug. We even commissioned the construction of machined-brass hypervelocity 9mm and .357 projectiles. Projectiles used in these tests ran from a low weight of 40 grains to a high of 255. Velocities ran from a low of 750 fps to a high of 2300 fps. The calibers used were .38 Special, 9mm, .357 Magnum, .45 ACP, and .45 LC. If it was out there, we tested it. If it wasn't out there and we thought it should be, we manufactured it.

We tested all of the ammunition to determine the following:

- Kinetic energy at the muzzle
- Momentum at the muzzle (using the IPSC Power Factor formula)
- Recoil energy
- Cartridge component compatibility with firearms used (lead, copper, and powder debris fouling)
- Penetration in 1-gallon water jugs
- Penetration through automotive windshields to location of driver
- Penetration through automotive rear windows to location of driver
- Penetration of car door
- Penetration of half-ton truck tailgate
- Penetration through brush
- Integrity of projectile path of travel after penetration
- Retained weight of projectiles after penetration
- Projectile deformation after penetration
- Consistency of expansion

- Night time muzzle flash
- Accuracy at 25 yards
- Accuracy at 50 yards

These tests revealed some interesting information. First, the .38 Special +P+ was a remarkably consistent nonperformer. We already knew that powder residue from this round was a disaster if it fell between the extractor star and the cylinder. Nothing would jam the revolver quicker than this combination. The tests proved that the +P+ load had the brightest muzzle flash signature of all the rounds tested, had the worst penetration potential on vehicle doors and windows, and was one of the least accurate rounds beyond 25 yards. It was capable of penetrating into one water jug but rarely penetrated through the back wall of the first jug.

The rounds that we were most interested in testing were those that touted performance based on extreme levels of kinetic energy derived from light projectile weight and hyper velocities. There was little doubt that these projectiles could be highly effective if conditions were right, but they lacked the robustness of performance demanded by our job description. While they penetrated automotive glass and doors like a laser beam, they rarely had enough retained energy to cause even superficial damage to the intended target. They were easily deflected by brush and easily deformed upon impact with anything other than a liquid mass. They tended to produce high muzzle blast and bright muzzle flash. They were also significantly less accurate than more conventional ammunition. Aside from their impressive hydrostatic performance, their only other redeeming quality was low recoil.

Our favorite from this class was the French Arcane or THV, as it is known here. This 40-grain pill left a 4 inch .357 Magnum with velocities in excess of 2300 fps and literally exploded water jugs. It was the only round that created significant amounts

of water vapor. Water vapor results from the velocity of the water that leaves the jug after impact. The higher the velocity of the water, the smaller the size of the water droplets. None of us had ever seen water vaporized by a handgun bullet to the extent that was evidenced with the THV. A more robust hypervelocity design was a 110-grain .357 and 9mm machined-brass hollowpoint Teflon-coated projectile. It had a velocity of 1550 fps from a 4-inch-barreled .357 and proved to be quite robust. It was an excellent penetrator and expanded quite reliably. Unfortunately, it was very unstable and had unacceptable accuracy at ranges in excess of 15 yards. We did not have the time to solve this problem and the round was dropped from our considerations.

Both of these rounds did convince me that there was good potential for a properly designed nondeforming high-velocity projectile for law enforcement use. I began working on what would become 15 years of developmental work on a new concept for projectile design. I will cover this in more detail at the end of the chapter.

The high-momentum rounds were the best penetrators in all tests, as was expected. Many of them penetrated to a fault, and it was easy to see the origin of the concerns expressed in the LEAA tests. Our biggest cause for concern was that very few of the hollowpoint designs expanded consistently when fired from 4 or 5 inch barrels. Their ability to expand was abysmal when fired from snub-nosed revolvers or compact semiauto pistols. Keep in mind that this was in 1984, and there have been dramatic changes in ammunition designs since that time. It was unnerving performance for projectiles that were designed for rapid expansion and low penetration as mandated by the LEAA tests.

The lesson learned here was that law enforcement ammunition must be tested to ensure that it will perform to expectations. Performance can never be taken for granted; variables such as the firearm's barrel length can quickly turn a premium expanding projectile into the world's fanciest ball round. As another example of this, we found that our current stock of .38 Special 158-grain lead hollowpoint ammunition was also extremely inaccurate at ranges in excess of 15 yards. This was the second most commonly used .38 caliber ammunition in law enforcement and was generally accepted as being an accurate round.

High-momentum rounds caused the least affect on the water jugs. While water is significantly more "solid" than gelatin, heavy low-velocity rounds slipped through the medium, causing very little disturbance. I would characterize the wounding effect of these rounds to be much like a knife wound. While potentially deadly, the immediate result of the wound may produce no visible effect on the person who has been shot. This can of course be very distressing if the person whom you have just shot is enthusiastically trying to kill you.

This impression is somewhat supported by my experience as a bow hunter. A 600-grain arrow traveling at 200 fps is a very high-momentum projectile that can quite easily achieve full penetration of a 500-pound animal. Yet every bow hunter knows that the first rule of conduct after a successful shot is to give the animal at least 30 minutes to lie down and expire. An immediate attempt to locate the fatally wounded animal can result in many hours and miles of tracking or the loss of the game altogether. I have great confidence in the lethality of high-momentum projectiles; I have little faith in their ability to cause any immediate incapacitation barring a direct hit to the central nervous system or heavy bone.

My partners Kent Williams and Bob Rogers saw things somewhat differently. Bob is pretty much a hopeless case. He is a dyed-in-the-wool .44 Magnum fan. He has always been

mystified as to why anyone would settle for less than a 300-grain bullet traveling at 1500 feet per second. He is the quintessential Border Patrol Agent and reasons that the kinetic energy required for serious social work begins at about 1,000 ft-lbs. with enough momentum to send bowling pins into orbit. You certainly can't fault this argument, but it would be a hard sell when considering the weaponcraft abilities of the average law enforcement officer.

Kent Williams favored well-balanced rounds that were traveling at the highest possible velocity but weighted toward momentum characteristics. He still maintains that one of the best rounds available to law enforcement is the .38 Special 158-grain +P semiwadcutter hollowpoint. This load, also known as "the FBI load," has an enviable record for success in spite of its low energy levels. Kent has affection for it based primarily on the quality of robustness. It is a round that will penetrate deeply and consistently through the human body regardless of clothing factors or the distance between the shooter and the target. It demonstrates moderate expansion but is not entirely dependent on expansion for effective performance. It is very accurate and has very mild recoil characteristics that allow for quick follow-up shots. While it is not a very reliable penetrator through motor vehicles, it is still one of the best penetrators in the .38 Special family. To paraphrase Kent, "At least you know what it will do if it hits someone. It's going to go deep." He has a point. (Bob holds that a .38 Special is just a .44 Magnum wondering what it's going to be when it grows up!)

This left us with the middle-of-the-road crowd. If you think about it, that should not be surprising. If projectile robustness is a primary concern, then one is driven toward a selection of ammunition that provides high kinetic energy balanced by sufficient retained energy

(momentum) to ensure penetration in a broad range of scenarios.

When it came right down to broad range performance with a well-balanced distribution of both kinetic energy and momentum, the .357 Magnum loadings in 125 through 158 grains were the hands-down performance winners. In .45 ACP loads, the 185 was clearly superior for law enforcement applications. They both performed well, but the 185-grain demonstrated more consistent expansion. The .38 Special and standard-velocity 9mm rounds were clearly substandard in performance when compared with the .45 ACP and .357.

The +P+ 9mm 115-grain JHP, or "Illinois State Police" load, was a different story. This round was clearly in the same performance category as the .357 Magnums and appeared to be slightly but measurably superior to the 110-grain .357 Magnum. The weakest characteristic of the high-velocity .357 family was the greatly reduced effectiveness of the projectiles after penetration of automotive glass and sheet metal. Our selection of ammunition for Service handguns was limited to the .38 Special and .357 Magnum. The three magnum rounds selected were still the most robust performers within this restriction.

1984 AMMUNITION RECOMMENDATIONS

Our final recommendations to Headquarters were these:

1. That the .357 Magnum 110-grain JHP replace the .38 Special 110-grain +P+ load for Service issue ammunition.
2. That agents be given the option of carrying either the Federal brand .357 125-grain JHP or the Winchester brand .357 145-grain STHP. Agents would have to pay for this ammunition out of their own pocket and would be required to qualify with it.

3. That agents be allowed to carry semiautomatic pistols of DA/SA or safe action design in calibers .45 ACP or .38 Super.

4. That no 9mm semiautomatic pistols would be authorized until the Service could acquire a contract for the ISP 115-grain +P+ load or its equivalent.

We had found that the 110-grain .357 clearly fell into the magnum performance level. It had the lowest recoil levels of any of the magnums tested, was very accurate, had a moderate flash signature, and actually outperformed the 145-grain STHP on penetration through brush and vehicles. While we did a great deal of soul-searching before settling on this recommendation, there was one factor that could not be ignored. Penetration.

We knew that the 110-grain .357 was capable of penetrating from 9 to 12 inches in 20 percent ballistic gelatin. This increased the depth of penetration as much as 50 percent over the .38 110-grain +P+ projectile. It was our decision to take a small step forward using the same weight projectile as our then current .38 load. We were willing to risk the personal stakes involved in an overpenetration incident because our tests had convinced us that this was highly unlikely with any of the .357 loads tested. At the same time, in the event that such an incident occurred, we felt we could defend our choice of the 110-grain .357 based on the fact that it used an identical weight projectile as the .38 but met the headquarters request for a significantly better penetrator than the .38 Treasury load.

We also knew that this was the round least likely to accelerate wear on our medium-framed Smith & Wesson and Ruger revolvers. We were not overly concerned about the optional loads because most of the agents who would be willing to absorb the cost of this ammunition tended to carry personally owned S&W L and N frame revolvers.

An interesting note is that with all of the tried and true performers, exotics, and custom made ammunition in the test, none of us had believed that the 110-grain .357 was even in contention. After our experience with the .38 110-grain, we still found ourselves reluctant in our consideration of the magnum 110. Fortunately, we approached the tests with open minds, and when the dust had settled we believed we had made the best possible recommendation. Funny what happens when you are just looking for the truth.

It surprised us to find that the Winchester Silvertips in both .357 and 9mm were outperformed by the 110-grain .357 Magnum. Keep in mind that the Winchester Silvertip hollowpoint was designed to be a very soft and easily expanding bullet in keeping with the LEAA recommendations. If one used the LEAA recommendations for selection, the Silvertip line was the best performing law enforcement ammunition in the world. While it was particularly weak on penetration of automotive cover when fired from an angle, it was still a good performer overall. It had mild recoil, a low flash signature, and was extremely accurate. The .357 145-grain STHP quickly became the round of choice for those agents who felt the money spent was the cheapest insurance they could buy. As noted earlier, all of the standard-velocity 9mm, including the 9mm Silvertip, were deemed to have insufficient muzzle energy for reliable performance.

While the .357 125-grain JHP is widely touted as the best man stopper ever built, it was interesting to see knowledgable agents opting for the Silvertip. These agents, many of them seasoned shooters, made this choice for two simple reasons: they knew that the recoil and muzzle blast characteristics of the Silvertip were a definite real-world advantage in a gun fight. Given the freedom of choice, they picked the round that enhanced their ability to fire accurately and recover quickly. Hitting the target is still the number one consideration for those who pack a gun for a living.

Our recommendations were accepted as proposed, and the Border

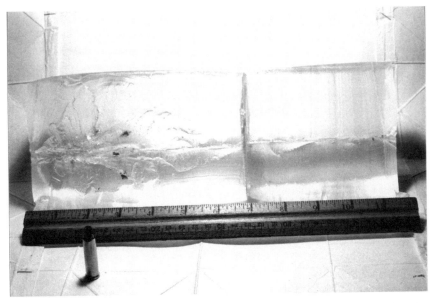

The INS authorized this .357 Magnum 110-grain S-JHP from 1986 to 1994. The 110-grain load was the most controllable of all the Magnums. Note the bullet frags at the 3 inch depth, consistently thrown from the main bullet path with the Remington scallop-serrated JHPs.

Patrol went back to the magnum and the optional semiautomatic pistols in 1985. Our decision to forbid the carry of 9mm semiautomatic pistols was to cause us no end of trouble, and it began immediately.

WHY NOT THE NINE?

For those of us who were on duty in the mid-1980s, the 9mm high-capacity semiautomatic pistols were hotter than pancakes at a hunter's breakfast. We suddenly had available to us a sidearm that would hold 15 to 20 rounds in one magazine. Agents had been settling for six in the gun, six in loops, and six or 12 in speed loaders. Now, they could carry that much right in a pistol that was compact, light, well-balanced, and virtually recoilless when compared to the .357 Magnum revolver. The obvious advantages of these pistols seemed to outweigh all other considerations. Some agents, anticipating the headquarters approval for the carry of personally owned semiautomatic pistols, had already purchased 9mm pistols for this purpose.

Many field agents were outraged by our ban on the 9mm pistols. While some were delighted to be able to carry semiautos in .45 ACP and .38 Super, the vast majority wanted to carry the nines. In spite of intense political pressure caused by the popularity of the nine, we stuck to our guns and headquarters backed us on this issue.

The problem was too obvious to avoid. The standard-velocity 9mm ammunition had almost identical kinetic energy and momentum levels of the .38 Special 110-grain load that we had just abandoned on the justification that it was dangerously underpowered. We had already established a new standard that stated that all Service ammunition would have to produce a minimum of 400 ft-lbs. of kinetic energy to qualify for duty use. We had also set a standard of a minimum Power Factor of 170 for those rounds that could not meet the kinetic energy minimum

The new Border Patrol ammo protocol can be used to select any general issue, police-duty load. With a minimum energy requirement of 370 ft-lbs. and a minimum Power Factor of 170, the Patrol has focused on the .40 S&W 155-grain JHPs. The Remington version is shown.

standard. There was simply no way we could approve the use of standard-velocity 9mm without violating our own firm conviction that this ammunition was inadequate for law enforcement purposes.

To compound the issue, we ran into problems with legal considerations regarding the use of +P+ ammunition in personally owned pistols. The firearms manufacturers were reluctant to approve the carry of this ammunition for fear of potential lawsuits. The ammunition manufacturers did not want to provide us with the ammunition without assurance from the firearms people that it could be used in their firearms. This situation would not be resolved until 1987.

The pressure continued to increase. No matter how many agents or administrators I explained it to, there were just too many people who could not seem to grasp that the number of rounds in a pistol did not determine the effectiveness of the ammunition fired from it. Fortunately, our people in headquarters held their ground. It was getting tougher all the time because now a company called Glock had introduced a polymer pistol that was proving to be one of the greatest pistol designs of the century. It joined the SIG 226 and the HK-P7, and I could feel the butts of these fine sidearms

driving the nails into my coffin. I was invited to sit down and talk guns with Gaston Glock in late 1985. I tried to explain our position to the great designer who, at that time, was manufacturing 9mm pistols exclusively. I damn near groveled at his feet and begged him to consider importing the 9mm x 21 that he was manufacturing for the Italians. I pleaded with him to chamber his pistol for the IPSC 10mm Short or the .41 Action Express. His reply? "I am sorry, but we cannot even keep up with the demand for our 9mm pistols." That was an undeniable truth for all of the manufacturers, and we both knew it.

THE FBI HANDGUN AMMUNITION TEST PROTOCOL

The pressure came off in 1986. I wish it hadn't happened the way it did. Most of us are familiar with it as the FBI Miami Incident. All of us can accept it as one of the greatest law enforcement tragedies in the history of this great country. Why did it happen? How did it happen? Was it a result of the failure of Agent Dove's killing shot with a 9mm Silvertip round that failed this team of dedicated agents? Was it a question of tactical error or choice of arms? Did it all hinge on the will of a dead man who refused to die? Was it just plain bad luck?

These are questions that have no complete answers. Each question we ask begs a thousand more to bury the question still unanswered. My opinion? I think we should get on our knees every day and implore a just and merciful God to protect us as we do our best to do our duty. Diligent and dedicated officers will lose their lives each and every day that we live. The greatest honor we can give them is to learn from their last living experience what we must know if we are to survive.

The deaths of Agents Grogan and Dove led to the most sweeping and dramatic changes in law enforcement that we have experienced in this century. Our training changed, our choice of firearms changed, our ammunition changed, and our perceptions of the challenges we face changed. I do not believe, as the cynics do, that good officers must die in order to effect change. I am however convinced that the honor we bestow upon fallen officers will always be manifested in the form of changes that improve our chances of survival for those who follow.

Among the many changes that we have experienced since this incident, the most dramatic and lasting is perhaps the changes to the way law enforcement ammunition performance is tested. Prior to the Miami shootout, all of us used ammunition that was either a product of the LEAA recommendations or ammunition that was designed primarily for hunting. There were no standards for law enforcement ammunition based on reasonable expectations of the performance that is required to ensure our safety. The FBI recognized this and immediately accepted the challenge to create such a system.

Special Agent in Charge John Hall, Chief of the FBI Academy Firearms Division, invited me to attend the first Handgun Ammunition Wounding Effectiveness Symposium held at the FBI Academy in Quantico, Virginia, in 1986. It was the formal beginning of a new day for all of us in law enforcement. The list of subject matter experts who occupied the dais read like a who's who in wound ballistics. There were agreements, disagreements, heads nodding yes and heads shaking no, friendships made, and enemies sworn. Most importantly, it was an opportunity to start anew. The symposium served as a symbolic declaration that the LEAA recommendations, sponsored by the Department of Justice in the 1970s, were finally being laid to rest. The Department of Justice was prepared to roll up its sleeves and try again.

THE FBI BALLISTIC TEST PROTOCOL IS BORN

The FBI test protocol is the best standard test for law enforcement handgun ammunition that has ever existed. It owes its excellence to the fact that it pits projectile dynamics against the real-world challenges of clothing and concealment barriers that are most commonly encountered in law enforcement shooting incidents.

Most importantly, the FBI took the time and effort to carefully document exactly how the tests would be conducted and what materials would be used and identify specific parameters for performance. By doing this, they created a standard that could be used and duplicated by ballistic laboratories anywhere in the world. Of equal importance is the fact that the tests are straightforward and can be conducted by individuals who do not have the luxury of working in high-tech laboratories.

While we had conducted similar tests in 1984, we had not used the painstaking scientific methodology required by the FBI. No one could have duplicated the tests we conducted because we had used junked vehicles, brush that grew in our geographic location, and firearms that we just happened to have available for the occasion. We had no computerized system for the storing of data and no easy way to continue our examination of new ammunition designs as they came onto the market. Ours was a one-shot deal that gave us the information we needed but could not define specific performance criteria for us or anyone else.

I owe no apology for this. The three of us who had performed these tests were full-time firearm instructors assigned to both the U.S. Border Patrol training program and the Federal Law Enforcement Training Center. All of our tests were conducted after hours and on weekends without compensation. Until the Miami tragedy, this is the way it was done by most agencies. The selection of firearms, ammunition, and related equipment rested very much in the hands of dedicated officers who were willing to suffer significant personal sacrifice in order to provide others with the tools they needed.

THE FBI TEST PROTOCOL CONTROVERSY

The FBI test protocol ran headlong into a wall of controversy. Without weighing the pros and cons of the controversy, I think it boiled down to a few simple considerations.

First, the FBI made a mistake, which they have since corrected, by attempting to define a wounding value for handgun projectiles. We are still a long way from being able to identify, empirically measure, and predict performance due to all the variables involved in the dynamics of incapacitation. The FBI wound value data was well intentioned but ill advised. Again, the FBI recognized this defect, and the data has been removed from its published test results.

The second problem with the FBI methodology was that it forced other agencies into a position of having to adopt the recommendations resulting from the test procedures simply because there was no other game in town. Now all agencies were back in the same boat they had been in as a consequence of the LEAA tests. Any selection of ammunition that did not perform well in the FBI tests was highly suspect even if it performed well in the applications for which it was intended. Personally, being well-read in the LEAA tests, I was overjoyed by the FBI reversal of the LEAA findings even though I was concerned about the FBI ammunition recommendations that resulted from its interpretation of test data. Now we had two reputable scientific methodologies that appeared to be diametrically opposed. I use the LEAA scientific data as a resource to justify kinetic energy as a factor for assailant incapacitation. I use the FBI test data as a resource for the justification of momentum as a similar factor in assailant incapacitation. What I recognize in both of these studies is that there is absolutely nothing wrong with the data that was acquired in these tests. The data is scientific, repeatable, and predictable. There is everything right and nothing wrong with this simple fact. So why all the controversy?

The controversy, which at times gets a little far to the right of heated debate, is not about the test procedures used in either of these scientific endeavors. The debate is solely about the manner in which the data was interpreted by the agencies involved. In this sense, both studies fail the end users to a significant extent. The interpretation of data from the LEAA studies left us extremely vulnerable in situations that demanded deep penetration to ensure suspect incapacitation. The FBI studies left us vulnerable in situation where the violent dispersion of high levels of kinetic energy might be required to ensure suspect incapacitation. In both of these studies, the parameters defining performance were weighted to a fault. We know this because the interpretation of test results creates obvious anomalies between known

projectile performance and the performance predicted by laboratory analysis.

As an example, FBI data published between 1989–1995 rates Swedish M-39 106-grain armor-piercing ball ammunition as having a higher wounding value (1.51) than the Remington Golden Saber .357 125-grain hollowpoint ammunition (1.19). I suppose there are those who might argue that these results are indeed correct, but those individuals are exceedingly difficult to locate. No one can argue the anomaly present in the interpretation of data that assigns the CorBon 9mm 115-grain JHP a wounding value of 0.00. Anomalies in the data interpretation from the LEAA studies are equally profound.

The truly important point here is that while interpretation of data can be bizarre and easily recognized as invalid, the data remains accurate, germane, and absolutely priceless to those of us who are burdened with the responsibility of securing the safety of front line officers. In my last three years of service to the U.S. Border Patrol and INS enforcement officers, I was responsible for ammunition selections that would be relied upon by almost 20,000 armed officers spread throughout the world. Believe me, it is a heavy burden and could not have been responsibly born if not for the dedicated efforts of the LEAA and FBI personnel who provided us with such an excellent foundation of scientific data.

To give you an idea of how close the FBI came to accurate data interpretation in what was an absolutely ground-breaking effort that broke all the rules and abandoned all established precepts, consider this:

There are only two basic changes needed to eliminate the bulk of the anomalies in the data interpretation. A reasonable and generous maximum depth of penetration for efficient handgun expanding ammunition design is around 14 inches. If the formula for adjusted volume had used

14 inches rather than 18 inches, most of the anomalies would disappear. (Remember that the FBI had arrived at the conclusion that lack of penetration was a primary causative factor in Miami. You can easily understand why they favored generous penetration in the equation.)

The second change is equally simple. While the FBI quite rightly established a minimum standard for acceptable penetration for procurement purposes, this minimum causes some confusion in the interpretive data. It is the minimum 12 inch penetration requirement in the tests that creates the curious characteristic of ammunition that cannot hurt you or might in fact actually make you feel better if you were to be shot with it. To cure your headache, take two aspirin or a double tap to the brain stem with a .22 caliber pistol and your headache will be gone! While we can amuse ourselves with this type of take on interpretation of data, the priceless data from which the interpretation is derived becomes obscured and discounted along with the interpretation. This is a mistake we can ill afford.

In a final but profound reflection on these two scientific efforts, I offer you the following:

The FBI seriously considered adopting the .45 ACP with a projectile velocity of between 1000 and 1100 fps. Its initial selection was the 10mm 180-grain JHP with a velocity of approximately 1000 fps. This was based on the firm conviction that momentum, not kinetic energy dispersion, was the key to projectile performance.

The LEAA study discounted momentum and credited the creation of a temporary cavity within the human body resulting from the dispersion of kinetic energy as the key to projectile performance. Everyone assumes that the LEAA recommendations placed the .38 110-grain +P+ load at the pinnacle of performance. It did not.

While slogging through the piles of data from the LEAA study, I came across the following statement found in "Ammunition for Law Enforcement: Part 1 Methodology for Evaluating Relative Stopping Power and Results," Technical Report ARBRL-TR-02199 dated October 1979 superseding interim memorandum report no. 323 dated December 1974.

"From both ricochet considerations and stopping power considerations, a velocity of approximately 335m/sec (1100 ft/sec) is most effective" (VII. Conclusions A.2)

"It is the location of the temporary cavity with respect to that of vital organs that produces varying degrees of incapacitation. The data show that optimal bullet mass is in the range of 158-170 grains. Combined with conclusion A and B, this mass range bullet in .45 caliber would produce an optimal bullet." (VII. Conclusions, C.)

Let's look at the actual difference in results between the findings of the LEAA and the FBI (chart below). Just for kicks, I will throw in the Border Patrol 1984 and 1990 test conclusions since we are historically notorious for being an exception to any established norm.

Folks, the LEAA study and the FBI study approached the same problem from diametrically opposed points of view *and arrived at the same conclusion!* The Border Patrol, using an approach that gave us the highest practical levels of kinetic energy with reasonably high attendant momentum, settled on the 155-grain .40 S&W at a velocity of 1170 fps. These amazing facts are not coincidence. I am firmly convinced that dedicated truth seekers will always arrive at similar conclusions. They are limited in

abilities, ignorant of the variables, overwhelmed by the complexities of the task, but somehow they get there. Ridiculing the seekers who are so vulnerable to criticism while on this journey is a cruel injustice and most undeserved. Hatcher, Bruchey, Burczynski, Kelsey, DiMaio, Niewenhous, Herring, Marshall, Corzine, Sanow, Fackler, Ragsdale, Alexander, McPherson, Benini, Godlin, Warren, Pi, Schluckebier, Dwyer, Zefiro, Michaud, and a thousand others, some well known and some not, are out there on the journey for all of us. I admire their courage, and it has been a privilege to work with so many of them.

To put a little icing on this cake, Evan Marshal and Ed Sanow have been attempting to extrapolate information regarding projectile performance using methodologies that are completely inconsistent with those used by any of the aforementioned agencies. Yet their conclusions are completely consistent with those of these other agencies. As kinetic energy increases, projectile effectiveness increases. This is true in virtually every caliber and projectile weight evaluated.

In a nutshell, four independent studies all seem to agree that a large caliber bullet weighing 155 to 180 grains driven at an average velocity of 1100 fps is a good starting point in the selection of law enforcement duty ammunition.

BORDER PATROL AMMUNITION, 1987-1995

In 1987 we were finally able to get the 9mm 115-grain +P+ ammunition. With contracts for this ammunition in place, we finally authorized the carry

of 9mm semiautomatic pistols. The Glock 17 and 19 and the SIG P-226 quickly became the weapons of choice for Border Patrol Agents around the country. While a small number of agents still purchased the SIG P-220 in .45 ACP and .38 Super, there was no question that the 9 ruled the Border. The Glock 17 was the most popular of the semiautomatic pistols, and for good reason. It was appreciably less expensive than the SIG, carried two additional rounds for a total of 18, and was more compact and lighter.

It had two other attributes that made it a very desirable tool. The first

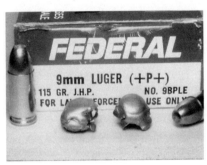

In 1987, the Border Patrol went to the 9mm 115-grain JHP in a +P+ loading. In 1994, it adopted the .40 S&W with a 155-grain JHP.

was the trigger. While the SIG had a conventional double action to single action trigger pull, the Glock safe-action trigger had a trigger pull that was consistent on each shot. The trigger pull on the Glock was also shorter and lighter. No one had to educate these agents about the advantages of such a mechanism. When you pit your wits and your life against heavily armed drug smuggler's every night, the advantages of such a trigger system leap right out at you.

The other remarkable advantage gained by the Glock is a result of barrel design. The Glock has polygonal rifling. This system causes an immediate increase in projectile velocities of anywhere from 30 to 50 fps. While this might not seem like much, many of the agents were well

Agency	Caliber	Weight	Velocity	Ke	Mo
LEAA	.45	165 gr. (avg.)	1100	443	162
FBI	.40	180 gr.	1000	400	167
USBP (84)	.357	110 gr.	1300	413	143
USBP (90)	.40	155 gr.	1170	471	181

aware that kinetic energy gain is a function of velocity squared. A 30 to 50 fps gain in velocity translated to a significant gain in energy for a handgun bullet. This was especially critical with the 9mm ammunition since even the +P+ configuration could drop below our 400 ft-lb. energy level requirement. A 115-grain 9mm +P+ fired from a conventional barrel might have a velocity as low as 1250 fps. with an attendant Ke of 399 ft-lbs. The exact same cartridge fired in the polygonal barrel of the Glock 17 might have a velocity of 1300 fps and a Ke level of 432 ft-lbs., well into .357 Magnum performance levels.

In fact, the Glock 17 loaded with 115-grain +P+ ammunition is perhaps the most formidable package of hand-held firepower ever devised. Our .357 Magnum 110-grain JHP loading had Ke levels in the area of 413 ft-lbs., well below the levels achieved by the Glock 17. What the Glock 17 gave our agents was the equivalent of an 18-round .357 Magnum with the recoil characteristic of a .38 Special that was far easier than a revolver to shoot and could be reloaded 200 percent faster. Little wonder that this gem of a pistol became an overnight favorite with our agents and other law enforcement officers throughout the United States! My sidekick and pistolero extraordinaire, Cliff Koenig, dubbed the pistol "Lethal Tupperware." He won numerous speed shooting competitions firing his stock Glock against all comers, including many who used high-speed compensated pistols sporting optical or electronic sights.

While all of this may sound great, it still begs the question of how well the 9mm +P+ and the 110-grain magnum fared in the real world. Both of these cartridges were outstanding performers. In the period from 1985 through 1995 we did not have a single failure to stop attributed to either of these cartridges although they were involved in numerous shooting

incidents as drug smuggling continued to escalate heavily along the Southwest border.

I recall one rather unusual incident involving the 110-grain magnum that is worth a retelling. I had just finished another gun magazine article warning about the perils of arming oneself with the 110-grain magnum. The distinguished author pointed out that the then new FBI protocol clearly demonstrated that this fast moving pill was not capable of penetrating to sufficient depths in the human body to cause any significant damage. I wish I could have hooked him up with the two Texas agents who relied upon it that very same day to drop an enraged longhorn range bull that was attempting to use them as hood ornaments for his 5 foot spread of horn. They estimated the weight of the bull at about 1,200 pissed-off pounds, and it was dropped when one of five shots fired found the heart. Both agents had two or more rounds left in their wheel guns at the conclusion of this encounter. They had no complaints about the stopping power of the light magnum load, though one of them did complain about a piercing pain in his butt every time he saw steak on his plate!

In another incident, the 9mm +P+ fired from the Glock 17 exemplified the attributes of both of these tools. Several agents were searching in thick cane brakes for a suspect whom they knew was armed with a machete. This suspect had already made it clear in the initial encounter that he was half a bubble off center and extremely dangerous. The agents knew that they were hunting for a tiger in the bush, and they had weapons drawn and ready. They knew that the suspect would attack if cornered, and he could be within a distance of less than 3 feet and they might not see him through the thick cover.

That's exactly what happened. The lead agent passed the suspect's concealment. After he passed, the

suspect burst from the cane and charged straight at the second agent with the machete already flung back for a murderous downswing. The agent had no time to think or aim. He hammered three quick shots at point-blank range with his back against the unyielding cane thicket. There was no escaping the onslaught. Fortunately, the quick trigger of the Glock combined with the smashing power of the 115-grain +P+ rounds did the job. The suspect fell dead at the feet of the agent and the machete fell harmlessly from his hand before the downswing was completed. The shooting report stated that the suspect had burst from concealment only 7 feet from the agent who dropped him. The first and third agents in the group were powerless to assist because of the thickness of the brush.

I am sure the suspect determined that his machete was a superior weapon under the circumstances. He had every right to expect that in the darkness, the thick cover, and the confusion, he could get in the middle of these agents and finish all three of them before they could get off an accurate shot. He received a quick education in the balance, control, and point-aiming capabilities of the Glock and the formidable power of the 9mm +P+ ammunition. For his efforts, he was summarily graduated and moved on to his first day in Hell 101.

TRANSITION TO THE .40 S&W

The revolver became obsolete for all but die-hard fans by the mid-1980s. The advent of the high-capacity 9mms had put the odds in favor of the person armed with one of these pistols. While there are all sorts of pithy quotes that extol the virtues of accuracy over volume, they just don't translate very well when it is raining lead—you can't remember in all the excitement if you have fired five or six, and you don't feeling lucky.

In 1990, Bob Rogers, Cliff Koenig,

and I were tasked with recommending a cartridge to be carried by all Border Patrol and INS enforcement officers. Once this cartridge was approved and a pistol procured for its use, all other sidearm authorizations would be rescinded. We were going to become a one pistol, one cartridge agency.

The need for this transition was urgent. Between 1985 and 1990, the personnel assigned to enforcement had doubled to almost 10,000 officers. Between 1990 and the year 2000 it would double again to 20,000. The logistics involved in training, firearms repair, and ammunition procurements would become totally unmanageable if we did not adopt a one gun, one ammunition policy.

Our recommendation was simple. When we tested various firearms and ammunition combinations for ergonomic compatibility, size, weight, kinetic energy, momentum, chamber pressure, magazine capacity, short and long-range capability, and the potential for use in a law enforcement carbine or submachine gun, one round stood head and shoulders above the rest. This was the .40 S&W 155-grain JHP. It was a compromise in the best possible sense of the word, for it brought to us a round that had the best of all worlds all wrapped up in one.

At that time, the law enforcement community was still heavily under the

The INS evaluated seven auto pistol calibers in eight different categories before selecting the .40 S&W 155-grain JHP. Dozens of gunfights have proved they made the right choice.

Cartridge	Bullet Weight	Velocity	Ke	Power Factor (M)
.45 ACP	185 grain	950 fps	371	176
.40 S&W	180 grain	930 fps	346	167
.40 S&W	155 grain	1170 fps	471	181
.357 Mag	125 grain	1425 fps	564	178

influence of the data interpretation coming out of the FBI ammunition tests. For this reason, the 147-grain 9mm and the 180-grain .40 S&W were the two most popular rounds in use by law enforcement agencies. So why did we take a different route?

The FBI was most cooperative in providing us with data from its tests. As we reviewed the data in conjunction with our own testing methodologies, we found that our results were very consistent with those of the FBI. What stood out quite dramatically for us was that the 155-grain .40 S&W provided us with everything we had been looking for. At that time we specified a 155-grain projectile at a velocity of 1170 fps from a 5-inch-barreled semiautomatic pistol. A quick look at both kinetic energy and momentum figures for this load as compared to the 185-grain .45 ACP, the 125-grain .357 Magnum, and the 180-grain .40 S&W tells most of the story. It should be noted that for this comparison, we were able to use actual ammunition loaded to FBI specifications in our test pistols. This gave us accurate velocity figures for firearms rather than velocities established through factory universal receivers and test barrels.

The 155-grain .40 caliber gave us .357 Magnum Ke levels and .45 ACP momentum levels all in one package. While the recoil level of this round is noticeably stiffer then the mild 180-grain load, it was a relatively easy transition for our officers to move from the recoil of the 110-grain .357 to that of the 155-grain .40 S&W.

It was also noteworthy to us that the energy levels demonstrated by the 155-grain loading gave us some

assurance that we would still have good performance when this round was fired from compact firearms with short barrels. This prediction has proven true.

The performance of the .40 S&W 155-grain load has met and exceeded all of our expectations. A review of autopsy and medical data and photographs combined with eyewitness accounts of suspect behavior after being hit with this round leaves me convinced that it is clearly superior to any other conventional law-enforcement expanding projectile in service today.

I have been at this business of ammunition evaluation since beginning of my law enforcement career in 1970. In all of the work that I have done and in all of the lessons I have had to learn, one fact stands out above all else: *ammunition is energy.* While we must consider projectile construction, the dynamics of terminal ballistics, the reliability of design performance, and many other equally necessary considerations, it is the pure essence of energy that makes it all work. *Projectiles must leave the barrel with enough energy to do the job that is required of them.* The less energy they start with, the less they can be trusted to perform reliably. I agree with the FBI that the use of the 9mm standard-velocity ammunition was a causative factor in the Miami tragedy. I will always believe that the ammunition failure was due to the lack of energy generated by the round more so than a flaw in projectile design. Agent Dove's well-aimed shot left the suspect clinically dead; he just did not die soon enough. This brings us back to the infernal questions of "stopping power" and "incapacitation," which I will get to a bit later. For whatever reason, they did not occur on that fateful day, and we have been working hard ever since to ensure that this tragedy is not repeated.

Everyone has an opinion as to what sufficient energy levels for handgun ammunition are, and here is my opinion. I believe that a projectile should have a minimum energy level of 400 ft-lbs. of kinetic energy. It should also have the highest level of momentum that it can achieve without sacrificing this minimum level of kinetic energy. Momentum is not nearly as critical as kinetic energy since penetration can also be achieved as a function of projectile design and material rather than weight. In my experience, the most consistent conventional projectiles are well above this minimum kinetic energy level. Projectiles that achieve kinetic energy levels of between 450 and 550 ft-lbs. have been proving their ability to incapacitate suspects for the better part of the last 50 years. This is not to say that handgun ammunition that generates kinetic energy levels higher than 550 ft-lbs. are somehow ineffective. As a broad generalization, the reality is that the higher the initial kinetic energy, the greater the chance for quick suspect incapacitation. The only reason we do not focus on these higher levels is because they generate far more recoil then the average officer can handle in a conventional JHP load. Bob Rogers can shoot the wings off Georgia sand gnats at 100 yards with his .44 Magnum while topping off his chaw of Redman, but even he will admit that this powerful pistol is a handful for a down and injured officer.

Note however, that I qualified the above statement with the term "conventional JHP load." The exciting news is that the future holds promise of loads that can generate these levels of kinetic energy utilizing projectiles of moderate weight that do not depend on expansion as a vehicle for energy dispersion. We'll get to these new munitions soon, but first, let's take a

look at the INS Ballistic Test Protocol and how we tried to address some of the issues that created problems for the LEAA and FBI.

THE INS BALLISTIC GELATIN PROTOCOL

In 1998 I moderated a Ballistic Gelatin Test Protocol Symposium at the INS National Firearms Unit in Altoona, Pennsylvania. I invited the best ballistic experts from all of the major ammunition manufacturers to attend. I also invited other subject matter experts, including Evan Marshall, Ed Sanow, and Tom Burcynski, to participate in this landmark event. The purpose of the symposium was to assist the INS in reviewing current ballistic test protocols and to make recommendations for the establishment of a test protocol for the INS.

I liked the FBI protocol so much that I used it as a basis for the INS protocol. The ballistic experts who had been working with this protocol for over 10 years had many valid suggestions for changes that they felt would enhance the INS version. I wrote a draft protocol and submitted it to this group of over 15 subject matter experts who had participated in the symposium. They took the time to give me invaluable assistance in fine-tuning the document. I completed the writing in November of 1998, and it became the official test protocol for the INS in 1999. This is now the standard for INS ammunition performance.

I would like to take this opportunity to thank all of the subject matter experts for their input and encouragement during the drafting of this protocol. I owe a special thanks to FBI Agents Wade Jackson, Harry Kerns, and Buford Boone for their assistance and encouragement as I went through the painstaking process. Although the INS protocol is significantly different than the FBI's, it provides both the INS and the FBI with empirical data that is equally

useful to both Department of Justice agencies. It was an exercise in cooperation that benefits both these sister agencies as well as all of the law enforcement agencies that depend on us for ammunition performance data.

The INS protocol uses several of the tests defined by the FBI protocol, but differs significantly from the FBI protocol in the parameters established for defining projectile performance. It also includes the documentation and evaluation of temporary cavitation in ballistic gelatin through the use of high-speed video and computerized volumetric measurement of this cavity. While the actual effect of temporary cavitation cannot be measured, the INS feels quite strongly that it cannot be ignored as a factor in temporary incapacitation of suspects.

The INS protocol uses the tests listed below and weights them according to our perception of their importance in actual confrontations. While we are every bit as convinced as the FBI that consistent and deep penetration through barriers is critical to projectile robustness, we also believe that the main emphasis on projectile construction must be measured in terms of effectiveness against the person being struck by the projectile. The INS tests are weighted to reflect this emphasis.

I have neither time nor space to detail all the specifics of the INS test protocol in this chapter. Those law enforcement officers who wish to review the protocol in detail may do so by requesting it on department letterhead from the NFU. Inquiries should be addressed to:

Director
INS National Firearms Unit
320 East Chestnut Ave.
Altoona, PA 16601

The INS test protocol is noteworthy in many respects but perhaps none more so than it creates a system that allows for the competitive evaluation of projectiles that do not

John Jacobs is shown measuring the wound cavity in ordnance gelatin during NFU ammo testing. The new INS protocol focuses on only three tests: bare gelatin, heavily clothed gelatin, and gelatin after auto glass.

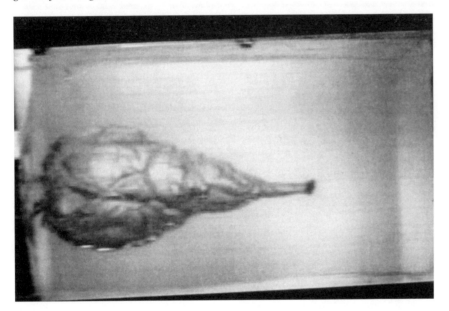

The INS measures the volume of the temporary stretch cavity as part of its ammo test protocol. The agency is convinced the stretch cavity is a key to stopping power. The cavity from a .357 Magnum 125-grain JHP is shown.

Test	Meas. & Max Pen	Weight (Value)
Depth of pen in bare 10% ballistic gelatin	9-12", 18" max	50%
Retained proj. weight	9-18", 18" max.	25%
Volume of temp cavity	Point of greatest volume	25%

depend on expansion for the delivery of effective penetration and kinetic energy dissipation in the target mass. Now the ammunition engineers are encouraged to examine projectiles that tumble, separate, or focus the destructive release of kinetic energy as a means of achieving suspect incapacitation. This is a major breakthrough in ammunition test protocol and is already leading to some very exciting changes in projectile dynamics. Although none of these new designs were able to outperform the excellent hollowpoints in the INS FY2000 ammunition tests, there is little doubt that they will equal or surpass hollowpoint designs in future tests. The fact that they were competitive but outperformed by expanding projectile designs in these tests confirms my belief that the INS protocol is valid. This test protocol insures that INS agents will receive the best ammunition that technology can produce and will not be "locked in" to traditional designs or mind-sets as they become obsolete.

In a nutshell, the INS protocol weighs three factors (see chart below). Note that for procurement purposes, a minimum depth of 9 inches and a maximum depth of 12 inches are used in performance evaluation formulas. Projectiles are allowed to penetrate to a depth of 18 inches but are not assigned value for this additional penetration.

Note that there is a balance established here between the need for consistent penetration and the presence of energy dissipation that may be a significant and positive factor in disrupting the central nervous system and/or the cardiovascular system. For those who argue that kinetic energy dispersion is not a proven incapacitation factor, we simply reply that they have never proven that it is not, and there is more than ample evidence to support consideration of the phenomenon. This being the case, it seems somewhat foolhardy to put all of one's eggs in the penetration basket.

The most significant difference between the FBI and the INS protocol is the *dynamic* measurement of volumetric displacement of gelatin during the formation of temporary cavities. This is achieved through the use of state-of-the-art high-speed video cameras that feed this data directly into a motion analysis computer station. The data resulting from this process includes volume and event-time data that should prove extremely valuable in documenting how the dynamics of kinetic energy dispersion effect human tissue.

Before leaving the NFU, I initiated research with the Aberdeen Test Center and the Southwest Research Institute. Either or both of these agencies may be able to devise a means of recording pressure measurements from the gelatin during projectile penetration. This combination of research data would greatly improve our ability to identify which projectiles are the best performers and, more importantly, why they perform well.

We broke through the "expanding projectiles only" barrier by removing the FBI measurements for

The INS ammo protocol has set a new minimum penetration distance for police ammo at 9 inches. Much of the ammo it prefers, like this 9mm 115-grain JHP +P+, penetrates less than 12 inches.

expanded diameter of the recovered projectile. In the INS test, penetration wound efficiency is determined by minimum requirements for the length and depth of multiple wound channels. The retained weight of projectile fragments must also meet minimum individual weight

requirements to be given value as effective wounding agents. This system appears to be quite workable based on preliminary test results.

We decided that a pass-fail criterion was the right methodology to use for testing ammunition robustness. The real question here is not how well the projectile performs after passing through barriers, but will the projectile successfully penetrate a suspect after passing through the barrier. The second consideration here is assurance that deformed projectiles will not manifest excessive penetration after striking a suspect on the far side of the barrier. Our third consideration is that all of the variables involved in trying to get a projectile to perform well on both the human body and on hard barriers is enough to drive an engineer to distraction. Our perception of the result of these conflicting design parameters is that projectiles are now being manufactured that perform well in the FBI barrier test to the detriment of their performance against a human target. As stated earlier, our decision was to consider projectile dynamics within the human body as paramount.

Most of the engineers and subject

One-third of the shots fired by Border Patrol agents are into windshields of smugglers trying to run down agents.

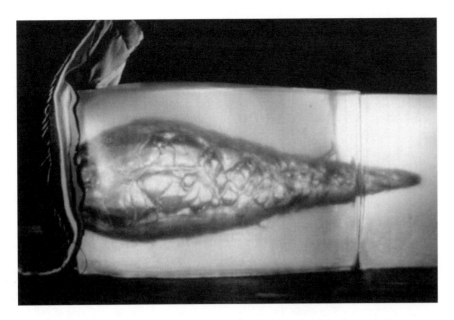

The INS gives a full 50 percent weighting to the gelatin test involving heavy clothes. Heavily clothed subjects are encountered in cold and hot climates alike.

matter experts who helped to build this protocol felt that the FBI test results over the last 10 years have shown that the sheet metal, plywood, and 20 yard tests are somewhat redundant and produce little additional data for the effort and expense required to complete them. For this reason, the INS dropped all but the sheet metal tests from the pass/fail penetration tests. I made every effort to insure that the INS would conduct all gelatin tests using identical materials and procedures as are used at the FBI laboratory. This allows the INS, which has the largest number of federal law enforcement officers and the greatest number of federal shooting incidents, to exchange and compare data with the FBI, which has the best law enforcement ammunition performance data base in the world.

One other thing. The INS protocol will produce the same "two aspirin" anomaly as does the FBI protocol due to our minimum penetration requirements. We wouldn't want our compadres at Quantico to suffer all that ridicule alone!

Finally, I did my best to ensure that the INS test protocol will remain dynamic. There are measures built into the entire process that mandate reexamination on a regular basis. The protocol encourages flexibility and change as new advancements are realized in ammunition technology. Initial tests using the INS protocol have already revealed some amazing advancements in both design and material technologies. I am convinced that there will be dramatic changes in ammunition in the very near future. I retired from the U.S.

Border Patrol in August of 1999 satisfied that I have done what I can to assure our agents that the INS is prepared for these changes.

INCAPACITATION: WHAT IT IS AND WHAT IT AIN'T

While arguments rage about what causes incapacitation and/or what works the best, the dismal reality is that it is difficult to find any significant number of people who agree on a definition for the beast. The words "incapacitation" and "stopping power" have so many different interpretations that any discussion of the topic must be prefaced by a definition. In 1986 Dr. Martin Fackler opined that the only true incapacitation was death. Evan Marshall, who recognized and tackled this monster before science was willing to admit it existed, tried to define it as a combination of cessation of aggression followed by collapse of the suspect before he could move a certain distance. There are probably as many definitions as there are subject matter experts in the field.

As both a procurement officer and a researcher, definitions have become of paramount importance to me. While we can dance around with vague concepts in a debate, concepts such as "stopping power," "frangible" bullets, and "nontoxic" primers just don't work for the simple reason that they do not exist. The word "frangible" is meaningless unless one can define exactly what one means by the term. This can only be done through clearly written performance requirements. Concepts such as "nontoxic" cannot be defined because the product does not exist. Try a box full of "nontoxic" primers on top of your Wheaties and you will quickly enter the world of chelation therapy! I'm prefacing my attempt to identify a rational definition of incapacitation with this discussion so that the reader might appreciate that this is no easy task.

Test	Pass/Fail	Minimum and Maximum depth of Pen.
Clothed Gelatin	9″ min.	18″ maximum
Auto Glass @ compound angle	9″ min	18″ maximum
Sheetrock	9″ min	18″ maximum
20 gauge sheet metal	9″ min	18″ maximum

In order to work with the concept of incapacitation for INS purposes, I first had to create a definition for us to work with. My approach is somewhat different from those used by others because I could not find a definition that I felt adequately described the phenomenon. I do not feel that the distance a person staggers after being shot is an adequate definition, although it has worked quite well for Marshall and Sanow. I think that a dead man is truly incapacitated, but it hardly describes the other 90 percent of assailants who are shot, cannot continue to fight, but survive their experience quite nicely.

From my point of view, any attempt to define incapacitation in terms of wound severity or location is off-track. Many are wounded, but few expire. If there is no identifiable constant in the equation, the definition will always collapse. Here then is incapacitation as I have attempted to define it:

Incapacitation is an event measured in the dimension of time. It cannot be measured in any other way because there is no constant with which to measure it. A person shot in the arm may instantly collapse in a state of complete unconsciousness. A suspect shot through the heart may fight like a lion for seconds that seem like an eternity.

The "event" measured in time must be the point(s) at which the suspect is unable to continue aggressive action. This is the only event that is appreciated by the officer(s) involved in the incident. All other "events" fall far short of this reasonable expectation. I felt that we must stay away from such descriptive words such as "temporary" or "permanent" because they complicate the issue of time. How much time defines "temporary"? How long does the suspect have to remain neutralized before the incapacitation can be termed "permanent"? If the suspect becomes instantly comatose and wakes up 30 years later, do we go back and

change the incident report to reflect that his incapacitation was temporary? You see the problem.

I define incapacitation as a cessation of aggression on the part of the assailant that can be reasonably attributed to a projectile impact on the assailant preceding the cessation of aggression. This cessation of aggression shall be categorized exclusively in terms of time as "immediate" or "delayed" and may be further described using the adjectives of "momentary" or "prolonged."

Any identifiable cessation of aggression, regardless of cause or duration, is always temporary in nature. Permanent incapacitation is not an attribute of injury or surrender. It is a condition of control achieved when the person of the suspect is handcuffed and/or otherwise secured from further potential for effective aggression.

Law enforcement officers who must use deadly force do so with only one goal in mind—to stop the aggressive actions of the assailant. There is no other consideration, and how this is achieved is a moot point. In a recent shooting incident in El Paso, the assailant was firing at agents when he was struck near the juncture of the neck and shoulder with a .40 S&W 155-grain JHP. The assailant immediately stopped shooting, then turned and ran approximately 100 yards before expiring from his wound. Using the above definition, this is clearly a successful incapacitation that can be directly attributed to the ammunition used in the incident. It was clearly the causative factor in the cessation of aggression.

In another earlier incident, I received a complaint from an agent who claimed that the 110-grain projectile was worthless because he had shot a suspect with the round at point-blank range. He stated that the surgeon had given him the recovered projectile and that it had failed to expand. When I asked him for further details, he stated that the round had

passed through the suspect's leather belt just above the right hip and had traveled through the viscera approximately 12 inches before coming to rest. When I asked him how the suspect reacted to the single shot fired by the agent, he waxed enthusiastic. "Oh," he said, "The guy collapsed on the spot and grabbed his stomach with both hands. He was in a lot of pain!" As I walked the agent back through the incident, explaining that the round had not expanded because the hollow cavity had seen service as a leather punch, and pointed out that the round had actually done everything he wanted it to do, he agreed that maybe it was OK ammunition after all!

I think the critical aspect of immediate or delayed incapacitation is found in the descriptive adverb of *momentary*. It is this concept that brings focus back to the issue of the efficacy of kinetic energy. As stated earlier, there are many incidents in which immediate incapacitation occurred but did not last any appreciable time. The important fact to remember is that any incapacitation, regardless of duration, may be just the break the officer needs to get the upper hand. This is extremely critical when the fight takes place at point-blank range, the range in which most officers are killed. Incapacitation lasting only a fraction of a second can prevent the assailant from delivering a timely and potentially fatal shot. It may additionally provide the officer with an opportunity to deliver one or more following shots to effect a prolonged (always temporary) state of incapacitation.

The immediacy of incapacitation is the primary measure of projectile performance in the law enforcement context. The value of this performance goal cannot be overstated. While the high-momentum round may achieve immediate incapacitation through a direct hit on the spinal column or brain, it rarely elicits immediate incapacitation with penetrations to other anatomical areas. It would certainly be incorrect to say or even imply that high-energy rounds always provide incapacitation. That just isn't true. What cannot be ignored is that they have a much better record of achieving immediate momentary incapacitation than do high-momentum rounds. I will debate this position with anyone and put a year's paycheck on my soapbox to boot!

Now some sharp fella out there is going to point out that the .38 Special 110-grain +P+ was a high-energy round and I have already admitted that it failed miserably. It failed us for the same reason I believe the standard-velocity 9mm failed so many others. If it doesn't leave the muzzle with enough energy to do the job, it isn't going to acquire it on the way to the mark. In fact, I believe this load would have been significantly more effective if it had performed to specification. It was supposed to have a velocity of 1200 fps, which would have given it a Ke of 352 ft-lbs. This falls well short of our mandatory 400 ft-lbs. level, but it is still significantly better than the 1050 fps and 269 ft-lbs. level of Ke that we got out of it. When kinetic energy levels are this low, you had better be using a high-momentum round or you are in deep trouble.

The requirement for immediate incapacitation is what truly separates law enforcement ammunition from military or hunting ammunition. The military objective is to remove opponents from the field of battle. Wounding is the best avenue to this goal since wounded soldiers need the assistance of other soldiers and medical personal. This further reduces the number of opponents. The military tactician is hardly concerned about the immediacy of incapacitation. The savvy hunter will use ammunition that penetrates through both sides of the game he is hunting. He knows that this will not only increase the blood flow from the quarry but will create a better blood trail for him to follow at his leisure. Again, the immediacy of incapacitation is hardly a concern.

Every hunter knows that knocking an animal off its feet with the initial impact of the round does not ensure a successful hunt. (Yes folks, the weight of a projectile may not knock a man off his feet, but the effect of energy dissipation within the human body damn sure can.) The average deer size animal will regain its feet and be off and running anyhow. It's to be expected. A second shot is nice if you can get it, but it's rarely critical.

It is very different for the law enforcement officer. *Immediacy is everything*. Our very lives depend on it. Delayed incapacitation is a disaster that has cost us the lives of too many of our fellow officers. We simply cannot afford it.

HANDGUN AMMUNITION OF THE FUTURE

The last quarter century has truly been a renaissance period for conventional hollowpoint projectile designs. Virtually every major manufacturer produces a premium design with breathtaking performance capabilities. The Federal Hydra-Shok, CCI Gold Dot, Remington Golden Saber, and PMC Starfire are but a few of these outstanding designs. Even the standard-grade hollowpoint munitions demonstrate a robustness and expansion consistency that was unheard of prior to the FBI Ballistic Protocol. For those who desire the ultimate in power, there are the +P and +P+ offerings of Cor-Bon that many consider to be the ultimate performers in this genre. These are great products, but time marches on, and all things must change. So it is with ammunition.

Small arms ammunition technology is poised at the threshold of breathtaking breakthroughs. Ammunition that was a pipe dream yesterday is today's reality. Within five years, conventional handgun and rifle ammunition as we know it will join the legions of antiquity; they will be

held in the same fond perspective of nostalgia as the black powder firearms of another time.

The age of composite projectile construction is upon us, and it appears to be a good thing. Lead is dead, and the wake is in full swing. Technological design, aided by computerized engineering and composite material technology, is already producing projectiles that promise to outperform conventional lead projectiles for all but the most demanding long-range competitive rifle disciplines.

I have already seen .40 S&W composite projectiles that weigh only 125 grains but have twice the robustness of the fabled .357 125-grain JHP. This proprietary round creates a temporary cavity that has at least 25 percent greater volume than the benchmark magnum and penetrates consistently to 12 inches or more in ballistic gelatin. The 357/125 struggles to break the 10 inch penetration level and seems rather inadequate in comparison. The level of recoil generated is less than any current .40 S&W load on the market.

I have seen ammunition designed as frangible for the purpose of increasing the safety margin in training and reducing toxic metal build-up on ranges that had accuracy every bit as good or better than some of the best conventional ammunition on the market. And I'm speaking of ammunition that I tested in the prototype stages of development!

Sinterfire, Powell River, Simunitions, Delta, Long Bow—these are just a few of the pioneers in this field. Many of them are working hand-in-hand with the major ammunition manufacturers to bring us some pretty fantastic offerings.

The changes don't stop here. Expanding ammunition design continues to improve in leaps and bounds, but the truly exciting news is the advent of ammunition that equals or exceeds the performance of these rounds and does not depend on the dynamics of expansion for their performance. I would like to share three of these designs with you.

First, because it is already a relatively old design but a harbinger of the future, is the FN SS-190 or 5.7 x 28. This diminutive bottleneck cartridge design has been around for awhile. What makes it noteworthy is that it is chambered in both the FN P90 submachine gun and a companion semiautomatic polymer pistol. It utilizes an alloy projectile with a hardened core that destabilizes and tumbles very quickly after impact with the target. This 31-grain projectile leaves the muzzle of the handgun at a blistering 2100 fps. This round has energy figures that fall below our recommended minimum, but I believe that the projectile design and upset characteristics give it high potential for immediate suspect incapacitation. In spite of the fact that it is a military ball design, it outperforms the temporary cavitation abilities of most law enforcement handgun ammo due to the fact that it tumbles immediately after entry into gelatin. It penetrates an average of 9 inches, the same as the .357 125-grain, which it handily outperforms. The characteristics of performance are far closer to those demonstrated by rifle ammunition.

The pistol holds 20 rounds in the magazine, is extremely accurate, and generates 25 percent less recoil than a standard 9mm 124-grain load. My first six shots at 25 yards from standing supported position with this fixed-sight pistol placed four shots touching and one shot slightly out of the group at each side. All six shots fell into a sub 1 inch group. Again, this was with a prototype pistol. Needless to say, Type III-A body armor proves utterly inadequate to stop this round. The P-90 submachine gun is so controllable that I can fire an entire 50-round magazine in the full automatic mode at a distance of 15 yards and keep all shots in the torso area of a Transtar II target . . . with the weapon fired while I am holding it one-handed butted

against my teeth! (Yes, I have a witness and a videotape to prove it!)

For law enforcement agencies that still maintain it is not good to issue ammunition that can penetrate an officer's own ballistic vest, I offer you this. With the Los Angeles bank robbery and the Carl Drega incidents behind us, the increased criminal use of ballistic armor is a documented certainty. The question is no longer, "Will my armor defeat my own ammunition?" but rather, "Will my ammunition defeat the armor of my adversary?" Arming our law enforcement officers with handguns and long arms that cannot defeat threat level III-A ballistic armor is irresponsible to the point of insanity. Unfortunately, more officers and civilians will die before this truth becomes self-evident.

Second on the list of dramatic new direction is the Quik-Shok design. This projectile is manufactured for handguns by the Triton Ammunition Corporation; shotgun slugs are manufactured by Magnum Performance Ballistics. These cartridges utilize a unique projectile that causes a controlled separation of the projectile into three well-defined independent projectiles *after* penetration into the body. It is particularly dramatic in the 12-gauge shotgun slug configuration. After observing the effect of this projectile in both ballistic gelatin tests and in wild hogs and deer, it is my humble opinion that it has the highest potential for incapacitation of any ammunition available to law enforcement today, bar none. It has the added advantage of reduced penetration due to the separation process. This is good news for tactical teams. Even in the event of full penetration, each individual projectile is significantly smaller in size and less lethal than a Foster or sabot slug design.

One of the major differences between this design and the Glaser and Mag-Safe projectiles that preceded it is the factor of robustness. Tom Burcyznski, the architect of the projectile, states that the depth of the

The only "controlled separation" load to meet INS standards for penetration and retained weight was the Triton .40 S&W 155-grain Quik-Shok. The load was specifically developed for the INS.

grooves in the sides of the projectiles determines how quickly or slowly separation will occur. This feature, combined with the hardening or softening of the projectile material, allows the manufacturer to build a projectile that can penetrate to whatever depth is desirable. Mr. Burcynski also designed the Federal Hydra-Shok and PMC Starfire bullets as well as numerous other patented designs. When he speaks, I listen.

Perhaps the greatest benefit of Burcynski's pistol cartridge design is the increasing cone-shaped path of travel of the three projectiles. In measuring the circumference of the area covered at 8 inches of travel through ballistic gelatin, the potential for striking a major organ, blood vessel, or the central nervous system is increased dramatically. This area is approximately 2.5 inches in diameter. At 10 inches it is roughly 4 inches in diameter. In other words, one centered shot will place projectiles within 50 to 75 percent of the entire 6-inch-diameter critical-center mass area of the human torso. While the multiple handgun projectile concept is not new, this is the only design that has good exterior ballistics, excellent initial penetration of the body, and an attendant explosive release of kinetic energy at the moment of projectile separation that takes place well within the body. When the depth of penetrations of the independent projectiles are combined, the penetration performance is 50 to 100 percent greater than conventional expanding designs. As an added bonus, this penetration occurs where it counts—in the first 12 inches of target mass.

While these premium projectiles for both small arms and shotguns carry a premium price, the price is well worth the performance. I am sure that other controlled-separation projectile designs will follow from these and other manufacturers. They are worth taking a look at.

RADIALLY DYNAMIC SOLID PROJECTILES

The final design that I want to discuss is one that I mentioned at the beginning of this chapter. I was absolutely captivated by the potential of solid nonexpanding projectile designs for handgun cartridges after our 1984 ballistic tests. The major problem inherent to the THV design was its lack of penetration. A second shortcoming of this round and most other handgun projectile designs is that their use of kinetic energy is very inefficient. The disruption of tissue caused by their release of kinetic energy is distributed uniformly in a spherical shape around the path of the projectile. It is commonly held and quite true that the energy dispersion characteristics of handgun projectiles does not overcome the elastic capabilities of most human tissue with the exception of the heart, kidneys, and liver. As a result, the only significant permanent damage that can be expected results from tissue destroyed due to direct contact with the projectile. The dynamics of reshaping a projectile designed for good exterior ballistic performance into one that will maximize tissue damage also requires the use of significant levels of projectile energy. This is a waste of energy in a projectile that barely retains enough

energy to cause incapacitation in the best of scenarios.

I started considering designs based on the THV and came to the following concept. I believed that the shortcomings of the THV and expanding projectiles could be eliminated through design. I discussed my ideas with several industry engineers and received positive but cautious feedback. I then contacted Charles Kelsey of the Devel Corporation and shared the concept with him.

I believed that if cutting edges (i.e., fins) were added to the lateral surfaces of the THV design along with increased projectile weight, several things might occur:

1. The lateral fins would cause cuts in any tissue that came in contact with the projectile.
2. If the space between the fins were designed properly, kinetic energy bleeding off the projectile would concentrate and direct both this energy and liquefied tissue directly into the cuts caused by the fins. This directed flow of energy and tissue would continue the cutting of the preweakened tissue. Since energy will follow the path of least resistance, the ball of energy observed in conventional projectile cavities should now be directed in a star-shaped lateral dispersion. In other words, the projectile would release energy in much the same manner as a shaped charge explosive. I felt this design might very well overcome the elasticity of human tissue and render plastic, i.e., permanent tissue damage beyond the actual wound channel of the projectile. If this permanent damage extended even an eighth of an inch beyond the wound channel, the net result would be a wound channel in any given caliber that was a minimum of 50 percent greater than the best performing expanding projectile!

3. Such a round, utilizing a controlled meplat diameter would easily penetrate to any depth desired while requiring far less weight than a conventional expanding projectile.
4. With the weight held down, velocities could be increased dramatically. This would result in even greater levels of kinetic energy available for tissue destruction.
5. If the meplat was designed with a sharp 90 degree edge completely around its circumference, the ability of the projectile to "grab" the target would be enhanced appreciably. This was of particular importance for handgun projectiles striking the human skull or materials used in automobile construction.
6. Since the projectile is designed to be nondeforming with high rotational speed, its straight-line path should have significantly greater integrity than expanding designs. Penetration of bone, muscle tissue, and internal organs would not deflect the round significantly from its intended path of travel.
7. The low weight and high velocity of the round would result in a very flat shooting projectile with good long range capabilities. This is an important consideration for the Border Patrol.
8. The low weight and high velocity of the round would create very controllable recoil characteristics and allow for better firearm control and quick multiple shot delivery.

Charles Kelsey immediately saw the potential for such a round and began independent development of the projectile assisted by engineer Ed Herring of the Remington Corporation. The first prototypes were delivered in 1986 and proved extremely promising. Remington declined further involvement with the project, and Kelsey continued development on his own.

Kelsey's final prototype design was tested in December 1999, and the results were outstanding. This projectile, weighing 155 grains in .45 caliber, was driven at velocities between 1140 and 1700 fps. A frontal shot on a wild hog produced an entry wound that was *2.25 inches in diameter!* Two other flanking shots on hogs revealed that at entry, one rib had been struck, but the ribs on each side of the penetrated rib were also shattered by the disruption of tissue as the round penetrated the chest wall. Penetration averaged about 18 inches in all rounds tested, including the .40 S&W 125-grain and a 9mm of approximately 100 grains. While the prototype driven at 1700 fps was obviously the most spectacular, the .45 ACP, .40 S&W, and 9mm loadings delivered identical performance on a reduced scale. No ballistics expert who has reviewed the results of these shots can recall ever seeing this magnitude of wounding from a handgun projectile.

While the damage caused by this design was impressive, Kelsey was not satisfied. He consulted with ballistic engineers at the Southwest Research Institue in San Antonio, Texas, and made one last modification to the design that provided a 7 percent increase in performance. The Sinterfire Corporation will manufacture the projectiles and the Black Hills Ammunition Corporation under the LEVED ammunition label will assemble the cartridge components.

This projectile meets all of the design parameters that Charlie and I had envisioned for it. I commend him on his patience and perseverance in bringing it to life and wish him every success with it. How well it will perform as a self-defense cartridge remains to be seen. I think it has excellent potential.

Perhaps the most significant and impressive characteristic of the controlled separation projectiles and the radially directed energy solids is the fact that both of these designs demonstrate massive tissue and bone damage beginning at the moment of impact and continuing to the point of rest of the projectile(s). I predict that this type of instantaneous damage to external and intermediate tissues as well as internal organs will translate to an improvement in the immediate incapacitation effect of law enforcement ammunition.

These are only three designs from an industry that has only just begun to break through the boundaries of conventional thinking. It seems as though new designs are appearing every day, and it is almost impossible to keep up with them. I couldn't do it even when it was my full-time job. That brings me to two final observations.

Self-defense ammunition cannot be tested in every firearm available for its use. Each and every type of ammunition that an agency considers for use must be fired from agency weapons under conditions that closely approximate job performance requirements. Only then can you be sure that the ammunition you select has a high potential to perform to your expectations.

The only reliable performance expectation that one can have of a self-defense handgun load is that it will not achieve the desired results on the first shot delivered. One of the most important questions I ask of agents who have successfully overcome their adversaries is this: "What caused you to stop shooting?" Their reply is the only other near constant I have found in all my years of research. Almost all of them stated, "I stopped shooting because I lost visual contact with the suspect. When I relocated the suspect, I could see that he was out of the fight." To paraphrase their experience, most of these agents maintained fire on their adversary and only stopped after the adversary collapsed and was no longer in their sights. In most cases, the fight was over in less than two seconds after the first shot fired by the agent. This does not allow time for cognitive thought or for assessments of the adversary's condition. Focus must be on maintaining a practiced and consistent aiming technique combined with disciplined trigger control. These are the elements that will win the day. I sincerely desire this most satisfactory result for all who are destined to face the ultimate challenge.

I would like to dedicate my efforts on this project to the memory of my good friend and fellow Border Patrol Agent Walter Panchison, FBI Agents Ben Grogan and Jerry Dove, and all the law enforcement officers who have joined the ranks of our most honored. May they rest in peace.

TABLE 25-1
HANDGUN AMMO USED BY THE U.S. BORDER PATROL

Date	Caliber & Load	One-Shot Stop
1924	.45 ACP 230 grain Hardball	62%
1939	.38 Special 158 grain Roundnose Lead	51%
1958	.357 Magnum 158 grain Softpoint	73%
1982	.38 Special +P+ 110 grain JHP	83%
1986	.357 Magnun 110 grain JHP	88-90%
1986	.357 Magnum 125 grain JHP	87-96%
1986	.357 Magnum 145 grain Silvertip	86%
1987	.38 Super 125 grain Silvertip	91%
1987	.45 ACP +P 185 grain JHP	93%
1987	.45 ACP 185 grain Silvertip	84%
1987	9mm +P+ 115 grain JHP	90-93%
1994	.40 S&W 155 grain JHP	88-97%

TABLE 25-2
USEFUL RANGE VERSUS CALIBER

Caliber & Load	Range in yards
9mm 115 gr. +P+ JHP	150
.40 S&W 155 gr. JHP	115
.40 S&W 180 gr. JHP	100
10mm MV 180 gr. JHP	90
10mm Auto 180 gr. JHP	140
.45 ACP 185 gr. JHP	80
.45 ACP 185 gr. +P JHP	110

TABLE 25-3
GRIP SIZE VERSUS CALIBER

Caliber & Pistol	Design Rating
9mm single row	excellent
9mm double row	excellent
.40 S&W single row	excellent
.40 S&W double row	excellent
10mm single row	very good
10mm double row	poor
.45 ACP single row	very good
.45 ACP double row	poor

TABLE 25-4
FELT RECOIL VERSUS CALIBER

Caliber & Load	Recoil	Energy Rating
9mm 115 gr. +P+ JHP	5.4	Excellent
.40 S&W 155 gr. JHP	8.3	Very good
.40 S&W 180 gr. JHP	7.8	Very good
10mm MV 180 gr. JHP	7.8	Very good
10mm Auto 180 gr. JHP	9.2	Poor
.45 ACP 185 gr. JHP	8.1	Good
.45 ACP 185 gr. +P JHP	11.0	Fair

TABLE 25-5
INS/NFU AMMO TEST PROTOCOL

Test One	Bare 10 percent gelatin
Test Two	Heavily clothed gelatin
Test Three	Windshield glass, 45/15 compound angle
Test Four	Wallboard, 2 sheets
Test Five	Sheet steel 18 gauge

* In all five tests, measure bullet penetration up to 12 inches and retained weight. Bullets must penetrate between 9 and 20 inches in all test phases. Range for all five tests is 10 feet.

TABLE 25-6
INS AND FBI AMMO PROTOCOL COMPARISON

	INS	FBI
Test media	BB-calibrated 10% gelatin	BB-calibrated 10% gelatin
Minimum penetration	9 inches	12 inches
Measurement range	9 to 12 inches	12 to 18 inches
Maximum penetration	20 inches	none
Wound cavity measured	temporary stretch cavity	permanent crush cavity
Current duty load	Remington .40 S&W 155 gr. JHP	Federal .40 S&W 165 gr. Med. Vel. Hydra-Shok
Nominal Velocity	1195 fps	950 fps
Muzzle Energy	492 ft-lbs.	331 ft-lbs.
Power Factor	185	157
Actual One-Shot Stops	93%	82%

TABLE 25-7
FUNCTIONAL RELIABILITY PHASE

ELEMENT	POINTS
Functional Reliability	**400 points**
Malfunctions	
0	400 points
1	280 points
2	Disqualified
Terminal Ballistic Performance	400 points
Depth of Penetration	
Bare Gelatin	60 points
Heavy Clothing	100 points
Auto Glass	40 points
Projectile Weight Retention	
Bare Gelatin	22 points
Heavy Clothing	38 points
Auto Glass	15 points
Temporary Stretch Cavity	
Bare Gelatin	125 points
Dispersion	200 points
Firearm	125 points
Test Barrel	75 points
TOTAL	1000 points

CHAPTER 26

INS Ammunition Barrier Penetration Comparative Evaluation

AUTHORS' NOTE: *This INS report is presented in its entirety and without edit or comment, with one exception. All references to the ability of any particular cartridge to defeat any threat level of soft or hard body armor have been deleted.*

INS Ammunition Barrier Penetration Comparative Evaluation
August 18–29, 1997

PURPOSE: This test was conducted for the following purposes:

To provide the Service with empirical data regarding the penetrative characteristics of ammunition after impact with a variety of common barriers that may be present in operational scenarios.

To provide the Service with empirical data that could be used to develop procurement specifications for controlled penetration .223 caliber rifle ammunition.

To provide the Service with empirical data regarding the comparative depths of penetration exhibited by Service duty ammunition for the 12 gauge shotgun, the 9 mm submachine gun, the .223 Rem. caliber carbine, and the .40 S&W caliber handgun when fired through common barriers.

HISTORY: This test was conducted as a result of concerns stated by INS Investigators. The Service did not have any empirical data regarding the penetrative characteristics of Service ammunition when used in an urban environment. INS Officers are uncertain as to what ammunition is most appropriate for use in different situations.

INS officers working in urban environments wanted to know if the penetrative characteristics of .223 ammunition are equal, lesser, or greater than other standard ammunition used by INS officers.

I. TEST PROCEDURES: The following information defines the procedures used for each test phase.

Preliminary Phase: 31 ammunition samples are listed by item numbers in this comparative evaluation. Item 8 was not tested in all phases due to projectile fragmentation that occurred as the bullet exited the barrel of the test firearm. Each ammunition was logged onto a computer data base prior to testing. Ammunition was categorized by manufacturer, caliber, weight, bullet type, and index numbers when available.

Velocity Test: Ten shots were fired for each ammunition sample through an Oehler Model 35 chronograph located 5 feet in front of the leading edge of the

The INS National Firearms Unit (NRU) is responsible for testing and selecting firearms and ammunition for 18,000 INS agents.

shooting bench. Chronograph screens were placed 5 feet apart with a verification screen between the front and rear screens. A black shield was placed between the muzzle of the test fire arm and the front screen of the chronograph. The ten shots fired for each item tested were used to establish a velocity average for the ammunition. All test shots were fired through the chronograph screens at the same distance and under controlled climactic conditions to ensure the validity of the test shot velocities.

Weight: All projectile samples were weighed on an RCBS Range Master electronic scale. The scales were calibrated before each session. The scales were re-calibrated at regular intervals during the weighing process to ensure accuracy. Sample projectile weights were recorded to the nearest whole grain. Recovered projectiles were weighed to the nearest one-tenth grain.

Gelatin Composition: The gelatin used was Kind and Knox Ballistic Gelatin (250-A) mixed to a 10% gelatin consistency as measured by weight. The mixing protocol consisted of heating the water to 180 degrees Fahrenheit, adding the gelatin, allowing the mix to cool to room temperature, and then curing the gelatin for a minimum of 24 hours at a temperature of 39.2 degrees. The gelatin was then removed from the containers, wrapped in cellophane to retain the moisture content of the gelatin, and replaced in the refrigerator. Refrigeration temperatures were monitored a minimum of six times per day when gelatin was under refrigeration.

The gelatin was calibrated with a 17 caliber BB at a velocity of 590 feet

From its Beretta 96D Brigadier pistol, the INS found the Remington .40 S&W 155-grain JHP to penetrate 12.75 inches in bare gelatin. The bullet expanded to .73 caliber and had a 100 percent weight retention.

The Remington .40 S&W 155-grain JHP penetrates 13.25 inches of gelatin after a double pane window and 14.25 inches of gelatin after angled auto glass.

per second +/- 20 feet per second. Penetration required in this test was 3.75 inches minimum and 4.725 inches maximum. All calibration shots were fired from a distance of 10 feet. All calibration and actual test shots were fired into gelatin blocks that had been exposed at room temperature for no more than 5 minutes.

All gelatin blocks were labeled with the time and date of mixing and all lots were used for testing within 36 hours after curing was completed. All gelatin blocks were wrapped to preserve moisture content prior to use.

Test Firearms: The firearms used in this test were as follows:

1. Colt M4/A1 carbine, 5.56 mm (.223 caliber with a 14.5" barrel.)
2. Colt 9 mm submachine-gun with a 10" barrel.

3. Remington 870 shotgun, 12 gauge with a 14" modified choke barrel.

4. Beretta 96D Brigadier pistol, .40 caliber with 4.72" barrel.

II. TEST PHASES: This evaluation was conducted in six test phases. A single block of gelatin measuring 13.5 inches in length was used in the bare gelatin test since industry protocol considers only the first 14 inches of penetration to be a factor in incapacitation. All other phases utilized as much gelatin as was necessary to capture each individual projectile fired. The additional gelatin was used to provide a gauge for determining the retained penetrative capabilities of projectiles after penetrating barriers.

The test phases are as follows:

Phase 1. Bare gelatin penetration test

Phase 2. Interior wall penetration test

Phase 3. Interior and exterior wall penetration test

Phase 4. Two pane window glass (untempered) penetration test

Phase 6. Automotive glass (tempered) penetration test

III DATA MATRIX CHARTS

Matrix One (Charts One through Six)

A Data matrix was prepared for each test Phase. Each ammunition item tested was listed in this matrix. Charts one through six are done in the matrix one format. Matrix one includes the following information:

1. Test Item Number: This is the number assigned to each ammunition tested.

2. Manufacturer: The name of the company under whom the ammunition is labelled. Some of the ammunition tested is jointed manufactured by two different companies.

During Border Patrol testing, the FN P90-fired 5.7 x 28mm 31-grain FMJ penetrated 13.5 inches of bare gelatin and 11.25 inches of gelatin after a double pane window. This caliber is now being used by tactical and patrol officers across the country.

From a Colt AR-15 M4, the Federal .223 Rem 40-grain HP penetrated 8.5 inches of bare gelatin. From a 20 inch Colt HBAR, this explosive bullet penetrated just 6.5 inches. This load produces the least penetration of any conventional bullet in the caliber.

3. Caliber: The measured diameter of the bullet tested in either fraction of inches or in millimeters as designated by the manufacturer.

4. Weight: The manufacturers specified weight for the bullet tested. Samples of all bullets were weighed to ensure that the manufacturers stated bullet weights were accurate.

5. Type: Bullets were classified using standard SAAMI designations for bullet type. Classifications were arbitrarily given

to ammunition that do not currently have established SAAMI designations. Appendix One provides the purpose and definitions for this category.

6. Firearm: Firearms were listed as Carbine, Shotgun, Submachine-gun and Pistol.

7. Barrel Length: The length of the barrel on the test firearm.

8. Average Velocity: The average velocity taken from a ten round sample of the test ammunition.

9. Test Velocity: The velocity recorded for the test shot fired for each individual phase of the test.

10. Retained Weight: The retained weight of the fired projectile to the nearest one-tenth of a grain.

11. Percentage of Retained Weight: The difference between the original weight of the projectile and the weight of the recovered projectile.

12. Projectile Diameter: An average of two or more measurements of the diameter of the recovered projectile.

13. Projectile Classification: A system developed to define the level of deformation of projectiles after recovery from the ballistic gelatin.

14. Gelatin Penetration: The depth of penetration of the projectile, or the largest remaining portion of the projectile by weight, into the ballistic gelatin.

15. Temporary Cavity Length (TCL): The length of the temporary cavity from the point where it became approximately twice the bullet diameter to the point where it became reduced to less than twice the bullet diameter.

16. Temporary Cavity Median (TCM): The point at which the mid point of the cavity occurred, measured from the front of the gelatin block.

The .223 Rem 55-grain HPBT penetrates 10 inches of bare gelatin. As an urban patrol load, this penetrates less than most handgun loads and produces 94 percent one-shot stops.

The .223 Rem 55-grain SP produces roughly the same penetration as the 55-grain HP. However, the wound profile is very different.

17. Temporary Cavity Diameter (TCD): The diameter of the temporary cavity measured at its point of greatest occurrence.

18. Fragment Location: The points at which significant bullet fragments came to rest in the ballistic gelatin as measured from the front of the gelatin block.

II. Test Measurements. The performance of the ammunition was measured in the following manner:

1. Each ammunition being evaluated was chronographed with a 10 round average used as the standard velocity for that ammunition.

2. Each ammunition being evaluated was chronographed when fired in the ballistic gelatin tests.

3. Each ammunition being evaluated was measured for depth of penetration into the ballistic gelatin. The heaviest portion of the bullet that exhibited the deepest penetration into the ballistic gelatin was use for this measurement.

4. Each gelatin block was photographed after impact of the test ammunition.

5. Each ammunition being tested had the heaviest remaining portion of the bullet weighed after extraction from the ballistic gelatin to determine retained weight.

6. Each ammunition being tested had the heaviest remaining portion of the bullet achieving deepest penetration into the gelatin measured for diameter. This measurement was an average of two or more measurements taken at the circumference of the forward end of the bullet. In cases involving only bullet fragments, the heaviest recoverable fragment was measured for diameter if a measurable diameter was present.

7. Each projectile was classified for type after extraction from the ballistic gelatin.

Phase One: Bare Gelatin Penetration

One round of each ammunition tested was fired across the chronograph and into the ballistic gelatin located fifteen feet from the muzzle of the test firearm.

The use of a [13.5"+] designation on Phase One charts and graphs indicates that the projectile passed completely through a gelatin block measuring 13.5 inches in length.

All necessary measurements were recorded to include:

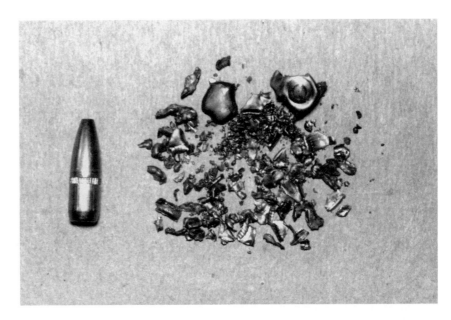

The .223 Rem 40-grain HP almost totally fragments in gelatin. Its controlled penetration and 96 percent one-shot stop rating make it an excellent choice for urban patrol.

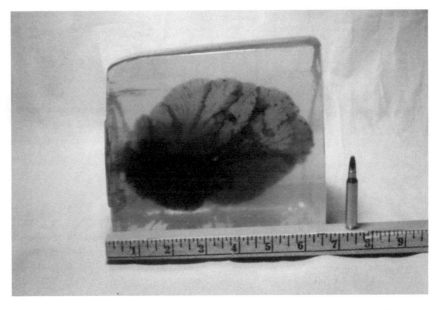

The .223 Rem Glaser 45-grain Safety Slug at 3430 fps totally fragments in bare gelatin. Number 12 birdshot shreds the first 6 inches.

a) The depth of penetration of the bullet in the gelatin block

b) The weight of the bullet or largest bullet fragment that exhibited the deepest penetration in the gelatin block

c) The diameter of the spent bullet

d) A photograph of the gelatin block with an identifying card and measuring scale before the bullet was removed from the gelatin block

e) A classification of the bullet or bullet fragment

Phase Two: Interior Wall Penetration Test

One round of each ammunition was fired across the chronograph and through two sheets of one half inch sheetrock placed three and one half inches apart before impacting the gelatin block(s) located four inches behind the second sheet of sheetrock and fifteen feet from the muzzle of the test firearm.

All necessary measurements were recorded to include

a) The depth of penetration of the bullet in the gelatin block.

b) The weight of the bullet or heaviest bullet fragment that exhibited the deepest penetration in the gelatin block.

c) The diameter of the spent bullet.

d) A photograph of the gelatin block with an identifying card and measuring scale before the bullet was removed from the gelatin block.

e) A classification of the bullet or bullet fragment.

Phase Three: Combined Interior and Exterior Wall Penetration Test

One round of each ammunition was fired across the chronograph and through a barrier placed in front of the ballistic gelatin. The round passed through the barrier designed to duplicate a combined interior and exterior wall. This barrier consisted of one sheet of one half inch sheetrock, a three and one half inch sheet of R11 rolled fiberglass insulation, one sheet of three quarter inch cellutex exterior insulation, one sheet of five eighth inch Homosote exterior sheathing, and one layer of exterior vinyl siding. Ammunition that passed through this barrier then impacted with a block(s)

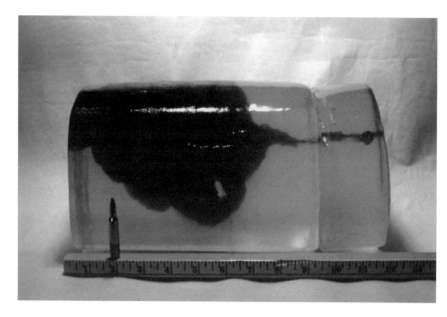

The .223 Rem 64-grain PSP is a popular police load. The Border Patrol found it penetrated around 12 inches of gelatin regardless of the barrier.

The .223 Rem 64-grain PSP is shown recovered from bare gelatin. This load has produced 95 percent one-shot stops.

of gelatin placed four inches from the barrier and fifteen feet from the muzzle of the test firearm.

All necessary measurements were recorded to include

a) The depth of penetration of the bullet in the gelatin block.

b) The weight of the bullet or heaviest bullet fragment that exhibited the deepest penetration in the gelatin block.

c) The diameter of the spent bullet.

d) A photograph of the gelatin block with an identifying card and measuring scale before the bullet was removed from the gelatin block.

e) A classification of the bullet or bullet fragment. Phase Four: Two Pane Window Penetration Test

One round of each ammunition was fired across the chronograph and through two sheets of one sixteenth inch thick, untempered, single strength window glass spaced two inches apart. The bullet then impacted with a gelatin block(s) located four inches from the rear pane and fifteen feet from the muzzle of the test firearm.

All necessary measurements were recorded to include

a) The depth of penetration of the bullet in the gelatin block.

b) The weight of the bullet or heaviest bullet fragment that exhibited the deepest penetration in the gelatin block.

c) The diameter of the spent bullet.

d) A photograph of the gelatin block with an identifying card and measuring scale before the bullet was removed from the gelatin block.

e) A classification of the bullet or bullet fragment.

Phase Six: Tempered Automotive Glass Penetration Test

One round of each ammunition was fired across the chronograph and through a sheet of tempered automotive windshield glass placed at a 45 degree angle to the path of the bullet. The bullet then impacted with a gelatin block(s) located four inches from the glass and fifteen feet from the muzzle of the test firearm.

All necessary measurements were recorded to include

a) The depth of penetration of the bullet in the gelatin block.

b) The weight of the bullet or heaviest bullet fragment that exhibited the deepest penetration in the gelatin block.

c) The diameter of the spent bullet.

d) A photograph of the gelatin block with an identifying card and measuring scale before the bullet was removed from the gelatin block.

e) A classification of the bullet or bullet fragment.

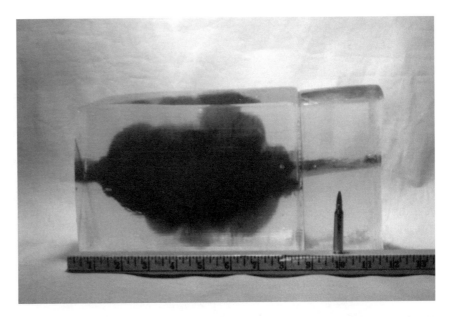

The .223 Rem 69-grain HPBT penetrates 12.75 inches of bare gelatin (shown) and 9 inches after auto glass. The 69-grain HPBTs have the best stopping power record in the caliber.

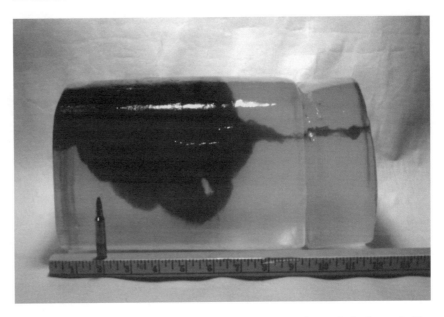

The .223 Rem 69-grain HPBT is shown recovered from bare gelatin. In nearly 80 shootings, this popular match load has produced 98 percent one-shot stops.

III. TEST RESULTS

It is worth noting that the 12 gauge buckshot loads out-penetrated the 155 grain .40 S&W caliber pistol loading in all but phase two of the test. The handgun bullet surpassed the buckshot loads by enough distance in this one phase to place it ahead of the buckshot loads in the category of combined total penetration depth. This type of anomaly can occur in any test scenario and emphasizes the need for careful review of all the test data rather than just the cumulative results of the test.

The test results indicate that there are significant differences in the penetration characteristics of different types of ammunition. A general synopsis of these characteristics are as follows:

12 Gauge Shotgun Ammunition
437 Grain Slug-The 12 gauge slug is characterized by deep penetration through barriers.

Tactical Buckshot Loadings-The buckshot loads are characterized by deep penetration through most barriers.

The 12 gauge shotgun loads were, in general, the deepest penetrating

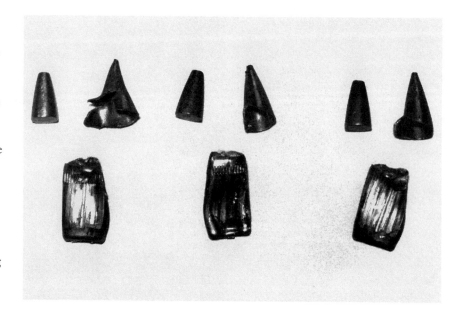

On impact with gelatin, the dual core, .223 Rem 62-grain M855 FMJ tumbles and snaps in two behind the steel penetrator. The result is rapid energy transfer and 96 percent one-shot stops. This FMJ bullet penetrates LESS than the 69-grain HPs.

rounds in these barrier tests. This is probably due to their unique characteristic of having very high energy levels generated at relatively low velocities with a projectile(s) that have high sectional density.

9 mm Submachine-gun Ammunition
The 9 mm Submachine-gun performance varied significantly depending on the type of ammunition used. It was the least predictable of all ammunition tested.

Officers who utilize the Service 9 mm submachine-guns should review the results of this test carefully and must be aware of the significant differences in barrier penetration that may occur when different types of Service 9 mm ammunition are used in the submachine-gun.

Pistol Ammunition
The .40 S&W 155 grain ammunition demonstrated deep penetration characteristics. In many cases it was only outperformed by the shotgun loads and two of the .223 rifle loadings that were designed specifically to provide deep penetration of barriers. It penetrated deeper than all other rounds tested on the interior/exterior wall test, and penetrated deeper than the special purpose .223 rifle rounds on the windshield test.

The depth of penetration of the .40 S&W ammunition is critically influenced by its capacity for expansion. If the bullet strikes soft tissue, it will generally exhibit moderate penetration due to expansion of the bullet. If the expansion cavity is filled with material from hard barriers, it will fail to expand and then exhibits very deep penetration characteristics. This tendency to penetrate deeply is also enhanced by the relatively low velocity and heavy sectional density of the bullet.

Rifle Ammunition
The Service .223 caliber 55 grain full metal jacket rifle ammunition (Item 18) displayed moderate penetration characteristics after passing through barriers. In most cases it was the least penetrative of all Service ammunition tested.

The inability of this ammunition to provide deep penetration after passing through barriers is due to the high initial velocity of the ammunition and the relatively light weight, low section density, and light construction of the projectile. These factors contribute to the rapid loss of energy exhibited in the test by this and most other, .223 caliber rifle ammunition tested.

APPENDIX ONE:
Projectile Classification:
Purpose: The purpose of projectile classification is to provide the researcher with information regarding the

characteristics of the recovered projectile. The size, diameter, and retained weight of a recovered projectile can be useful in an evaluation of the effectiveness of a particular projectile when compared with other projectiles fired under the same controlled conditions. Different projectiles may demonstrate the same level of penetration in ballistic gelatin but retain significantly different levels of weight, size, and diameter as they pass through the gelatin. The INS National Firearms Unit maintains that all projectiles fired from Service firearms have the potential of inflicting disabling injuries to the person struck by the projectile(s) regardless of the size, shape, or weight of the recovered projectiles(s). The INS National Firearms Unit further maintains that projectiles that retain their original mass will, in most cases, be more effective than projectiles that fragment. The NFU perception is that law enforcement ammunition must be able to perform consistently in a wide variety of situations. While fragmenting projectiles can be highly effective in some situations, they do not perform well in many other situations. In most applications, INS officers need ammunition that can be relied upon to provide consistent performance in a wide variety of situations. There are however, specific circumstances identified within INS Program activities where fragmenting ammunition may be highly desirable. The NFU will continue to evaluate a wide variety of ammunition to ensure that INS Program needs are met.

The following classifications are designed for comparative use only. The INS National Firearms Unit does not include wound values or predictions of wounding effectiveness in ballistic reports.

Conclusions regarding the effectiveness of ammunition must be based on a balanced consideration of several factors. These factors include the ballistic performance of ammunition, reliable functioning of the ammunition in Service firearms, officer interface with the firearm/ammunition system, and the ammunition performance parameters required by the INS Program that will be utilizing the ammunition.

Projectile Classification Definition:

Full Projectile (FP): A full projectile is any recovered projectile that retains 90% or more of its original weight.

Hyper-expanded Projectile (HEP): A hyper-expanded projectile is a recovered projectile that retains more than 50% but less than 90% of the original projectile weight.

Diametric Fragment (DF): A diametric fragment is any recovered projectile that weighs less than 50% but more than 20% of its original weight. It will retain a measurable symmetrical diameter.

Non-Diametric Fragment (NDF): A non-diametric fragment is any recovered projectile that retains less than 50% but more than 20% of its original weight but does not retain a measurable symmetrical diameter.

Fragment Shard (FS): A fragment shard is any recovered projectile that retains less than 20% of the original projectile weight. Fragments shards may, or may not, retain a measurable symmetrical diameter.

TABLE 26-1
NFU-LIMITED PENETRATION TESTS

August 18-September 10, 1997
Test Phase One-Bare Gelatin Test

Ammo Mfg.	Cal.	Wght.	Type	Firearm	Ret. Wght. gr.	% Ret. Wght.	Proj. Dia. in.	Proj. Class	Gel. Pen. in.
Rem	9mm	115 gr.	JHP	SMG	91.1	79	.410	HEP	13.5
Fed	9mm	124 gr.	HSJHP	SMG	48	39	.375	DF	13.5
Fed	9mm	124 gr. +P	HSJHP	SMG	47.7	61.4	.400	HEP	12.5
Rem	9mm	115 gr. +P	JHP	SMG	89.6	78	.570	HEP	11.5
Rem	.40	155 gr.	JHP	Pistol	155.0	100	.730	FP	12.75
Fiocchi	.223	41 gr.	FR	Carbine	15.2	37	.223	DF	10.25
Win	.223	33 gr.	FR	Carbine	6.1	19	.230	FS	6.5
Sim	.223	36 gr.	FR	Carbine	10.0	28	.245	NDF	9
Rem	.223	40 gr.	JHP	Carbine	12	30	n/a	NDF	8.5
Rem	.223	50 gr.	POLYBT	Carbine	13.9	28	.233	DF	6.25
Blkhills	.223	50 gr.	POLYV	Carbine	12.2	24	n/a	NDF	6.25
Win	.223	50 gr.	STNOS	Carbine	13.1	26	.220	DF	13
Rem	.223	55 gr.	PSP	Carbine	30.2	55	.390	HEP	10.25
Rem	.223	55 gr.	PLHP	Carbine	26	47	.455	NDF	10
Fed	.223	55 gr.	JSPTAC	Carbine	53.3	97	.425	FP	13.5
Fed	.223	55 gr.	BTHP	Carbine	22.7	41	.360	DF	10
Win	.223	55 gr.	FMJ	Carbine	52	95	.223	FP	9
Blkhills	.223	55 gr.	SP	Carbine	33	60	.355	HEP	11.75
Blkhills	.223	60 gr.	SP	Carbine	34.2	57	.348	HEP	12.5
Rem	.223	62 gr.	HP-M	Carbine	41.8	67	.480	HEP	11
Win	.223	64 gr.	JSP	Carbine	57.6	90	.510	FP	12.25
Blkhills	.223	68 gr.	HP-M	Carbine	42.1	62	.243	HEP	13.25
Rem	.223	69 gr.	BTHP	Carbine	41.7	59	.245	HEP	12.75
Blkhills	.223	75 gr.	HP-M	Carbine	42	56	.400	HEP	13
F.N.	5.7x28	31 gr.	FMJ	SMG	31.0	100	.220	FP	13.5
Rem	.72	437 gr.	HP	Shotgun	434.2	99	.900	FP	13.5
Rem	.33	406 gr.	TAC-8	Shotgun	none rec.	none rec.	.320	FP	13.5
Fed	.33	486.5 gr.	TAC-9	Shotgun	490	100	.330	FP	13.5
Delta	.223	45 gr.	COP	Carbine	45	100	.223	FP	14.25
Win	.223	45 gr.	JKTFR	Carbine	16.6	37	.295	DF	11.5

TABLE 26-2
NFU-LIMITED PENETRATION TESTS

August 18-September 10, 1997
Test Phase Two-Interior Sheetrock Wall Test

Ammo Mfg.	Cal.	Wght.	Type	Firearm	% Ret. Wght.	Proj. Dia. in.	Proj. Class	Gel. Pen. in
Rem	9mm	115 gr.	JHP	SMG	100	.350	FP	18.75
Fed	9mm	124 gr.	HSJHP	SMG	98	.480	FP	19.5
Fed	9mm	124 gr. +P	HSJHP	SMG	99	.60	FP	13
Rem	9mm	115 gr. +P	JHP	SMG	100	.620	FP	12.75
Rem	.40	155 gr.	JHP	Pistol	100	.40	FP	19.25
Fiocchi	.223	41 gr.	FR	Carbine	18	.190	FS	9.75
Win	.223	33 gr.	FR	Carbine	frag	frag	FS	2.75
Sim	.223	36 gr.	FR	Carbine	27	.250	DF	8.25
Rem	.223	40 gr.	JHP	Carbine	23	.40	NDF	4.25
Rem	.223	50 gr.	POLYBT	Carbine	47	.450	DF	7.75
Blkhills	.223	50 gr.	POLYV	Carbine	38	.438	DF	7.5
Win	.223	50 gr.	STNOS	Carbine	26	.233	DF	12.5
Rem	.223	55 gr.	PSP	Carbine	72	.610	HEP	8.75
Rem	.223	55 gr.	PLHP	Carbine	43	.388	DF	10
Fed	.223	55 gr.	JSPTAC	Carbine	96	.512	FP	16
Fed	.223	55 gr.	BTHP	Carbine	51	.520	HEP	8.25
Win	.223	55 gr.	FMJ	Carbine	87	.304	FP	11.75
Blkhills	.223	55 gr.	SP	Carbine	60	.60	HEP	9.5
Blkhills	.223	60 gr.	SP	Carbine	47	.483	DF	8.75
Rem	.223	62 gr.	HP-M	Carbine	59	.545	HEP	9.75
Win	.223	64 gr.	JSP	Carbine	80	.495	FP	13.25
Blkhills	.223	68 gr.	HP-M	Carbine	76	.655	HEP	10.75
Rem	.223	69 gr.	BTHP	Carbine	n/a	none	FS	12
Blkhills	.223	75 gr.	HP-M	Carbine	17	none	FS	10
F.N.	5.7x28	31 gr.	FMJ	SMG	100	.220	FP	9
Rem	.72	437 gr.	HP	Shotgun	100	.80	FP	21.5
Rem	.33	406 gr.	TAC-8	Shotgun	100	.32	FP	21
Fed	.33	486.5 gr.	TAC-9	Shotgun	92	.33	FP	18
Delta	.223	45 gr.	COP	Carbine	100	.223	FP	22.5
Win	.223	45 gr.	JKTFR	Carbine	13.5	none	FS	7.5

TABLE 26-3
NFU-LIMITED PENETRATION TESTS

August 18-September 10, 1997
Test Phase Three-Interior/Exterior Wall Penetration

Ammo Mfg.	Cal.	Wght. gr.	Type	Avg. Vel. fps.	Test Vel. fps.	Ret. Wght. gr.	% Wght.	Proj. Dia. in.	Proj. Class	Gel. Pen.
Rem/9 mm/115 gr/JHP	9mm	115	JHP	1263	1263	115	100	.570	FP	16
Fed/9 mm/124 gr/HSJHP	9mm	124	HSJHP	1179	1192	121	98	.540	FP	13.25
Fed/9 mm/124 gr +P+/HS	9mm	124 +P	HS	1304	1292	122.1	98	.640	FP	12.5
Rem/9 mm/115 gr +P+/JHP	9mm	115 +P+	JHP	1403	1396	115	100	.590	FP	13
Rem/.40/155 gr/JHP	.40	155	JHP	1189	1219	155	100	.40	FP	24
Fiocchi/.223.41 gr/FR	.223	41	FR	3098	2971	8	19.5	n/a	FS	6.5
Win.RA/.223/33 gr/FR	.223	33	FR	3540	2919	6.7	2 pcs	n/a	FS	4.75
Simun/.223/36 gr/FR	.223	36	FR	3149	3091	14.0	39	.223	DF	9.5
Rem/.223/40 gr/JHP	.223	40	JHP	3129	3129	8.0	20	NDF	NDF	8.5
Rem/.223/40 gr/JHP	.223	50	POLYBT	2932	2908	n/a	n/a	n/a	FS	9
Rem/.223/50 gr/POLYBT	.223	50	POLYV	2989	2991	11.4	23	NDF	FS	7
Blkhls/.223/50 gr/POLYV	.223	50	STNOS	3043	2898	12	24	.223	DF	11
Win/.223/50 gr/STNOS	.223	55	PSP	2845	2872	23.4	43	.38	DF	9.25
Rem/.223/55 gr/PSP	.223	55	PLHP	2783	2795	27.5	50	.40	HEP	10.25
Rem/.223/55 gr/PLHP	.223	55	JSPTAC	2730	2719	47.1	86	.42	HEP	15
Fed/.223/55 gr/JSPTAC	.223	55	BTHP	2918	2884	20.6	37	.33	DF	10.75
Fed/.223/55 gr/FMJ	.223	55	FMJ	2973	2770	47.1	86	.223	FP	12
Blkhls/.223/55 gr/SP	.223	55	SP	2801	2770	25	45	.34	DF	10.5
Blkhls/.223/60 gr/SP	.223	60	SP	2624	2564	38.4	64	.44	HEP	10.25
Rem/.223/62 gr/HPM	.223	62	HP-M	2530	2477	49.0	79	.42	HEP	11.25
Win/.223/64 gr/JSP	.223	64	JSP	2479	2513	54.4	85	.490	FP	12
Blkhls/.223/68 gr/HPM	.223	68	HP-M	2541	2558	44.27	65	.50	HEP	12
Fed/.223/69 gr/BTHP	.223	69	BTHP	2584	2502	44	64	.50	HEP	12.75
Blkhls/.223/75 gr/HPM	.223	75	HP-M	2511	2460	39.6	53	.53	HEP	14.25
FN/5.7x28/31 gr/FMJ	5.7x28	31	FMJ	2426	1390	31.0	100	.223	FP	9.75
Rem/.72/437 gr/HP	.72	437	HP	1384	1122	433.3	99	.790	FP	22.5
Rem/.33/406 gr/TAC8	.33	406	TAC-8	1120	1044	400	98	.33	FP	15.24
Fed/.33/486.5 gr/TAC9	.33	486.5	TAC-9	1053	2921	484.4	99	.33	FP	20.75
Delta/.223/45 gr/COP	.223	45	COP	2921	2872	29.9	66	.223	FP	18.5
Win/.223/45 gr/JKTFR	.223	45	JKTFR	2935		7.7	17	.223	FS	9.25

TABLE 26-4
NFU-LIMITED PENETRATION TESTS

August 18-September 10, 1997
Test Phase Four-Double Pane Window Test

Ammo Mfg.	Cal.	Wght. gr.	Type	Avg. Vel. fps.	Test Vel. fps.	Ret. Wght. gr.	% Ret. Wght.	Proj. Dia. inches	Proj. Class	Gel. Pen.
Rem/9 mm/115 gr/JHP	9mm	115	JHP	1263	1280	115	100	.420	FP	18
Fed/9 mm/124 gr/HSJHP	9mm	124	HSJHP	1179	1186	124	100	.650	FP	11
Fed/9 mm/124 gr +P+/HS	9mm	124 +P	HS	1304	1303	121.4	98	.750	FP	10
Rem/9 mm/115 gr +P+/JHP	9mm	115 +P+	JHP	1403	1427	115	100	.675		9.75
Rem/.40/155 gr/JHP	.40	155	JHP	1189	1177	155	100	.650	FP	13.25
Fiocchi/.223.41 gr/FR	.223	41	FR	3098	3121	8.1	20	.198	FS	9
Win.RA/.223/33 gr/FR	.223	33	FR	3540	3513	n/a	n/a	n/a	FS	3
Simun/.223/36 gr/FR	.223	36	FR	3149	3148	10.0	28	.250	NDF	7
Rem/.223/40 gr/JHP	.223	40	JHP	3129	3152	5.4	14	.290	FS	5
Rem/.223/40 gr/JHP	.223	50	POLYBT	2932	2902	n/a	n/a	n/a	FS	5
Rem/.223/50 gr/POLYBT	.223	50	POLYV	2989	2972	n/a	n/a	n/a	FS	4.5
Blkhls/.223/50 gr/POLYV	.223	50	STNOS	3043	2995	12.0	24	.255	NDF	8.5
Win/.223/50 gr/STNOS	.223	55	PSP	2845	2803	14.8	27	.520	NDF	9
Rem/.223/55 gr/PSP	.223	55	PLHP	2783	2803	24.8	45	.415	DF	8
Rem/.223/55 gr/PLHP	.223	55	JSPTAC	2730	2749	44.8	82	.370	HEP	13.75
Fed/.223/55 gr/JSPTAC	.223	55	BTHP	2918	2886	14.4	26	.420	NDF	5.5
Fed/.223/55 gr/FMJ	.223	55	FMJ	2973	3036	10.8	20	.250	FS	10.5
Blkhls/.223/55 gr/SP	.223	55	SP	2801	2805	19.5	36	.380	NDF	8.5
Blkhls/.223/60 gr/SP	.223	60	SP	2624	2664	29.6	49	.480	NDF	9.25
Rem/.223/62 gr/HPM	.223	62	HP-M	2530	2565	26.7	43	.375	DF	9.75
Win/.223/64 gr/JSP	.223	64	JSP	2479	2506	49.0	77	.575	HEP	10.5
Blkhls/.223/68 gr/HPM	.223	68	HP-M	2541	2561	26.5	39	.375	NDF	11
Fed/.223/69 gr/BTHP	.223	69	BTHP	2584	2583	33.5	49	.450	NDF	9.25
Blkhls/.223/75 gr/HPM	.223	75	HP-M	2511	2538	45.0	60	.500	HEP	12.25
FN/5.7x28/31 gr/FMJ	5.7x28	31	FMJ	2426	2417	29.3	95	.229	FP	11.25
Rem/.72/437 gr/HP	.72	437	HP	1384	1415	431.3	99	.890	FP	20.5
Rem/.33/406 gr/TAC8	.33	406	TAC-8	1120	1131	417.5	100	.32	FP	16
Fed/.33/486.5 gr/TAC9	.33	486.5	TAC-9	1053	1058	508.1	100	.33	FP	14
Delta/.223/45 gr/COP	.223	45	COP	2921	2895	16.2	36	.238	NDF	13.25
Win/.223/45 gr/JKTFR	.223	45	JKTFR	2935	2874	6.0	13	.20	FS	8.75

TABLE 26-5
NFU-LIMITED PENETRATION TESTS

August 18-September 10, 1997
Test Phase Six-Windshield Test

Ammo Mfg.	Cal.	Wght. gr.	Type	Avg. Vel. fps.	Test Vel. fps	Ret. Wght. gr.	% Ret. Wght	Proj. Dia. inches	Proj. Class	Gel. Pen.
Rem/9 mm/115 gr/JHP	9mm	115	JHP	1263	1278	108	94	.560	HEP	12
Fed/9 mm/124 gr/HSJHP	9mm	124	HSJHP	1179	1184	96.8	78	.520	HEP	10.75
Fed/9 mm/124 gr +P+/HS	9mm	124 +P	HS	1304	1315	103.2	83	.530	HEP	10
Rem/9 mm/115 gr +P+/JHP	9mm	115 +P+	JHP	1403	1426	94.7	82	.593	HEP	12.25
Rem/.40/155 gr/JHP	.40	155	JHP	1189	1183	141.5	91	.615	HEP	14.25
Fiocchi/.223.41 gr/FR	.223	41	FR	3098	3098	6.8	17	.205	FS	8
Win.RA/.223/33 gr/FR	.223	33	FR	3540	3565	n/a	n/a	n/a	FS	2
Simun/.223/36 gr/FR	.223	36	FR	3149	3109	7.1	20	.270	FS	4.5
Rem/.223/40 gr/JHP	.223	40	JHP	3129	3147	n/a	n/a	n/a	FS	5
Rem/.223/40 gr/JHP	.223	50	POLYBT	2932	2938	3.6	7	.160	FS	5.25
Rem/.223/50 gr/POLYBT	.223	50	POLYV	2989	3033	n/a	n/a	n/a	FS	4
Blkhls/.223/50 gr/POLYV	.223	50	STNOS	3043	3008	12.3	25	.270	NDF	9.5
Win/.223/50 gr/STNOS	.223	55	PSP	2845	2845	8.3	15	n/a	FS	7
Rem/.223/55 gr/PSP	.223	55	PLHP	2783	2770	21.1	38	.50	NDF	6
Rem/.223/55 gr/PLHP	.223	55	JSPTAC	2730	2780	no rec pro	n/a	n/a	FS	12
Fed/.223/55 gr/JSPTAC	.223	55	BTHP	2918	2978	21.3	39	.455	NDF	8
Fed/.223/55 gr/FMJ	.223	55	FMJ	2973	2936	10.9	20	.373	FS	8
Blkhls/.223/55 gr/SP	.223	55	SP	2801	2786	13.3	24	.380	DF	7
Blkhls/.223/60 gr/SP	.223	60	SP	2624	2672	n/a	n/a	n/a	FS	10
Rem/.223/62 gr/HPM	.223	62	HP-M	2530	2543	24.8	40	.450	NDF	7.25
Win/.223/64 gr/JSP	.223	64	JSP	2479	2539	20.6	32	.470	DF	10
Blkhls/.223/68 gr/HPM	.223	68	HP-M	2541	2553	35.6	52	.412	HEP	8
Fed/.223/69 gr/BTHP	.223	69	BTHP	2584	2571	34.6	50	.450	HEP	9
Blkhls/.223/75 gr/HPM	.223	75	HP-M	2511	2511	23.1	31	.440	NDF	10.25
FN/5.7x28/31 gr/FMJ	5.7x28	31	FMJ	2426	2457	27.4	88	.245	FP	8.25
Rem/.72/437 gr/HP	.72	437	HP	1384	1355	390.7	89	.90	HEP	19.5
Rem/.33/406 gr/TAC8	.33	406	TAC-8	1120	1133	368.8	91	IN	HEP	17
Fed/.33/486.5 gr/TAC9	.33	486.5	TAC-9	1053	1040	409.1	84	IN	HEP	13.75
Delta/.223/45 gr/COP	.223	45	COP	2921	2794	13.3	30	.250	NDF	11.25
Win/.223/45 gr/JKTFR	.223	45	JKTFR	2935	2859	3.9	9	.175	FS	4

CHAPTER 27
Actual Street Results

We have not included any shooting incidents involving either .22 Long Rifle or .25 ACP. Both of these loads are dismal stoppers, and including examples of successful stops with them would give a false sense of confidence that is totally unjustified.

We have included at least one failure in each caliber due to repeated requests by readers for this information.

The bullet at left was removed at autopsy. The one at right was recovered from calibrated 10 percent gelatin. Gelatin is a guideline; it is not the Holy Grail!

.32 ACP

As has been cited before, the .32 Silvertip has produced good, though not spectacular, results. I first started to pay attention to this round when Larry Seecamp paid me for some consulting work with a Seecamp .32 Auto. This little pistol is a genuine precision piece of equipment that can easily be concealed in the palm of your hand. It will be interesting to see if the Hydra-Shok, Gold Dot, and Golden Saber offerings in this caliber will eventually overtake the Silvertip.

● ● ● ● ●

Never a large man, age had caused him to shrink even further. His old-fashioned rimless glasses gave him a bookish air, and no one was surprised to learn he was an accountant by profession. He had been a young accountant in 1943 when Nazi troops had marched into his town. They quickly rounded up all the Jews and marched them away. While other townspeople discussed what had happened, he quietly walked home, changed clothes, took a hunting rifle from the closet of his den, and walked in the direction he had seen his fellow citizens go.

Hearing German voices around the bend three miles from town, he turned and cut through some heavy brush. He finally crept close enough to see a number of his former citizens laying dead in the field. He also observed three soldiers raping a teenaged girl he recognized from his neighborhood. After quietly loading his bolt-action rifle, he killed the three soldiers with three shots. He then helped the young girl get dressed and directed her to go directly to his house and tell his wife to hide her.

Realizing he would need weapons, ammunition, food, water, and a good pair of walking shoes, he stripped the German soldiers of anything of value. One of those items was a Walther .32 ACP pistol. He walked for several days before finding a resistance group and joining the war against the invaders. A year later, he learned his family had been shot for harboring a Jew. He soon gained the nickname "The Terrible One" and gave the Germans no quarter.

Twice he was taken prisoner by the Gestapo and twice he escaped, leaving dead Germans behind. When the war ended, he was awarded medals by several countries because of his tireless efforts to keep downed fliers out of German hands. The American government was so impressed they allowed him to immigrate to this country.

He graduated from an Ivy League school with an advanced degree in accounting and opened an office in a major eastern city. A few years later he met and married a women and eventually had two daughters. His wife resisted the names he had chosen until he told her one was the name of his daughter who had been murdered by the Nazis and the other was the name of the Jewish girl they had tried to save.

As time went by he noticed that the neighborhood where he had located his office had started to deteriorate. He didn't understand what the young men were doing on the street corners, but he recognized a prostitute when he saw one. He had been confronted one night by two young men, but something in the look he had given them had caused them to look elsewhere for a victim.

Realizing that a look might not always be sufficient to deter trouble in the future, he went to the attic and removed a small box from inside a large chest. Unlocking it, he removed an object from an oil-stained rag—the Walther .32 ACP. He reminisced for a moment before slipping the pistol in his briefcase. Realizing that the only ammunition he had for it was 20 years old, he stopped at a local gun store and purchased a box of Winchester Silvertip hollowpoints. The clerk told him that some gun writer was saying it had worked well in actual shootings but that he personally thought that was a bunch of crap, but it was all he had.

The accountant also purchased a cleaning kit and left quietly. During his lunch break, he locked his office door and carefully cleaned and then loaded the pistol. He was about to put it back in the briefcase when he thought better of it and placed it in the small of his back where he had carried it so many years before. It was almost 7

Winchester's .32 ACP Silvetip breathes new life into a long neglected caliber. These two were recovered at autopsy from an individual breaking into an elderly widow's apartment.

Moderate deformation didn't prevent these two rounds from penetrating to reach vital organs.

P.M. when he completed his duties and headed for home.

While waiting for his regular bus, he became aware of a group of young men in baggy clothes standing behind him. They started shoving each other back and forth until one of them bumped into the accountant. He asked them to be more careful and their response was quick and obscene.

He chose to avoid a confrontation and walked two blocks to the next stop. While waiting there, the same group of men approached, quickly surrounded him, and taunted him, asking what was in his briefcase. He tried to ignore them but one grabbed his case and tried to pull it out of his grasp. He took a quick step and tripped the young man, getting back

possession of his case. The punk jumped to his feet and, producing a stream of obscene comments, pulled a knife from his pocket and lunged at the accountant.

The man put his left arm up to take the slash while he produced the Walther with his right. Seeing the gun the young man hesitated, but taking courage from the derisive comments of his buddies, he attacked the older man again.

It was the last act of his life as the man fired. The round struck the assailant in the chest, tearing the aorta. He bled to death before medical attention arrived.

The accountant was questioned by police but released without being charged. The police intended to confiscate the pistol, but a phone call from Washington, D.C., changed their mind, and it was returned to its owner with an application for an unrestricted concealed weapon permit.

● ● ● ● ●

A single mother, she worked midnights at a big city insurance firm. This schedule allowed her to be home with her young children. She generally packed a lunch and ate at her desk because she had concerns about the safety of the neighborhood. One particular night she had taken her kids to a movie and realized too late that she only had enough lunch meat for their lunch in the morning.

A level-headed person, she slipped a .32 auto into her coat pocket just in case. It was shortly after 3 A.M. when she finished a project and decided to walk to a nearby all-night restaurant for a bowl of soup. The streets were deserted as she walked quickly to the eatery. She finished her soup, had a second cup of coffee, and headed back to work. She had almost reached the night entrance when she realized she was being followed. She pushed the bell for the night watchman and waited. She heard the footsteps of the approaching watchman when a hand grabbed her and spun her around. She was confronted by a large white man who said, "I've been looking for a whore all night and your it," while exposing himself.

She tried to explain to the man that she was a data entry clerk, not a prostitute. His response was to rip her blouse and slap her. She turned to see the night watchman standing inside the door, making no effort to come to her aid. She reached inside her coat, pushed the gun against the attacker's chest, and pulled the trigger.

The man tore the gun from her grasp and started to point it at her when he fell to his knees and died. The Silvertip slug was recovered from the liver, where it had a recovered diameter of .41 caliber. The woman was charged with a misdemeanor unregistered gun possession charge, but a judge dismissed the case. These days she always makes sure she has plenty of lunch meat at home.

• • • • •

The bicycle courier in a large city was a fitness freak with a secret. A Ph.D. candidate in history, he was the first of six generations in his family who had not chosen law enforcement as a career. He had, however, inherited a healthy sense of skepticism. Tucked inside his fanny pack was a Colt .32 automatic. His bicycle was his most prized possession, and after its predecessor had been stolen he vowed it wouldn't happen again.

It was a beautiful spring day, and he had stopped for a veggie pita at a small strip mall. His bike was leaning against a nearby wall as he enjoyed the weather, his lunch, and the women who walked by. He was in the process of disposing of his trash when he noticed three young men examining his bike.

As he approached the trio, one asked him, "Your bike?" When he responded that it was, the same young man said "Not any more!" and produced what homicide

investigators later determined was an unloaded .25 auto.

The courier's response was immediate and deadly. He produced the .32 from his Uncle Mike's fanny pack and, chambering a Silvertip JHP, shot the armed bicycle thief in the upper chest. Pointing the pistol at his companions, the courier said, "Next?" but they turned and fled.

The Silvertip was recovered from the heart at autopsy. The courier's pistol was confiscated, but since two of the three responding homicide investigators had worked with his dad and brothers, prosecution for an unregistered handgun was not seriously considered.

When they were finished with him at Homicide, he rode his bike to his father's house and said, "Pop, I need another pistol."

• • • • •

It had been one of those days. The shift sergeant had put him on radar patrol but his radar unit was inoperative. When he asked for a replacement, he was told to just estimate their speeds and write tickets anyway. When he indicated he wasn't going to perjure himself, he was reassigned to a foot patrol by the docks. This was a well-known punishment tour, since the only place he could relieve himself was in the alley and there was nowhere to eat.

He got two cans of soda and took them with him to his assignment. Concealing them behind a metal trash container, he thought he would at least have something to drink later. He was wrong.

Four hours into his shift he decided to take a break and have a can of soda. He returned to his hiding place but they were gone. Cursing his luck under his breath, he realized he heard voices. Walking toward the location of the sounds, he found two derelicts consuming his Cokes. "Hey, that's my Coke!" he exclaimed. "____ you, cop" was their response. As the

officer grabbed the closest man, he was struck in the chest. Looking down he saw a butcher knife in the hand of the other man. It had entered the officer's shirt but slid harmlessly across his soft body armor. Before he could grab the knife the man struck again, this time stabbing him in the right biceps.

He tried to pull his 10mm duty pistol but found his right hand wasn't working properly. As the man lunged again, the officer pulled a Beretta Tomcat .32 auto from his left front pocket and emptied it at the knife-wielding miscreant. The man took three steps and slid to the ground. The officer stuck the Beretta in his waistband long enough to get his portable radio out and call for help. The paramedics almost lost the officer due to massive blood loss, but he recovered, though nerve damage forced him to take a premature retirement.

His attacker had been struck once in the left lung and had expired in the emergency room of a nearby hospital. The recovered round showed moderate deformation.

• • • • •

Born and raised in the big city, he saw no logic in living anywhere else. He had graduated with a Ph.D. from a major east coast university and then returned to his hometown to teach at the college level. He had spent 25 years at one of the city's most prestigious universities before "retiring" to an inner city community college.

The smaller institution was excited to get someone with such impressive credentials, and he was happy for the change of environment, as his wife had died a year before his scheduled retirement. The memories contained in their original apartment were too painful, so he had given his children almost all of its contents and moved closer to his new institution.

While he was fully committed to the exciting pace of the city, he was not prepared to become a victim, so he carried the .32 auto his father had taught him to shoot on summer vacations long ago. His grandfatherly exterior was belied by an unwavering conviction that if he who had been raised in a poor black home could rise above racism at a time when neither legislation or social focus had been there to assist him in his struggle to gain an education, others certainly could in much more benign times.

Since he lived alone, he was perfectly willing to stay late in his office to be accessible to his students. He found that a necessity since his classes were rigorous and demanded a level of study unheard of at this school.

He was engrossed in reading a student's paper when he realized it was 1 A.M. and time to go home. Throwing a bunch of papers into his briefcase, he checked to make sure the pistol was secure in the outside pocket. He exited the building and walked slowly toward the subway, noticing that winter was on its way and wondering how many more he would see.

He had almost reached the subway entrance when he heard a car pull up alongside. He steadfastly ignored it until some one yelled, "Hi nigger! What you got in that briefcase?" The academician ignored it until he heard a car door open. He turned to his left and saw three young white males exit the vehicle. He placed his briefcase on the right side of his body and quickly removed the pistol from its place of concealment. The street was not well lit and his harassers did not see the pistol.

"Leave me alone" was all he said, and the sole survivor remembered he said it with surprising calmness. The young men started to run toward the professor, and he opened fire. He told responding homicide investigators he had simply locked his arm like his father had taught him and pressed the trigger.

Two of the three were dead at the scene with Silvertips in their respective hearts, while the third took one round through his mouth. The professor had his pistol confiscated

An undercover narcotics officer carried a .32 auto in an ankle holster "just in case." This prudent planning saved his life when suspicious druggies searched him and took his Glock .40 auto.

and, when his three-year contract with the school expired, it was not renewed because he was considered too reactionary. I recently had the pleasure of attending his 90th birthday, and while he is somewhat frail his mind is as sharp as ever.

.32 ACP Silvertip Failure

There were a number of reasons why he shouldn't carry a gun. First, he was breaking the law. A commercial driver, he passed through many states and cities that had very restrictive laws regarding the possession of a handgun. Second, his wife was rabidly antigun. Third, he was a terrible shot and didn't like to practice.

He had convinced himself that the mere exposure of the gun would stop hostilities. He would be fatally wrong.

He was near the end of a three-day haul when he stopped for diesel fuel. When he was done, he pulled the rig to a parking area to clear the pumps for other truckers. He then went inside to get some nachos and a soda. He was walking back to the rig when he saw movement out of the corner of his eye. It was a white female in hot pants and a halter top. Noting that she was obviously one of the whores working the interstate truck stops, he walked a little faster hoping to avoid contact.

The prostitute cut him off and asked if he wanted "a date." He politely declined, but the woman grabbed his arm and demanded his wallet. Looking down he saw the straight razor. Pulling the small auto, he told the woman to leave before she got shot. Her response was rapid and terminal—she slashed his throat. Holding his throat, he emptied the pistol at her before bleeding to death. Responding troopers found her propositioning another trucker. A close examination revealed she had been shot in the arm, stomach, and thigh. She was too high on cocaine to even notice.

.380 ACP

The rookie officer had learned a number of lessons from the veteran street cop who was his first partner. Some had been easy, others rather hard. He had learned that body armor wasn't optional and that the key to survival was common sense and staying alert. He also learned the value of redundancy and carried an extra set of handcuffs, a second smaller flashlight, and a Walther PPK loaded with Federal Hydra-Shok hollowpoints in a Kramer ankle holster.

As a rookie, he was assigned to the graveyard shift in an active district. He worked a patrol area that had the dubious distinction of leading the city in homicides and drug arrests. He and his partner had been given information from homicide teams that a transvestite named Bubbles had murdered a customer who had discovered the "woman" he was having sex with had been born with the first name of Isaac.

They had been kept busy with a constant stream of radio runs for most of the night. Shortly after 5 A.M., they had the opportunity to stop for breakfast. There was only one place they could eat at that hour of the morning. It was considered a neutral location by both cops and miscreants, and the unwritten rule was that no one would commit a crime on the premises and no would be arrested there.

While they were waiting for their food, the training officer suggested that the rookie get the reports he had done earlier in the tour of duty so they could review them for errors. The rookie saw a trio of transvestites across the street as he went out to the vehicle but paid little attention to them.

Calling back in service, the rookie mentioned the trio to his training officer. They drove down to the corner to see if the wanted subject was there. Purposely going the wrong way on one-way street, they crept toward the location in question. The rookie soon noticed the same trio he had seen near the restaurant. "That's her!" said the training officer, pointing at the tallest of the three. The rookie was incredulous. "Bubbles" was at least 6' 5", 300 pounds, and ugly as sin with a cheap blonde wig and size 12 high heel shoes. "How could anyone mistake that for a woman?" he asked his trainer. "Who knows? Watch yourself. These beauties are usually armed."

As the patrol unit pulled up, the transvestites gave them what was designed to be a casual look. As the officers exited their vehicle, the trio separated and started to walk away. The officers grabbed the wanted subject and told "her" to assume the position. They were searching Bubbles when one of the other prostitutes produced a Ruger .357 Magnum revolver from a purse. The first round took the rookie in the middle of his vest and he went down. The second round missed both officers, but the third struck the training officer in the lower left side. The rookie was in the process of drawing his .40 Glock when Bubbles grabbed his gun and wrestled it away from him. Without thinking, the cop grabbed his PPK and shot Bubbles. Turning to the Ruger-armed prostitute, he emptied his .380 and watched the transvestite drop the Magnum and collapse.

Bubbles was rushed to the emergency room, where the Hydra-

Winchester Silvertips produce consistent expansion in human tissue. This one was used to prevent the kidnapping of a drug dealer's son.

Superior designed bullets like Hydra-Shok give smaller calibers a big boost in the stopping power race. This one was used by an undercover narcotics cop to save her life.

Shok slug was removed from his lung in surgery. He recovered to stand trail. The other prostitute was DOA—the Hydra-Shok was removed at autopsy from the left ventricle of the heart. The other rounds had missed.

• • • • •

He drove a garbage truck for a living and was a man of rather simple tastes. He liked football, Coors beer, and deep-dish pizza. He hated dogs, and after being severely bitten he had bought a .380 auto off a guy in the bar he frequented. He later bought a couple of boxes of Hydra-Shok ammo and practiced with it on the far side of the dump. He figured if he could hit a scurrying rat, he could hit a vicious dog.

He was working a double shift on a hot summer day when he noticed what he thought was a pile of clothes next to several trash cans in the alley. When the object moved he figured it must be a dog, so he pulled the pistol from his coveralls and chambered a round. He saw the small leg then and realized it was a child. She was probably 6 years old and had been beaten. When he asked who did it, the girl didn't answer but pointed behind him. He turned to see a man in his 40s with a baseball bat. The man menaced him with the bat and yelled, "I told the little _____ that if she wet her bed again I'd whup her. Now get out of here before I take the bat to you!"

The garbage truck driver thought about it for a moment and realized that there were four-legged dogs and two-legged dogs. "Leave her alone, you piece of trash," he responded. The child beater lunged at him and he fired. The round struck just above the right nipple, coursed downward, and lodged in the liver. He dropped the bat, sat down, and said, "You _____. You killed me!" He was right.

• • • • •

The Asian immigrant had worked hard in his store after emigrating to this country. It was almost 11 years before he was able to earn enough money to bring over his wife and children from their Communist country. Things were still iffy, but they worked hard and enjoyed the benefits of a free country.

His oldest daughter worked in the store while attending a local community college. Incredibly beautiful, her presence had increased sales dramatically as young men would stop by for a can of soda and then return for a candy bar and then again for something else. Most of them seemed harmless, but he was concerned about one who wore a lot of gold, drove a new car, and had a beeper and a cell phone. He didn't

While producing only moderate expansion, these two .380 Silvertips carried the day when a plainclothes vice cop was attacked by a razor-wielding prostitute.

The Starfire .380 JHP expands well and penetrates deeply enough in actual shootings.

know a lot about crime in his adopted country, but he knew a punk when he saw one.

Returning from the post office, he was walking in the store when he saw the punk say something to his daughter that caused her to blush and move away. He ordered the young man to leave his store and not return. The man just sneered and left.

Several weeks later, the store owner was moving stock in the back when he heard his daughter raise her voice. Walking quickly, he saw his daughter pinned against the counter by the same fancy dressed punk. He grabbed the young man and pulled him off his daughter, slapping him repeatedly across the face. The young man staggered back and pulled a nickel-plated .25 auto from his waistband. "Old man, I'm going to kill

you and then give your daughter the best sex she's ever had."

"Leave my father alone," he heard his daughter say. She was holding the .380 auto that was kept behind the cash register. "Ah, Beauty," the young man said, "I was only kidding about your father. Put the gun down and I'll leave." When the young woman lowered the pistol, the punk shot her father and then spun toward her. He didn't quite make it. She fired three times. One .380 Hydra-Shok struck him in the chest and penetrated both lungs and the heart. The expanded bullet was recovered under the skin on the far side. The young woman was not charged and 16 months later married an Asian lab technician who had responded to the scene.

• • • • •

The private duty nurse worked for a wealthy client who lived in an exclusive neighborhood. Unfortunately, much of the area surrounding this enclave had deteriorated severely. She shared the around-the-clock duties with another nurse like herself. Both had children, but they were grown and gone. Both lived alone: one divorced, the other widowed.

Having worked the midnight shift her entire career, she preferred the 7 P.M. to 7 A.M. tour, while her co-worker liked the other one. They had worked this assignment for five years and were both comfortable with the other's level of competency and especially pleased with the salary.

The midnight nurse had three sons; two were federal law enforcement agents and the third was a prosecutor. All had tried to get their mom to really retire and come live with one of them. When she refused repeated requests, they got her a Walther PPK stainless steel .380 auto and an unrestricted carry permit. All three sons had taken her shooting until they were satisfied with her level of competency. She carried the pistol in

This Remington .380 JHP saved the life of a wheelchair-bound housewife during a home invasion. The bullet was recovered from the left ventricle of the criminal's heart.

A Remington .380 JHP that was used by a rural gas station attendant to save a life.

an inside-the-waistband holster because her client kept the house cool and she always wore a sweater.

She was an hour short of finishing her shift when her co-worker called and said she was sick and wouldn't be in. She volunteered to find a replacement, but the midnight shift nurse told her she'd rather work a triple shift since there was ample time to nap before the weekend nurses came on-duty.

Thirty-six hours later she turned her patient over to one of the weekend nurses. Realizing she wasn't as young as she once was, she headed to the bus stop. While standing there, she wasn't paying attention to her surroundings until it was almost too late. Two young men and an older woman were engaged in an argument over some money. She turned to see what was

A Federal 90-grain JHP that expanded well in human tissue.

This Federal .380 90-grain Hydra-Shok JHP was a fight stopper

going on and saw one of the men knock the woman down. Before she could get up they started to kick her.

The nurse pulled her pistol and ordered the men to stop. One turned and started to laugh until he saw the gun. "Bobby, she's got a gun!" His partner turned and grinned. "That ain't a real gun. Take it away from her and get her purse."

As the miscreant approached the nurse, she pointed the gun just below his throat and pulled the trigger. The man took two steps, fell to his knees, then fell face forward on the ground. As the second perpetrator turned to run, the nurse said "No!" and he stopped immediately. She helped the woman up and told her to go for the police. "Go for the police? You murdered my son and you want me to go for the police? My boys wanted some money for drugs and they got a little excited, that's all."

The nurse was astounded and put the pistol away when the police turned the corner. She was charged with involuntary manslaughter but acquitted at trial. Her client dismissed her because of the controversy, and she finally accepted one of her sons' offer to live with him. Today she focuses her attention on her grandchildren rather than IVs.

.380 Hydra-Shok Failure

The victim in this incident was a utility employee who managed several field workers. He had agreed to advise another supervisor regarding a problem employee at another branch of the company. A survivor of the Korean War, he had carried a Colt .380 automatic loaded with Hydra-Shok hollowpoints in his briefcase. The gun, loaded with ball ammo, had once saved his life just north of Seoul.

He arrived at the branch office and met with the supervisor for 45 minutes. The supervisor asked him if he would mind meeting with the employee. Since the worker in question had no history of violence he agreed. It would cost him his life.

Neither supervisor knew that earlier that day the employee's wife had served him with divorce papers. He decided to commit "suicide by cop." Lacking the courage to shoot himself, he took an unloaded .45 auto to work in his waistband. He entered his supervisor's office and they began

No, hollowpoints don't always expand, but both of these penetrated deeply enough to reach vital organs and end a bank robber's spree.

.380 hollowpoints don't expand every time, but this one still stopped the bad guy.

A .380 Starfire that stopped a rape.

to discuss their concerns. The meeting started on a friendly note, but when the worker's supervisor began to explain to him that unless there was an improvement he would be fired, the man produced the gun and told the supervisors that he intended to kill them and then himself. The supervisors tried to reason with him, but he became more and more agitated. While his supervisor tried to talk to him, the other man slowly reached into his briefcase for his pistol

He had just removed it and was in the process of chambering a round when the distraught employee struck him in the head with the .45. Knocked to the floor, he dropped the gun. The employee dropped his .45 and lunged for the .380. The two men struggled for the gun for several minutes. The other supervisor fled the room. The owner of the .380 felt his fingers being pried off the gun. Realizing it was pointed at his assailant, he pulled the trigger four times.

He felt his attacker collapse so he let go of the gun. It was a fatal error. The disgruntled worker, who had absorbed four Hydra-Shoks, picked up the gun and shot the supervisor once in the chest, killing him. He then pointed the gun at himself and a single Hydra-Shok to the brain ended the incident.

The four rounds recovered at autopsy had been found in the thoracic cavity, and all had expanded nicely.

.38 SPECIAL, 2 INCH BARREL

In these days of titanium and stainless steel weapons, the officer's blue finish S&W Model 38 lightweight revolver was considered rather pedestrian. He really didn't care what others thought. After all, he carried a 10mm Glock when everyone else in his small department carried a Beretta .40.

He further broke convention by carrying the 10mm off duty. The .38 snub was strictly for second usage, and he avoided the temptation to carry it off duty on muggy summer days. It was loaded with Winchester 158-grain lead hollowpoint +P loads. Other officers thought the recoil abusive and carried other loads in their .38 snubs, which they did carry off duty.

Assigned to court on this particular day, he went to the locker room to change into his uniform. A couple of officers poked fun at him as he put on his ballistic vest and strapped the holster containing his .38 snub to his ankle. "Court ain't Bosnia, kid!" one of the officers shouted as he left.

He was there to testify in a shoplifting case and hoped to be done by noon so he could get a nap before reporting for his 12 hour shift. In the same building there were courts that heard divorce and other civil matters. Because there had never been an incident at court, security was almost nonexistent.

Court had taken a 15 minute recess prior to his testimony, so he

While this round produced modest expansion when fired from a 2 inch .38 Special, the 129-grain Hydra-Shok struck a holdup man in the chest and he was DRT (dead right there).

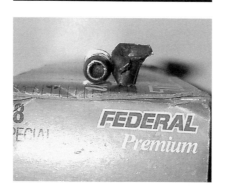

The Federal Nyclad 125-grain .38 Special hollowpoint standard-pressure load produces virtually identical results to the +P offerings and is much more pleasant to shoot. This one was fired from a 2-inch-barreled Ruger by a female officer after a stoppage had occurred in her 9mm.

walked to the lobby to get a bottle of juice from the vending machine. He was searching his pocket for the right change when he heard screaming from a nearby courtroom. He ran to the courtroom and took a quick peak. What he saw was a man holding a gun to the head of an obviously terrified woman. He could hear the man screaming that his wife wasn't going to get his kids and house; she was going to get a bullet.

He grabbed a bystander and told him to run across the street to the police station and let them know what was happening. He started to draw his

10mm when he realized that the man would notice his holster was empty, so he knelt and withdrew his .38 snub and held it behind his back with his nondominant hand.

Entering the courtroom, he held up his dominant hand and asked, "What's the problem?" "The problem is that this _____ and her lawyer think they're gonna rape me and they're wrong!" the gunman responded.

"Look, buddy," the cop responded, "You got to think this through. The police station is just across the street and the sheriff's office is two buildings down. Besides, if you kill them, who's going to take care of your kids?"

"It won't be that _____!" the man responded and cocked what appeared to be a .357 Magnum. Realizing that this incident wasn't going to be resolved peaceably, the officer started to sidestep so that he could get a clear shot at the gunman. He was almost in position when the gunman fired at the attorney. Raising the .38 snub, the officer fired twice. The first round struck the gunman on the left side, penetrated his body, and stopped under the skin on the far side. The second one missed.

The gunman dropped his revolver and fell to the floor. He was rushed to a local hospital, where surgery saved his life. The recovered slug weighed 137 grains and had a diameter of .53 inch. The man was charged with and convicted of attempted murder. The officer received an official reprimand since second guns were not approved in his department.

• • • • •

She had lived alone after her husband's death from cancer. She enjoyed her flower and fruit garden. Her children had made repeated requests for her to leave the old neighborhood that had begun to deteriorate. Her response was always the same—she had raised her family in

A Remington .38 125-grain JHP +P that worked well from a 2 inch barreled revolver.

Federal's .38 Special Nyclad hollowpoint produces good results from a 2 inch barrel.

Cor-Bon's .38 Special 158-grain LHP + expanded well in an actual shooting from a 2 inch barrel during a parking dispute.

that home and she intended to die there. She was almost right.

Although she was a simple farm girl, she was aware of crime and watched the news every night as she ate dinner. Her husband had a gun that he had kept behind the counter of his neighborhood grocery store. She kept it in the nightstand next to her bed. It was a S&W Model 64 revolver with a 2 inch barrel. Loaded with Winchester lead hollowpoints, it gave her a measure of comfort at night.

While the neighborhood had gone downhill, her house stood out with a fresh coat of paint, manicured lawns, and well-organized gardens. It wasn't long before the local knuckleheads had began to notice. They became convinced that the house had to contain a lot of valuable items and decided to break in the following night.

They waited until the lights had gone out at 11 P.M. and attempted to gain entrance through a basement window. They were unsuccessful because the woman's late husband had installed heavy mesh screens on the inside of all the basement windows shortly before his death. The attempt, however, had awoken the widow. She listened carefully and almost dismissed it, but then she put her robe on, removed the revolver from the nightstand, and sat at the top of the stairs with the gun in one hand and a cordless phone in the other.

She had just about decided to go

back to bed when she heard a window break on the back porch. She heard several individuals climb through the window and walk toward the stairs. One said, "The old _____ sleeps upstairs. Let's take care of her and then we'll have all the time we need." She realized they were too close for her to use the phone now, so she waited in the dark.

When she heard the fourth step from the top squeak she pointed the handgun downstairs and opened fire. The house was filled with screams and running. She called 911 then and gave the requested information to the police.

She waited in the dark until she saw the flashing lights and then flipped on the light switch. At the bottom of the stairs lay the body of one of the home invasion team. Another one was found by responding officers two blocks away trying to run on a broken leg.

A Winchester 158-grain lead hollowpoint was recovered at autopsy, while three were removed during surgery from the bad guy with the broken leg. Three days later a body was found with another one of the widow's slugs in it. When asked by their commander what they were going to do with this women, the homicide dick suggested making her the rangemaster.

The woman was not charged despite protests by various community groups who felt this African-American

widow had gotten away with murder by shooting three white gangbangers.

• • • • •

A real estate agent, she had been sexually assaulted by a "customer" at a house showing some 10 years before. It had taken a lot of therapy for her to overcome her fears and go back to work. She had, however, not returned to work alone. In her purse was a Colt Detective Special loaded with Winchester 158-grain lead hollowpoints, a can of Mace, and an HKS speedloader containing an additional six rounds of lead hollowpoints.

She had called her husband and told him she would be late, as a couple were coming into the office to look at some photos of possible homes. The "couple" consisted of a sexual predator and his girlfriend. She got her kicks from watching her boyfriend torture, rape, and murder other women. They had found that real estate agents were often easy prey.

The couple was dressed nicely enough, but something seemed wrong to the agent. She greeted the people, seated them, and then excused herself. In the lunch room, she removed both the gun and Mace from her purse and placed them in the rather voluminous pockets of the stylish jacket she was wearing.

As she sat down at her desk, the

woman said, "Nice blouse. Why don't you take it off?" The agent was so stunned she could only say, "What?" "Take off the blouse and the bra too," the man ordered, producing a large folding knife and opening it slowly. The agent flashed back to her earlier sexual assault and pulled the gun. "You're dead!" the agent yelled and shot both of them.

Responding officers found the agent stabbing two corpses with an empty canister of Mace in her hand. The unloaded snub, 12 spent casings, and an empty speedloader lay at her feet. She had hit her attackers with 10 out of 12 rounds. Finally calmed down by a female officer, she was admitted to the psychiatric ward at the local hospital. It was several months before she was released. By then the homicide investigators had ruled it a justifiable homicide and returned her .38 snub to her.

The 10 rounds had an average recovered diameter of .53 inch and an average recovered weight of 131 grains. The woman left real estate to become a counselor at a women's center.

• • • • •

It was a bitterly cold day, and he was grateful that traffic was light. The state road he was patrolling was extremely icy, and 25 mph was all he could achieve with control. He was five hours into his shift when he came over the hill and saw the car in the ditch. He cursed his luck at having to deal with someone who hadn't paid attention to the conditions.

The problem was that the driver of the car was an escaped murderer who wanted to put as many miles as possible between him and the sheriff's department he had escaped from. The deputy's .357 Magnum was stuck in his waistband. He had probably hoped a good Samaritan would stop but he didn't expect a state trooper.

The trooper looked at the vehicle in the ditch, but the window was fogged over. As he started down the ditch he slipped and fell. The fall saved

his life. As he was sliding down the ditch the car door flew open and the killer opened fire. Both rounds struck the officer's ballistic vest, but the impact from the 125-grain Magnum loads were extremely painful. Focusing past the pain, he reached for his own Magnum but realized it was pinned under him. Shoving his left hand into his heavy winter coat pocket, he retrieved his second gun and opened fire. The first round missed, but the second one struck the bad guy just above the left nipple.

The escapee slid down on the car seat, started to sit up, then died. The slug was recovered from the liver, where it had a diameter of .48 inch and a weight of 128 grains. The trooper received the Medal of Valor for his response after being shot. Today he's federal agent with counterterrorist responsibilities and still carries a second gun loaded with Winchester lead hollowpoints.

• • • • •

The intern working the emergency room of a major urban hospital had already been a victim of crime, being robbed of his expensive laptop computer. His response was a visceral one—he bought a .38 snub and used some political connections to get a concealed weapons permit. He left it in his locker at work and stuck it in his waistband before he went home.

It had been a quiet shift, and at 4 A.M. he decided to walk down the block for breakfast. He was out of the hospital before he remembered the gun and returned for it. It would be a life-saving decision.

He enjoyed the scrambled eggs and Canadian bacon and then headed back to work. He was almost back to the hospital when a man walked out of the shadows and asked, "Hey buddy, you got a buck?" When the doctor replied he didn't, the man produced a knife and said, "Then give me all your money!"

The intern produced the snub, shoved it against the man's chest, and

fired. The holdup man staggered backward, sat down, and died. Responding paramedics found the intern giving CPR to a corpse. The slug weighed 157 grains and had a diameter of .50 inch when recovered from the spinal column.

The intern was not prosecuted but was terminated by the hospital. Today he manages his family finances on Wall Street and carries a .38 snub under his $3,000 suits.

Winchester .38 Special 158-grain Lead Hollowpoint Failure

The security guard had been hired away from his employer by a customer. His new employer was a wholesale jeweler. While he carried a handgun, he wanted some backup.

On the day of the incident, the guard decided against his Glock Model 19 since it didn't fit well under his new suit. He stuck the .38 snub in his waistband and five extra rounds in his back pocket. It would prove to be a critical mistake.

His employer was transporting $300,000 worth of gems to a business deal. They took a cab downtown and met one customer for lunch. The guard sat two tables away and constantly scanned the crowd. After lunch, his employer decided to enjoy the weather and walk the three blocks to deliver the gems.

The guard recognized two men wearing business suits from the restaurant but made the connection too late. One produced a gun and shot his employer three times. The guard produced his .38 snub and shot both holdup men, but they returned fire. He took three bullets and collapsed. The employer was DOA and the security guard underwent emergency surgery. He survived but is confined to a wheelchair.

.38 SPECIAL, 4 INCH BARREL

While the agency he did armed courier work for restricted its people to the .38 Special revolver, it did not restrict ammunition. Having read of Cor-Bon's performance in *Street Stoppers*, he bought several boxes and practiced on a regular basis. His duty gun was a Ruger GP-100 .357 Magnum revolver. He had chosen the Magnum because he knew that the +P loads wouldn't wear it out, and he carried two speedloaders of 125-grain .357 Magnums if things ever reached critical mass.

His regular routine was to reload and maintain ATM machines. He was at his third stop for the day and was busy adding money to the machine when he noticed a man walk up to the drive-up window with something in his hand. The teller ignored him, so the courier assumed that he was trying to conduct a transaction at the wrong location.

He returned to his work when he heard someone approach the ATM. Looking up, he saw the same man who had tried to transact business at the window. The man held out his hand and said, "I need change for a hundred dollar bill." The courier started to reply that he couldn't give change when he realized what the man had in his hand was not money but a piece of paper with "$100" written on it in red crayon. When he told the man it was not real money, the citizen replied that of course it was and pulled a large bundle of the same sort of "money" out of a shoulder bag. "Look pal," the courier replied, "I don't have time for this. Take your money inside and they'll change it for you."

The man's eye's got large. "You don't understand. It's a worldwide conspiracy! Everywhere I go they tell me my money's worthless! They don't understand the creatures from the fourth Moon of Venus gave it to me!"

Realizing he was dealing with a severely disturbed individual, the courier said, "Look there's a new bank at the hospital. You go there and they'll change your money." It was the wrong thing to say. The man suddenly

Federal's +P 129-grain Hydra-Shok load was used by an armed courier to stop a determined robber. The courier was armed with a 4 inch Smith & Wesson Model 19 revolver.

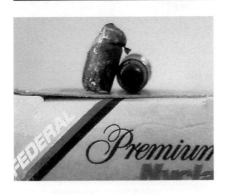

The Federal Nyclad .38 Special 158-grain SWC NYPD load doesn't work better than round-nose lead in shootings.

produced a butcher knife from the bag and stabbed the courier in the upper left chest. Falling to the ground, the courier pulled his revolver and fired one shot before he passed out.

The courier received surgery to repair nerve and muscle damage. The assailant received surgery to remove most of his liver. The recovered slug weighed 88 grains and had a recovered diameter of .61 inch

• • • • •

Concerned about the long hours his wheelchair-bound younger brother spent at home alone in their inner city apartment, the young black officer had a bought a Smith & Wesson Model 64 stainless steel .38 Special

revolver to enhance his sibling's safety. It was loaded with Cor-Bon 115-grain +P+ JHPs and stuffed in one side of the chair.

There had been a number of forced entries in their building, so the officer had purchased a cordless phone his brother could have wherever he went in the dwelling. The officer had also remodeled the bathroom to accommodate the wheelchair. It would save his brother's life.

The younger brother had rolled himself into the bathroom and pulled himself on to the toilet when he heard someone try the door to the apartment. He started to reach for the chair, but the noises stopped and he relaxed.

He was using the toilet when the door was kicked open suddenly. He lunged for the chair and gained partial control of the revolver before losing his balance and falling to the floor. Two scruffy looking white males entered the apartment. "Look Bobby," one said to the other, "We got us a crippled nigger. Let's break his neck and rip this place off." The resident reached up to the chair and his fingers brushed the Pachmayr grip of the revolver. He reached again and pulled it to the floor. Fortunately it landed on the carpet in front of the toilet.

As the two men stood in the doorway of the bathroom, the young man raised the revolver and said, "Go away!" They smiled and started to enter the bathroom. He opened fire, emptying the revolver. The bad guys collapsed on top of him, pinning him to the floor. Both were dead by the time his brother arrived home from work. None of their neighbors had responded to his calls for help. They moved the next day.

One of the assailants had taken three hits in the thoracic cavity, while the other had taken one round in the heart. The four rounds averaged .62 inch and weighed 91 grains. The family of one of the dead burglars tried to sue the officer for failing to train his brother, but a judge threw the case out.

Remington .38 LHP +P 158-grain load expands well in human tissue.

Federal's .38 147-grain +P+ has been a spotty performer on the street.

This Nyclad .38 Special 125-grain +P hollowpoint ended a bar fight.

• • • • •

He had lived a rather simple life, driving a tow truck and listening to classical music. He had graduated from a major university with a degree in music. Wounds he had received in Vietnam had ended his piano career, but he took such events philosophically and kept his sense of humor.

Because he responded to calls for assistance at any hour of the day or night, he had purchased a used Smith & Wesson Model 10 revolver. Asking the dealer for an ammo recommendation, he was handed a box of Cor-Bon 115-grain ammo.

The telephone woke him up at 4 A.M. It was a request for a tow, and the location was a rural, unpaved road in the nearby foothills. It took him an hour to get there and a find a new Lincoln in a ditch. The two young men waiting by the car didn't seem to fit the vehicle, but he didn't think that was his business. He should have.

He was in the process of hooking up to the Lincoln when he heard loud heavy metal music blaring from his truck. He walked back to his vehicle and turned down the radio, smiling at his two customers as he said, "I'm sorry, but I only listen to classical music."

"____ you!" one of the young men said and grabbed the tow truck driver by the throat.

The driver quickly spun loose and removed both men from his truck forcibly. They were young but were

The Remington .38 Special 125-grain JHP +P works well out of a 4 inch barrel.

city soft. As they lay there puking up their guts, he got his tow line and retracted it into the rig. He walked to driver's side of the rig and said, "Don't ever call me again, boys."

He was closing the door when they opened fire with the guns they had stolen along with the car. The first two rounds stopped in the door, but the third struck the driver in the side, glanced off a rib, and tunneled around the outside of his body before exiting. Grunting with the pain, he grabbed the .38 from under the driver's seat, pushed the door open, and returned fire.

One of his attackers screamed and fell while the other turned and ran into the darkness. The truck driver called the police on his car phone, then crept out into the darkness and waited. When the cops showed up, he left the gun under a bush and walked out with his arms high in the air. He was

handcuffed until law enforcement personnel sorted it all out.

A SWAT team found the second suspect early the next morning. He made the fatal mistake of opening fire with a .25 auto at an officer armed with a 9mm submachine gun. The one who had fallen at the scene had taken one round that had entered over the right nipple and been found just under the skin on the far side. Its recovered weight was 72 grains and recovered diameter was .57 inch

The truck driver was absolved of any criminal responsibility, but his handgun was not returned. He replaced it with a Colt AR-15. Today, several years later, he still drives his tow truck, lives alone, and listens to classical music.

• • • • •

Unlike all the other police agencies in the area, they not only still used revolvers but were restricted to the .38 Special. Their chief had retired from a federal agency. He had carried a .38 Special for 30 years, and if it was good enough for him it was good enough for his people.

After lengthy negotiations he had allowed his people to carry second guns, but they also had to be .38 Special. Since there was only one load available when he had been an agent, he hadn't specified the type of ammunition.

The officers had quietly loaded their second guns with a variety of hollowpoint offerings. Many had taken to carrying a 4-inch-barreled revolver under the uniform jacket when the weather permitted. The officer in question carried a 4 inch Taurus .357 Magnum revolver loaded with Cor-Bon 115-grain +P+ ammo in a shoulder holster. The gun in his duty holster was loaded with round-nose lead, but the HKS speedloaders on his belt also contained Cor-Bon JHPs.

It was two days before Thanksgiving, and the officer was working the midnight shift. He had responded to a holdup at a gas station just off the interstate. The station attendant had given him a description of two males armed with handguns in a purple sports car.

The officer assumed that the suspects had probably gotten onto the interstate, so he switched over to the state patrol frequency and put out the information. Three hours later the dispatcher reported that a state patrol unit was in pursuit of a black Mustang. Assuming correctly that this could be his wanted pair, he joined in pursuit. Within minutes, however, the trooper reported he had lost the car on a back road. When the dispatcher asked the trooper if he had a license number, there was no response. Repeated inquiries failed to contact the trooper, and the officer responded to his last known location at a high rate of speed.

The officer came over the crest of the hill and saw the trooper laying next to his unit. He notified the dispatcher that he had an officer down and to send paramedics and a state patrol supervisor. As he knelt next to the trooper, the downed officer moved his head slightly and whispered, "The vest stopped the round. I think they're in the ditch behind my car. I had my AR-15 on the front seat. I think they took it." The officer quickly looked inside the unit and apprised responding units that the officer was okay but the suspects were believed to still be in the area and were known to be armed with an AR-15 and other weapons. Pulling his second gun, he

Federal's .38 Special 158-grain lead hollowpoint +P offering is an excellent street performer. This one was used by an off-duty court officer to defend himself from an angry participant in a divorce proceeding.

removed the trooper's .40 caliber pistol and handed it to him. "Stay put. If you hear gunfire, haul yourself into the ditch and wait for help."

The officer then crept to the back of the state unit and took a quick peek. He thought he saw movement in the ditch, so he went prone and extended his gun. A couple of seconds went by before he recognized the muzzle of an AR-15 being pushed through the brush. Aiming just above it, he fired two quick rounds. He heard some one yelp and the rifle disappeared.

A moment later, he heard some one yell, "I'll get you for killing him, you _____." A male jumped up with the AR-15 and opened fire. The officer emptied his second gun and rolled back, grabbed a speed loader, and reloaded. There was no further response from the ditch, but he waited for backup. When responding units got there, they searched the ditch and found both subjects dead. The first had been hit twice in the forehead, while the second had taken one Cor-Bon JHP in the upper chest. The recovered slug weighed 72 grains and was .51 inch in diameter.

• • • • •

The woman had two real passions in her life: running and her son. An

architect, she had survived a bitter divorce and hard-fought custody fight. Her ex-husband, a graduate from an Ivy League law school, had used all his family's money and prestige in an attempt to get custody of his son but had failed. He still had private detectives follow her in an attempt to find something to overturn the judge's decision, but the last thing she was interested in was another relationship.

She and her son lived in a large home north of the city. It was not the home she had lived in while married. That one contained too many memories of a very wealthy man who was a mean drunk.

Her early morning routine was always the same—she'd drop off her son at preschool, then jog 10 miles before getting ready for work and taking the train into the city. The one thing that separated her from the other professionals on the train was the gun. Her dad, a small town judge, had survived an assassination attempt by having it when he needed it. That had impressed her deeply, and when she returned home from his funeral she quietly removed it from his desk drawer.

She carried it in a leather bag next to an expensive lap top computer. No one ever expected that such a well-educated, sophisticated woman could possibly have a weapon. If people had known they would have assumed that it was because of her ex-husband. They would be wrong. There was a man that loitered in front of her place of employment who worried her. He looked respectable enough, but there was just something about him that pushed her apprehension button.

When she worked late occasionally, she would have a neighbor pick her son up and keep him until she got home. This particular night it looked like she would be quite late, so she called her friend and asked if her son could spend the night. Solving that problem, she returned to her project. An hour later she realized a solution to the problem that had been frustrating her. She looked at her watch and realized that she could finish the project on her laptop and if she hurried she could catch the last train home.

She was rushing out of the office building for the train station when a hand reached out of the shadows and grabbed her. She screamed and turned to see the man she had been concerned about. He had a large knife in his hand and said, "Just the laptop, _____!"

"Just let me get some important papers out of the bag and you can have the computer," she pled. Instead of papers her hand grasped the .38 and withdrew it. She fired through the computer bag and its contents. The round struck her assailant in the left lung and he immediately dropped to the sidewalk.

The slug had a recovered diameter of .46 inch and a recovered weight of 72 grains. The computer company's "no questions asked" warrantee was only honored after a lot of questions and a phone call from a homicide investigator. Her ex-husband used the incident in an attempt to gain possession of his son, but the judge laughed him out of court.

.38 Special Cor-Bon 115-grain JHP +P+ Failure

It had been one of those days. His year-old car had failed to start and he was 20 minutes late for work. Already angry, his sergeant then assigned him to work with the laziest guard on his shift. The guy complained about everything. He even ridiculed his partner for purchasing his own hollowpoint ammunition and speedloaders for the company-issued revolver. The fact that he had purchased his own soft body armor was an even greater focus of ridicule.

It was after 2 A.M. when they decided to break for lunch. Tired of his partner's constant carping, he told him he had to go to the bathroom and took his lunch with him. He sat on the floor of the men's room and ate his tuna salad in silence, wondering when the

local police department would complete his background investigation so he could get out of this dead-end job.

He was throwing the remains of his lunch away when he heard a muffled noise. He ignored it until he heard the same sound and recognized it as a gun shot. He pulled his .38 revolver, turned off the bathroom light to avoid silhouetting himself, and stepped outside. He walked toward where his partner had been eating, and his walk quickly turned into a run as he saw his partner laying on the ground. He was within 10 feet of the body when he was shot. He staggered back and realized the vest had done its job. He took cover and waited. He saw some movement in the shadows and yelled, "Halt!" His command brought more gunfire. He aimed at the place where the muzzle flashed and fired three shots. Getting behind cover, he reloaded and waited. After a few minutes he remembered the "panic button" on his belt and pushed it.

When more guards responded, they searched the area and followed a blood trail to a fence. Three days later a man staggered into the hospital. He had taken two Cor-Bon JHPs in the chest and finally decided to have it looked at.

He had been shot with his partner's gun after the inattentive guard had been struck with a brick from the front while sitting down!

Note on .38 Special Loads Performance from a 4-inch Barrel

The top two performers in this barrel length are both +P+ loads, and many users worry about the wear and tear on their weapons. The Remington .38 Special 125-grain Golden Saber +P JHPs are working just as well and are extremely accurate in my Ruger GP-100 .357 Magnum revolver.

9MM LUGER

His brother in law was a cop, so he was able to get several boxes of Federal's 9BPLE 9mm for his Glock

17. A salesman for a software company, he spent a lot on the road and had grown concerned over the escalating violent crime rate in several of the cities he traveled to.

Carry permits were impossible to get, but a concealment holster wasn't. He carried his Glock in a Kramer IWB holster over his right hip. It had been there for several years and its presence had become most comforting.

He got up early and prepared for a busy day. He had no idea that it would almost be his last.

He had stopped at three locations and decided to squeeze in one more sales call before lunch. He parked his car in the alley to avoid paying a parking lot. Returning from the call, he was walking up the alley to his car when he noticed the driver's side door slightly ajar and a young man in the backseat. "Get out of my car!" the salesman yelled. The intruder backed out of the car, turned, and rushed at the owner with a tire iron in his hand. Dropping his sales case, he produced the Glock, placed the front sight in the middle of his attacker's chest, and pulled the trigger three times. The young man staggered and collapsed. Although rushed to the hospital, he died during emergency surgery.

Two of the rounds had missed,

Winchester 9mm 147-grain Ranger Talon is a favorite of those who advocate heavy bullets and deep penetration. This one ended the career of a holdup man wearing body armor. It entered between the panels and stopped under the skin on the far side after penetrating the heart.

The Remington 147-grain brass-jacketed Golden Saber hollowpoint breathed new life into this bullet weight. This one was used by a big city cop to end a gas station holdup.

The career of a thief who specialized in stealing luxury cars was ended by this Winchester 9mm 147-grain Silvertip.

Winchester 9mm Silvertip produces excellent results in actual shootings. These rounds were recovered from the chest of a cop killer.

Remington's 124-grain JHP +P is rapidly becoming a popular law enforcement/self-defense choice. This one ended a standoff with a hostage taker at a school.

Speer Gold Dot 9mm 124-grain bonded hollowpoints produce superior expansion in people. This one was recovered from the heart of a car thief.

Federal's 9mm Nyclad 124-grain hollowpoint has shown good results in actual shootings. This one stopped a drug dealer armed with a machete.

The Winchester 9mm 115-grain +P+ JHP was originally developed for the Illinois State Police and selected by Evan Marshall when he was Firearms and Tactics Instructor for the Special Response Team of the Detroit Police Department. It has worked extremely well in actual shootings.

Federal's original 9mm was a superior 147-grain load. Unfortunately, "improved" versions feature a much smaller cavity. An off-duty "peace keeper" shot an AK-47 armed terrorist with this one.

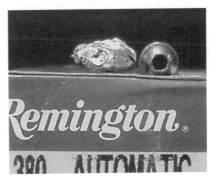

Remington's 9mm 115-grain +P+ JHP is an excellent stopper. This one ended an attempted car jacking.

ACTUAL STREET RESULTS

but one +P+ slug was recovered resting against the spine. It had a weight of 99 grains and a diameter of .65 inch. The salesman was charged with possession of an unlicenced pistol and sentenced to 30 days in jail. Fired from his firm, he now works in the natural gas industry and still carries a handgun.

• • • • •

A cop in a nice middle and upper class community enjoyed the fact that he could raise his kids in a town with superior schools but chaffed at the lack of action. His department issued Glock 17 and 19s. Their issue ammo was the Federal 115-grain JHP +P+ load. Each officer also had a 12-gauge shotgun and the option of carrying an AR-15 in their patrol unit. Second guns were allowed, though not encouraged. Officers were also given option of carrying off duty, though most did not "because nothing ever happened in _____!"

The cop in question did carry off-duty and preferred his Model 17 in a De Santis concealment rig. While other officers poked fun at him, he just shrugged it off.

He had been working on his lawn and realized he needed some more grass seed. He had gotten into his pickup and had backed almost all the way out of the driveway when he realized he didn't have his Glock. He stopped, smiled to himself, and went back into the house to get it.

At the store he bought two bags of seed and headed for his truck. He heard the argument before he actually saw the participants. A man and a woman, both in their mid-30s, were screaming at each other. He placed the bags in the back of his truck and watched for a moment. When the man slapped her, the officer decided to intervene. He walked closer, identified himself as a police officer, and told the man to stop.

The man suddenly reached into the open window of his vehicle. The officer saw the stock of a long gun and

took cover, producing his Glock in the process. He ordered the man to freeze, but he continued to pull the weapon. He yelled, "I'll kill this cop and then I'll kill you, you stupid _____!" The officer placed the front sight in the middle of the man and fired four shots. The first three were high and missed, but the fourth struck the left arm. The round penetrated the arm, entered the thoracic cavity, and penetrated both lungs and the heart before finally lodging in the other arm. The man collapsed and was dead before the paramedics arrived.

The officer was cleared in the shooting and returned to duty a couple of weeks later. The chief called him in and spent a number of hours discussing the matter. His final comment was, "Well, at least it was done in typical _____ fashion. That was a $4,000 engraved over-and-under shotgun he tried to shoot you with."

• • • • •

He was sitting on the edge of a hospital gurney having stitches put in his left hand. He had been in the process of arresting a drunk when the man's equally inebriated wife cut him with a kitchen knife. He had knocked her out with one bloody punch and then arrested both of them. The stitches really upset him, as he was a member of his department's SERT team that had a raid planned the next night. He could flex his hand, but it was obvious he couldn't fulfill his role as the shotgun man.

He went to the briefing anyway. The team leader took one look at his hand and just shook his head. The officer looked so disappointed that the team leader told him he could work perimeter security if he felt comfortable relying on his Beretta 9mm. The officer, who had led the committee that had chosen the Beretta pistol and Federal 9mm +P+ ammunition, just grinned.

The team entered their van and

headed out for the raid's location. The injured officer was dropped off with two team members armed with submachine gun. He found a place of cover behind a large oak tree and waited. When he heard the team start their countdown, he drew his pistol and waited. He heard the dull thump of stun grenades and then the noise of high-caliber rifle fire.

Knowing that the team was only equipped with submachine guns and shotguns, he started to rise from his position. Another perimeter team member grabbed him, "We're perimeter security. Stay put. The guys out front have plenty of help!" He heard the MP5s on full auto then and knew it was going bad. One of the other men with him had night vision on and whispered," I've got movement out the back! One suspect with a long gun." The officer couldn't see him yet, but the other perimeter officer launched a parachuted flare to illuminate the rear.

He saw the man then. He was running directly toward their position with an AK-47. The officer was about to issue a verbal challenge when he heard a report over the radio that three officers were down. The officer placed his front sight just above the bad guy's weapon and fired three rounds. It was later determined that the first round struck the magazine of the rifle, making it incapable of firing beyond the round in the chamber. The man fired the one round and then pulled the cocking lever several times. The officer yelled for him to drop the weapon, but the man continued to try to chamber a round.

This time the officer fired twice. The first round missed, but the second struck him in the rib cage. It was removed at autopsy from the severely shredded liver. It had a recovered diameter of .68 inch and a recovered weight of 101 grains.

• • • • •

The officer looked at his alarm

The Orlando, Florida, Police Department recently adopted the Ranger Talon 127-grain JHP +P+ and have been happy with the results from the street.

A Black Hills 9mm 115-grain JHP that expanded and glanced off a rib before penetrating the liver.

Two Federal 9mm 124-grain Nyclad hollowpoints show the difference in resistance between soft tissue and muscle

Speer's Gold Dot bullet is a superior design. This standard-velocity 9mm 115-grain BHP was used overseas to end a terrorist attack.

These Remington 124-grain Golden Saber 9mm brass hollowpoints were used by a plainclothes officer to stop two felons with one shot each.

Remington's 9mm 147-grain brass hollowpoint should be the first choice of those who prefer this bullet weight in 9mm.

Highly controversial when first introduced, the Black Talon line produces moderate expansion and deep penetration. This 147-grain 9mm offering was used by a state trooper to kill a knife-wielding drunk.

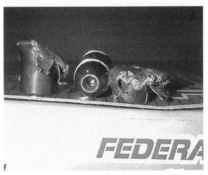

Federal's 9mm 115-grain JHP +P+ has long been a superior stopper in this caliber. These two rounds were fired by a SWAT cop who had responded to a bank alarm.

This Federal 9mm 124-grain +P+ Hydra-Shok was used by an internal affairs investigator to stop a sexual assault.

clock and remembered that today was the day he had promised to take his kids to a nearby amusement park. They got up, showered, dressed, and went downstairs to make breakfast. His family loved his blueberry waffles, and he enjoyed making them.

His wife and kids were climbing into their van when he went back upstairs to get his Glock 9mm. He smiled at himself but took it nonetheless.

The day was hot, but the family had a great time. His teenage daughters even got him to ride the latest super roller coaster. They laughed at their dad when he screamed right along with them. They left the park at 6 P.M., and the rest of the family soon fell asleep on the drive home.

They were less than 20 miles from home when he noticed a police car on a vehicle stop. Like most cops he slowed down to make sure his brother officer was okay. The officer had stopped a car full of young men in beach attire. He had gotten less than 100 yards when he looked back and saw the officer laying on the ground being stomped. He pulled his car to the curb and yelled to his wife while handing her the cell phone, "A cop back there is being assaulted. Call 911 and give them a physical and clothing description of me! Don't let the kids leave the car!" He started to run to the officer's assistance when he was shot in the leg. Falling to the ground, he pulled his Glock and fired at his attacker. The first three rounds missed, but the fourth ended this cop killing in progress. It entered just above the left nipple and stopped just under the skin of his back. Its recovered diameter was .65 inch, and it had a recovered weight of 104 grains.

The leg wound had created permanent nerve damage and the officer had to take a duty disability retirement. Today he works in a bait and tackle shop and rides the latest, fastest roller coaster with his grandchildren.

• • • • •

He had retired as a big city homicide investigator and moved up north. He enjoyed the woods and especially the low population density of his county. Still a realist, he carried his Beretta 9mm in a Milt Sparks Summer Special. His department had carried a 124-grain JHP load, but he had traded for a box of Federal 9BPLE while attending a homicide class and, now that he was not controlled by departmental regulations, that's what his pistol was loaded with.

He had a daily routine. He would get up and fix breakfast for him and his wife. After breakfast he would do the dishes, put on his Nikes, and take the dog for a walk. His dog, Felony, was an older black retriever that had started to show his age lately. When they first started these walks, the dog would run ahead and smell everything. Now he just walked along slowly, and his owner had slowed his pace to match the dog's progress.

They had reached their goal, the gas station/convenience store, where he picked up the daily paper from the city where he had worked for so many years. He was inside paying for the paper when he heard the dog bark. Since the dog rarely did so, he quickly walked outside just in time to see a shabbily dressed young man kick his dog. "I wouldn't do that if I was you, boy!" The young man's response was obscene and racial: "Why don't you take your nigger ____ and your nigger dog and go somewhere else!"

The retired detective just smiled, but a wiser man would have realized it was a warning. He called the dog and they left. He was about a quarter mile down the road when he heard the pickup truck accelerating toward him. He turned and looked to see the same young man bearing down on him. Pulling the dog out of the way, he drew the Beretta and aimed it at the truck.

When the driver showed no signs of slowing down or swerving back onto the pavement, he fired three rounds. All three penetrated the windshield, and one caught the man just above the sternum. Though the truck continued on its way, it was being driven by a dead man.

The round was recovered at autopsy from the spinal column. It weighed 89 grains and had a recovered diameter of .63 inch.

The local sheriff was a bit harsh with the man until a couple of retired white detectives who had worked homicide with him took the sheriff to a "Come to Jesus meeting" and the shooting was quickly ruled a justifiable homicide.

Federal 9BPLE Failure

It was typical day where he lived, overcast and threatening to rain. In spite of that, he wheeled his motorcycle out of the garage and zipped up his leather jacket. A motorcycle cop by profession, he couldn't get enough of it. His first wife had left him over the job and his interest in two-wheeled vehicles. The leather jacket covered a SIG P226 loaded with Federal +P+ 115-grain JHPs in a Bianchi thumb-break holster.

He had planned to ride north of the city, stop for lunch, and return home in time to shower, change, and ride the department's cycle for eight hours. He would never make it. He was on the return portion of the trip when he saw a car pulled off the road. The hood was up and a young woman was looking under it. It was a trap, but he didn't see it.

He got off his bike and walked up to her. "Got a problem?" He didn't see the knife until it was too late. She slashed him across the stomach. Staggering back, he pulled the SIG and opened fire. He hit her twice with a department-mandated double tap and stood frozen while she cut his throat. She was killed by responding officers a quarter mile away with the bloody knife in one hand and the SIG in the other.

.357 MAGNUM

He belonged to a small agency that did not provide a handgun for its officers. All the other officers had bought semiautomatic pistols, but he carried the same .357 Magnum his dad had for 30 years on the state patrol. It had saved his father's life twice, and he was a firm believer in luck. While his father's agency had mandated 158-grain jacketed softpoint ammo, his was loaded with Federal's 125-grain jacketed hollowpoints. A large city in his state has used this load for years with superb results, and that was good enough for him.

He was working the afternoon shift and had written two tickets when he realized he didn't have any more. He had pulled up to the city hall and walked around to the rear of the building to the police entrance. He noticed the door ajar and wondered about that since regulations required it be locked after the building was closed. He walked into the report room and saw someone's hand-held radio and report book. He heard the toilet flush, and the only female officer in the agency walked out. They exchanged greetings and he reminded her to keep the door locked.

He signed out some tickets and was leaving when she asked him, "Do you know the _____ family very well?" He responded that they were a bunch of pathetic losers except for Junior, but since he was in the state prison, they had become a minor problem. "Well, they told me tonight that Junior got paroled and will be home tomorrow."

The officer reflected on the last time he and Junior had crossed paths. It had taken the full contents of an OC cannister and repeated application of a PR-24 before Junior had submitted to arrest. It was only after Junior had been treated in the hospital that the officer was notified that he was wanted for shooting a cop in the south end of the state. He had to admit that he was not surprised that Junior had

Federal's .357 Magnum 125-grain JHP, the King of the Hill. It produces superior results on the street, though some complain about its "failure" in gelatin.

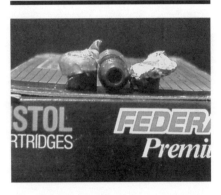

The Federal .357 Magnum 158-grain Nyclad hollowpoint produces good penetration with reasonable expansion.

only served 5 years of a 20 year sentence for attempted murder. He considered judges, defense attorneys, and parole boards to be all part of the same gene pool.

The rest of the shift was uneventful, and he went home and crawled in bed. Since he lived alone he had the habit of getting up when the mood struck him. He was laying in bed at 8:15 A.M. trying to decide whether he should get up or roll over when the phone rang. It was the chief. "We got a possible problem. I sent _____ out to the _____ family farm on a disturbance. When he didn't answer the radio, I sent _____ out and she hasn't called in either." The officer advised the chief that Junior had been paroled and that they had better call the sheriffs's department

and state patrol for backup. Since the officer lived five miles closer to the _____ family than the PD, he told the chief he would take his own car from home. He put his vest on, grabbed his uniform and gun belt, and left. He called the chief on his cell phone and gave him the number, advising him he would take it with him when he left the car.

He turned down the rural road and saw the two police vehicles parked in front of the house in question. Both driver side doors were open, and he noticed the shotgun rack on one was empty. He called the chief on his cell phone and apprised him of the situation. He advised the chief to have all backup units respond without lights and siren and asked for paramedics to respond to a nearby location.

He exited his car and proceeded through the corn field. He had gotten within 75 yards of the house when he saw the two officers. Both were laying behind a utility shed with guns drawn. He pulled his Magnum and crept closer. He called to the two officers and ran to their location. The male officer had a large bruise on his head. He explained that when he had arrived, the father of the family had informed him that Junior came home, got high on crystal meth, and started beating his mother. When the officer asked him if Junior was armed his response was that he had some little pistol. The officer had removed the shotgun from the rack and was coming around the house when Junior hit him with a brick, took his shotgun, and fled into the house.

The newly arrived officer took one of the other cop's hand-held radios but found he couldn't transmit successfully from their location. Dialing the chief on his cell phone, he told him what was going on and asked the chief to get the sheriff's SWAT team activated. He told the other two officers that he was going to work his way around the house so that Junior couldn't outflank them.

He had made his way to a barn

behind the house when he heard gunfire. He took a quick peek and saw Junior shooting at the other officers. Taking careful aim, he cocked the Model 28 and fired once. Junior collapsed and was dead by the time the paramedics arrived. The 125-grain jacketed hollowpoint penetrated the right arm and chest cavity and lodged under the skin on the far side of the left arm. It weighed 91 grains and was .67 inch in diameter.

• • • • •

It wasn't that hard of a decision. While both his dad and grandfather had been lawyers, his great grandfather had been one of the more notorious gunman of the Old West. It wasn't that much of a stretch to enter the executive protection business. He was adept in the martial arts and skilled with a variety of impact weapons and firearms.

He worked for a small, reclusive firm that catered to the needs of high-risk clients. He had met one of their people in a martial arts class, had gone in for an interview, and was hired a few weeks later. On the range they smirked at his choice of weapons, but he controlled the 4 inch Magnum with ease. He proved equally adept with a wide variety of shoulder weapons.

He was overseas working a client whose risk level was so high that the country's notoriously antigun stance had been modified so the team could be heavily armed. He had worked his shift and was returning to his hotel room when he decided to run downstairs and buy a newspaper. The shop in the lobby was closed, so he walked down the street. He found a newsstand that featured English language papers and purchased two.

He was returning to the hotel when two men slammed him against the wall and tried to search him. "Get his gun," one said to the other prior to any search, and the agent realized this wasn't a random strong arming. Spinning away from his attackers, he

Federal's .357 Magnum 158-grain Hydra-Shok penetrates deeply and produces fair expansion. This one stopped a road rage participant.

A Federal .357 Magnum 158-grain Nyclad shot from a 2 inch gun to save the life of a backpacker.

produced the 4 inch .357 Magnum and ordered them in their native tongue to freeze. Both men ignored the command and reached under their jackets. The agent fired one round at each of his attackers and returned to the first one, but they were both down.

He spent several hours in the local jail before somebody from the team and a high-ranking counterterrorist agent from the host country showed up and had him released. He sought permission to attend the autopsy, and his request was granted. His interest was not ballistic but forensic. He fingerprinted both dead men and sent the cards to a friend in a federal law enforcement agency. Both men were identified as members of _____, the terrorist group that had targeted his client. He sent me the recovered

slugs a year later. They had an average weight of 102 grains and an average diameter of .68 inch.

• • • • •

He was the senior man on an armored car crew. The employer issued Smith & Wesson Model 64 .38 Specials, but he had purchased a Model 65, a virtual clone with one important advantage—it was chambered for .357 Magnum, not .38 Special. The loops on his duty belt carried the company-issue .38 Special 125-grain JHP loads, but the gun contained six rounds of Federal .357 Magnum 125-grain JHPs.

In spite of the fact that he was senior man on the crew, he hated being cooped up in the truck in nice weather, so he would do most of the deliveries himself. It was a mild spring day as they stopped for a delivery in a shopping mall. He got the hand truck out and loaded several banks of coins designated for a video arcade. It made an impressive looking pile, but the total value was less than $3,000.

He was wheeling the money toward the mall when he was approached by two older men who asked the location of a particular store. He turned to point toward an information board when one of the men struck him on the side of the head with a handgun. The force of the blow drove him to his knees and he was drawing his gun when the other subject put a gun to his chest and fired. The round glanced off his vest but rode down his gun arm and exited above his wrist.

Unable to remove his weapon with his dominant hand, he reached across his body with his nondominant and fired the Magnum with his little finger. The combination of recoil and poor grip caused him to drop the gun, but it was enough. The man who had shot him turned and started to run before collapsing.

The round was recovered during surgery. It weighed 96 grains and had a recovered diameter of .69 inch. The second man escaped but was captured later. Both men were convicted of armed robbery, and the shooter was also convicted of attempted murder. The guard was suspended for 30 days without pay and a reprimand was put in his personnel file.

• • • • •

He had left his native country in the Middle East and emigrated to the United States. Working night and day for several years, he was able to bring a number of his family to his new homeland too. He owned three stores, all of them in the inner city. He was honest and charged prices considerably lower than some of the grocery stores in the area.

Crime and violence had always been a problem, and under the counter of each of his stores were virtually identical Ruger GP-100 revolvers loaded with Federal 125-grain JHP ammo. Next to each revolver was a cell phone preprogrammed to dial 911. Only his sons were allowed access to the guns.

The owner was returning to one of his stores with a bank bag full of change and cash when he noticed two men loitering in front of the premises. He didn't pay a whole lot of attention to them, as there was always someone loitering there. He entered the store, waved at his son, and waited to be buzzed into the secure area containing the cash register and liquor. He had opened the door and started in when he felt a knife against his neck. "Give me the money or I'll cut your useless Arab throat! We want the money in the register too!" The man told his son to give him the money in the register and the money under the counter too. It took a moment for the son to realize what his father was saying. "Are you sure?" the son asked in Arabic. The father replied also in Arabic, "Yes, give him what he deserves!"

The son put the money in a bag and then reached under the counter.

Remington's .357 Magnum 125-grain JHP has produced excellent results in this caliber. These two rounds were recovered from the body of a drug addict who had stolen a gun and gone on a rampage.

Starfire .357 Magnum 150-grain JHP that produced excellent expansion when fired from a 4 inch barrel into the heart of a robber.

Before the holdup man had time to react, he produced the gun and fired. The first round missed and the holdup man slashed the father's throat, missing the jugular. As the father fell to the floor, the holdup man turned to escape and the son's second shot struck him in the middle of the back, severing the spine. He was DOA at a local hospital. The recovered round weighed 102 grains and had a diameter of .61 inch.

• • • • •

Driving a truck for a major delivery service, much of his route was over a large rural area. He had started carrying a .357 Magnum in a bag because he had been attacked twice by large dogs running in a pack. Plastic surgery had minimized the physical scars, but not the emotional ones.

He looked at the map again but couldn't find _____ Road. He stopped at a corner store and asked for directions. The owner laughed and told the driver that people around there called it a different name and the county had changed the name awhile ago.

The driver then got back in the truck and went to the location. The box was big, heavy, and obviously of superior construction. As he struggled to carry it to the house he saw a man exit a vehicle parked in front. "Hi" he said to the driver, "I see you got my package." Suspicious, the driver asked for identification. "ID?" the man asked and laughed. "Hell buddy, I live here."

The man's response only made the driver more suspicious. He informed the man that unless he could produce identification with the address on it, he would return the package to the warehouse. The man's smile faded as he produced a large folding knife. "Either you give me that package or I'll cut your throat and take it!" The driver dropped the box and ran for his truck. The man folded his knife and started to pick up the box but stopped when he looked up and saw the driver holding the Magnum.

"Step away from the box!" the driver demanded. "You gonna shoot me over some little ole box?" the man asked? "Get away from the box!" the driver demanded again. The man took a step and the driver retreated. Thinking the driver was indecisive, the man opened the knife and started to wave it. It was a fatal mistake.

The driver continued to retreat until he was backed up against the side of the truck. Realizing he had nowhere to go, he raised the revolver to eye level and cocked it. The knife-wielding man continued to advance and the driver fired. The round struck him just above the right nipple, pierced the heart, and was found under his T-shirt. It had a recovered weight of 108 grains and a recovered diameter of .72 inch.

The driver was fired for the unauthorized possession of a handgun. In response he sued his ex-employer for failure to provide for his safety. The company settled out of court for enough money that the former driver bought a beachfront cabin on a small lake in the south. On a high shelf above the front door is a .357 Magnum revolver loaded with Federal 125-grain JHP ammo.

Federal .357 Magnum 125-grain JHP Failure

Assigned to an overseas security detail, he carried a Beretta 9mm on duty. In his off-duty hours, however, he carried a Smith & Wesson Model 66 .357 Magnum with 4 inch barrel. He was not confident that auto pistols were reliable anyway, and when he had two stoppages during qualification it only confirmed his suspicions.

He worked a four-day, 10 hour a day rotation. He enjoyed the three days off in a row and had bought a good 35mm camera and several lenses. He had developed into a decent photographer and had several albums filled with his work.

He had heard that in a far part of the city there was some ancient architecture so he headed out that way. He was not aware that this part of the city was the site of several tribal skirmishes. He had located the buildings he wanted to photograph and began taking pictures when he heard an argument break out behind him.

He turned to see two men in tribal dress arguing over an emaciated cow. He turned back to his work and was reloading the camera when he heard a scream. Turning, he saw one man holding his chest while the other was waving a bloody knife. Pulling his .357, he told the man to drop the knife. The knife wielder's response was to advance on the American. He fired three times and lowered the weapon. To his horror the man with the knife continued to rush him, stabbed him in

the stomach, then ran away, leaving his knife embedded in him.

The victim was lucky that the police drove by shortly after the stabbing and rushed him to a nearby hospital. Emergency surgery and an aggressive program of antibiotics saved his life. His attacker was found three days later wandering the streets with three 125-grain slugs in his chest and legs.

.357 SIG

He had resisted his department's conversion from revolvers to semiautomatic pistols. He was perfectly content with his .357 Magnum revolver loaded with 125-grain JHPs. It had saved his life on the roof of a hotel several years before. He now carried the high-capacity 9mm but had little faith in it.

When the .357 SIG appeared on the scene, he lobbied his chief incessantly until he threw up his hands and allowed the officer to purchase and carry his own handgun in this caliber. Having relied on the Federal 125-grain JHP in his revolver, his choice of ammunition was an easy one.

A few years later, when the SIG P239 became available in this caliber he bought one for off-duty carry. Its flat, compact, lightweight package made an ideal concealment option. With a spare magazine it gave him 15 rounds of serious ammunition, and it was much more pleasant to shoot and easier to control than the .357 snub he had carried formerly.

It was a typical Saturday for him. His wife had a list of things for him to do, and he rushed to get them done before Notre Dame football started. He didn't care who they were playing—he just wanted to see them get defeated soundly.

He drove to the local strip mall and began his search for some replacement handles for a chest he had been refinishing. Unfortunately, it had been hand made and was not a standard width. After several minutes

of frustrating search, he explained his problem to the manager. He was taken to the back of the stock room and shown several drawers of assorted items. "If I got what you're looking for, it's in there," the manager said. The officer opened the drawers and saw they contained a hodgepodge of items. He alternated looking in the drawers and looking at his watch as kick-off time approached.

He was measuring a likely prospect when he heard loud voices from the front of the store. Walking toward the front he saw a large man gesturing at the manager and yelling, "I'm telling you that the _____ check is good!" The manager explained that he had taken a check from him before and it had been returned stamped "NSF," and although the manager had called and written him, he had never made it good.

The man then reached across the counter and grabbed the manager by the throat. The officer ran forward and told him to stop. Instead the man grabbed an inexpensive screwdriver from a bin at the register and stabbed the officer in the chest. Pulling his SIG, he fired three rounds. Two missed, but the third struck the 300 pound man in the upper chest. He yelled "Ah, _____!" and died.

The officer walked to the paramedic's vehicle but went into cardiac arrest on the way to the hospital and almost died. Hours later in the recovery room, he turned to his wife and asked, "Did Notre Dame lose?"

The slug was recovered from the back, 2 inches to the right of the spine under the skin. It had a recovered weight of 104 grains and a recovered diameter of .62 inch.

• • • • •

The man tended to be reclusive. His wife had died a few years before and his kids were grown and moved away. They kept in close contact, and he would visit them while on business

A cop's life was saved by this Remington .357 SIG 125-grain JHP.

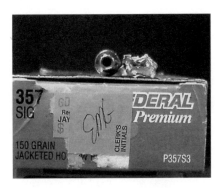

Federal's .357 SIG 150-grain JHP produces deep penetration in people.

trips. He ran an antique store in town, and many people wondered about his sexual orientation because they never saw him in the company of a woman.

He was aware of the speculation but didn't care. He had retired after 20 years of military service, most of it in special operations. He had jumped into Grenada but had lost buddies due to what he considered the ineptitude of the military planners, so he pulled the pin. He had looked forward to decades of buying and selling antiques with his wife, but breast cancer had taken her quickly.

He had always preferred a cash business and routinely carried large amounts. He had obtained an unrestricted concealed weapons permit. Now he was in a gun store shopping for just the right handgun. Looking at the various offerings in the store, he had recalled with fondness the .357 Magnum he had carried in a lot of the world's hot spots. After more than an hour of evaluation, he chose a compact Glock in .357 SIG and six boxes of ammunition.

Driving to an abandoned dump outside of town, he found his finely honed handgun skills were still in place. He loaded the gun with Federal 125-grain JHPs and stuck it in his waistband. He returned home and ordered a holster, belt, and mag pouch from the same source his SpecOps unit had used—Kramer Leather. Over the next year or so he would travel extensively and practice regularly.

One Friday evening he was waiting in his shop for an out-of-town customer to arrive. This particular customer specialized in china and silver with royal family crests. He had acquired a complete set of picnic china and silverware from the royal family of a minor European country. It was in superb condition, and the collector had promised him a bonus for accommodating his late arrival. It was shortly after 9 P.M. when the shop door opened, but it was not his anticipated visitor. Two young men entered. "May I be of service?" the owner asked. The taller of the two mimicked his question and said to his buddy, "The faggot wants to know if he can be of service!"

The owner recognized them then. They always hung out around the city square drinking and harassing people. "Look," he said, "why don't you two come back some other time?" The shorter one's response was to grab a plate on display and smash it. The man came around from behind the counter then, grabbed him in a pain compliance hold, and was escorting him to the door when the taller one punched him in the back. He took a couple of steps before realizing he had been stabbed. He threw the one he had ahold of to the floor with a judo move and turned on the second one with his Glock drawn.

The assailant waved the knife and yelled at him to drop the gun before he sliced off an intimate portion of his anatomy. The owner's response was to shoot him. The knife-wielding man took two steps backwards, collided with the counter, and collapsed.

His attacker was rushed to the hospital, where emergency surgery saved his life, but not his ability to walk. He is currently spending 10–15 years in state prison confined to a wheelchair. The recovered round weighed 94 grains and had a recovered diameter of .55 inch.

• • • • •

He didn't consider it that big of a deal, but his wife was extremely upset. He had accepted a reassignment to Narcotics. He tried to explain to her that his role was that of training sergeant, that he wouldn't be doing raids, and he wouldn't be working undercover. "You'll find some way to get back on the street! Haven't we been through enough hell?"

His wife's question referred to a fatal shooting he had been involved in. An alderman's son tried to rob him when he was working the decoy unit, and the officer killed him. The alderman used his influence to get a grand jury empaneled, and it was almost two years before the sergeant was exonerated and returned to duty.

He had taken the assignment because it was a training position that included a department vehicle to drive to and from work. Additionally, being assigned to narcotics meant he was not restricted to the department-issue 9mm Glock. He had bought a full-size SIG pistol chambered for the .357 SIG and loaded it with Federal 125-grain JHP ammo.

He spent the next two years sharpening the unit's raiding and shooting skills. Finally, he decided he ought to go on an occasional raid to make sure people were doing what he trained them to do. Of course he didn't bother to tell his wife of his plan.

The raid in question involved a drug dealer who tended to shoot at cops. The planning session started at 7

A.M. and lasted two hours. The raid team suited up and entered two leased vans. They proceded to a point near the raid, where they went over the plan one last time. The training sergeant was taking the place of the rear security officer and was armed with a 12-gauge shotgun with 14 inch barrel and attached light.

The entry went smoothly. The occupants were secured and the drugs and cash seized. The only disappointment was that the main dealer was not present. What they did not know was that he had a lady friend next door. The training sergeant had slung the shotgun and was making some notes when the door was jerked open and the drug dealer rushed in with a 10mm pistol in his hand.

Realizing he could never get the shotgun in action in time, he dropped his notebook and started to draw his SIG. He took two 10mm rounds in the vest before he could complete the draw, but the steel plate absorbed most of the shock. He brought his gun to eye level and fired twice. One round missed, but the other struck a heavy gold medallion the dealer wore around his neck. It penetrated the jewelry and was recovered at autopsy from the left ventricle of his heart. It weighed 82 grains and had a recovered diameter of .64 inch.

Six months later he was promoted to lieutenant and assigned to the Communications Division, where to his wife's delight he stayed.

• • • • •

A big city emergency room doctor, he had watched his grandparents shot down by the secret police in his homeland simply because they were Christians. He had escaped from the land of his birth and eventually was able to immigrate to the United States. Extremely bright, he had won a full tuition scholarship to an Ivy League college and later to a prestigious medical school.

He still viewed the police with a

This Remington .357 SIG 125-grain JHP ended a custody dispute.

Remington .357 SIG 125-grain JHP load that was used by a narcotics cop to stop a rifle-armed drug dealer.

degree of suspicion but had developed a cordial if not friendly relationship with the officers who conveyed people to the hospital. While none of them shared his passion for bird watching, they found him to be especially helpful with injured children.

It was a cold fall day when he went to the large park in the center of town with binoculars, a thermos of hot soup, and a Glock chambered for .357 SIG. He had to stand by helpless when his relatives had been murdered and had decided long ago it would never happen to him.

He kept track of the birds he saw by speaking into a compact and very expensive cassette recorder. After a few hours he stopped for some soup. He was listening to his taped notes when he realized he wasn't alone. He looked up to see two young men approaching. Something about the

way they walked caused him concern.

"Watcha doing, pal?" one asked. He responded that he was watching birds. Jerking the recorder out of the doctor's hand, he turned to his buddy and said, "Bet we could record some fine tunes on this, huh?" When the doctor asked for his recorder back, the two individuals laughed at him.

"Please leave me alone and give me my recorder back," the doctor pleaded. The two young men grabbed him and, after stripping off his binoculars, started to take his wallet. He pulled the gun then and emptied it at his two attackers. Both went down and died right there. One was hit with five .357 SIG Federal 125-grain JHPs, while the other had taken just one. The single hollowpoint had entered just below the left nipple and was found in his leather jacket at the morgue. It weighed 112 grains and had a recovered diameter of .71 inch.

The doctor was exonerated at a coroner's inquest and returned to his duties at the hospital. Today he is a pediatric specialist in a western state.

• • • • •

He had been in court all day and was exhausted. He had a couple hours to nap before working the 8 P.M. to 4 A.M. shift in the anticrime unit. He had been asleep for about 15 minutes when the phone rang. It was his mother, and he spent the next 20 minutes getting advice on how to find a wife. He had sat down with his mom several months before and explained to her that he was gay, but she just considered it a phase. After all, her four other sons were all married with children.

He hung up the phone, realizing that his mother's inane and ludicrous comments had given him a headache and he wouldn't get any more sleep. He showered, shaved, and donned his usual garb for work—soft body armor, handcuffs, sweatshirt, jeans, .357 SIG pistol in a De Santis belt holster, and Walther PPK in an Uncle Mike's ankle holster.

The bus was crowded, but he tuned it all out. Maybe his brothers could convince his mom; he certainly couldn't. He looked up and realized he had traveled past his stop. He got up and pulled the cord. He was only four blocks from his stop, so he decided to walk. After all, he was just one more Hispanic male in a predominantly Hispanic neighborhood.

He stopped for a bottle of apple juice and wandered back to the magazine rack. Looking through the selection of gun magazines, he didn't notice the three young men enter the store, but he became alert when the usually noisy store became silent. Crouching, he pulled his duty weapon and his badge. He made his way down a far aisle and knelt before taking a quick peek.

The three were at the register and the clerk was emptying its contents into a paper bag. Regretting his decision not to buy a cell phone, he waited and hoped they would just take the money and leave. Unfortunately, when one of the robbers demanded the money in the back, the clerk's eyes got wide and, calling the one holdup man by name, said, "_____, why are you doing this?" It cost him his life—he took both barrels of a shotgun in the chest. As the man broke the shotgun open to reload it, the officer shot him twice in the upper back. The other two robbers turned and opened fire. The officer chose the man closest to him and gave him one .357 SIG in the upper chest. The third man threw his gun down.

Hearing sirens, he ordered the uninjured holdup man on the floor while he held his gun by his side and displayed his badge. The shotgun-armed thug was dead at the scene, while the one who had taken a single round and collapsed on the spot died en route to the hospital. The single survivor was convicted of felony murder and given the death penalty.

The Federal hollowpoint had a recovered diameter of .65 inch and a recovered weight of 107 grains.

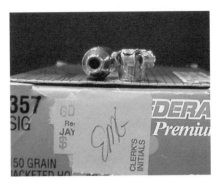

This Federal .357 SIG 150-grain JHP ended the career of a purse snatcher. It produced moderate expansion and deep penetration.

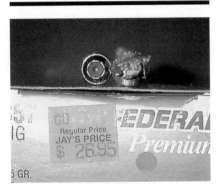

A Federal .357 SIG 125-grain JHP that produced good expansion and appropriate penetration when fired from a SIG compact auto. This one was recovered from the right lung at autopsy.

Federal .357 SIG 125-grain Failure

His dad was thrilled when he had chosen horticulture as a major in college. The older man owned a chain of extremely successful nurseries located in several states. He was less than pleased when, upon graduation, his son borrowed $100,000 and set up his own organic fruit orchards.

The young man's efforts soon became successful, and he bought more land and hired more employees. He married, had several kids, and looked on his career choice with satisfaction. Then life took a turn for the worse when his wife was abducted, raped, and murdered. This case was never solved.

About a year later, he started to get threats of arson if he did not pay off some individuals in the area. Being a practical man, we went to a local gun shop and purchased a Glock chambered for the .357 SIG cartridge and four boxes of Federal 125-grain jacketed hollowpoint ammunition. A local cop worked for him part time, and the officer instructed him at the range until he felt his employer was competent with the pistol. The boss had not explained why he wanted to learn how to shoot. If he had, the officer told investigators he would have tried to talk him out of it.

The man made an appointment with his intended extorters at 2 A.M. behind an abandoned drive-in theater. He had no intent of paying. Investigators had to piece together what happened after the fact. Apparently, he had offered the extortionists a bag supposedly containing the payoff. In fact it contained three copies of the Sunday *New York Times*. It is not clear who fired first, but the orchard owner was at some point hit three times with .45 ACP 230-grain hardball and fell where he stood.

The two felons were found three blocks away in a vehicle. Both were dead. One had been hit three times in the upper thoracic cavity, while the other took one round to the throat and a second to the groin. The two individuals were identified as convicted felons who had been sentenced to 20 years for prior convictions but had been paroled after 7 years because of time off for good behavior!

.40 S&W

His department had originally issued a deep-penetrating 180-grain JHP for the new .40 S&W pistols. Unfortunately, while it had produced spotty results in actual shootings, the rangemaster had gotten his ego tangled up in its selection and they had stumbled along until his retirement. His replacement had done a lot of ammunition testing and selected the Remington 165-grain Golden Saber as the new duty load. They had not had any shootings with it, but that was to change.

He was assigned as a school security detail during the school year and to a nearby mall during the summer. He had attended the end-of-year luncheon at the school and stopped by the mall to let its security personnel know he would be in the following day and to obtain a radio to carry in addition to his department portable.

He walked to his unmarked car and was backing out of his parking space when he saw people running from the lot across the street. He drove across the street and headed toward the location people were running from. He saw the man then. He was dressed in bib overalls and nothing else, and he was armed with a long-barreled shotgun. The officer promptly notified the dispatcher of his location and that he had a man with a gun.

He had intended to wait for backup because he didn't have a long gun, but the man ended that plan when he opened fire. The officer exited his vehicle and drew his .40 pistol. Using the engine block for cover, he reported shots fired at his location and then ordered the man to drop his gun. The man's response was to turn slightly and open fire on the officer. The officer took cover, changed location, and engaged the attacker. His first three rounds missed, so he changed locations and engaged the man again.

This time his attacker fell to the ground. The officer covered him until backup arrived. The man was conveyed to a local hospital, where he expired in the emergency room. One Remington 165-grain Golden Saber was recovered from the thoracic cavity. It had a recovered diameter of .72 caliber and weighed 141 grains.

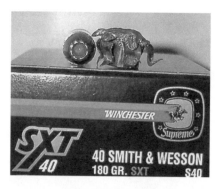

A Winchester .40 S&W 180-grain Ranger Talon that produced good results in an actual shooting. This one penetrated a car windshield and the felon behind it.

The Speer .40 S&W 180-grain BHP is a consistent performer. These two rounds were used by a businessman to stop a holdup of his shop.

Winchester .40 Ranger XST 180-grain loads that ended the career of a holdup team.

A dentist in a small town, he had grown up and attended dental school in a major urban center. He had been a victim of crime on several occasions there, so he had bought a .40 Glock auto and loaded it with Golden Saber 165-grain JHPs. At first he carried it in a shoulder bag, but eventually he purchased an inside-the-waistband holster.

After graduation he accepted a position in a small town. Because of the low crime rate there, he unloaded his Glock and put it in a locked case. At first things were fine, but he found that some people were a bit unfriendly. He decided that it was because the last town dentist had been born there and had practiced for almost 40 years. He didn't realize that his Japanese ancestry had anything to do with it. After all, he had been born in the United States, as had his parents. His dad had fought in Italy during World War II while his family had lived in an internment camp. But that was ancient history, he thought. He would turn out to be tragically wrong.

It started with a dead cat on his porch. He didn't think much of it and buried it in the field he owned adjacent to his rural home. A week later he found the words "Dirty Jap" scratched into the side of his Japanese import car. He mistakenly thought the comment referred to the car, not him.

A week later the phone calls started. First there was no conversation, just heavy breathing. Again he decided that someone had dialed a wrong number, since he was single and lived alone. Then the calls turned obscene and racial. Finally, the dentist took his Glock from its secure location, loaded it, and started carrying it. He always wore a coat and tie, so no one noticed the pistol. While treating his patients it was locked in his desk drawer. He reasoned mistakenly that no one would bother him in his office because of the presence of his receptionist, dental assistants, and a steady stream of customers.

Remington .40 S&W 180-grain JHPs show performance typical of "first generation" loads in this caliber.

This Federal .40 S&W 135-grain Hydra-Shok Personal Defense load worked well out of a 4 inch barrel.

These three Federal .40 S&W 180-grain JHPs were recovered from the same body. Left to right: stomach, heart, and lung.

Speer's .40 S&W 155-grain BHP is producing excellent results in actual shootings. This one was used by an off-duty federal agent to stop a rape. It was recovered from the large intestine at autopsy.

The Speer Gold Dot 180-grain .40 S&W works well. The round on the left was recovered from 10 percent calibrated gelatin. The round at right was recovered from an uncalibrated hoodlum.

Speer's superior bullet design shows excellent expansion even after passing through a door and heavy clothing into the chest of a child molester.

An art thief was stopped with this Federal .40 S&W 180-grain Hydra-Shok.

Norma .40 S&W 155-grain JHP that put a stop to a wife beater.

A .40 S&W Black Hills 180-grain JHP.

A string of bar stickups came to an end with this Remington .40 S&W 165-grain Golden Saber.

A Black Hills .40 S&W 155-grain hollowpoint that stopped an assault.

This Winchester .40 S&W 180-grain JHP stopped a home invasion.

Remington's .40 S&W 165-grain brass hollowpoint is a superior stopper in this caliber. This one was used by a barber to stop the holdup of his shop.

This Remington .40 S&W 155-grain JHP worked well in a gunfight between a security guard and jewelry store robbers. It was recovered at autopsy.

A drug agent shot this Winchester .40 S&W 155-grain Silvertip round from a compact Glock to save his partner's life. Recovered from the lung at autopsy.

He was treating his last patient when he heard the front door open. Suddenly a man yelled, "So_____, you work for that dirty Jap now! Are you _____ him too?" The dentist quickly entered his office, unlocked his desk, and retrieved the Glock. He was hurrying toward the waiting room when he heard his receptionist scream. Running now, he entered the waiting room.

His receptionist was on the floor with blood running down the front of her blouse. He saw the man then. He was a white male in his 70s. "You _____ Jap. This is for my brother Billy who died on Iwo Jima!" He raised the knife then and rushed the dentist, who responded with four rounds from the Glock. The attacker

collapsed on the floor. The dentist instructed his assistant to dial 911 and then attempted to treat his receptionist, but she died in the paramedics vehicle on the way to the hospital. The attacker survived and was judged insane and committed to a mental institution. During his hospital stay, one Golden Saber was recovered near his heart. It weighed 152 grains and had a recovered diameter of .67 inch.

The dentist still practices in the same town, but both he and his new wife carry .40 Glocks loaded with Golden Sabers every day.

• • • • •

He was a parole officer whose agency issued a .38 snub but had no

policy on second guns, so he carried a Beretta 96D loaded with 165-grain Golden Sabers. Most of his co-workers thought he was nuts, but he didn't care.

He had spent a frustrating day trying to track down one of his clients. His last possibility was the man's great aunt who lived in public housing. He found her apartment and knocked. The elderly woman who answered the door was obviously senile, and the answers to his questions were nonsensical.

He turned to leave and was halfway down the hall when the door opened quickly. He turned to see the elderly woman standing in the doorway with a lever-action rifle. She yelled, "My daddy told me the only thing to do with you KKK members was to kill you!" The man responded that he was African-American just like her. It had no effect and she opened fire, striking the parole officer in the upper left chest. He fell to the floor in extreme pain. He was vaguely aware of the woman's approach as he pulled the Beretta, pointed it in her direction, and emptied it. He then passed out.

He woke up in the hospital. He had suffered major muscle and nerve damage and had to retire. The elderly woman hadn't been as fortunate. She was DOA at a local hospital. One Golden Saber was recovered from her back near the spinal column. The recovered slug weighed 142 grains and had a diameter of .69 inch

• • • • •

A member of a state law enforcement agency, he lacked confidence in the department's issue .40 caliber load. They had selected a deep-penetrating 180-grain JHP that was supposedly a superior round for penetration of motor vehicles. His brother-in-law owned a junkyard, so he took a wide variety of loads out there and shot a number of vehicles. His testing showed that the 165-grain Golden Saber penetrated just as well as the issue load and did better against windshield glass.

When his department refused to even look at the photographs he had taken and the bullets he recovered, he simply went home and loaded his duty pistol with Golden Sabers. Two weeks later he was called by a local agency to assist in a drug raid. The wanted suspect was a notorious outlaw biker who ran a crystal meth lab. Since he was a regular user of his product he was considered extremely dangerous.

The trooper accepted the loan of a tactical vest with ceramic insert and followed the local cops to a rendevous point. The sheriff's SWAT team was present and would handle the entry. The trooper was assigned to the evidence recovery team after a state

A Federal .40 S&W 155-grain Hydra-Shok fired from a carbine through a windshield that ended the career of a child molester.

Starfire .40 S&W 155-grain JHP that stopped an assault by an abusive father.

hazardous material unit had checked the safety of the premises.

The entry went without incident, but when the SWAT team exited with several prisoners, the primary suspect was not among them. While the hazmat team searched for dangerous chemicals, the state officer wandered off to urinate. He was thus engaged when he heard a noise in a nearby barn. Zipping up, he pulled his pistol and went to investigate. He heard more movement and laid down in the weeds.

A couple of minutes later, the primary suspect emerged from the barn with an AK-47 and a tactical vest. The officer raised his pistol and waited. As the suspect raised the rifle to shoulder level, the officer aimed just below the drug dealer's arm and fired. The dealer screamed and emptied the rifle as he fell. The officer took two

AK hits to his vest, but the ceramic plate stopped the rounds.

The dealer was pronounced dead at the scene. At autopsy the bullet track had gone through both lungs and was found embedded in the kevlar on the far side. It weighed 142 grains and had a recovered diameter of .74 inch

• • • • •

He drove a volunteer fire truck in his local community and sold pharmaceuticals state-wide for a major firm. The father of five children, he called home every night before they went to bed. He had stopped for the night at a motel. After unpacking he found that the motel's phones were temporarily out of order. He had noticed a small strip mall down the road and decided that a mile walk would do him good.

Changing into casual clothes and athletic shoes, he picked up his briefcase, removed a Smith & Wesson .40 caliber pistol, and stuck it in his waistband. A few years before he had been kidnaped by two junkies who thought because he sold drugs he would have narcotics in his sample case. When all they found were birth control pills and vitamins, they had beaten him severely.

He walked slowly, enjoying the fresh mountain air and evergreen trees. After reaching the mall and calling his kids, he noticed a parked car just off the road on his way back to the motel. Walking by it, he heard a woman plead, "Please, no!" He turned and walked closer and saw a partially clothed woman struggling with two men. Pulling the pistol, he jerked the door open and yelled, "Freeze!" He saw the gun then, a sawed-off .22 rifle. Before he could bring the .40 to bear, he was shot twice. He returned fire, emptying the pistol into the car.

He staggered back to the mall and a store owner dialed 911. Responding deputies and paramedics treated him and then responded to the car. All three occupants were dead. An autopsy determined that the woman had received a non-life-threatening wound from the salesman's .40 but had been killed by a .22 through the left eye.

One of the rapists had taken four rounds of 165-grain Golden Saber. The other had taken one in the right arm, which proceeded through the chest and was recovered from the other arm. It had broken several bones and had a recovered weight of 119 grains and a diameter of .59 inch.

.40 S&W 165-grain Golden Saber Failure

His dad had told him that the pen was mightier than the sword, and he had followed that advice and made a comfortable income writing paperback books under a variety of pen names. He had no delusions about having a #1 best seller, but his income was sufficient so that he and his family could live in a neighborhood where the homes cost $250,000+. His wife taught at a local community college, while all three of their kids attended college out west.

His wife's responsibilities included night classes and office hours, so he often ate dinner with his Jack Russell terrier. Afterwards they would take a walk; then the dog would settle down with a rawhide chew toy as he balanced the computer on his lap while watching cable TV.

Most of his works were crime and cop related so he had become friends with a number of detectives and even spent two weeks with the SWAT team a couple of years ago. They had convinced him that he should have at least one gun in the house. His wife had been raised on a turkey farm in the southwest and possessed none of the antigun phobia's so prevalent in academia. He had bought a Glock Model 22 and two cases of Remington 165-grain Golden Saber. The SWAT team instructor taught him how to use it, and it rested, loaded, on top of an antique china cabinet.

He looked up from his laptop and realized his wife should have been

home an hour ago. He called her cell phone without success, and then tried her office with similar results.

Worried, he put the Glock in his laptop bag and he and the dog jumped in his SUV. Arriving on campus, he saw his wife's car parked in its usual spot. He relaxed and walked down the hall to her office. The lights were off, but he thought he heard a noise inside. He knocked on her office door but got no response. He remembered that he had a key for it on his key ring and inserted it in the lock while removing the Glock from the bag. He pushed the door open and found a woman laying on the floor. He quickly determined it was not his wife, but he was unable to revive the unconscious woman.

He quickly dialed 911 and went to find his wife. He searched the faculty lounge and found her keys on the floor. He opened the door to the women's rest room and called his wife's name. He heard a groan and opened the stall to find her laying on the floor, severely beaten. He ran back to a phone and called 911 again. He also called campus security and reported the incident to them.

He was trying to comfort his wife when he heard a loud, hysterical laugh outside the rest room. He pulled the Glock and waited. The SWAT instructor had been adamant—take a position and maintain it while waiting for the authorities. The door started to open and he aimed the pistol carefully. The door opened to reveal a former co-worker of his wife. He was covered in blood and had a large hammer.

"Drop the _____ hammer!" he yelled. The man just grinned and raised it over his head. The writer placed the front sight in the middle of the man's chest and emptied the pistol. His attacker grunted, dropped the hammer, turned, and ran away.

Responding officers found the writer holding his wife and trying to comfort her. After a lengthy hospital stay both she and the other woman

recovered. Their attacker was found seven blocks away from the college, dead in the doorway of a business. Six slugs were recovered from his upper torso. They had a recovered weight of 146 grains and a recovered diameter of .68 inch. Tests run after the autopsy failed to find the presence of drugs or alcohol.

10MM

As the chief, he felt free to carry whatever firearm he wanted, and what he wanted was a full-sized Glock 10mm loaded with Cor Bon 150-grain JHP ammo. The department's issue gun was a full-sized Glock loaded with Cor Bon's .40 S&W 165-grain JHP load. He had given his officers the option of carrying something else, but they all seemed content with the .40.

Although his agency was a rural one, a portion of the main north-south interstate went through his community. His agency had made a lot of money off of drug forfeiture stops on the federal highway. The funds had been used to buy a variety of items, including in-car cameras and body armor. Their most recent purchase was .223 rifles that the chief preferred to shotguns.

With 70+ officers, the chief spent most of his time bogged down in administrative matters. A former big city tactical unit supervisor, he still craved action. He would get it sooner than he thought.

He looked up from the never-ending flow of paperwork to realize it was 1:30 P.M. and he still hadn't eaten lunch. He decided to head out to a restaurant just off the interstate where they made a really good Reuben sandwich. Unlike most chiefs, he wore his vest daily and demanded that his officers do the same. It would safe his life and that of a waitress.

He pulled in the parking lot and locked his cruiser. While his predecessor had driven an unmarked car, he preferred to drive the same vehicle his people did. He sat in the corner with his back against the wall. He had not survived 18 years in the big city by being careless.

After placing his order, he sipped his soda and waited for his sandwich. The waitress placed an order in front of a large man in bib overalls. "Hey," he yelled, "I ordered the chicken fried steak, not the meat loaf!" The waitress apologized and picked up the plate, but the man called her an obscene name as she went back to the kitchen.

The chief got up and walked slowly to the man. "There's no need to get so excited over a simple mistake." Without turning around the man told him to go to hell. The chief took the man by the arm and jerked him off the stool. "If you can't behave you can eat elsewhere," the chief told him. He didn't see the gun until it was too late. The man shoved a large-bore revolver against his chest and pulled the trigger.

Staggering back, the chief pulled his 10mm and fired twice. The man turned, took a couple of steps, and collapsed. "You should have minded your own business. The _____ is my ex-wife, and I was gonna kill her and myself. Nobody innocent would have got hurt!" He died there, right on the floor of the restaurant.

The gun the chief had been shot with was a single-action revolver loaded with full-power .41 Magnum ammunition. The round fired by the chief was recovered from the left lung at autopsy. It had a weight of 117 grains and a diameter of .71 inch.

• • • • •

He was an avid IDPA competitor and a pharmacist by profession. Unlike many of his buddies who competed in this sport, he could afford to shoot factory ammo. He shot the same round in competition—150-grain Cor-Bon hollowpoints loaded in a Glock 10mm pistol. He had chosen it because it was quite accurate in his pistol and because he had contacted me to see what load in this caliber was working best on the street.

This Winchester 10mm Silvertip stopped a robber's attempt to separate an off-duty officer from her money.

The Remington 10mm 180-grain JHP combines deep penetration and good expansion. This one was used to stop a drug dealer.

I had also recommended a Kramer IWB holster, belt, and mag pouch as the best system for carrying a full-sized pistol concealed comfortably. He had ordered a slightly larger jacket from the pharmacy chain he worked for and no one ever noticed the pistol and spare mag. He had an unrestricted concealed carry permit and carried everywhere, even in church.

He normally worked the afternoon shift at the 24-hour drugstore where he was employed, but the midnight pharmacist had called in sick and he agreed to work a double shift. It had been fairly slow and he was working his way through a pile of the latest gun magazines.

He heard the bell at the counter ring and stepped forward to wait on a new customer. The man in his mid-20s was clean shaven and well groomed, but he seemed extremely nervous. He stuttered as he told the pharmacist the prescription was for his wife who went by her professional name. When the pharmacist asked to see his driver's license he was handed an expired one from another state. When he asked for another piece of ID, the man became angry. "Just fill the _____ prescription or I'll take it somewhere else!"

When the pharmacist suggested he do that, the man turned and stomped out. The pharmacist returned to his magazines and a cup of coffee. About an hour later, the bell rang again and the same man stood at the counter. He smiled sheepishly, "I'm sorry I blew up. My wife strained her back and she's in a lot of pain." The pharmacist smiled but repeated his request for more ID and this time the man complied, handing him a U.S. passport.

When the pharmacist went to the computer and entered the physician's name, a bright red warning flashed indicating that the doctor in question had been robbed of several prescription pads and that any prescriptions written on one would have to be verified with his office before being filled. He looked at the clock and realized that no one would be in the doctor's office at 4:37 A.M. Scrolling down the page he found specific instructions not to call the doctor after 12 A.M.

He returned to the counter and said, "I'm sorry, but I can't fill this prescription without verifying it with the doctor. And he won't be available until 9 A.M." He tried to hand it back to the man, but he knocked it away. "Look I appreciate your frustration . . . ." The words trailed off as he saw the .38 snub in the man's hand. Well, the pharmacist thought as he raised his hands, I always knew this day would come and it seriously looks like today's the day.

The man ordered the pharmacist to put all the narcotics into a small shopping basket and to hurry. As the pharmacist turned away he unbuttoned his jacket. He started to bend down and, after placing the basket on the floor, he pulled the Glock and spun into a kneeling position. He ordered the man to freeze, but instead he started to bring the snub to bear. The pharmacist fired one round, but the man disappeared from view before he could fire the two additional rounds he had planned.

He quickly scrambled the long way down the pharmacy counter to maintain cover and came around the front with his gun in position. He quickly realized that his assailant was dead. The round had struck him approximately 4 inches below the throat. It was recovered at autopsy and weighed 127 grains and had a recovered diameter of .80 inch.

The pharmacist was fired, but he sued and got his job back when it was revealed that this individual had murdered at least one person during each of his prior felonies.

• • • • •

A civilian employee of one of America's armed forces, he had served in a number foreign posts. Some had been very pleasant, but his current one was both unpleasant and dangerous. He had bought a S&W Model 1076 10mm pistol, a shoulder holster, and two boxes of Cor-Bon 150-grain JHP ammo. Since he traveled on a diplomatic passport his luggage and person were not subject to search.

He wore a photographer's vest that he had bought from Banana Republic because he could carry the small tools that he used in his job without carrying a tool box. It also concealed his gun and holster with ease.

He parked the four-wheel drive in front of the remote location and looked at the work order. Grabbing a handful of parts, he exited the air-conditioned vehicle and walked into the extremely hot and humid reality of his assignment. As he approached the building, he was searching through his

A Cor-Bon 10mm 135-grain JHP that penetrated the rear of a motor vehicle and killed the driver of a getaway car.

keys for the right one when he realized the door was ajar.

While this was not a top security location, it was a violation of security for the door to be unlocked. Besides, the building was air conditioned and who in his right mind would leave such comfort for this hell hole?

He was about to chew the technician out when he saw the blood on the doorstep. He dropped the fuses and pulled the pistol. He had almost decided he was over-reacting when he saw the two men standing over the tech. "Freeze," he yelled in the local dialect. The two men turned and smiled. "American no shoot" one of them said in English as they advanced toward him.

They were wrong, dead wrong. Using a solid Weaver stance, he fired three times, two at the man closest to him and one at the man behind. Both men collapsed, and he waited for several minutes before approaching them. He recharged the pistol and then moved forward. Both of the natives were dead, but fortunately the tech was only stunned.

The tech wanted to call the embassy but the shooter refused. Instead he called the Minister of the Interior, whose computer he had upgraded for free using excess parts from his supply. The minister listened carefully and told him to stay put. An hour later they heard a helicopter approaching. It was from the host

nation and was occupied by the minister, a judge in formal black robes, and a doctor. The doctor pulled out a Polaroid camera and photographed both bodies. The judge conveyed a coroner's inquest and within 15 minutes had absolved the shooter. The doctor handed him three recovered slugs from an impromptu autopsy. Two had been recovered from the first man's chest, while the third was recovered from the heart of the second. It weighed 132 grains and had a recovered diameter of .77 inch.

When the tech protested that the U.S. embassy ought to be notified, the minister told the tech that he was aware that Americans considered his country's heat to be oppressive and its ways backward, but if the tech wanted to involve the embassy he would be happy to request that this specific tech serve two tours of duty in his country, back to back.

Six months after this event, I received a package containing a formal autopsy report, photos, and three recovered slugs that had been carefully soaked in bleach to kill infection.

• • • • •

She was a single mom with three small kids who had decided to enter law enforcement at age 30. It hadn't been easy to complete against "kids," but she had done it. She had finished first in her class academically, second in defensive tactics, and third in firearms.

Upon graduation she had taken a job with an agency near the small farming community she and her kids lived in. Her dad had given her two gifts for graduation: a Second Chance vest and a Glock 10mm pistol with three high-capacity magazines. He was a homicide investigator for the state police and carried a compact version of the same pistol. When she asked about ammunition, he went to his gun safe and removed three boxes of Cor-Bon 150-grain JHPs.

She spent the next two years learning her trade. Most of the male

STOPPING POWER

cops were generally supportive, but a few were suspicious of their first female co-workers. One in particular had been verbally abusive until her dad paid him a visit without her knowledge. After that the abuse stopped, although he was less than friendly.

She was on patrol when she heard her former tormentor receive a radio run to a familiar location on a domestic disturbance. She had been there before and both times pepper spray and batons had been employed to bring things under control. She pulled up as the other officer was exiting his vehicle. He turned to her and said, "The last thing I need is your backup." She noticed that his baton ring was empty and that there wasn't an OC cannister on his belt. She decided to drive a couple of blocks away and wait. Her caution would save his life.

It was perhaps five minutes later when she heard an excited call on the radio. Recognizing the voice, she responded to her former location. She exited the vehicle and walked quickly to the slightly ajar front door. Pulling her 10mm, she took a quick peek inside and gasped involuntarily. The officer was on the floor trying to pull a butcher knife out of his leg, while a man was assaulting him with an axe handle. Putting her front sight in the middle of the man's chest, she pulled the trigger twice and he immediately fell. She ran to the officer's side and was calling on her hand-held radio when she was struck on the head by the wife. She fell on her side and was trying to bring her pistol to bear when the male officer fired his .45 auto five times. The woman collapsed on top of her, dead.

Responding officers found the two former adversaries hugging and weeping. The male officer had to retire due to the severe nature of his injuries, but the female officer was back at work within weeks. The man she had killed had been struck once in the chest, and the 10mm slug had been

This Cor-Bon 10mm 180-grain JHP put an end to a serial rapist's career.

• • • • •

recovered from his spinal column. It had a diameter of .71 inch and weighed 111 grains.

• • • • •

He looked at the clock at city hall and realized his wife was almost an hour late and he was worried. She was a very punctual and always called when she was delayed. He checked his cell phone again, but it was working properly.

At least she has a gun in the car, he thought. The center console in their SUV was roomy and contained a Glock 10mm pistol, a spare magazine, an OC cannister, and a small flashlight. She had practiced with it on several occasions and had commented how pleasant it was to shoot.

His wife was aware of the pistol, but she couldn't get to it. She had seen a small boy wandering on the rural route she was taking. When she stopped and asked him where he lived, he pointed up the hill at a dilapidated trailer. She had driven him up the hill and held his hand while she knocked on the door. An elderly man opened the door and, seeing the boy with a stranger, uttered a string of curses and kicked at him. When the woman jerked the boy out of harm's way, the man grabbed her and dragged her inside. The stench was overpowering, and there was garbage and dirty clothes everywhere.

The man had tied her to a kitchen chair and had cut off all her clothes with a pair of scissors. He was obviously intoxicated and made repeated threats to rape her. She asked the man if she could go to the bathroom. "It's plugged up. I just go outside," he responded. "Can I go outside, please?" she pleaded. "Okay, but don't try to run away or I'll put the dogs on you. Go right there by the car so I can keep an eye on you."

As she squatted next to her car she placed one hand near the handle. She had locked the door, but her vehicle featured keyless entry and she carefully punched in the code. Finishing, she stood up and suddenly jerked the door open and jumped inside. Thinking she was simply going to lock the door, the man reached inside the trailer and grabbed an axe.

He rushed the car and started beating on the glass with the heavy implement. The first blow cracked the glass and the second shattered it. As he reached inside to grab her, she stuck the Glock against his chest and fired. He stepped back, called her an obscene name, and tried to swing the axe again when he collapsed.

After waiting for what seemed like an eternity but was only eight minutes on her wristwatch, she exited out the passenger side. With the gun at the ready, she slowly came around the front of the vehicle. The man was laying on his back, whispering that he could not feel his legs. She went inside, found a relatively clean blanket to wrap herself in, and called her husband on the car phone. Responding officers and paramedics found her sobbing with a small boy on her lap.

The round was found in the emergency room inside the man's clothing. It had severely damaged the spinal cord before exiting. It had a recovered diameter of .67 inch and a recovered weight of 113 grains. The man was convicted of abduction of both the woman and the little boy but died of a heart attack prior to sentencing.

10mm Cor-Bon 150-grain JHP Failure

The snow had been falling for three days and the snow plow driver was exhausted. He and all his co-workers hadn't been home since the storm started. Catching an hour's sleep here and there just wasn't enough.

He'd driven the truck for almost 30 years and was quickly reaching the conclusion it was time to retire. He thought he had seen everything, but three years earlier he had witnessed the murder of a police officer and had stood by helpless because he was unarmed. The next day he went to a local gun shop and bought the biggest handgun they carried, a S&W Model 1076 10mm, and loaded it with Cor-Bon 150-grain JHP ammo.

He had been a competitive pistol shooter in the service and had used a pistol in Korea to save his life. He took the gun out in the woods and shot it on several occasions until he felt confident that he was proficient with it. He carried it loaded inside a soft pistol case that rested in the bottom of a large soft-sided bag he had carried for years.

He opened the bag looking for some granola bars and a can of juice. His hand brushed the case and he thought about using it on himself for a millisecond, but he just laughed and kept searching. Finding the snack and drink, he turned up the radio. He hated heavy metal music, but the noise kept him awake.

Partially refreshed, he put the truck in gear, lowered the blade, and went back to work. He had plowed about three miles when he decided to turn around in the mouth of a housing development. He saw the woman then, lying face down in the snow. He jumped out of the truck and saw that she'd been shot, a grazing wound on the right side of her head. He dragged her to the truck, called his dispatcher, and requested the police and paramedics. The woman gained consciousness then and started to yell, "My boy, My

boy!" pointing at the house where she had been found laying in front of. Thinking she was worried about her son, he removed the pistol from its case and ran toward the house. He had almost reached the door when a teenage boy exited the house covered in blood. He didn't see the knife until the young man stabbed him with it. Looking down, he saw the knife in his side. He raised the pistol and shot the young man three times. The assailant went to his knee's and then incredibly pulled another knife and stabbed the driver in the leg.

The driver shot him in the top of the head then. He started back to the truck but collapsed in the snow. The paramedics reached him and hurriedly loaded him and two others found inside the house. An officer rode along and was able to get a statement from him. His heart stopped twice, but they were able to revive him.

The young man had gone on an unsuccessful killing spree because his mother had banned him from the computer for two weeks. He had shot his mother with a single-shot 20-gauge shotgun. When he couldn't find any more shells, he used knives on his father, younger sister, and the plow driver. All had survived, although the driver suffered permanent damage to his leg, which forced his retirement. Today he's retired and spends his days fishing year round. In both the boat and ice fishing shack rests a scruffy bag. Among granola bars and cans of juice lies a Taurus .44 Magnum loaded with Cor-Bon JHPs.

.41 MAGNUM

He was raised to mind his own business and for years that had not been a problem. He lived outside of one of the largest cities in his state, although by eastern standards it wasn't very big. He kept to himself and rarely went to town. He had inherited significant wealth from his father, who had been an inventor all his life. Although each one had not been super

successful, taken together the dollar amount was impressive.

Though he had never had to work, he had obtained a Ph.D. in paleontology and spent the days digging in the land around his large spread. He certainly didn't dress like he was wealthy, and the only outward sign that he had any money at all was a new four-wheel drive pickup truck. It contained the obligatory gun rack with a Ruger scope-sighted rifle. He didn't hunt, but he was always on the outlook for predators.

Under his Levi jacket was something no other paleontologist he knew wore—a Smith & Wesson 657 .41 Magnum revolver loaded with Winchester Silvertips. The left hand pocket contained an additional 12 rounds of ammo. Several years before he had stopped to assist what he thought was a stranded motorist but turned out to be two pot smoking fools. He had beaten the snot out of them but decided he was getting too old to roll around in the dirt like some teenager.

He had only made three concessions to living in the late twentieth century—the Internet, satellite TV, and cell phones. The Internet enabled him and his wife to keep in touch with their kids. He bought the satellite because he was an NFL addict, and the cell phones were in case either one of them broke down somewhere.

His wife was European and old enough to remember the German occupation of her country, so she was decidedly more comfortable with a house full of guns. She routinely wandered their property with a 9mm Beretta on her belt.

He had gone into town for a few supplies and made the trip as brief as possible. Every time he went there he thought it had gotten worse. Paying for his items in cash, he opened a wallet full of money and extracted a $20 from among a wad of $100s. Two young men observed this and followed him out to his truck. They tailed him as he drove out of town and decided they'd not only get his money but his truck and rifle too.

He stopped at a four-way intersection about two miles out of town when he heard a horn honking. Looking in his rear-view mirror, he saw two young men in some kind of sports car waving at him. More city folk lost, he thought, and pulled over to the shoulder. As the young men pulled alongside they yelled, "Maybe you can give us directions?" The other one added, producing a .22 pistol, "Might as well throw in the truck and your wallet too!"

They both laughed, overly impressed with their attempt at humor. "I don't want any trouble. Why don't you boys just go back to town and rent a dirty movie or something?" Their response was short and obscene, accompanied by a lot of gesturing with the pistol. "OK," he replied, "I'll give you what you need."

The .41 Magnum was out, aimed, and discharged before either of the two holdup men had a chance to react. He slowly climbed out of his truck to verify what he had suspected; they were dead. He made two phone calls—the first to his wife telling her he'd be a bit late and the second to the sheriff.

The sheriff rolled with paramedics, evidence technicians, and the local prosecutor. Recognizing the two dead men, he said, "Well it was just a matter of time before one of my boys or some honest citizen would send these two to Hell."

The man closest to the paleontologist had taken five rounds, while the one behind the wheel had taken one. It was recovered at autopsy from the lining of the driver's side door. It weighed 144 grains and had a recovered diameter of .69 inch. Three of the five rounds that had struck the closest miscreant had penetrated the car door before lodging on the far side of his body just under the skin.

• • • • •

This Federal 210-grain .41 Magnum JHP ended a career criminal's life.

Remington .41 Magnum 210-grain SWC. Evan Marshall once thought this was the ultimate police load. He was wrong.

He was a big city criminal investigator who had been underwhelmed when his department switched from the .38 Special revolver to a .40 caliber semiautomatic pistol. He had carried a .41 caliber pistol for years in the form of a Mag-Na-Port customized S&W Model 57 revolver.

Having loaded his sidearm with Silvertip hollowpoints, he felt perfectly content with his choice. While 99 percent of his time was spent investigating homicides and officer-involved shootings, those he arrested were often looking at death row.

He had worked 24 hours straight and gone home to sleep for three hours, shower, and change clothes. Returning to work, he was somewhat refreshed but he felt like he was getting too old for this routine. They were looking for a team of drug

enforcers that had opened fire on their intended target while he stood on a densely populated street corner. They wounded their target but killed an older man and an 11 year old girl.

He contacted a number of his informants and had offered them a get-out-of-jail-free card—his business card with a notation on the back for any arresting officer to call him before processing the person in possession of the card. It took awhile, but he finally got a lead from "Bullseye," a crack addict.

With three other investigators, he made a rendevous with five members of the SWAT team. He had requested two teams, but the sergeant explained that the rest of the unit was tied up with a nasty hostage situation. Distributing mug shots, he explained that the three wanted men were heavily armed and extremely dangerous. The team opted for shotguns and M16s since the bad guys were known to wear soft body armor.

The investigator and his partners waited for the SWAT team to make the entry. The flash bangs went off and then the gunfire erupted. Pulling his .41 Magnum, he rushed through the open door. He saw the muzzle flashes from across the room and returned fire, emptying his gun. He reloaded and fired three more rounds before the gunfire stopped.

The team flex-cuffed all the suspects even though two were obviously dead. One had taken multiple .223 hits to the head, while the second had taken one Silvertip just above the vest. It was removed at autopsy, where it weighed 156 grains and was .64 inch in diameter. The third felon was tried, convicted, and given the death penalty.

• • • • •

He worked for a rural utility company and spent a lot of time on the road. He had a cassette player to listen to the Broadway tunes he loved so much. He realized he didn't have a

This Federal .41 Magnum 210-grain JHP ended a home invasion.

This Winchester .41 Magnum 175-grain Silvertip stopped a motorcycle thief.

very good voice, but working by himself, no one complained. He also kept a Ruger Redhawk in .41 Magnum in a gym bag. He carried it because he occasionally came across deer that had been hit by a car and left to die. He also carried it because you just never know.

He had been on the road for 14 hours repairing a number of service interruptions. The first had been caused by a drunk driver who had clipped a utility pole, while the second and third appeared to be inferior insulation. He had complained repeatedly about foolish cost-cutting measures but with little effect.

His radio crackled, so he pulled to the side of the road and wrote down the details of his next call. Someone had been using a junction box for target practice. Fortunately, he had the correct type of box in the back of his truck. He pulled up to the location and realized the box had been struck several times by high-powered rifle fire.

He was getting his gear out of the truck when he heard someone yell, "It's a waste of time 'cause I'll shoot the new one as soon as you leave!" The utility worker turned and saw a man smiling standing on the other side of a solid waist-high fence. He thought the man was kidding, so he returned the smile and asked, "Now, why in the hell would you want to do that?"

The man screamed, "Because Satan told me to!" and produced a

lever-action rifle and opened fire. The utility worker turned and ran for the truck. His first thought was the radio, but the second shot reminded him of the Ruger. He had the door partially open when he was struck in the ankle. The pain was incredible and he was barely able to snatch the bag before collapsing on the road. He grabbed the pistol and rolled over. The man was reloading the rifle when the utility worker shot him.

The 170-grain Silvertip entered the sternum and was recovered from the spinal column in surgery. The man survived but today is confined to a wheelchair. The utility worker underwent amputation of his ankle and foot. After extensive therapy he was able to return to work with an artificial limb. He had been suspended for 90 days for possession of a firearm at work.

The recovered slug weighed 129 grains and had a diameter of .62 inch. Today, in addition to the Ruger .41, the driver carries a folding-stock Ruger Mini-14, because you just never know.

• • • • •

A sergeant with a large sheriff's department, he had been "grandfathered" in when his department had switched from revolvers to semiautomatic pistols. He was able to keep his Model 57 .41 Magnum as his duty weapon. It was backed up by three HKS speedloaders filled with Silvertip JHPs and a Taurus snub also chambered for .41 Magnum.

He regretted that his promotion meant what seemed like an endless stream of paperwork. He was still young enough to crave the excitement of high-speed chases and other adrenalin pumping activities, but these days he spent more time justifying these type of activities by his subordinates.

He decided that he needed to get away from the paperwork for an hour

or so and went on patrol. It was getting dark and he wanted to check to see if his patrol units were running the teenagers out of the county park and locking the gate like they were supposed to. They considered it a minor nuisance, but then they didn't have to answer the complaints by those residents who lived near the park.

By the time he got to the park it was dark. He pulled up to the locked gate and was backing around to leave when he thought he saw a light in the trees. He exited his vehicle and walked across the graveled parking lot. He heard a noise but couldn't identify it. He heard it again and stopped. Listening intently, he heard someone very faintly calling for help. He called the dispatcher on his hand-held and asked for backup and a paramedic team.

Turning his Mag Lite on, he saw a young woman laying on the ground, naked. She had been beaten, and when he touched her she said, "Please don't rape me again!" He identified himself as a police officer and she started to sob. He tried to obtain a description of the attacker, but the woman was hysterical. He notified the dispatcher of his situation and waited. She asked him to turn off the light because of her embarrassment.

They waited in the dark for eight minutes when he heard voices coming down the hill. She gasped and he whispered for her to be quiet. He drew his .41 and waited. The voices got louder and he was able to decipher the conversation. "I'm telling you, we got to find the _____! If we don't she'll ID us to the cops. I'll cut her throat and we'll split!"

The sergeant turned on the flashlight and saw the men, both of whom were carrying hunting knives. "Weasel and Butter, drop the _____ knives!" He had recognized the two men as local knuckleheads he had arrested repeatedly but never for anything this serious. Suddenly one of them yelled, "We gotta kill the cop too!" and started to run toward the sergeant. The punk had taken only a few steps when he took a Silvertip through the left nipple. He screamed and collapsed. The other one just stood still, making chopping motions in the air with his knife.

"Butter, drop the knife or I'll kill you just like I did Weasel!" At the mention of his name, the wounded suspect sat up and told his partner, "Don't just stand there, cut their _____ throats and help me get to the hospital. I feel like I got a hornet's nest inside my chest!" The second suspect started to run toward the sergeant and met the same fate. This round was just a little to the right of mid line and was recovered in surgery.

The sergeant got to his feet, kicked the knives away from the two men, and handcuffed them together. Informing the dispatcher of his situation, he carried the woman to the patrol vehicle and wrapped her in a blanket he retrieved from the trunk. He carried the first aid kit back and attended to the two rapists until responding paramedics took over the treatment. Both survived and were convicted of sexual assault and sentenced to the state prison.

The recovered slugs had an average weight of 142 grains and an average recovered diameter of .65 inch. The sergeant was transferred to the Administrative Division, where his days are spent with endless piles of paperwork.

• • • • •

It looked like rain for sure, and he wondered if it would hold off until his tour of duty was over. Walking foot patrol in the warehouse district was not his idea of police work. He was a lean, mean, fighting machine, and here he was checking tractor trailer rigs for breaking and entering.

He checked row after row of vehicles without incident when he saw the door to one open. He pulled his .41 Magnum and flashlight and looked inside. Seeing nothing unusual, he started to close and lock the door when he heard footsteps behind him. He turned and saw a man walking toward him. The man looked like a truck driver, but something didn't seem right so instead of holstering his weapon he simply lowered it to his side.

The man asked him if there was something wrong. The officer turned slightly to point at the trailer when the man pulled a .38 snub and shot him. Hoping the vest had worked, the officer pointed the Magnum and opened fire. The man stepped back, fell to his knees, and died.

Responding personnel found the young officer sitting on the ground staring at the base of a .38 Special jacketed hollowpoint protruding from the Kevlar. His attacker lay nearby dead. One Silvertip JHP was recovered from his heart at autopsy. It weighed a 159 grains and had a diameter of .65 inch.

Two weeks later the officer resigned his position. Today he teaches high school history, although he still has the .41 Magnum. When his wife asks him about it, he just smiles and says, "It's a reminder of times past."

Winchester .41 Magnum 170-grain Silvertip Failure

An avid exercise devotee, he preferred an inner city gym where a large group of eastern European emigrees focused on lifting heavy weights, Greco-Roman wrestling,

steambaths, and vodka. He would skip the vodka but enjoyed the rest.

His dad had been a member of one of the original U.S. Navy UDT groups in Vietnam. A surprisingly quiet, introspective man, his dad always carried at least one handgun. His preference ran to a pair of customized .41 Magnum revolvers. He liked the idea of a big-bore weapon, but the .45 ACP loaded with ball had failed him twice in combat.

When he found out his son was frequenting a gym in such a shabby neighborhood, he convinced him to buy a .41 Magnum and load it with 170-grain Silvertip ammunition. They had some sessions at the range until his dad was convinced he was competent.

His trendy gym bag contained the usual complement of equipment and clothing, plus a Smith & Wesson Model 57 revolver in a Seven Trees holster. Next to it were two HKS speedloaders containing 12 extra rounds of ammo.

He had won the first two wrestling matches but had been beaten soundly in the third. He took some steam and then declined the vodka for what must have been the hundredth time. Walking to the bus stop, he felt refreshed and ready to deal with the pressures of his job as a stockbroker.

At first he didn't pay much attention to the woman at the bus stop. She was nicely dressed and carried a large shoulder bag. He soon realized that she was talking to someone. Looking around, he realized that she wasn't talking to him and there was no else present.

Suddenly she jumped back, pulled a claw hammer from her bag, and yelled, "Get away from me, you devil!" She swung at him then, but he sidestepped the blow. He tried to reason with her, but her reaction was to reach in the bag with her other hand and produce a cleaver. Backing away as quickly as possible, he pulled the revolver from the bag and ordered her to stop. The presence of a gun failed to stop the woman's demented attack. He shot her once, but it had no apparent effect. He shot her three more times and took a cleaver blow to the shoulder for his efforts. She then took a few steps backward, vomited blood, and died.

It took 29 stitches to close his shoulder wound and IV antibiotics to stop the infection. All four rounds were recovered from her left lung at autopsy. They had an average weight of 152 grains and an average diameter of .67 inch.

His dad visited him at the hospital and chewed him out. "How many times did I tell you! Four rounds puts 'em down!" When he responded that he had shot her four times, his dad pointed out that 1 + 3 does not equal 4 on the street.

.44 SPECIAL

He walked into the local gun store with a new concealed carry permit in his pocket. He wasn't quite sure what he wanted to buy, but he knew he needed another gun. He ended up with one of Smith & Wesson's new titanium .44 Special snubs and three boxes of Silvertip .44 Special hollowpoints.

A trip to the range proved the gun accurate, but the recoil could only be described as stiff. He loved its light weight, and it soon replaced the SP-101 in his fanny pack. Accompanying it was a speedloader, an OC cannister, and a Benchmade folding knife. Because of an old football injury, he found it painful to jog, so he would take long walks with Homer, a large dog of unknown breed that his son had brought home one day. Although he displayed the same lack of intellect as his namesake from the television show, he was affectionate and loyal.

He had to change their usual route due to a construction project that was replacing the sidewalks. He didn't trust the dog in the street so they went a different way. His substitute route took him past a

vocational center that he hadn't realized was there. Checking his pedometer, he realized that he had covered half his usual distance. He decided to return the way he had come.

He was walking by the vocational center, when he heard someone yell, "That's the ugliest dog I've ever seen!" Turning, he saw three young men standing next to a car drinking beer. He just smiled and kept walking. He had taken about three steps when a beer can hit the dog. He turned and said, "There's no need for that." One of the young men made an obscene gesture. Shaking his head, he just kept walking. He had thought the incident was over but as he reached the corner he heard a car accelerating down the street.

He recognized it as the same car the young men had been leaning against. He stepped behind a large tree, drew the revolver, and held it behind his back. Too late he realized the dog hadn't followed him. He called for it, but Homer just stood there and was run over. The car quickly braked and its occupants jumped out. "Now that we've killed that stupid dog, we're gonna kick your ____!" He noticed that one of them had a baseball bat. He produced the revolver and ordered them to halt. They were either too stupid or too stoned to be scared. He shot the one with the bat, who fell to the ground and started to scream. The other two came to their senses and fled on foot. He reholstered the snub, closed up his fanny pack, and waited for the cops.

The first unit on the scene called for paramedics, and the man surrendered his pistol, fanny pack, and concealed weapons permit. He was held for a few hours before being released. It was ruled a justifiable shooting. The bullet was recovered from the large intestine during surgery. It had a recovered weight of 187 grains and a diameter of .60 inch.

• • • • •

He had paid a premium price for a Smith & Wesson Model 29 during the Dirty Harry craze. He had carried it loaded with magnum loads until he had seen Silvertip .44 Specials in a gun shop. When his department allowed its personnel to carry a personally owned 9mm semiauto, he stuck with the .44. He just didn't trust auto pistols and considered the 9mm anemic.

His younger partner had teased him regularly and with a degree of malice. He called him "Wyatt" and would ask what Doc Holiday was really like. Finally he told the youngster that he could cool it or get his butt kicked. The look on the senior partner's face caused him to stop, but by then the nickname had stuck.

They were responding to a disturbance call at a local convenience store when the dispatcher radioed a second time and informed the officers that shots fired were now being reported at that location. "Stop at the corner!" he told his younger partner. The officers exited their vehicle just as two young men with handguns exited the premises dragging a wounded accomplice.

The officers ordered the men to stop, but the felons opened fire. "Wyatt" placed the red ramp in the middle of one target's chest and fired. He was swinging to the right as his younger partner opened fire. By the time he got his sights aligned, his partner was reloading. He again fired one round and tracked back to the first felon, but he was down.

He grabbed the portable from his partner's belt and informed the dispatcher that they had three suspects down and they needed a supervisor, the shooting team, and paramedics.

All three were conveyed to a local hospital, where they recovered after extensive surgery. One had been shot by the store clerk with a .45 ACP before the officers arrived. The second one had taken six rounds of 147-grain 9mm JHP and one round of .44 Silvertip. The final holdup man had taken one .44 Special Silvertip in the

This Winchester .44 Special Silvertip put an end to a felon's career.

A Federal .44 Special 200-grain LHP that stopped a felony in progress.

kidney, where it had a recovered weight of 181 grains and a recovered diameter of .51 inch.

• • • • •

He had inherited the gun from his uncle. It was a Smith & Wesson N frame .44 Special revolver with a 4 inch barrel. He loaded it with the ammo that came with the gun and stuck it in a nightstand. Since he lived alone, he didn't worry about anyone finding it. He worked as a civil engineer for a local government bureau and often took his work home on his Gateway laptop.

He wasn't antisocial, but his wife had died some 30 years before just two weeks after they had married. He had dated occasionally but never found another woman who made him laugh like she had. The house was exceptionally neat, and his office at work mirrored his attention to detail.

He had ridden the bus home, thrown something in the microwave, and booted up his laptop. He was engrossed in his latest project when the microwave signaled dinner was ready. He went upstairs to use the bathroom and wash his hands. He had just flushed the toilet when he heard glass breaking. Going to the nightstand, he withdrew the revolver, dialed 911, laid down at the top of the stairs, and waited. Fifteen minutes later, the police arrived. He put the gun away and went downstairs to meet them.

They found a basement window broken, and though the officers searched thoroughly, they didn't find anyone. The officers advised that some kid had probably just thrown a rock. He cleaned up the glass and, realizing it was too late to get another piece made, removed the shards and boarded up the window.

It was almost midnight when he decided to end his work day, go upstairs, and get ready for bed. As was his occasional evening ritual, he spent a moment looking through their wedding album and wondered what might have been. Realizing that it was late, he closed the book, set his alarm, and turned out the light.

Something woke him up and he looked at the clock. It was 2:30 A.M. He then recognized the sound of wood being pulled away from the basement window. He grabbed the pistol and called 911. Creeping downstairs, he walked to the door leading to the basement stairs and sat in the corner to wait for the police. He then heard steps on the stairs and raised the revolver.

He heard the door being opened. Grasping the pistol with both hands, he fired two rounds. Someone screamed and fell down the stairs. He grabbed the phone and this time told them there had been a gunshot at his house. He heard sirens approaching and placed the gun next to his laptop. He met the officers at the door and told them an intruder was shot in the basement. The officers and paramedics rushed past him and down the stairs. The paramedics came back upstairs shortly, shaking their heads. The homeowner broke down then, sobbing. It was a few minutes before he realized there was an officer standing next to him. As he looked up at the policeman, he realized he was holding a bag. "I wouldn't shed too many tears!" He showed him the contents of the bag, which included handcuffs, a gag, and a can of lighter fluid.

"You would of been the fifth

person these animals would have tortured." A single .44 Special Silvertip was taken from the back of the burglar. It had a recovered weight of 167 grains and a recovered diameter of .58 inch.

• • • • •

A retired minister, he spent his time working in his fruit orchard and occasionally assisting the man who had replaced him. He seemed dedicated enough, but you always had to watch the young ones. He laughed at that thought, as he realized the man he replaced some 30 years ago had held the same opinion.

While he was a gentle and kind man, he was a realist. He had served as a U.S. Army medic in Vietnam and soon realized that neither the Viet Cong or NVA felt that his duties exempted him from being shot. He had found himself carrying not only medical supplies but an M16 and .45 ACP pistol. He had regretted the necessity of using both but had promised his future wife he would return home.

Unknown to his parishioners, he had kept a pistol in his office for his entire ministerial career. It was a Charter Arms Bull Dog loaded with Winchester Silvertip ammo. It had been a comforting presence when people had shown up late at night for counseling or assistance. While he had never needed it, he would periodically shoot and clean it. Its recoil was brisk, but it felt comforting in his hand.

It was almost midnight when the phone rang. It was his successor, asking for advice. He had two men in his office who were asking for help, and he needed the older man's input. He dressed quietly without waking his wife. Walking past his office downstairs, he felt strangely uneasy. He went to the desk and slipped the handgun in his coat pocket.

I must be getting old, he thought, but he didn't put the gun back. He walked to the church since it was just two blocks away. He was about to knock when he remembered he still had a key. He let himself in and was walking toward the office in the back when he heard angry voices. He stood quietly, straining to make out the conversations, but he couldn't. He slipped his shoes off and walked closer. "Where's the _____ money?" he heard a man demand. "Yeah, where's the money?" a second man asked.

He crept closer and saw them then. They had his successor duct taped to a chair, and it was obvious he had been beaten. He was instantly filled with the same quiet rage that he had experienced when he came upon Viet Cong murdering wounded GIs. He had shot them until he ran out of ammo.

He entered the room with the gun extended and ordered the men to put their hands up. They turned and saw a gray-haired old man stooped with age, and they made a critical mistake— they didn't look at his eyes. They both lunged at him, but you can't jump faster than a bullet.

He dialed 911 and then freed the minister. The younger man knelt next to the two wounded holdup men. "Aren't you going help me to minister to them?" he asked. "I gave them the sacraments they deserved!" the older man responded.

Both men underwent surgery and recovered to stand trial. One bullet was removed from the subject's left lung and had a recovered weight of

This Remington .44 Special SWC was deformed when it struck bone. These rounds saved the life of a night watchman.

177 grains and a recovered diameter of .51 inch. The other slug was left inside the bad guy, as it was decided it would do more damage to remove it than to leave it in place.

• • • • •

It had been a busy day, and it wasn't getting any quieter. A big city cop, he had been deluged with calls about a man with a sword terrorizing the neighborhood. He and has partner responded repeatedly with other units but they had never been able to find the guy.

The eighth time they got the run, no one else showed up. The same woman they had met each previous time was screaming and gesturing wildly. Both cops had decided they were dealing with a nut case, something their city had no shortage of. Then they saw the blood and quickly changed their minds.

Drawing their weapons, they entered the apartment building and started to search. Hearing screams from the second floor, they ran upstairs and were confronted by a Caucasian male dressed in a black karate suit holding a samurai sword. Before the officer could react he was struck with the edged weapon. His vest stopped the blade, but the impact caused him to drop his gun and fall to the floor. His partner fired at the subject but missed. He was slashed on

the leg and also collapsed. He was struck again and started to scream. His partner pulled his second gun, a Taurus .44 Special snub, and opened fire. The first two rounds missed, but the third one struck the would-be samurai in the chest. He dropped the sword, turned, and sat down screaming for medical attention.

Emergency surgery saved the felon's life, and the bullet was removed from the right kidney. It weighed 183 grains and had a diameter of .51 inch. The officer who had been cut on the leg was forced to retire, while the other one continues his career to this day.

Winchester .44 Special Silvertip Failure

He had been second-guessed to death and had decided to quit. His partner had been killed during a bank robbery when the officer had failed to shoot the holdup man because of innocent bystanders in the way. The officer's widow had told him she understood, but no one else seemed to.

He was on his way downtown to turn in his papers. A high-ranking official had made it possible for him to take a stress-related retirement so he wouldn't lose his pension. Part of the retirement process involved the issuance of a concealed carry permit, so he was armed with his off-duty weapon: a Smith & Wesson Model 624 .44 Special revolver loaded with Winchester Silvertips.

Several hours later after completing all the necessary paperwork, he walked out of police headquarters with a retired badge and ID card. He and his wife had talked about moving to _____ to be near his parents. He stopped at a hardware store to get some paint and other items to refurbish their house, making it ready for sale.

He was walking to his car when he realized he had forgotten to get a small paintbrush he needed. He put his purchases in the trunk and returned to the store. He was standing in line when the cashier told the man in front of him that he hadn't given her enough money for the items he intended to purchase. The man got loud and obscene. "Hey buddy, there's no reason to act like that," the newly retired officer said. When the man continued, he put his hand on the jerk's shoulder. Before he could react the man spun quickly and struck him on the jaw with a hammer he had placed on the counter. The pain was excruciating, and he went down to one knee. The man hit him again on the collarbone and he heard it break.

He drew his revolver and emptied it at the attacker, but the man ran and got in his car. Another customer got the license number, and officers from another agency arrested him 12 hours later. He was conveyed to the hospital because he had three Silvertip slugs in his right lung. They had an average recovered weight of 182 grains and an average recovered diameter of .53 inch.

While recuperating from his injuries, he was amazed to see many of the same officers who had been so judgmental before show up on their days off to paint and fix up his house so it could be sold. Today, the retired officer and his family live on three acres in the rural area of a southern state.

.44 MAGNUM

The private investigator had purchased a nickel-plated S&W Model 29 and wore it in a shoulder holster. He actually thought it was a little hokey, but it seemed to impress his clients. He personally liked it better than several semiautos he owned. He happened to shoot it very well and felt comfortable with those big silver bullets.

He was working a nasty divorce case with several of his operatives. One had asked for time off to attend his sister's wedding, so he was filling in on the surveillance duties. He checked the log and video and still cameras and sat down for the shift. The location was

the house of an alleged female lover of the client's wife. It had been in place for several weeks without a single appearance by her. He was seriously considering shutting down this part of the operation, but the husband insisted that there was something going on that would enhance his claims.

He was almost halfway through the shift when he saw the wife's silver car pull up in the driveway of the house in question. She approached the door and rang the bell. She gave a friendly embrace to the woman who came to the door. He noticed, however, that they quickly went upstairs. Turning on the video camera with the night vision attachment, he soon found that the husband was absolutely right. He made sure the camera was operating properly and returned to his book.

He looked up to see the door open and the wife leave the house. He took several photos with the digital camera and shut off the night vision gear. The rest of the shift was uneventful, and toward the end he made copies of both the digital and video images and put them in his briefcase. When his relief showed up, he went out the back door of the rented house and walked through the alley. He had walked about 30 feet toward his parked SUV when two men stepped out of the shadows.

"All we want is the case," one said and showed him the large knife. The PI replied that the videotape and floppy disc were in his suitcoat pocket. He reached inside and threw the case in the first man's face as he pulled the .44 and shot the man with the knife. He turned to the second, who quickly raised his hands and said, "The _____ said this would be the easiest $500 I ever made!"

Holding the second man at gunpoint, he dialed 911 on his cell phone. The police and the paramedics arrived shortly and took over. The knife-wielding subject was rushed to a major trauma center, where he survived several hours of surgery. The

This Remington .44 Magnum 240-grain JHP got inside a vehicle and hit the driver

recovered slug had a weight of 182 grains and a diameter of .77 inch. The two suspects testified against the wife, and she was convicted of conspiracy charges and received a minimal divorce award.

• • • • •

When his partner asked why he carried a .44 Magnum instead of the department-issue .45 Auto, his response was because nobody made a .50 Magnum. Times had changed, and while there were more powerful handguns available he stuck with his 6 1/2 inch barreled Model 29 loaded with Silvertip .44 Magnum hollowpoints. He carried 12 additional rounds in loops on his duty belt.

They patrolled what they both referred to as "the armpit of the city." Both of African-American extraction, they took a very realistic view of life. They both wore body armor and carried second guns. The gun rack between the seats carried a 12-gauge shotgun, and the trunk contained an additional shotgun and a privately owned Ruger Mini-14.

They were looking for a pair of particularly brutal rapists. Not content with sexual assaults, they had severely beaten their victims after the women had complied with the thugs' sexual demands. Only one victim had given a description, and it was so vague as to be almost useless.

They were looking for a red car

A Remington .44 Magnum JHP that worked well in defeating car jacking.

A .44 Magnum 210-grain Silvertip that stopped a purse snatcher.

with the rear license plate held on with only one screw. It might have a cracked windshield and might be occupied by two white or Hispanic males. The officers hoped for the best, but they were not optimistic. When they spotted an orange car occupied by two light-complectioned African-Americans, they felt that they were probably not the right guys, but they could always use an entry for their activity report.

Turning on the overhead lights and giving the siren a brief yelp, they directed the vehicle to the curb. As they exited their patrol car, one officer said to the other, "Don't get yourself shot. It creates so much paperwork." His partner just smiled and put his hand on the butt of his .44 Magnum. As the one officer walked past the rear of the vehicle, he pointed to the rear license plate that was held by only one screw.

After a brief conversation with the driver, who could not produce a valid operator's license, the officers ordered both occupants out of the vehicle. "What the _____ for?" the passenger asked. "He was driving. Take his sorry soul to jail. I don't care!" The officer opened the passenger side door to extricate the man and was doing so when the driver reached across and shot him in the face. The officer was on the way to the ground when he fired one shot at the passenger.

His partner opened fire on the driver, striking him multiple times with .45 ACP hollowpoints. He called for a supervisor and paramedics, indicating that his partner and two suspects were down. Running to the other side of the vehicle, he found his partner sitting and spitting blood. He had taken a .22 Long Rifle round in the mouth. It had broken two teeth and exited out his cheek but had done no serious damage.

As paramedics extracted the two wounded men, they found that both were sitting on a total of 12 rocks of crack cocaine. The driver died in emergency surgery from five rounds of .45 ACP 230-grain JHP ammo, while the passenger had one .44 Magnum Silvertip removed from his left arm, where it had ended up after traversing both lungs. It weighed 181 grains and was .76 inch in diameter. He recovered to strand trial for attempted murder. They were not the rapists they had been searching for.

• • • • •

He had driven a big city delivery truck for 30 years and had recently retired. He had bought an obscure stock called Microsoft years before and had found himself financially set. Being a bit of an iconoclast, he continued to drive a cab. He had two constant companions: a portable CD player and a S&W Model 629 .44 Magnum customized with a 3 inch barrel and round butt. It was loaded with six rounds of Winchester Silvertip ammunition and rode in a backpack that sat next to him on the seat.

After moving out west, he bought a luxury SUV and a pair of expensive cowboy boots. His eastern accent was often the focus of some good-natured teasing, but because he kept to himself and didn't pry into other people's lives he soon fit in. He maintained two old habits—the constant sound of a CD player in his car and the .44 Magnum. It had been moved from the backpack to a large pocket on the driver's side door.

No one where he lived was frightened by the sight of a handgun in his car.

He made a daily trip downtown to pick up several newspapers and magazines. He devoted his life these days to what he had always wanted to do: read. The UPS driver made a delivery from a major online bookstore at least once a month. His wife complained about living in a four bedroom bookcase, but she wasn't serious.

Two years after moving out west, he decided to drive down to a major western city to attend a writer's convention. He had always harbored a secret desire to write poetry. His wife had no desire to spend even 15 minutes in any big city, so she stayed behind. She gave him a "shopping list" that included a beret, turtleneck sweater, and sandals so that he could be a real poet.

He left the revolver in its usual resting place but draped a small towel over it. He was about 120 miles from his final destination when he saw a car pulled over on the shoulder with the hood up. He stopped to see if he could be of assistance and found a man and a woman staring at the engine.

He exited his vehicle and asked if he could be of help. The man's response was startling. "Well," he smiled, "this car we stole in Cody crapped out on us, so I guess we'll have to take yours!" The retired truck driver looked down and saw a 9mm pistol in the man's hand.

Federal's .44 Magnum 240-grain Hydra-Shok.

This Federal .44 Magnum Hydra-Shok ended a car jacking.

"Let's go back to your car. I'll drive you four or five miles into the desert and by the time you get back we'll be long gone." Somehow the retiree didn't believe him. "You drive," the man told him and pointed to a dirt road that led to nowhere.

After 15 minutes, the man told him to pull over and get out. The look on his face told the former truck driver that his future could be measured in seconds if he didn't do something. He asked his captor if he could get a bottle of water from the small cooler between the seats. When the man told him he could, he raised the lid with his right hand. The felon looked down into the cooler to examine its contents. Thus distracted, he didn't see the .44 until it was too late. Not taking any chances, he simply shot the man in the chest. The noise was excruciating in the confined space of the SUV, and the stench as the dying man lost control of his bowels was overwhelming.

He drove back to the interstate, but the woman was gone. He waited almost two hours before a state patrol unit came by. He missed the convention, but a police investigation cleared him of all charges.

The round was recovered from the spinal column with a diameter of .76 inch and a weight of 186 grains. The dead man was later identified as a wanted felon.

• • • • •

She was a plainclothes investigator assigned to a special squad within the Sex Crimes Unit that handled the sexual molestation of juveniles. While her partners all carried .38 snubs, she carried a S&W Model 29 .44 Magnum loaded with Winchester Silvertip magnum loads.

When the squad went to the range for their semiannual qualification, much of the kidding quit because she shot it very well indeed. She had taken her job very seriously and shot the Magnum every other week. She would practice with three-quarter strength reloads her boyfriend made up for her and then finish up with 18 rounds of Silvertip on multiple targets.

She had been called in on her day off because of a particularly nasty case. Two young children had been sexually molested in the same neighborhood, and another was missing. The first two were undergoing surgery at a local hospital, but the third child had not been found. The suspect, identified as a relative of one of children, was also missing.

They were on the street looking for the suspect when the dispatcher instructed them to switch to the tactical frequency. They were advised that a state patrol unit had the suspect's vehicle stopped and the suspect was holding the missing child at gun point. It took almost 15 minutes for the Sex Crimes Unit to arrive at the scene. As they exited their vehicle, they noticed that a sniper was taking a position on the roof of a nearby building.

The female member was trained as a hostage negotiator, so it was suggested that she try to resolve the problem. Unenthusiastic about face-to-face negotiation, she realized that in this case it was the only viable alternative.

She talked to him for over three hours but reached the conclusion that the situation was going down the toilet. She had given the agreed upon hand signal for the sniper to take the

shot, but nothing happened. She gave it again, and then decided if the child was going to be saved she would have to do it herself.

She asked the man if he would like a cigarette and he agreed. She walked closer with a pack of cigarettes extended in her right hand. When the man reached for the pack, she raised the Magnum in her left hand and shot him through the sternum. He immediately collapsed and she grabbed the child and ran. Expecting either to be shot at or for other officers to shoot him again, she was surprised when neither happened.

The man was rushed to a nearby trauma center, where they saved his life but not his mobility. A quadriplegic, his days of child molestation are over. The recovered slug weighed 184 grains and had a recovered diameter of .80 inch. The SWAT sniper was reprimanded and transferred to patrol, and he and the Sex Crimes investigator broke up shortly after the incident.

• • • • •

The bush pilot carried a .458 Winchester Magnum in his plane and a long-barreled .44 Magnum in a shoulder holster. He enjoyed the outdoor aspect of his job but sometimes the clients were a bit much. He had to admit, though, that the job of flying these self-absorbed people in and out of remote locations was preferable to spending time in the bush with them.

He had a couple days off and flew down to a major city to buy some new clothes. After making his purchases, he took a cab back to where he had left his float plane moored at a dock in the harbor. At the last minute, he decided to walk down to a local café for a large bowl of moose chili before heading back.

He walked back to the plane after finishing his meal, where he found the passenger door ajar. He looked inside and noticed that the hard case containing his rifle was gone. He started up a nearby alley and saw a young man holding something behind his back. He yelled at the man and saw what he was holding then—his rifle. Since he routinely carried it with a loaded magazine and empty chamber, the pilot pulled his .44 Magnum and ordered the young man to lay the rifle down. Instead, he started to work the bolt so the pilot fired twice.

One round missed, but the other one struck the thief in the left side and spun him around. The pilot grabbed his large first aid kit from the plane and treated him until the paramedics arrived. The young man was conveyed to the hospital, where he was operated on successfully. The recovered slug weighed 198 grains and had a recovered diameter of .82 inch.

.44 Magnum Silvertip Failure

Day in and day out, it was the same old crap. People brought their cars in after they'd neglected to respond to warning lights or tell-tale indications or noises. Then they expected him to solve a $500 problem for $39.95.

He loved working on cars but hated arguing with people. His dad had been a career master mechanic for a major German automobile manufacturer, and he had inherited his father's pride in his work. It was incomprehensible to him that people could question his integrity, and it made him angry.

He had a gun in his desk, a Ruger Red Hawk .44 Magnum Revolver loaded with Winchester Silvertip JHP ammo. It was there in case of a robbery, and there had been a number in their area. He, however, focused on carburetors, not crime.

He was working late so that he could take a couple of days off for fishing. He had two deep-rooted passions—his grandchildren and fishing. His oldest grandson had turned 5, and he was going to take him on his first overnight fishing trip.

He heard a knock on the office door, but ignored it. The shop hours were clearly posted, and it was long past closing time. After 5 minutes of continuous banging, the shop owner got up and jerked open the door. "What in the hell do you want?" The man in the doorway shoved a pistol in his face and screamed, "What I want is every _____ penny in the place or I'll shoot you!"

The owner told him to be calm and he'd get what he needed. What he was referring to was the .44 in the desk drawer. He opened his wallet and gave the man the $300 he had withdrawn for the fishing trip. "There's more in the desk. I'll get it for you."

The owner reached into the desk, but the robber suddenly got suspicious. "Back away. I'll get it!" Holding his hands up, the shop owner said, "Look, the drawer's a little tricky. I didn't want to get you stressed out." The holdup man nodded his agreement and motioned toward the desk. The owner reached in the drawer and almost had the gun out when the robber realized what was happening and opened fire. He emptied the gun without effect while the owner fired three shots in response.

The robber turned and fled, dropping the money. The shop owner was wiping blood off his $300 when the cops arrived. They took a report and put out a broadcast. The next morning he took his grandson fishing.

Four days later the holdup man was killed trying to ply his trade in a

liquor store clerked by a retired cop. At the autopsy they found not only the cop's 125-grain JHP but two fully expanded .44 Magnum Silvertip slugs in his large intestine.

.45 ACP

He had decided that supervisors really were like diapers—always on your backside and full of crap. He had been a cop for 20 years, and this hot shot sergeant with a Masters degree and eight years total on the job was making his life miserable.

He decided that his only chance for relief was to find a felon wanted by somebody downtown. Anybody who was wanted by Homicide, Holdup, or Sex Crimes would have to be conveyed to headquarters, and the resulting paperwork and meeting with investigators would take up most of a day and there was nothing the boy genius could do about it.

He and his partner called Homicide and found a local knucklehead that was wanted as a material witness. It would have to do, so they started hunting him. Fortunately, the radio was relatively quiet and they spotted him just before noon. He was standing on a corner talking to a major drug dealer. The dealer was too cool to run and his lawyer was sharp enough to keep his client out of the slam unless he did something incredibly stupid.

Their guy ran sometimes, but today he was following the dealer's example and just stood there. The officers exited their vehicle, walked to their target, and asked him if he thought it was going to rain. Taken aback, he said, "What the _____ do you mean, is it going to rain?" The officers smiled and the older one said, "Well, we were going to go golfing after work, but I think it's going to rain." The man's response was to tell the officers what they could do with their golf clubs.

Shaking his head, he said, "Little P, now you've done it. You're under arrest for rude verbiage. Put your hands up."

Unfortunately, the officers had received bad information. Their "material witness" was the shooter and he wasn't going anywhere. The younger officer saw the 9mm first and yelled "gun!" He lunged for it but missed and took a 9mm round through the shoulder.

His partner pulled his S&W 4506, but the other officer was in the way. Stepping to the right, he brought the gun to bear and opened fire. The first round missed, but the second one struck the killer in the chest and he went down. Responding paramedics did their best, but the man expired en route to the hospital. The round was recovered from under the skin on his back. The Federal 230-grain Hydra-Shok had a recovered weight of 204 grains and a recovered diameter of .72 inch.

The best part of the whole incident was that both officers were assigned out to Homicide for two weeks and had almost no contact with the "boy genius."

•••••

He had spent 27 years as a member of his state's highway patrol and had never had to fire his handgun other than on the range. Retired for several years, he carried a lightweight Colt Commander that had been tuned for carry use by noted pistolsmith Karl Sokol. Strictly a carry gun, it had night sights, a 4 pound trigger, and all the sharp edges taken off, and it was modified to feed the Federal 230-grain Hydra-Shoks hollowpoints he favored.

He worked part time driving cars to various airports for a rental car company. It kept him just busy enough to break the routine of farming the few acres he kept in vegetables.

He was returning a vehicle to a major urban airport, and they had a car for him to drive back to where his personal car was parked. He had never informed the rental car company of the fact that he carried on a daily basis.

The Winchester .45 ACP 230-grain Ranger Talon produces deep penetration and moderate expansion. This one was used by an interstate truck driver to prevent the hijacking of his rig.

This Federal .45 ACP 185-grain JHP penetrated a car door and the rapist behind it.

This Remington 230-grain brass-jacketed Golden Saber produced excellent results from a compact auto pistol deployed by a computer repair man.

They knew he was a retired highway patrolman and if they couldn't figure out the obvious, he didn't feel the need to enlighten them.

He had missed the exit for the rental car return and pulled on the shoulder to look at the airport map to see if there was another exit or if he would have to go completely around the airport. He was trying to figure what to do when he was struck from behind by another vehicle. He got out to see the extent of the damage and found himself looking down the barrel of a sawed-off .22 rifle. The two men quickly put him in the trunk without searching him, and he pulled his .45 and waited. He discovered that this vehicle had a trunk release inside the compartment.

After 15 minutes by his watch, the car pulled over and stopped. He heard someone exit the rental car and another vehicle pull in behind his. As the trunk lid swung up, he shot both of his abductors. Climbing out of the trunk, he searched both wounded suspects and threw the sawed-off rifle in the trunk of the rental car. He drove for almost three miles before he came to a gas station and called 911.

Responding officers and paramedics followed him down the rural road, where they found the two abductors trying to sit up. Both had been shot once. They were conveyed to a local hospital, where the bullets were removed during surgery. One was recovered from the kidney and weighed 221 grains, with a diameter of .68 inch, while the other was removed from the second felon's liver and had a recovered weight of 205 grains and a diameter of .77 inch.

•••••

He was a security guard at a site for sensitive corporate documents who patrolled his area with dedication and thoroughness. A retired Marine, there was only one handgun he considered carrying—a Colt Government Model .45 ACP. His son, a sheriff's deputy,

These Federal .45 ACP 185-grain JHPs produced varied results when fired into the same bad guy from a compact auto.

The Remington .45 ACP 185-grain JHP offers deep penetration and good expansion. This one was used on a drug dealer.

This Remington .45 ACP 185-grain JHP +P wsa used by a retired fireman to stop two holdup men.

Federal's .45 ACP 185-grain Hydra-Shok +P produced deep penetration and moderate expansion when used to put down a shotgun-armed holdup man.

This Black Hills .45 ACP 185-grain BHP saved the life of a rural officer whose closest backup was 62 minutes away!

This Federal .45 ACP 230-grain Hydra-Shok was fired from a compact Glock by a cab driver who was tired of being robbed.

Federal's .45 ACP 230-grain Hydra-Shok load has a long record of superior results. An undercover cop shot a felon with this one during an attempted drug rip-off. It was recovered resting against a rib on the far side.

Winchester's .45 ACP 185-grain Silvertip has long been derided by some. These two were recovered at autopsy from the thoracic cavity of a home invasion team member.

Cor-Bon's .45 ACP 185-grain JHP produces excellent expansion in human tissue. This was recovered from the right lung of a prison escapee.

STOPPING POWER

had convinced him to replace military ball with Hydra-Shok.

He worked the midnight shift by preference so that he could tend to his garden and fish. The documents he guarded were a potential target for corporate espionage, though past thefts had been carried out by computer hackers. Nonetheless, he believed in giving eight hours work for eight hours pay.

While other guards read the paper or watched TV, he patrolled constantly and was the constant source of amusement. He didn't care what they thought and only went into the guard's office to use the bathroom and get his sack lunch from the fridge.

It was shortly after 3 A.M. when he started to hear a lot of static on his radio. He called for a radio check but did not receive a response. Driving to the office, he exchanged the radio and went back on patrol. The rest of his tour of duty was uneventful, and he left for home. While driving home at the prescribed speed limit, a car suddenly appeared in his rear view mirror and honked and flashed its lights. Since there was no shoulder for him to pull off, he simply motioned them past. They pulled out and roared by, but instead of continuing on they slowed down to 10 miles per hour below the speed limit.

The guard braked some more, but the car in front slowed even further. He reached into his bag and quickly chambered a round in the .45 ACP. The car in front of him suddenly stopped, and he attempted to shift the manual transmission into reverse, but the car stalled.

The occupants of the car exited and started beating on his windows with baseball bats. The guard was unable to start his car and realized that the glass was starting to give on the driver's side, so he slid to the far side and displayed the pistol. They continued to beat on the glass and when it gave way, he fired three rounds. He saw two men run back to their car and escape. He exited the

passenger side and came around to find a young man in his 20s laying in the road suffering a single gunshot wound to the upper chest.

The man was conveyed to a local hospital, where he survived lengthy surgery. The recovered slug weighed 198 grains and had a diameter of .71 inch. The man had an extensive record of vicious assaults.

• • • • •

It was hot even for the desert—111°F and no relief in sight. The officer turned the air conditioning up another notch. The vehicle's cooling system really helped, but he couldn't help but debate the wisdom of body armor under such conditions. He patrolled a low-crime rural area where nothing ever happened and had considered removing his vest on several occasions over the last week but hadn't quite convinced himself yet. His ambivalence would save his life.

He had stopped for a soda and shared his views on the heat with the store clerk. He finished and bought a six pack of soda and an inexpensive Styrofoam cooler, which he filled with ice and carried out to his patrol vehicle. A half hour later he stopped to remove another soda and found to his dismay that three of the cans had leaked out their contents. Since there was nothing in the soft plastic cooler to damage the cans, he made a U-turn and drove back toward the store.

He walked in with the cooler in his hands, but the clerk was nowhere to be seen. He started to walk toward the stock room when an unfamiliar person appeared. "Where's Bob?" the officer asked.

"Oh, he quit last week," was the response.

"Too bad," the officer replied. "He owed me $20." The officer turned around and started to walk out casually but his mind was racing. It was Bob who had sold him the soda and cooler some 40 minutes before, and he knew it was about to hit the fan.

The officer turned then. "Oh, you could do me a favor." The man asked what he needed and the officer produced his SIG P220 pistol. "You can put your hands up!" As he was focusing on the suspect, a second one stepped out of the storeroom and shot him with a 12-gauge shotgun. Fortunately, the Kevlar stopped the birdshot with ease. Unfortunately, the holdup man's rock band T-shirt did not impede the officer's 230-grain Hydra Shok round. He handcuffed the original suspect and called for assistance. When his backup arrived, they searched the premises and found the clerk dead out back.

In spite of a 47 mile ride to the hospital, the suspect survived, though without the continued use of his legs. The recovered slug weighed 178 grains and had a recovered diameter of .72 inch.

• • • • •

The teenage girl had been the continuing victim of an uncle who had started molesting her when she was 11. She had been moved to another state and was living with a distant cousin who she thought her uncle was unaware of. She was wrong.

The cousin and his wife who had taken her in were patient and caring. He was a CPA who served as a reserve deputy, while the wife was a full-time corrections officer. They were both competitive shooters and owned a number of firearms. One of those was a house gun, a Ruger P90 .45 ACP pistol loaded with Hydra-Shok ammunition. It was on top of an expensive china cabinet in the dining room.

The girl had gradually begun to live a normal existence. It had been almost a year and with the help of loving relatives and a caring therapist she had made great progress. She always got home before her cousin and his wife so she could do her homework and start dinner. She had just put the noodles in boiling water when the doorbell rang.

She opened the door without

A Speer .45 ACP 230-grain BHP that was used by an off-duty cop to prevent the abduction of his young daughter by a pedophile.

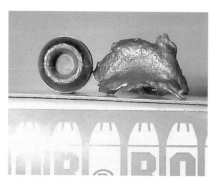

Cor-Bon's .45 ACP 200-grain JHP was recovered from the left lung of a rapist high on heroin.

Black Hills .45 ACP 230-grain uses the Gold Dot bullet. This round penetrated a car windshield before killing the driver.

This Starfire .45 ACP 230-grain JHP stopped a boat thief.

The Winchester .45 ACP 230-grain Black Talon is favored by those who consider deep penetration important.

Remington .45 ACP 185-grain Golden Saber fired from a Marlin carbine.

A road rage incident was stopped with this .45 ACP Remington 185-grain Golden Saber +P load.

Speer's .45 ACP 185-grain Gold Dot shot from a compact auto stopped a car theft.

This Speer .45 ACP 185-grain bonded hollowpoint penetrated a car windshield and stopped a road rage episode.

thinking and was confronted by her worst nightmare—her uncle. She screamed and ran for the phone but never made it. He knocked her down and was tearing her clothes off when the corrections officer arrived home. Seeing the door open, she sensed something was wrong and entered the back door. Hearing the screams, she grabbed the Ruger and entered the living room.

She ordered the man to stop, but he reached down and produced a .380 auto, saying, "You're next you stupid _____!" She fired three rounds, but only one hit its intended target. It entered above the left nipple and coursed downward. Recovered from the large intestine in surgery, it weighed 207 grains and measured .70 inch.

Today the former molested girl is married and pregnant with her first child.

Federal .45 ACP 230-grain Hydra-Shok Failure

All things considered, it had been a pretty good day. He had closed three construction jobs and was looking forward to the commission checks. He would never get to spend them. He left work after 7 P.M. and called his girlfriend on his cell phone. He shared his success with her and suggested they celebrate by having dinner at her favorite Italian restaurant. He asked if she could meet him there. When she agreed, he called and made a reservation for 8 P.M.

On his way to the restaurant, he stopped by the gun shop and picked up his Glock .45 with its newly installed night sights. He loaded it was 230-grain Hydra Shoks and stuck it in his briefcase. He purchased it because he had once had his laptop stolen from his hand, and when his next round of bids came up, his competition somehow managed to come in $1 less on each one.

He stopped to get his girlfriend a dozen roses, and as he walked out of the florist and started to enter his vehicle, he was approached by a man who asked him for directions. When

he started to provide them he felt something pressed against his stomach. Looking down, he saw a knife against his stomach. He told the man not to get excited and that he had money in his bag. He reached in the bag and wrapped his hand around the gun. He started to pull it but the man stabbed him before he completed the draw. Gasping, he pulled the gun and opened fire. He looked down and realized the gun was empty, with the slide locked back.

He staggered into the florist and collapsed. He died on the way to the hospital, but witnesses gave a detailed description of his attacker. The man was caught two days later with three Hydra-Shoks in his stomach. They had an averaged recovered weight of 200 grains and an average recovered diameter of .71 inch.

.45 COLT

He belonged to a public safety agency whose director had resisted the pressure to change to semiauto pistols, though he allowed his personnel the option of carrying a larger caliber revolver or auto pistol as long as it wasn't a magnum or used jacketed hollowpoint ammunition.

He had settled on a S&W Model 25-5 loaded with Federal lead hollowpoint ammunition. He still carried it when assigned to the Investigative Division, even though they only handled minor cases on university property. Serious crimes were handled by the city police where the university was located. While it was located in the core of the city, the school's crime rate was extremely low, and at least half of the detectives were going to graduate school on duty.

He was attending his Terminal Masters Seminar when his pager went off. The number was the office number followed by 911. He had never seen this signal before and immediately called the office from a hallway phone. He was told that one of their officers had been shot and that the gunman

was hiding in an underground parking structure on campus. Realizing the parking lot in question was less than a block away, he responded to the location at a fast walk.

He notified the parking lot attendant and was informed that a man matching that description had entered in a vehicle 15 minutes before and that the car had not returned. The detective relieved the parking attendant by trading shirts with him and notified the office of the situation. They informed him that the city SWAT team was responding and would be there within 45 minutes.

He took the seat in the booth and waited, watching the various TV monitors in front of him. He had placed his duty weapon on the desk and covered it with a newspaper. Fifteen minutes went by before the suspect and vehicle in question came down the ramp. Smiling, the detective stood up and held the gun by his side. The man handed him the ticket and a five dollar bill. "I'm sorry," the detective told him, "I don't have enough change. If you can wait I'll have them bring some. It should only take 5 minutes or so."

The man frowned and shook his head, "Nah, I'll come back later. I've got to get to work."

"Wait a minute. I might have enough change in my wallet and then you won't have to come back." The detective reached in his back pocket but what he produced was his badge. Bringing the gun to bear, he yelled, "Police! Freeze!" but the man started to accelerate away. The officer fired three times and the car lurched once and rolled to a stop.

Responding officers and paramedics found the man wounded though alive. He was conveyed to a nearby trauma center, where a single Federal lead hollowpoint was removed from his left lung. It had a recovered weight of 196 grains and a recovered diameter of .49 inch. The other two rounds had penetrated the vehicle and were imbedded in the dash.

A devoted cowboy action competitor, he enjoyed dressing up in western garb and competing almost every weekend with his Ruger Vaquero .45 Colt and lever-action carbine in the same caliber. He had completed his most successful competition yet, winning his first trophy for a third place finish.

Putting his gear away, he loaded his single-action revolver with Federal lead hollowpoints and stuck it on the top of his gym bag and zipped it almost closed. He also changed out of his western clothing and put on a T-shirt, Levis, and cowboy boots.

He drove his new compact 4x4 pickup, carefully adhering to the speed limit. He signaled and looked before pulling into the exit lane. He had not seen anyone and had made the lane change when he heard the screeching of tires, honking, and profanity. The other driver had been in his blind spot and he turned and gave an apologetic shrug. The other driver was not pacified, however, and pulled along side swearing and gesturing. The cowboy shooter yelled I'm sorry, but the man reached down, grabbed a hammer, and waved it in a threatening manner. He then swerved his car, striking the compact pickup.

The cowboy competitor jammed on his brakes and pulled to the side of the freeway. He had no sooner stopped then he was struck in the rear by the same road rage disciple. He grabbed the bag then, unzipping it as he exited his damaged pickup.

He pulled the revolver and told the man to stop, but he rushed him with the hammer. He cocked the revolver, but the man was on top of him. He fired with the muzzle jammed against his chest. His attacker collapsed and died right there.

The slug was recovered at autopsy with a weight of 192 grains and a diameter of .51 inch. The competitor was charged with illegal transportation of a loaded handgun and given probation.

A Winchester .45 Colt 225-grain Silvertip used by a rural delivery man to stop a holdup.

This 225-grain .45 Colt Silvertip stopped an unwanted sexual advance.

Today he has a concealed carry permit and relies on a compact .40 Glock.

• • • • •

He followed in his father's footsteps, but while his dad sold men's hats, he sold business software. His dad had traveled for 30 years and had never gone a mile without his Colt New Service revolver. He had passed it on to his son, and the only change that had been made had been the replacement of round-nose lead ammunition with Federal lead hollowpoints.

It resided in a worn leather bag that had been his dad's also. He routinely carried it into the premises he visited and into his motel at night. Having just completed a grueling 18 hour day, he pulled into the motel, registered, got his key, went to his room, and collapsed on his bed. He had

almost dozed off when he realized the brown bag was laying on the front seat.

Groaning, he stood up and went back to the car. He removed the bag, returned to his room, and laid back down on the bed. He was woken several hours later by somebody beating on his motel door. "I know you're in there with another man. I'll kill you!"

"Go away, you fool! There's nobody in here but me!" When the man continued to beat on his door he called the front desk, explained the situation, and asked them to call the police.

The beating stopped for a minute or two, and the salesman relaxed. The door burst open then and there stood an obviously intoxicated individual armed with a fire axe. Not hesitating, the salesman pulled the big Colt from the leather bag and opened fire. The man yelled, turned, took two steps, and collapsed.

The man was conveyed to a local hospital where a single Federal lead hollowpoint was removed from his left arm after it had penetrated both lungs. It had a recovered weight of 178 grains and a diameter of .51 inch. The salesman was arrested for possession of an unregistered handgun and jailed for 15 days.

• • • • •

His dad had told him years before that doing favors for some people could be a dangerous process, and he was beginning to think the old man was right. He had changed assignments with another officer and so far he had been shot at twice and assaulted with a baseball bat. He wondered what tonight would bring. Putting on his uniform, he pulled his duty weapon down off the shelf and secured it in its holster. While many members of his department carried big-bore revolvers, his was the only custom one. It was a S&W Model 28 .357 Magnum converted to .45 Colt with a 5 inch bull barrel. The action was incredibly smooth and light and it was loaded with Federal lead hollowpoints. An additional 12 rounds resided in HKS speedloaders on his belt.

Strapping on a lightweight .38 snub as a second gun, he was ready for duty. After roll call, he climbed on his patrol vehicle and pedaled off. At 42, he wasn't sure about this bike patrol, but he had already lost 15 pounds, though his posterior had not gotten used to the hard seat.

In his regular patrol area people were friendly and supportive, but the area covered by his temporary assignment was not the same. People looked at him suspiciously, and few would wave or say hello. It was almost noon when he realized his rear tire was low so he pedaled to a nearby gas station. He dug a quarter out of his pocket and filled his tire, then decided to get a soda and introduce himself to the gas station owner.

He walked into the office and noticed no one was there. He paused for a moment and then heard conversation in the rear office. He selected his soda and took a sip while waiting to pay for it. He waited a couple of minutes while finishing his soda. He then decided to knock on the office door, pay for his soda, and leave.

He knocked on the door and it swung open. He didn't see the gun in the man's hand until it fired. In spite of being less than 3 feet from his attacker, the round missed. Pulling his weapon, the officer fired two rounds and the man dropped his gun and screamed repeatedly until he died.

The officer thought he had interrupted a robbery, but the man with the gun was there because he was convinced the station owner was sleeping with his wife. His mistake cost him his life. The round was recovered at autopsy and had a weight of 188 grains and a diameter of .52 inch. The officer still works bike patrol but is back in his old area where Hispanic residents don't look at a Hispanic officer with the same suspicions Caucasians do.

• • • • •

The man had retired to the west and spent his time camping and hunting with a Springfield 03 rifle. Other than the addition of a 6X scope, it was the same as when he bought it 40 years before. He had taken every head of game that he ever wanted with it. He also carried a S&W long-barreled revolver chambered for .45 Colt. A former cop, he had carried a handgun for 27 years and felt naked without one.

He had been out in the country for two weeks and needed to go into town for supplies. Since his wife had died three years before in a house fire, he rarely shaved or cleaned up while in the brush. Securing his rifle in the back of his Range Rover, he headed to the market.

He made his purchases and decided to stop for gas before heading back to his camp. He was filling his tank when he heard someone say, "That's an awful fancy car for a bum like you!" He turned and smiled. "I don't think a bum could afford the payments on this puppy." The young man who had made the nasty remark didn't say anything but frowned and turned back to the task of filling his older model sedan.

When the young man finished, he walked over and, smirking, said, "I've never kicked the _____ out of no eccentric millionaire!"

"Look, sonny, why don't you just go mug an old lady or something. I'm not a millionaire. I just worked hard and saved my pennies." The young man walked away, and he thought the incident was over. He started to enter his vehicle when he noticed the punk extracting a rifle from his vehicle.

He pulled his revolver as the young man struggled to extract the long gun from it case. "Freeze," he shouted, but the knucklehead continued to tug on the gun, yelling, "I'll kill you, you _____!" The lever-action rifle was almost clear now. Well, the man thought, you didn't survive a career as a drug enforcement agent by letting people point guns at you, and fired twice. The first round

struck the rifle and knocked it out of the young man's grasp. The second one struck him in the left arm and he went down.

The round was removed during emergency surgery. It had penetrated the arm, entering the chest cavity above the rib cage, and was removed under the skin on the far side. It had a recovered weight of 156 grains and a recovered diameter of .48 inch.

.45 Colt Federal Lead Hollowpoint Failure

He had been carrying a .38 snub for self-defense purposes for years but decided he needed something bigger. Not comfortable with semiautomatic pistols, he was looking for a large-bore snubby. He found it at a local dealer and loaded it with Federal lead hollowpoints.

His daughter was in the hospital with an appendicitis attack that had ended in surgery. His wife stayed in the room with her and had asked him to get her some cash, as she only had $7 in her wallet. He walked down to the lobby but discovered the ATM there wanted a hefty fee for his business. He saw a branch of his bank just two blocks away and decided to enjoy the pleasant spring evening.

He approached the machine and was engrossed in using it when he was struck from behind. Falling to his knees, he felt a man grab his wallet and start to run. He pulled his snub and emptied it at his attacker.

Responding paramedics conveyed him back to the hospital he had just left. He had a broken arm and a large bruise on the back of his head. He was in the process of asking a nurse to call his daughter's room and tell his wife he was in emergency when he heard someone yelling at the top of his lungs, "I need help! Some SOB shot me while I was using the ATM!" He looked to see his attacker staggering into the treatment area with his wallet in his left hand. He had taken four lead hollowpoints and walked the two blocks to the hospital. They had an average recovered weight of 191 grains and an average diameter of .49 inch.

CHAPTER 28

Trends in Ammunition

There are currently a number of trends in ammunition for handguns, shotgun, and rifles. Unlike the trends from the Dark Ages (mid-1980s to mid-1990s), the trends from the late 1990s are all good.

HANDGUNS

In handgun ammo, it now seems that cops and civilians alike want bullets that actually expand *and* penetrate, not just penetrate. It also seems that the bizarre penetration pendulum has swung back to the center position. No longer are penetration distances of 18 to 20 inches acceptable, as the intellectuals and academia wanted in the 1980s. Now 9 inches is an acceptable minimum, and penetration in excess of 15 inches is considered clearly excessive.

Credit for this enlightened change of thinking goes to two places. First, to computer whiz Steve Fuller. He compared the street results from Evan Marshall with the gelatin results from the same loads from Ed Sanow. When all of the so-called experts were saying 12 inches of penetration in gelatin was an ideal minimum, Fuller had the intellect, guts, and audacity to say penetration depths greater than 8.4

inches actually result in less stopping power. This flew in the face of strong rhetoric from the FBI and the International Wound Ballistics Association (IWBA), which held the theory that 12 inches was the minimum acceptable penetration for a police bullet.

Fuller proved that police bullet performance peaked at 8.4 inches. He further proved that the performance was nearly flat, or nearly identical, for bullets that penetrate from 8.4 to 12.8 inches. Fuller's work was controversial

The reign of the deep penetrator, subsonic hollowpoint is over. The heavy bullet weights and slow velocities will continue but these bullets will expand more and penetrate less. Today, few defensive and police-oriented JHPs penetrate deeper than 15 inches of bare gelatin.

and directly opposed to conventional wisdom, but it was confirmed and applauded by the real gunfighters in law enforcement.

Second, credit goes to the Border Patrol agents with the National Firearms Unit of the Immigration and Naturalization Service (INS). In 1987, with much fanfare, the FBI established 12 inches as the minimum bullet penetration in 10 percent gelatin along with no maximum. In 1990, with no fanfare whatsoever, the INS adopted different penetration standards than its Department of Justice cousin. In the same barrier and gelatin tests popularized by the FBI, the Border Patrol established a minimum of 9 inches and a maximum of 20 inches.

The INS is the largest federal law enforcement agency in the U.S. and the third largest police department behind only the New York City Police and the Los Angeles Police. Most significantly, the INS experiences more armed confrontations than any federal agency, including the FBI, Marshal's Service, Customs Service, BATF, and Secret Service. In fact, INS agents, led by the Border Patrol, are involved in more gunfights than all other federal agencies combined. The Border Patrol did not seek to influence

The minimum and maximum penetration limits in bare gelatin are changing to agree with what we see on the street. Minimum numbers like 8.4 inches and 9 inches make more sense than 12 inches. The .38 Special +P+ 110 grain JHP is shown at 10 inches.

Evidence of a change in thinking from late energy release to medium energy release is the new Winchester Ranger Talon. As late energy release Black Talon loads, they ended up at the bottom of the stopping power results. As medium energy release loads, they outperform the top-rated Hydra-Shok in gelatin and living tissue alike.

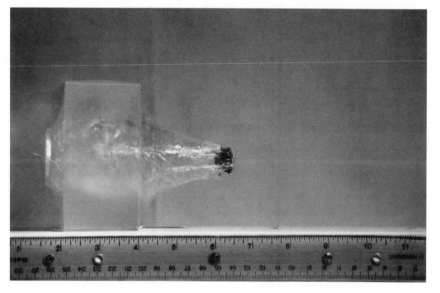

The trend of the future will be to focus on the effects of the temporary stretch cavity. The effort started in the mid-1970s has been restarted by the U.S. Border Patrol in the late 1990s. The Winchester .40 S&W 165-grain Ranger Talon is shown.

Evidence of the trend away from low-energy, subsonic hollowpoints comes from CCI-Speer. The company dropped this .40 S&W 165-grain medium-velocity Gold Dot and rereleased it as a full-power 1170 fps load. The new 500 ft-lb. 165-grain Gold Dot will produce 90 percent one-shot stops compared to 82 percent for the wimp load.

city, county, and state police departments like the FBI did. As a result, its position on wound ballistics was almost unknown.

In the late 1990s, under the leadership of NFU Director Gary Runyon and Deputy Director John Jacobs, the INS took steps to update the FBI ammo protocol. This time, they made their hard work public.

While the FBI ammo test protocol still has merit, its minimum and maximum penetration distances never had merit. The trend in handgun ammo is away from the FBI 12 inch minimum and no maximum to the Border Patrol 9 inch minimum and 20 inch maximum.

The change from a 12 inch minimum to a 9 inch minimum now allows hollowpoint bullets to actually

expand. This, in turn, transfers more energy to the target. This changing standard also allows bullets with higher initial energy, which also results in more energy transferred to the target. All of this clearly results in ammo with more stopping power.

The best possible example of this thinking is a direct comparison of the two .40 S&W duty loads used by the FBI and the INS at the turn of the century. The FBI uses a Federal 165-grain medium-velocity Hydra-Shok at

950 fps packing 330 ft-lbs. of energy. This load, specifically developed by and for the FBI, produces 83 percent one-shot stops. The INS uses a Remington 155-grain JHP at 1145 fps packing 479 ft-lbs. of energy. This load, developed by Remington for the INS but available to all shooters, produces 88 percent one-shot stops. Other 155-grain loads produce one-shot stops up to 93 percent, but the contract was awarded on a performance-modified but low-bid basis.

Further evidence of this change in thinking is the Winchester line of Ranger SXT ammo. As released in the early 1990s, it was heralded as late-energy-release ammunition. Unfortunately, its design earned the Black Talon and, later, the Ranger SXT the absolute basement for stopping power results compared to other loads. In the late 1990s, the ammo was significantly redesigned for more rapid expansion, faster energy release, and less penetration. The result is T-series ammo that is as good as the best JHPs available.

Even more evidence of a trend away from low-energy, deep-penetrator subsonic loads and the influence of the FBI and IWBA comes from CCI-Speer. The company made a politically incorrect but market-driven change to its .40 S&W 165-grain Gold Dot. Originally, it was a 975 fps, medium-velocity load. The medium-velocity version of the .40 S&W 165-grain JHP was demanded by the FBI, the same folks that popularized the 9mm 147-grain subsonic JHP. This time, however, local law enforcement caught on to the faults of the .40 S&W medium-velocity 165 grain JHP much faster than they did the 9mm 147-grain subsonic JHP.

As a result, CCI-Speer recently dropped the medium-velocity Gold Dot, citing lack of law enforcement demand. Cops everywhere wanted the 1050 to 1150 fps versions of the 165-grain bullet. CCI-Speer completely redesigned its 165-grain Gold Dot as a full-power load. The high-velocity

version has solved problems with police departments whose officers experienced weapon stoppages and lack of expansion from the .40 S&W medium-velocity 165-grain JHPs.

Other clear trends in law enforcement are toward the so-called "tactical" bullets. These are bullets that are specifically designed to perform well in soft tissue after first defeating windshield glass and car bodies. The FBI gets the credit for objectively demonstrating that bullets can perform very differently in bare gelatin and in gelatin after having passed through tactical barriers. Specifically, the agency proved for all to see that many hollowpoints will not expand at all after striking heavy clothes and that many JHPs fail to penetrate enough after first striking auto glass. This, in turn, has resulted in an array of bullets that have been designed to expand and penetrate the same whether or not they strike barriers first.

The first step in total weight retention was to reduce the amount of lead fragments that break off from the expanded mushroom. The second phase in total weight retention is to prevent the jacket from separating from the lead core even after impacts with tactical barriers like windshields and thermopane glass.

The CCI-Speer Gold Dot, while marketed as a bonded JHP, was the first of the true tactical bullets. Its jacket will not separate after impacting glass. The Federal Tactical was the second bullet specifically designed to perform well after these barriers. The Remington Golden Saber Bonded was next, followed by the Winchester Partition Gold.

All these bullets give up a certain amount of soft tissue wound ballistics to more than gain in stopping power after tactical barriers. As a result, these loads were at first only used by tactical teams, be they SWAT, SRT, STAR, ERT, CIRT, or any other acronym. The trend, however, is for these so-called tactical bullets to be used as a

The trend in defensive and police bullets, with two exceptions, is to high retained weights. Federal redesigned its 9mm 124-grain +P+ Hydra-Shok (old, left and new, right) with this in mind. The exceptions are the "controlled separation" bullets like the Triton Quik-Shok and the new generation of reduced hazard hollowpoints.

general duty load. Road deputies with the Marion County, Indiana, Sheriffs Department use the Federal .40 S&W 165-grain Tactical JHP. Troopers with the Indiana State Police are planning on using the Winchester .40 S&W 165-grain Partition Gold hollowpoint.

The Salt Lake County, Utah, Sheriff is one agency using the Federal 180-grain Tactical as its duty load. The Strike Force with the Montgomery, Alabama, Police uses the 165-grain Tactical. The 165-grain Tactical is loaded to a nominal velocity of 1050 fps, roughly 75 fps faster than a medium-velocity load. This means it produces the same rearward slide velocity as the 180-grain JHPs around which the .40 S&W auto pistol was designed.

This trend among cops will continue, and it is generally a good thing. Specifically, it is a great idea for state police, highway patrol, and rural sheriffs departments. It is okay for urban sheriffs departments but questionable for metro police departments who seldom shoot into vehicles. And it is an outright bad idea for school cops, housing cops, transit cops, courtroom security, and other officers in densely populated patrol areas. These officers need the more wound ballistics and the less

Now that most hollowpoints can defeat heavy clothes and still expand, the ammo industry is tackling an even tougher problem: expansion and penetration after glass. Every major ammo maker has some sort of bonded or partition "anticar" handgun bullet. Ammo companies are still looking for the right balance of stopping power and tactical penetration.

penetration that comes from more conventional JHPs. In this regard, the higher energy Gold Dots and Partition Golds may be better overall choices than the Tactical JHPs and Golden Saber Bonded JHPs.

In stark contrast to the cops, civilian shooters looking for home defense and personal carry ammo are not best served by this tactical ammo. The only crossover load is the CCI Gold Dot. Otherwise, civilian carry—and that includes police backup and off-duty—is best served by the higher energy hollowpoints or one of the frangibles. The best of these is probably the Triton Quik-Shok. These

scenarios call for uncompromised stopping power and rarely involve tactical barriers or the need for penetration deeper than 9 inches.

RIFLES

This trend to tactical handgun ammo has spilled over to tactical rifle ammo. The two top loads in this area are the Federal Tactical and the Winchester Fail-Safe. These loads defeat tactical barriers and still fly true to the target and then expand in the soft tissue. These loads are slowly replacing hollowpoint boat-tail match bullets among tactical teams. The

reason the acceptance has not been faster, in spite of superb terminal ballistics, is the only moderate accuracy from these tactical loads. A typical match bullet may shoot 1/2 MOA while a typical tactical bullet is closer to 1 1/2 MOA. As the accuracy from tactical bullets improves, so will their acceptance by law enforcement.

Another rifle ammo trend in law enforcement is the so-called "hostage rescue" loads. The .308 Win 168-grain HPBT Match penetrates up to 22 inches of gelatin. With hostages present, that may be too much. Marketed under a variety of names, they produce just 10 to 12 inches of penetration from .308 Win ammo. Like the tactical loads, the hostage rescue loads also suffer from only modest accuracy. The race is on to get an explosive hollowpoint to shoot as good as a match bullet. Watch for Black Hills Ammunition to lead the way with this kind of ammo.

Expect more and more companies to offer three kinds of loads for the .308 Winchester and four kinds for the .223 Remington. In .308 Win/7.62 NATO, these three loads are 1) a pure match load involving something like the Sierra Match King, Nosler J4, or Hornaday Match, 2) a tactical load to give the best in-flight stability after thermopane glass and, 3) the so-called hostage rescue hollowpoint bullets, where the penetration is limited to 12 inches of gelatin or less. Expect the accuracy of both the tactical bullets and the reduced-penetration hollowpoints to approach that of match bullets.

In .223 Rem/5.56 NATO, the four loads are 1) a pure match load like the Federal 69-grain Match King, 2) a general-purpose patrol load like the Winchester 64-grain softpoint, 3) a deep penetrator load like the Winchester 62-grain FMJ Ranger, which is really the dual-core M855 grain military ball with a front core made of steel, and 4) a very controlled penetration load for use in heavily urbanized scenarios like the Federal 40-grain hollowpoint.

In the future, expect the ammo companies to improve the accuracy of their tactical rifle bullets to match levels. Also expect match-grade hostage rescue loads for the .308 Win that penetrate no more than 12 inches of gelatin.

The future of police shotgun ammo is reduced-recoil loads. These allow a greater first-shot hit probability due to less tendency to flinch and faster follow-up shots due to less muzzle rise. World class instructor Clint Smith gets almost no muzzle rise from a reduced-recoil load even from a 14 inch shotgun.

SHOTGUNS

In shotgun ammo, the trend continues to be toward low recoil, reduced recoil, or tactical shotshells. All of this is good. In the late 1980s, Remington was the first to introduce a reduced-recoil, rapid-recovery, 12-gauge buckshot load. This was a nine-pellet 00 buck load at trap load velocities. In the 1990s, Federal and Winchester followed suit with reduced-velocity 00 buck loads. Then this spilled over to reduced-velocity rifled slug loads from all the shotshell makes. This, in turn, led to reduced recoil, reduced pellet count, 00 buck loads (eight pellets versus nine pellets) and further reduced slug loads.

In all these cases, the reduced buckshot and slug loads proved to have plenty of penetration in gelatin and against typical barriers. The real surprise occurred in 1998 when Evan Marshall released some of his shotgun statistics. The most one-shot stops for a 12-gauge buckshot load turned out to be the reduced recoil, nine-pellet 00 buck. Acceptable penetration distances compared to full-power loads was one thing. Superior stopping power from the tactical buckshot was quite another. However, the tactical 00 buck proved to be more effective in actual shootings than full-power 00 buck and far more effective than full-power #4 buck loads. The tactical slugs offer two advantages over full-power slugs: much less recoil and less excessive penetration. Among reduced-recoil slugs, the Winchester version expands the most and penetrates the least.

Another big trend in the ammo industry is reduced hazard, nontoxic, or low-lead ammunition. This includes the use of composite bullets for police duty use. This was covered in detail in Chapter 20.

CHAPTER 29

Updated Shooting Results

What follows are the latest shootings results with two additional pieces of information: average recovered diameter and average penetration. Both of these figures refer to results in human targets. I realize that these will often not square with many cherished beliefs, but the collection of this data has often demolished some of my own.

Abbreviations

		HP	hollowpoint	PD	Personal Defense	
		HS	Hydra-Shok	PP	Power Point	
BH	Black Hills	HSP	hollow softpoint	Rem	Remington	
BT	Black Talon	JHP	jacketed hollowpoint	RNL	round-nose lead	
CB	Cor-Bon	JSP	jacketed softpoint	SF	Starfire	
Fed	Federal	LHP	lead hollowpoint	ST	Silvertip	
FMJ	full metal jacket	Mil	military	SWC	semiwadcutter	
GD	Gold Dot	mv	medium velocity	Win	Winchester	
GS	Golden Saber	Ny	Nyclad			

.22 LONG RIFLE

LOAD	TOTAL	STOPS	%	ARD	AP
1. Quik Shok HP	10	4	40	na	6.7"
2. CCI Stinger	465	178	38	.28"	7.3"
3. Fed HP	722	214	30	.26"	8.8"
4. Win HP	654	196	30	.29"	9.6"
5. Rem HP	988	296	29	.25"	9.1"
6. Win solid	1644	348	21	.22"	11.8"

.25 ACP

LOAD	TOTAL	STOPS	%	ARD	AP
1. Win expanding pt.	204	55	27	.30"	8.9"
2. Win FMJ	2804	673	24	.25"	10.4"
3. Rem FMJ	2221	511	23	.25"	10.9"

.32 ACP

LOAD	TOTAL	STOPS	%	ARD	AP
1. Win ST	151	99	66	.41"	9.2"
2. Fed HS	23	14	61	.44"	9.3"
3. CCI GD	10	6	60	.42"	9.9"
4. Win FMJ	203	99	49	.32"	11.1"

.380 ACP

LOAD	TOTAL	STOPS	%	ARD	AP
1. Fed HS	96	68	71	.56"	9.4"
2. Cor Bon JHP	42	30	71	.59"	8.8"
3. Triton JHP	10	7	70	.58"	9.1"
4. Fed JHP	178	123	69	.55"	8.7"
5. Win ST	103	70	68	.51"	8.2"
6. Rem JHP	75	52	67	.49"	9.7"
7. CCI JHP	78	52	67	.48"	9.2"
8. Fed FMJ	231	127	55	NA	10.9"

The Federal .380 Hydra-Shok is the top street performer in this caliber.

A PMC Starfire .380 JHP that saved the life of a small-town cab driver.

This Winchester .380 ACP Silvertip ended the career of a drug rip-off man.

This PMC .380 Starfire JHP ended a robbery.

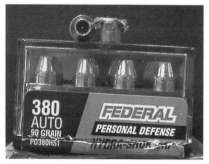

This Federal .380 Hydra-Shok ended a gunfight when it was deployed from an officer's second gun.

This Winchester .380 Auto Silvertip hollowpoint stopped a vicious assault by an assailant armed with a baseball bat.

.38 SPECIAL-2" BARREL

LOAD	TOTAL	STOPS	%	ARD	AP
1. Win LHP +P	145	97	67	.51"	11.6"
2. Fed LHP+P	160	107	67	.52"	11.2"
3. Rem 125-gr. JHP+P	126	84	67	.56"	10.9"
4. Rem LHP+P	111	74	65	.52"	11.5"
5. Fed 129-gr. HS	77	50	65	.56"	10.2"
6. Fed 125-gr. +P	145	94	65	.49"	11.7"
7. CCI 125-gr. +P	72	46	64	.44"	11.2"
8. Rem 125-gr. GS+P	11	7	64	.58"	10.3"
9. Fed 147-gr. HS+P+	59	38	64	.60"	12.2"
10. Win 125-gr. +P	75	47	63	.51"	8.6"
11. Fed Nyclad 125-gr.	46	29	63	.56"	10.4"
12. Fed Ny 125-gr. +P	32	20	63	.59"	9.8"
13. Fed 158-gr. SWC+P	261	129	49	.36"	14.5"
14. Fed 158-gr. RNL	421	208	49	.357	17.1"

The .38 Special 158-grain lead hollowpoint has been around for a long time. This one was used by a U.S. citizen in South America to end a robbery attempt.

A PMC Starfire .380 JHP that saved the life of a small-town cab driver. This .38 Special Starfire 125-grain JHP stopped a car thief.

This .38 Special Starfire 125-grain JHP stopped a car thief.

This Federal +P .38 Special Nyclad hollowpoint was used to end a domestic squabble. Fired from a 6 inch Ruger, it was recovered at autopsy just short of the spinal column.

A Starfire .38 Special 125-grain +P hollowpoint that was used by an off-duty cop to stop a burglary.

.38 SPECIAL-4" BARREL

LOAD	TOTAL	STOPS	%	ARD	AP
1. Cor Bon 115-gr.+P+	41	33	80	.62"	11.4" *
2. Win 110-gr. JHP+P+	49	39	80	.64"	12.1"
3. Rem 125+P GS	10	8	80	.68"	12.4"
4. Fed 158+P LHP	401	305	76	.63"	12.9"
5. Rem 125-gr. +P	206	157	76	.66"	13.5"
6. Fed 125-gr. +P	264	190	72	.60"	12.7"
7. Rem 158-gr. LHP+P	173	119	69	.64"	12.9"
8. Fed 147-gr. HS+P+	72	59	69	.66"	13.8"
9. Win 110-gr. ST+P	142	98	69	.65"	12.7"
10. CCI 125-gr. JHP+P	93	62	67	.64"	11.8"
11. Fed 129-gr. HS+P	86	58	67	.61"	10.7"
12. Rem 95-gr. JHP+P	167	110	66	.56"	13.1"
13. Fed 158-gr. SWC+P	393	194	49	.36"	15.1"
14. Fed 158-gr. RNL	592	288	47	.357"	17.1"

* no longer in production

.357 SIG

LOAD	TOTAL	STOPS	%	ARD	AP
1. Fed 125-gr. JHP	24	22	92	.62"	12.3"
2. CCI 125-gr. JHP	11	10	91	.66"	12.6"
3. Win 125-gr. JHP	10	9	90	.64"	12.8"
4. Rem 125-gr. JHP	19	17	89	.61"	13.2"
5. Fed 150-gr. JHP	13	11	85	.58"	15.2"

Federal's .357 SIG 150-grain JHP produces moderate expansion in people.

A child molester was put down with this Remington .357 SIG 125-grain JHP.

This Federal .357 SIG 125-grain JHP worked well in a police shooting.

.357 MAGNUM

LOAD	TOTAL	STOPS	%	ARD	AP
1. Fed 125-gr. JHP	641	615	96	.74"	11.1"
2. Rem 125-gr. JHP	431	414	96	.58*	12.3"
3. CCI 125-gr. JHP	183	170	93	.69"	13.1"
4. Fed 110-gr. JHP	280	251	89	.71"	11.2"
5. Rem 110-gr. JHP	71	63	89	.65"	10.9"
6. Win 125-gr. JHP	101	88	87	.72"	10.4"
7. Fed 158-gr. HS	78	68	87	.66"	13.8"
8. Win 145-gr. ST	100	87	87	.64"	14.2"
9. Fed 158-gr. Ny	76	64	84	.61"	13.5"
10. Rem 125-gr. mv	45	37	82	.68"	12.2"
11. Rem 158-gr. JHP	65	53	82	.64"	14.7"
12. Win 158-gr. SWC	120	93	78	.49"	16.2"

* routinely throws off secondary projectiles

Long ridiculed by some, the Federal .357 Magnum 125-grain JHP continues to succeed where it counts—on the street.

Remington .357 Magnum 125-grain JHP has worked well even when fired from revolvers with 2 inch barrels.

An off-duty detective received this result from his .357 Hydra-Shok round fired from a short-barreled revolver at an armed robber.

Federal's .357 158-grain Nyclad hollowpoint stopped two holdup men with two rounds.

9MM LUGER

LOAD	TOTAL	STOPS	%	ARD	AP
1. Fed 115-gr. +P+	189	172	91	.71"	13.9"
2. Win 115-gr. +P+	150	135	90	.73"	13.6"
3. Win 127-gr. BT+P+	86	77	90	.68"	14.2"
4. Rem 115-gr. +P+	80	72	89	.64"	15.6"
5. Fed 124-gr. HS+P+	95	85	89	.67"	14.1"
6. Speer 124-gr. GD+P	74	65	88	.71"	13.6"
7. Cor Bon 115-gr. +P	51	45	88	.73"	11.2'
8. Rem 124-gr. GS+P	14	12	86	.67"	13.9"
9. Fed Nyclad 124-gr.	265	220	83	.69"	14.3"
10. Fed 124-gr. HS	243	202	83	.67"	14.5"
11. Win 115-gr. ST	421	349	83	.64"	13.7"
12. Fed 115-gr. JHP	382	317	82	.56"	13.6"
13. Rem 115-gr. JHP	265	217	82	.58"	14.3"
14. Speer 115-gr. JHP	121	97	80	.59"	14.6"
15. Fed 135-gr. HS	334	267	80	.52"	14.9"
16. Fed 147-gr. HS	304	240	79	.51"	17.1"
17. Fed 147-gr. JHP	71	55	78	.62"	18.3"
18. Win 147-gr. BT	259	203	78	.53"	16.3"
19. Win 115-gr. FMJ	315	221	70	.35"	17.5"

Winchester's 147-grain 9mm Black Talon is the favorite of the deep penetration crowd. The 127-grain +P+ Ranger Talon works significantly better. Two bullets jammed together on the right are the ultimate double tap.

Black Hills ammunition is starting to be seen in actual shootings on a regular basis. This 9mm JHP was used by a deputy sheriff. The round went through the driver's side door, then the arm, both lungs, and the heart. It was found under the skin on the far side.

This Speer 9mm 124-grain +P Gold Dot BHP was used by a retired cop to save the life of a neighbor. It penetrated the storm door of a house and was recovered just short of the spinal column.

Recovered bullets can be misleading. These two penetrated the passenger side door before killing a terrorist wielding a submachine gun.

These Remington 9mm 147-grain Golden Sabers produced excellent results from a 9mm carbine. A police officer ended a botched robbery with them.

Winchester's 9mm 147-grain Ranger Talon produces remarkably consistent results. These three rounds are from three separate shootings.

The 9mm Silvertip was the villain of the FBI Miami shootout, but it has shown good results in actual shootings. This one stopped an ex-wife armed with a shotgun.

Winchester's 9mm 127-grain +P+ Black Talon has become an excellent choice in this caliber. This one was used by a state trooper to end a standoff at a toll booth.

Federal's 9mm 124-grain Hydra-Shok has been the issue round for several agencies. These two were recovered at autopsy from the body of a would-be cop killer.

.40 S&W

LOAD	TOTAL	STOPS	%	ARD	AP
1. Rem 165-gr. GS	146	137	94	.70"	13.9"
2. CCI 155-gr. GD	59	55	93	.67"	14.2"
3. Fed 155-gr. HS	88	82	93	.73"	13.6"
4. Fed 155-gr. JHP	139	124	89	.68"	11.8"
5. CB 135-gr. JHP	56	50	89	.74"	10.9"
6. CB 150-gr. JHP	40	35	88	.71"	11.3"
7. Rem 155-gr.	41	36	88	.63"	12.9"
8. Win 155-gr. ST	106	93	88	.74"	11.2"
9. Fed 180-gr. HS	65	57	88	.66"	15.6"
10. PMC 155-gr.	49	42	86	.65"	13.9"
11. GD 180-gr.	63	54	86	.63"	12.6"
12. CB 180-gr. JHP	21	18	86	.71"	11.4"
13. GS 180-gr.	78	67	86	.63"	12.7"
14. SF 180-gr.	51	43	84	.61"	14.2"
15. BH 180-gr.	44	37	84	.67"	13.3"
16. Fed 180-gr.	100	84	84	.65"	13.1"
17. Win BT 180-gr.	157	132	84	.68"	15.8"
18. Win 180-gr.	159	132	83	.61"	14.3"
19. Fed HS 165-gr.	112	93	83	.51"	16.8"
20. Win 180-gr. FMJ	94	67	71	.40"	19.2"

The .40 S&W 180-grain BHP works well on the street. A bayonet-armed drunk was stopped by this one.

A store owner used a Black Hills .40 S&W 180-grain Gold Dot hollowpoint to end an attempted holdup. The weapon was a Kahr .40 auto.

Silvertips expand too quickly and underpenetrate? These two .40 S&W 155-grain slugs were found 15.7 and 16.2 inches inside a holdup man.

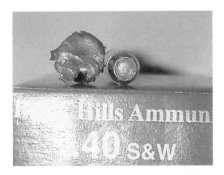

A Black Hills .40 S&W 155-grain BHP that was used by a judge to stop the abduction of a neighbor.

This Speer .40 S&W Gold Dot 180-grain BHP entered a car and killed the occupant.

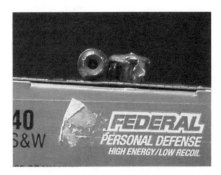

Federal .40 S&W 135-grain Hydra-Shok stopped a domestic violence attack when fired from a compact auto.

Remington's .40 S&W 165-grain jacketed Golden Saber is producing superior results. This one was used by a pediatrician to stop a car jacking.

Winchester 180-grain JHPs show expansion potency of first-generation .40 S&W loads. This one ended the career of a drug dealer.

A citizen armed with a Ruger .40 carbine loaded with Federal 155-grain Hydra-Shoks brought a quick end to a criminal's career.

The Federal .40 S&W 180-grain JHP has been a steady performer. This one ended an attempted assassination.

The Federal .40 S&W 180-grain Hydra-Shok is an excellent heavy bullet load in this caliber. This one put an end to a bar holdup.

This incident ended well, even though the Winchester .40 S&W 155-grain Silvertip was shot from the short barrel of a compact auto.

10MM

LOAD	TOTAL	STOPS	%	ARD	AP
1. CB 150-gr.	10	9	90	.82"	11.1"
2. Fed 155-gr.	20	18	90	.73"	12.4"
3. Win ST 175	64	56	88	.76"	10.8"
4. Fed 180-gr. HS	57	49	86	.66"	12.9"
5. Fed 180	45	38	84	68"	13.4"
6. Win 180	59	48	82	.63"	14.6"
7. Rem 180	48	29	81	.67"	13.7"

Lightweight bullets don't penetrate deeply enough, right? This Cor-Bon 135-grain 10mm JHP was found 16.7 inches inside a bad guy!

.44 SPECIAL

LOAD	TOTAL	STOPS	%	ARD	AP
1. Win ST	70	53	76	.58"	13.8"
2. Fed LHP	45	33	73	.63"	14.5"
3. Win RNL	52	34	65	.44"	18.8"
4. Rem RNL	20	13	65	.44"	18.5"

This Winchester .44 Special Silvertip JHP was taken from a holdup man.

.44 MAGNUM

LOAD	TOTAL	STOPS	%	ARD	AP
1. Win 210-gr.	71	65	92	.81"	16.3"
2. Fed 180-gr.	49	44	90	.72"	15.6"
3. Rem 240-gr.	43	38	88	.62"	16.7"
4. Win 240-gr.	52	45	87	.67"	16.2"
5. Win 240-gr. SWC	56	46	82	.49"	19.4"
6. Fed 240-gr.	66	53	80	.58"	18.1"
7. Rem 240-gr. LFN	55	42	76	.44"	20.7"

.41 MAGNUM

LOAD	TOTAL	STOPS	%	ARD	AP
1. Win 170-gr. ST	61	55	90	.68"	14.9"
2. Win 210-gr. JHP	40	32	80	.59"	16.3"
3. Rem 210-gr. SWC	57	43	75	.43"	17.9"
4. Win 210-gr. SWC	43	32	74	.44"	17.4"

This Remington .44 Magnum 240-grain JHP ended a domestic dispute.

This Federal 240-grain .44 Magnum Hydra-Shok stopped a plane theft.

An abduction was foiled with this Winchester .41 Magnum 175-grain Silvertip.

This Federal .41 Magnum 210-grain JHP ended a robber's career.

.45 ACP

LOAD	TOTAL	STOPS	%	ARD	AP
1. 230-gr. HS	173	166	96	.76"	13.9"
2. 185-gr. GS	83	80	96	.69"	12.4"
3. 230-gr. GD	45	42	93	.68"	12.2"
4. Rem 185-gr. +P	77	71	92	.74"	12.9"
5. CB 185-gr.	20	18	90	.78"	11.1"
6. 230-gr. GS	10	9	90	.73"	12.9"
7. Fed 185-gr.	128	112	88	.71"	11.6"
8. CCI 200-gr.	139	122	88	.73"	12.4"
9. 230-gr. BT	96	84	88	.75"	13.9"
10. 185-gr. ST	121	106	88	.78"	11.5"
11. Fed 185-gr. HS	78	69	88	.67"	12.9"
12. Fed 165-gr. HS PD	38	32	84	.59"	14.7"
13. Rem 185-gr.	145	117	81	.64"	13.6"
14. Rem 230-gr. FMJ	151	94	62	.45"	19.1"
15. Win 230-gr. FMJ	209	130	62	.45"	19.9"
16. Fed 230-gr. FMJ	215	134	62	.45"	20.4"

This .45 ACP Remington 230-grain Golden Saber shot from a compact auto stopped an emotionally disturbed person wielding a sword.

Speer Gold bullets are consistent performers. This .45 ACP 185-grain BHP was used by a citizen to stop a home invasion at a neighbor's house.

Federal's .45 ACP 185-grain Hydra-Shok produces good expansion and adequate penetration in actual shootings. This one ended a car jacking attempt.

A .45 ACP Gold Dot fired at a measured 170 meters did not expand, but it stopped a sniper armed with a scoped sighted rifle.

Remington's .45 ACP 185-grain JHP load produced modest deformation in the large intestine and excellent expansion in the heart.

The Federal .45 ACP 185-grain Hydra-Shok +P doesn't work as well as the 230-grain Hydra-Shok.

The Federal .45 ACP 230-grain FMJ doesn't always live up to the myth.

A shooting spree came to an end thanks to this Winchester 230-grain .45 ACP +P.

A Winchester .45 ACP Silvertip that penetrated a glass window before killing a man armed with a rifle.

Starfire .45 ACP 230-grain JHP that put an end to an attempted B&E.

Speer's .45 ACP 185-grain Gold Dot closed out a 30-year criminal career.

Remington's .45 ACP 185-grain +P Golden Saber works well on people.

Winchester's .45 ACP 230-grain Ranger Talon demonstrates deep penetration and good expansion in actual shootings. This one went through three layers of clothing before killing a holdup woman.

These Federal .45 ACP 185-grain JHP show how terminal performance can depend on the resistance met. The two rounds on the left were recovered from the stomach, while the round at right was recovered from the liver.

The Federal .45 ACP 230-grain Hydra-Shok is a superb stopper even from compact auto pistols. This one, fired by an off-duty special agent, stopped a vicious assault from a martial artist armed with a butterfly knife.

.45 COLT

LOAD	TOTAL	STOPS	%	ARD	AP
1. Fed 225-gr. LHP	36	29	81	.51"	14.9"
2. Win 225-gr. ST	45	36	80	.58"	13.1"
3. Win 255-gr. RNL	21	15	71	.45"	16.8"
4. Rem 250-gr. RNL	10	7	70	.45"	18.3"

A cop killer was hit with this .45 Colt 225-grain Silvertip.

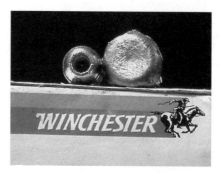

This Winchester .45 Colt 225-grain Silvertip expanded well in soft tissue.

.30 CARBINE

LOAD	TOTAL	STOPS	%	ARD	AP
1. Win 110-gr. HSP	43	38	88	.42"	T&T*
2. Fed 110-gr. JSP	63	55	87	.44"	20.9"
3. Fed 110-gr. FMJ	27	22	81	.30"	T&T*
4. Win 110-gr. FMJ	20	16	80	.30"	T&T*
5. Mil issue **	1033	826	79	.30"	T&T*

* through and through—routinely exited human target
** various arsenals; for informational purposes only

.223 REMINGTON

LOAD	TOTAL	STOPS	%	ARD	AP
1. Rem 69-gr. JHP	40	39	98	.32"	16.9"
2. Win 69-gr. match	38	37	97	.37"	18.5"
3. SS109	283	272	96	2-pieces	15.7"
4. Fed 40-gr.	162	156	96	fragmented	9.8"
5. Fed 52-gr. match	37	35	95	2-pieces	9.4"
6. Win 64-gr. PP	21	20	95	fragmented	9.1"
7. Win 52-gr.	41	39	95	fragmented	8.8"
8. Fed 55-gr. JHP	112	105	94	fragmented	9.2"
9. Win 55-gr. JSP	41	38	93	2-pieces	10.4"
10. Fed 55-gr. Nosler	27	25	93	.38"	11.8"
11. Win 55-gr. FMJ	123	113	92	2-pieces	12.3"
12. Fed 62-gr. JHP	48	44	92	fragmented	9.7"
13. Rem 55-gr. JSP	36	33	92	2-pieces	8.7"
14. Rem 55-gr. FMJ	46	42	91	2-pieces	10.3

.30-30

LOAD	TOTAL	STOPS	%	ARD	AP
1. PMC 150-gr. SF	44	42	95	53"	19.6"
2. Win 150-gr. JHP	83	78	94	.57"	23.4"
3. Rem 170-gr. JHP	10	9	90	.48"	T&T*
4. Fed 150-gr. JSP	29	26	90	.43"	T&T*

* through and through—routinely exited human target

.308 WINCHESTER

LOAD	TOTAL	STOPS	%	ARD	AP
1. Rem 168-gr. match	40	39	98	2-pieces	24.7"
2. Mil 168-gr. match	124	122	98	na	T&T
3. IMI 168-gr. match	213	209	98	2-pieces	25.1"
4. Fed 168-gr. match	112	110	98	2-pieces	24.9"
5. Win 168-gr. match	28	27	98	2-pieces	23.8"
6. BH 168-gr. match	38	37	97	2-pieces	22.7"
7. Fed 165-gr. TBBC *	40	38	95	.58"	T&T

* Trophy Bonded Bear Claw

A Federal 12-gauge sabot slug that penetrated a car and a felon.

This Winchester 12-gauge LE slug produced massive soft tissue damage.

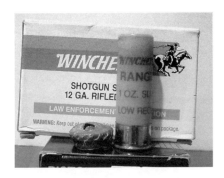

This Winchester 12-gauge slug ended a standoff.

A bar holdup was halted with this Winchester 12-gauge low-recoil slug.

12-GAUGE SHOTGUN-00 BUCKSHOT

LOAD	TOTAL	STOPS	%	ARD	AP
1. Win 2 3/4"	238	228	96	na	11.3"
2. Fed 2 3/4" *	124	119	96	na	14.5"
3. Rem 3"	47	45	96	na	11.9"
4. Rem 2 3/4"	299	269	90	na	12.6"
5. Rem 3" **	10	9	90	na	15.4"
6. Fed 3"	28	25	89	na	13.9"
7. Fed 2 3/4" ***	35	31	89	na	15.4"

* tactical buckshot—reduced recoil load for law enforcement
** nickel-plated buckshot
*** magnum load, 12 pellets

12-GAUGE FEDERAL PERSONAL DEFENSE

LOAD	TOTAL	STOPS	%	ARD	AP
1. Fed #2 shot	42	36	86	na	11.2"

12-GAUGE #4 BUCKSHOT

LOAD	TOTAL	STOPS	%	ARD	AP
1. Fed 3" Mag	81	76	94	na	15.2"
2. Win 2 3/4"	163	143	88	na	13.6"
3. Rem 2 3/4"	156	137	88	na	14.8"
4. Fed 2 3/4" Mag	32	28	88	na	15.8"

12-GAUGE SLUG

LOAD	TOTAL	STOPS	%	ARD	AP
1. Win 2 3/4"	89	88	99	1.09"	15.8"
2. Fed 2 3/4"	65	64	98	1.1"	18.1"
3. Rem 2 3/4"	62	61	98	1.2"	16.3"
4. Fed 2 3/4" Sabot	34	33	97	.89"	T&T
5. Rem 2 3/4" *	61	59	97	1.14"	16.3"

*reduced recoil load for law enforcement

COMPACT PISTOL DATA
(SHORTER THAN 4" BARREL)

9MM

LOAD	TOTAL	STOPS	%	ARD	AP
1. Rem 115 +P+	26	23	87	.59"	12.6"
2. Rem 124 +P GS	50	43	86	.52"	12.2"
3. Win 127 +P+	20	17	85	.51"	12.8"
4. Speer GD 124 +P	55	47	85	.56"	11.6"
5. Fed 115 +P+ JHP	49	41	84	.63"	11.2"
6. Fed HS 124 +P+	62	52	84	.64"	12.4"
7. Fed Ny 124	44	36	82	.56"	13.1"
8. Win 115 +P+ JHP	88	72	82	.50"	13.8"
9. Fed HS 124	25	20	80	.52"	12.6"
10. Win ST 115	40	32	80	.55"	11.1"
11. Fed 115 JHP	54	43	80	.56"	11.5"
12. Rem 115 JHP	49	39	80	.50"	12.8"
13. Fed HS 147	74	59	80	.46"	13.9"
14. Fed HS 135	10	8	80	.53"	10.9"
15. CB 115 +P	10	8	80	.59"	10.2"
16. Win BT 147	84	66	79	.47"	15.3"
17. Win 115 FMJ	24	14	58	.35"	17.2"

.40 S&W COMPACT

LOAD	TOTAL	STOPS	%	AD	AP
1. Rem GS 165	61	54	89	.68"	12.6"
2. Speer GD 155	18	16	89	.65"	11.9"
3. CB 135	9	8	89	.69"	10.4"
4. Fed HS 155	24	21	88	.69"	12.6"
5. Fed HS 180	30	26	86	.59"	12.9"
6. Rem GS 180	25	21	84	.62"	12.2"
7. Fed 180	32	27	84	.67"	12.9"
8. Fed 155	22	18	82	.54"	11.1"
9. Rem GS 180	15	12	80	.51"	12.8"
10. Win BT 180	34	27	79	.47"	14.2"
11. Win 180 JHP	46	36	78	.46"	13.9"
12. Win FMJ	28	17	61	.40"	16.7"

10MM

LOAD	TOTAL	STOPS	%	AD	AP
1. Win ST 175	28	24	86	.69"	12.4"
2. Fed HS 180	19	16	84	.61"	13.2"
3. Fed 180	11	9	82	.63"	13.9"

.357 SIG

LOAD	TOTAL	STOPS	%	AD	AP
1. Rem 125	11	10	91	.67"	12.8"

.45 ACP

LOAD	TOTAL	STOPS	%	AD	AP
1. Rem GS 185	39	35	90	.62"	11.3"
2. Fed HS 230	28	25	89	.68"	12.9"
3. Rem 185+P	18	16	89	.64"	10.8"
4. Win ST 185	27	23	85	.67"	10.2"
5. Win BT 230	26	21	81	.69"	13.1"
6. Fed 230 FMJ	15	9	60	.45"	14.2"
7. Win 230 FMJ	34	20	59	.45"	13.7"
8. Rem 230 FMJ	14	8	57	.45"	14.2"

CHAPTER 30

First Shootings

The photos in this chapter are of the first shootings with several loads. All of them met my criteria for a stop. While one shooting is hardly enough to hang your hat on, I thought readers would be interested in these early results.

First shooting with Speer Gold Dot .357 SIG 125-grain brass hollowpoint. This one was used by a SWAT officer to stop a heavily armed robber.

Federal's EFMJ load has a silicone-like plug under the nose to enhance deformation. This one, a first shooting, worked very well on a miscreant who brought a hatchet to a gunfight.

First shooting with Federal .40 S&W 165-grain Tactical load by a Midwest cop to stop the murder of a fellow police officer. This round penetrated the windshield and then the felon's thoracic cavity. It was recovered from the back seat.

This first shooting shows that Winchester's 9mm 115-grain JHP "controlled expansion" offering provides deep penetration with modest expansion.

First shooting with Remington Golden Saber 147-grain brass hollowpoint. A drug-enraged homeless man was struck twice in the upper thoracic cavity.

First shooting with Starfire 95-grain JHP. This one stopped a robbery attempt at an ATM.

First shooting with a Starfire .38 Special showed good results from a 2 inch barrel.

First shooting with a Black Hills .357 SIG 125-grain BHP.

First shooting with a PMC 240-grain .44 Special.

First shooting with a Remington 9mm 147-grain Golden Saber from a compact auto pistol.

First shooting with a PMC 165-grain JHP.

First shooting with Black Hills .45 ACP 230-grain load that penetrated the rear window of an SUV and stopped a car jacker.

First shooting with this Norma .40 S&W 155-grain JHP produced deep penetration and good expansion.

PMC's 95-grain 9mm load produces good expansion and penetration. This one stopped a home invasion. It is the first shooting with this load.

CHAPTER 31

Overseas Shootings

The following shootings are from an overseas source accumulated over a 15-year period. It has taken several years to translate, analyze, and correlate. They are from a special operations police group in a very active venue where gunfights were an almost weekly occurrence and coroner hearings were often held at the shooting's site and completed in 30 minutes!

9MM

LOAD	TOTAL	STOPS	PERCENTAGE
Win 9mm 115-gr. ST	96	81	84
Win 9mm 115-gr. JHP +P+	67	61	91

.357 MAGNUM

LOAD	TOTAL	STOPS	PERCENTAGE
Win 158-gr. SWC	73	58	79
Win 125-gr. JHP	153	135	88

12 GAUGE 00 BUCKSHOT

LOAD	TOTAL	STOPS	PERCENTAGE
Win 2 3/4"	40	38	95

.223 REMINGTON

LOAD	TOTAL	STOPS	PERCENTAGE
Win 55-gr. FMJ	111	101	91

9MM SUBMACHINE GUN

LOAD	TOTAL	STOPS	PERCENTAGE
Win 115-gr. FMJ	38	28	74

CHAPTER 32

"Stopping" Power

by John Farnam

"Here is the ultimate manstopper!" shrieks the headline. "A pocket-full of dynamite!" "A fist-full of raw brawn!" "The caliber the bad guys dread most!" "When your life's at stake!"

Such are the routine salutations affronting anyone who picks up a typical contemporary gun magazine. One can only wonder how germane any of these headlines are to the everyday lives of suburban, middle-class 12 year olds who comprise the bulk of the gun-journal-reading constituency. Sadly however, such yellow journalism seems quintessential to today's gun press. Such articles are little more than infomercials, and the advice one gleans is seldom of any practical use.

Absent the hype and pyrotechnics, I would like to discuss the various legitimate considerations a serious adult must take into account when he/she is trying to decide what handgun caliber to select for bona fide defensive purposes.

Handguns are instant, reactive, defensive weapons. They are designed to provide an adequate defense against a close, violent, potentially lethal, and unexpected personal attack. Good handgun ammunition is designed so that it quickly and decisively cripples human targets at close range. Of course, the operator must do his part—that is, persuade all bullets to impact in the vital area of the attacker's body. The "vital area" on a human body for handgun bullets is a

John Farnam wants the defensive handgun to incapacitate a person within three seconds at least 50 percent of the time. He gives an "excellent" rating to the .357 Magnum (shown), the .40 S&W, the .45 ACP, and the .357 SIG.

10 x 8 inch rectangle, with the long axis starting at the base of the collar bone just below the throat and extending downward several inches below the base of the sternum.

"Lethality" is not, by itself, a critical factor. An effective handgun round, upon impact, promptly cripples the target. That capability is fundamental and foremost. Whether or not the person struck by the bullet(s) ultimately dies from the resultant wound(s) is not particularly important, although experience has shown that crippling ability and lethality are inexorably linked.

By way of a useable definition, for a handgun round to thus be "effective," one hit on a human target in the vital area will deanimate that person within three seconds of impact at least 50 percent of the time. Any caliber or round of ammunition that consistently fails this test is considered ineffective and is thus not recommended for serious defensive purposes. To get significantly more effective than that, one would have to select a shotgun or rifle. Because of a handgun's relatively small size, its effectiveness is exceedingly limited.

The problem is, of course, that this "test" cannot be administered under laboratory conditions. In making judgements with regard to the effectiveness of bullets, velocities, and calibers, all we have to rely on is data collected from written and verbal narratives of actual shootings. Unhappily, because of legal, administrative, and other human factors, none of this data is particularly credible. Add to that the fact that the circumstances surrounding domestic, defensive shootings are always so diverse that one must exercise extreme caution when drawing conclusions with regard to ammunition performance, particularly when such conclusions are derived from only a few incidents.

Laboratory ballistic experiments conducted on clay, jelly, "computer people," and other nonliving, contrived test mediums are fascinating, but it is anyone's guess as to how significant (if significant at all) the results of these experiments really are. Sometimes, the overenthusiastic proponents of such research presume that their mission is to fabricate reality rather than measure it. That is, they consistently get their conclusions mixed in with their suppositions!

The shape, diameter, configuration, velocity, and construction of handgun bullets are all factors that contribute to the ultimate terminal performance of a particular round. Of those factors, no one can really say which is most important. With autoloading pistols, however, we can definitely say that feeding reliability is important, indeed critical. The best performing projectile in the world is still utterly unacceptable if it does not feed through the pistol reliably.

If a bullet is designed in such a way that it is inclined to change its shape subsequent to impact so as to expand from its original caliber, the amount and degree of tissue destruction will certainly be amplified. In addition, when bullets expand consistently, the probability of through-and-through penetration will be reduced. Also, ricochets from

Farnam's guidelines for weapon selection include terminal performance, controllability, and gun size. Most of all, the auto pistol must cycle reliably. He gives an "excellent" reliability rating to the .40 S&W, the .45 ACP (shown), and the .357 SIG and a "superior" rating to the 9mm.

projectiles so designed are less likely to be damaging than are those from solid projectiles. All other things being equal, those are all desirable attributes. Does that mean that hollowpoint projectiles are more effective than solid ones? Generally, yes. However, to reiterate, if one is using an autoloader, reliable feeding takes precedent over terminal ballistic performance.

I've heard it said that hollowpoint ammunition may expand sometimes in living, human tissue, but not very often. That allegation is not fair and not true. Ammunition manufacturers have labored diligently to match velocity and bullet construction in such a way as to insure reliable expansion in living, human tissue, and they have been largely successful. Modern high-performance handgun ammunition that is designed to expand does so in almost every instance, and bullets recovered from human tissue invariably bear that out. What is subject to debate is how important all that expansion really is.

The bottom line is we will probably never really know much about "stopping power," and for researchers to quarrel about it endlessly is pointless and counterproductive, although such public dissension does fill the pages of gun magazines to the delight of publishers and others who stand to profit therefrom.

In the domain of domestic defensive handguns, there are the large weapons, referred to as "main" guns, and there are the small "backup" guns. A main gun is the one a person would go for first. A backup gun is one's last defense when his main gun becomes inoperative or is taken away. Professional gunmen routinely carry backup guns.

A backup should be chambered for at least .38 Special or .380 Auto and should be strictly top quality. Under most circumstances, the .380 Auto is the smallest caliber one should consider for a backup gun. Pip-squeak calibers (mouse guns) are killers but not assault breakers. Don't bet your life on one if you can help it.

Typical not-recommended backup gun calibers—.22 rimfire, .25 ACP, and .32 ACP—are too underpowered to bother with. Many guns chambered for these calibers are trashy and unreliable. In fact, I do not know of any defensive handgun chambered for .22 rimfire that is reliable enough to recommend. Much of the commercially produced .22 rimfire ammunition is so dimensionally inconsistent that even well-made handguns will not feed and fire it reliably.

With regard to main gun calibers, even with the most powerful, rapid multiple hits are often necessary to quickly deanimate an attacker. One must be fully prepared and able to hit the attacker several times, regardless of the gun/cartridge combination used. That means, of course, the main gun must function reliably.

Here is a chart reprinted from my book on the subject of defensive handgunning. It may provide you with useable guidance in selecting a defensive handgun. As you can see, your ultimate selection will be the product of several compromises. You won't get every desirable feature in one package. The most devastating gun/cartridge combination in the world will be of little use to you if it is too big and bulky to be carried on a regular basis and you therefore don't have it with you at the moment it is desperately needed. On the other hand, the mouse gun you do have with you may well fail to cripple your attacker even though you strike him repeatedly in the vital area. Between these two extremes, I trust you'll find something you can live with and that will work for you. With any luck, you'll never know if your decision was a sound one!

TABLE 32-1
COMPARISON OF SERIOUS HANDGUN CALIBERS

Caliber	Feeding Reliability	Availability	Terminal Performance	Controllability	Gun Size & Weight
.380 Auto	good	fair	fair	excellent	excellent
9mm	superior	excellent	good	superior	excellent
.38 Special	n/a	excellent	good	excellent	excellent
.38 Super	fair	poor	good	excellent	fair
.357 Magnum	n/a	good	excellent	poor	fair
.40 S&W	excellent	good	excellent	good	good
10mm	poor	poor	superior*	fair	fair
.45 ACP	excellent	excellent	excellent	fair	fair
.357 SIG	excellent	fair	excellent	excellent	good
.400 C-B	good	poor	superior	good	fair

* Superior terminal performance from the 10mm Auto is ONLY realized in its full power, full-performance loadings, which are, unfortunately, difficult to find. Most ammunition currently manufactured for the 10mm has been reduced to 40 S&W ballistics. These "wimp 10" loadings, as they are called, were first introduced by the FBI, because agents complained about the recoil from the full-power loads. The Medium Velocity 10mm loads have since become standard.

One-Shot Stop Percentages

.22 Long Rifle

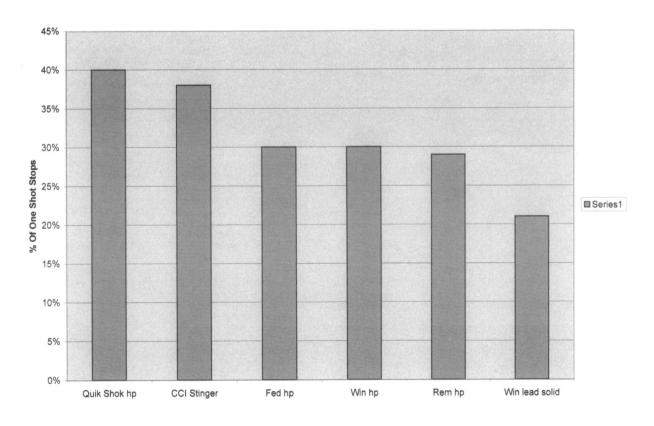

.25 ACP

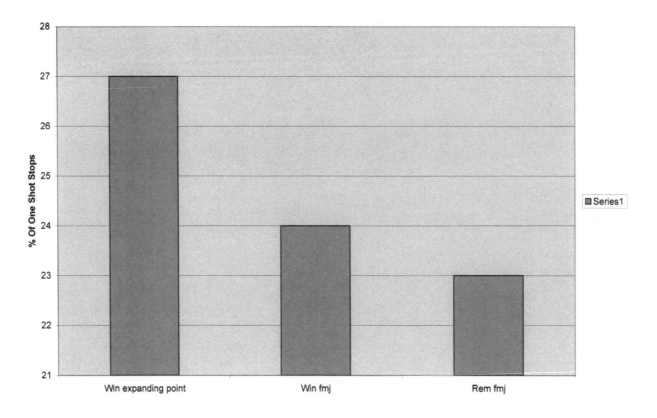

.32 ACP

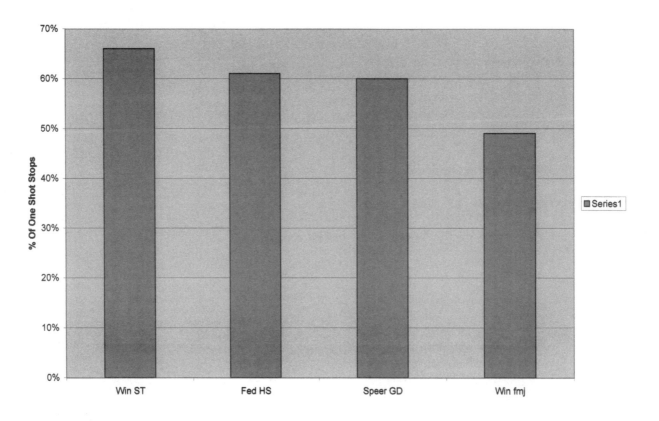

STOPPING POWER

.380 ACP

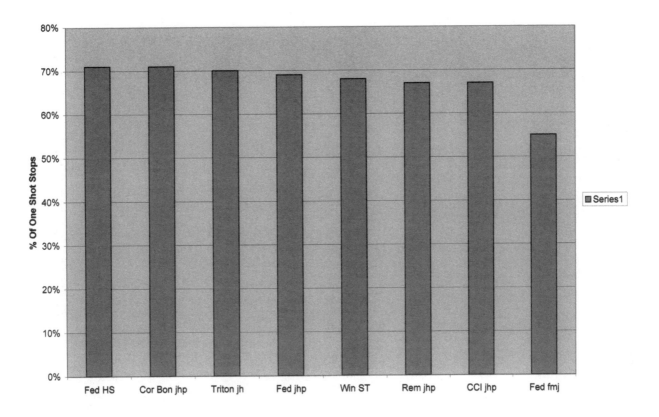

.38 Special-2″ Barrel

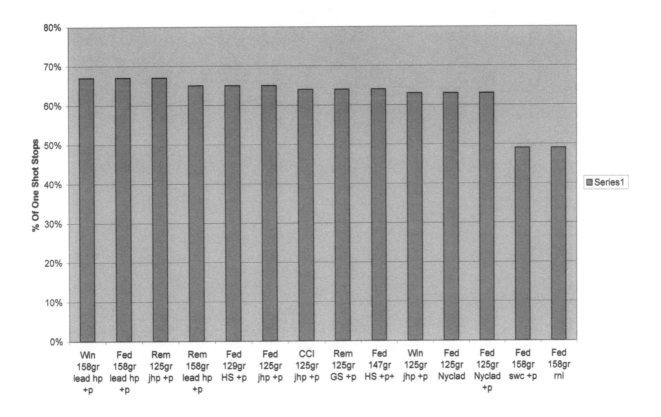

.38 Special-4" Barrel

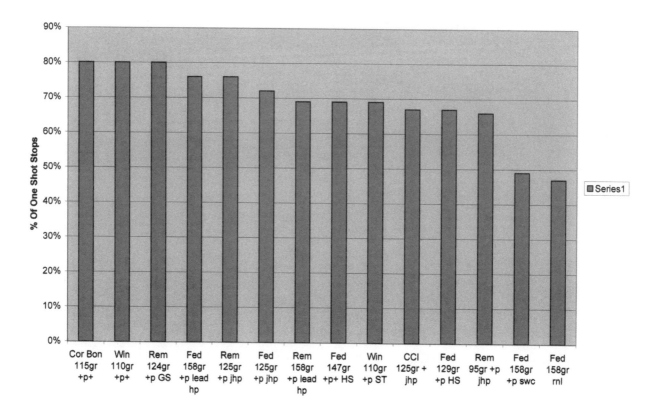

9MM Compact Auto

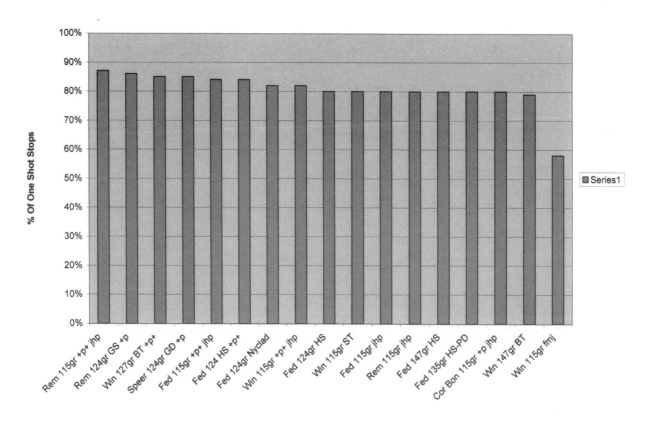

STOPPING POWER

9MM

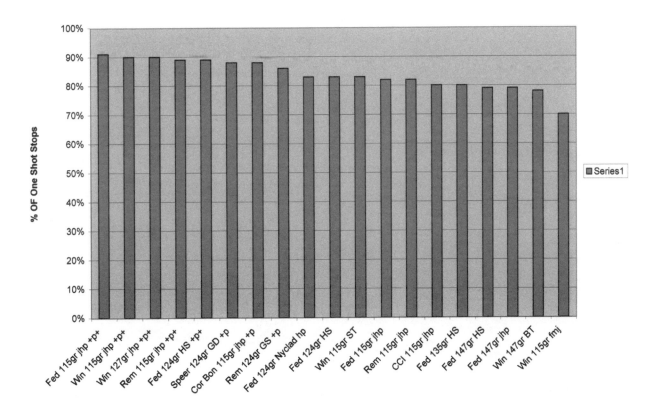

.357 Magnum

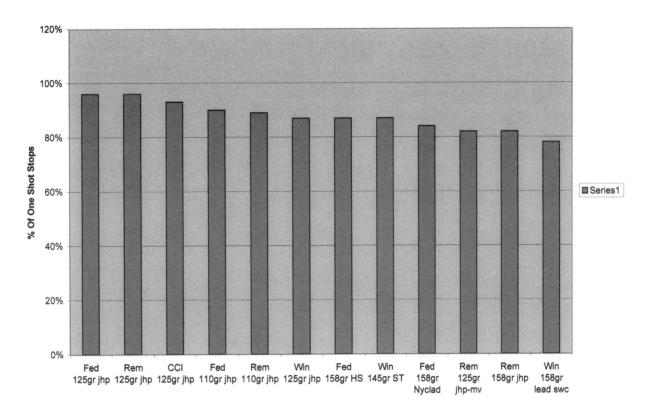

.357 SIG Compact

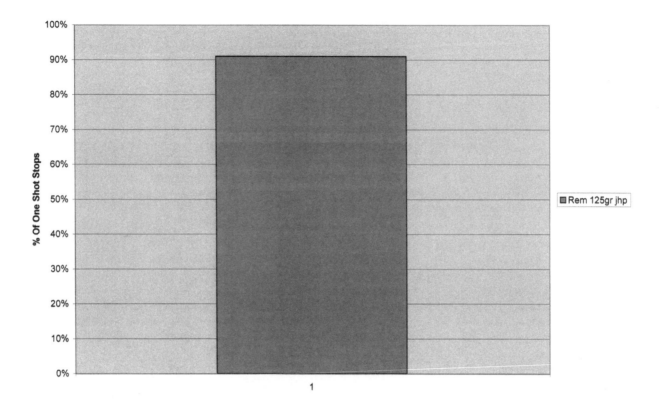

.357 SIG

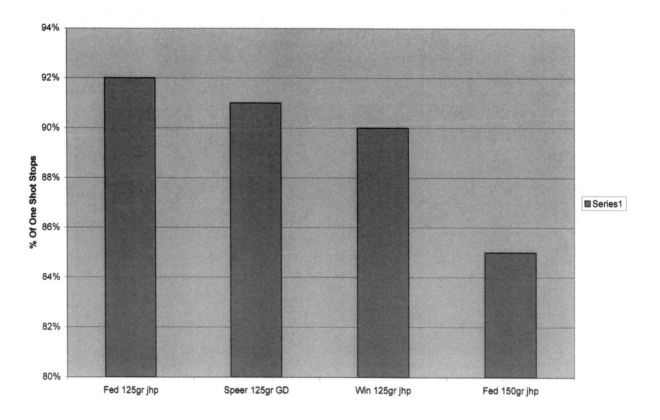

STOPPING POWER

10MM

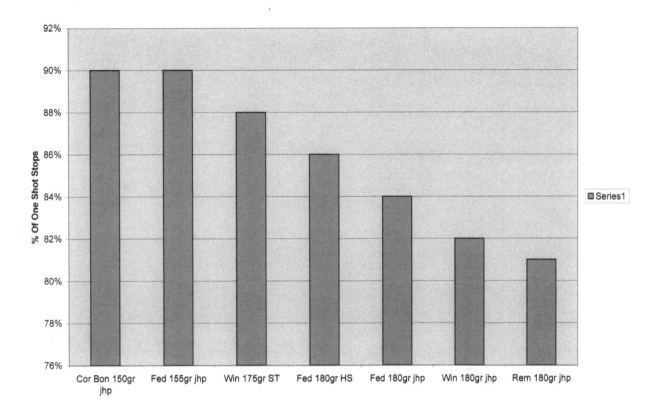

.40 S&W Compact Auto

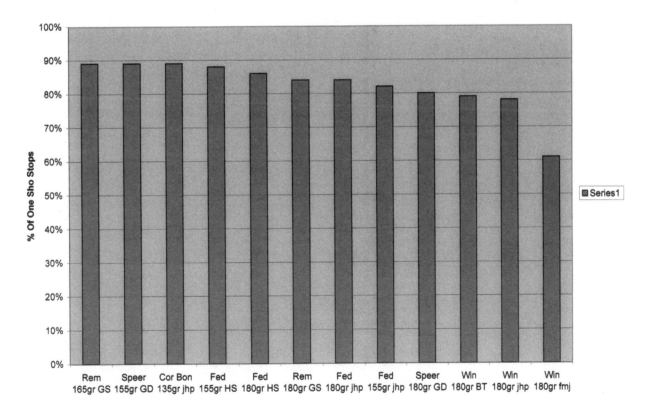

.40 S&W

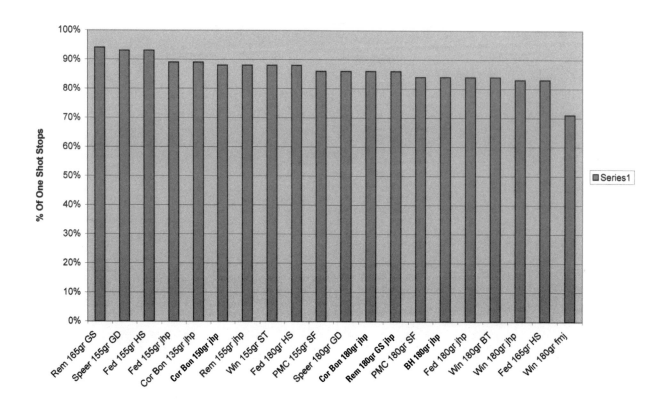

.41 Magnum

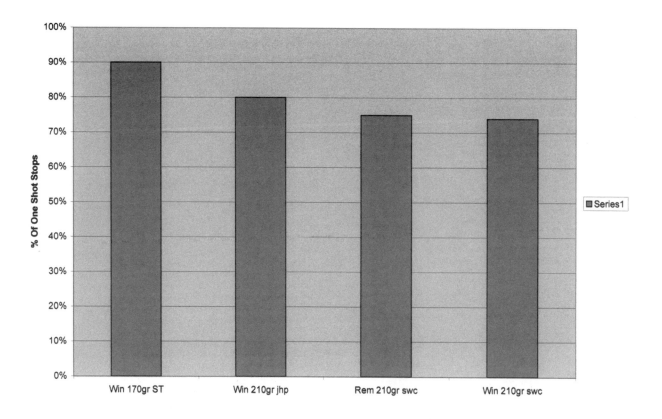

STOPPING POWER

.44 Special

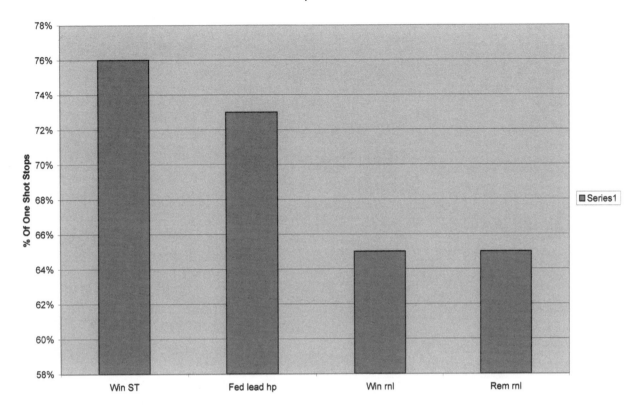

.44 Magnum

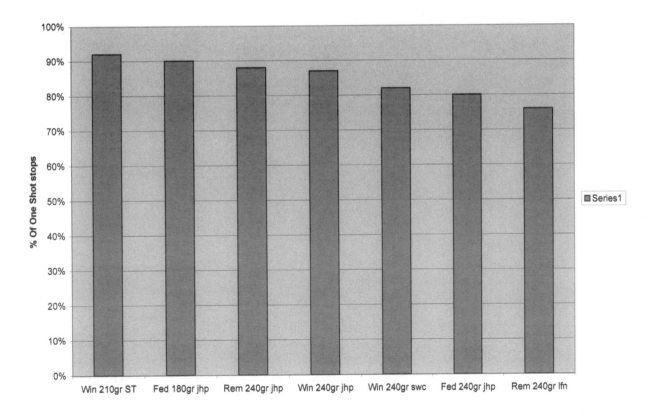

.45 Colt

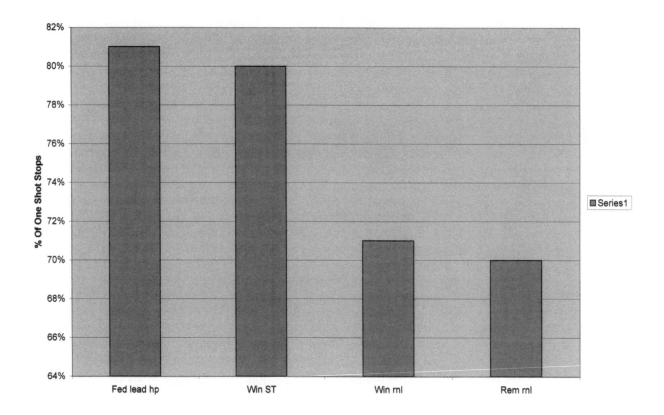

.45 ACP Compact Auto

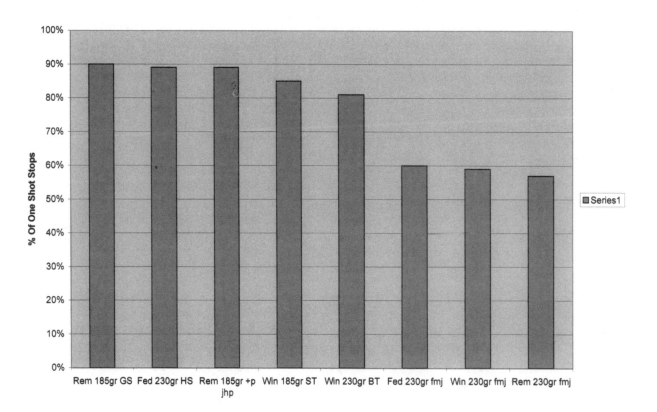

.45 ACP

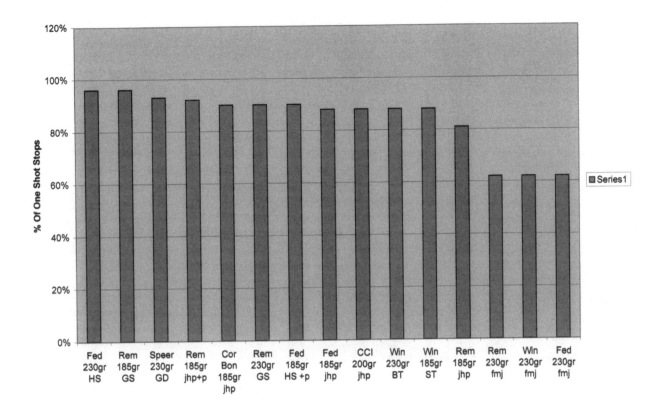

Caliber Comparison

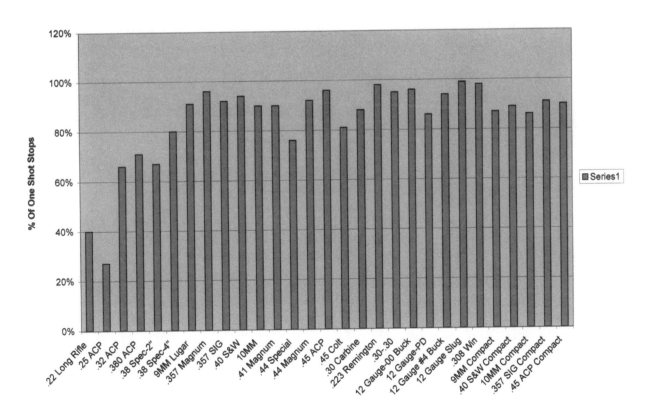

Full Size vs. Compact Auto

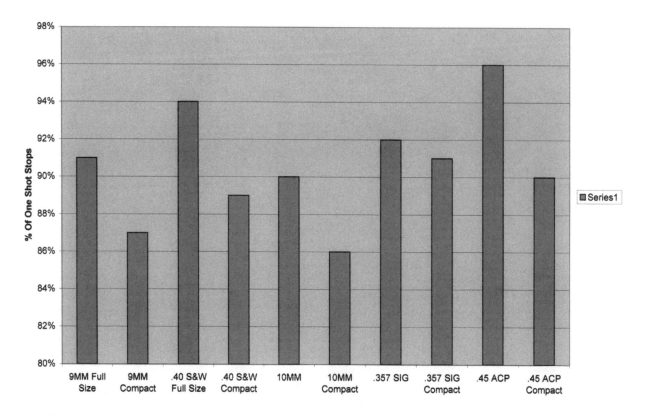

.223

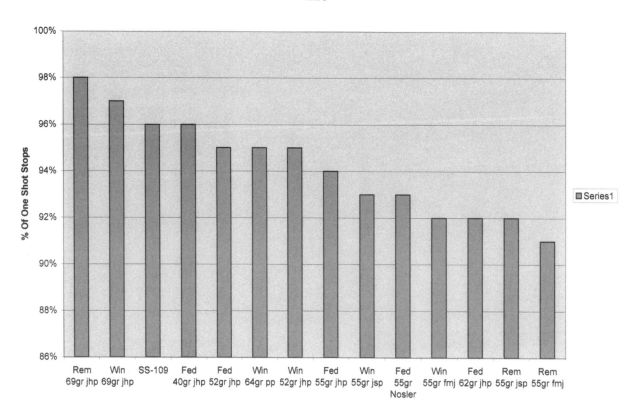

STOPPING POWER

.30 Carbine

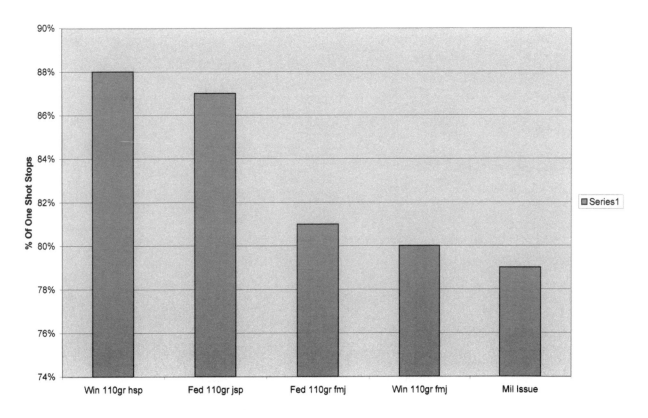

.30-30 Winchester

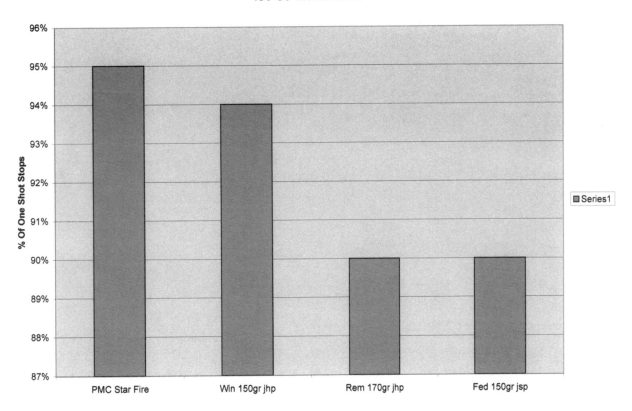

.308

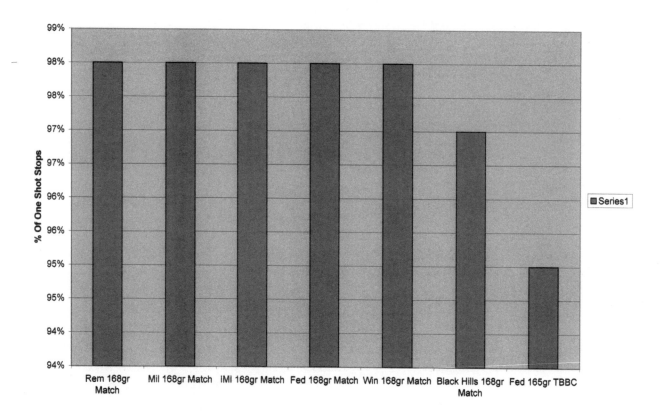

12 Gauge 00 Buck Shot

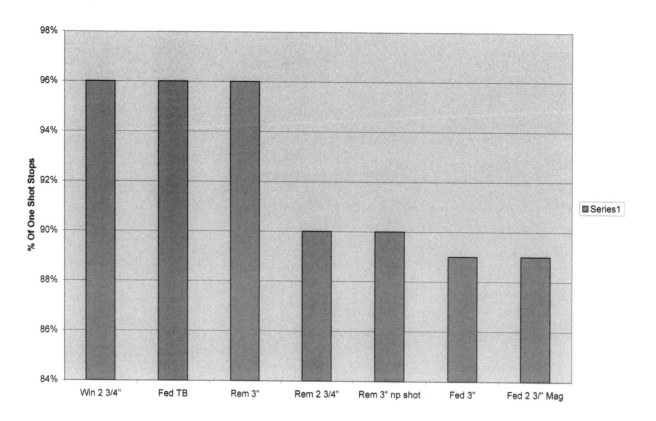

STOPPING POWER

12 Gauge #4 Buck Shot

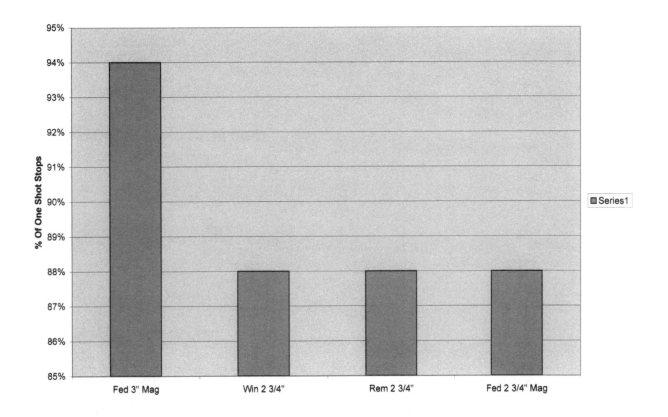

12 Gauge Slug

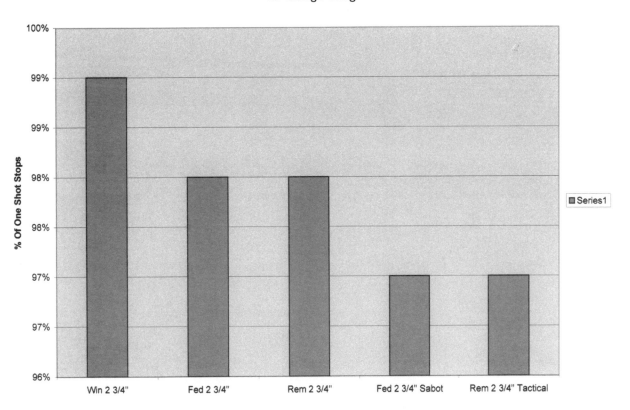

About the Authors

EVAN MARSHALL

Evan Marshall is currently employed as a Special Weapon and Tactics trainer for a federal agency with counterterrorist reponsiblities. He retired from the Detroit Police Department after 20 years service with the rank of Sergeant. His assignments included Tactical Unit, Crime Scene Investigation, Homicide, and the Special Response Team.

Marshall attended college at Brigham Young University, Stanford University, and the University of Southern California before graduating with a BA in History from Wayne State University. He later returned to school and obtained a Masters Degree in Criminal Justice from the University of Detroit.

He has been a guest lecturer at a number of agencies and organizations and has trained groups as diverse as the Federal Air Marshals and the U.S. Army Special Reaction Teams. He wrote the first magazine column solely devoted to the subject of officer survival and is widely recognized as one of the founders of the modern officer survival movement.

Evan Marshall and his wife are the parents of seven children and grandparents of ten. They live in Midland, Michigan, where they are active in their church. He has been widely published in the law enforcement and firearms press over the past 25 years.

Evan Marshall

EDWIN J. SANOW

Cpl. Ed Sanow is the senior reserve deputy and a 14 year veteran with the Benton County, Indiana, Sheriff's Department, where he holds a single unit status. He is a state-certified Firearms Instructor with a Distinguished Expert firearms rating. Sanow is a Team Leader with the Benton County Multi-Agency Response Team. He is also one of the most active patrol officers in the county, holding records for the most traffic citations issued in one year and the most cocaine seized during a vehicle stop. He serves as the Field Training Officer for the reserve force.

Sanow has a Bachelor of Science degree from Purdue University. In addition to the Indiana Law Enforcement Academy In-Service Training, he is a multiple course graduate of Clint Smith's Thunder Ranch, Massad Ayoob's Lethal Force Institute, and John Farnam's Defense Tactics Institute. He is a certified Glock armorer.

In addition to being the co-author

Ed Sanow

with Sgt. Evan Marshall (ret.) of the books *Handgun Stopping Power* and *Street Stoppers*, Sanow is the author of over 1,000 articles on ammo and stopping power in magazines like *Handguns, Gun World, S.W.A.T., Combat Handguns, Fire!* (Belgium), *Law and Order, Police, Police Marksman,* and *Law Enforcement Technology.*

Sanow has popularized the use of ordnance gelatin to evaluate bullet performance and predict stopping power. He has been an expert witness in both civil and criminal cases, including capital murder, on the topics of ammunition and gelatin wound profiles. Sanow has toured the major ammo factories, including Remington, Winchester, Federal, CCI-Speer, Hirtenberger (Austria), Georgia Arms, the original Hydra-Shok Corp., and Cor-Bon.

Sanow was a guest lecturer at the 1998 INS/NFU (Border Patrol) Ammunition Protocol Symposium. He has been a staff instructor at ASLET, IALEFI, and GALEFI training conferences. He was a commentator on the History Channel's series "Working Wheels" and a commentator on the Law Enforcement Television Network series "Winning Armed Encounters." He has served as an ammunition consultant to major ammo companies and major police departments alike. In October 2000, Sanow became the editor of *Law and Order* magazine.

TOM BURCZYNSKI

Tom Burczynski grew up in the rolling hills southwest of Watkins Glen, New York, an area that abounds with game and where shooting was almost a daily activity. He first became interested in ballistics at age 17 after being introduced to handloading by his brother, Mike. After attending Mohawk Valley College, he took a position with Westinghouse Electric Corporation as a cathode ray tube technician. It was during his employment there, while studying

mechanical engineering and metal fabrication techniques, that he invented the Hydra-Shok bullet. Six years later, he became involved in a water well drilling company, during which time he invented a self-actuating drilling bit, perfected Hydra-Shok, and invented the Starfire bullet.

After obtaining patents on the Hydra-Shok design, Tom collaborated with a local businessman and formed the Hydra-Shok Corporation, serving as vice president. He invented an automatic ejection system to mass produce the bullet and, soon after, Hydra-Shok ammunition was marketed as a rapid-expanding, semiexotic round sold directly to dealers and police departments. Less than a year later, Hydra-Shok had become the official duty round of the U.S. Department of State in .38 Special and .357 Magnum. Seven years later, the patent rights were licensed exclusively to PMC/Eldorado in 1990.

Since then, several patents have been issued covering various forms of his latest design, Quik-Shok. Exclusive manufacturing rights to this design have been negotiated for centerfire, rimfire, and shotshell. In 2000, Burczynski's latest invention, the Expanding Full Metal Jacket, was put into production by Federal.

Burczynski has developed 44 bullet designs from his home-based company, Experimental Research, along with more than 80 nonballistic inventions. Currently residing in Montour Falls, New York, he is still actively involved in ballistic research and development and patent development, does consulting work, and is always seeking sharp investors to share in the inevitable profits that will be made from his inventions.

JOHN FARNAM

John Farnam is a Viet Nam combat veteran and a former Wisconsin Sheriff's Deputy. Farnam is one of the top defensive firearms instructor in the nation. He

popularized the use of computer-controlled, Duel-A-Tron shoot/no shoot, reaction targets in firearms training across the country.

Farnam teaches the pistol and revolver as well as anyone in the country, but his real specialty is Special Weapons. He is without peer in his shotgun training and teaches a wide variety of submachine gun techniques not found at the "corporate" schools. He is one of the few instructors competent to teach handgun, shotgun, rifle, and submachine gun.

Farnam has personally trained thousands of federal, state, and local law enforcement officers, many private security agencies, and hundreds of civilians. He has authored dozens of articles for magazines like *S.W.A.T.*, three books on tactics and techniques, several handgun manuals, and a model Use of Force Policy. He has also produced numerous training videos. His most recent book, *The Farnam Method of Defensive Rifle and Shotgun Shooting*, has become the standard text on the subject.

JOHN JACOBS

John Jacobs began his law enforcement career with the Burlington, Vermont, Police Department in 1970. From 1972 to 1978, he served as Chief of the Richmond, Vermont, Police Department. In 1978, he joined the U.S. Border Patrol and was top gun in his Nogales, Arizona, Border Patrol Academy class. By 1984, he rose to the rank of Senior Border Patrol Agent. He transferred to the Firearms Division at the USBP Academy located at the Federal Law Enforcement Training Center (FLETC) in Glynco, Georgia, where he served as instructor and course developer.

Jacobs wrote all of the INS/Border Patrol ammo and firearms procurement documents and conducted all of the testing. He also wrote the first INS semiautomatic pistol specifications. The resulting double-action-only pistol was the first to be used by the federal government.

Jacobs collaborated in the development of the USBP Agent Survival Course. He wrote and produced all of the shoot/no-shoot judgement video scenarios. Jacobs also wrote the INS semiauto pistol Transition Training Course as well as the FLETC generic semiauto pistol and Glock pistol lesson plans. He pioneered the use of reactive targets and Simunition training at FLETC. He also developed the USBP Firearms Instructor's Training Program. While at FLETC, Jacobs worked with Remington and Federal to pioneer the development of reduced recoil 12-gauge buckshot loads.

In 1992, Jacobs wrote the proposal and the organization plan establishing the INS National Firearms Unit. While with the NFU as a Senior BPA, he served as an Instructor/Course Developer and wrote the Field Officers Integrity Training Program. In 1996, Jacobs was promoted to Assistant Director of the INS/NFU. In this capacity, he wrote and advised on National Firearms Policy issues, supervised all ammunition procurement, wrote all ammo test and evaluation procedures,

and performed research and quality assurance testing. He was one of the driving forces behind the new INS/NFU ammo test protocol.

KEITH JONES

Keith Jones is a 30 year veteran of law enforcement with a highly diversified police and security background. He has served as a police officer with the medium-sized Newark, Ohio, Police Department. As a member of their pistol team, Jones was a two-time competitor at the Police PPC Nationals held annually in Jackson, Mississippi. He also served with the large, urban Indianapolis, Indiana, Police Department. Jones was one of IPD's first five Field Training Officers at the beginning of that landmark program, circa 1976.

Jones has been a road deputy with a small, rural sheriff's department and a security officer with a large, metro sheriff's department. He has served as the town marshal in a small Indiana community, a police position which carries the broadest statutory and enforcement powers under Indiana law. He has received meritorious commendations from each police department he has served.

Jones is a survivor of four police-

action gunfights, three while armed with a revolver and one when deployed with a shotgun. Significantly, the ammo used by Jones in two of these scenarios was .38 Special non +P 158-grain round-nose lead, the least effective load in the least powerful duty caliber. The other handgun load was a softpoint. Jones thus speaks with profound authority when it comes to surviving a gunfight by controlling the variables before and during the fight and not by the pursuit of a magic bullet.

Jones is one of very few officers to become an Indiana Law Enforcement Academy-certified "survival tactics instructor." He is currently a deputy sheriff with the Marion County, Indiana, Sheriff's Department. He is a frequent speaker to police and civic groups on the topics of survival tactics, chemical agents, domestic violence intervention, and law enforcement history and heritage.

A gunfight veteran himself, Keith has researched the dynamics of both armed and unarmed close-quarter combat all during his long career. He has attended after-action autopsies, reviewed and reconstructed armed encounter scenarios, and interviewed gunfight survivors all over the United States.